D1458123

DATE

LABOR ECONOMICS

Consulting Editor:

Albert Blum
Michigan State University

LABOR ECONOMICS

Roy B. Helfgott

*Newark College
of Engineering*

**RANDOM HOUSE
NEW YORK**

First Edition
987654321

Library of Congress Cataloging in Publication Data

Helfgott, Roy B
  Labor economics.

  Includes bibliographies.
  1. Labor supply—United States. 2. Industrial
relations—United States. 3. Labor economics.
I. Title.
HD5724.H38   331 .0973   73-18116
ISBN 0-394-31535-9

Manufactured in the United States of America. Composed by Cherry Hill Composition,
Pennsauken, N.J. Printed and bound by Halliday Lithograph Corp., West Hanover, Mass.

*To the memory of
my parents*

PREFACE

A cursory glance at the daily newspaper should bring home to students the importance of labor economics and industrial relations. Stories of strikes, civil rights demonstrations, litigations concerned with alleged job discrimination, levels of employment and unemployment, and the latest developments on the inflation front abound. A discussion of these topics alone justifies a book on labor economics.

One major aim in writing this text was to overcome the dichotomy that is typical of many labor textbooks: either concentration on the institutional aspects of the subject—unionism, collective bargaining, labor law—to the neglect of basic economic theory; or focusing on the theory but ignoring the institutional features. My aim has been to integrate economic theory and institutional aspects and to show how they interact to explain events. A second aim was to make the subject of labor economics alive to the student by indicating its relevance to major issues of our time: inflation, unemployment, the urban crisis, and equal employment opportunity. A third aim was to avoid writing the typical voluminous labor economics textbook. This book is shorter than almost all others. Its chapter introductions serve to weave a unifying thread through the book; chapter summaries highlight the material covered in each chapter; and bibliographies provide interested students with sources of further information.

This book attempts to explore the free labor market in all its aspects. Although written from the perspective of the economist, it is also concerned with interdisciplinary matters such as class structure and attitudes toward work. The rise and growth of unionism, its extent, structure, philosophy, and practices are scrutinized and related to basic economic-technological-political forces. Collective bargaining and labor law are thoroughly discussed, and attention is given to the newest development—labor-management relations in public employment.

The book next probes basic subjects of labor economics, tracing theories of wages, culminating in the marginal productivity theory. The interaction between economic and institutional forces in wage determination is stressed. Wage structure, both internal and external, is examined, as are industry, occupational, regional, and union-nonunion differentials. Special attention is focused on the problem of inflation, including the relationship between productivity and real wage gains, hypotheses that seek to explain rising money wages, and U.S. incomes policies from the guideposts of the 1960s through the various phases of the Nixon administration's New Economic Policy.

Unemployment, the unemployment insurance system, the Keynesian critique of neoclassical theory, the Employment Act of 1946, and the structural transformation–aggregate demand debate are analyzed. The subject of working time is also explored, including such recent developments as the 10-hour day, 4-day week. The problem of economic security for workers, the Social Security system, private pension and welfare programs, workmen's compensation, and occupational safety and health are examined.

A distinctive feature of the book is a chapter devoted to labor in an urban environment, which focuses on imbalances in the urban labor market as a major factor in the present urban crisis. Other chapters are devoted to equal employment opportunity—efforts to improve the status of blacks and women in the labor market—and to manpower policy—a review and appraisal of recent manpower programs.

I have striven to be up-to-date in my coverage. Since many topics are subject to differing interpretations, I have sought to present the varying viewpoints dispassionately but have not attempted to hide my own views on any subject.

I must express my appreciation to those who have helped make this book possible. In twenty-five years of experience in industrial relations and labor economics as a student, researcher, teacher, and consultant, and working with both labor and management, I have gained much knowledge from many people whom it is impossible to acknowledge individually. A special note of appreciation goes to Industrial Relations Counselors, Inc., for permitting me to use material that I helped to prepare while in its employ. I am also grateful to Irene Pierce, Mary Ann Sarrus, and Carol Williams for typing various drafts of the manuscript. Finally, I should like to thank Professor Albert A. Blum of Michigan State University, who not only inveigled me into writing the book, but more importantly, read the entire manuscript and offered many worthwhile suggestions for its improvement, as did Professor Morrison Handsaker of Lafayette College and Professor Robert Bowers of Michigan State University. I assume full responsibility, however, for the ideas expressed herein and any errors.

May, 1973   Roy B. Helfgott

CONTENTS

LABOR ECONOMICS

1 THE LABOR FORCE

Some 90 million Americans, better than two out of every five men, women, and children in the nation, are in the labor force—that is, they are working or actively seeking work. Five out of every six workers, moreover, work for someone else rather than for themselves, and receive remuneration in the form of wages and salaries. Labor economics, the subject of this book, is that branch of the discipline of economics which focuses on the exchange relationship between employees and employers, thus employing the normal tools of economic analysis to determine both the allocation of labor among industries, occupations, firms, and regions and the prices that must be paid for labor.

But the peculiar nature of labor, the fact that it involves the services of human beings, does not permit the labor economist to rely solely upon the normal tools of economic analysis. He must also examine the institutions, such as employer and worker organizations, that have been created by human beings to see how they affect the workings of the labor market. As a result, with respect to human and organizational behavior, he depends on the findings of such other disciplines as sociology, psychology, history, and political science, which he must then, as an economist, relate to the basic economic questions.

In a privately organized economic system, labor is allocated and its price determined primarily through the institution of a free labor market. Each of the members of the U.S. labor force is free, within the limits of his needs and abilities, to elect the occupation at which he wants to work, to choose the firm for which he works, and even to decide for himself whether to work or not. He may, moreover, change his mind and quit his present job to seek a different one. He may move from one part of the country to another, as he sees fit; there are no internal passports to restrict his mobility, and all a worker needs to change his job is to find some other employer who is willing to hire him.

It was not always thus, and in this opening chapter we shall briefly trace the process by which a free labor market emerged, examine the essence of a free labor market, and look back into American history to discover the types of unfree labor that once existed. Having done this, we shall focus our attention on the nation's labor force—past, present, and future—in terms of total numbers; its distribution among industries; and its composition by occupation, sex, age, education, and race.

3

Emergence of a Free Labor Market

Slavery

The free labor market is of rather recent vintage. For most of man's history work has been organized in other fashions: free men usually worked for themselves, mainly as farmers and shepherds, and those who performed labor for others generally did not have the option of choosing their employment, nor were they paid wages for the work performed. The oldest means through which one man performed labor for another was slavery; indeed, slavery is an ancient human institution that has persisted into modern times.[1]

Serfdom

Although slavery had been an important feature of the Greek and Roman civilizations and had persisted in Europe into the Middle Ages, it then declined in importance in the Western world, disappearing in England by the thirteenth century and in other countries within the next few centuries. In its stead did not come freedom, but feudalism, a new form of economic organization that depended upon a different form of servitude—serfdom—for its labor. Feudalism was the institution through which the agricultural economy of Europe was operated, and at its center was the manorial estate owned by the feudal lord and worked by his hundreds of serfs. Each feudal manor was a self-contained economic, governmental, and religious unit. It raised its own food and had some auxiliary workshops to produce tools and weapons, as well as its own court and chapel.

Under feudalism, three categories of people existed: nobles, clergy, and commoners. The organization of work was a fixed status system, into which one was born, and it involved mutual obligations. The major group of commoners, the serfs—or, as they were known in England, villeins)—who labored in the fields or workshops, although not slaves, were bound to the manor. A second category of rural workers, the freemen, had greater rights, were not tied to the land, and were more like tenant farmers. Both villeins and freemen, however, had to perform labor for the lord or turn over a share of their crops to him (later paying him in money); in return, in an age in which law and order were poorly developed, the lord and his knights provided them with physical and some degree of economic security. The feudal division of labor was summed up in the saying "The House of God is tripartite. Some work, some fight, some pray."[2]

---

[1] An interesting account of unfree labor can be found in E. H. Phelps Brown, *The Economics of Labor* (New Haven: Yale University Press, 1962), pp. 9–19.

[2] Herbert Heaton, *Economic History of Europe* (New York: Harper & Bros., 1936), p. 55. As Muller has observed, however, this division of society by medieval writers omitted "merchants and townsmen; but it was these men without status and an anonymous 'middle' class—who made over the whole society. They developed the money economy that undermined the feudal system, helping the peasants to emerge from serfdom and the kings to dominate the barons" (Herbert F. Muller, *The Uses of the Past* [New York: Oxford University Press, 1957], p. 256). Because they were not part of the feudal system, the Jews were an important part of this middle class from the very beginning.

Merchant Guilds

The rise of trade created a need for an institution to operate the trade, and starting in the eleventh century the merchant guilds arose. These organizations of traders were not tied to the feudal manors but were located in the towns, particularly the seaports of Europe and those places along trade routes that could best be defended from invasion by enemies. The people who lived in the towns, of course, had originally come from the feudal manors, and included former serfs who had bought their freedom. The towns, too, secured their freedom from the feudal manors and became self-governing communities.

Craft Guilds

The collection of merchants in favorable spots soon caused artisans to collect there; since people from the manors came to the towns periodically to trade, the artisans found it easier to make their sales there, too.[3] The craftsmen also saw a need for mutual solidarity, and thus a second form of guild—the craft guild—arose in the towns in western Europe starting in the twelfth century. Each craft guild was granted a charter, which bestowed upon it a monopoly of production rights in a particular region for a particular product or service, such as woolens, silks, furs, locksmithing, and carpentry.

The guilds were largely self-regulated, and entrance into them was strictly controlled. A boy would become an apprentice of a master craftsman, with whom he would live and from whom he could learn the trade. After serving his apprenticeship, usually for five to seven years, the craftsman would become a journeyman, who was paid a daily wage (the word "journeyman" derives from the French *journee*, or worker paid by the day). Journeymen in turn might become master craftsmen, if they could show that they had sufficient funds to make good any damage done to customers' goods, possessed the equipment needed, and had sufficient skill,[4] the test for which consisted of submitting an elaborate example of one's work—a "masterpiece." Not all journeymen became masters, because some lacked the funds, the skill, or both. The guilds were monopolies that limited entrance into the trade and controlled prices and production.

The Domestic System

The craft guilds were dominant through the sixteenth century, but after that, as the pace of industrial activity quickened, they disappeared. This was partly due to internal dissension, but mainly to the extension of the market and the rise of the nation-state, which permitted the growth of industry in the countryside, outside their spheres of control. Industry, instead of being conducted in masters' workshops, was now conducted in the artisans' homes, a system of

[3] Henri Pirenne, *Economic and Social History of Medieval Europe* (London: Routledge & Kegan Paul, 1961), p. 44.
[4] Heaton, *op. cit.*, pp. 215–216.

production that became known as the "domestic" system. Weavers, for instance, owned the looms on which they wove cloth and kept them in their houses. Industry was organized by merchant employers, who provided the artisans with raw materials—for which reason the system was also referred to as the "putting-out" system—and who marketed the finished products. Under this system, however, the functions of employer and employee were separated, for the person who actually produced the item did not own it and did not sell it.

The Factory System

With the further extension of the market, the domestic system soon gave way to the factory system, in which a large number of workers were concentrated under one roof, cooperating under centralized control in the manufacture of products. The factory permitted savings in transportation of raw materials and finished products, as well as discipline of the workers and control of the quality of the product. With the advent of the Industrial Revolution, the factory became indispensable, for power-driven machinery was too big for a home and too expensive for the individual worker to buy. Industry, however, continued to be conducted in the countryside as long as the main source of power was water, but when it was replaced by steam power factories began to be set up in the cities, where a large mass of people could be concentrated.

The factory wrought an entire revolution in terms of man and his work. First, it separated home and workshop and forced people, literally, to "go" to work. Second, by concentrating a mass of people under one roof it inevitably made the relationship between employer and employee an impersonal one. Third, power-driven machinery entailed a further separation of the functions of employer and employee because now the former also owned the tools, converting him from a merchant employer to a capitalist captain of industry. As Karl Marx pointed out, under capitalist industrialism the worker had only his labor power to sell. To Marx this was a great tragedy that demanded the overthrow of capitalism, but to defenders of the new economic order it spelled a degree of freedom for the individual worker that he had not previously enjoyed.

Sources of Labor

Obviously, some of the former craftsmen had become the wage earners of the new form of organization of work, but this would hardly have been a sufficient supply of labor for the burgeoning industrial system. In order to understand where the bulk of the workers, or labor force, for the new factories came from, we must retrace our steps, focusing on England's economic history. Under feudalism, the problems of controlling the serfs, extracting sufficient labor from them, and preventing their escape led the lords gradually to convert their status to that of tenant farmers. The freemen had their own strips of land, plus the right to graze their livestock on the common pastures.

With the rise of trade, England's major export became woolen manufactures, and to obtain wool it was necessary to raise sheep. Farming lands, therefore, were converted to sheep grazing, and this was done by evicting tenants (former serfs, in most cases) where possible and by enclosing the common lands that the tenants had used.

The newly displaced farmers were joined in the migration to the burgeoning cities, where they found work in the factories that were being opened, both by former farmers who had become artisans in the domestic system and by the surplus of farm laborers that had been created by population growth. There was a carrot as well as a stick, for the relatively high wages in industry, as compared to earnings in agriculture, also acted to attract farm workers to the factories. Even so, labor conditions in the early days of industrialism were very harsh—long hours, strict discipline, low wages—and they improved only gradually. Over the long run, however, industrialization has brought very high standards of living, undreamed of two hundred years ago.

The Essence of a Free Labor Market

Free labor has a special meaning, and it became an indispensable feature of the free-enterprise, laissez-faire economic system that arose in the last quarter of the eighteenth century. The liberal economic philosophy that emerged with the publication in 1776 of Adam Smith's *An Inquiry into the Nature and Causes of the Wealth of Nations* was based largely on the eighteenth-century view of natural immutable laws. Among its key elements were the principles of individual initiative, with each person attempting to maximize his benefits; private business operated for profit; competition among many firms, none of which was of dominant size; and the exchange of goods in a free market through the use of money.

A "market," thus, is a place where goods and services are exchanged through the medium of money and in which, because of competition, prices tend to uniformity; that is, no one will pay more for an item if he can get it for less from someone else and no one would offer his product or service for sale at a lower price than another buyer would offer. Under economic liberalism the labor market, too, was a "free" one; that is, workers were not bound to an employer, but could change jobs whenever they wanted to in response to pressures they might be under or desires to increase their benefits. Similarly, employers were free to hire whomever they pleased, had no obligations to their employees other than paying them for the work performed at the competitive price dictated by the market, and could dismiss them whenever their services were no longer required.

Under an industrial system, in order to manufacture goods one must have the elements that go into producing the goods. These "factors of production" are land, labor, and capital. Land, in its broadest context, means not only the site for a plant, but includes the raw materials—metals and minerals, forest products, agricultural products—that are used in producing manufactured goods, plus the fuel and energy for carrying out the production process. Capital refers to capital goods, that is, goods that are used to produce other goods, such as the physical plant, its machinery and equipment. By themselves, land and capital cannot produce goods, for this requires the exertion of human effort; thus, labor is the third indispensable factor of production.

Under the industrial capitalist system, therefore, labor became a factor of production that was combined by entrepreneurs with the other factors of production—land and capital—to produce goods and services for sale. As an input to the production process, labor itself became a commodity to be bought and sold. The individual worker was free to sell his services to the highest bidder, and the employer was free to purchase those services for the lowest price he could obtain. The actual price of labor was determined, of course, by the market—at the point, that is, where the supply of a particular type of labor was balanced by the demand for it.

Hence a labor market existed whenever prospective employers and employees met to negotiate the purchase and sale of human services. The relationship between employers and employees became an impersonal, purely exchange relationship, unfettered by any obligations or status arrangements aside from paying what the balance of supply and demand required. Indeed, Kenneth Boulding has defined economics as the subject that "specializes in the study of the total social system which is organized through exchange and deals with exchangeables,"[5] and labor economics merely concentrates on the exchange relationship with respect to the labor factor of production.

An exchange economy tends to specialization, because this permits the individual production unit to become expert in one line and hence to be able to produce more units of output per unit of input. The producer who specializes in one type of production then exchanges his product for the specialized production of another firm. This in turn leads to a division of labor, which enables each worker to perfect some particular operation or skill. The division of labor also allows the greater use of capital equipment, for machines can be devised that will perform simple tasks.

Under an agricultural order a man might be a farmer, a priest, a merchant, or a craftsman, such as a carpenter or shoemaker, but under industrialism, with its specialization and division of labor, hundreds, and later thousands, of new occupations arose. As Adam Smith pointed out, however, the division of labor is limited by the extent of the market. That is, if one pair of shoes were to be made, it would be uneconomical to divide the work among many people, for one man could do it more cheaply; but if a thousand pairs of shoes were to be produced, then it would be cheaper for many men, each specializing in one particular operation, to produce the shoes. Thus, as economic growth took place and mass markets developed, work was more

---

[5] Kenneth E. Boulding, *Economics as a Science* (New York: McGraw-Hill, 1971), p. 123.

finely broken down, and individual workers found themselves doing more and more restricted tasks.

Unfree Labor in the American Colonies

By the time the American colonies were settled in the seventeenth century, feudalism was a thing of the past in England, so it never took hold on this side of the Atlantic Ocean; indeed, one of the foremost attractions of North America was the opportunity to become an independent farmer. Yet the colonial labor force was not primarily a free one. Many people lacked the means to pay for passage from Europe and indentured themselves to someone who would advance the fare for them; that is, they agreed to work for that person for a specified period of time to cover the money advanced. In addition to these redemptioners, often called "free-willers" because they had chosen to indenture themselves, some people were "kidnaped" and sold into servitude, and about fifty thousand convicts were sent to labor in the colonies.[6] Free men convicted of offenses in the colonies themselves could also be bound into servitude as their punishment, and debtors were often forced into servitude to satisfy their debts.

An indentured servant, although treated as property, had all legal rights except those specifically abridged by his indenture agreement, and he could even take his master to court for violation of their contract. The servant worked for board and lodgings but no pay, although there might be a payment in cash or kind, known as "freedom dues," at the conclusion of the period of service. He had to work for his master for a period of years, from two to seven; at the end of that period of service, however, he became a free man and part of the free labor supply of the colonies. Thus, although a significant part of the early colonial labor force was composed of white indentured servants, whose treatment was often harsh, their period of unfree labor was limited.

Another group of unfree workers, however, was not as fortunate, for their status was that of slaves. Unlike the white indentured servant the black slave, taken forcibly from Africa, had no legal rights other than those which were specifically granted to him by law. A slave's children also became slaves and the chattel property of the master, and there was no limit on his period of servitude unless his particular owner, of his own free will, decided to grant him freedom.

The institution of slavery is the greatest blight in American history, and it lasted longer than the practice of indentured servitude, which passed out of existence during the first few decades of the nineteenth century. Slavery, however, continued for almost a century after the Declaration of Independ-

---

[6] For a full description of the status of labor in the colonies, see Richard B. Morris, *Government and Labor in Early America* (New York: Columbia University Press, 1946), which has been the source of much of the material on indentured servitude covered here.

ence, and became an important economic institution with the growth, in the southern states, of the plantation system for raising such staple crops as tobacco, sugar, rice, and—much later—cotton.

The absence of large estates in the northern states made slavery unprofitable there, and this fact, combined with the opposition of free labor to slave labor and a drive for freedom by various religious groups on humanitarian grounds, led to its decline and early abolition in the North. Slavery did, however, persist and spread in the South, particularly following Eli Whitney's invention of the cotton gin, which made cotton production profitable and led to the widening search for new cotton lands. Time and again, conflicts between the North and the South over the extension of slavery into new territories threatened to dissolve the Union, and finally, in an act that precipitated the Civil War of 1861, the southern states, mainly to preserve the "peculiar institution" of slavery, attempted to secede from the Union.

Theoretically, the Thirteenth Amendment to the Constitution, which abolished involuntary servitude, made the blacks part of the nation's free labor supply, but in the South, where the greatest number of former slaves was concentrated, this was not the case for a long time to come. When initial attempts at wage labor failed to be profitable, the plantation system was replaced by sharecropping, a new system of labor that put the tenant farmer, either black or white, in a situation similar to that of the tenant farmer of the late medieval period in England and gave the planters superior control of their labor force than if they had used free labor.[7] With the decline in agriculture, the blacks moved to the northern urban centers, where they did become part of the free labor supply, but the white attitude toward them and their abilities has prevented them from fully enjoying the fruits of that freedom until this day.

The Labor Force

Since labor is a factor of production, the size of the aggregate labor supply is a key determinant of the amount of goods and services that an economy can produce. Of course, labor is not the sole determinant, because the amount and kinds of tools that men work with (capital) is also of extreme importance. Yet it is obvious that, with a given amount of capital, more workers can produce more goods and services than fewer could, so the size of the labor supply is also an important determinant of how much capital can be produced.

The size of the aggregate supply of labor depends upon the decisions of individuals, and in a free labor market the supply of labor consists of all those people who seek and are capable of performing work, either for themselves or for others, for remuneration. The hours that they are willing to work

---

[7] Barrington Moore, Jr., *Social Origins of Dictatorship and Democracy* (Boston: Beacon Press, 1966), p. 147.

and the effort with which they work also constitute part of the supply of labor, but we shall leave these subjects until later and focus instead on the number of people in the labor force.

The definition of the labor force essentially boils down to those ready, willing, and able to work. Thus, both those employed and those who are unemployed but looking for work are counted as being in the labor force. This concept of the labor force, then, is one that links work only with the market economy and ignores all other types of work, such as taking care of one's own home and going to school.

The "total labor force" consists of all persons classified as employed or unemployed, plus the members of the armed forces. The "civilian labor force" is comprised of all the employed and the unemployed. The 87 million in the labor force in 1971 included 84 million in the civilian labor force and 3 million in the armed forces. Our primary concern in this book is with the civilian labor force, and when we discuss the labor force it is that component to which we shall be referring.

Data on the labor force are gathered by the Bureau of Labor Statistics (BLS) of the United States Department of Labor through a monthly survey of 47,000 households. The statistics are reported in the bureau's publication, *Employment and Earnings.* The survey sample concerns those persons sixteen years of age and over who are not in institutions, such as mental hospitals and prisons. According to the answers provided by the persons in the survey sample, they are classified as either in the labor force or not in the labor force; the latter group consists primarily of housewives, retired persons, and students.

The type of attachment that individuals have to the labor force differs. Of the 84 million members of the civilian labor force in 1971, 72 million were full-time workers, and almost all of the other 12 million were part-time workers by choice. Many women, older people, and students, who do not want full-time employment, either work part time or seek part-time jobs, and so they are included in the labor force. The fact that they are only part-time workers, however, means that the effective labor supply is not equivalent to 84 million people, and might better be measured by the total number of hours worked.

Data on the labor force are collected as of a given moment in time, but people's circumstances and inclinations change from one point in time to another. The labor force, therefore, is not static, and within any given year people will be entering and leaving it at various times. A person who was working at the beginning of the year may retire during its course because he has reached the age of sixty-five. Students graduating from school in June will not have been in the labor force until then, but will seek jobs following graduation. Housewives may enter the labor force during those months in which their children are in school, but return to home chores during the summer vacation period and then go back into the labor force in September when the new school year starts. College students, on the other hand, will not be members of the labor force during the school year, but may very well seek jobs during the summer vacation.

The data do not reflect all individual decisions—as, for example, when one person drops out of the labor force but another enters it, for the two cancel each other out. The monthly data, however, do reflect net movements of people in and out of the labor force, and those net movements are significant. The figure of 84.1 million in the civilian labor force in 1971, thus, is an average for the year, but the actual number varied from one month to another, ranging from a low of 83.1 million in June to a high of 85.3 million in December.

Sources of Labor Supply

There are three major determinants of the size of the labor force at any given time: the size of the total population, the age composition of that population, and the participation rate (the percentage of the total group that actually seeks work) of the segments of the population. As a result of the operation of these three factors, the labor force of the United States, which was about 85 million at the start of the 1970s, is expected to expand to 100 million by 1980. This will come about because more workers will be entering the labor force (41 million) than will be retiring from it (26 million). Five out of every six of the 41 million additional workers will be young people getting out of school and seeking their first jobs. These youngsters—34 million of them—will be supplemented by 6 million women returning to the labor force after caring for their young children, and by 1 million immigrants. Let us now look at each of the three factors that determine the size of the labor force.

Population Size

The first and most important determinant of the labor supply is the size of the total population of the nation. The tremendous growth in the labor force of the United States in the past century, from 13 million in 1870 to 85 million in 1970, is explained primarily by the phenomenal increase in the nation's population. In this same time period the United States went from a nation of under 40 million people to one of 205 million people.

Natural increase, that is, the excess of births over deaths, partially accounts for this population surge, but for the first one hundred fifty years of U.S. history, until restrictive legislation was enacted in the 1920s, immigration from abroad accounted directly for better than one-third of the growth. Each wave of immigrants in turn had children who became part of the natural increase in population; there is no question, therefore, that had it not been for free immigration, the United States today would be a nation only a fraction of its present size, and its labor supply would be much smaller than it is.

Whether or not the population will continue to rise at the same rate as it has since World War II is questionable. The tremendous increase in the birthrate in the 1950s seemed to have peaked around 1957, and it has dropped since then. Changing attitudes toward marriage, the role of women in society, and preservation of the environment may indeed continue to hold down or still further lower the birthrate, but the nation still seems to be a long way from the zero population growth that some people advocate. Continued growth in the size of the labor force, therefore, can be anticipated, even though the rate of increase may diminish.

Age Distribution of the Population

The age distribution of the population is a second factor determining the size of the labor force. Babies and young children are not yet capable of performing work, and many older people no longer are. The greater the proportion of people who are very young or very old, therefore, the fewer there are available to the labor force.

Labor Force Participation Rates

The third factor explaining labor force size is the participation rate, that is, the percentage of the potential labor force who actually work or seek work. Obviously, almost all married men in the prime working ages of twenty-five to fifty-four are in the labor force (98 percent), but the same compulsions to earn a living do not apply to other sectors of the population. In 1971 61 percent of the total noninstitutional population sixteen years of age and over was in the labor force, and this percentage has not varied very greatly historically. A number of countervailing forces, however, have operated to maintain stability in the aggregate labor force participation rate through time. The participation rate of some groups in the population has risen, that of other groups has fallen, and the net result has been remarkable total stability.

One hundred fifty years ago it was not uncommon for a boy to start his lifetime work career at the age of nine or ten, but legislation regulating and prohibiting child labor, the extension of free public education, and changing social attitudes as the nation grew richer have virtually ended participation of the very young in the labor force. A reflection of this change is the fact that statistics on the working population used to be gathered for those ten years of age and older, but this lower age limit was later raised to fourteen; in 1967 it was raised again, this time to sixteen years. The lengthening of the period of schooling, moreover, keeps many young people from entering the labor force before their early, or even mid-, twenties. Thus, less than half of the sixteen- and seventeen-year-olds, and less than two-thirds of the eighteen- and nineteen-year-olds, are in the labor force, and many of those who are in the labor force are only part-time workers.

The labor force participation rate of older persons has also declined. In most cases a man used to work until he became too physically infirm or died, but over the years, particularly since the enactment of social security legislation in the 1930s and the spread of private pension systems in the 1950s and 1960s, older people have tended to choose retirement in preference to continued work. And even where older people might want to continue on the job, they often encounter compulsory retirement policies of their employers, usually at age sixty-five. Whereas at the turn of the century two out of every three men sixty-five years of age and over were still in the labor force, today less than one out of three are. In terms of total labor supply, however, retirement of a large portion of older workers has been balanced by an increase in the average life span; the average person, therefore, spends as many years in active employment as before.

One segment of the population—females—has increased its participation rates significantly, and this has greatly augmented the labor supply and counterbalanced the decline in participation of young and old males. Formerly, the role of women was considered to be in the home, but today two out of every five females sixteen years of age and over are in the labor force, and women account for more than one out of every three workers.

Influences on Labor Force Participation Rates

Changing attitudes toward the nurturing of children, retirement for the elderly, and the role of women have had important influences on the participation rate in the labor force. These attitudes in turn have developed within a context of economic growth and rising income. Since people value leisure as well as income, it requires an increase in the latter to induce some people to give up the former. As wages rose, therefore, many women were induced to seek work instead of remaining at home. At the same time higher earnings for family breadwinners reduced pressure to send the children to work at an early age. And as affluence increased further, the nation could afford to transfer a greater share of income to the elderly in the form of pensions, thus inducing more of them to quit the labor force.

Another important influence on the labor force participation rate, and hence on the supply of labor, is the demand for labor. When the labor market is tight—that is, when there are more jobs available than workers to fill them—employers offer higher wages, special work time schedules, and other inducements, which tend to draw housewives, retired people, and teenagers into the labor force. This is exactly what happened during World War II: in the four years between 1940 and 1944 the total labor force rose by the spectacular figure of 10 million, and the percentage of the potential labor force (the total noninstitutional population) that actually participated rose from 56 to 63. Similarly, when the labor market loosens up and employers begin laying off workers, some of those workers simply drop out of active search for another job and return to their former status as housewives, students, or retirees. Thus, as World War II came to an end the total labor force dropped by 5,330,000 in the one year between 1945 and 1946.

A result of this expansion and contraction of the labor force in response to the demand for labor is that the monthly unemployment figures do not necessarily accurately reflect the immediate condition of the economy. Thirty years ago, for instance, the hypothesis was advanced that the labor force expands as male workers are laid off during a decline in overall economic activity because their wives and children go out to seek jobs in order to provide some income for the family.[8] Others, however, have advanced the completely opposite thesis, that the labor force contracts as the economy declines because some workers become too discouraged to seek new jobs and simply drop out of the labor market.

There is some evidence to support the first proposition—the "additional workers" thesis—in individual cases. After having studied the data from a sample of the 1960 census, Bowen and Finegan concluded that for every hundred male household heads who become unemployed, six to eight "additional" wives may enter the labor force.[9] On the other hand, they found that school-attending sons of unemployed fathers do not drop out to seek work.[10]

The fact that some wives join the labor force when their husbands become unemployed need not contradict the "discouraged worker" thesis; while some wives of unemployed husbands may be induced to seek work, members of families not affected by unemployment may be induced not to seek work. The effect of higher unemployment on labor force participation will be the net result of these two contradictory movements, and the evidence is greater that the net effect is in favor of the discouraged worker hypothesis. In fact, Dernburg and Strand estimated that the net effect in the decade 1953–1962 was for one person to leave the labor force for every two who lost jobs,[11] but this probably exaggerates the net effect. Bowen and Finegan, in comparing labor force participation by married women in different labor market areas, found that the higher the unemployment rate in an area, the lower the proportion of married women who work or seek work.[12] Similarly, Mincer found that labor force participation is directly affected by short-run variations in the level of aggregate demand, and he attributed this fact primarily to the behavior of "secondary" workers.[13] Unlike the family breadwinner, these secondary workers—mainly the young, the old, and women—only supplement family income, and thus enter and leave the labor force depending upon the availability of jobs.

In spite of the growth of this secondary labor force, at any given time

---

[8] W. S. Woytinsky, *Three Aspects of Labor Dynamics* (Washington, D.C.: Social Science Research Council, 1940).

[9] William G. Bowen and T. Aldrich Finegan, *The Economics of Labor Force Participation* (Princeton: Princeton University Press, 1969), pp. 147–149.

[10] *Ibid.*, pp. 399–401.

[11] T. F. Dernburg and K. T. Strand, "Hidden Unemployment, 1953–62: A Quantitative Analysis by Age and Sex," *American Economic Review*, March 1966, pp. 71–95.

[12] Bowen and Finegan, *op. cit.*, pp. 178–180.

[13] Jacob Mincer, "Labor Force Participation and Unemployment: A Review of Recent Evidence," in Robert A. Gordon and Margaret S. Gordon, *Prosperity and Unemployment* (New York: Wiley, 1966), pp. 73–112.

about two out of every five persons sixteen years of age and over are not in any way attached to the labor market. Who are the nonparticipants in the labor force and why do they not seek work? In an attempt to answer these questions, the Department of Labor did a sample survey of the 53.3 million persons who were not in institutions but were also not in the labor force in 1968.[14] Of the total, 33 million, or 60 percent, did not seek work because of home responsibilities, and, as expected, almost all of them were women. Another 7 million, 13 percent of the 53.3 million, were going to school, 95 percent of these between the ages of sixteen and twenty-four and equally divided between men and women. About 5.5 million, or 10 percent of the nonparticipants, were not seeking work because of retirement or old age, and 4.3 million, 8 percent of the total, because of either ill health or disability. Of the 1 million persons who were classified as "not wanting a job at present," most of them could have cited other reasons for nonparticipation, particularly old age. Only 700,000 were not in the labor force because they believed it was impossible for them to find a job—"discouraged workers." It must be remembered, however, that 1968 was a year of relatively abundant employment opportunities; in years of higher unemployment more workers may drop out of active pursuit of a job because they become discouraged about prospects for finding one.

Industrial Distribution of the Labor Force

People generally prefer some income to no income and more income to less income. Workers, therefore, gravitate to those industries in which there are job openings and which offer the best pay and working conditions. Thus, those industries which are expanding output in response to consumer demand for their goods or services will also probably be growing in numbers of employees. Employment, however, may not be rising as fast as production, because productivity—the output per input of labor—may also be increasing as a result of technological innovation. Since consumer tastes change over time, since new products are developed, and since productivity increases at different rates among industries, the industrial distribution of the labor force shifts over the years.

The Decline of Agriculture and Mining

The changing distribution of the labor force is most obvious with respect to agriculture. When the United States was founded, the majority of people— about 80 percent—were engaged in agriculture, but today less than 10 percent are. This tremendous shift away from farming is due to two factors: (1) the demand for agricultural products and (2) the productivity of the industry.

---

[14] Paul O. Flaim, "Persons Not in the Labor Force: Who They Are and Why They Don't Work," *Monthly Labor Review*, July 1969, pp. 3–14.

To understand the demand aspects, it should be remembered that the basic wants of man are for food, clothing, and shelter. Since food is a basic need of man, he must satisfy it first before purchasing less essential products. In economics terminology it is said that the demand for food, the major agricultural product, is inelastic; that is, people, having satisfied their basic needs for it, do not purchase much more food as a result of cither their incomes going up or the prices of food products declining. The increase in demand for agricultural products, therefore, is largely limited to the increase in the population.

The second factor is even more important in explaining the decline in the agricultural work force, for, as a result of the substitution of capital for labor on the farms, farm output per worker has been increasing much faster than in the rest of the economy. In the years since World War II, for example, labor productivity in agriculture has risen 5.7 percent per year, but productivity for the entire economy only about 3 percent. Since the 5.7 percent annual rate of increase in productivity (output per man-hour) was accompanied by only a 1.4 percent increase in farm output, people have been moving out of agriculture; the average annual net out-migration was 1.3 million for the decade of the 1940s, 1 million in the 1950s, and 750,000 in the 1960s.[15] This out-migration has been most pronounced among young people, who have left farms for the greater opportunities in other industries, usually in urban areas.

The decline in the number of people involved in farming, however, is a phenomenon only of the twentieth century. Until the early years of the twentieth century the rapid increase in the nation's population caused an absolute increase in the number of people engaged in agriculture as owners, tenants, or laborers. As a percentage of total employment, however, agriculture had declined steadily, from three out of every four persons at the time the nation was established to one out of two by the 1850s. The total number of people engaged in farming reached its height of 11.5 million in 1906,[16] but by then farm workers represented only slightly more than one out of every three members of the labor force. Since then the decline has been absolute as well as relative, as the rate of population growth tapered off and productivity growth increased. In the six and one-half decades since 1906, agricultural employment has dropped by 70 percent, and the 3.4 million employed in agriculture in 1971 equaled only 4.3 percent of total employment.

Another primary industry that has suffered severe reductions in employment is mining; its labor force today of under 700,000 is half a million below what it was half a century ago. The substitution of petroleum and

---

[15] C. E. Bishop, "The Need for Improved Mobility Policy," in John A. Delahenty (ed.), *Manpower Problems and Policies* (Scranton: International Textbook Company, 1969), p. 244.

[16] Stanley Lebergott, *Manpower in Economic Growth* (New York: McGraw-Hill, 1964), p. 512.

natural gas for coal as a fuel and the rapid increase in mining productivity are the main reasons for this trend.

The Rise of Manufacturing and Other Industries

Employment in manufacturing, on the other hand, increased steadily as the nation became more and more of an industrial power. By 1840 500,000 people were employed in manufacturing; by 1860, 1.5 million; by 1890, 4.5 million; and by 1910, over 8 million. In 1969 manufacturing employment was almost double the 10.5 million it had been in 1919. Manufacturing, however, has also enjoyed rapid increases in productivity as a result of improved technology, and in relative terms manufacturing employment peaked at the conclusion of the First World War at about 27 percent of the labor force; as Table 1.1 shows, by 1968 it was only 25 percent.

Focusing on what has transpired in the past half century, we find that the figure of 4 million people employed in contract construction is about double what it was in 1919, and the 4 million in finance, insurance, and real estate is about three and one-half times the number employed in each in 1919. Employment in wholesale and retail trade has done almost as well, climbing from 5 million to 16.5 million people. Transportation and public utilities, with an employment of 4.5 million, however, have grown barely 20 percent since 1919. The most dramatic increases in employment have been in services (including business and repair services, personal services, entertainment and recreation services, and professional and related services) and government; the former has grown fivefold since 1919 to 11.75 million, and the latter four and one-half times, to 12.25 million by 1969.

The Shift from Goods Producing to Service Producing

The general picture that emerges is that of a relative, and in some cases absolute, shift of employment away from those industries that produce goods (mining, contract construction, manufacturing, and agriculture) to those that produce services (wholesale and retail trade, transportation and public utilities, finance, insurance and real estate, service, and government). Again, there are two basic explanations of this trend. In the first place, as Americans have grown richer they have found that their incomes allow them to buy the physical goods they want and still have money left to spend on other things, such as vacations, eating out, going to beauty parlors, and the like. Second, it has been easier, up to now, to substitute machines for people in goods-producing than in service-producing industries. Productivity in most goods-producing industries, therefore, tends to rise more rapidly than in most service-producing industries; more automated machinery permits factories to turn out more products than formerly, but the barber, with his comb and scissors, cuts no more heads of hair today than he did ten, twenty, or fifty years ago.

These trends, moreover, are expected to continue into the future. As can be seen in Table 1.1, the Department of Labor estimates that between 1968 and 1980 there will be an increase in employment of more than 30 percent in service-producing industries but only 9 percent in goods-producing industries.[17] In fact, two goods-producing industries—agriculture and mining —are expected to continue their absolute declines and to contract by 1 million more jobs during the decade of the 1970s. Manufacturing, which is expected to provide 2.25 million additional jobs by 1980, will actually be growing more slowly than during the 1960s, and thus will fall from 25 percent to 22.5 percent of total employment. Among the goods producers, only construction is expected to show a more rapid rate of employment growth in the decade, raising its share of total employment from 5 to 5.5 percent. As the Labor Department points out, "This modest employment expansion, overall, for goods-producing industries, in the face of an overall healthy increase in output, reflects, of course, their rising productivity."[18]

Table 1.1 Changes in Employment by Industry Sector,[a] 1968 (Actual) and 1980 (Projected), (in thousands)

Industry Sector	1968		1980		Change	
	No.	Percent	No.	Percent	No.	Percent
Goods producing						
Manufacturing	20,125	24.9	22,358	22.4	+ 2,233	+11.1
Agriculture	4,154	5.1	3,188	3.2	− 966	−23.4
Construction	4,050	5.0	5,482	5.5	+ 1,432	+35.4
Mining	646	.8	590	.6	− 56	− 8.7
Total[b]	28,975	35.9	31,618	31.7	+ 2,643	+ 9.1
Service producing						
Service industries	15,113	18.7	21,080	21.2	+ 5,967	+39.5
Trade	16,604	20.6	20,487	20.6	+ 3,883	+23.4
Transportation, communication, and public utilities	4,524	5.6	4,976	5.0	+ 452	+10.0
Finance, insurance, and real estate	3,726	4.6	4,639	4.7	+ 913	+27.2
Government	11,846	14.7	16,800	16.9	+ 4,954	+41.8
Total[b]	51,813	64.1	67,982	68.3	+16,169	+31.2
Grand Total	80,788	100.0	99,600	100.0	+18,812	+23.3

[a] Based on the projections for a services economy and a 3 percent unemployment rate; slightly different 1980 figures are projected for a durable economy and a 4 percent unemployment rate.

[b] Subtotals will not always add exactly because figures are rounded to the nearest tenth.

SOURCE: U.S. Department of Labor.

[17] "The U.S. Economy in 1980: A Preview of BLS Projections," *Monthly Labor Review*, April 1970, pp. 3–34.

[18] *Ibid.*, p. 17.

Figure 1.1   Nonagricultural Payroll Employment by Industry, 1953 to 1972

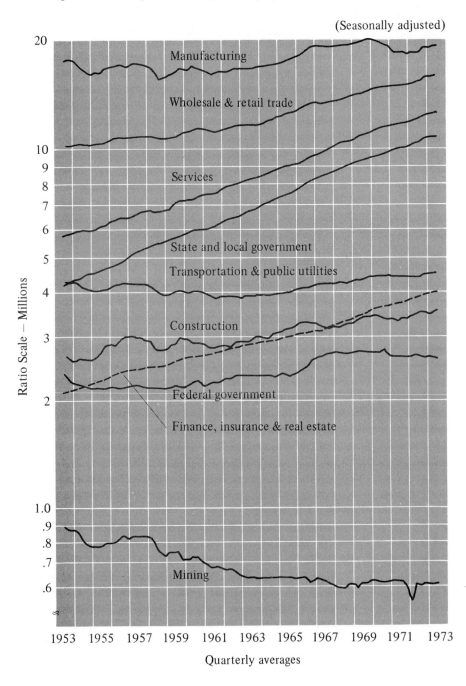

(Seasonally adjusted)

SOURCE: U.S. Bureau of Labor Statistics

The dramatic shift of employment into the service-producing industries will continue. In the early 1900s only three out of every ten workers were in these industries, but by 1950 five out of ten were, by 1965 six out of ten were, and by 1980 almost seven out of every ten workers will be. Among the service-producing industries, that of transportation, communication, and public utilities, while growing by 400,000 employees, will decline relatively, due both to the continued drop in railroad employment and to the expected high increase in productivity in public utilities and communications. Employment in the trade and finance, insurance, and real estate industries will expand about as rapidly as total employment, as the introduction of electronic data processing, vending machines, and the like slow down their growth of recent decades. Services, not enjoying rapid technological change that would boost their productivity, but benefiting from the growth in population and income, will increase employment 38 percent as people expand their demand for medical, educational, and other services. The fastest-growing service area will be health services, jobs in which will grow almost 90 percent, from 800,000 in 1968 to 1.5 million by 1980. Government employment, which grew 4.5 percent a year from 1960 to 1968, will continue to expand, but only at a 2.8 percent rate and almost entirely at the state and local government levels.

Composition of the Labor Force

Not only do jobs shift from one industry to another, but vast changes also take place within the labor force, as people respond to structural changes in the economy and their views of proper roles to play in society are altered. These changes in the composition of the labor force include its occupational structure, the male-female ratio, age structure, educational attainment, and race. Each of these will be examined briefly.

Occupation

The kinds of work that people do has changed drastically over the years. As we have seen, in colonial days four out of five people were farmers or farm laborers, but by 1900 only 20 percent of the "gainful workers" (a slightly different concept from "labor force," but close enough to permit comparisons from one period to another) [19] were farmers or farm managers and 17.5 per-

---

[19] Under that definition, persons who had gainful occupations, whether or not they were pursuing them at the time of the census, were included in the labor force. Today people who have ceased seeking work, even temporarily, would not be counted in the labor force, but, in the earlier period, as long as they reported a gainful occupation they would have been. On the other hand, people who have recently left school to seek their first jobs are included in the labor force under present definitions, but many of them would not have been counted in the earlier period because they had no gainful occupations. Even so, the gainful worker statistics are considered to be a generally reliable measure of long-term trends in the labor force.

cent farm laborers.[20] The absolute decline in agricultural employment during this century reduced the proportion of people who were either farmers or farm laborers to one out of five by 1930, and to less than one out of ten today. As can be seen in Table 1.2, the number engaged in farming will drop by almost another 1 million by 1980, as machines continue to replace men in the production process; as a percentage of total employment, farmers and farm workers will decline from 4.6 in 1968 to 2.7 in 1980.

Table 1.2 Occupational Employment, 1968 (Actual) and 1980 (Projected) (in thousands)

	1968		1980		Change	
Occupation	No.	Percent	No.	Percent	No.	Percent
White-collar[a]	35.6	46.5	48.3	50.8	+12.7	+35.7
Professional, technical, and kindred	10.3	13.6	15.5	16.3	+ 5.2	+50.5
Managers, officials, and proprietors	7.8	10.0	9.5	10.0	+ 1.7	+21.8
Clerical	12.8	16.9	17.3	18.2	+ 4.5	+35.2
Sales	4.6	6.1	6.0	6.3	+ 1.4	+32.6
Blue-collar[a]	27.5	36.3	31.1	32.7	+ 3.6	+13.1
Craftsmen and foremen	10.0	13.2	12.2	12.8	+ 2.2	+22.0
Operatives	14.0	18.4	15.4	16.2	+ 1.4	+10.0
Nonfarm laborers	3.6	4.7	3.5	3.7	− .1	− 2.8
Service workers	9.4	12.4	13.1	13.8	+ 3.7	+39.4
Farm workers	3.5	4.6	2.6	2.7	− .9	−25.7
Total	76.0	99.9	95.1	100.0	+19.1	+25.1

[a] Subtotals will not always add exactly because figures are rounded to the nearest tenth.

SOURCE: U.S. Department of Labor.

The decline in farming has also meant a decline in the proportion of the labor force that is self-employed, since farmers were the largest group of independent businessmen. Even so, there are still large numbers of people who are independent entrepreneurs, including professionals, such as physicians and lawyers; craftsmen who do repair and contract work, such as plumbers and electricians; and the proprietors of small, unincorporated businesses, such as retail stores. As a result of the drastic decline in the number of people who run their own farms, however, the vast majority of participants in the labor force—five out of every six—are employees who work for an organization, private or public, that pays them wages or salaries for their contribution to its mission. Half of them, moreover, work for large organizations—those which employ a hundred or more people—and more than a third work for very large organizations—those which employ a thousand or more people.

---

[20] Gertrude Bancroft, *The American Labor Force* (New York: Wiley, 1958), p. 209.

Figure 2.6 Employment in Nonfarm Occupations, 1958 to 1972[a]

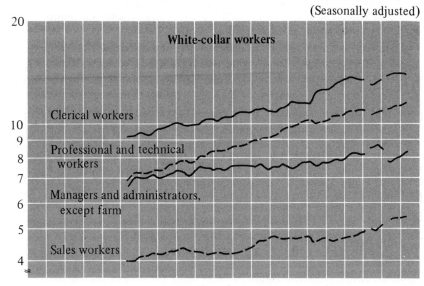

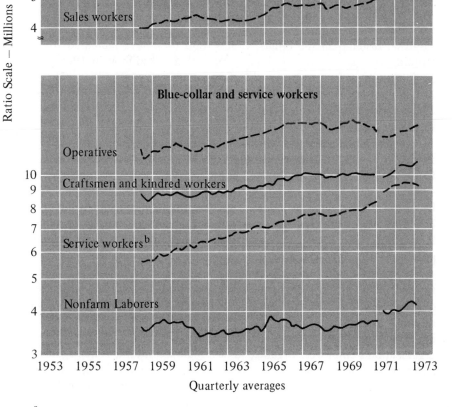

Quarterly averages

[a] The breaks in series in 1971 stem from the reclassification of occupations introduced in January and from a questionnaire change concerning "major activity" introduced in December.

[b] Excludes private household workers.

SOURCE: U.S. Bureau of Labor Statistics

Indeed, it is this group of wage and salary workers and their behavior in the labor market that is the focus of our attention in this book.

The United States is the world's leading manufacturing nation, but precisely because of this it has shifted from a production to a service economy. The tremendous increase in productivity has led to a need for relatively fewer workers in direct production, and the gains in government employment, in indirect production, and in the service sectors of private industry, both profit and nonprofit, have given rise to vast new employment opportunities in white-collar occupations. In 1900 about two in five of the working population were engaged in manual occupations—as craftsmen, operatives, and nonfarm laborers—and less than one in five had white-collar jobs—professional, managerial, clerical, and sales jobs.[21] The white-collar group of occupations, however, has been growing most rapidly for more than half a century, and by 1956, for the first time, white-collar occupations outnumbered blue-collar ones; by 1980 the ratio will be better than 3 to 2. In fact, as Table 1.2 shows, white-collar occupations will account for about half of all employed workers.

Within the white-collar group, professional jobs—engineers, technicians, teachers, physical and social scientists—have been growing, and are expected to grow, faster than the others. Since 1890 they have increased in number tenfold, from less than 1 million to more than 10 million in 1968. By 1980 professionals will jump by another fifty percent to 15.5 million. The growth in this high-talent manpower results from population growth, the expansion of the national economy, the spread of science and technology, and the urbanization of the population.

A second category of white-collar occupations—managers, officials, and proprietors—comprising one out of every ten workers in 1968—will continue to grow about as fast as total employment. Within this category, however, significant changes have been taking place. As the size of the business unit has grown, the number of independent proprietors has declined but the number of salaried managers has expanded rapidly. The decline in the number of farms, of course, has contributed significantly to the historic drop in the number of self-employed proprietors.

Although managers and officials are employees of the corporation, they represent the stockholder owners, and therefore, in most of our discussions of labor relations, they will not be considered part of "labor." Managers are responsible for directing the affairs of the organization, and one of their most important functions is the management of the firm's work force. When an organization's employees organize, as we shall see later, it is management that negotiates the terms and conditions of employment with the unions that represent those employees. Thus, although in labor relations we make a clear distinction between labor and management, in analyzing the nation's labor force we consider managers as one type of occupation.

The largest single group of white-collar employees is composed of those

---

[21] *Ibid.*, p. 35.

who hold clerical jobs in offices, factories, and warehouses. A century ago there were very few clerical workers, because record keeping was incidental to the main job of business—producing goods and services. As the American economy became more complex, and as both larger business units and government intervention into business affairs became more common, record keeping, management planning, and control operations increased in importance. With the proliferation of paper work within the American economy, clerical jobs grew phenomenally, from less than 1 million in 1900 to 5 million in 1940 and 12.8 million—or one out of every six jobs—in 1968. Although clerical jobs will continue to grow faster than total employment in the 1970s, it will be at a slower rate than in the 1960s, as rapid technological developments in the field of computers, office equipment, and communications devices become more widespread in application. These technological changes, moreover, will reduce the need for some types of clerical jobs—those involved in filing, payroll, inventory control, and customer billing—while expanding the need for others—clerical personnel to prepare computer inputs.

The expansion of trade and the greater attention paid by business to the selling of the myriad of products and services that it turns out increased the demand for sales personnel, whose numbers rose from 1.25 million in 1900 to 3.5 million in 1940 and 4.5 million in 1968. By 1980 there will be 6 million sales jobs, which will continue to account for somewhat above 6 percent of the labor force.

As the United States developed into a great industrial power, blue-collar jobs expanded, but, with the onset of a period of slow economic growth in the mid-1950s, blue-collar employment actually started to decline in absolute numbers. Then, as the American economy began to expand more rapidly after 1963, blue-collar jobs began to increase again—but much more slowly than white-collar and service ones. Thus, although there will be 3.5 million more blue-collar workers in 1980 than there were in 1968, they will decline relatively, to less than one out of every three workers.

The most skilled occupations within the blue-collar group—craftsmen, foremen, and kindred workers—will be growing most rapidly, from 10 million in 1968 to 12.2 million in 1980, an increase of 22 percent, slightly less than the expected 25 percent increase in total employment. The growth among operatives, basically semiskilled workers, will only be 10 percent, from 14 million to 15.4 million, dropping this occupational category from one out of every five and one-half jobs to only one in seven. These types of occupations had historically been the ones that had grown most rapidly as the United States became a great manufacturing nation and made such great technological innovations as the assembly line, the hallmark of mass production. In more recent years, however, technological innovation has changed in character from further mechanization to automation, and this has meant a reduction in the need for direct production work and an increase in maintenance and technical employment.

Completely unskilled work has been even more adversely affected, and by mechanization as well as automation. At one time a good deal of the handling of materials within a factory depended upon human brawn: men lifted apparatus, shoveled sand and other raw materials, and wheeled things from one place to another, all by manual labor. Over the years, however, the handling of materials has been mechanized through such devices as forklift trucks, conveyor belts, and buckets that automatically tip liquids into pots. As a result, the need for laborers has been declining for many decades, both in absolute numbers as well as in relative terms. Thus, although the Labor Department anticipates a rise of 2.25 million in manufacturing employment by 1980, it expects no change in the number of nonfarm laborers—3.5 million —and a further decline in their share of employment, from 4.7 to 3.7 percent.

As population has grown, income has increased, business activity has expanded, and people have had more leisure time, the American economy has become increasingly service oriented, and so service types of jobs (a broad classification encompassing occupations as diverse as waitressing and police work) have grown rapidly, from 2.5 million in 1900 to 7 million in 1940 and 9.5 million in 1968. The kinds of service jobs have changed even more; in 1900 half the service workers, almost all women, were private household workers, but today only one in six is employed in domestic service. A further 40 percent increase in service jobs will bring the total number in service occupations to over 13 million by 1980.

Sex

One of the most dramatic shifts in the composition of the labor force has been the influx of women into it. Mechanical aids that have relieved homemaking chores—refrigerators, washing machines, vacuum cleaners, and easy-to-prepare foods, for instance—combined with changing social attitudes toward the role of females in our society, have greatly augmented the supply of female labor. At the same time the commercialization of activities formerly conducted at home, such as the making of clothes, led to a vast increase in the demand for women workers. Women have responded to this demand, particularly as salaries have risen, by entering the labor force in increasing numbers.

Thus, after World War I, it became commonplace for young women to go to work following graduation from high school and college. But, after a few years, with the onset of marriage and childbearing, women would retire from active employment and remain housewives the rest of their lives. Since World War II, however, the distinctive new trend has been for women to reenter the labor force when their children are grown, and until a few years ago the most rapid increases were taking place among women forty-five to sixty-four years of age. The growing drive by women for complete status equality with men can be seen in the fact that, in the last few years, labor force participation rates have been increasing sharply among women twenty to forty-four, even when they are mothers of preschool-age children. Of the 18.5 million wives who were working in 1970, over 10 million were mothers.

As a result of these trends, today four out of every ten women are working, double the proportion (two out of ten) in 1890. The continuation of these trends means that by 1980 more than half the women eighteen to twenty-four years of age and those thirty-five to sixty-four will be active participants in the labor market. Only in the case of women twenty-five to thirty-four, the prime years of childbearing, will less than half be in the labor force, but, even among this group, 46.5 percent will be.[22] The 31.5 million female workers in 1970 constituted 36 percent of the total labor force; in the 1980s 37 million female workers will comprise 37 percent.[23]

Age

The age composition of the labor force has also undergone significant change over time. As we have already seen, the very young and the old have become declining proportions of the nation's labor supply. In 1890 over 37 percent of youngsters fourteen to nineteen years of age were in the labor force, but by 1955, despite the increasing tendency of girls to work, only 29 percent were. With the rise in the school-leaving age and the decline of the employment of youngsters in even part-time work, data are no longer collected for those under sixteen.

Increasing longevity has led to an increase in the number of older citizens: in 1900 there were only 1.5 million persons sixty-five years old, but by 1970 there were close to 20 million. Yet only 3 million older persons, about 15 percent of the total, remain in the labor force, reflecting the spread of and rise in government and private pensions. At the same time the upsurge in the birthrate that began in the 1940s has meant more children both absolutely and as a percentage of the total population. The fact that there were more children and more oldsters meant that there were relatively fewer people in between; the percentage of the population in the prime working ages, twenty through sixty-four, dropped from 59 in 1940 to 51 by 1970. That this has not reduced the supply of labor, and that 40 percent of the total population continues to be in the labor force, is explained by the increased participation of women.

The age composition of the labor force changed significantly during the 1960s as the young people who had been born in the 1940s, when the birthrate started to rise, began to seek their first jobs. In fact, more than half of the labor growth during the 1960s was accounted for by young people under the age of twenty-five. By 1970, however, the age structure of the population

---

[22] Sophia C. Travis, "The U.S. Labor Force: Projections to 1985," *Monthly Labor Review*, May 1970.

[23] Finegan points out, however, that most projections of U.S. labor force participation rates have seriously underestimated the rise in rates for women during the years since World War II, and he believes that this is still the case. If he is correct, then women will comprise a larger portion of the labor force in 1980 than the 37 percent projected by the Bureau of Labor Statistics. See T. Aldrich Finegan, "Labor Force Growth and the Return to Full Employment," *Monthly Labor Review*, February 1972, pp. 29–39.

had stabilized, and young workers will account for only a little over one-quarter of the labor force growth of the 1970s. Indeed, the most rapidly expanding age group during this decade will be the twenty-five to thirty-four group.

This changing age structure of the labor force should help to ease some of the adjustment problems that were common in the last decade, when young people under twenty-five years of age were flooding the labor market. The economy had a rough time absorbing all those inexperienced young people, who themselves were less firmly attached to the labor force and more prone to engage in job-hopping and the quitting of jobs that seemed uninteresting. Their very high rates of unemployment became a source of social tension, particularly in urban slums. With relatively fewer of them entering the labor market each year during the 1970s, it should be easier to slot them into meaningful jobs—assuming, of course, that the nation experiences satisfactory rates of economic growth. Generally high unemployment rates in the early 1970s, for example, were accompanied by continuing severe employment problems for young workers.

The fact that the twenty-five through thirty-four age group should be the most rapidly expanding might also be good news for employers and the nation, because by the time a person has reached this age bracket, he is more likely to have settled down; established a firm attachment to the labor market; and, because of growing family responsibilities, be more concerned with job tenure, income security, and career development. Those in this age group who would be seeking rapid advancement in their careers would also benefit by the relative decline, from 40 to 35 percent, of workers in the key age group, thirty-five to fifty-four. This growth of the twenty-five through thirty-four age group, however, could present new problems for employers if some of the ideas of the youth rebellion of the late 1960s persist among these workers—a subject we shall discuss further in the next chapter.

The relative decline of the thirty-five through fifty-four age group could result in shortages of experienced skilled workers in some sectors. In fact, among male workers this group will hardly increase in size at all, a continuing reflection of the low birthrates of the 1930s, the depression decade. Male workers in the forty-five through fifty-four category, the source of management leadership, will drop absolutely by 300,000. This shortage of potential male executives should not only allow younger men to move up faster, but should help to open managerial ranks to heretofore discriminated-against minority and women workers.

Education

Labor force participation tends to rise with the number of years of schooling completed, and another significant and continuing trend in the labor force is its rising educational level. In fact, the spread of universal education has been coincident with the rise of an industrial economy, for even the most unskilled factory laborer must be able to read simple instructions in order to operate a piece of machinery properly.

More advanced technology, such as automation, demands of employees still more advanced educational backgrounds and levels of skill. This need has been reflected in the higher educational attainment of American workers over time. In 1942 the median number of years of schooling completed by workers aged eighteen and over was 10.4, but by 1970 it was 12.4. Rising educational attainments can be seen most dramatically by comparison of different age groups: thus, in 1970 workers sixty-five years of age and over had completed 9.6 years of school; those between fifty-five and sixty-four, 11.8 years; those between forty-five and fifty-four, 12.3 years; those between thirty-five and forty-four, 12.4 years; and those under thirty-five, 12.6 years. In 1950 only 35 percent of the population fifteen years old and over had graduated from high school; by 1960 41 percent had; by 1970, 48 percent had; and by 1980, 56 percent will have. The relative increase in college graduates is even greater. Of the population twenty years old and over, 6 percent had graduated from college in 1950; the percentage was 7.5 in 1960, 9 in 1970, and by 1980 it will be 11.3 percent.

The rising educational level of the labor force is also linked with the changes in occupation. The shift into white-collar work, particularly professional and technical occupations, has been a key factor in this advancing educational attainment. In fact, the amount of schooling that people have rises as the occupational ladder is ascended: for example, the median number of years of school completed in 1970 was 16.3 for professional and technical workers; 12.7 for managers, officials, and proprietors; 12.6 for clerical and sales workers; 12.1 for craftsmen and foremen; 11.3 for operatives; 10.5 for nonfarm laborers; and only 8.6 (1967 data) for farm laborers.

Race

The proportion of blacks in the labor force is also rising. The increase in black workers is due to higher birthrates, and so it will be most marked among the teen-age and young twenties group. While the number of white workers will grow by one-fifth between 1968 and 1980, the number of black workers will rise by one-third, to a total of 12 million.

Labor force participation rates differ substantially between whites and blacks: it is lower among black males and higher among black females. While 80 percent of white males sixteen years of age and over were participants in the civilian labor force in 1970, only 76.5 percent of blacks and other races were.[24] When educational attainment, age, and marital status are taken into account, however, most of the difference in labor force participation between white and black men in the prime working ages, twenty-five through

---

[24] *Manpower Report of the President, 1971* (Washington, D.C.: U.S. Government Printing Office, 1971), p. 209.

fifty-four, disappears.[25] The fact that there are significant differences in educational attainment and marital status between blacks and whites means, however, that fewer of the former participate in the labor force. Much of that lower participation may reflect the "discouraged worker" syndrome, as black males who suffer long spells of unemployment simply give up the search for jobs as hopeless.

Although the lower labor force participation of black men is of recent origin, black women have always had a higher labor force participation rate than white women. Low earnings of black men and the much higher proportion of families headed by females have forced more black women to seek work. Thus, half of black women sixteen years and over, but only 42.5 percent of white women, were in the labor force in 1970. The differences between white and black women in labor force participation, however, are declining as working outside the home has become more common for white women. At the same time it is assumed that as black men find better employment opportunities opening up to them, black women will be under less pressure to work. Thus, by 1980 it is projected that only 47 percent of black women will be in the labor force, while the percentage of white women will have risen, so that the two rates will be almost the same.

Summary

As we have seen in this chapter, the free labor market had emerged in England by the eighteenth century as part of the development of a laissez-faire, private-enterprise economic system. Capitalist industrialism, however, brought a sharp distinction between worker and employer, with the former being dependent upon the latter for his opportunity to earn a livelihood, but with the employer owing the worker nothing more than remuneration for the services provided. The employer-employee relationship, thus, was a purely pecuniary one, without status connotations, and workers and employers were free to break those relationships as they saw fit and to form new ones.

Under this exchange relationship labor became a factor of production, which employers combined with the other factors of production—land and capital—to produce goods and services for sale to consumers. Free labor became the dominant institution through which work was performed in the United States, but in the early years of the nation indentured servitude was important, and until a century ago southern agriculture utilized slave labor. Even after slavery was abolished, however, the former black slaves, as well as other ethnic minorities, suffered from discrimination in the labor market.

Two out of every five persons in the United States, and three out of every five noninstitutionalized persons sixteen years of age and older, are in the labor force; that is, they either have jobs or are seeking work. The labor force has grown as the population has expanded, but the particular groups

---

[25] Bowen and Finegan, *op. cit.*, pp. 51, 52.

comprising that labor force have changed dramatically, as the participation rates of young and old males have declined while that of women has risen sharply. The labor force, however, is not constant, even within a given year, but expands and contracts at different times as members of the "secondary labor force"—housewives, students, and older people—enter and leave the job market.

The employments of the labor force have also changed quite dramatically in the past two hundred years. The big shift was away from agriculture and into industrial pursuits, but in recent years it has been from goods-producing to service-producing industries. Higher incomes for the population and a more rapid increase in productivity in the goods-producing industries explain these shifts in employment. These shifts have been accompanied by changes in the occupational structure of the labor force, with relatively fewer people being needed for direct production jobs but more for jobs that are indirectly related to the actual turning out of goods and services. This has meant a shift from blue-collar to white-collar occupations, and from unskilled to skilled ones.

The labor force has also been changing in structure in terms of sex— becoming more female—and in terms of age—having fewer very young and very old members—and one of the most dramatic trends in the labor force has been its rising educational level. Also, differentials in birthrates have meant an increase in the proportion of the labor force that is black.

BIBLIOGRAPHY

Bancroft, Gertrude. *The American Labor Force.* New York: Wiley, 1958.

Boulding, Kenneth E. *Economics as a Science.* New York: McGraw-Hill, 1970.

Bowen, William G., and Finegan, T. Aldrich. *The Economics of Labor Force Participation.* Princeton: Princeton University Press, 1969.

Delahenty, John A. *Manpower Problems and Policies.* Scranton: International Textbook Company, 1969.

Easterlin, Richard A. *Population, Labor Force, and Long Swings in Economic Growth.* Princeton: National Bureau of Economic Research and Princeton University Press, 1968.

Gordon, Robert A., and Gordon, Margaret S. *Prosperity and Unemployment.* New York: Wiley, 1966.

Heaton, Herbert. *Economic History of Europe.* New York: Harper & Bros., 1936.

Lebergott, Stanley. *Manpower in Economic Growth.* New York: McGraw-Hill, 1964.

Long, Clarence D. *The Labor Force Under Changing Income and Employment.* Princeton: National Bureau of Economic Research and Princeton University Press, 1958.

Manpower Report of the President. Washington, D.C.: U.S. Government Printing Office, annually.

Moore, Barrington, Jr. *Social Origins of Dictatorship and Democracy.* Boston: Beacon Press, 1966.

Morris, Richard B. *Government and Labor in Early America.* New York: Columbia University Press, 1946.

Muller, Herbert F. *The Uses of the Past.* New York: Oxford University Press, 1957.

Pirenne, Henri. *Economic and Social History of Medieval Europe.* London: Routledge & Kegan Paul, 1961.

Wolfbein, Seymour L. *Employment and Unemployment in the United States.* Chicago: Science Research Associates, 1964.

Woytinsky, W. S. *Three Aspects of Labor Dynamics.* Washington, D.C.: Social Science Research Council, 1940.

"The U.S. Economy in 1980: A Preview of BLS Projections," *Monthly Labor Review,* April 1970.

2 WORKERS AND EMPLOYERS

With the separation of the functions of employer and employee and the emergence of a frce labor market, labor became, as we have seen, a commodity to be bought and sold—an exchange relationship that was, however, complicated by the peculiarity of the commodity, which embodied human effort. Inanimate objects, such as chairs and tables, may be bought and sold without reference to their feelings or attitudes, because they have none. Labor power, however, is derived from human beings, who do have attitudes and feelings; as a result, no matter how impersonal the market tries to make it, the exchange does involve interpersonal relations. In order to help us understand the evolving economic relationship between labor and management, therefore, we shall focus our attention in this chapter on the social structure and on matters of status and attitudes. We shall examine the concept of class structure, the changes in management ideology, why American labor has not developed along European class struggle lines, differences in attitudes among social classes, and worker attitudes in today's affluent society.

Class Structure

The Nature of Social Classes

All human societies have a social system in which groups of people are differentiated from one another in terms of status. These groupings, known as social classes, differ from one another in their mode of living.[1] This can be seen quite clearly in terms of residence; in every city there are some neighborhoods that are considered to be lower class, others that are working class, some that are middle class, and still others that are upper class. The Lower East Side of New York, for instance, has been known as a lower-class neighborhood for a century, even though its particular residents have changed, while Grosse Point, Michigan, is a wealthy upper-class suburb of Detroit in which many of the automobile executives live.

Classes also differ from each other in the way their members dress and speak, and in the amount and kinds of education they have. Members of a particular class, moreover, tend to behave differently toward members of

---

[1] Many of the basic concepts expressed here were absorbed by the author in courses on social stratification with Professor Emeritus Carl Mayer of the Graduate Faculty of the New School for Social Research some years ago, and links with the stratification concepts formulated by Max Weber will be apparent.

other classes than toward members of their own class. This is most evident with respect to connubium—intermarriage—and commensuality—social intercourse. Most people tend to associate with others who are more or less in the same type of life situation as they; segregation at work by occupation and at home by residence, of course, promotes this social class separation.

Differences in mode of living need not imply higher and lower, as does a class structure, so something more must be involved. A social class, therefore, can be defined as a portion of society that is marked off from the rest by social status. Such social status gives its possessor a degree of prestige, honor, influence, and power, regardless of his personal qualities, and it emanates from the fact that a society evaluates some things more highly than it does others. In the words of Talcott Parsons, "Stratification in its valuational aspect, then, is the ranking of units in a social system in accordance with the standards of the common value system."[2]

Evolution of the Capitalist Class Structure

As we saw in the last chapter, under feudalism the class structure was tripartite: nobility, clergy, and the masses of peasants. Since in feudal society land ownership, military exploits, and religion were viewed as the most important aspects of life (as exemplified by the feudal lord, who owned land, conducted military campaigns, and was a "defender of the faith"), the nobility and the clergy formed the upper classes and the rest of the people comprised the lower class. In France this tripartite social structure was formalized into the three estates of aristocracy, clergy, and common people.

A social system can exist as long as the fundamental assumptions of what is important to the society are shared by all classes. When this is no longer the case, the system must break down and be replaced by a new one, which will reflect the new values of the society. Thus, with the growth of trade and industry and the decline in importance of agriculture, the rise of rational and scientific thought and the decline in importance of religion, and the rise of the national state and the decline in importance of individual military leaders, the social system of feudalism was destined to be replaced by a new one with a different class structure.

Given the importance of industrial development and capital accumulation under the new capitalist economic system, the rising entrepreneurs and wealthy people constituted the new upper class. Those who did not possess wealth and did not engage in business—the workers—became the new lower class. It should not be thought that the change in the economic structure resulted in an immediate change in the social system; on the contrary, it took a long time for society to rearrange its ideas about what things were more

---

[2] Talcott Parsons, "A Revised Analytical Approach to the Theory of Social Classes," in Reinhard Bendix and Seymour Martin Lipset (eds.), *Class, Status, and Power* (Glencoe, Ill.: Free Press, 1953), p. 93.

important than others and hence worthy of high social status. The transition from the old class structure to the new took place very gradually—and not without difficulty, as the old upper classes were reluctant to recognize their own demise. In Britain the displacement of the old social system was accomplished without too much of a national convulsion, but in France it took the bloody revolution of 1789 to displace the aristocracy and the clergy and assert the dominance of the bourgeoisie.

The new social structure also differed from the preindustrial one in its degree of rigidity. Under the old order a person's social status was fixed, being determined at birth; one was born either a noble or a commoner. Although the church allowed some to rise in status, commoners usually filled the lower positions, such as parish priests, with the upper clergy coming mainly from the aristocracy. The social structure of capitalism, by replacing status relationships with exchange relationships, permitted much greater social mobility and the rise of people to higher status. Under a status relationship, one could not change the fact of his birth, but under an exchange relationship, which emphasized free competition, it was possible for an individual, regardless of what his father had been, to enter a business, accumulate wealth, and shift to a higher social class. Talent in production became much more important than a background of titles and proper manners. Indeed, as capitalist industrialism grew in England most of the new industrial entrepreneurs were commoners, many coming from fairly humble backgrounds, rather than from the aristocracy.

Although the new economic and social order was an open one allowing people with initiative and good fortune to ascend the social ladder, it did not reduce the distance between the upper and lower classes. Those who accumulated capital exercised power, lived in luxury, and looked down from their lofty heights upon the mass of workers whose lot was grinding poverty and obsequiousness.

The Marxist View

Viewing this scene in England in the middle of the nineteenth century, Karl Marx, who identified social classes strictly in terms of the functions performed in the production process, believed that a struggle had to take place between the capitalists who owned the means of production and distribution and the propertyless workers. Marx foresaw as inevitable the victory of the workers in this struggle, and the replacement of private ownership of the means of production and distribution (capitalism) by social ownership (socialism), as well as the establishment of a "classless" society. Before the workers triumphed, however, they would suffer continued impoverishment, and, moreover, there would be a polarization of the classes, with the mass of the middle classes being ground down into the working class.

The history of Western capitalist industrialism, however, has not borne out Karl Marx's predictions. There is no question but that the rich have gotten richer, but so have the poor. As capital was accumulated and industry poured out goods and services, the capitalists discovered that they needed customers to buy their products and that higher wages enabled workers to become those customers. Thus, rather than the increasing impoverishment of the working class, we have had its "embourgeoisement," as higher incomes enabled workers to move up to what had once been considered middle-class modes of living.

The economic rise of the working class has been most evident in the United States, where the average worker today has an automobile, refrigerator, good medical services, paid vacations, and retirement on a pension when he gets old. Indeed, the AFL-CIO discovered a few years ago that the typical trade unionist was a homeowner in the suburbs with many of the same attitudes as his middle-class neighbors. It is not surprising, therefore, that in 1970 George Meany, president of the AFL-CIO, warned the Democratic party that it would lose worker support if it moved to the left because, according to Meany, trade unionists today are middle class, concerned about law and order, disturbed by violence, and more conservatively oriented than in the past.[3] In 1972 Meany delivered on that promise, and the AFL-CIO refused to endorse George McGovern, the Democratic candidate for President, because he was considered too far to the left.

The lower class that we have in the United States today is not composed of the workers but of those who, because they lack education or skill and suffer from discrimination, cannot get the jobs that would permit them to break into the working class. Some social scientists have become fearful that, unless something is done to allow these people to move up to working-class status, we shall produce a permanent underclass in this country.[4] At the same time many members of the present working class feel threatened by attempts to inject members from the lower class, especially when they are black, into their factories and neighborhoods, and this helps to explain their movement to the political right.

Not only was Karl Marx wrong with respect to the economic fate of the working class, but he also misjudged the fate of the middle class. The middle class has not disappeared, and in fact a whole new middle class of salaried professional and semiprofessional white-collar workers has grown up and expanded. A Marxist might say that, since these people do not own the means of production and distribution but work for those who do, they are really members of the working class. Class status, however, does not derive solely from a person's role in the production process; occupation, education, and other factors are also determinants. Since white-collar workers do not see their employee status as the determinant of their social status, their attitudes make the whole difference between the Marxist prescription and reality.

---

[3] *The New York Times*, August 31, 1970.

[4] See, for instance, Gunnar Myrdal, *Challenge to Affluence* (New York: Pantheon, 1962).

Factors Mitigating Class Conflict

Unlike Europe, where the workers became class conscious and large numbers of them adhered to Marxist doctrines, the United States has been notably free of overt class conflict. Obviously, the favorable economic status of the working class has been important in reducing class conflict; while Marx may have said that the workers had "nothing to lose but their chains," this has not been true for most of them. The existence of a large middle class also serves to mitigate class conflict in the United States, because workers are not continually confronted with very sharp differences in life styles between themselves and the upper classes.

Class conflict has also been mitigated by the fact that the channels of upward social mobility have been kept open and indeed widened over time. Just as high a proportion of people rise from "rags to riches" today as ever before in history—though rags have become less common. While it may be less easy to become "one's own boss" today, a new channel of upward ascent has developed as a result of the change in the nature of the business organization. The small, independent, personally owned and operated business has to a great extent been replaced by the large corporation, owned by thousands, and even millions, of absentee stockholders and operated by professional salaried managers, who are recruited on the basis of ability. Thus, it is no longer necessary for a person to accumulate capital and start his own business to become an executive and move into an upper class; he can get a managerial position within a large corporation upon graduation from college and push his way to the top.

Managers can come from all walks of life, for education, the chief means of rising into management, has become increasingly available to everyone. Although most managers come from families whose economic and social position is well above average, Warner and Abegglen found that more business leaders today come from lower social ranks than formerly.[5] According to their findings, by 1952 15 percent of the top executives of American businesses had come from manual laborer families. Similarly, a more recent study of the nation's occupational structure by Blau and Duncan found that "the relative opportunities of underprivileged Americans with manual origins to move up into the top stratum are particularly good compared to those in other societies. Nearly 10 percent of manual sons achieve elite status in the United States, a higher proportion than in any other country."[6]

Social mobility, however, need not be measured solely by the few who rise from the bottom to the top, for there is a wide spectrum of opportunities in between. It is true that few laborers' sons may become corporation executives, but many of them may move into the rapidly expanding white-collar middle class. Indeed, it is possible to trace the rise of successive immigrant

---

[5] W. Lloyd Warner and James C. Abegglen, *Big Business Leaders in America* (New York: Harper & Row, 1955).

[6] Peter M. Blau and Otis Dudley Duncan, *The American Occupational Structure* (New York: Wiley, 1967), p. 435.

groups from a concentration in unskilled factory jobs to higher-level occupations and out of central city slums into middle-class suburban communities within a generation or two. The continued expansion of the American economy and the shift from direct production work to white-collar types of occupations, of course, have helped make this possible.

The social mobility of the United States, however, has been limited largely to those whose skins are white. For a long time, in fact, the black American was not integrated at all into the social structure. At first he was a slave, and not even considered to be a full person. (The Constitution counted slaves as three-fifths of a person for purposes of determining congressional representation.) Even after the abolition of slavery, white prejudice continued to confine blacks to a separate social status based solely upon their race, rather than upon their wealth, occupation, education, or other attributes. In terms of the social structure, blacks were relegated to a separate caste; that is, their social status was determined by their birth and could not be changed by anything they did.[7] Within the separate caste, however, blacks had their own class structure, but no matter how high a person might rise within it, he was treated in the larger society as inferior to any white. Although this separate caste status has not yet disappeared, and some social scientists fear that we may confine a large portion of the black community to a permanent underclass, there are signs that blacks are beginning to be considered part of the overall social structure.

Management Ideology

The fact that the socioeconomic system in the United States has been an open one does not mean that everyone has been treated the same under it. In a recent study of industrialism throughout the world, Professors Kerr, Dunlop, Harbison, and Myers advanced the idea that industrialization is always introduced into a society by a minority group, whether a dynastic elite, as in Japan in the nineteenth century, or a group of revolutionary intellectuals, as in Russia and China in the twentieth.[8] In the Western capitalist nations, particularly Britain and the United States, it was the rising middle class that pioneered industrialization. The ideology of this new class emphasized economic individualism and material progress.

Management's Harsh Attitude Toward Workers

This ideology, which was born in England, reached its heights in the United States and remained strong here after it had waned in Britain.[9] In this country,

---

[7] Illustration of this caste status is contained in John Dollard, *Caste and Class in a Southern Town* (Garden City, N.Y.: Doubleday Anchor Books, 1957).

[8] Clark Kerr, *et al., Industrialism and Industrial Man: The Problems of Labor and Management in Economic Growth* (Cambridge, Mass.: Harvard University Press, 1960).

[9] For a full exposition of this thesis, see Reinhard Bendix, *Work and Authority in Industry* (New York: Wiley, 1956). Chapter 5, "The American Experience," is the source of much of the discussion that follows.

it was rooted in the Protestant ethic, emphasizing the ideas of getting ahead through hard work and the survival of the fittest. These social ideas, when combined with the economic concepts of laissez faire and individual initiative, meant that each business owner should be free to run his enterprise as he saw fit without interference from either government or workers. The employer's authority in the factory was almost absolute, and this was justified, according to the doctrine, because of his success, and thus his proven abilities. Following this line of reasoning, it was natural to conclude that the workers were not the equal of the employer, and therefore should be in a subservient position.

The harsh attitude of management toward its employees was further reinforced by the widening gap in backgrounds between the two as the composition of the industrial work force changed. Between 1880 and 1910 the United States enjoyed an economic expansion as rapid as that of any industrialized country in a comparable period of time. The labor force more than doubled in size, from 17.4 million to 36.3 million, and a much larger portion of it was employed in manufacturing.

Great technological breakthroughs were made in this period, such as the adoption of the Bessemer process for the making of steel, and factories were better organized and run, utilizing mechanical conveyances and power-driven cranes. In the process machinery was introduced that was able to substitute for skilled labor, and this mechanization created a need for large numbers of workers to do unskilled and semiskilled heavy labor in factories. The pace of industrial development was so rapid that the native-born labor supply could not meet its needs, and industry sought immigrants to augment it. Net annual immigration during the decade 1881–1890 was 524,661; it dropped to an annual average of 467,846 during the 1890s because of a prolonged depression, but it mounted to 869,536 during the first decade of the twentieth century. The source of factory workers was a new one; until then immigrants had come mainly from the countries of northern and western Europe, particularly the British Isles, but beginning in the 1880s there was a heavy influx of people from southern and eastern Europe.

From the beginnings of the nation, each new immigrant group had been looked upon with disdain by its predecessors; thus, in the late 1700s Benjamin Franklin doubted that good Americans could ever be made of the Germans who were settling in Pennsylvania. The attitude of the native American owners and managers of industry, who were overwhelmingly of white, Anglo-Saxon Protestant (WASP) stock, was even more condescending to the former peasants—often illiterate, largely Roman Catholic, and speaking strange languages—who became the mass of their unskilled employees. The idea developed that "micks," "Hunkies," "Polacks," and "wops," as the immigrants were derogatively called, were ignorant and susceptible to inflamed passions, so it was up to their betters—the managers of industry—to keep them in line. Thus, factory discipline was harsh, employees possessed no rights, and they could be, and often were, dismissed for the slightest infraction of the rules.

Gradual Change in Management's Attitudes

As managers sought to increase labor productivity, they found it necessary to become concerned with the human as well as the machine problems of industrial plants. The need to positively motivate workers as well as to threaten them was seen. Where formerly workers had been viewed as inefficient and unwilling to exert themselves unless driven by management, Frederick W. Taylor and his disciples in the "scientific management" school proposed to elicit the cooperation of the workers in the production process through financial incentives for greater output. In the process managerial ideology began to change, and the new outlook stressed the duties of managers as well as their prerogatives, and the granting of financial rewards in place of exhortations to workers.

Following the First World War, managerial ideology underwent further change, particularly under the influence of the new field of industrial psychology. What emerged was an approach according to which workers' behavior could be controlled by means of changing the environmental stimuli. It was discovered that better lighting, musical backgrounds, and occasional rest periods would help to achieve greater productivity. As management became more concerned with the well-being of its employees, an era of "welfare capitalism" dawned.

As a result of the famous Hawthorne experiment conducted at a Western Electric facility near Chicago, it became evident that workers were interested in aspects of a job other than the amount of money it provided. In that experiment, a group of assemblers under study increased their output as the physical conditions of the job were improved, which was what had been hypothesized. The social scientists conducting the investigation were perplexed, however, when output continued to go up even though physical conditions were worsened. They finally realized that the workers were responding to the attention being focused on them and to the esprit de corps that had developed in their group.[10] Management began to see that a worker sought, in addition to decent pay and working conditions, the respect of others, and that he wanted to be somebody other than an unidentified human unit in an industrial organization.

The new "human relations" approach, spearheaded by Elton W. Mayo, undermined the former view of employees as "rabble" that had to be firmly controlled by management. It stressed the scientific selection, training, and placement of employees as well as their motivation. Instead of either just pushing workers harder or offering them more money for increased output, management was obliged to provide an environment in which employees would want to cooperate.

All of these approaches, though differing from one another, left the initiative to management. Then, in the 1930s, in addition to the changes tak-

---

[10] A full report of the Hawthorne experiment is contained in F. J. Roethlisberger and William J. Dickson, *Management and the Worker* (Cambridge, Mass.: Harvard University Press, 1939).

ing place within management thinking, came the external force of union organization of the production workers in basic industry. Now, the employees asserted their right to share in decision-making with respect to wages and working conditions, and management's arbitrary authority was further curtailed.

Both management and labor, moreover, had been changing during the period of this evolution of the relationship between them. Native-born Americans with high-school educations, rather than illiterate immigrants, now made up the majority of workers, and they could not be subjected to the kind of treatment their fathers had accepted. In place of the self-made entrepreneurs of the earlier era, management had become a virtual profession, the practitioners of which were trained in colleges and universities specifically for administrative positions in large, bureaucratic corporations. While in school they had absorbed much of the recent findings of the behavioral sciences, which they later tried to apply within the large corporations. At the same time a good deal of university research was focused on the human problems of large organizations.

The net result of these various trends is that management, although still responsible for maintaining industrial discipline, must do so in a fair manner; if it does not, the individual worker, if he is a member of a union, can charge a violation of the collective bargaining agreement and obtain redress of management's action. But even where workers are not organized, they are usually treated fairly by management, because our nation's democratic ideology has also filtered into the work place, infecting both employees and managers. Instead of simply threatening and cajoling workers, we find many large companies today attempting to create the type of environment in which employees will be motivated to produce more through making their jobs more interesting, informing them of changes that are to take place, listening to what they have to say, and even experimenting with democratic participation.

American Exceptionalism

Although there is a heritage of conflict between labor and management in the United States, the relationships between the two have evolved quite differently than in Europe. A very clear indication of this is the absence of a strong Marxist tradition or the development of political parties along class lines in this country. This is in sharp contrast to Europe, where political parties were organized along class lines and where social democratic and labor parties became the spokesmen for the workers in the nineteenth and early twentieth centuries. Today those parties, though less Marxist than they used to be, still represent the workers in western Europe, but in France and Italy they have been replaced as the major spokesmen by Marxist-Leninist Communist parties.

A similar development seemed to be under way here as the Socialist party of the United States, formed in 1901, grew in importance before the First World War. By 1911 Milwaukee, Wisconsin, and Schenectady, New York, had Socialist mayors; Socialists were in the state legislature of New York, Massachusetts, Pennsylvania, Minnesota, and Rhode Island; and Wisconsin sent a Socialist to Congress.[11] But, since the major political parties were not ideological, they could adopt some of the Socialists' rallying cries, though not their demand for socialism, and thus win back voters from them. This is precisely what happened, and the Socialist party reached the height of its popularity in 1912 when its candidate for President, Eugene Victor Debs, polled 6 percent of the national vote. After that the Socialists declined, and at no time did they pose a serious challenge to the Democrats and Republicans, nor did they gain any wide support from organized labor. The Communist party, which arose in the 1920s, achieved much less electoral success, and even its growing important influence in a number of CIO unions was attributable to its members hiding the fact that they were Communists.

The German sociologist, Werner Sombart, was so fascinated with this difference between the United States and the other industrial countries that, early in this century, he posed the serious scholarly question, "Why is there no socialism in America?" There is no simple answer to Sombart's question, but a whole series of facts that help to explain this American exceptionalism.

The Absence of a Feudal Tradition

The absence of a feudal tradition in the United States was very important. For one thing, it allowed the democratic ethos to develop more fully in the social sphere and thus prevented class lines from becoming rigidly fixed. The American class system has been accurately described as "a finely-graded continuum of strata rather than a series of sharply separated ranks with little mobility between them."[12] Class differences were fairly strong on the eastern seaboard in the nation's formative period, and there were even proposals by Alexander Hamilton and others to establish an American aristocracy. The influence of the frontier, however, ran counter to this, for on the frontier, where everybody was exposed to the same dangers and hardships, and people had to be willing to help one another, it was difficult to impose religious conformity, authoritarian government, unduly restrictive economic arrangements, or sharp social distinctions.

The absence of a feudal tradition also deflected class conflict in the political arena. In Europe each group of "commoners" had to fight for the right to vote, which was first won by the middle classes (property owners) and only much later extended to the workers. In the United States the workers obtained the franchise early in American history, and, by the time the socialist doctrine was gaining adherence in Europe, universal manhood suffrage had

---

[11] Thomas R. Brooks, *Toil and Trouble* (New York: Delta, 1965), p. 103.
[12] Bernard Barber and Lyle S. Lobel, " 'Fashion' in Women's Clothes and the American Social System," in Bendix and Lipset, *op. cit.*, p. 326; reprinted from *Social Forces*, December 1952.

become commonplace in the United States, and winning the right to vote did not provide a cause for labor political solidarity.

The Availability of Free Public Education

Class differences in outlook have also been mitigated by the spread of universal free education and the dominance of the public school. In Europe education, at least beyond the first few years of schooling, was limited to the upper and middle classes. The securing of education, therefore, was a rallying cry for worker political solidarity. In contrast to Europe's "class" education, on the other hand, the United States, by the middle of the nineteenth century, before the growth of a large industrial working class, had adopted "mass" education.

Not only was education available to the children of workers, but they went through the same school system as that of the children of other social classes. Although the older, established wealthy families sent their sons to a few exclusive eastern private schools, most of the sons of the poor, the middle class, and the working class attended the public schools. The administrators and teachers in the public schools were themselves middle class, and thus all social status groups were molded in their very early years by the same set of social values.

Economic Opportunity and Rising Living Standards

Perhaps the most important explanation for the failure of socialism to take firm root lies in the opportunity for personal betterment that existed in this country, and that was the major factor attracting immigrants from Europe. From the very beginning America was a virgin territory with land available, and so people were able to become independent farmers. Those who were not drawn to the land found jobs in business and industry available in the growing cities of the nation.

Economic factors interrelated with the social and political ones to deflect class antagonism. The shortage of labor that plagued this country from the very outset never allowed the conditions to which workers were subjected to be as bad as they were in England during the early period of industrialization. American capitalism has been, at least until recently, more dynamic than that of most European nations, and the rapid economic growth of the country provided sufficient opportunities for people to advance themselves, or at least see their sons better off than they had been. While few became capitalists, the sons of yesterday's unskilled worker were likely to have obtained some degree of skill and thus a higher status and income, as the unskilled jobs were left to a new wave of immigrants. The continual rise in the standard of living that was shared by all sectors of society, as the mass market accompanied mass production, prevented conflict over the division of the economic pie; the various groups each received a larger piece of a bigger pie even if its share remained the same.

People Belong to Groups Other than Social Classes

A final explanation of the absence of overt class conflict lies in the fact that people are members of groups other than social classes, and in terms of American political behavior some of these allegiances have proved to be stronger than class solidarity. One of the most significant of these other divisions of American society has been geographic, with people identifying themselves as "easterners," "westerners," or "southerners."

At one time sectional feelings ran so high in this country that we suffered a civil war between the North and the South, and for almost a century afterward southern workers, sharecroppers, rich farmers, and businessmen, despite conflicting economic and social interests, were united in voting the straight Democratic ticket. Until the post–World War II period, the solid Democratic South was broken only in 1928, when many southerners balked at voting for Alfred E. Smith for President because he was a Roman Catholic. Only recently has a two-party system begun to emerge in the South; even so, sectional feelings, particularly over the race issue, continue to run so strong that southern third-party candidates have carried a number of southern states in the presidential elections of 1948 (J. Strom Thurmond) and 1968 (George C. Wallace). Sectionalism, moreover, has not been confined to the South, but has simply been less vehement in the Northeast, Midwest, and West.

Americans, with the exception of the Indians, all being of immigrant stock, have also preserved strong ethnic and religious ties. These ties were reinforced politically as the big city machines, usually Democratic but sometimes Republican, organized the newcomers into voting blocs that were integrated into their patronage structures. To this day elections are analyzed in such terms as the "Italian vote," the "Irish vote," the "Jewish vote," and the like, for ethnic patterns continue, though apparently with diminishing force, to supersede economic and social affiliations. Thus American politics has been an amalgam of class, sectional, ethnic, and other interests, rather than being based solely on socioeconomic status and interests.

Differences in Attitudes among Social Classes

Although all social classes in the United States share a basic set of common values, there are also differences in their outlooks upon life. Keeping in mind that not all members of a particular social class share the same outlook, we can discuss some differences between the outlook of the majority of one class and that of most of those in another social class. The basic difference, for instance, between the working and middle classes is, in the economist's terms, that they discount the future at different rates; that is, workers tend to be more "now" oriented and middle-class people more "future" oriented. This flows directly from the difference in their life prospects. The young blue-collar worker, taking his first job upon graduation from high school, looks forward to higher earnings and upgrading to higher job levels, but he cannot anticipate any fundamental change in his lifetime career. His earnings, moreover, although increasing as he moves to higher job grades, will move in a rather narrow range, and the increases in his standard of living will depend fundamentally on the nation's economic growth.

The middle-class youngster is in a different situation. First of all, he is much more likely to attend college, thus sacrificing present income for the prospects of higher income later in life. Secondly, his entire approach to an occupation tends to be more career oriented; that is, his first job is viewed as the beginning of a career of successive advancement. He may thus be willing to work for very low pay at the outset, as does the young medical intern, because this is part of his further training and paves the way for success in his chosen field. This discounting of the future at a higher rate affects all aspects of the middle-class person's life: he is more likely to postpone marriage and child-rearing lest they interfere with his long-term prospects.[13] His earnings during his lifetime will cover a significantly wider range than those of the working-class person, and at their height may be three or four times (in real terms) his starting salary.

Differences in earnings in turn help to shape differing styles of life for their recipients. In 1963 the average gross weekly earnings of production workers was $99.63, but the average annual salary of the five highest-paid positions in each of a group of the fifty largest corporations was $148,553.00,[14] or thirty times higher. Of course, most managers do not earn anywhere near what the top five company officials do, but still it is much more than what the average blue-collar worker earns; in that same year, for instance, the starting salary for university graduates with the degree of Master of Business Administration, the vast majority of whom entered corporate management, was $8,982, considerably more than most blue-collar workers were receiving after many years on the job.

Although blue-collar workers have narrowed the earnings differential between themselves and white-collar workers, they still lag behind. For all nonfarm occupations, those in white-collar jobs earn considerably more than blue-collar and service workers, as can be seen in Table 2.1. Professional and managerial workers had the highest annual median incomes in 1969. In fact, blue-collar workers—craftsmen, operatives, and laborers—had lower annual incomes than all categories of white-collar workers, with one exception: craftsmen earned more than clerical workers.

The very differences in earnings means that workers and managers will rarely have any contacts off the job, for each lives in his own socioeconomic neighborhood, which, with today's suburbanization, may be separated by many miles. Indeed, they may even have few contacts on the job, for the

---

[13] In recent years, however, many middle-class youths have rejected the values of parents and sought immediate, rather than postponed, gratification; interestingly, we have dubbed this the "now" generation, but whether or not this will be of long-run significance is difficult to predict.

[14] Wilbur G. Lewellen, *Executive Compensation in Large Industrial Corporations* (New York: National Bureau of Economic Research, 1968), pp. 123, 177.

Table 2.1 Percentage Distribution of Earnings and Income of Four-person Husband-Wife Families, by Major Occupational Group, 1969 (in thousands)

Major occupational group	Number	Percent distribution						Median income
		All families	Under $5,000	$5,000–6,999	$7,000–9,999	$10,000–14,999	$15,000 and over	
EARNINGS OF FAMILY HEAD								
All nonfarm occupations	7,032	100.0	6.6	14.5	34.5	30.2	14.2	$ 9,464
White-collar workers	3,542	100.0	4.2	9.3	28.8	33.0	24.9	10,721
Professional and managerial	2,671	100.0	3.8	7.5	24.4	35.0	29.4	11,540
Clerical	489	100.0	4.7	18.3	50.7	22.0	4.3	8,500
Sales	382	100.0	5.7	10.2	31.4	32.7	19.9	10,175
Blue-collar workers	3,194	100.0	8.3	19.0	41.3	27.9	3.5	8,466
Craftsmen	1,594	100.0	5.1	15.0	38.3	36.5	5.2	9,258
Operatives	1,364	100.0	10.1	21.4	45.6	20.9	2.0	8,068
Laborers	236	100.0	19.6	31.9	37.0	10.6	0.9	6,891
Service workers	296	100.0	16.9	28.4	29.4	23.0	2.4	7,538

SOURCE: Robert L. Stein and Janice Neipert Hedges, "Blue-Collar/White-Collar Pay Trends: Earnings and Family Income," *Monthly Labor Review*, June 1971, Table 7, p. 21.

individual production worker tends to interact mainly with his foreman, the lowest level of management, and occasionally with such higher-level supervisors as department heads and plant managers, but virtually never with higher-ups in company headquarters. The sheer size of large corporations and the geographic dispersion of their facilities contribute immeasurably to this physical separation of workers and managers.[15]

Role differences between management and worker, as well as economic and class differences, contribute to their varying outlooks, particularly on the job. The manager of a corporation acts as a trustee, in effect, for its owners, and as such he must be concerned that the company earn profits. In order to maximize profitability, the manager attempts to increase the efficiency of operations through the introduction of better production flows, new machinery, and new organizational structures, and in the process he is continually changing the existing situation in the work place.

The worker, occupying a different position in the organization, looks at things from his own vantage point. He is not opposed to the company's earning profits, recognizing that a profitable company can better assure him job security and afford to pay him higher wages. Yet, since his fundamental concerns are job security and income maintenance, when management introduces technological and organizational change he may resist it, not because he is opposed to more efficient operations, but because these pose a possible threat to his existing job. Even where jobs are not threatened, change may upset existing work groups, to which individuals have become attached and which have become a source of support for them. Thus, while managers tend to be concerned with business growth and firm profitability, workers are more concerned with being members of stable work groups, having an opportunity to display workmanship, and maintaining a decent standard of living; the result is a conflict between change and efficiency on the one hand and stability and security on the other.

Worker Attitudes in an Affluent Society

In recent years the nation has become both aware of the emergence of a new set of attitudes toward life on the part of younger people and concerned with the "generation gap." Much of the intergenerational attitude conflict has been centered on the college campuses, but there is growing evidence that young workers also see things differently than do their elders. With the heavy influx of young workers into the labor force in recent years, both management

---

[15] This problem is not limited to corporations, but is also true of the unions that represent the workers. Thus, an amusing anecdote traveled the labor-management circuits a few years ago, when David J. McDonald, then president of the United Steelworkers of America, AFL-CIO, and Benjamin Fairless, president of United States Steel Corporation, in the interests of promoting better labor-management relations, conducted a joint tour of a number of U.S. Steel plants. According to this story, as they walked through one of the mills, the workers kept turning to one another and asking, "Which one is McDonald?"

and union leaders have been startled by the different aspirations and interests that they have begun to express.

First of all, there is evidence of a continuing decline of belief in the old Protestant ethic of hard work and thrift. People in general have become more consumption and less production oriented, a factor especially pronounced among workers in routine, uninteresting jobs. The attitude of these workers toward work is "instrumental"; that is, it is viewed as providing income with which to enjoy life outside the plant rather than having an intrinsic value in and of itself. Since work does not provide satisfaction, they seek recognition, status, and creative outlets in their homes, with their families, and in their outside activities.[16]

Second, having grown up since the Great Depression, young people take full employment for granted and are less concerned with sticking with a job once they get one. Having fewer family responsibilities, they are less concerned with security and more willing to gamble by giving up good jobs for other prospects. Most companies have become acutely aware of this change as a result of an increase in employee absenteeism and turnover, which is very expensive in terms of recruitment, selection, and training costs. Both young blue-collar and white-collar employees, particularly managers themselves, have greatly increased turnover rates.

Third, in an increasingly affluent America, workers tend to value time off more highly than heretofore. Young workers in particular are less job and more leisure-activity oriented. While union leaders, in response to the demands of their older members, have pressed employers for higher pensions and other benefits, the cry from young workers has been for a shorter work week, more holidays, and longer vacations. A clear example of this change in worker attitude can be seen with respect to overtime work. Many plants have had a good deal of labor-management conflict over the fair sharing of overtime, as every employee wanted to be assured of his opportunity to earn extra pay. In the last few years, however, conflict has arisen over the refusal of employees to work overtime and their insistence on the right to reject overtime work. Indeed, the issue of voluntary overtime was a major issue of union-management confrontation in the 1973 collective bargaining negotiations in the automobile industry.

The desire for leisure, and the ability to enjoy it, has been heightened by increasing incomes. In the late 1960s it was estimated that about 15 million, or 30 percent, of all families had incomes of $10,000 or more, but by 1975 that bracket will contain 26 million, or roughly 47 percent of all families. A number of blue-collar worker families are already in that category, and as average hourly earnings rise, the proportion in the over $10,000 group grows. This affluence, when combined with rising educational and skill levels, leads to resentment on the part of blue-collar workers over the continued distinc-

---

[16] For an exposition of this theme, see William A. Westley and Margaret W. Westley, *The Emerging Worker* (Montreal and London: McGill–Queen's University Press, 1971).

tions between themselves and white-collar employees. For example, the high-school graduate who is a machine operator on the plant floor fails to understand why he should be paid by the hour while the high-school graduate operating an office machine in the plant office should be salaried. Such distinctions make even less sense to the hourly-paid computer console operator being handed tapes to run by a salaried technician.

The better education of the young worker, moreover, makes him reluctant to work at the routine and dirty jobs commonly associated with the assembly line of the mass production industries. Indeed, the automobile manufacturers have been troubled by the difficulty of recruiting and retaining workers for such types of jobs. The higher status of white-collar work and the more attractive working conditions of nonmanual jobs, including less susceptibility to layoff, tends to draw labor to them and away from factory jobs. The attitudes toward assembly line work have not changed—they have always been negative—but the ability of workers to find alternatives has. As reported by Chinoy, despite their dislike for their jobs, assembly workers used to be attracted to them by the high wages and encouraged to stay in them because of family responsibilities,[17] but three decades of full employment and the expansion of the nongoods-producing industries and nonmanual jobs made younger workers less inclined to put up with dull, routine jobs. As a result, companies have been forced to explore means of increasing job satisfaction through job enlargement and enrichment.

The rebellious spirit of our time has also affected younger workers. They are less willing to do things merely because that is "standard operating procedure," but tend to question orders with which they disagree. As a result, disciplinary problems have risen in many companies as young workers have become a major share of the plant work force. Young, better-educated workers, furthermore, are not willing to abide by regulations that they have had no voice in determining. Just as college students have been demanding a voice in establishing college policy, so young workers have begun to insist that their unions fight for joint decision-making on matters of plant operating policy, an area that management has heretofore considered basically its sole prerogative.

The young also tend to be more militant and less willing to wait for a gradual solution of problems. This is most evident in the attitude and behavior of young blacks, Puerto Ricans, Chicanos, and Indians, who have often resorted to "direct action" to receive immediate redress of grievances, but it also is true of young white workers. Within industry it is the young workers who are often the "hotheads," demanding strike action if employers do not meet all their union's demands and willing to engage in wildcat strikes (strikes not authorized by the union leadership), rather than using the slower procedure of processing a grievance, when they object to a particular manage-

---

[17] Eli Chinoy, *Automobile Workers and the American Dream* (Garden City, N.Y.: Doubleday, 1952).

ment action. Union leaders, moreover, are no more capable of handling the young worker than are most managers.[18]

These trends in industry can be explained partially with A. H. Maslow's theory of a hierarchy of human needs.[19] In his view, once a lower need is fairly well satisfied, a man can be motivated only by a desire to satisfy the next higher need. According to Maslow, these needs in ascending order are:

1. Physiological needs (food, clothing, shelter)
2. Need for safety from danger, threat, and deprivation
3. Social needs (association with one's fellows, friendship and love)
4. Ego needs (self-esteem, self-respect, respect of one's fellows, status)
5. Need for self-fulfillment through development of one's powers and skills and chance to use creativity

Following this line of reasoning, we can conclude that since workers have physiological, social, and ego needs, they will respond in terms of output only if the firms provide sufficient opportunity to realize these needs. Therefore, managers have attempted to establish a work environment that enables employees to meet their basic needs through adequate wage and fringe arrangements. Since these physiological needs are well satisfied today, managers must turn their attention to meeting workers' higher needs: their social needs through group efforts in the work situation, their ego needs through rewards to innovation, and their need for self-fulfillment through the introduction of greater creativity into the work they do. To the degree that this is not possible because of the nature of much of the work, money will have to be a substitute, and managers will have to contend with worker dissatisfaction and turnover.

The changing attitudes of workers will become more pronounced in time, as more young people, born since the Great Depression of the 1930s right through into the rebellious 1960s, take their place in the work force. Worker insistence on having a greater voice in determining the rules and regulations by which they are governed in the work place will probably mesh with the behavioral approach of modern management that visualizes participation as meeting the needs of the enterprise as well as the employee,[20] and, while it is difficult to predict what the outcome of all this will be, it is clear that the new attitudes will have a profound effect upon the relationships between labor and management and that these will be much different in the future than they have been in the past.

---

[18] See, for example, Peter Henle, "Organized Labor and the New Militants," *Monthly Labor Review*, July 1969, pp. 20–25.

[19] A. H. Maslow, "A Theory of Human Motivation," *Psychological Review*, July 1943.

[20] For the growing management literature propounding this view, see, for example, F. J. Roethlisberger, *Management and Morale* (Cambridge, Mass.: Harvard University Press, 1941); Mason Haire (ed.), *Modern Organization Theory* (New York: Wiley, 1959); Douglas McGregor, *The Human Side of Enterprise* (New York: McGraw-Hill, 1960); and Alfred J. Marrow, David G. Bowers, and Stanley E. Seashore, *Management by Participation* (New York: Harper & Row, 1967).

Summary

The emergence of the new economic system of capitalism was accompanied by a rearrangement of the social structure, under which the capitalists constituted a new upper class and the workers the new lower class. Karl Marx foresaw that this would mean a class struggle from which would emerge a new socioeconomic system known as socialism, but the history of Western capitalist industrialism has not borne out his predictions. Even so, differences in class status meant differences in attitudes and behavior patterns among classes, and a higher evaluation of the wealthy, property-owning people.

The precepts of laissez-faire economics and class attitudes resulted in rather harsh treatment of workers by management in the nineteenth century, but this was gradually modified as new concepts of "scientific management," human relations, and the motivational theories of the behavioral sciences gained headway. The absence of a mass socialist movement in the United States also reduced the conflict between workers and employers, at least in the political sphere, as labor turned to winning a fairer share rather than attempting to overturn the existing economic order. Even so, differences in attitudes and behavior patterns between workers and middle-class managers persist, mainly in terms of the different rates at which they discount the future, the workers being more "now" and the middle classes more "future" oriented. Role differentiation also makes workers more security conscious, while managers work for higher company profits, and a conflict between innovation and stability results.

As the United States has become more affluent, worker attitudes have changed accordingly, and these changes are most pronounced among the young, who have not experienced either depression or harsh treatment at the hands of management. Workers are more consumption than production oriented, take full employment more for granted, and value leisure very highly. At the same time young workers are less willing to accept rules that management has set down for them but that they have had no voice in shaping. The routine nature of many types of jobs alienates workers from their work, but the ability to find other jobs leads many of them to quit such jobs; management, as a result, has been forced to seek means of enriching jobs. These changing attitudes are bound to have a profound effect on employee-employer relationships, but it is difficult to discern precisely what that will be.

BIBLIOGRAPHY

Bendix, Reinhard. *Work and Authority in Industry.* New York: Wiley, 1956.
Bendix, Reinhard, and Seymour Martin Lipset (eds.). *Class, Status, and Power.* Glencoe, Ill.: Free Press, 1953.
Blau, Peter M., and Otis D. Duncan. *The American Occupational Structure.* New York: Wiley, 1967.
Brooks, Thomas R. *Toil and Trouble.* New York: Delta, 1965.

Chinoy, Eli. *Automobile Workers and the American Dream*. Garden City, N.Y.: Doubleday, 1952.

Dollard, John. *Caste and Class in a Southern Town*. Garden City, N.Y.: Doubleday Anchor Books, 1957.

Gomberg, William, and Arthur B. Shostak (eds.). *Blue-Collar World*. Englewood Cliffs, N.J.: Prentice-Hall, 1964.

Henle, Peter. "Organized Labor and the New Militants," *Monthly Labor Review*, July 1969.

Kerr, Clark, John T. Dunlop, Frederick Harbison, and Charles A. Myers. *Industrialism and Industrial Man: The Problems of Labor and Management in Economic Growth*. Cambridge, Mass.: Harvard University Press, 1960.

Lewellen, Wilbur G. *Executive Compensation in Large Industrial Corporations*. New York: National Bureau of Economic Research, 1968.

Marrow, Alfred J., David G. Bowers, and Stanley E. Seashore. *Management by Participation*. New York: Harper & Row, 1967.

Maslow, A. H. "A Theory of Human Motivation," *Psychological Review*, July 1943.

McGregor, Douglas. *The Human Side of Enterprise*. New York: McGraw-Hill, 1960.

Myrdal, Gunnar. *Challenge to Affluence*. New York: Pantheon, 1962.

Roethlisberger, F. J., and William J. Dickson. *Management and the Worker*. Cambridge, Mass.: Harvard University Press, 1939.

Warner, W. Lloyd, and James C. Abegglen. *Big Business Leaders in America*. New York: Harper & Row, 1955.

Westley, William A., and Margaret W. Westley. *The Emerging Worker*. Montreal and London: McGill–Queen's University Press, 1971.

Work in America. Report of a special task force of the secretary of Health, Education, and Welfare. Prepared under the auspices of the W. E. Upjohn Institute for Employment Research. Cambridge, Mass.: The MIT Press, 1972.

3 THE RISE OF UNIONISM

The free labor market, in which workers exchanged their physical and mental effort for wages, was a mixed blessing from their point of view. While it granted them the freedom to enter into or to refuse to enter into an exchange relationship with any particular employer, their ability to do so and the price at which their labor was exchanged depended upon supply and demand conditions over which they had no control. Today wages might be relatively high because employers sought workers, but tomorrow they could suddenly be driven down by the appearance of additional workers or because employers no longer wanted as many, at least not at the former wage. This did not seem to be fair as far as the workers were concerned, because neither their skills nor efforts had changed. Workers, moreover, were not anxious to compete with each other for available jobs. Finally, as the historian Herbert F. Muller has pointed out, under the free market "they were free to sell their services, and free to starve if they found no buyer."[1]

The free labor market had not been in existence very long before workers discovered that by banding together they could counter some of its adverse effects upon them and strengthen their power in effecting an exchange relationship with their employers. In fact, one theory of unionism sees it as a worker reaction against the free labor market.[2] According to the late Professor Tannenbaum's theory, capitalism, by destroying the status system of the Middle Ages and atomizing the workers, cut them adrift in an uncharted sea. Unions arose, therefore, to give workers a new sense of security, status, and mooring within a social group.

The Tannenbaum thesis is not widely accepted, and in the next chapter we shall examine other theories of unionism, but it is clear that unionism was a reaction to the free labor market, which in many ways ran counter to its basic precepts. In this chapter, therefore, we shall examine briefly the rise of unionism in the United States, its development through the nineteenth and twentieth centuries, its status today, and some of the principles and practices of American unions.[3]

---

[1] Herbert F. Muller, *The Uses of the Past* (New York: Oxford University Press, 1957), pp. 267–268.

[2] Frank Tannenbaum, *A Theory of the Labor Movement* (New York: Knopf, 1951).

[3] The major sources of union history, particularly for the earlier periods, are: John R. Commons *et al., History of Labour in the United States* (New York: Macmillan, 1918); Harry A. Millis and Royal E. Montgomery, *Organized Labor* (New York: McGraw-Hill, 1945); Selig Perlman, *History of Trade Unionism in the United States* (New York: Augustus M. Kelley, 1950); Philip Taft, *Organized Labor in American History* (New York: Harper & Row, 1963); Norman J. Ware, *Labor in Modern Industrial Society* (Boston: D. C. Heath, 1924).

The Advent of Local Craft Unions

The history of trade unionism in the United States is coterminous with the history of the nation. Although there are records of sporadic labor action even earlier, the first unions of any strength arose in the 1790s. These unions, known as "societies" or "bodies" at first, arose among the skilled artisans in the towns, who comprised the bulk of the nation's free labor supply at that time.

According to the famed labor historians Sidney and Beatrice Webb, many unions in England had their origin in the gathering of the journeymen "to take a social pint of porter together,"[4] and this was also true in the United States. When the craftsmen got together in their taverns, the inevitable conversation about work would eventually focus on their grievances against the masters, and pretty soon someone would suggest that, if the journeymen were to act as a group, they could force the masters to do their bidding. Thus, a few societies of such trades (hence the term "trade unionism") as carpentry, shoemaking, tailoring, and printing arose in such major cities as Philadelphia, Baltimore, and New York. These early unions attempted both to establish the prices that the journeymen were to be paid (most work was paid for on a piece rate basis) and the hours of work and to regulate apprenticeship (thus controlling the supply of labor).

The most interesting thing about the origin of unionism, as Norman Ware concluded, was that it did not originate among the oppressed members of the wage-earning class nor because of oppression. A second conclusion of Ware's is that unionism did not originate in the machine, large-scale production industries and, therefore, was not conditioned originally by the Industrial Revolution. On these two points there is little dissent among scholars, but many disagree with his third point, that no changes in property relations or in market conditions explain the beginning of trade unionism. According to the Webbs, it was when the master craftsman, in response to a growing market, became a capitalist producer, employing a larger number of journeymen, who became merely hired hands with little prospect of rising to master status, that trade unionism began to appear.[5]

Ware also put forth two other hypotheses with respect to the early unions. The first was that trade unions were first organized where the balance of power lay with the workers. Thus, when the journeymen presented a united front to the masters and threatened a "turnout" (strike) unless their demands were met, the masters were at their mercy and had to accede. Secondly, the early unions were organized for "pure and simple" trade purposes—wages, hours, apprenticeship regulation—and there was no labor philosophy.

The early unions were thus quite powerful, but the balance shifted to the employers when they, too, learned to band together against the journeymen's

---

[4] Sidney Webb and Beatrice Webb, *The History of Trade Unionism* (London: Longmans, Green, 1920), p. 23.

[5] *Ibid.*, pp. 11–26.

demands, when economic downturns reduced the demand for labor, and when machinery was introduced that diluted the skills of the craftsmen. (Another factor heavily contributing to the shift in the balance of power was court decisions against unions, a topic we shall examine in Chapter 5.)

Not all of these early craft locals were permanent bodies; on the contrary, they tended to arise when economic forces favored the workers and become quiescent when conditions were more favorable to the employers. Very few of even those that had a more or less continuous existence, however, were able to survive the economic dislocation following the War of 1812, particularly the flow into the country of cheaper British goods, and then the panic of 1819.

Unions and the Reform Movement

The period 1827–1833 saw labor concentrate its activities in the political rather than in the economic sphere. Workingmen's parties appeared in such cities as Philadelphia and New York, and, although some scholars have questioned the "labor" nature of these parties, they did have support from the urban artisans and they fought for many issues that were to the interest of workingmen. Among the issues in their platforms were free schools, universal manhood suffrage, direct election of public officials, and abolition of imprisonment for debt. Such issues, although of great concern to workers, were also of broad public interest; others, however, were more specifically wage-earner oriented, such as mechanics lien laws, factory regulation, the ten-hour day, and the elimination of competition from woman, child, and convict labor. These parties, notably the Workingmen's party of Philadelphia, scored some initial successes, but their demands were gradually absorbed by the major parties, and with their reforms achieved they disappeared.

It should not be thought that all of labor's energies were concentrated in the political arena, for local craft unionism also grew in this period. Unions were formed by weavers, blacksmiths, cigar makers, and other craftsmen. By 1836 these unions were established in every major city, and records indicate that there were fifty-eight of them in Philadelphia, fifty-two in New York, twenty-three in Baltimore, sixteen each in Boston and Newark, fourteen in Cincinnati, thirteen in Pittsburgh, and seven in Louisville. As before, these unions continued to fight for higher wages, shorter hours, union control of apprenticeship, and the closed shop, whereby only union members would be hired, giving the union monopoly control of the supply of a particular type of labor.

The one thing that the unions could not yet overcome, however, was adverse economic conditions. Workers were more inclined to stick together when jobs were plentiful, and employers were more likely to accede to union demands when orders were in hand, because profits could be earned by fulfilling those orders. Thus, unions usually did well in times of prosperity, but when slack times set in, workers, since they needed jobs in order to feed their families, started to break ranks and agreed to work for wages below union scale. In a very loose labor market, therefore, a union could do little to protect its members or preserve their standards, so members ceased paying dues and the unions disappeared. This is what happened to most of the local craft unions when the panic of 1837 struck. The rise of unions in periods of prosperity and their decline in depression, thus, is a recurring theme of American labor history until the 1920s.

Good times eventually returned in the 1840s, and local craft unions arose again. The prosperity of the 1840s was more sporadic than consistent, however, and in that economic atmosphere a number of schemes for reshaping the socioeconomic system were able to flourish. Charles Fourier's theory of organizing society into small, cooperative communities, basically agricultural but with their own workshops for producing industrial goods, was put into practice in Brook Farm, Massachusetts; Robert Owen's founding of New Harmony, Indiana, as a cooperative society was another such attempt. Such "utopian" experiments were largely ignored by workers, though there were some ventures, such as the organization of consumer and producer cooperatives owned by customers and workers, that were more successful.

The Rise of National Craft Unions

Local craft unions existed throughout the decade of the 1840s, but they made no dramatic gains and their history has been drowned out by the clamor of the utopians. New developments in unionism did emerge in the 1850s, and to understand them we should view what was happening in the economy. The period 1840 to 1860 was one of rapid industrial development. The value of manufactured products more than doubled between 1840 and 1850, from $483 million to $1 billion, and then almost doubled again by 1860, rising to $1.9 billion. Population was also growing, from 17 million in 1840 to 23 million in 1850 and to 31.5 million in 1860, and a greater percentage of that population was living in urban areas. Vast improvements in transportation— first turnpikes and canals and then railroads—began to tie the nation together. As a result, commodity markets were becoming nationwide.

With the widening of the markets for the products that workers helped to manufacture, local craft unionism was no longer sufficient to maintain wage standards. Until this time workers in Philadelphia, for instance, did not have to worry about lower wages being paid in Pittsburgh, because the high cost of transporting goods over the Allegheny Mountains more than compensated for any wage differential; as long as their union could control wages in Philadelphia, they could ignore what was happening elsewhere. But, when the railroad brought the cost of transportation down to a fraction of its former level, wages being paid in Pittsburgh, Boston, New York, and elsewhere were as important to workers in Philadelphia as the wages being paid to the local unions in those cities. The glass industry serves as a good example of the impact of improved transportation: it cost $10.00 to ship a hundredweight of glass from Pittsburgh to Philadelphia in 1800, only $1.25 after the completion of the Pennsylvania Canal System in the 1830s, and by 1853 the railroad had reduced the cost to only $.40 to $.50.[6] The result was that local craft unions began to join together in national unions in order to better standardize wage rates.[7]

The first permanent national craft union, the National Typographical Union (now known as the International Typographical Union because, like other national unions, it has locals in Canada) was organized in 1852. The next year saw the formation of the Journeyman Stonecutters Association of North America, and soon there were national organizations of hat finishers, machinists, molders, locomotive engineers, cigar makers, and blacksmiths. By 1860 there were more than twenty national unions.

The 1860s and 1870s: Renewed Union Growth and Subsequent Decline

Some of the national unions that had been formed in the 1850s collapsed when the business depression of 1857 set in, and in others the weaker locals became ineffective. The initial impact of the Civil War, with its economic dislocation, was also adverse for trade unionism, but as the war continued unions began to grow. Wartime is generally favorable to union growth, because the labor market is tight and employers are willing to meet union demands rather than face possible shutdown of facilities. Wartime situations are usually accompanied by inflation, too, and workers flock into unions to try to win wage increases to keep pace with rising living costs.

All these factors prevailed during the Civil War, and local unions began to grow at a rapid rate once more. A local union of workers in a craft was usually affiliated with two other bodies: it joined with locals of other crafts in its community in a federation known as a "local trade assembly"; and it joined with local unions of its own craft from different cities into a national union.

In this early period the trade assembly was an important union institution. Not only were the local unions of a city represented in it, but workingmen's clubs and reform societies as well. It was mainly a spokesman for labor interests, particularly in the political arena, but it occasionally engaged in collective bargaining and aiding strikes. With the expansion of the market and the rise of the national union its importance declined, but not before an unsuccessful attempt was made in 1864 to form a national federation of local trade assemblies.[8]

---

[6] William Bining, "The Glass Industry of Western Pennsylvania, 1797–1857," *Western Pennsylvania Historical Magazine*, December 1936, pp. 255–265.

[7] The fact that the labor market was also larger than a single city, as some craftsmen traveled from one to another in search of work, also encouraged the local unions to unite into national ones. The most comprehensive work on the subject is Lloyd Ulman, *The Rise of the National Trade Union* (Cambridge, Mass.: Harvard University Press, 1955).

[8] Norman J. Ware, *The Labor Movement in the United States, 1860–1895* (New York: Appleton, 1929), p. 2.

A second attempt to form a national organization representing all labor groups was made in 1866 with the establishment of the National Labor Union. It had a heterogeneous membership that included local trade assemblies, national unions, and reform organizations, but the local trade assemblies predominated. The National Labor Union flourished briefly, but it was more politically reformist in character than unionist, and it ceased to exist after converting itself into the National Labor and Reform party in 1872.

The first federation of the national unions, the National Industrial Congress, a primarily economic rather than political body, came into being in 1873. That was a fateful year, however, because in it another panic occurred, ushering in some half dozen years of depression. Only eight of forty-one national craft unions were able to survive, and by 1878 total trade union membership, which had been 300,000 in 1873, was down to 50,000. Under the adverse economic conditions the National Industrial Congress also passed quickly from the scene.

The hard times of the 1870s kindled a good deal of violence in American labor relations. In the Pennsylvania anthracite coal mining region, when worker solidarity broke down in the face of mass unemployment, attempts were made to preserve union standards among the Irish miners through force and intimidation by the so-called Molly Maguires, the leaders of whom were eventually hanged for murder on the basis of evidence collected by a Pinkerton detective who had infiltrated their ranks. The most widespread violence, however, occurred in the railroad industry in 1877, when a lowering of wages by the railroads erupted into a strike that spread across the country, resulting in the use of federal and state troops to crush it.

The Knights of Labor

By 1879 the business cycle had moved once more into the prosperity phase, and unionism again started to grow. This time, however, one national organization, the Noble Order of the Knights of Labor, predominated. The Knights of Labor, which had begun in 1869 among Philadelphia tailors, had originally been modeled on the Masons and Knights of Pythias. It expanded to take in other trade assemblies, as the local craft unions were known, as well as "mixed" assemblies, that is, local unions of workers in different crafts and industries. Local assemblies were unified in district assemblies, and in 1878 a General Assembly was established at the top.

From a very modest beginning, the Knights suddenly became a major labor organization when they scored a victory in a strike against Jay Gould's Wabash Railroad in 1885. Within one year, 1885–1886, the Knights' membership increased sevenfold, to over 700,000. Never before in American history had so many workers been organized.

The decline of the Knights of Labor was almost as rapid as its ascent, for by 1890 membership had dropped back to 100,000. A constellation of factors helps to explain the demise of the Knights. The failure to secure the eight-hour day, its loss of some key strikes, and a growing employer opposition to unionism, all played a role. Public opinion turned antilabor following the Haymarket affair of 1886, in which a bomb exploded among Chicago policemen trying to break up a legal, peaceful rally protesting the fatal shooting of four McCormick Works strikers, and for which a group of German anarchists were convicted of conspiracy, even though there was no evidence to link them directly with the bombing.

But the very structure and philosophy of the Knights contributed heavily to its downfall. The national craft unions resented its reformist philosophy, its centralization of power in the General Assembly, and most of all its mixed assemblies of workers in different trades, and they formed a new organization in opposition to the Knights.

The Birth of the American Federation of Labor

Actually, the new organization had been formed in 1881 as the Federation of Organized Trades and Labor Unions by a few national unions that had survived the panic of 1873 and some new ones that had arisen. The national unions were very much in the tradition of the New Model Unions that arose in Britain in the middle of the nineteenth century. The New Model was characterized by a permanent dues-paying membership which gave it financial stability, and centralized and businesslike administration. This type of unionism spread among the craftsmen and skilled workers, who could afford high dues and who came to be looked upon as the "aristocracy of labor" in England.[9] The same became true in the United States.

In 1886 the organization merged with some craft unions that had seceded from the Knights of Labor, changed its name to the American Federation of Labor, and began its long history as the dominant labor group in the United States. The AFL was a hardheaded group bent upon improving the conditions of its members within the existing socioeconomic order rather than attempting to reshape that order. The stress was on economic activity, with each union attempting to control jobs and regulate wages in an occupation through the monopolization of a scarce resource—the skills of its members.

The basic unit of the federation was the autonomous national craft union representing the workers of a specific skill. The greatest benefit that a union received from joining the AFL was the granting of a charter conferring upon it an exclusive jurisdiction of organizing. This jurisdiction, which was in the nature of a private franchise, was supposed to assure the particular union that all other AFL unions would recognize its exclusive right to organize workers of the occupation; in cases of jurisdictional disputes between AFL affiliates, the parent body would have the power to adjudicate. When industrial unions, such as the United Mine Workers, which covered workers in a specific industry regardless of occupation, arose, they were given the exclusive right to

---

[9] Allan Flanders, *Trade Unions* (London: Hutchinson's University Library, 1952), p. 13.

organize workers in that industry (except, of course, where some craft union could lay claim to certain skilled workers). The UMW was allowed an industrial form of organization largely because of the relatively isolated communities in which mining was conducted, and the AFL continued to favor the organization of workers along occupational lines.

The new American Federation of Labor, under the leadership of Samuel Gompers, who was its president, save for one year, from its founding until his death in 1924, did not make any startling progress in its first decade of existence. The Knights of Labor, which was still powerful, engaged the AFL in an active struggle for labor leadership, and it was not until the AFL won out in the New York cigar trade in 1890 that its victory was assured. But even that triumph over the Knights brought no flood of members into the AFL unions, largely because of the intensifying resistance of business to the spread of unionism. The most powerful union of that day, the Amalgamated Association of Iron, Steel, and Tin Workers, which represented the skilled workers in the steel industry, was broken by the Carnegie Steel Corporation in a bloody struggle at Homestead, Pennsylvania, in 1892, a defeat so decisive that unionism made no comeback in the steel industry for forty-five years.

Perhaps the most important factor in the union tribulations at that time was the economic depression that began in 1893; the hard times and loose labor markets that resulted were, as always, inauspicious occasions for workers to join unions. Managements, moreover, took advantage of the situation to launch counterattacks upon unionism, and labor suffered another disaster in the railroad industry. A new industrial-type union, the American Railway Union, saw its membership skyrocket to 150,000 within one year of its founding, only to be destroyed the very next year, 1894, in a violent strike in support of the workers of the Pullman Sleeping Car Company. Railway management received the wholehearted support of the United States government, which attached mail cars to the sleeping cars and then sent federal troops in to break the strike because it was interfering with the U.S. mails. A court injunction against the strike for interfering with the free flow of interstate commerce finally broke its back, and the ARU president, Eugene Debs, was sentenced to prison for violation of the injunction.

The Gay Nineties were obviously far from gay on the labor-management front, but there were also some bright spots. In 1891 the first real and complete collective bargaining agreement between the employers in an industry, in this case the stove foundry industry, and the national union representing its production workers was concluded. Despite the labor-management travails that followed, this agreement is regarded as the beginning of both a stabilized union movement and genuine collective bargaining between labor and management.

The AFL managed to stay intact despite the depression and the growing employer hostility, and it eschewed participation in the election of 1896, in which the progressive forces rallied to the banner of the Democratic candidate, William Jennings Bryan. By 1897, as the depression approached its end, the AFL unions found themselves with 265,000 members, about the same number that they had had when the federation had been founded. Thus, all that the AFL could claim in its favor was that it had managed to survive.

The Expansion of the AFL

With the return of prosperity, however, the existing unions began to expand their memberships, and a number of new national unions came into being. Many more unions, moreover, were able to negotiate agreements with employer associations. In fact, as the prevalence of collective bargaining spread, the five years from 1898 through 1902 became known as the "honeymoon period" of labor-management relations.

By 1900 the membership of the AFL unions had climbed to 584,000, double the number of three years earlier. Within the next four years it tripled again, and the AFL could boast of 1,676,000 members in 114 national unions, 828 local trade and federal unions (local unions chartered directly by the AFL because there was no national union that had jurisdiction over their trade), 549 city central bodies, and 29 state federations. There was no question but that the American Federation of Labor was a powerful force, one that could speak without serious challenge as the "voice" of American labor, at least that part of it that was organized.

The success of the AFL can be attributed primarily to its pragmatism. In place of some vague pronouncements about abolishing "wage labor," its constituent national unions sought, just as the local craft unions of a century before had, to raise their members' wages by organizing all the workers of a given occupation and thus monopolizing that sector of the labor supply. Then, instead of attacking the capitalists, they sought to enter into agreements with them governing the wages and hours of, and conditions for, employees. And, rather than dissipating a great deal of energy in national politics and cooperative ventures, they concentrated most of their efforts in the economic arena, where the most immediate payoffs for union members lay.

Too often the success of the AFL is used to disparage its predecessors, but that is unfair. Despite its failure, the Knights of Labor had put labor on the map, and had reached groups that had never been reached before, including unskilled immigrant workers, whom the AFL largely disdained.[10] As Grob has clearly shown, however, the clash between the Knights of Labor and the AFL was inevitable, in that they represented two distinct tendencies within labor ranks.[11] The Knights were in the tradition of reform dating from the Jacksonian era, and were intent upon abolishing the wage system and replacing it with producer cooperatives, their structure of mixed assemblies having been erected for these reform purposes. The trade unions, on the other hand,

---

[10] Ware, *op. cit.*, pp. xiii–xviii.

[11] Gerald N. Grob, *Workers and Utopia* (Evanston, Ill.: Northwestern University Press, 1961).

accepted the existing economic order, but sought to gain higher wages, shorter hours, and job control within it. Accepting the workers' wage status, the trade unions sought to build local organizations on a craft basis, through which they could conduct collective bargaining with employers to improve the job conditions of their members. Viewed in this light, the demise of the Knights was inevitable and the goals of the AFL much more realistic.

Internal and External Opposition

Its accommodation to the realities of the labor market enabled the AFL to dominate the labor scene for close to half a century, though not without internal and external opposition. First of all, by 1902 the employer attitude toward unionism had again stiffened. Fearing that unionism was growing too strong, many of them broke off relations that they had formerly established, and for the next decade there was increasing labor-management strife. This was the period in which the ideas of scientific management were gaining their foothold in industry, and union resistance to efficiency measures, which became associated in their minds with speedups and rate-cutting, only intensified hostility.

Many employers perfected union-busting tactics—including the circulation of blacklists of pro-union employees and the use of vigilante groups against union organizers—and unions responded with their own strong-arm methods. Some court decisions undermined union weapons in the struggle with management. With labor on the defensive, the growth of unionism slowed considerably, and the AFL unions in 1914 had 2 million members, an increase of only 20 percent in the decade.

Meanwhile, labor was undergoing internal conflicts, too. For one thing, there was never unanimity within the AFL concerning its policies. The socialists generally led the opposition that sought a greater emphasis on political action and on organizing the less skilled workers in basic industry, and one group of socialists and industrial unionists (chiefly the Western Federation of Miners) formed a rival organization in 1905—the Industrial Workers of the World.

The IWW—whose members were popularly known as "Wobblies"— was a form of revolutionary unionism, proclaiming that it "was building the foundation of a new society within the shell of the old." The IWW advocated syndicalism—the ownership and operation of industry, not through central government, but by the workers in each industry. It achieved some notable success in organizing migrant workers in western mining and logging and in attracting immigrant unskilled workers in eastern factories; two famous strikes that it conducted were in the textile industry, in Paterson, New Jersey, and Lawrence, Massachusetts. The IWW, however, was more concerned with conducting the struggle against capitalism than in cementing collective bargaining rights, and many of its victories turned out to be very ephemeral. Splits occurred within it over the issues of political versus direct action and industrial unionism versus class warfare. Finally, the IWW suffered from adverse public reaction and severe governmental persecution, particularly because of its opposition to U.S. involvement in the First World War; many western states passed antisyndicalist laws, by which IWW leaders were sentenced to prison, and by the 1920s it had ceased to exist as an effective force. It did, however, leave a heritage of industrial unionism that was acted upon effectively some decades later.

World War I: Labor Resurgence

The industrial unrest of the years preceding the war led to the appointment of a federal industrial commission to study labor-management relations. The commission's report was favorable to collective bargaining, and helped pave the way for the creation in 1913 of a Department of Labor on the cabinet level and the insertion in the Clayton Act of 1914 of clauses supposedly exempting labor from the antitrust acts.

World War I provided a favorable atmosphere for a new surge of union growth. The cutting off of immigration from Europe tightened the labor market, and the relative shortage of labor, when combined with high profits, made employers more willing to recognize unions and to agree to their wage demands. With a friendly national administration, that of Woodrow Wilson, the railroad brotherhoods, representing engineers, firemen, conductors, and trainmen, were able, in 1916, to get Congress to pass the Adamson Act, which established the basic eight-hour day for rail operatives.

When the United States entered the ranks of the belligerents, labor cooperation was sought in the national mobilization effort. Since the AFL had a record of conservative and able leadership, it was given representation on the wartime bodies that were established. Samuel Gompers, for instance, was a member of the Advisory Commission to the Council of National Defense and the National War Labor Board. In return for labor's pledge not to conduct strikes in industries vital to the war effort, employers promised not to abrogate their collective bargaining agreements.

As in most war situations, unions did very well during the First World War. The basic eight-hour day spread through the American economy, and trade union standards were used as a yardstick by the War Labor Board in settling labor-management disputes. The most important trend, from the union point of view, was a rapid rise in membership. In five years AFL membership doubled, reaching 4,079,000 in 110 national unions by 1920; including unions that were not affiliated with the AFL, such as the railroad brotherhoods, total union membership went over the 5 million mark that year. Unionism spread into sectors of the American economy from which it had been absent heretofore, and there was a significant growth of unions organized on an industrial basis; that is, their memberships were composed of the workers in a given industry regardless of occupation.

Postwar Decline in Unionism

After the war, when the controls that had artificially held down prices were removed, prices started to rise rapidly. The union response was a demand for higher wages, but with wartime profits gone employers were actually attempting to reduce their labor costs. The stage thus was set for renewed labor-management strife, and the signal for battle was issued by the National Association of Manufacturers in 1919, when it launched an "open shop"—which in practice meant a "closed to unions" shop—campaign. In addition, in most cases the specter of radicalism that followed the Bolshevik takeover in Russia rallied public opinion against the unions.

Then, in 1921, a two-year depression set in. The employers took advantage of the economic situation to press their open-shop drive, and unions encountered greater court repression. The result was a drastic falloff in union membership, from 1920's high of 5 million to 3.6 million in 1923, with the sharpest drops occurring in the areas that had only recently been organized, particularly in manufacturing.

In 1923 prosperity returned, but this time there was a twist in history as far as unionism was concerned, for, unlike former prosperity periods, trade union membership did not grow in the period 1923–1929; in fact, union membership declined a further 200,000 in the face of a 3 million increase in nonagricultural employment. Those were sad days for those who favored worker organization, for basic industry was untouched by unionism. Under the influence of the human relations movement, American management was attempting to improve conditions on the job and extend benefits to workers, and in so doing prove to them that unions were not necessary to their welfare. Many companies, moreover, gave their employees a semblance of collective representation through the formation of worker councils or employee representation bodies; these groups, however, were not independent of management influence and control.

In view of this, and of the fact that workers enjoyed a rise in real earnings as wages rose somewhat and the cost of living remained fairly steady during this period, unions found it difficult to organize the employees of the large manufacturing companies. In some industries in which unionism had once been strong, industry migrated from older centers of production to other regions, and in others technological changes eliminated the need for skilled workers. An example of this is the glass industry, in which unionism had been very strong, but when machinery was invented that replaced the skilled workers, the Glass Bottle Blowers Association and the American Flint Glass Workers Union fell upon hard times, and the once powerful union of flat glass workers disappeared altogether. A number of AFL unions were also racked by internal dissension as the Communists, through their Trade Union Education League, tried to gain control of them. Some unions also found themselves infiltrated by racketeering elements, and this served to further besmirch the reputation of organized labor.

Despite all these unfavorable conditions, there were many people both inside and outside the AFL who believed that greater progress in organizing workers could have been made. To them the prime reason for the AFL's failure to effectively counter the power of the giant corporations in the mass production industries lay in what they regarded as its structural and functional obsolescence. By this they meant the ineffectiveness of the federation as a central body, particularly its dependence upon its constituent unions for major organizing activity and the continued reliance on the craft form of organization. Their voices were raised in vain at AFL conventions, however, for the craft unions, jealously guarding their autonomies and jurisdictions, had a majority of the votes to prevent any change.

The Great Depression

On October 29, 1929, "Black Thursday," the stock market came crashing down from its dizzy speculative heights, and within a few months it was obvious that the "era of permanent prosperity" had come to an end. In its stead came the era of the Great Depression. Production and employment dropped drastically, and while the business cycle was not new to the United States, the severity of this depression was fantastic. By the time the bottom was hit in early 1933, the national income had been cut in half and fully one-fourth of the labor force was unemployed. Trade union membership declined further, of course, and the AFL unions went from 2,961,000 in 1929 to 2,127,000 in 1933.

The situation in the 1930s is hard for anyone reared since 1940 to imagine, but, to say the least, there was great mass misery.[12] Businesses that had been efficient and profitable organizations yesterday found that no one wanted their products today. Workers who had been diligent and faithful found themselves out on the street without jobs as their employers' orders disappeared. At first private charity carried the load of caring for the needy, but as the numbers of these swelled the funds were exhausted, and there were no government programs of welfare to help, either. Worst of all, nobody could explain what had happened or why, and what was to be done about it. The only things that came from the White House were pious pronouncements from President Hoover to the effect that "prosperity was around the corner," but it appeared that the block had no end.

The depression also had profound sociopsychological effects upon the nation. The morale of the business community was broken. After all, the self-confidence of business that it could run its affairs unfettered by government regulations or uninhibited by union interference had been based upon a record of achievement: continual progress in material betterment that had given the American people the highest standard of living in the world. But

---

[12] Descriptions of the period can be found in Dixon Wecter, *The Age of the Great Depression* (New York: Macmillan, 1948), and Studs Terkel, *Hard Times* (New York: Random House, 1970).

the early 1930s were hardly a period of pride in accomplishment, and businessmen, like everyone else, hardly knew what to do about the depression. The faith of the public, particularly the middle class, in laissez faire was shaken to its foundations, and the miseries that large segments of the working class were suffering made them psychologically ripe for unionization; after all, the situation almost fit Karl Marx's dictum that they "had nothing to lose but their chains."

The election results of 1932 showed that there had been defections from the Republican to the Democratic ticket in all segments of the population; even many businessmen deserted "their party" to cast their votes for Roosevelt. Although the 1932 Democratic platform had been little different from that of the Republicans, except to charge them with the sin of having unbalanced the budget, Roosevelt caught the mood of the people during the campaign, and began to talk about the vast changes that were necessary. When he took office on March 4, 1933, in the midst of the nation's worst banking crisis, the stage was set for dramatic changes. As FDR's New Deal unfolded, these changes came swiftly, one succeeding the other, and among them was bound to be a vast rearrangement of traditional labor-management relations.

The Rise of Industrial Unionism

Among the first moves of the new administration was passage of the National Industrial Recovery Act, section 7a of which said that labor had the right to organize and bargain collectively with management. Although there was an absence of effective enforcement, unions took advantage of 7a and of the generally friendly government policy to rebuild their ranks; John L. Lewis, for example, sent his organizers into the mining towns with the message, "President Roosevelt wants you to join the union."

A number of unions were quite successful in their organizing efforts. Membership in the United Mine Workers (UMW) skyrocketed from 50,000 to 500,000 in less than two years. Other unions making significant gains included the International Ladies' Garment Workers' Union (ILGWU) and the Amalgamated Clothing Workers of America (ACWA). Structurally these unions were not typical of the AFL, in that they organized all workers in their industries, even if local unions were based on specific crafts, as in the case of the garment unions. Furthermore, unions were often arising spontaneously in factories in basic industry, and, not knowing what else to do with them, the AFL made them federal locals. Federal locals were affiliated directly with the AFL, and covered workers in industries or occupations over which no existing national union had jurisdiction. Between June and October 1933 alone, the federation chartered 584 directly affiliated federal unions with 300,000 members, more than in any other comparable period.[13] These federal locals, too, were composed of all workers in the plant regardless of occupation.

---

[13] Millis and Montgomery, *op. cit.*, p. 193.

The industrial unionists within the AFL were of the opinion that the federation's policies with respect to the granting of new charters and the apportionment of the membership of federal locals among the national craft unions were deterring union expansion. They believed that the time was ripe for major breakthroughs in basic manufacturing, but that this could be accomplished only if the factory workers were organized on an industrial basis, which the craft unions opposed. A compromise between the two forces was effected at the AFL's 1934 convention, but following the 1935 convention, in which the craft unions, which still commanded a majority of the votes, refused to renounce their claims to the workers in the new industrial locals, a group of AFL unions formed the unofficial Committee for Industrial Organization (CIO).

The new CIO, under the leadership of John L. Lewis, president of the United Mine Workers, launched organizing drives in a number of industries, displaying a militancy and aggressiveness that had long been absent from unionism. Taking advantage of the mood of the times, a friendly administration both in Washington and in many states, and the recently passed Wagner-Connery National Labor Relations Act, which declared that employers must recognize and bargain collectively with unions freely chosen by a majority of their employees, the CIO achieved some startling successes. In some cases, employers acquiesced very quickly to union demands for recognition; having suffered a number of years of very poor business, they did not want to be involved in strikes that would disrupt production just when orders were beginning to mount. Others, though not happy about unionism, recognized it as inevitable, particularly since the force of the law now supported it.

All sections of the glass industry—flat, containers, and pressed and blown ware—were organized or, in some cases, reorganized, with relatively little serious labor-management confrontation. In other industries, however, particularly those in which there was no history of collective bargaining and in which management had no experience in dealing with unions, employers seemed determined to resist the encroachment of unionism. To this end they unleashed antiunion propaganda campaigns, hired spies to infiltrate unions and report on their activities, and used armed guards forcibly to keep union organizers from the gates of their plants. Such employer tactics were often quite successful in preventing organization of their facilities.

Labor found a counterweapon, however, when striking rubber workers in Akron, Ohio, instead of leaving the plant to mount picket lines outside, simply "sat down" at their work places. This "sit-down" strike effectively prevented management from operating the plant with nonstrikers. The sit-down strike spread quickly and often spontaneously, and it was the device through which the CIO won its possibly greatest victory, organization in the automobile industry.

In early 1937 strikes had erupted in many General Motors plants, and the autoworkers in Flint, Michigan, occupied GM facilities. Both sides prepared to do battle as GM demanded the use of the National Guard to oust the strikers, who were possessing their property illegally. Michigan governor Frank Murphy was friendly to labor and feared, moreover, that a bloodbath would ensue if attempts were made to eject the strikers forcibly. When the top management of General Motors recognized that the choice was between violence and bloodshed on the one hand, and recognition of the union on the other, it agreed to recognize the union as representative of its employees in seventeen struck plants. It was a great union victory, and in a few weeks the membership of the United Automobile Workers (UAW) doubled, rising from 100,000 to 200,000.[14] Although the sit-down strike was subsequently declared to be unconstitutional by the Supreme Court, and labor abandoned its use, it had played a vital role in the extension of unionism in this period.

The AFL had looked askance upon the formation of the Committee for Industrial Organization, viewing it as a form of dual unionism and a violation of decisions that had been arrived at democratically. When the affiliated unions that had formed the committee refused to cease their activities, the AFL suspended them and, in 1938, formally expelled them. By this time, however, the CIO, flush from its victory in the automobile industry, and having been recognized voluntarily and without a violent struggle by the United States Steel Corporation, had a membership of a little over 4 million, which made it larger than the AFL.

Attempts at reunification of the two union federations foundered on the issue of inviolability of the newly organized industrial unions, since the craft unions still believed that the skilled workers belonged in their ranks; but the AFL was willing to concede that there were "certain industries where the industrial form of organization would apply."[15] Although one of the original unions that had helped to form the CIO, the International Ladies' Garment Workers, returned to the AFL ranks in 1940, the newly organized industrial unions, composed mainly of semiskilled workers in large-scale manufacturing —such as the automobile, steel, rubber, electrical, and textile industries—had no loyalty to the AFL and its craft traditions, and were thus prepared to go their own way. CIO head John L. Lewis, moreover, was not ready to abdicate leadership and become just another vice-president of the AFL. Thus, upon the expulsion of the committee's unions from the AFL, the CIO converted itself to a full-fledged separate federation of unions, the Congress of Industrial Organizations.

Warfare between the AFL and the CIO

A period of interunion warfare between the AFL and CIO ensued. Many employers who were willing to recognize and bargain with the unions chosen by their employees found themselves victims of this interunion rivalry, for when they recognized a union affiliated with one of the federations, they might be subjected to picketing and other harassment by unions from the

---

[14] Thomas R. Brooks, *Toil and Trouble* (New York: Delta, 1965), p. 185.

[15] Millis and Montgomery, *op. cit.*, pp. 216–218.

other. Unionism itself, however, as the AFL and CIO vied with each other to organize more workers, seemed to be spurred by the division in labor's ranks.

In the process of this struggle, the structure of many AFL unions began to change. In order to more effectively compete with their CIO rivals, they began to organize all workers in a plant, regardless of occupation. This switch in policy was spurred by decisions of the National Labor Relations Board, created by the Wagner Act. The board seemed to favor industrial over craft unionism, and it controlled and conducted plant elections to determine which union represented the employees.

The intense organizing efforts of the 1930s resulted in the reorganization of those sectors of the economy in which unionism had formerly existed and organization for the first time of such basic manufacturing industries as automobiles, steel, rubber, and electrical equipment. Within six years more than 3.5 million members were added to labor's ranks, and by 1939 total membership stood at 6.5 million. With the revitalization of the AFL, it again asserted its dominance as the largest union group, with 3,878,000 members, while the CIO, with some unions leaving it when it became a rival federation and and as the business downturn of 1938 eroded employment in manufacturing, dropped to 1,838,000; there were also 840,000 members of unions unaffiliated with either federation.[16]

World War II: The Extension of Unionism

World War II, as was true of previous war periods, provided another golden opportunity for union expansion. War production zoomed, millions of men entered military service, and the depression became a memory (though a bitter one), as idle plants were replaced by three-shift operations, and idle men by severe labor shortages and many hours of overtime work at premium pay rates. An entire panoply of special agencies was established to coordinate the war effort—the War Production Board, the Office of Price Administration, the War Labor Board—and labor received representation on them.

In the interests of promoting the war effort, both the AFL and the CIO offered "no-strike" pledges for the duration. Both prices and wages were regulated, the latter by the National War Labor Board, which adopted the "Little Steel Formula," by which wage rates were allowed to rise 15 percent, or equal to the increase in consumer prices between January 1941 and May 1942. Although prices continued to rise after that, worker discontent was deflected by the presence of overtime work, as a result of which earnings actually rose faster than prices.

---

[16] Membership figures are from Leo Troy, *Trade Union Membership, 1892–1962* (New York: National Bureau of Economic Research, 1965), p. 8. According to the data of the Bureau of Labor Statistics, union membership in 1939 was 9 million, 2.5 million higher than the Troy estimate, which is based upon those paying full-time dues, whereas the BLS relied on union reports of their memberships, which in 1939 probably included workers represented even though not paying union dues.

As could be expected, unionism expanded greatly during the war, particularly now that the law required employers to bargain collectively. Between 1939 and 1945 the unions added another 6 million members, and collective bargaining became a permanent institution in most of basic industry. The one issue that threatened to upset labor-management peace was that of union security. The unions, fearful that employers might take advantage of their no-strike pledge to undermine their majority status as new workers flocked into factories, insisted that all employees be required to join the union. Many employers, on the other hand, were opposed on principle to forcing employees to join a union against their will; to have agreed to the union shop, moreover, would have amounted to a betrayal of those employees who had remained loyal to management and resisted unionization during the period of the organizing drives. The potential threat to uninterrupted production was removed when the War Labor Board found a novel compromise solution: the "maintenance of membership" shop, whereby all those who joined the union would have to remain members for the duration of the agreement, but those who refused to join could remain outside union ranks. Both sides accepted the compromise, for it protected the union sufficiently against employer undermining, while not violating employer principles.

The Postwar Period: Employer Reconciliation to Unionism

After victory over the Axis powers was achieved in 1945, many people, including most labor leaders, feared that there would be an inevitable postwar economic depression. To union leaders, the best protection against such an event would be the maintenance of worker purchasing power, which was threatened by the elimination of most overtime work. Unions, therefore, demanded wage increases of up to 30 percent at the very time that employers feared a reduction in profits with the end of cost-plus government war contracts. The result was a series of industry-wide strikes that spread across the economy in late 1945 and in 1946.

Despite the failure of the national Labor-Management Conference, which was called at the conclusion of hostilities by President Truman to map out a program of labor-management peace, industry did not attempt to rid itself of unionism as it had following World War I. Instead it settled for some redressing of the balance of bargaining power through the passage of the Taft-Hartley Labor-Management Relations Act of 1947. With the reconciliation of most of American management to unionism and collective bargaining, trade union membership continued to grow in the postwar period, reaching 17,316,000 in 1953.[17]

Thus, despite the division in labor's ranks, union membership in 1953 was equal to 34.5 percent of nonfarm employment and 27.6 percent of the total civilian labor force. But the mid-1950s appeared to be the high-water

---

[17] *Ibid.*, p. 18. According to the Bureau of Labor Statistics' estimate, membership was half a million higher—17,860,000.

mark of unionism, because after that union membership began to ebb, at least as a percentage of employment. The division in the House of Labor was no longer paying dividends in union growth, and forces were afoot that were to lead to unity between the AFL and the CIO.

The AFL-CIO

The basic reasons for the continued existence of two separate labor federations had largely dissipated over the years. AFL charges of Communist influence in the CIO dissolved when the latter expelled, in 1949 and 1950, ten affiliated unions for being Communist party-dominated. In the early days of the split the CIO had been more politically active than the AFL, but by 1952 both groups had political committees, through which they actively supported the Democratic presidential candidate, Adlai Stevenson. Even the basic structural difference between the two had been modified, for by the 1950s many old AFL craft unions, such as the International Association of Machinists and the International Brotherhood of Electrical Workers, had spawned large industrial sections.

A series of coincidences in November 1952 paved the way for eventual merger of the two organizations. First, the first Republican administration in twenty years was elected, and the unions feared that it might usher in an antilabor era. Secondly, within a few weeks of the election the presidents of both federations, William Green, who had succeeded Samuel Gompers as head of the AFL in 1924, and Philip Murray, who had taken John L. Lewis's place as head of the CIO in 1940, died. Their successors, George Meany in the AFL and Walter Reuther in the CIO, immediately set out to unify the two organizations. The first step toward this goal was the signing, in 1953, of a no-raiding agreement, by which sixty-five AFL and twenty-nine CIO affiliates promised not to try to steal members from each other.

The CIO, having cleansed its house of Communist influence, believed that it was high time that the AFL cleanse itself of corruption, but the AFL had always refrained from doing so on the basis of the autonomy of the national unions. The second step toward unity came, therefore, when the AFL reversed this historic refusal to act and expelled the racket-ridden International Longshoremen's Association (ILA) at its 1953 convention. Early in 1955 a committee, the Joint Unity Committee, was set up by the two federations and began meeting to work out the details of the merger. Under the guidance of Arthur Goldberg, who was then the CIO's legal counsel, a new constitution was written. On December 5, 1955, the two federations were formally united into one labor federation, the American Federation of Labor and Congress of Industrial Organizations (AFL-CIO), into which came all the former AFL and CIO unions intact.

The new 16 million-strong AFL-CIO started life with great expectations, which are yet to be realized. The extension of unionism into areas of the economy and geographic regions in which it was not strong, such as office work and the South, had been thought to be a possibility through unity, but no significant organizing efforts were launched. Others anticipated that the AFL-CIO would become the champion, not only of the organized workers, but of the underprivileged as well. Instead, increasing friction developed between minority groups and the unions—particularly, but not exclusively, those in the building trades—as the pace of black militancy mounted. Clearly, the problems besetting organized labor in this period were more fundamental than merely division into two separate federations.

One of the major problems besetting the unions was the extent of corruption within its ranks. The glare of public attention usually fell upon the union leader who helped himself to union funds or who took a payoff from an employer for allowing him some leeway from contractual standards. This type of problem was endemic, however, and not limited to unions; banks also suffer from occasional dishonest officers. The more fundamental problem was that, with the expansion of unionism to a dominant force within many industries, underworld elements could use it as a vehicle through which to gain substantial control; the problem was particularly acute in the small-scale, highly competitive industries.

Given the autonomy that each national union enjoyed, the only thing that the AFL-CIO could do with a corrupt union was to threaten it with expulsion unless it reformed itself. Once the union was expelled, the only thing that the parent body could do would be to attempt to create a rival national union in that jurisdiction. A few smaller affiliates were cajoled into reforming themselves as a result of AFL-CIO threats of expulsion, and, when the International Bakery and Confectionery Workers organization was expelled, a rival American Bakery and Confectionery Workers' Union was created. A more fundamental problem was faced, however, when Senate hearings uncovered widespread wrongdoing in the International Brotherhood of Teamsters, the largest single union in the AFL-CIO. When the IBT failed to act against corruption in its ranks, the 1957 convention of the AFL-CIO voted to expel it. The AFL-CIO, however, was in no position to create a serious rival to the giant union. The expulsion, therefore, had little impact on the Teamsters, which continued to make gains, and many AFL-CIO unions, despite admonitions to the contrary, continued to forge alliances with the IBT, being dependent upon the truck drivers for support in organizing campaigns and strikes.

The membership of the AFL-CIO dropped dramatically, from 16.1 million in 1957 to 13.9 million in 1958. The loss of the Teamsters was only part of the explanation, for the former CIO unions dropped half a million members that year with the setting in of the most serious post–World War II economic recession. Union membership failed to grow, and even declined close to another million during the next few years, as employment in manufacturing dropped. Labor leaders were most vociferous in denouncing "automation" as the culprit, but, as we shall see later, the more fundamental cause was that the nation was undergoing a period of slow economic growth, and the unions were unable to penetrate into the areas of the economy in which employment was expanding.

With the resumption of a faster rate of national economic growth beginning with the tax cut of 1964, employment in goods-producing industries, the backbone of union membership, once again expanded. With the escalation of the war in Vietnam, labor markets tightened, living costs rose, and unions were again in a favorable situation to add members and win larger demands from employers. Besides, the latter part of the 1960s saw a significant breakthrough of unionism into public and nonprofit private employment, major growth areas in terms of jobs. According to the Bureau of Labor Statistics, between 1966 and 1970 union membership climbed 1.6 million, to a new high of 20.7 million. Employee associations, such as those of civil service employees, which do not regard themselves as unions but do represent their members in bargaining with management, had 1.9 million members in 1970, bringing the total organized to 22.6 million. Despite gains in organizing workers in new areas, however, AFL-CIO membership actually dropped .3 million in this period, to 15.9 million, as a result of the defection of the United Automobile Workers, which, with the Teamsters gone, had become its largest affiliate.

American trade unionism thus entered the decade of the 1970s at the pinnacle of success in terms of absolute numbers. As a percentage of non-farm employment, however, union membership continued to decline from the heights it had reached in the mid-1950s, and by 1970 it was down to 27.4 percent. With the addition of employee associations, the percentage would be 30.1 percent of nonfarm employment. Divisions within organized labor's ranks, moreover, had reasserted themselves, but not on the scale of former periods. Clearly, if trade unionism were not to become a smaller spokesman for American employees, it would have to spread into the faster-growing, nongoods-producing sectors of the economy, and there were distinct signs of progress in these areas. Further discussion of this subject will be left to the next chapter.

Practices and Principles of American Unions

No review of the history of American trade unionism, no matter how brief, would be complete without seeking to determine the threads of continuity. The most obvious element of continuity is the constant focus of trade unions on matters related to workers' jobs. American trade unionism conforms quite closely to the Webbs' definition of trade unionism as a permanent combination of employees for the purpose of improving the condition of their working lives.

Despite ephemeral periods of political reformism, and even brief minority excursions into revolutionary unionism, the bulk of American unionism has been "bread and butter" oriented. From the days of the first local craft unions in the 1790s to the giant national unions of today, the stress has been on achieving better wages, hours, and working conditions. Of course, today's elaborate negotiations with employers cover many more items than they once did—as, for instance, pensions, welfare funds, and limitations on the employer's right to subcontract work—but all these items are part and parcel of assuring union members greater security in their jobs, better standards on their jobs, and protection from risks of old age and sickness when they leave their jobs.

Organized labor in this country, like business, has no long-range philosophy. What it seeks was summed up neatly by Samuel Gompers more than half a century ago in the phrase, "More, more, and more," and as long as the American economy has grown, labor has been able to achieve that goal. If that goal seems to be nothing more than crass materialism, labor is hardly to be blamed, for in this respect it has been as American as apple pie. Only those intoxicated with Marxist ideology who thought that somehow greater virtue abided with the working class than with the "bourgeoisie" have been disillusioned by union behavior. Even when Communists controlled unions, they remained in power not by behaving differently from the "pure and simple" trade unionists, but by acting exactly like them; few members of their unions were at all favorably disposed to communism, yet they reelected their leaders because they brought home the bacon of higher wages and better working conditions.

Although collective bargaining has been the focal point of their endeavors, unions have also engaged in political activity. Unlike unions in Europe, however, they have not created a working class party but have supported legislation (and candidates) put forth by the Democrats and Republicans that was considered to be favorable to labor's interests. Again, it was Samuel Gompers who many years ago supplied the slogan and rationale of labor in politics that is still basically true today: "Reward your friends, and punish your enemies."

Since 1952, however, when both the AFL and CIO formally endorsed Adlai Stevenson, the Democratic candidate for President, the unions have drawn closer to that party. In every presidential election except 1972 the AFL-CIO, through its Committee for Political Education (COPE), has actively supported the Democratic party nominee. In many communities, moreover, there has developed a strong interconnection between organized labor and the Democratic party; in the state of Michigan, for example, the Autoworkers are a major element in the party.

Although whom labor endorses for President of the United States or for a Senate seat gets most of the notoriety, more political activity is concentrated at the city, county, and state levels than on the national scene. Much of this political activity is an adjunct to union collective bargaining efforts on behalf of their members, concerned with such matters as building codes that ensure that only union members can perform certain work.

The stress on the interests of their own members has been both the strength and the weakness of organized labor: its strength in that such a stress has prevented dissipation of energies in other directions and has enabled unions to win gains for their members, its weakness in that it has prevented unions from speaking for a broader segment of the population, for those gains have sometimes been obtained at the expense of other elements of the public. Moreover, the exclusiveness of some unions has meant that some segments of the population have not had an opportunity to share the gains won, as exemplified by the paucity of blacks and other disadvantaged in the higher-wage skilled trades.

Summary

Workers looked upon the free labor market as at best a mixed blessing, for the freedom that it gave them with respect to entering into an exchange relationship with employers came at the expense of their having to compete among themselves for jobs. The workers, therefore, sought to protect themselves against the vicissitudes of the market by banding together into associations that became known as trade unions, through which they attempted to regulate the wages that they would be paid.

Unions first arose in each city among the skilled artisans, but, as improvements in transportation widened product markets, the local craft unions had to unite into national unions if they were to be able to standardize wages and working conditions. A number of attempts were also made to form national federations of unions, but none was of lasting success until the rise of the Knights of Labor in the 1880s. The Knights were more interested in replacing the wage system of the free labor market with producer cooperatives than in improving the status of workers as wage earners, and its success was short lived. In its stead arose the American Federation of Labor, which was to be the dominant labor group for half a century. The AFL unions sought neither revolution nor reform, but to raise the wages of their members by monopolizing the labor supply and entering into agreements with employers governing the wages, hours, and work conditions.

The AFL continued to make progress, reaching its high point during and right after World War I, but then employers counterattacked and union membership fell during the 1920s, even though nonagricultural employment was growing. Then the Great Depression of the 1930s set in, and union membership declined still further as unemployment skyrocketed to 25 percent of the labor force. But the election of 1932 brought into office a national administration that was friendly to labor, and under these conditions there was a new upsurge of union growth.

The new union locals, however, were organized mainly on an industrial basis; that is, they represented all the workers in a plant, regardless of skill. Fearing that the AFL would later attempt to divide the new unions among the craft unions, the industrial unionists, under the leadership of John L. Lewis, launched the Committee for Industrial Organization. The CIO achieved some notable victories in organizing basic industry, and, upon expulsion of its member unions from the AFL, converted itself into a rival labor federation, the Congress of Industrial Organizations. In the ensuing struggle for dominance between the AFL and CIO, union membership climbed to new heights and was further augmented during World War II.

Unlike the situation after World War I, when World War II came to an end employers did not try to rid themselves of unionism, but they did receive some redress of powers through the enactment of the Taft-Hartley Act in 1947. Union membership continued to grow, hitting a high-water mark in the mid-1950s, after which it began to slip, despite the unification of the AFL and CIO into one labor federation. Then, in the mid-1960s, as the rate of national economic growth moved upward once again, union membership began to rise again in absolute numbers, but as a percentage of nonagricultural employment it continued to decline from the heights that had been reached in the mid-1950s.

Whatever the differences among American unions today, they all accept the free labor market and focus their activities on achieving better wages, hours, and working conditions for their members through collective bargaining with employers. Organized labor, however, has become very active in political affairs, taking positions on broad local, national, and international issues, and actively supporting candidates (usually Democrats) for office.

BIBLIOGRAPHY

Commons, John R., *et al. History of Labour in the United States.* New York: Macmillan, 1918.

Galenson, Walter. *The CIO Challenge to the AFL.* Cambridge, Mass.: Harvard University Press, 1960.

Goldberg, Arthur J. *AFL-CIO, Labor United.* New York: McGraw-Hill, 1956.

Gompers, Samuel. *Seventy Years of Life and Labor.* New York: Dutton, 1925.

Grob, Gerald N. *Workers and Utopia.* Evanston, Ill.: Northwestern University Press, 1961.

Lorwin, Lewis L. *The American Federation of Labor.* Washington, D.C.: Brookings, 1933.

Millis, Harry A., and Royal E. Montgomery. *Organized Labor.* New York: McGraw-Hill, 1945.

Muller, Herbert F. *The Uses of the Past.* New York: Oxford University Press, 1957.

Perlman, Selig. *History of Trade Unionism in the United States.* New York: Augustus M. Kelley, 1950.

Taft, Philip. *Organized Labor in American History.* New York: Harper & Row, 1963.

Tannenbaum, Frank. *A Theory of the Labor Movement.* New York: Knopf, 1951.

Terkel, Studs. *Hard Times.* New York: Random House, 1970.

Troy, Leo. *Trade Union Membership, 1892–1962.* New York: National Bureau of Economic Research, 1965.

Ulman, Lloyd. *The Rise of the National Trade Union.* Cambridge, Mass.: Harvard University Press, 1955.

Ware, Norman J. *Labor in Modern Industrial Society.* Boston: D. C. Heath, 1924.

Webb, Sidney, and Beatrice Webb. *The History of Trade Unionism.* London: Longmans, Green, 1920.

4 UNION ORGANIZATION AND STRUCTURE

Now that we have surveyed the rise of unions in the United States, we shall, in this chapter, try to examine some of the aspects of unionism, so that we shall be better able to understand its impact on the exchange relationship between employee and employer. First of all, we shall discuss some theories of why unionism has arisen and the factors that explain its growth. Secondly, we shall find that unionism is not spread evenly throughout the economy, and we shall examine its extent—by industry, occupation, and geographic area. American unionism, we shall find, has largely been limited to blue-collar workers in transportation, construction, mining, and manufacturing; but since these are no longer rapidly growing areas of employment, union membership as a percentage of the labor force has been declining. Next, we shall probe into the structure of unionism at its various levels, from the place of work up to the AFL-CIO. Fourthly, we shall look at the growth areas of unionism today, as represented by the organization of government employees; and finally we shall consider the prospects for the development of large-scale white-collar unionism.

Factors Explaining Union Development

Economic theory historically made no provision for the rise of unionism, and even today many traditional economists continue to see unionism strictly as an artificial interference with the operation of a free labor market. Yet, as we have seen, unionism is almost coterminous with the advent of the free labor market, and even Adam Smith, the apostle of laissez faire, observed a tendency on the part of both workers and employers to combine for their mutual advantage. The almost natural tendency of workers to combine can be found in those countries in which unionism has been legally abolished by government—and where unions reappear as soon as repression eases.

The Marxist View of Unionism

One theory of unionism emanates from the revolutionary philosophy of Karl Marx. According to the Marxian analysis, a class struggle takes place between the workers, who own only their labor power, and the capitalists, who own the means of production and distribution and upon whom the workers are dependent for their livelihood. The conflict between labor and capital is inevitable, because, according to Marx, the profit of the employer is really "surplus value" that is withheld from the workers. This conclusion emerges from Marx's identification of human effort as the source of all value; hence, profits are really unearned and rightfully belong to the workers. Furthermore, Marx hypothesized that there was a natural tendency for the rate of profit to decline, and, in order for the capitalists to maintain their profits, they would have to take more and more "surplus value"; thus the position of the workers would deteriorate, increasing impoverishment.

In the Marxian view, all this was inherent in the capitalist system so unions could do little to ameliorate the conditions of the workers. Marx, however, was pro-union, seeing them as a means of mobilizing the workers for the revolutionary struggle to replace capitalism with socialism. We cannot here analyze all of Marx's theory, but it is clear that the reality of capitalist development has not conformed to it, and that his theory of unionism, therefore, is an inadequate explanation. In recent years an interesting countertheory has been propounded, which sees a revolutionary potential in unionism only in the transition period when workers are emerging from agriculture; in this stage, the revolt is really one' against industrialism rather than capitalism, and once industrialism takes hold that revolutionary potential is gone and unions turn to improving workers' conditions under the existing economic arrangements.

Job-Conscious Unionism

Theories of the rise of unionism that were quite similar were formulated in Britain by Sidney and Beatrice Webb and in the United States by John R. Commons. According to these theories, unionism arose in response to a widening of the product market, which led to a separation of the interests between journeymen and employers.[1] Workers formed unions as a means of protecting themselves from the impact of product market competition upon their job standards. Commons' view of unionism was a part of his broader analysis of the economy, which has come to be known as "institutional economics." Rejecting the concept of the free, impersonal market, Commons saw the need for the various economic groupings in society, including labor, to form organizations to advance their interests, with the government maintaining a balance between the competing groups.

Commons' student and colleague at the University of Wisconsin, Selig Perlman, extended his concept of job-conscious unionism. According to the Perlman thesis, the role of unionism is to abolish competition among workers for jobs so that the marginal employer does not set labor standards.[2] Perlman saw the labor market as one in which jobs were scarce relative to

---

[1] Sidney Webb and Beatrice Webb, *The History of Trade Unionism* (London: Longmans, Green, 1920); John R. Commons *et al., History of Labour in the United States* (New York: Macmillan, 1918); and John R. Commons, "American Shoemakers, 1648–1895," in *Labor and Administration* (New York: Macmillan, 1925), pp. 219–266.

[2] Selig Perlman, *A Theory of the Labor Movement* (New York: Augustus M. Kelley, 1949).

the supply of labor, and since the supply of labor cannot be easily reduced, wages would be driven down as workers competed among themselves for the available jobs. Unions, practicing business methods and avoiding the siren songs of intellectuals for a reform of existing economic institutions, would allocate jobs among workers and then protect those jobs. Thus, by taking labor out of competition, unionism would give workers a greater sense of security in the midst of scarcity.

Other theories of unionism have been propounded, such as that of Tannenbaum, referred to in the introduction to the last chapter, which sees unionism as a reaction against worker atomization and as a means of restructuring a social system for workers. In the United States, however, the Commons-Perlman thesis of job-conscious unionism has become the most widely accepted one. It has not been without its critics, particularly with respect to Perlman's theory of the psychology of workers,[3] but it is the most accurate description to date of the functioning of unionism in this country.

Dunlop's Industrial Relations System

A more recent attempt to elaborate a theory, not only of unionism but of labor-management relations in general, has been made by John Dunlop, according to which:

> An industrial-relations system at any one time in its development is regarded as comprised of certain actors, certain contexts, an ideology which binds the industrial-relations system together, and a body of rules created to govern the actors at the work place and work community.[4]

In Dunlop's typology there are three sets of actors: (1) a hierarchy of managers, who are responsible for issuing instructions to the second set of actors; (2) a hierarchy of workers, who may or may not be organized; and (3) specialized government agencies, concerned with workers, enterprises, and their relationships. The actors in the industrial relations system interact within a context composed of the technological characteristics of the work place and work community, the market or budgetary constraints that impinge on the actors, and the locus and distribution of power in the larger society. Within any given context, the actors establish rules for the work place and the work community. Although each of the sets of actors has its own ideology, these ideologies must be compatible enough so as to permit a common set of ideas that recognize an acceptable role for each.

The Dunlop theory is broad enough to permit the encompassing of the Commons-Perlman thesis of unionism as an integral part of the American industrial relations system: unions are interested primarily in the allocation of jobs and the establishment of wage rates for those jobs; management has

[3] Charles Gulick and Melvin K. Bers, "Insight and Illusion in Perlman's Theory of the Labor Movement," *Industrial and Labor Relations Review*, July 1953, pp. 510–531.
[4] John T. Dunlop, *Industrial Relations Systems* (New York: Holt, 1958), p. 7.

come to recognize the unions' right to represent workers with respect to jobs; and government sets guidelines in which this job-related, labor-management relationship takes place. Dunlop's theory does not imply that all unions and managements must behave in the same manner; on the contrary, differences in labor-management relations among industries, and over periods of time, are to be expected because of variations in their technological, economic, and political contexts. For example, most unions in durable-goods manufacturing industries fight for the use of the principle of seniority in the allocation of jobs when they are scarce, thus giving greatest protection to the workers with the longest service. And since in the seasonal clothing industries seniority would give a few workers an inordinate share of job opportunities, the unions insist upon equal division of the work among all employees. In both cases the unions are job conscious, but the differing technological and economic contexts lead them to favor different approaches to job allocation.

Union Organization and Structure

Before turning to the factors that influence union growth and the prospects of unionism's being extended into new areas, let us briefly review some facts about union organization and structure.

Workshop Level

Analyses of union organization and structure typically concentrate on the national unions and the AFL-CIO, which is only proper, since they are important decision-making institutions in our economy today. Too often, however, they completely omit any reference to the immediate work place, and this is unfortunate. A worker in a factory, mill, mine, warehouse, or office may belong to a national union affiliated with the AFL-CIO, but this fact is usually of less immediate concern to him than his own work group within his place of work.

The very low percentage of union members who attend meetings is often cited as proof of membership lack of interest, yet in their study of local unions Sayles and Strauss found that work groups do keep apprised of local events by having one of their number attend each meeting to guard their particular interests.[5] Kuhn found that work groups can be very important centers of decision-making within the work place, and that they use the grievance procedure to engage in "fractional bargaining" with shop floor management on behalf of their own specific interests; higher management and union officers, who think that they negotiate the work standards, may not even know what is taking place.[6]

Even in the absence of such overt and concentrated action on the part of

---

[5] Leonard R. Sayles and George Strauss, *The Local Union* (New York: Harper & Bros., 1953).

[6] James W. Kuhn, *Bargaining in Grievance Settlement* (New York: Columbia University Press, 1961).

work groups, the day-to-day informal decisions of work groups may be as important to the productivity of an establishment and to the earnings of the workers as the agreements negotiated higher up the line. Workers can informally decide to "slow down" or "speed up" their efforts, a type of behavior that is often most visible where incentive systems are in operation.

Unions do, however, attempt to formalize these informal work groups through the election of shop stewards to represent each of them, or a group of them, in presenting employee grievances to management. Where work places are small and a local's membership is composed of employees from many establishments, the union may establish a formal substructural organization for the workshop. Each printing establishment under agreement with locals of the International Typographical Union, for example, will have its own "chapel" of ITU members. And in many unions regular membership meetings are held as part of the governmental process of the sublocal groups, and shop meetings are usually well attended.[7]

To the individual union member, particularly in factory situations, the shop steward is the union; thus, he has a dual role in that he represents the union to the membership and the membership in dealings with management. Plant management, in turn, recognizes the importance of this representational role by allowing stewards time away from their work duties without loss of pay when performing that role, and very often it grants them superseniority as protection against layoff. Shop stewards are elected by the union membership, and in contrast to higher officials, who may stay in office for many years, there is a more rapid turnover of stewards as the workers on the shop floor become dissatisfied with their performance.

The Local Union

The basic unit in the structure of labor unions is the local. It is the body to which the individual member belongs directly and to which he pays his dues. In many ways a local union is like a private club, and indeed, in the early days, the locals were as much fraternal organizations as unions. Many local unions continue to behave like fraternal societies, having committees to visit sick members, sending flowers when there is a death in the family, and the like; others, however, have become very impersonal, limiting their activities directly to work-related matters.

There are more than 70,000 local unions in the United States. Since total union and employee association membership is almost 22 million, this means that the average local is composed of 300 members. But the average hides a wide range of difference, for these are many small locals of but a few dozen people, and others of many thousands, such as the 30,000-member Local 32B, Service Employees, in New York City, and the 29,000-member Local 600, UAW, to which the production and maintenance workers of the Ford Motor Company's River Rouge complex belong.

---

[7] Jack Barbash, *American Unions: Structure, Government, and Politics* (New York: Random House, 1967), p. 50.

Locals may be organized on an occupational or industrial basis. In the former type, common in the building trades, they will cover all the organized workers of a particular occupation—for example, electricians, plumbers, and painters—in a given geographic area regardless of the place of work. Where locals are organized on an industrial basis, they may be composed of all production workers, regardless of occupation, from one particular department of a plant, the entire plant, or a complex of plants. Thus, all the production and maintenance workers at the River Rouge complex of the Ford Motor Company belong to Local 600, United Automobile Workers. When individual plants are too small to justify separate locals for each of them, the workers from a number of establishments in a community will belong to one local: Local 174, UAW, is composed of workers in the many machine shops on Detroit's west side.

Each local union is governed according to its own constitution and by-laws, consonant with the constitution and by-laws of the national union of which it is a part. The local officers may be full-time paid officials or part-time ones—workers in the industry. Full-time officials are common in multi-employer situations, and they generally consist of a manager and a staff of business agents. The officers of the union, including the executive board composed of members actively working in the trade, are elected periodically by the membership.

Although the local meeting is the supreme authority, few members (about 5 percent) attend except at crucial times, such as the time of negotiating new agreements with employers. Some members do not attend simply because they would prefer not to belong to the union at all, but have to because their work place is covered by a union shop agreement. To most members, however, the union is regarded as a type of insurance: you pay your premiums (dues) so that it will be there to help you when you need it, but you do not become active in its affairs.

The constitution provides for membership control, and while some locals are run very democratically, others resemble feudal fiefdoms, in which the members must kowtow to the leadership. Some locals, whether internally democratically run or not, discriminate against minority groups, often keeping them from becoming members and, as a result, from obtaining jobs in the trade. Exclusive membership policies are more typical of craft locals, where the union attempts to insure a monopoly of job opportunities to those who are already members. In such situations, when more labor is needed the local may issue "temporary work permits" to newcomers, but still deny them the right to membership and thus to permanent jobs.

The autocratic or discriminatory situations are more typical, though not the exclusive preserve, of craft locals, where the union can subvert democratic procedures through its control of the allocation of jobs. In a skilled trade, employers normally call the union business agent when they need workers, and it is his control over job assignments that may permit him to build a powerful political machine and squelch opposition to the local's leadership. On occasion, business agents have used their economic power for self-aggrandizement, forcing workers to pay for job assignments or employers to pay them for receipt of an adequate supply of skilled labor. In the main, however, unions are probably no less honest or democratic than most other institutions in the nation. The Landrum-Griffin Act of 1959, moreover, guarantees union members certain rights and insists that local unions conduct elections every three years at a minimum. (We shall examine the legal aspects in the next chapter.)

A local union typically belongs to a city central body and to a state federation, if it is affiliated to a national union belonging to the AFL-CIO. Two types of local unions are not affiliated with national unions, either independent or part of the AFL-CIO. The first type consists of the federal locals that are affiliated directly with the AFL-CIO. There are about 300 such local unions with about 62,000 members, and they represent workers in a craft or industry over which no national union has jurisdiction. When there is a sizable number of federal locals representing similar types of workers, they may combine to form a new national union. This happened among AFL federal locals in the chemical industry, which joined together in 1941 and were chartered as the International Chemical Workers Union.

The second type is the local union that is affiliated with neither a national union nor the AFL-CIO, but is completely independent.[8] A local independent union represents the workers in one plant; there are numerous such unions in the petroleum refining industry, some of which had emerged from employer-sponsored employee representation plans of the 1920s. When employer domination of unions was outlawed by the Wagner Act, most "company unions" disappeared, but some became locals of the new CIO unions, such as the United Steelworkers of America, and others became genuinely independent both of the employers and other labor organizations. In 1970 there were 537,000 members in such unaffiliated local unions.

National Unions

The vast majority of the 70,000 locals are affiliated with one or another of the 185 national, or more precisely international, unions, since most have locals in Canada. Although the locals were originally more important, in most cases today the national union is the dominant force within the union structure: it is autonomous even if affiliated with the AFL-CIO, it has power over the locals comprising it, it generally is responsible for new organizing efforts, and it plays a vital role in collective bargaining, which is the major function of American unions. Even where locals do their own collective bargaining, they are dependent upon services from the national union, for it is the latter that has the legal staff, research department, and very often the skilled negotiators to assist the local.

---

[8] For descriptions and analyses of such unions, see Leo Troy, "Local Independent Unions in the American Labor Movement," *Industrial and Labor Relations Review*, April 1961; and Arthur B. Shostak, *America's Forgotten Labor Organization* (Princeton, N.J.: Industrial Relations Section, Princeton University, 1962).

Just as in the case of locals, national unions vary greatly in size, from the twenty-five-member (six of whom are in Canada) International Association of Sideographers, AFL-CIO, to the 1.8 million International Brotherhood of Teamsters. The typical national union has fewer than 100,000 members, but the fourteen largest unions, each with more than 400,000 members, had 53 percent of total membership in 1970. Table 4.1 lists the twenty-seven largest unions, each with 200,000 or more members, and their reported memberships in 1970.

Table 4.1 The Largest National and International Unions, 1970

1. Teamsters (Ind)	1,829,000	15. Operating Engineers	393,000
2. Automobile Workers (Ind)	1,486,000	16. Clothing Workers	386,000
3. Steelworkers	1,200,000	17. Government (AFGE)	325,000
4. Electrical (IBEW)	922,000	18. Plumbers	312,000
5. Machinists	865,000	19. Electrical (IUE)	300,000
6. Carpenters	820,000	20. Musicians	300,000
7. Retail Clerks	605,000	21. Railway Clerks	275,000
8. Laborers	580,000	22. Transportation Union	263,000
9. Meat Cutters	494,000	23. Rubber	216,000
10. Hotel & Restaurant	461,000	24. Letter Carriers	215,000
11. State, County	444,000	25. Painters	210,000
12. Ladies' Garment	442,000	26. District 50 (Ind)	210,000
13. Service Employees	435,000	27. Teachers	205,000
14. Communications Workers	422,000		

Source: *Directory of National Unions and Employee Associations 1971*, Bureau of Labor Statistics, Bulletin 1750, Table 9, p. 75

Rivalry between national unions with competing jurisdictions no longer pays off in terms of adding members to their ranks. The administrative costs of servicing members, moreover, have become too high for many smaller unions to bear. As a result, a number of unions are merging in order to pool their strength and to enjoy administrative economies of scale. In the future, therefore, there will probably be fewer, but larger, national unions.

In terms of structure, unions are typically divided between craft and industrial, but this is an oversimplification, for many have lost their purity as one or the other. Even the term "industrial" hardly conveys the true status of many unions, which today are actually multi-industrial; that is, they organize the production and maintenance workers in a number of different industries. The full name of the 1.5 million-member Autoworkers—United Automobile, Aerospace and Agricultural Implement Workers of America—indicates three of the industries the union covers, but it also organizes workers in machinery manufacturing, electrical equipment, and other industries; indeed, a study conducted during the 1950s found the UAW to have had representation rights in thirty-six industries.[9]

[9] Neil W. Chamberlain, "The Structure of Bargaining Units," *Industrial and Labor Relations Review*, October 1956.

A number of unions that were originally purely craft are today an amalgam of craft and industrial units. The Teamsters is virtually a "general" union today, representing workers of many varied occupations in a host of different industries. The fourth largest union in the nation, the International Brotherhood of Electrical Workers, was for many decades confined to organizing the skilled electricians in the building trades. When the CIO arose and began to organize workers in the electrical equipment manufacturing industry, the IBEW broadened its jurisdiction in an attempt to compete. As a result, the IBEW today not only has skilled electricians in its ranks, but also 400,000 workers in factories producing electrical equipment (about 45 percent of its membership is reported to be in the electrical machinery industry). In fact, this former AFL craft union has more industrial worker members than its fellow AFL-CIO affiliate, the International Union of Electrical Workers (300,000 total membership), and the independent United Electrical Workers (163,000 members). (The IUE had been formed by the CIO in 1949 when it expelled the UE for being Communist dominated.)

Not only do the national unions differ in total number of members and structure, but also in terms of the number of locals of which they are comprised. At one extreme, eighty-eight national unions have under one hundred locals each, while, at the other, five have two thousand or more locals each.[10] Indeed, more than half of all locals are affiliated with only eighteen national unions, each having one thousand locals or more.

Size and diversity of membership force many national unions to establish intermediate bodies between themselves and the locals. According to Barbash, the intermediate body "represents a consciously rational effort to adapt organization to function by remedying defects in the organizational relationship among locals, or between locals and the national union."[11] Thus, a local may belong to a number of intermediate bodies.

Typically, for purposes of easing administrative burdens and providing better services to the locals in an area, a national union will have geographic subdivisions—New England, South Atlantic, and so on. Unions that are multi-industry in membership will also tend to set up subdivisional bodies in each industry to deal with the problems specific to it, and unions dealing with very large corporations may have subdivisions for dealing with specific companies. Multioccupational unions may have occupational subdivisions as well. One union, moreover, may have various of these subdivisional types of structure: thus, the United Automobile Workers is divided into geographic regions; has departments covering industries, such as aerospace and agricultural implements; departments for bargaining with very large companies, such as Ford and General Motors; and, in order to provide a greater say to its minority of skilled and white-collar members, special occupational departments.

Some unions are highly centralized, but in others the actual locus of power rests with intermediate bodies or with the locals themselves. Local

---

[10] *Directory of National Unions and Employee Associations 1971,* Bureau of Labor Statistics Bulletin 1750, pp. 86–87.
[11] Barbash, *op. cit.,* p. 55.

autonomy is more common in the craft unions, in which collective bargaining is usually conducted by the local unions with the employers in their particular labor market. In basic manufacturing, however, skill is less important, and competitive pressures are associated with the product market, which may be regional or national in scope. The industrial unions, therefore, tend to be more centralized in order to deal effectively with national multiplant companies and to enforce uniform labor standards throughout the nation.

Just as unions differ in their degrees of centralization, they also differ with respect to how democratic they are, but there is no necessary correlation between democracy and local autonomy. A union with highly centralized policies may be fairly democratic, as for example the United Automobile Workers, whereas one with local autonomy may, in practice, amount to a loose federation of feudal baronies, as has been the case in some of the old craft unions. With the exception of a handful of unions, such as the Typographers (ITU) and the Teachers (AFT), unions do not have organized two-party systems. And although it is difficult to coalesce an opposition capable of ousting an incumbent administration, in the last few years hotly contested elections have replaced the presidents in a number of large unions, including the Steelworkers (USA), Electrical Workers (IUE), State, County, and Municipal Employees (AFSCME), Teachers (AFT), and Mine Workers (UMW).

A good deal of the problem of union democracy lies with the lack of interest and participation on the part of the rank and file. Lipset has concluded that only those unions which fulfill many functions related to the status and leisure time of their members have high membership participation and involvement, for example, the International Typographical Union and Actors' Equity. In his view, although most unions are not internally democratic, their activities in protecting the economic and political interests of their members within the larger society help to sustain political democracy in the larger body politic.[12]

In most national unions the convention, to which all locals elect delegates more or less in accordance with their size, is the final authority. It establishes the union's policies with respect to internal affairs, collective bargaining, and the external environment, including national and local legislation. The convention—or in the case of those unions using direct vote of the membership, the referendum—elects the national officers of the union (president, secretary-treasurer, and executive board), who administer its affairs and carry out the broad policies voted at the convention.

The AFL-CIO

Most union members—about three out of every four—belong to the AFL-CIO, but, as we have seen, their connection with it is rather indirect. They

---

[12] Seymour Martin Lipset, "The Political Process in Trade Unions: A Theoretical Statement," in Walter Galenson and Seymour Martin Lipset (eds.), *Labor and Trade Unionism: An Interdisciplinary Reader* (New York: Wiley, 1960), pp. 236–238.

belong to the 64,000 local unions that are affiliated with the 120 national unions, which are, in turn, affiliated directly with the AFL-CIO. (The major national unions that are independent include the Autoworkers, which quit the AFL-CIO because of dissatisfaction with its activities; the Teamsters, which was expelled for corruption; the United Mine Workers; and some unions that had been expelled from the CIO for Communist domination in 1949–1950.) In addition, there are about three hundred federal local unions that are affiliated directly with the federation.

Just as national unions have intermediate bodies, so likewise does the federation, through its close to 750 city central bodies and 51 state federations (50 states plus Puerto Rico) and through its trade and industrial departments, which arose to coordinate the efforts of the various craft unions in particular industries. Thus, there are departments covering the construction industry, the maritime trades, the railways, and the metal trades. When the AFL and CIO merged in December 1955, the former CIO unions sought to maintain their identity by organizing a department known as the Industrial Union Department within the AFL-CIO; former AFL affiliates with industrial structures were also invited to join the IUD, and today it is just another department of the merged federation. These departments, plus the Union Labels Department, report to the Executive Council of the AFL-CIO.

Since not all national unions can be represented in the top administration of the AFL-CIO, they are accorded some recognition through the General Board, which consists of the members of the Executive Council plus a principal officer of all the national unions and the heads of the constituent departments. The General Board meets at the call of the president, but it has little more than advisory powers.

The supreme legislative body of the AFL-CIO is the convention, which is held every two years, to which the member unions send delegates, and at which the number of votes are apportioned according to the per capita dues paid. The actual governing body between conventions is the Executive Council, which is composed of the president, the secretary-treasurer, and thirty-three vice-presidents (all of whom are usually presidents of national unions) elected by the convention. The Executive Council meets at least three times a year to chart the federation's policy within the broad guidelines established at the convention.

The members of the Executive Council are also divided into committees. The standing committees are appointed by the president, and they deal with such important problem areas as organization, political education, international affairs, education, economic policy, research, and public relations, monitoring the activities of the administrative departments of the AFL-CIO covering these areas. Figure 4.1 illustrates the organizational structure of the AFL-CIO.

The AFL-CIO constitution requires that affiliated unions be free from communism, corruption, and discrimination, but, since the national unions are autonomous, the powers of the federation to discipline recalcitrants are

Figure 4.1   Structure of the AFL–CIO

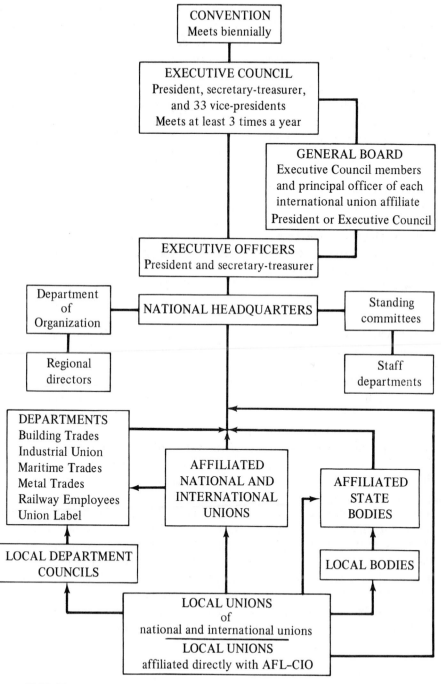

SOURCE: U.S. Department of Labor

limited. It can use moral suasion and even sanctions to influence the policy of its constituent unions, but, if a union fails to comply with AFL-CIO policy, it can, as a last resort, only be expelled as occurred in the case of the Teamsters on the issue of corruption. Communism has not been a problem since the CIO expelled a number of unions two decades ago, and while no union has been disciplined for discriminatory practices, the federation has been active in promoting civil rights and has had some success in getting unions to admit blacks and other minorities on an equal basis.

Although the AFL-CIO does not engage in collective bargaining, it does provide some limited help to the unions through its research activities and through coordination of activities in some instances in which a number of unions are bargaining with one employer or group of employers. The federation, however, does act as an arbiter of jurisdictional disputes between unions, making the decision when two or more unions disagree over which one's members are entitled to specific types of work or to which union a group of workers are supposed to belong. For example, of 1,171 cases filed under its Internal Disputes Plan between 1962 and 1971, only 17 decisions were rejected by the losing union, and in those cases sanctions were imposed by the Executive Council.[13]

Two areas in which the AFL-CIO plays important roles are organizing and representing labor in national and international affairs. The AFL-CIO is not as active in organizing as was the old CIO, but it has an organization department that generally works with national unions or nascent unions, such as the councils for farm workers and professional employees, to extend unionism to new areas. National leaders look to the AFL-CIO when they want to know how "labor" stands on an issue, and federation representatives participate on commissions, both governmental and nongovernmental, from the United Fund drive to economic and foreign policy advisory bodies.

The AFL-CIO also represents American labor in international affairs. For many years it was a mainstay of the International Confederation of Free Trade Unions, a body encompassing noncommunist, nondenominational (not tied to any church) union federations from about one hundred countries, but quit that organization in 1969 over disagreements with its policies and procedures. The AFL-CIO is the chief American labor group in the International Labor Organization, an intergovernmental body encompassing labor, employer, and government representatives, the aim of which is to improve labor standards throughout the world. (The AFL-CIO, however, has been boycotting the ILO in recent years because of disagreement with it and has used its influence to get Congress to refuse to vote U.S. financial support of the international body.) The federation itself directly supports union efforts in other countries and encourages resistance to communism and fascism.

---

[13] BLS Bulletin 1750, p. 66.

Factors Influencing Union Growth

Economic Factors

Having examined some leading theories of why unionism arises and the structure of unions in the United States, we shall now look at those factors which explain why unions grow, reach a plateau, or decline. One major and obvious influence on union growth emerged from our historical survey of unionism—the business cycle. As we have seen, throughout the nineteenth century unions arose and grew during periods of prosperity, but declined drastically during periods of depression.

Fluctuations in union membership, however, cannot be explained entirely by the business cycle; in the 1920s, a period of prosperity, union membership declined, and in the depressed 1930s it rose dramatically. On the other hand, the influence of the business cycle should not be discounted: between 1957 and 1958, as the third and deepest post–World War II recession set in, total union membership dropped by 1 million, and the losses were heaviest among the unions representing workers in the cyclically sensitive durable-goods manufacturing industries. With the resumption of rapid economic growth in the mid-1960s, union membership began to climb once more.

National Crisis

One theory of union growth correlates it with periods of crisis in the nation, whether of economic depression or war. This conclusion was reached by Irving Bernstein after studying the patterns of union growth in the sixty-year period from 1884 to 1944. In his view, the most important short-run influence on union growth is a time of disaster such as war or social upheaval, both of which are favorable to union membership expansion.[14]

Political Factors

Union membership growth is also heavily influenced by political factors, particularly the legal climate. The application of the criminal conspiracy and restraint of trade doctrines restricted union growth in the first half of the nineteenth century, and the issuance of court injunctions against labor activities, until restricted by law in 1932, constrained its growth thereafter. The great upsurge in unionism that occurred in the 1930s probably would not have been possible except for the change in government policy from one of antagonism or neutrality to one of openly favoring the spread of unionism and collective bargaining.

According to Rezler, the most important factor in explaining union growth is not social crisis, as claimed by Bernstein, but the attitude of the

---

[14] Irving Bernstein, "Union Growth and Structural Cycles," *Proceedings of the Seventh Annual Meeting* (Madison, Wisc.: Industrial Relations Research Association, 1954), pp. 202–231.

political party in power during the crisis;[15] thus unions tend to expand if the Democrats rather than the Republicans are in office. Of course, once unions became powerful, they were in a position to help determine government policy to the point where a return by government to a blatant antiunion position would be political suicide for the party attempting it.

Sociopsychological Factors

Sociopsychological factors are also important influences on union growth. As discussed in Chapter 2, a native-born, better-educated labor force, indoctrinated in democratic principles, was less inclined than were immigrants to accept whatever management had to offer, and wanted a voice in determining the conditions under which it would work. Also, the insecurities of the 1930s and the dispelling of the notion of business infallibility played roles in making workers psychologically ripe for unionization.

The Role of Leadership

Finally, the role of union leadership cannot be overlooked. It is doubtful that the CIO would have made as much progress as it did, and indeed if it would even have come into being, had it not been for the drive and determination of John L. Lewis. Within the mass production industries, moreover, there was in the 1930s a core of potential leaders among young blue-collar workers —men such as the Reuther brothers in the automobile industry and James Carey in the electrical industry—who responded to the CIO and to the more favorable climate for unionization ushered in by the New Deal.

A Composite of Influences

Thus, each of the influences on union growth is important, and none can be considered in isolation, for they interact with one another. John L. Lewis, for example, had been around in the 1920s, but not only did he not organize extensively, but his own United Mine Workers declined precipitously in membership. In the favorable political and sociopsychological climates of the 1930s, however, Lewis was able to assert the leadership that brought unionism to the basic industries. Similarly, although unions are dependent upon the economic and political climate, today they are powerful forces in shaping that climate. Increases in unemployment, which tend to reduce union membership, bring vigorous political responses from the unions, and whatever administration is in office moves rapidly to counteract any serious downturn in the economy.

That many factors influence union growth is underscored by recent research. Ashenfelter and Pencavel, using multiple regression analysis, have attempted to quantify the importance of a number of factors.[16] According to their results, among the more important variables affecting union growth are

---

[15] Julius Rezler, *Union Growth Reconsidered* (New York: Kossuth Foundation, 1961), p. 8.

[16] Orley Ashenfelter and John H. Pencavel, "American Trade Union Growth: 1900–1960," *Quarterly Journal of Economics*, August 1969, pp. 434–448.

changes in the rate of prices, employment changes in unionized sectors, the extent of unionization, and the political climate as measured by the Democratic party strength in Congress.

Not only are the factors explaining union growth multiple, but, as Blum has contended, a factor that encourages growth in one period may actually deter it in another, when the technological-economic-political context is different.[17] For example, in the 1930s social unrest stemming from the deep economic depression led workers to join unions as a means of redressing their grievances and achieving some degree of economic security. In today's climate, however, a severe economic recession might very well lead to a type of social unrest that would result in workers following right-wing, antiunion causes. Even in the absence of depressed economic conditions, many workers were drawn to third-party candidate George Wallace in the presidential election of 1968, and political polls showed heavy worker support for the Conservative party candidate for the United States Senate in New York State in 1970, as many workers considered the Democratic and Republican candidates too liberal.

The Extent of Unionism by Industry

While overall economic and political factors help to explain fluctuations in total union membership, the forces operating in specific product and labor markets are important in explaining why some industries and areas are more heavily organized than others. Let us start by examining the extent of unionism by industry. Although precise data are lacking, the Bureau of Labor Statistics has ranked industry groupings by degree of union organization, as follows:[18]

75 percent and over
Ordnance
Transportation
Contract construction
Transportation equipment
Fabricated metals
Paper
Electrical machinery

50 percent to less than 75 percent
Mining
Primary Metals
Food and kindred products
Apparel
Petroleum
Manufacturing
Rubber
Telephone and telegraph
Chemicals
Miscellaneous manufacturing
Tobacco manufactures

Furniture
Stone, clay, glass products
Federal Government
Printing, publishing

25 percent to less than 50 percent
Electric, gas utilities
Leather
Lumber
Machinery
Nonmanufacturing

Less than 25 percent
Textile mill products
Government
Instruments
Service
Trade
State and local government
Agriculture and fishing
Finance

---

[17] Albert A. Blum, "Why Unions Grow," *Labor History*, Winter 1968, pp. 39–72.
[18] BLS Bulletin 1750, p. 81.

According to the BLS estimates, three-fifths of the employees in manufacturing were unionized, but only one quarter of those in nonmanufacturing and, including employee associations, about one-third of those employed by government were. Even within nonmanufacturing, the groups organized are those that are regarded as blue-collar, such as truck drivers and railroad workers in transportation; miners in mining and quarrying; and carpenters, electricians, and the like in construction. Indeed, despite recent gains among government and other white-collar employees, there is no question but that American labor union membership remains fundamentally a blue-collar phenomenon.

Although manufacturing accounts for less than 30 percent of total nonagricultural employment, it accounts for fully 40 percent of total union membership. The rise of unionism in manufacturing was, of course, a result of the great organizing drives of the CIO in the 1930s, because until then union membership had been largely concentrated in mining, construction, and transportation.[19] Manufacturing, on the other hand, was largely nonunion, except for printing and clothing, and unionism in even the latter declined precipitously during the 1920s.

Within manufacturing, there are wide variations in union membership by industry that are related to product and labor market forces. Generally, it is the production and maintenance workers in the large-scale, multiple-plant firm, heavily-capitalized industries that are best organized, and this is even more true when the industry is concentrated in a particular geographic area. Thus, the most highly organized manufacturing industry is transportation equipment, the largest segment of which is the automobile industry, heavily concentrated in and around Detroit, Michigan.

The textile industry stands in sharp contrast with automobiles as far as unionization is concerned, for less than one-fourth of the potential membership is organized. From the days of the industry's founding in the early nineteenth century, textiles had been geographically concentrated in the Northeast, particularly New England, but also in New York, New Jersey (Paterson had been the silk and dyeing center), and Pennsylvania (Reading had been the hosiery center). Cotton textiles had moved South in the post–Civil War period so that plants could be closer to the source of raw materials. By the 1920s much of the rest of textile production had joined the southward trek, for by then the old, multistoried northern textile mills had become technologically obsolete, and the South offered cheap land sites for constructing modern plants with up-to-date machinery, abundant and cheap labor, and communities that were willing to provide financial inducements for locating there. The shift of the textile industry southward also enabled it to escape unionism, to which it had been subjected in the North. The textile unions have found it very difficult to organize southern mills, each of which usually is the dominant business in a town, recruiting its labor force from the abundant supply of former farm

---

[19] Leo Wolman, *Ebb and Flow in Trade Unionism* (New York: National Bureau of Economic Research, 1936), p. 7.

workers and having a friendly local political administration and police force, which are generally antagonistic to unions.

Even in the absence of employer or community hostility, unions find it difficult to organize small-scale industries unless they are dependent upon skilled labor, or are concentrated in one geographic area, as is the apparel industry in New York City. Small-scale industries that mainly employ less-skilled workers and are widely distributed geographically are less subject to union organization. Since unskilled workers may be easily replaced, they often fear that overt union activity may cost them their jobs. Lightly capitalized plants are highly mobile, and employers threatened with unionization of their work forces, which may force noncompetitive wage rates upon them, may be induced to relocate; under these conditions, employees are often wary of joining a union. Employees in small plants may also not feel the same need as workers in large factories for a union to represent them in dealing with management, because personal relationships still exist between them and their managers, and they believe that they can talk directly and easily to the boss when there is a problem. Finally, many unions are less aggressive about organizing small plants because the costs of serving the members in them may be much greater than the dues to be collected.

The increasing number of women in the labor force has also added to the problems facing unions. Women comprise only one-fifth of total union membership,[20] just half of their percentage of the civilian labor force. Many female employees are secondary wage earners or transient employees, and so are less concerned with labor standards. Most observers believe that the lack of career orientation on the part of women makes them resistant to union organizing efforts,[21] but Bernstein disagrees. He ascribes the relatively low rate of unionism among women to the industries and occupations in which they work rather than to their sex.[22] The fact that the major unions—ILGWU and ACWA—in the relatively well-organized apparel industries are more than three-fourths female would indicate that women are capable of being unionized.

In a recent review of the literature on union growth, Ginsburg sees the advent of new technology and industrial structure and the impact on the structure of the labor force as the most important explanations of changes in total union membership and the fate of specific unions.[23] Employment in the

---

[20] If employee associations are added, then the female proportion of membership is closer to one-fourth, since their membership includes large groups of female employees in government.

[21] See, for example, Jack Barbash, "The Labor Movement in the Changing Industrial Order," in *Labor-Management Relations: The Forensic Quarterly*, May 1965, p. 105; and Joseph Shister, "The Direction of Unionism 1947–1967—Thrust or Drift," *Industrial and Labor Relations Review*, July 1967, p. 581.

[22] Irving Bernstein, "The Growth of American Unions, 1945–1960," *Labor History*, Spring 1961, pp. 131–157.

[23] Woodrow Ginsburg, "Review of Literature on Union Growth, Government and Structure—1955–1969," in Woodrow L. Ginsburg *et al.*, *A Review of Industrial Relations Research*, Vol. 1 (Madison, Wisc.: Industrial Relations Research Association, 1970), p. 207.

industries in which union membership has been concentrated—manufacturing, construction, and transportation—has been growing more slowly than employment in other industries. Thus, although union membership hit an all-time high of 20.7 million in 1970, it represented a smaller percentage of the employees in nonagricultural establishments, declining steadily from 33.4 percent in 1956 to 27.4 percent in 1970. Unless unionism can break into new industries and occupations, therefore, it will become increasingly less important in our economy, an idea we shall examine later in this chapter.

The Extent of Unionism by Region

The extent of unionization varies geographically as well as industrially. Table 4.2 gives a breakdown of union membership in 1970 by state, showing that the large states have the largest memberships, but not necessarily in proportion to their nonagricultural employment. In fact, the spread of union membership as a percentage of a state's nonagricultural employment is quite wide, ranging from 43, or close to one out of two, in West Virginia, a coal-mining region, down to only 7.8 percent, one out of thirteen, in North Carolina, a center of textile production.

Table 4.2 Union Membership by State, 1970[a]

State	Total Membership (in thousands)	Membership as a percentage of Employment in Nonagricultural Establishments
1. West Virginia	221	43.0
2. Michigan	1,195	40.2
3. Washington	434	40.0
4. Pennsylvania	1,617	37.2
5. Ohio	1,413	36.3
6. Missouri	594	35.9
7. Illinois	1,548	35.7
8. Indiana	657	35.6
9. New York	2,555	35.6
10. Nevada	66	32.8
11. Wisconsin	482	31.4
12. Oregon	218	30.7
13. California	2,137	30.5
14. Montana	60	29.9
15. New Jersey	768	29.5
16. Minnesota	378	28.9
17. Hawaii	82	28.1
18. Kentucky	250	27.3
19. Alaska	25	27.1
20. Rhode Island	89	26.1
21. Massachusetts	573	25.6
22. Connecticut	290	24.2
23. Maryland–D.C.	463	23.3
24. Delaware	48	22.6
25. Iowa	186	21.1

State	Total Membership (in thousands)	Membership as a Percentage of Employment in Nonagricultural Establishments
26. Utah	75	20.9
27. Tennessee	274	20.6
28. Colorado	152	20.5
29. Alabama	204	20.3
30. Idaho	38	18.5
31. Louisiana	193	18.4
32. Maine	61	18.4
33. Arkansas	95	17.9
34. Nebraska	86	17.9
35. Wyoming	19	17.7
36. Arizona	96	17.6
37. New Hampshire	45	17.3
38. North Dakota	28	17.2
39. Virginia	245	16.7
40. Kansas	112	16.6
41. Vermont	24	16.2
42. Georgia	251	16.2
43. Oklahoma	124	16.1
44. New Mexico	43	14.8
45. Texas	523	14.4
46. Florida	299	13.9
47. Mississippi	76	13.2
48. South Dakota	21	11.9
49. South Carolina	81	9.6
50. North Carolina	137	7.8
Membership not classifiable	108	–
United States	19,757	27.9

a States are ranked by union membership as a proportion of total employment in nonagricultural establishments.

SOURCE: Bureau of Labor Statistics Bulletin 1750, Table 18, p. 84.

To a very large degree, the extent of unionization in a state has been a reflection of the composition of its industry. As Troy has pointed out with reference to 1953, "... highly unionized states were those with a large proportion of total employment in building, transportation, and manufacturing, while, as a rule, states low in organization had a smaller proportion of employment in those three industries."[24] Since 1953, however, manufacturing has grown in a number of the southern states, yet their degree of unionization has remained low. Of course, what manufacturing industries are located in a state is still an important factor in determining the degree of unionization. When large, northern-based corporations such as United States Steel establish branch plants, the labor standards in these factories are usually very similar

[24] Leo Troy, *Distribution of Union Membership among the States, 1939 and 1953,* Occasional Paper 56 (New York: National Bureau of Economic Research, 1957), p. 25.

to those elsewhere, and management makes little effort to prevent their being organized by the unions that are powerful in the corporation's other plants. The states in which unionism is weakest are North and South Carolina, where the most important manufacturing industry is textiles, an industry that is largely unorganized, as we have already seen.

In small-scale industries, unionization in the South is often much more difficult than it is in other regions of the nation. The clothing industry, in which unionization has a relatively long history, has become less well organized as it has migrated southward from its original centers in New York, Chicago, and other major northern urban areas. As the author of this book found in a study of the location of the women's and children's apparel industries, "the ILGWU has run into its most formidable opposition in its attempts to unionize the rapidly growing apparel industry in the South. In this area it has met roadblocks of right-to-work laws, organizer licensing requirements, town fees for signing up new members, and outright physical violence by local law enforcement agencies."[25]

In his study of southern unionism, Marshall concluded that union growth is related to the industrial composition of a particular region, the size of the establishment, the presence of branch plants of national companies, the occupational mix, and the location of an establishment in an urban rather than a rural center.[26] Marshall believes that until now the largely nonunion textile industry has been the psychological key to organizing the South, since the industry is concentrated heavily in that region, which remains a bulwark against union penetration into many communities. The South, however, is diversifying its economic base and becoming more like other parts of the country. Marshall, therefore, sees such factors as the changing composition of employment and the migration out of agriculture, which reduces the southern labor supply, as favoring union growth in the future. In fact, he sees unionism growing faster in the South than elsewhere, with a narrowing of the gap between the extent of unionism in the South and elsewhere but with equalization with the rest of the country a long way off. The evidence of recent years appears to be bearing out this prediction: unionism has been growing more rapidly in the South, yet it remains very far behind the levels achieved in the rest of the nation.

Government Unionism

While three out of every five potential members in manufacturing are unionized, in government the ratio is only one out of three. Moreover, the changing industrial mix of the nation has been working against the unions's maintaining,

---

[25] Roy B. Helfgott, "Women's and Children's Apparel," in Max Hall (ed.), *Made in New York: Case Studies in Metropolitan Manufacturing* (Cambridge, Mass.: Harvard University Press, 1959), p. 90.

[26] F. Ray Marshall, *Labor in the South* (Cambridge, Mass.: Harvard University Press, 1967).

no less increasing, their share of the labor force. In Chapter 1 we saw that the Department of Labor's projections of employment by industry sector found manufacturing falling from 24.9 percent of the total in 1968 to 22.4 percent by 1980, and all goods-producing industries dropping from 35.9 to 31.7 percent. Thus, even if unions were to maintain their share of each industry, they would have a significantly smaller share of total employment by 1980 because of the interindustry shifts in employment. Indeed, this has been occurring since the mid-1950s, and unions have been most unhappy about this trend, to the point that many have spoken of a "crisis" in unionism similar to that of the 1920s.[27]

If American unionism is to avoid a significant decline in its importance, one area into which it would have to move with increasing vigor is government, which has been the fastest-growing area of employment. In 1922 there were only 2.5 million government employees, constituting one out of every ten nonagricultural employees. By 1970 there were 12.6 million employees of government, equaling better than one out of six nonagricultural employees. By 1980 government employment is expected to total 16.8 million.

Historically, with a very few exceptions unionism has been very weak among public employees. In some cases, employees secured their jobs through political patronage and so looked to the party clubhouse for redress of any grievances they might have. With the decline of the political machine and the rise of the merit system in public employment, employees became civil servants, and as such usually enjoyed tenure of appointment and very good labor standards relative to most of private industry. Under neither the patronage nor merit systems, however, did public employees feel a great need to belong to a union for job protection, salary improvement, or grievance redress.

With the rise of unionism in private industry, starting in the 1930s, many government employees found themselves losing out relatively as unions won wages, pensions, and health benefits that were often superior to those of civil servants. This was particularly true in periods of inflation, because the unions in private industry could, through periodic collective bargaining, boost wages to keep up with rising prices, but legislatures were typically much slower to act, and many public employees suffered declines in their real earnings. Tenure of office also sometimes proved to be quite ephemeral, as new administrations got rid of civil servants by "abolishing their jobs." Moreover, as government services expanded, relations between employees and public management became more impersonal, and the individual employee often considered himself neglected, caught in a mesh of bureaucratic red tape, and unable to secure redress of grievances.

---

[27] See, for example, Solomon Barkin, *The Decline of the Labor Movement* (Santa Barbara, Calif.: Center for the Study of Democratic Institutions, 1961); and Solomon Barkin, "Is There a Crisis in the American Trade Union Movement? Yes," in Solomon Barkin and Albert A. Blum (eds.), "The Crisis in the American Trade Union Movement," *Annals of the American Academy of Political and Social Science* (Philadelphia: American Academy of Political and Social Science, November 1963).

The climate seemed to be right for unionization of public employees, yet progress came very slowly. In a few large, heavily unionized cities, such as Philadelphia and New York, unions did begin to make progress in organizing civil servants. The major problem that all public unions faced, however, was that government failed to recognize their right to engage in collective bargaining, though a few jurisdictions permitted them a sort of advisory role. Then in the 1960s, first the city of Philadelphia and then New York agreed to enter into formal collective bargaining agreements with unions chosen by the majority of employees in city departments to represent them. New York City adopted a labor relations code patterned after New York State's "little Wagner Act," enacted in the 1930s to govern labor-management relations in private industry.

Probably the most important boost given to government employee unionism came in the Kennedy administration. The federal government had long conceded the right of employees to organize and bargain collectively, but aside from the independent Tennessee Valley Administration, few agencies had any formal procedures through which union recognition and collective bargaining could take place. Then in 1962, following the recommendations of a study commission headed by then Secretary of Labor Arthur Goldberg, President Kennedy issued Executive Order 10988, which provided rules whereby a union could obtain recognition as spokesman for employees of a government agency and greatly encouraged collective bargaining between the unions and the agency administration. Finally, effective January 1, 1970, Executive Order 11491, issued by President Nixon, simplified recognition procedures for unions and still further facilitated collective bargaining in the federal government.

The upsurge in unionism among public employees can be seen in the figures on changes in union membership between 1956 and 1970. According to the data collected by the Bureau of Labor Statistics, in 1956, 915,000, or 5.1 percent of total union membership, were in government.[28] In 1962 the number had grown to 1.2 million, 7.0 percent of total membership, and by 1970 to 2.3 million, 11.2 percent of total membership. If the membership of employee associations is added, we find that 4.1 million government employees are organized, and this is equal to 18.1 percent of all organized employees.

The figures for some individual unions are even more impressive. Between 1952 and 1970 the major union of nonfederal employees, the American Federation of State, County, and Municipal Employees, quintupled its membership, from 85,000 to 444,000, thus becoming the eleventh largest union in the nation. By 1970 the major union of federal employees, the American Federation of Government Employees, had grown seven and one-half times larger than it had been in 1952, 325,000 members compared with 48,000 of eighteen years earlier. The American Federation of Teachers increased its membership four times in the period, from 50,000 to 205,000. Even that

---

[28] Harry P. Cohany and Lucretia M. Dewey, "Union Membership among Government Employees," *Monthly Labor Review*, July 1970, p. 15.

hardly tells the story of unionism among teachers, because in this period the affiliates of the National Education Association began to convert themselves from pure and simple professional associations to collective bargaining agencies. Indeed, there have been numerous contests between the AFT and NEA concerning who should bargain for teachers in various communities, and the NEA affiliates have been as active in conducting strikes as have AFT locals. If the NEA membership were added to that of the AFT, there would be more than 1 million unionized teachers.

Another focal point of unionism among government employees has been the post office, in which 80 percent of the employees are union members. Examining what transpired between 1952 and 1970, we see that the National Association of Letter Carriers had a membership jump from 95,000 to 215,-000. A second large union of postal employees, the United Federation of Postal Clerks, had 162,000 members in 1970. Various other unions brought the membership for all postal unions to 670,000.

The gains in public employee unionism, however, are far from universal. First of all, they are much more pronounced within federal service than they are in state and local. By 1970 more than one-half of all federal employees were union members, reflecting the encouragement that had emanated from Executive Order 10988. On the other hand, less than 25 percent of state and local government employees are members of unions or associations ("near-unions" such as civil service associations, policemen's benevolent associations, and the like, which negotiate with government agencies on behalf of their members). Unionism among state and local government employees is still confined to a small, but growing, minority. As in the case of total union membership, that of government employees is not distributed evenly among the states, being generally highest east of the Mississippi River and north of the Mason-Dixon line.

Part of the explanation of the variations among states in the degree of public employee unionism lies in the different attitudes taken by governments toward collective bargaining by their own employees. More than twenty states now have legislation extending bargaining privileges to public employees, but other states and cities continue to restrict public employee bargaining—a subject we shall examine in Chapter 7.

Prospects for White-Collar Unionism

Public employment is not the only virgin territory inviting union expansion. Another is the private, but nonprofit, sector of the economy. The types of problems here are quite similar to those in government, and the developments in public employment will probably serve as a model for this sector.

Unionism is growing in the private nonprofit sector, which is itself growing rapidly. Teachers in private schools are organizing, just as are teachers in public schools. The rapidly expanding health services field, too, has seen a spate of union activity. Employees in hospitals, including the professional staffs—nurses and laboratory chemists—and the nonprofessionals—from ward attendants to dishwashers—have been unionized in many areas. The 180,000-member American Nurses Association has virtually converted itself into a full-fledged union, its state associations seeking recognition as the collective bargaining representative of its members. In many cases unionism, or the threat of it, has raised the pay of hospital workers from among the lowest in the community to comparable with private industry. Many states are enacting special legislation to govern labor-management relations in hospitals, particularly in order to find substitutes for the strike, which would claim the sick as its chief victims.

One extremely large and continually growing field that unions have eyed is that of white-collar employment. As we saw in Chapter 1, by 1956 the number of workers classified as white collar had for the first time surpassed those considered to be blue collar. Indeed, the United States has become a service, rather than a production, economy—the first service economy in the world.[29]

The gains in unionism among government employees have brought large numbers of white-collar workers into their ranks. In fact, 41 percent of all union members in government are listed as white-collar employees (with association membership, the ratio rises to 62 percent), compared with much smaller percentages in private employment: 4 percent in manufacturing and 21 percent in nonmanufacturing. The three largest "white-collar" unions in private industry are the Retail Clerks International Association (RCIA); the Communications Workers of America (CWA), which represents the telephone employees; and the Railway, Airline, and Steamship Clerks. The latter two are in the transportation and public utility fields, in which unionism has long been powerful. Although the RCIA has made impressive gains in recent years, bringing its membership over 600,000, it, together with the other unions in this field, represents less than 25 percent of the total employment in retail and wholesale trade.

While teachers and nurses may be turning toward unionism, even if in the guise of a professional association, another large group of professionals—engineers—has failed to respond to calls for organization. There are a few isolated engineering unions, but the Engineers and Scientists of America (ESA), a federation of independent engineering and scientific unions, went out of existence in 1961. A more recent attempt at unionization was started in 1969, with the founding of the independent Council of Engineering and Scientific Organizations (CESO). This is a loosely structured group with nine affiliates claiming to represent 50,000 engineers, scientists and technicians in aerospace, electronics, and government. The AFL-CIO is also anxious to bring more engineers and scientists into its ranks, and in 1967 seventeen unions, representing 400,000 white-collar professional employees, formed the

[29] Victor R. Fuchs, *The Service Economy* (New York: National Bureau of Economic Research, 1968), p. 1.

Council for Scientific, Professional, and Cultural Employees (SPACE). Whether CESO and SPACE will be any more successful than previous associations remains to be seen.

If unions have made only modest inroads in organizing white-collar workers generally, they have achieved even less success in private offices. The union with major jurisdiction in the field, the Office and Professional Employees International Union, with a total membership of 82,500 in 1970, remains a small AFL-CIO affiliate. Of course, office workers are also members of other unions, but still the total is unimpressive, for, according to the estimates of Benjamin Solomon and Robert K. Burns,[30] of the union potential of 9.1 million clerical workers in 1960 only 1.6 million, or 18 percent, were organized, and most of these workers were not in offices but were performing clerical tasks in factories or warehouses. Of the 5.4 million clerical workers who were office workers, they estimated that union membership in 1960 was barely 500,000, and there is no evidence of a significant increase since then.

A number of observers saw technological change, and the change in the white-collar employee's environment and conditions of work that were presumed to stem from automation, as new factors that would spur unionism.[31] Among retail workers, Harrington found that the change in the nature of work did make them more ready to accept unionism.[32] On the other hand, in a study of the impact of the computer in the office, this author did not see it as increasing the prospects for office unionism.[33]

The preponderant view still seems to be rather dubious of major union strides among white-collar employees in private industry. The fact that the vast majority of office employees are women, many of whom intend to stay in the labor force only a few years, coupled with the decent treatment by management that prevents the development of deep-seated employee grievances and the individualistic bent of most white-collar employees are cited as reasons for such a conclusion. But hard and fast conclusions with respect to social phenomena cannot be reached. In 1930, for instance, few observers foresaw the tremendous growth of factory unionism that took place within the decade, and the same could be true of white-collar unionism in the 1970s.

For one thing, a further narrowing of pay differentials between white- and blue-collar workers could become an incentive for the former to join

---

[30] Benjamin Solomon and Robert K. Burns, "Unionization of White-Collar Employees: Extent, Potential, and Implications," *Journal of Business*, April 1963, pp. 141–165.

[31] Barbash, "The Labor Movement in the Changing Industrial Order," *op. cit.*, p. 104; Ida R. Hoos, "When the Computer Takes over the Office," *Harvard Business Review*, July–August 1960, pp. 102–112; Everett M. Kassalow, "White Collar Unions in the United States," in Adolf Sturmthal (ed.), *White-Collar Trade Unions* (Urbana: University of Illinois Press, 1966), pp. 356–359; and Lawrence Williams, "How Automation Affects the White-Collar Clerical Employee," in *Computer Technology—Concepts for Management* (New York: Industrial Relations Counselors, 1965), pp. 17–29.

[32] Michael Harrington, *The Retail Clerks* (New York: Wiley, 1962).

[33] Roy B. Helfgott, "The Computer and Prospects for Office Unionism," *Quarterly Review of Economics and Business*, Spring 1969, pp. 19–28.

unions. The experience of the period of 1949 to 1955, however, when clerical salaries rose only two-thirds as fast of those of operative and kindred workers, indicates that lagging paychecks do not necessarily lead to unionization.[34] With the increase in the percentage of labor forces in the white-collar category, there may be pressure to reduce their numbers when the volume of business declines; if white-collar employees become increasingly susceptible to layoffs, the search for job protection could also be a prod to unionization.

Perhaps most important will be the impact of unionization in other areas. In explaining the startling upsurge of factory worker unionism in the mid-1930s, Daniel Bell termed it growth "by eruption, extension and enforcement."[35] It is, therefore, quite possible that widespread organization of white-collar employees in government could provide the type of union eruption that could encompass office employees in its extension phase. Should this happen, then unionism will become an even more important decision-making institution in the American economy than it is today. If not, unions will be fortunate to maintain their current share of the labor force.

Summary

Since unionism acted as an interference with the operation of a free labor market, some explanation of why it arose was needed, and the theory that best fits American unionism is that of the job-conscious unionism propounded by Commons and Perlman. According to that theory, since jobs are scarce relative to the supply of labor, the function of unionism was to prevent workers from competing among themselves for the available jobs and thus to hold wage rates above what the labor market would have set.

Although unionism is a powerful force in the economy, it is much stronger in some sectors than others, and the basically blue-collar workers in manufacturing, transportation, construction, public utilities, and mining are the backbone of American unionism. Even in these industries, however, unionism is more prevalent in the large establishments, and small-scale industries, except where they are geographically concentrated in one area, are more poorly organized. Similarly, unionism is not distributed equally among regions, but is stronger in those in which manufacturing, transportation, construction, and mining are important industries; the South remains the weakest region of union strength.

The basic unit in the structure of labor unions is the local, to which the member belongs directly and which services him in his daily dealings with work-place management. The dominant force, however, is the national unions to which the locals are affiliated. The national union is generally responsible

---

[34] Albert A. Blum, "The Prospects for Office Employee Unionization," *Proceedings of the Sixteenth Annual Meeting of the Industrial Relations Research Association* (Madison, Wisc.: Industrial Relations Research Association, 1963), pp. 183–185.

[35] Daniel Bell, "Discussion—Union Growth and Structural Cycles," *Proceedings of the Seventh Annual Meeting of the Industrial Relations Research Association* (Madison, Wisc.: Industrial Relations Research Association, 1954), pp. 231–241.

for new organizing efforts, and it plays a vital role in collective bargaining, which is the major function of American unions. Greater centralization is typical of the industrial unions, where competitive pressures are associated with the product market, but local autonomy is more common in the craft unions, where collective bargaining is usually conducted by the local unions with the employers in their particular labor markets. Most of the national unions, in turn, are affiliated with the AFL-CIO, which is the major spokesman for organized labor in national and international affairs.

Interindustry shifts in employment, particularly the shift from goods-producing to service-producing industries, however, have threatened the power of organized labor. If union membership as a share of the labor force is not to decline further, unions will have to make significant organizing gains in the nongoods-producing industries. One such area in which unions have made significant gains in recent years has been government. They have also scored membership gains among employees in the health care field and in other private, nonprofit employment. The vast majority of white-collar workers in private industry, particularly the office employees, remain solidly non-union. The extent of union growth in the future, therefore, will depend to a large extent on the ability of unions to bring white-collar employees into their ranks.

BIBLIOGRAPHY

Barbash, Jack. *American Unions: Structure, Government, and Politics.* New York: Random House, 1967.

Barkin, Solomon, and Albert A. Blum (eds.). "The Crisis in the American Trade Union Movement," *Annals of the American Academy of Political and Social Science.* Philadelphia: American Academy of Political and Social Science, November 1963.

Blum, Albert A., *et al. White Collar Workers.* New York: Random House, 1970.

Bureau of Labor Statistics. *Directory of National Unions and Employee Associations 1971.* Bulletin 1750. Washington, D.C.: U.S. Government Printing Office.

Dunlop, John T. *Industrial Relations Systems.* New York: Holt, 1958.

Galenson, Walter, and Seymour Martin Lipset (eds.). *Labor and Trade Unionism: An Interdisciplinary Reader.* New York: Wiley, 1960.

Ginsburg, Woodrow. "Review of Literature on Union Growth, Government and Structure—1955–1969," in *A Review of Industrial Relations Research,* Vol. 1. Madison, Wisc.: Industrial Relations Research Association, 1970.

Kuhn, James W. *Bargaining in Grievance Settlement.* New York: Columbia University Press, 1961.

Marshall, F. Ray. *Labor in the South.* Cambridge, Mass.: Harvard University Press, 1967.

Perlman, Selig. *A Theory of the Labor Movement.* New York: Augustus M. Kelley, 1949.

Sayles, Leonard R., and George Strauss. *The Local Union.* New York: Harper & Bros., 1953.

Solomon, Benjamin, and Robert K. Burns. "Unionization of White-Collar Employees: Extent, Potential, and Implications," *Journal of Business*, April 1963.

Sturmthal, Adolf (ed.). *White-Collar Trade Unions.* Urbana: University of Illinois Press, 1966.

Troy, Leo. *Distribution of Union Membership Among the States, 1939 and 1953.* Occasional Paper 56. New York: National Bureau of Economic Research, 1957.

5 GOVERNMENT REGULATION OF LABOR-MANAGEMENT RELATIONS

Although the exchange relationship between labor and management involves those two actors in the industrial relations system, it is also heavily influenced by the third actor—government. The behavior of government toward the other two actors helps to determine the context in which their relationship takes place, and is itself a reflection of the ideology governing the industrial relations system. In this chapter our focus will be on the actions of the third party—government—with respect to the relationship between the other two parties—management and labor. We shall, therefore, explore the legal setting in which labor-management relations take place, tracing the evolution of American public policy from that of viewing unions as inimical to the public welfare to that of actively favoring unionism and collective bargaining as the cornerstone of national labor policy.

Unions and Economic Development

The early attitude of government, as evidenced through court decisions, was decidedly unfavorable to unions and their activities. To understand why this was the case, we must focus attention on the history of economic growth, particularly industrial development.

In the early period of a nation's economic development, the stress is on capital formation. The way in which a nation can accumulate capital is to consume less than it produces, save the surplus, and then convert it into capital goods to be used in further production. Immediate increases in consumption, therefore, would come at the expense of capital formation and, in the long run, detract from a nation's ability to increase real incomes.

Since a major aim of unions is to extract wages that are higher than they would otherwise be, most countries have looked unfavorably upon them and restricted them in the early stages of economic development. In the United States, as we shall see shortly, the doctrines of criminal conspiracy and restraint of trade hindered union development. In Britain, Parliament in 1799 and 1800 passed the Combination Acts, forbidding union activity. In the Soviet Union, a centrally planned rather than a market economy, Joseph Stalin destroyed the unions' capacity to act as unions, that is, to represent the interests of the workers who were their members, when he undertook rapid industrial development under the first Five Year Plan in the late 1920s.

Even in the absence of the need for rapid capital accumulation, the very philosophy of laissez-faire economics, which dominated American thinking for so long, left no room for trade unions. The emphasis was on exchange in a free, competitive market, in which no firm was of large enough size to affect the price of a commodity. And, if no firm was to be able to affect the price of a commodity, it was equally obvious that no combination of workers should be able to affect the price of labor, which should be determined through the interaction of supply and demand. Since the raison d'être of a union is precisely to effect a different price than would be arrived at through the normal working of the market, unionism ran directly counter to the economic philosophy of early capitalism. Moreover, it was reasoned that, if a union could raise the price of labor, this would in turn force employers to charge the public higher prices for the commodities or services they produced.

Application of the Criminal Conspiracy Doctrine

Armed with this introductory background, we shall perhaps be better able to understand the rationale behind the attitude taken by government, through the courts, toward unionism. As we saw in Chapter 3, unions first arose in the 1790s among the skilled artisans, who were able to use their relative scarcity to force the masters to grant them higher pay scales. One of the earliest of those unions, the Journeymen Boot and Shoemakers of Philadelphia, suffered a severe legal setback in a court decision of 1806.

Unlike Britain, where Parliament enacted legislation—the Combination Acts—against unions and their activities, the United States Congress ignored developments in labor-management relations. In the absence of statute law, the courts still had to make decisions on what was permissible and what was not, and they fell back upon the common law, that body of legal decisions established over a long period of time that became precedents for dealing with similar matters. American common law, of course, had been inherited from British common law, which in turn dated back to medieval times, when feudalism bound serfs to the land and artisans were governed by guild regulations. The philosophy of that common law supported concepts of private property and freedom of enterprise.[1]

The well-organized Philadelphia Cordwainers (Shoemakers) had, in 1805, presented their employers with a demand for a new schedule of piece rate prices, the alternative being to face a "turnout," as a strike was called in those days. The employers, facing growing competition from outside Philadelphia as improved transportation physically extended the market for boots and shoes, feared a loss of business should they agree to the journeymen's demands, yet realized that not to agree meant a shutdown of their production. Their way out of this dilemma was to seek redress in court.

The employers could not have hoped for a better decision, for the Pennsylvania court, applying the common law, convicted the leaders of the strike

---

[1] Ronald A. Wykstra and Eleanour V. Stevens, *American Labor and Manpower Policy* (New York: Odyssey Press, 1970), p. 11.

of engaging in a criminal conspiracy; that is, they had gotten together in order to commit an unlawful act. In instructing the jury, Judge Levy had stated, "A combination of workmen to raise their wages may be considered in a twofold point of view: one is to benefit themselves, the other is to injure those who do not join their society. The rule of law condemns both." The ruling that a "combination to raise wages" was an illegal conspiracy was a severe blow to unions, because that is precisely what a union usually is— a group of workers seeking to increase their bargaining power vis à vis their employer through combining together.

A second aspect of common law invoked against unions was that forbidding restraint of trade. Although this was supposed to prevent business monopoly, it was also used particularly after the 1840s against unions, if their actions injured the public by cutting off its normal access to a commodity market, as a strike does; if it hampered freedom of competition among employers; or if it prevented an employer's access to the labor market, as picketing does.

A significant change in public policy toward unions, from one of outright hostility to one of limited tolerance, emerged from a Massachusetts court decision of 1842. In the case of *Commonwealth v. Hunt*, the Massachusetts Supreme Court refused to apply the doctrine of criminal conspiracy to a union that struck to enforce a closed shop. Chief Justice Shaw stated that ". . . a conspiracy must be a combination of two or more persons, by some concerted action, to accomplish some criminal or unlawful purpose, or to accomplish some purpose not in itself criminal or unlawful by criminal or unlawful means." He reasoned, however, that, as long as the intent of workers in striking was merely to improve their conditions, it was not illegal, even if it resulted in some incidental harm to the employer. In other words, concerted action by employees might have justifiable objectives and therefore might be perfectly legal, even if not liked.

Commonwealth v. Hunt is considered to be a landmark in labor law. Although it did not completely end the use of the conspiracy doctrine, according to Gregory, "common-law conspiracy has never again played a prominent part in the control of labor unions by American courts, although it was used occasionally after the Civil War to break up strikes."[2] As we shall see, however, the courts fashioned new concepts that served to thwart union activities.

The Injunction

In place of the conspiracy doctrine, the courts began to rely more heavily on the concept of restraint of trade in their handling of union activities. The actions of organized workers were legal only if they were designed to advance

---

[2] Charles O. Gregory, *Labor and the Law* (New York: Norton, 1958), p. 29.

their own interests and not to harm those of the employer, and as long as such actions were not harmful to the public, that is, if they did not unreasonably restrain trade. A union, however, could be accused of restraining trade if its actions harmed the public by blocking its normal access to a commodity market. Hampering free competition among employers or preventing an employer from having free access to the labor market (through an insistence upon the closed shop; that is, not permitting him to hire anyone who was not a member of the union) could also be considered as restraining trade.

If an employer was of the opinion that a union action, such as a strike, was designed to harm him by, say, violence that would destroy his physical property or even by merely reducing his profit expectations, he could apply to a court for redress. The judge could then "enjoin" such an action, that is, prohibit the union from engaging in it. There are three types of injunctions. The first was a temporary restraining order, which a court can issue, without consulting the accused party, in order to prevent irremediable damage. The ex parte restraining order has a time limit of five days, after which, following a preliminary hearing, the court can order a temporary injunction. Following a comprehensive hearing, a judge can issue a final or permanent injunction.

The injunction proved to be a very effective weapon against unions, and its use spread widely in the last quarter of the nineteenth century as unions grew in size and importance. Since trial by jury does not apply to courts in equity, the judge determined the facts in each case himself. Judges, moreover, were notoriously antiunion, for, after all, most of them came from the same social class as the employers, and they were imbued with the same ideas of laissez-faire economics and the rabble theory of workers. Besides, even if one judge were not of this frame of mind, the lawyer for the employer could always find one who was. The appeal against an injunction, moreover, cannot be based on the judge's interpretation of the facts, but only by claiming that he had abused his discretion, something that was most difficult to prove and that judges of higher courts were reluctant to concede. Finally, if one refused to obey an injunction, he could be held in contempt of court, with punishment left to the discretion of the judge.

The widespread use of the injunction in labor relations came about as a result of a novel interpretation by the American judiciary of the concept of property. Obviously, in a private-enterprise economy property rights must be protected, and it is perfectly logical to have a judicial remedy to prevent destruction of physical property. Thus, if someone has threatened to set fire to your home, and he sets off toward your house with a can of gasoline, a judge must be able to enjoin his further actions along these lines without delay. But unions were seldom accused of attempting to destroy employers' physical property; their actions, however, were often enjoined because the courts interpreted "property" as being the business of the employer. Again it is obvious that, if a union conducts a strike against an employer, it will damage his business, possibly irreparably. It was this interpretation of intangibles as property that formed the basis for enjoining union actions. In contrast to the American judiciary, the British courts refused to issue injunctions in labor disputes, because they considered the injunction as designed only to prevent harm to irreplaceable tangible property interests.[3]

Most injunctions in labor disputes were not of the permanent type, but either temporary restraining orders or temporary injunctions. But in labor-management relations that was all that was needed, particularly since most injunctions were quite sweeping in nature, barring a union from all organizational activities while leaving the employer free to fire union members. Even if the union were not broken during the period of the injunction through the discharge of union sympathizers, it was difficult, once a strike was halted, for a union to rekindle worker enthusiasm to have another try at it later. In most instances an injunction simply broke the strike and spelled victory for the employer over the union.

Antitrust Laws

When the courts first began to issue injunctions in labor disputes, they had to rely on the common law prohibition of restraint of trade because there was no statute law on the subject. Soon, however, they were able to base their actions on statute law. In this instance, too, it was a rather novel interpretation of statute law that provided the new basis for court action, for the law had been enacted for other purposes than the control of labor relations.

The Sherman Act of 1890

In the last quarter of the nineteenth century there was a great movement within American industry to combine in order to secure the advantages of monopoly control over product markets. Among the devices used was the trust, which was a combination of corporations whose stock was assigned to a board of trustees for unified business control. The Standard Oil trust, put together by John D. Rockefeller, dominated the petroleum industry, and other trusts controlled production in the sugar, whiskey, and cottonseed oil industries.

A great hue and cry arose, and the nation became genuinely alarmed at the "trustification" of American business. Congress reacted in 1890 by passing the Sherman Anti-Trust Act, which prohibited combinations in restraint of interstate or foreign trade, forbade monopoly or the attempt to monopolize, and provided that one who suffered as a result of violation of the act by another party could sue and collect triple damages from him.

Although the Sherman Act had been intended to deal with business monopoly rather than activities of labor unions, some lower courts did apply it in labor cases. Eugene Victor Debs, for instance, was sentenced to prison for violation of a circuit court injunction against the American Railway

---

[3] *Ibid.*, p. 97.

Union's strike of the Pullman Palace Car Company in 1894. The court had ruled that the ARU activity was a conspiracy in restraint of trade under the Sherman Act, but, when the union leaders appealed their conviction to the Supreme Court, it avoided ruling on the applicability of the Sherman Act, finding the defendants guilty on other grounds. The Supreme Court's ruling in the Debs case, however, did validate the use of the injunction by federal courts in labor disputes.[4] In 1908, however, the Supreme Court, in the famous Danbury Hatters case, declared that unions and their activities were subject to antitrust prosecution.

The Danbury Hatters Case

The hat industry was one of the early ones to be organized, and Danbury, Connecticut, the center of production, became a "union town." There were, however, a few firms that resisted unionization by the United Hatters Union (AFL), and among them was Loewe and Company. In order to bring the recalcitrant firm into line, the union, in 1902, launched a strike and boycott against it. The strike was not very effective, because the company was able to continue to operate, but the boycott, by which the Hatters' Union warned dealers not to handle Loewe products and asked union members throughout the country not to buy Loewe hats, was more effective. Encouraged by the American Anti-Boycott Association, one of the employer groups formed to counteract unions at the turn of the century, Loewe filed action against the union in the United States District Court, alleging that the union's boycott was a violation of the Sherman Act and that the company had sustained losses of $88,000 as a result of that violation.

The case (*Loewe v. Lawlor*) finally reached the Supreme Court in 1908, and the Court sustained the claim of Loewe and Company, finding that the union action—the strike and boycott—was a conspiracy in restraint of trade under the Sherman Act. The Court's reasoning was that the union was pursuing an unjustifiable purpose, that of hurting the company, by interfering with its shipment of goods in interstate trade. Triple damages were assessed against the union, and a later decision held that the individual members of the union were liable for the money. The American Federation of Labor, however, conducted a national campaign that raised the funds to pay the fine, and thus saved the hat workers from losing their homes and savings.

From a legal point of view, the Supreme Court had stretched the meaning of the Sherman Act in applying it to unions. The act was supposed to apply to those who sold commodities in interstate commerce, and the restraint was in the nature of a control over supply and price. The union, however, dealt only with labor services, and was not directly attempting to affect the price of hats. In the opinion of one labor law expert, Professor Gregory, the Supreme Court was in error in holding that Congress meant any interference

---

[4] Wykstra and Stevens, *op. cit.*, p. 41.

with interstate commerce when it used the words "restraint of trade" in the Sherman Act. "What this may be, then, is another instance of judicial interference with the development of national economic policy—a matter properly for the sole concern of Congress."[5]

From an economic point of view, the Court's interpretation of the act as applying to the tactics of unions in attempting to further their ends ran counter to the very reason for the existence of unions. The dominant American theory of unionism—the Commons-Perlman thesis—was that the function of unions was to take labor out of competition, that is, to prevent workers from having to compete with one another for available jobs and thus having the marginal employer determine the wage rate. A union that won collective bargaining rights for a group of workers in an industry could maintain the labor standards achieved only if it were able to extend those standards to the rest of the firms in the industry. If it were not able to do so, then the nonunion firms, by having lower labor standards, would have a competitive advantage over the unionized firms, and thus threaten to undermine the union's gains. By restricting the ability of unions to use strikes and boycotts to bring the nonunion firms into line, therefore, the Court undermined the unions' ability to take labor out of competition and to maintain its gains in those sectors of an industry in which it had been able to organize the workers and win concessions from employers.

The Clayton Act of 1914

Under these circumstances, the alarm of the AFL at the extension of the Sherman Act to union activities is understandable, and efforts were exerted to have Congress reverse this trend. Relief seemingly came in 1914, under a Democratic administration, when Congress passed the Clayton Act as an amendment to the Sherman Act. The Clayton Act was designed to tighten restrictions on business monopoly practices by prohibiting price discrimination, tying contracts, and intercorporate stockholding and interlocking directorates that would substantially lessen competition. In terms of labor unions, it seemed that the act said that the antitrust laws were not to be applicable to labor. Section 6 of the Clayton Act declared that the labor of a human being is not a commodity or article of commerce, and that nothing should be construed to forbid the existence of unions, nor should labor combinations be held to be combinations in restraint of trade under the act. Section 20 stated that peaceful means, such as the primary boycott and peaceful assembly, are legal.

Court Interpretations of the Law

Union leaders were ecstatic, and Samuel Gompers, president of the AFL, hailed the Clayton Act as labor's Magna Charta. The joy, however, was

---

[5] Gregory, *op. cit.,* p. 209.

short lived, for in 1921, in the case of *Duplex Printing Press Company v. Deering,* the Supreme Court interpreted the Clayton Act adversely from the union point of view. Of the four firms manufacturing printing presses, Duplex was the only nonunion one, and the International Association of Machinists (IAM) was unable to organize its employees. On the one side, this represented a case of workers' freedom of choice as to whether or not to belong to a union. On the other side, this was a classic situation in which the labor standards established in the unionized sector of an industry were threatened by the lower standards of the nonunion sector, because the latter enjoyed a competitive advantage over the former. Under pressure from the unionized employers, therefore, the union undertook a boycott of Duplex presses; union members were instructed not to work on Duplex presses, customers were advised not to buy them, and truckers were warned not to transport them.

The company's response was to seek an injunction to bar the union from interfering with its sale and distribution of products. A lower court granted a temporary injunction, a higher court vacated it, and the case moved eventually to the Supreme Court. The Court, in a split decision, agreed that labor was not a commodity, but that this in no way meant that the actions of labor unions could not restrain trade. Most experts agreed with the Court's interpretation of Section 6 of the Clayton Act, but there was dissent with respect to Section 20. That section had barred injunctions in labor disputes between an employer and employees, but the Court interpreted this very narrowly to mean only disputes between an employer and *his* employees. It ruled that since the union actions involved other than Duplex employees, an injunction could be granted. The Court ignored the fact that the workers in the unionized plants had a direct interest in what transpired in nonunion establishments, and interpreted the Clayton Act to mean that only those union activities which were legal before its enactment were protected by it. As a result of the Duplex case, the unions found themselves right back under the antitrust acts and prohibited from using secondary pressure to protect the labor standards won in the unionized sectors of an industry.

The thrust of the Supreme Court's attitude toward union activities was further demonstrated in the Coronado Coal Company cases, which involved a violent strike against nonunion coal operators by the United Mine Workers. The Court ruled that a union could be held to be in restraint of trade if, through its activities, it sought to restrict the flow of interstate commerce. Since preventing the operation of struck facilities is the purpose of all strikes, the Court's decision came close to declaring all strikes to be restraints of trade. The Court, however, did not want to go this far, for it recognized the legitimacy of strikes by a union against an organized employer because of an impasse in collective bargaining; it simply wanted to restrict the ability of unions to extend organization to nonunion establishments through secondary pressures.

The Anti-Injunction Act

The ambiguity of the Supreme Court's decisions, however, placed all union weapons in legal jeopardy, and the injunction became an ever more formidable employer counterweapon. After half a century of the courts' enjoining union activities as restraints of trade, the reaction toward the abuse of this important legal device finally led to congressional action. In 1932, in the depths of the Great Depression, a bill dealing with injunctions in labor disputes, sponsored by two progressive Republicans, Senator Norris of Nebraska and Representative La Guardia of New York, was passed.

The Norris–La Guardia Anti-Injunction Act of 1932 placed severe restrictions on the federal courts in the issuance of injunctions in labor disputes, and declared national labor policy to be that of giving workers the right to organize and bargain free of employer restraint. Section 4 of the act prohibited the issuance of injunctions against workers ceasing work, thus affirming the right to strike. It also barred enjoining the normal accompaniments of a strike, such as publicizing it, assembling peaceably, and the like. Section 4 of the act, in effect, made all of labor's normal, peaceful weapons legal.

This section also forbade a federal court from issuing an injunction against a worker's being a member of a union, thus making the so-called yellow-dog contract unenforceable. The yellow-dog contract was a device used by employers in their attempt to prevent unionization. It required potential employees, as a condition of employment, to sign an agreement that they would not join a union. The importance of this device was not that the individual worker would have been sued for breach of contract if he later joined a union, but that it was used to prevent unions from attempting to organize workers who had signed such agreements. This was the essence of the Supreme Court's ruling in *Hitchman Coal and Coke Company v. Mitchell* (1917), in which it declared that a court of equity could issue an injunction restraining attempts to organize employees bound by promises not to join a union. This was reversed by Norris–La Guardia, which banned the issuance of injunctions against inducing, without fraud or violence, other persons to strike, picket, assemble legally and the like, regardless of any previous promise to the employer.

Section 5 declared that anything that one person could do legally could not be considered illegal if it were done in combination with others. Section 6 stated that one individual could not be held responsible for the actions of another. Section 13 defined a labor dispute in the broadest possible manner, "regardless of whether or not the disputants stand in the proximate relation of employer and employee," thus recognizing that unionized workers had a valid interest in the labor standards of unorganized firms.

A number of states, particularly the larger industrial ones, emulated the federal government and passed "little Norris–La Guardia Acts," restricting their state courts from issuing injunctions in labor disputes. A revolution in national labor policy had taken place, for the government was no longer going to act as an ally of employers resisting unionism, but henceforth would be neutral, leaving the evolution of labor-management relations to the parties themselves.

The Norris–La Guardia Act thus set the stage for a voluntary collective bargaining system in the United States along the lines of the one that had developed in Britain. In Britain the Combination Acts, restricting union organization, were repealed in 1824–1825; the government retreated from active interference in labor-management relations; and British employers voluntarily accommodated themselves to unions and collective bargaining in the second half of the nineteenth century. It seemed that this might be the path that the United States would follow in the second third of the twentieth century, but it turned out to be otherwise.

The National Industrial Recovery Act, 1933

Some people allege that voluntarism was never given a chance in the United States because government quickly intervened on the side of the unions. It is true that the federal government did intervene in 1933 to attempt to foster unionism and collective bargaining, but, as we shall see, without compulsion upon employers. On the contrary, it was the failure of employers to accommodate themselves to the realities of modern industrialism, in which workers wanted a voice in the determination of the conditions under which they worked, that led to compulsion.

The opportunity to evolve a voluntary system of industrial relations presented itself in 1933 when one of the first emergency measures to deal with the depression—the National Industrial Recovery Act—was passed by the new Roosevelt administration. The NIRA sought to encourage economic recovery by allowing the firms in each industry to get together to establish codes of fair competition. Section 7a of the act declared that employers were not to interfere with the attempts of workers to organize and to bargain collectively, but it provided no effective remedies for their failure to comply. Indeed, as we saw in our review of union history, a number of industries, such as coal mining and clothing, were reunionized in this period, and in others unionism and collective bargaining gained ground for the first time.

In most of basic manufacturing, however, employers continued to oppose unionism and to fashion new techniques with which to prevent organization of their work forces. Employee representation plans, by which the workers in an establishment elected representatives to meet and discuss problems with management, but which were not independent of management control, were encouraged by employers, and they grew in number. As disclosed by a Senate investigation (La Follette Committee), some employers used spies to keep themselves informed of unionization attempts by employees, discharged pro-union employees, and hired armed guards to keep union organizers away from their plant gates.

The Wagner Act

Even before the National Industrial Recovery Act was declared unconstitutional in the Schechter Poultry case, the friends of labor in Congress had begun to draft legislation that would add teeth to the requirement that employers recognize and bargain collectively with unions. Thus, when the NIRA was found to be unconstitutional by the Supreme Court in 1935, legislation to replace Section 7a was ready. In 1935, therefore, Congress passed the National Labor Relations Act (NLRA), known popularly as the Wagner Act (its chief sponsor being Senator Robert Wagner, Democrat of New York), which legally protected collective bargaining and forced employers to recognize and deal with unions chosen by a majority of their employees. A complete revolution in national labor policy had taken place within a few years, as the government switched from actually, through the courts, discouraging unionism, to actively, through statute law, encouraging it.

Earlier Railway Labor Legislation

The change in national labor policy was not completely without precedent, for there had been previous legislation regulating labor-management relations in the railroad industry. As early as 1888 a law was passed providing for voluntary arbitration of railway labor disputes. A more significant piece of legislation was the Railway Labor Act of 1926, which was designed to establish stable labor-management relations on the nation's railroads. The act established a system of mediation, arbitration, and fact-finding as the means of preventing labor-management disputes from leading to strikes and disruptions of rail service. In an attempt to prevent the spread of "independent" (often company-dominated) unions, the act provided that the parties had the right to choose their collective bargaining representatives without "interference, influence, or coercion." The RLA thus forced railway management to recognize the railroad brotherhoods and bargain with them. The RLA was amended in 1934 to further strengthen free choice by employees of bargaining representatives by detailing a list of unfair labor practices barred to employers.[6]

The Reasoning behind the Wagner Act

The Wagner Act, however, was of much greater significance, because it applied to all of interstate commerce with the major exception of agriculture. (Government employment was also exempt.) The Wagner Act was premised on the idea that the exchange relationship between the individual worker and the employer, grown to the size of a giant corporation, left the former at a serious disadvantage unless he could combine with his fellow workers. Behind this idea, that union organization was good and that employees must

---

[6] Herbert F. Northrup and Gordon F. Bloom, *Government and Labor* (Homewood, Ill.: Richard D. Irwin, 1963), p. 316.

be free to organize, lay a purchasing power theory of depressions: that part of the reason for the depression that had set in in 1929 was that increases in wages had lagged behind gains in productivity during the decade, and that, therefore, the workers did not have sufficient income to generate an effective demand for the goods and services that the nation was capable of producing. By organization, however, the workers would have the power to win higher wages from employers.

The framers of the Wagner Act also believed that industrial unrest flowed from employer resistance to unions, and that collective bargaining was the best way of insuring labor-management peace. In order to accomplish its purpose of promoting collective bargaining, the act declared a number of practices to be unfair and forbade employers from engaging in them, provided a procedure by which employees could choose to be represented by a union, and established administrative machinery by which the act's provisions would be enforced.

Provisions of the Wagner Act

Section 7 of the act states that "employees shall have the right to self-organization, to form, join, or assist labor organizations, to bargain collectively through representatives of their own choosing, and to engage in concerted activities, for the purpose of collective bargaining or other mutual aid or protection." Since the main obstacle to unionism and collective bargaining was employer opposition, employers were forbidden to engage in the following unfair labor practices:

1. To interfere with employees in the exercise of rights guaranteed by the act
2. To dominate an employee organization
3. To discriminate against employees on the basis of their membership in a union
4. To discharge or otherwise discriminate against an employee because he has filed charges or given testimony under the act
5. To refuse to bargain collectively with a union chosen by a majority of their employees

In one fell swoop the act gave the individual employee freedom of action with respect to union representation, abolished the employee representation plans and other forms of company unions that employers had created to ward off legitimate unions, and forced employers to recognize and deal with unions chosen by their employees. What unions had been unable to accomplish on their own was now to be accomplished through the agency of government compulsion.

To administer the act, the National Labor Relations Board, with quasi-judicial powers, was created. The NLRB was to investigate complaints of unfair labor practices, issue cease and desist orders against them, and enforce its orders in the courts. It was also to conduct secret ballot elections to determine if the employees in an "appropriate bargaining unit" wished to be represented by a particular union.

Reaction to the Wagner Act

The Wagner Act stimulated new organizational efforts on the part of the unions, and its passage virtually coincided with the formation of the CIO. Despite the Wagner Act, employers in many basic industries intensified their resistance to union organization, partially on the assumption that the act would be held to be unconstitutional. The question of its constitutionality reached the Supreme Court in 1937 in the case of *National Labor Relations Board v. Jones and Laughlin Steel Corporation,* but by then the Supreme Court had changed sufficiently in membership and outlook that, by a 5–4 vote, it declared the law valid. After that, some employer opposition to unionism began to crumble, and, under the protection of laws, the membership of unions skyrocketed and collective bargaining spread through American industry.

The Wagner Act was avowedly pro-union in its intent, but its framers could not have foreseen what the consequences would be. It would be only fair to say that, in the main, they were pleased with its results, for collective bargaining spread through industry, but there were some aspects of the act and its interpretation by the NLRB and the courts that would not have pleased them. For one thing, it did not lead to the industrial peace that had been sought, for unions and employers unused to collective bargaining could not easily reach settlements, and many strikes occurred. Secondly, Congress obviously could not have foreseen either the split in the labor movement that developed when John L. Lewis launched the CIO or some of the unfortunate consequences that this might have. There developed instances, for example, in which an employer, in compliance with the Wagner Act, would recognize and bargain with a union chosen in an NLRB election by a majority of his employees, only to find pickets at his gates from a rival union. Under the terms of the Norris–La Guardia Act, moreover, he could not obtain an injunction to halt the rival union's action against him.

Even the AFL was far from satisfied with the workings of the Wagner Act, for it was unhappy with the NLRB's determination in many cases of what constituted an "appropriate bargaining unit." When the act was passed there had been no CIO, but it came into being almost immediately, and it sought to organize workers industrially—that is, all production and maintenance workers in a plant regardless of skill—whereas the AFL unions sought to organize workers on a craft basis. There were continual charges that the NLRB's determinations of the bargaining unit favored industrial unionism to the detriment of the AFL craft unions; that is, the NLRB would not allow the skilled workers to vote separately on which union they wanted to represent them, but included them within the more comprehensive unit of all production and maintenance workers, of which the skilled workers formed only a minority. Since the craft unions could not, in many cases, even secure an election among the workers in their jurisdiction, many of them, as we have seen, also began to organize all workers in a plant in order to counter their CIO rivals effectively.

There were continual attempts to amend the Wagner Act, but, because of the long history of employer opposition to unionism, the majority in Congress turned a deaf ear to their proposals. Only during World War II was legislation restricting unions adopted. Although both the AFL and CIO had offered "no strike" pledges in order to further the war effort, John L. Lewis had called strikes in coal mining. Congress responded in 1943 by passing, over President Roosevelt's veto, the War Labor Disputes Act, which provided for thirty days' notice of intention to strike in plants involved in war production and for government seizure of struck facilities. This act, however, was only for the duration of the war.

When World War II ended, therefore, national labor policy was still embodied in the Wagner Act of 1935, and a number of Supreme Court decisions of the period had granted unions virtual immunity from the antitrust acts. Yet pressure had been building up for some change, because many people had come to believe that the scales had been tipped too far in labor's favor. A number of states had passed laws redressing what were considered to be the consequences of the Wagner Act, and the courts had ruled that the very tight restrictions on what employers could say to their employees during an organizing campaign, which the NLRB found to be interference with freedom of employee choice, were violations of employers' rights of free speech. Furthermore, the spate of national strikes in major industries during 1945 and 1946 turned public opinion toward placing some restrictions on union activity.

The Taft-Hartley Act

The elections of 1946, which produced Republican majorities in both houses of Congress for the first time since 1928, provided the votes for altering national labor policy. Many bills were introduced, but the final legislation bore the names of the chairmen of the Senate and House of Representatives Labor Committees, Senator Robert Taft (R., Ohio) and Representative Fred Hartley (R., New Jersey). The new law was passed, over President Truman's veto, in 1947, with the majority of both Democrats and Republicans in Congress supporting it. The new Labor-Management Relations Act, known more generally by its sponsors' names as Taft-Hartley, was a thoroughgoing series of amendments to the Wagner Act, the aim of which was to achieve a better balance in national labor policy.

To the unions, passage of the Taft-Hartley Act signaled a new assault upon labor similar to that experienced at the end of World War I; indeed, CIO president Philip Murray labeled it a "slave labor" act. To some employers, it seemed to promise greater freedom from unionism. Both groups, however, were wide of the mark in their appraisal of the act, for, although it did place restrictions on unions, it continued to feature collective bargaining at the center of national labor policy. Responsibility for administering the act remained with the National Labor Relations Board, but the board's composition and powers were changed somewhat, in order to separate judicial and enforcement functions and to speed up its processing of cases.

Provisions of the Taft-Hartley Act

To redress what was considered to be an imbalance of power between labor and management, the Taft-Hartley Act amended the provisions with respect to employer unfair labor practices. For one thing, it stated that the expression of arguments and opinions by employers prior to a representation election shall not constitute an unfair labor practice, or be "evidence" of one, if such expression contains no threat of reprisal or promise of benefit. Furthermore, the definition of "employer" was changed so that a firm could not be charged with having committed an unfair labor practice because of the actions of minor supervisory employees.

The concept of unfair labor practices was extended to activities of unions, and unions, as well as employers, were forbidden to restrain or coerce employees in the exercise of their rights guaranteed by the act. The obligation to bargain in good faith, which under the Wagner Act had been placed upon employers, was also extended to unions. This provision was inserted because there had been instances of unions presenting demands to employers on a take-it-or-leave-it basis, with the unions being unwilling to consider any employer arguments.

The old issue of secondary pressure—that is, an attempt by a union to bring pressure on a company by having the employees of other companies refuse to handle the first company's goods—arose again. Taft-Hartley outlawed all types of secondary boycotts, and provided furthermore that the General Counsel of the National Labor Relations Board must seek an injunction to bar secondary boycotts. In order to protect small employers, who found themselves at a disadvantage when confronting large and powerful unions, the act made it an unfair labor practice to coerce an employer or self-employed person to join a union. To deal with the problem of employers facing strikes by one union if they recognized another one, the act made a strike called by one union against an employer who, in conformity with the law, had recognized another one, an unfair practice. It banned jurisdictional strikes by declaring strikes to be unfair when called to replace another union for work assignments. If, in a dispute over work assignments, the unions cannot reach agreement, then the NLRB determines the dispute.

Unions could also be charged with having committed an unfair labor practice if their initiation fees were excessive, or for causing an employer to pay for work not performed. The effect of this latter so-called antifeatherbedding provision was largely obviated by the Supreme Court's ruling that as long as some work is performed, whether necessary or not, the union cannot be held to have violated the law. Thus, the practice of the International Typographical Union of forcing newspapers to pay printers to set type that would not be used (bogus) was found to be legal.

The history of employer opposition to trade unionism had made the American unions very security conscious, and the device that they had perfected for ensuring employer compliance with labor standards was the closed shop, whereby the employer could hire only members of the union. Employers, however, argued that their freedom of access to the labor market was denied by the closed shop, since they could hire only members of a particular union. The Taft-Hartley Act, therefore, outlawed the closed shop and made it an unfair labor practice for a union to demand one. It did, however, permit the union shop, under which the employer might hire anyone he pleased, but every new worker would have to join the union within thirty days of employment. If a union secured a union shop, however, it could force an employer to discharge a worker for his failure to offer to pay his dues.

It could have been said that the Taft-Hartley Act was trying to be fair to both sides on this issue—granting employers free access to the labor market and unions a high degree of security—except that the act contained a way out of the union shop arrangement, too. Section 14b permitted the union shop unless the particular state in which the establishment was located had a stricter ban on compulsory membership. A number of states (nineteen today), located in the South or rural Midwest, have adopted so-called "right-to-work" laws banning all forms of compulsory membership, including the union shop. Attempts since 1947 to have 14b repealed have failed.

The unions' resentment of the act was particularly vehement with respect to its provisions governing the union shop and voting by strikers. Under the Wagner Act, persons who went on strike over economic issues and had been replaced by newly hired workers could vote in a subsequent plant representation election along with their replacements. Taft-Hartley changed this by eliminating the right of replaced strikers to vote. The unions feared that employers might use this provision of the law to attempt to "bust" unions. They reasoned that an employer, through obstinate behavior in collective bargaining, could provoke a union into calling a strike, hire new workers in place of those on strike, and then request an NLRB election to decertify the union as bargaining agent as not being representative of his new employees. Although there is no evidence of any widespread attempt by employers to do this (largely because high to full employment did not permit the easy replacement of striking employees), President Eisenhower, during his term of office, referred to the provision as a potential "union-busting" technique, and the prohibition on voting by strikers was repealed in 1959.

In many respects the Taft-Hartley Act was a product of experience; that is, it dealt with problems that had arisen subsequent to the Wagner Act. In 1935 the nation had not been overly concerned with the problem of communism, but by 1947 the United States was engaged in a "cold war" with the Soviet Union, and there was deep concern with the fact that a number of unions were headed by persons who were either avowedly communists or surreptitiously so. The new act, therefore, required union officers to sign affidavits that they were not members of the Communist party in order for their unions to be able to file cases before the National Labor Relations Board.

Another problem that could not have been foreseen at the time that the Wagner Act was adopted was that of strikes that could prevent an entire vital industry from operating. By 1947, however, a number of large national strikes had occurred, and Congress was concerned with how to prevent disruptions in vital production or services. The Taft-Hartley Act, therefore, contained emergency disputes provisions that enabled the President to delay a strike that might imperil the national health or safety. (These provisions will be examined more fully in Chapter 7.)

A number of other Taft-Hartley provisions restricted unions, too. Among these was a requirement that unions file reports on their constitutions, by-laws, and financial accounts. Unions were forbidden to make contributions in elections for federal political office, and were also denied the right to sole administration of welfare funds that were based upon employer contributions. Union dues could no longer be deducted from the employee's pay by the employer unless the employee had given written consent to that effect. Moreover, employers were not required to bargain with unions of supervisory employees, and most of these unions, such as the Foreman's Association of America, which had represented the foremen at the Ford Motor Company, collapsed.

The Effects of Taft-Hartley

Despite the great union outcry against the Taft-Hartley Act as representing an assault upon labor and collective bargaining, unions continued to grow following its passage. While the act may have put further impediments in the way of new organizing on the part of weak unions, it had little effect on strong unions, to the disappointment of those who thought that the act would deal adequately with what they considered to be the inordinate amount of power that labor could wield. In Taft-Hartley Congress had sought to outlaw all secondary boycotts by making it an unfair labor practice to conduct secondary strikes or picketing. The unions, particularly the International Brotherhood of Teamsters (IBT), however, discovered loopholes in the law, described by a former chairman of the National Labor Relations Board, Guy Farmer, as "wide enough to drive a truck through."[7]

If employers were unhappy with the court interpretations of the law and the loopholes that had developed in the ban on secondary boycotts, they

[7] Guy Farmer, *Strikes, Picketing and Secondary Boycotts Under the Landrum-Griffin Amendments* (New York: Industrial Relations Counselors, 1960), p. 10.

seemed powerless to change the situation, because Congress was not in the mood to examine the whole question of labor law. However, congressional investigations, begun in 1957, of corruption in the labor-management field provided an atmosphere for consideration of new legislation. The Senate hearings, under the direction of Senator McClellan (D., Arkansas), exposed instances of union officials engaging in coercion, violence, and denial of rights to their members.[8] A parade of witnesses offered testimony detailing how small employers were being victimized by unions through the use of secondary boycotts and extortion picketing. Other witnesses gave evidence of employers interfering with the rights of their employees by signing "sweetheart contracts" with corrupt union leaders and by bribing union officials through the intermediary of labor "consultants."

The Landrum-Griffin Act

The resulting public outcry against these exposures of corruption forced Congress to act, and the AFL-CIO itself cooperated in proposing reform, but the legislation that emerged was not to the unions' liking. The resulting legislation, the Labor-Management Reporting and Disclosure (Landrum-Griffin) Act of 1959, dealt primarily with internal union affairs, but it also contained provisions that sought to tighten up some of the Taft-Hartley prohibitions on union activities with respect to employers. Title VII of Landrum-Griffin, for instance, curtailed organizational picketing, hot-cargo agreements, and secondary boycotts.

Labor-Management Relations

To deal with the problem of "sweetheart agreements," whereby an employer, in return for "favors" to some union officials, would be permitted to sign a contract with the union that provided standards far below what other unionized workers were receiving elsewhere, Title II of Landrum-Griffin required that employers file annual reports on their payments to unions, union officers, shop stewards, employees of unions, employees or employee committees, and labor consultants. Title V, moreover, expanded the types of payments that were to be considered as criminal rather than civil offenses. Extortionate picketing, that is, putting a picket line in front of an establishment unless the employer agrees to pay money to a union official, was made a federal offense.

A main thrust of the Landrum-Griffin Act was to close the loopholes with respect to secondary boycotts. First, the coverage of the act was broadened to include the industries covered by the Railway Labor Act. Secondly, the act declared that a union could not induce individual employees to engage in secondary pressures. Thirdly, the act prohibited hot-cargo clauses (recognition of the right of employees not to handle struck goods) in labor-manage-

---

[8] Northrup and Bloom, *op. cit.*, p. 146.

ment agreements, with exceptions permitted for the construction and clothing industries, in which special circumstances exist. Employers, moreover, could sue unions for the damages caused by strikes in violation of a collective bargaining agreement or for secondary boycott violations.

Recognition picketing was restricted, too. Recognition picketing was a device used by unions in their attempts to organize nonunion establishments where they did not have a majority of the workers as members. Theoretically, such a picket line was supposed to be a means of informing the workers of the union's interest in organizing them, but in practice it was often an attempt to induce the employer to recognize the union, even if his employees did not want to join it. Under Landrum-Griffin, recognition picketing was banned if an NLRB election had been held at that establishment within one year; thus, a union that failed to get a majority of the employees to vote to have it represent them could not immediately put a picket line in front of the establishment in a new attempt to win recognition, but had to wait a full year. Recognition picketing was also prohibited where another union had been recognized as the bargaining agent of the employees.

While Landrum-Griffin was largely aimed at curbing union power, one provision of it was designed to curb a potential union-busting technique. Taft-Hartley had denied economic strikers who had been replaced by new employees the right to vote in NLRB representation elections, but Landrum-Griffin declared that workers who had gone on strike over economic matters retained their right to vote in any NLRB election conducted within twelve months of the start of the strike.

Internal Union Affairs

Titles I through V of the Landrum-Griffin Act of 1959 deal with internal union affairs, imposing new obligations on unions and their officers. With respect to internal affairs, the law required that all unions adopt constitutions and by-laws and file them with the Secretary of Labor. These union-governing statutes must detail the requirements for membership, the procedures for financial assessments, and the rules governing discipline of union members. Unions must also file financial reports, which must be open to inspection by all members.

Restrictions were placed upon union officials, holding them accountable to strict standards of fiduciary responsibility. Embezzlement of union funds was made a federal crime, and union members were granted the right to file suit if they thought that a union was failing to take proper action against an officer accused of embezzlement. The act also prohibited loans by a union to its officers of more than $2,000. Furthermore, persons who had been convicted of serious crimes or had been members of the Communist party were denied the right to hold union office for five years after their release from prison or resignation from the Communist party (which latter provision was later declared to be unconstitutional by the Supreme Court). Finally, severe penalties were decreed for violations of these provisions of the act.

Title III of the act restricted the imposition of trusteeships by unions. The trusteeship is a legitimate device used by national unions to prevent undemocratic practices or corruption by local union officers; an accused local would lose the right to conduct its own affairs, and would be placed in the hands of a trustee designated by the national union. In some cases trusteeships were necessary in order to handle the assets of a local that had ceased to function because the plant it had covered had gone out of business. The trusteeship device, however, had been abused by some unions, which had used it to stifle local autonomy, quell opposition, and consolidate power in the hands of the national union and its officers. The Senate hearings had disclosed, for example, that 113 of the 892 locals of the Teamsters were under trusteeship. The act, therefore, declared that unions must file reports on all trusteeships and that trusteeships must be limited to assuring the performance of collective bargaining agreements, to the prevention of corruption, to the restoration of democratic procedures, or to the carrying out of the legitimate objectives of the union—for example, caretaker trusteeships for inactive locals. Furthermore, a member may protest a trusteeship, at which point the Secretary of Labor would investigate its legitimacy, and if he found it to be illegitimate he could file suit in court to end it. Finally, a trusteeship had to end after eighteen months, unless the union could prove that its continuance was necessary.

Title I of the act was designed to protect the individual union member by establishing a bill of rights. It provided for equal rights to nominate candidates for union office, vote in elections, attend meetings, and participate in union affairs. It declared that union members have the right to form oppositions to the incumbent administrations subject only to "reasonable rules," and that union dues and assessments can be raised only by secret ballot for locals or by convention for national unions. Union members must be given notice and fair hearing in disciplinary cases. There are, however, no criminal penalties for violations of Title I.

In a further move to strengthen union democracy, Landrum-Griffin established standards to ensure fair elections. A national union must elect its officers at least every five years, either by convention or referendum. Locals must hold elections at least every three years, and they must be conducted by secret ballot. Intermediate bodies must hold elections at least every four years. The law requires that there be a reasonable period in which members can make nominations for union offices and that candidates receive equal treatment in the union newspaper and other means of communication. Furthermore, no union monies may be spent on any candidate's behalf. A union member who believes that election procedures have not conformed to the law must first pursue the matter through the union's channels, but if he fails to be satisfied he may carry his complaint to the Secretary of Labor, who will investigate it and, if he finds evidence of wrongdoing, proceed to court.

Evaluation of Landrum-Griffin

With any piece of legislation, its proponents often find that it did not correct all the abuses for which it was intended, and this is true with respect to Landrum-Griffin. Moreover, while Congress legislates, it is left to the NLRB and the courts to interpret that legislation in specific cases, and that interpretation can alter congressional intent. It has been charged, for instance, that the NLRB has eroded the Landrum-Griffin restrictions on boycotts and picketing.[9]

Based upon a study of NLRB and court cases, Brinker concluded that certain secondary activity is still legal in spite of the tightening of the law by the Landrum-Griffin amendments.[10] The courts have read two exceptions into the secondary boycott prohibition: (1) the "ally" doctrine, that is, if the neutral employer is not really neutral but is closely tied to the struck one, then secondary pressures may be exerted on him; and (2) where the secondary employer is a corporate affiliate of the struck one, a union may exert pressure on it. Despite these exceptions to the ban on secondary boycotts, Landrum-Griffin has severely restricted unions in their use of pressure on neutral employers. In fact, Archibald Cox, former Solicitor General of the United States, has argued that, because of the law's restrictions on boycotts and picketing, increased protection is required against employer interference, coercion, and restraint of employees in the exercise of their rights of self-organization.[11]

With respect to the other aspect of Landrum-Griffin, that dealing with union internal democracy, the law seems to have had significant impact. Since its passage the incumbent administrations in a number of unions have been ousted from office. How much of this has been due to the law is questionable, but Barbash believes that the requirements giving candidates for office rights on distribution of campaign literature and access to membership lists, and the prohibition on using union dues to support one candidate, have been important.[12] In the case of the International Union of Electrical Workers, the new president took over in 1965 only after an investigation by the Secretary of Labor had disclosed an improper count of the votes by the incumbent administration, and the 1972 election in the United Mine Workers was actually conducted by the U.S. Department of Labor.

There is no agreement, however, on the impact of Title I, the "Bill of Rights of Members in Labor Organizations," on the functioning of unions and the protection of members' rights. One of those contending that the act

---

[9] *The Changing Climate in Labor Law* (New York: Industrial Relations Counselors, 1963).

[10] Paul A. Brinker, "Ambulatory Picketing Since 1958," *Labor Law Journal*, February 1971, pp. 80–88.

[11] Archibald Cox, *Law and the National Labor Policy* (Los Angeles: Institute of Industrial Relations, University of California, 1960), p. 22.

[12] Jack Barbash, *American Unions: Structure, Government, and Politics* (New York: Random House, 1967), p. 99.

has had little significant impact is Soffer, who finds that it "does not alter drastically the internal union power balance between union leaders and members."[13] A study of forty-three major union constitutions revealed that no important changes had to be made in order to conform with the act's requirements, but that union procedures with respect to discipline had been modified.[14]

A major area in which the LMRDA has had an impact was with respect to trusteeships. In 1959 there had been 487 trusteeships, but by March 1962 the number had declined to 187. According to Soffer, the removal of the incentive to establish trusteeships has been the outstanding contribution of the act; trusteeships have become only a last-resort device, and most of them today are "defensive" in character, that is, to help carry out the requirements of the law or to serve as a caretaker for locals being disbanded because of plant closings.[15]

Another area of impact was that of election procedures in unions. A study of the Office of Labor-Management Policy Reports found that, following the act, three-quarters of the unions amended their constitutions with respect to election procedures for local union officers.[16] In general, according to Ginsburg, there is a consensus "that the Act contributed to making members far more aware of their individual rights relating to appeals, freedom of speech, and participation within their union, and the protection of the law for such rights."[17]

Summary

We can close our review of the legal climate in which labor-management relations take place by referring to a five-phase typology of its evolution.

First, until the middle of the nineteenth century, roughly coincident with the decision in *Commonwealth v. Hunt,* the legal climate was such as to discourage workers from combining to improve their labor standards. Since unionism ran counter to the concepts of a laissez-faire economy, and given the stress on capital accumulation in the early stages of economic development, unions were considered inimical to the public welfare. Unions were liable to court prosecution as illegal conspiracies, and, in their application of

[13] Benson Soffer, "Collective Bargaining and Federal Regulation of Union Government," in Marten Estey, Philip Taft, and Martin Wagner (eds.), *Regulating Union Government* (New York: Harper & Row, 1964), p. 92.

[14] Philip Ross and Philip Taft, "The Effect of the LMRDA upon Union Constitutions," *New York University Law Review,* April 1968, pp. 305–334.

[15] Soffer, *op. cit.,* pp. 111, 112.

[16] *Union Constitutions and the Election of Local Union Officers,* U.S. Department of Labor (Washington, D.C.: Government Printing Office, 1965).

[17] Woodrow Ginsburg, "Review of Literature on Union Growth, Government and Structure—1955–1969," in Woodrow L. Ginsburg *et al., A Review of Industrial Relations Research,* Vol. 1 (Madison, Wisc.: Industrial Relations Research Association, 1970), p. 249.

the common law, the courts were the principal formulators of this national labor policy.

Following *Commonwealth v. Hunt,* and continuing through the first third of the twentieth century, union organization was tolerated. Collective bargaining, however, remained only a privilege and not a protected institution. In this period the courts were very restrictive of union actions, and enjoined many of them as restraining trade, first on the basis of common law, but after passage of the Sherman Act of 1890 on the basis of statute law.

A third era seemed to dawn with the passage of the Norris–La Guardia Act of 1932, which restricted the federal courts in the issuance of injunctions in labor disputes. The federal government ended its role of intervention in labor-management relations on the side of the employer, and the stage was set for the development of a voluntary system of industrial relations. But employer failure to reach accommodation with trade unionism resulted instead in a government-imposed collective bargaining system.

The Wagner Act, therefore, ushered in a fourth phase of national labor policy, in which government encouraged unionism and collective bargaining. Although the Taft-Hartley Act of 1947 redressed some of the imbalance in labor relations (on the side of unions by then), it did not alter the basic compulsion to engage in collective bargaining. In fact, Taft-Hartley put the government further into the labor-management relations arena with new controls over the bargaining process and prescriptions as to the content of agreements between the parties.

With Landrum-Griffin a fifth phase of national labor policy has emerged. While it continues some of the intent of Taft-Hartley to place limitations and qualifications on union activities, it opens a new era by bringing the internal workings of unions under government regulation. This was virtually inevitable, because once the government had made it national policy to encourage union growth and to force employers to bargain with unions, and it was made legal for workers to have to join unions whether they wanted to or not in order to retain their jobs, the government, in effect, had established a type of public franchise that demanded some protection for those subject to it.

This review of the legal climate is hardly closed, for there are many issues still outstanding. We shall, however, postpone looking at some of them until Chapter 7, turning next instead to the collective bargaining relationship between labor and management.

BIBLIOGRAPHY

Barbash, Jack. *American Unions: Structure, Government, and Politics.* New York: Random House, 1967.

Brinker, Paul A. "Ambulatory Picketing Since 1958," *Labor Law Journal,* February 1971.

Cohen, Sanford. *Labor Law.* Columbus: Charles E. Merrill, 1964.

Cox, Archibald. *Law and the National Labor Policy.* Los Angeles: Institute of Industrial Relations, University of California, 1960.

Estey, Marten, Philip Taft, and Martin Wagner (eds.). *Regulating Union Government.* New York: Harper & Row, 1964.

Farmer, Guy. *Strikes, Picketing and Secondary Boycotts Under the Landrum-Griffin Amendments.* New York: Industrial Relations Counselors, 1960.

Ginsburg, Woodrow L., E. Robert Livernash, Herbert S. Parnes, and George Strauss. *A Review of Industrial Relations Research,* Vol. 1. Madison, Wisc.: Industrial Relations Research Association, 1970.

Gregory, Charles O. *Labor and the Law.* New York: Norton, 1958.

Millis, Harry A., and Emily Clark Brown. *From the Wagner Act to Taft-Hartley.* Chicago: University of Chicago Press, 1950.

Northrup, Herbert F., and Gordon F. Bloom. *Government and Labor.* Homewood, Ill.: Richard D. Irwin, 1963.

Ross, Philip, and Philip Taft. "The Effect of the LMRDA upon Union Constitutions," *New York University Law Review,* April 1968.

Wellington, Harry W. *Labor and the Legal Process.* New Haven: Yale University Press, 1968.

Wykstra, Ronald A., and Eleanour V. Stevens. *American Labor and Manpower Policy.* New York: Odyssey Press, 1970.

6 COLLECTIVE BARGAINING

According to classical economic theory, the exchange relationship between workers and employers was supposed to take place in a free labor market, in which the forces of supply and demand would be determinant. Classical theory, however, did not foresee the rise of the large business organization or of combinations of employers and workers. The reality in large sectors of the modern industrial economy is that the terms and conditions of employment of workers are set through negotiations between combinations of workers—unions—and employers, many of whom are either large enough by themselves to affect the price of labor or who also act through employer associations. This process of negotiation of the terms and conditions of employment has become known as "collective bargaining," and in this chapter we shall examine the institution of collective bargaining, in terms of its extent, the legal setting in which it takes place, its structure, the grievance procedure that has emerged from it, the industrial conflict that takes place when it fails to achieve accommodation between the parties, and the theories that have been advanced to explain its operation.

The Extent of Collective Bargaining

To most college students, collective bargaining must seem to be a rather remote institution, since few of them expect to have the terms and conditions of their employment following graduation determined by it. If this is the case, then why is so much attention focused on collective bargaining? There are a number of answers to this question. First of all, as we have seen, some 20 million employees in the United States are union members whose terms and conditions of employment are determined through collective bargaining. While a minority of the nation's labor force, those 20 million are concentrated in manufacturing, transportation, and public utilities, all key segments of the economy. Moreover, collective bargaining itself is spreading into new areas, such as hospitals and public employment. Since the union shop, whereby all workers in the bargaining unit are required to join the union, is far from universal in organized establishments, many more workers are covered by collective bargaining agreements than are members of unions.

But many workers who are not covered by collective bargaining actually have the terms and conditions of their employment influenced significantly by collective bargaining. In industries in which some firms are organized and others are not, the nonunion ones generally are able to remain so by matching the gains achieved through collective bargaining in the organized firms. There is a similar relationship within firms with respect to the unorganized sectors of their work forces. Thus, in the typical large manufacturing company, pay and fringe benefit adjustments for nonunion salaried employees are usually commensurate with those which management agreed to in collective bargaining with the unions representing the production workers. Finally, even enterprises in areas of the economy in which very few of the employees are union members cannot ignore developments achieved elsewhere, and the wages and benefits of these employees are heavily influenced by what organized workers have achieved through collective bargaining.

The Legal Setting

One of the great paradoxes of the United States is that, while it clung longer and more tenaciously to the spirit of laissez faire in the labor market, today government plays a more important role in the industrial relations system here than it does in almost any other industrial nation. In fact, as we saw in the last chapter, the deep involvement of government in labor-management relations stems from the resistance by American business to unionism and collective bargaining. Thus, the law of the land protects the right of employees to form unions through which to bargain collectively with their employers.

The law also requires that the parties bargain in "good faith." The formal rules laid down by the National Labor Relations Board to implement this requirement seem quite simple: there should be face-to-face meetings between labor and management, held at reasonable times and places; there must be notification by one party, sixty days prior to contract expiration, of its desire to modify the terms of the existing agreement; during those sixty days, no changes are to be made in present terms and conditions; and, upon request of either party, formalization of the agreement reached by written contract. In practice, however, interpretations by both the NLRB and the courts of the simple requirement that the parties bargain in good faith have drawn the government deeply into the entire collective bargaining process, both as to how the parties should conduct their negotiations and the subjects about which they must bargain.

Although the Taft-Hartley Act states that the law does not compel either party "to agree to a proposal or require the making of a concession," management spokesmen have charged that pressure to make concessions inevitably derives from existing NLRB rules with respect to good-faith bargaining. A leading case has been that of the General Electric approach to bargaining, which has become known as "Boulwarism" after Lemuel Boulware, a former GE vice-president for industrial relations. Based upon extensive research, GE would make a firm offer to the union and then refuse to make concessions in its detailed bargaining proposal except on the basis of new information or changes in the facts used in drafting the proposal. Union leaders bitterly condemned the GE approach to bargaining, not because it resulted in niggardly increases in wages and benefits, but, on the contrary, because it left nothing for the union "to win" from management during negotiations.

In the usual labor-management negotiations, the union makes demands upon the employer that surpass its expectations of achievement; the employer makes counterproposals below what he expects to grant; and the two parties then bargain until a point somewhere between their original positions is reached that is mutually satisfactory to them. The GE bargaining approach, however, did not follow this pattern. The International Union of Electrical Workers (IUE) therefore formally charged that the bargaining table conduct of the General Electric Company in negotiations amounted to a refusal to bargain in good faith. In 1964 the NLRB ruled for the union, stating that the company did not leave the union room for bargaining gains and thereby devitalized the bargaining process and eliminated consideration of union proposals. In 1970 the Supreme Court refused to review the case, thus upholding the NLRB decision, but in the interim the company, following a strike in 1969–1970, had retreated from the Boulware approach.

The government not only regulates how the parties should conduct their bargaining, but also the subjects about which they must negotiate. Not all subjects, however, fit into the same mold, and, indeed, three different categories of bargaining subjects have been evolved:

1. Mandatory subjects (those about which the parties must negotiate or face charges of refusing to bargain in good faith).
2. Prohibited subjects (those which the law says the parties may not enter into, regardless of their own wishes). About the only subjects of any consequence that fall within this area are the prohibitions written into the Taft-Hartley Act of closed shop (only union members may be hired) or preferential hiring agreements (union members are hired before nonunion workers), the Landrum-Griffin Act ban on hot-cargo clauses (union members need not handle struck goods), the use of welfare funds for other than specified purposes, and the Civil Rights Act prohibition on racial discrimination.
3. Nonmandatory subjects (those which the parties may bargain about, but not to the point of impasse, such as union procedures with respect to strike votes by their members). Even though the subject is not a prohibited matter of bargaining and either party is allowed to raise it in negotiations, for one party to insist on continuing to bargain on the issue to the point of a work stoppage would make it guilty of an unfair labor practice.

The most important bargaining subjects are those that labor and management must negotiate, and from the time of its inception the NLRB has specified what these subjects are. With the passage of the Taft-Hartley Act, the authority of the board to do so was, in effect, confirmed by Congress; the law declared that the duty to bargain attaches to any matters that come within the area of wages, hours, and other terms and conditions of employment. Again, this may sound obvious, but people can and do disagree on precisely what it covers, and over the years the definition of "wages, hours and other terms and conditions of employment" has been expanded to include such matters as (1) fringe benefits (vacations, retirement and pension plans, group insurance plans, profit-sharing plans, Christmas bonuses, employee stock purchase plans); (2) union security and check-off of dues; (3) plant practices; and (4) company-owned housing.

Employers contend that the broad definition of bargaining areas permits unions to encroach upon what management regards as its prerogatives. They have been very concerned, for example, with a 1964 Supreme Court ruling, in *Fibreboard Paper Products Corporation v. NLRB,* that an employer must bargain with the union over subcontracting whenever subcontracting may result in the termination of jobs or impairment of the bargaining unit.[1] The company had ceased performing one phase of its operations, farming it out to another company, which was able to do the work more cheaply. In the view of the employers, subcontracting is a management right that should not be subjected to joint decision-making with the employees. As the unions see it, however, bargaining about subcontracting is necessary in order for the union to fulfill its function of protecting the jobs of its members.

The issue of union encroachment on management rights is not a new one, but has been present since unions arose. When unions first asked for a voice in the establishment of wages and hours, employers claimed that that would be an "unwarrantable encroachment on their rights as employers." A long and hard road has been traveled since then, and today collective bargaining is firmly established in the United States, but as one observer has stated: "Its frontiers are constantly expanding under the pressure of the most powerful, militant, and dynamic labor union movement the world has ever known."[2]

The Bargaining Process

Collective bargaining negotiations usually take place between "professionals," men with long experience in the field. Union officials, of course, develop expertise, and most are shrewd bargainers who are familiar with the technology and economics of the industry whose employees they represent. In large companies, management officials schooled in labor relations are the chief spokesmen for their companies. Very small firms may be members of employer associations that employ professional negotiators, or often they may hire a lawyer or other skilled negotiator for the purpose. Both sides, moreover, will include experts in various subjects, such as industrial engineering, pensions, and economics, on their negotiating teams.

---

[1] *Fibreboard Paper Products Corp. v. National Labor Relations Board,* 379, U.S. 203 (1964).

[2] Selwyn H. Torff, *Collective Bargaining—Negotiations and Agreements* (New York: McGraw-Hill, 1953), p. 4.

The negotiating process may take weeks or even months, and the teams meet often to exchange proposals and counterproposals. Small subcommittees from each side may be appointed to study specific subjects, particularly when they involve technical details, such as changes in a pension program. Some bargaining sessions may be public, but, as the parties get down to "hard bargaining," they tend to retreat behind closed doors. Although the negotiating process may be spread over an extended period, the most serious bargaining takes place as the contract expiration date approaches and the parties face the prospect of a strike.

Unless agreement on a new contract is reached by then, a strike normally occurs, for only occasionally, as when the parties are very close to a settlement, will the union extend the old contract beyond its expiration date, and then only for a few days. In most unions the agreement reached must be ratified by the membership before it can take effect. Similarly, in multi-employer bargaining, the agreement will be subject to the entire employer group's ratification.

In contrast to the usual process of last-minute deadline negotiations, the steel industry during the 1960s followed what amounted to a system of continuous consultation and study before bargaining. In an attempt to establish better labor-management relations following a 116-day strike in 1959, the steel companies and the United Steelworkers jointly set up a Human Relations Committee to study the problems facing the parties. Through serious study of problems and continual meetings, the committee played an instrumental role in securing peaceful contract settlements in the next two negotiations. In fact, the committee seemed to have been too successful, for many union members believed that it was neglecting their interests and turning the bargaining function over to hired technicians; as a result, after 1965 the Human Relations Committee disappeared.

In the United States collective bargaining results in a written agreement, usually of fixed duration, commonly two or three years, which is a formal, legal document, enforceable the same as any other contract. It is signed by the local union and the national union on one side, and by the employer on the other. The agreement may be a short one of only a few pages, but others, such as that between the General Motors Corporation and the United Automobile Workers, may consist of several hundred pages, detailing all the subjects covered. Let us now turn our attention to the typical subjects covered in collective bargaining.

The Subject Matter of Bargaining

Wages

Although the scope of collective bargaining has expanded, the question of wages remains the key one. American unions usually negotiate rates for jobs. This is very different from most European countries, in which national, industry-wide collective bargaining fixes minimum rates, and sometimes establishes varying rates for male and female and for adult and juvenile workers. In this country, however, minimum wages are left to the government, and the collective bargaining between union and employer establishes the actual wage rates to be paid. The rate is fixed for the particular skill or type of work, no matter who performs it. There may be single rates—for example, $2.95 for Assembler A—or rate ranges—$2.85 to $3.10 per hour for Assembler A— with individual workers proceeding through the range over time.

Although most wage rates are time rates (so much per hour), in some industries there are incentive wage rates. The highly organized garment industries for many decades have had piece-rate methods of wage payment, by which workers are paid by the number of items produced, for example, dress pleats sewn. At the beginning of each new style season, union and management officials negotiate the new piece rates. A number of metalworking industries, such as steel and machinery, have many production workers on incentive pay. In these cases the collective agreement will regulate how the time study is to be conducted, and provision is often made for guaranteed minimum rates and for payments for periods of "down time," that is, periods of machine breakdown and other disruptions in production for which the employee is not responsible.

Typically, the renegotiation of an agreement that has run out will provide for an increase in wage rates, time or piece. Some agreements also provide for cost-of-living wage increases during the life of the agreement. These operate either through an escalator clause, which automatically raises wages in line with increases in the Bureau of Labor Statistics' Consumer Price Index, or through a wage-reopening clause in the contract, which permits the union to bargain for higher wages after the CPI increases by a certain percentage. Wages, hence, are increased sufficiently to compensate for any increase in the cost of living, thus enabling workers to maintain their real wages, that is, to be able to continue to buy as much goods and services as before.

Employers have been attempting to negotiate cost-of-living wage increases out of their labor contracts. Since business firms must agree to supply customers with products at fixed prices, they are loath to leave one major area of their costs—labor—out of their control. For example, it takes a couple of years to build a hydroelectric generator, but the price is fixed at the time that the order is placed; if, in the period in which production is taking place, the cost of labor should unexpectedly go up, the company might find that it has lost money on the sale.

A second type of automatic wage increase—an annual improvement factor—came into being in the UAW–General Motors agreement of 1948. Such increases are not based upon increased productivity from the employee's own effort or even the improved productivity within the particular firm or industry, but on the average annual productivity increase of approximately 3 percent that the United States economy has been enjoying over the long run. Where the contract provides for an annual improvement factor, the workers will receive an increase in wages of, say, 12 cents per hour, every year. Such increases enable workers to enjoy higher real wages and improve their standard of living in line with the growth of the nation's economy.

Working Time

The federal Fair Labor Standards Act sets a basic forty-hour week for the nation, with one-and-one-half times regular rates of pay for overtime hours. Some unions, through collective bargaining, have been able to secure even shorter work weeks. The Ladies' Garment Workers, for example, have had a thirty-five-hour week in many branches of the industry for the past forty years. Most agreements also provide for time-and-a-half pay for any hours over eight in a day, for work outside of scheduled hours, and for Saturday work as such; double time for Sunday work; and triple-time pay for certain holidays.

Workers also receive various forms of premium pay for working certain hours. Most agreements provide some form of call-in pay; thus, if a worker is called in to work by his employer, he generally receives four hours' pay, whether the employer has that much work for him or not. And those employees that work the undesirable shifts—4 P.M. to midnight or midnight to 8 A.M.—receive shift differentials, that is, extra pay over and above the normal rates for their jobs. Many agreements also provide for paid rest periods, of ten to fifteen minutes, during the work day.

Job Security

A major emphasis of union activity is to protect the jobs of members. In a dynamic business economy, customer orders do not come in with regularity all the time, and it has been common in the United States for firms to lay off production workers when they are not needed. In order to prevent arbitrary decisions by management, unions have evolved the system of seniority as the fairest means of determining who is to be laid off when business becomes slow. Most labor-management agreements, therefore, provide that the last worker hired is the first to be laid off, and those with the longest service are the last to be let go. Similarly, when business picks up employees are recalled to work on the basis of their years of service. Seniority thus is a method of allocating scarce job opportunities among workers.

The seniority unit, however, varies. Where skills vary, it most likely will be by occupation or department, but where the mass of workers are semi-skilled, and thus can easily take over one another's jobs, seniority may be plant-wide. Whatever the seniority unit, most unions prefer layoffs to work sharing when business is slow, but some unions do permit the reduction of the work week to thirty-two hours before layoffs commence. Only in such seasonal industries as clothing, as already pointed out, do the unions insist upon equal division of work, instead of layoff, when the trade is slow; otherwise, some workers would have so little work that they could not earn a decent living.

The principle of seniority is also widely used with respect to benefits. The amount of pension that a worker receives at retirement and the number of weeks of vacation to which he is entitled while working normally increase with his years of service. Seniority also plays a role in promotions, but management tends to resist having it be a sole criterion, claiming that ability should also be a factor.

Collective agreements protect workers against disciplinary layoffs and arbitrary discharge by the employer. The employer must prove that there is "good cause" for a discharge, as defined by the collective agreement, before he can discharge an employee. Workers who believe that they have been unfairly disciplined, moreover, may appeal management action through the grievance procedure.

In multiplant companies, workers from plants that are permanently closed down may be given the right to transfer to other plants of the company. Where business conditions dictate the permanent layoff of workers, many collective agreements provide that they receive severance pay to compensate for the loss of the job. Such payments are based upon age and length of service.

Fringe Benefits

The big area of expansion of collective bargaining since World War II, when wages were controlled, has been in various welfare programs for workers. These additions to pay, known as "fringe benefits," including supplements to pay and paid time off, amounted in 1971 to 30.8 percent of payroll or $1.22 per payroll hour, according to a survey of large companies by the U.S. Chamber of Commerce.[3] Although smaller employers do not tend to offer as attractive employee benefits, "fringes" have become an important part of the total compensation of all workers.

Most collective agreements provide for various forms of hospital, surgical, and weekly sickness and accident benefits. Workers are also generally covered by group life insurance policies.

Pension plans spread widely throughout American industry as a result of the negotiations in the automobile and steel industries in 1949. The latter negotiations followed a Supreme Court ruling in the Inland Steel case that such matters as pensions and compulsory retirement were mandatory subjects over which employers had to bargain.[4]

Workers in the basic steel, automobile, cement, and rubber industries, and in other industries as well, also receive supplemental unemployment benefits for the periods during which they are laid off, for up to one, or even

---

[3] *Employee Benefits 1971* (Washington, D.C.: Chamber of Commerce of the United States, 1972).

[4] *Inland Steel Co. v. National Labor Relations Board*, 170 F. 2d 247 (7th Cir. 1948).

two, years, depending upon length of service. Such benefits are financed by employer payments to a special fund, and together with state unemployment insurance benefits they provide some laid-off workers with close to their normal take-home pay. In recent years short work-week benefits have been included.

Union Security

The history of employer opposition to trade unionism has made American unions extremely security conscious. The collective agreement, therefore, usually begins with a paragraph in which the employer recognizes the union as the exclusive bargaining agent for specified groups of his employees. Beyond that, unions often insist upon a union shop, whereby all employees must join the union within a specified period, usually thirty days, of their hire.

Although forcing workers to join a union seems to run against the principle of individual freedom, unions justify their insistence upon the union shop on the basis of majority rule, opposition to "free riders," and the claim that it facilitates union responsibility and prevents employer discrimination between union and nonunion members. They see union government as analogous to civil government, in which no one can opt out of citizenship or of paying taxes. Moreover, they contend that if unions are to be able to live up to agreements, they must have the power to discipline all those who are subject to the agreement.

Many people are opposed on principle to compulsory union membership, seeing it as a denial of a worker's freedom to choose whether or not he wants to join. Others see the union shop as allowing union leaders to ignore their members' wishes, since the latter cannot display their unhappiness with the union by withholding their dues. It is also claimed that compulsory unionism often compels a worker to support a policy that may be injurious to him, as when the union's winning of a large wage increase leads to his unemployment.

The opposition to compulsory union membership has been enacted into law in a number of southern and midwestern agricultural states. These so-called right-to-work laws forbid the union shop, whereby workers must join the union, and even the "agency shop," whereby those workers who do not wish to join the union must contribute a sum equal to membership dues in return for the services that the union, by law, must provide all workers in the unit.

Despite the debate on the legitimacy of compulsory membership, most employers have found it expedient not to resist the demand for union security, and union shop arrangements or some lesser form of it—such as the maintenance-of-membership shop, whereby no one need join the union but those who do must remain members for the duration of the contract—are provided for in 75 percent of labor-management contracts.[5] Many collective agreements also provide for the checkoff, whereby management deducts union fees from

---

[5] *Monthly Labor Review*, January 1960, p. 26.

the employee's pay and turns the money over to the union. From the employer's point of view, the checkoff may be highly preferable to the disruptions of production that might stem from union shop stewards roaming the plant trying to collect dues from employees.

Management Rights

Just as the union seeks to ensure its security in the collective bargaining agreement, management, too, seeks to protect areas of decision-making as belonging exclusively to management. This issue of what rights are the exclusive preserve of management has always been an area of contention between labor and management. In 1945, at the conclusion of World War II, President Truman called a conference, the Labor-Management Conference, to chart the readjustment to a civilian economy. The conference, however, ran into a major roadblock when the unions refused to draw a line recognizing certain functions as management's prerogatives and agreeing not to cross that line. This is not to say that American unions do not recognize management prerogatives, for they certainly do, but what they recognize as an area of unilateral decision-making by management today they may come to regard as a subject for collective bargaining tomorrow, because they have come to see it as necessary to advance the interests of their members.

In view of what management regards as union invasion of its prerogatives, it attempts to prevent further incursions through a management's rights clause in the labor agreement. Such clauses may be quite detailed, specifying that the management has the sole right to decide on such matters as the operation of its plants, determination of the processes and materials to be used, establishment of production standards, and determination of the products to be manufactured. Other companies prefer shorter clauses that simply state that "all matters not specifically covered by this Agreement are vested fully and solely in the Company."

Whether detailed or not, employers adhere to the doctrine of management's residual rights. According to this concept, employers consider that management rights are relinquished only to the extent evidenced in the contract. In other words, unless the contract specifically makes a subject a matter of bargaining between union and management, it remains the exclusive preserve of management. The doctrine of residual rights, however, has been eroded through arbitration decisions, which have been upheld by the courts.

The Grievance Procedure

Contract Administration

Too often, members of the public think that collective bargaining is something that takes place between labor and management only every two or three years when new contract terms are negotiated. Contract negotiation, however, has been likened to that part of the iceberg of collective bargaining that shows above the surface, for, once agreement is reached and the contract is signed, it must be enforced. It is the grievance procedure provided for in the agreement that regulates the day-to-day, in-plant, labor-management relations. The grievance procedure provides a peaceful means of settling the disputes concerning the administration of the labor contract that do and must arise in today's complex industrial life. Disputes arise between the parties in four major areas: (1) the meaning of the terms agreed upon in negotiations; (2) the proper application of general terms to particular situations; (3) new matters that arise that were not covered by the basic agreement but call for solution; and (4) making local adjustments and modifications in the basic multiplant agreement to fit specific locations.[6]

The right of employees to present grievances to their employers is recognized by law. A grievance arises any time that a worker feels aggrieved and believes that he has not been treated justly according to the terms of the labor-management agreement. For example, the agreement may read that promotion is to be by seniority as long as there is no significant difference in ability; management may promote the less senior man on the basis of his ability, but the passed-over worker may claim that he is as capable as the other man and therefore entitled to the promotion. Other areas in which grievances are likely to arise include penalties imposed upon employees in disciplinary cases, wage rates for new and changed jobs, incentive wage-rate adjustments because of the use of different materials, and the imposition or distribution of overtime work.

Employee grievances are presented by a union official, usually called a "shop steward" in factory situations. The shop steward is elected by his fellow workers in the plant, and it is his job to investigate, present, and attempt to settle employee grievances. Should he and the foreman not be able to settle a problem, then it goes up the steps of the grievance procedure ladder. Although the number of steps in the ladder will vary from one industry or company to another, a typical one might be as follows: steward and foreman; chief steward and department head; union grievance committee and personnel manager; and union business agent, who is a full-time official, and plant manager. When none of them can settle the matter, then it is usually referred to arbitration.

The handling of grievances takes place during working hours, and it is quite common for the employer to pay the steward for the time lost from his plant job in handling grievances. Speed is essential in handling grievances in order to prevent unnecessary delays and the festering of sore spots. The grievance procedure is one of the most important aspects of labor-management relations, for settlement of disputes affects morale in the plant. Indeed, some students of labor-management relations believe that the processing of worker grievances is the most important function of modern unionism.

---

[6] Neil W. Chamberlain and James W. Kuhn, *Collective Bargaining* (New York: McGraw-Hill, 1965), p. 141.

To the individual worker the grievance procedure is extremely important, since it affords him protection against arbitrary managerial practices. To the worker, the shop steward represents the union. Since he rarely comes into contact with higher union officials, he depends upon the steward to protect his interests within the plant. Stewards who fail to satisfy their constituencies are quickly replaced at the next elections; in fact, turnover of stewards is quite high. Recognizing the importance of the role, most unions conduct training sessions for shop stewards so that they are competent to handle grievances. Similarly, management normally trains plant foremen so that they, too, are knowledgeable about the labor-management agreement and the processing of grievances.

The grievance procedure is valuable also in that it builds up, through a series of decisions that become precedents for the future, a body of shop law that supplements the actual written agreement between the parties. The grievance procedure, furthermore, enables the parties to discover the weak spots in their agreement that warrant correction in the next negotiations. But the major advantage of the grievance procedure, of course, is that it permits the adjustment of disputes between labor and management without disruption of production and earnings.

Arbitration of Unresolved Grievances

The use of arbitration as the final step in the grievance procedure is common today in the United States. Arbitration consists of submitting a dispute over which the parties cannot reach agreement to a supposedly impartial third party for settlement. More than 90 percent of labor-management agreements provide that, if a grievance cannot be resolved by the parties, the dispute must be submitted to arbitration with both sides being bound in advance to accept the decision. The arbitrator is limited to deciding the case on the basis of the existing contract, and he has no authority to alter or add to the terms of that agreement.

Most agreements provide for ad hoc arbitration; that is, an arbitrator is selected by the parties to rule in a single case or specific group of cases. In some industries, however, arbitrators are appointed on a permanent (equivalent to the length of the collective bargaining agreement) basis. Such permanent arbitration is common to the automobile industry, in which there is an umpire to settle disputes between each of the companies and the UAW, and to the garment industry, in which there is an impartial chairman for each subsection of the industry.

The advantages of the single permanent arbitrator are that he becomes familiar with the agreement and the personalities on both sides of the bargaining table, that his decisions will be consistent with one another, and that, after the initial selection, no time is lost in choosing an arbitrator. On the other hand, the use of temporary arbitrators enables the parties to select different types of specialists to adjudicate different types of disputes: for example, an industrial engineer might be chosen to settle incentive wage disputes and a local respected clergyman to handle disputes involving human relations conflicts.

Some agreements limit the arbitration of grievances. Under the General Motors–UAW agreement, for instance, the umpire may not order changes in wage rates, or decide disputes over speed of operations, or fix penalties in disciplinary, layoff, or discharge cases. If the parties cannot come to an agreement in disputes over such matters, the union has the right to strike. As another example, the "International Laws," or union rules governing printing shop working conditions, are usually exempted from arbitration in agreements signed by the International Typographical Union.

Despite the widespread use of arbitration, both union and management would prefer decisions reached by direct negotiations between them to the rulings of an arbitrator. The parties reason that the arbitrator, no matter how good, does not know the industry and its complexities as well as they do. Moreover, there is always a lurking fear that an arbitrator may try to "split the difference" between the parties, instead of deciding a case on its own merits. Finally, continual resort to arbitration may indicate a breakdown in the collective bargaining process, because in most instances the parties should be able to settle grievance disputes amicably themselves, leaving only the more intractable ones to arbitration.

The Structure of Bargaining

As we have seen, the law requires the employer to recognize and bargain with unions representing his employees in an "appropriate bargaining unit." In a perceptive analysis, Chamberlain has pointed out that there is no single notion of the bargaining unit, but a multiplicity of units.[7] He distinguished the following:

1. Informal work groups, the members of which are unified by a set of common aspirations. These are not normally involved in collective bargaining, except, as Kuhn has pointed out, when work groups use the grievance procedure to wring special favors from plant management, a process he termed "fractional bargaining."[8]
2. Election district, that is, the appropriate bargaining unit as determined by the National Labor Relations Board, through which employees, by majority decision, determine for themselves whether or not they want union representation.
3. Negotiating unit, that is, the scope of the parties actually engaged in collective bargaining across the table. In practice, the negotiating unit

---

[7] Neil W. Chamberlain, "Determinants of Collective Bargaining Structure," in Arnold R. Weber (ed.), *The Structure of Collective Bargaining* (New York: Free Press of Glencoe, 1961), pp. 3–19.

[8] James W. Kuhn, *Bargaining in Grievance Settlement* (New York: Columbia University Press, 1961).

may be larger than the election district. For example, a union may organize a number of plants of a company, one at a time, as a result of which each is an "appropriate bargaining unit," but the union actually negotiates one agreement with the company that covers the production workers in all its plants.

4. Unit of direct impact, that is, the group that is affected by a particular bargaining agreement, even though members of that group are not direct parties to it. A union may thus negotiate a contract with one company, after which the other companies in that industry agree to similar terms.

Negotiating Units

As we saw in the last chapter, policies of the National Labor Relations Board have affected the election district, but less so the actual negotiating units. Labor and management are free to determine, largely by mutual agreement, whether a given set of negotiations will cover a number of "appropriate bargaining units" (election districts), or only one; a number of employers, or only one. Unions and employers are also each free to establish associations that permit the coordination of bargaining activities in order to achieve common objectives.

In the United States today there is a wide variety of actual bargaining structures. These range from negotiations that cover the employees of such varied units as a specific department within a plant, or all production and maintenance workers within a plant, a company, or even an industry, to negotiations that cover workers in a particular craft in a labor market area.

Where a union controls the supply of labor to employers, as it does with skilled craft groups, economists have discerned a tendency for bargaining to become coextensive with the relevant labor market.[9] Thus, small employers who must compete with each other for workers of a particular skill, such as plumbers, will tend to bargain together through an employers' association with the union representing those workers. In practice, craft-type bargaining is usually limited to where the labor market and the product market have the same scope, as in the building trades.

Where the mass of employees is semiskilled and organized in industrial unions, the actual negotiating unit tends to become coextensive with the competitive market for the product.[10] Product markets, once limited to particular geographic areas, have, as a consequence of relatively reduced transportation costs, expanded to cover vast regions or even the entire nation. Unions, therefore, have sought to widen the geographic coverage of the actual negotiating unit in order to equalize wages and working conditions, and thus prevent their members from competing against each other for available work.

---

[9] Clark Kerr and Lloyd H. Fisher, "Multi-Employer Bargaining: The San Francisco Experience," in Richard Lester and Joseph Shister (eds.), *Insights into Labor Issues* (New York: Macmillan, 1948), pp. 25–61.

[10] *Ibid.*

The Extent of Different Types of Bargaining Units

Close to 150,000 different labor-management agreements exist in the United States. The vast majority of these cover workers in a single plant, so the predominant negotiating unit is small. However, while most units may be small, most workers are covered in large units. According to the Bureau of Labor Statistics, "major" units are those covering one thousand or more workers, and among them the single plant is not the predominant type of negotiating unit.

As a result of a trend toward centralization, less than one-third of all major collective bargaining negotiations, involving only one out of eight workers, covers the employees of a single plant.[11] Single-employer multiplant bargaining is the most typical form; 36 percent of major agreements, involving 40 percent of the workers, are of this type. In the automobile industry, for example, negotiations between General Motors and the United Automobile Workers cover the production workers in all GM plants; negotiations are also company-wide between the UAW and Ford and Chrysler.

Multi-employer bargaining, on a local, regional, or national basis, is more typical of nonmanufacturing than manufacturing. It is common in trucking, railroads, retail trade, and hotels and restaurants. In manufacturing, multi-employer bargaining is generally the practice in small-scale industries, such as apparel, lumber, furniture, and printing. In these cases a union will bargain with the employers through their association. A few large-scale industries, however, also conduct negotiations on a multi-employer basis. In the basic steel industry, for instance, the United Steelworkers of America bargains with the dozen or so largest producers as one group.

When the collective bargaining unit is multiplant, the national union usually negotiates directly with company management. The resulting master agreement establishing basic wage and fringe benefit standards for all plants of the company is usually supplemented with separate subsidiary agreements covering working conditions in each plant. The latter are negotiated between the locals and plant management, in consultation with national union leaders and company management.

Not only is there wide variety in the actual bargaining structures established by labor and management in specific situations, but there is also change in these structures as conditions change and the parties seek new and better methods for achieving their bargaining goals. For example, union locals in a given labor market may seek, through their international union or district council, to coordinate their bargaining with employers in the area. Similarly, employers wishing to avoid union whipsawing tactics (whipsawing refers to the technique employed by some unions to wring a concession from one employer by threatening to strike him while his competitors continue to operate and, after he has acquiesced, to try to force a second employer to

---

[11] "Major Union Contracts in the United States, 1961," *Monthly Labor Review*, October 1962, p. 1136.

grant the same or even more or face a strike) may attempt to coordinate their bargaining activities, and perhaps negotiate as a single group.

Coalition Bargaining

In order to enhance their bargaining power with large companies, unions have sought, in recent years, to engage in coordinated or coalition bargaining. According to the AFL-CIO's Industrial Union Department, which has promoted this approach:

> In coordinated bargaining, several locals whose contracts expire over a short period of time band together and jointly prepare a list of major economic demands which each presents to the company. As local negotiations progress, additional meetings are held to discuss strategy and agree on a minimum package which will be acceptable. When one local has secured this minimum pattern, it does not accept it until all locals have obtained a similar offer from the company.
>
> In some of the coordinated bargaining committees, a steering committee made up of representatives of the coordinating locals is established to participate in all negotiations. These representatives of other unions sometimes have been able to contradict statements made by company representatives concerning practices in home plants. The ultimate goal of coordinated bargaining is to force companies to negotiate major economic items on a national level.[12]

Economists have defended industry-wide bargaining on the basis of the Commons-Perlman thesis that the function of unionism is to take labor out of competition. Unions have evolved coordinated bargaining to better strengthen their power vis à vis individual companies, in which more than one union represents the employees. In some cases, however, such bargaining has gone beyond industry limits, for many of the companies with which the unions are attempting to achieve coalition bargaining are multiproduct, as well as multiplant, firms. Differences in wages and working conditions between plants manufacturing different products are quite legitimate, and often necessary because of differences in market conditions for the products. Thus, the United Rubber Workers has negotiated one set of wages and working conditions with the rubber manufacturers for their tire and tube plants and another for their rubber footwear plants. Such a procedure does not violate the Commons-Perlman thesis, because the lower-paid footwear workers are not in competition with the workers in the tire and tube plants; the wage differentials, moreover, are essential to continued operation of the footwear plants, the products of which face more elastic demand curves.

Coalition-coordinated bargaining faced a major test in 1967 in the copper industry, when a coalition of unions led by the United Steelworkers demanded company-wide negotiations in place of the former separate negotiations for

---

[12] *Collective Bargaining Negotiations and Contracts*, 14;33 (Washington, D.C.: Bureau of National Affairs, 1965).

each mine or mill. The coalition of twenty-six unions remained on strike for eight months in their attempt to obtain collective bargaining agreements with the same expiration dates and identical wage increases for all employees of a company. The strike was finally ended when the parties accepted proposals of a panel headed by Professor George W. Taylor that compromised the bargaining unit positions. In place of the negotiations by individual units, one bargain was to be struck for all establishments within a company in a specific industry; that is, negotiations were to be company-wide, but based on three different industries: copper mining, lead and zinc mining, and metals fabrication. The solution thus recognized that the different industries in which the companies were engaged had distinct market conditions and that it was essential to preserve different labor standards in each.

Revolts against Overcentralized Bargaining

A fundamental conflict arises between the unions' drive for centralization of collective bargaining in order to standardize employment conditions and the desire of union members to have a say in the bargains that are effected. There is evidence that many union members fear that the process of bargaining is being taken out of their control. Some unions have been wracked with internal disputes stemming from membership disenchantment with a centralized bargaining structure. In some cases there has been a veritable "revolt of the locals" against the international union leadership over local plant grievances that have been lost sight of by both management and union leaders engaged in national bargaining. Within many industrial unions, skilled workers have objected to policies that tend to favor the majority of semiskilled members and ignore their particular situation.

Centralized bargaining tends to focus exclusively on economic matters, but, in a society of growing affluence, workers have become increasingly concerned with the physical aspects of their jobs. Such subjects are usually referred to as "noneconomic," since they do not provide any additional compensation to employees, but they do involve costs to the employer. In recent years there have been a number of disputes over plant administration and work rules: in the 1961 and 1964 automobile industry negotiations, for instance, company production was disrupted by local strikes over plant working conditions after the national union had reached agreement with the companies on wages and benefits. At General Motors production standards, job classifications and duties, wage inequities, equalization of overtime, pay for time not worked, relief time, working conditions, and representation issues were some of the more important categories into which local plant problems fell.[13] In 1965 steel industry negotiations, the local issues also dealt with working conditions and included items such as better parking facilities, in-plant

---

[13] E. Robert Livernash, "Special and Local Negotiations," in John T. Dunlop and Neil W. Chamberlain (eds.), *Frontiers of Collective Bargaining* (New York: Harper & Row, 1967), p. 35.

facilities, in-plant feeding, and improvement of atmospheric conditions (dust, fume, and smoke control).[14]

In most unions the membership must ratify all new agreements, but this was usually a perfunctory vote. In recent years, however, union leaders have found it increasingly difficult to "sell" negotiated agreements to their members at the plant level, and this in turn has made it less easy for management to reach agreement with national union leaders. In some unions national administrations have been voted out of office by memberships that had reached the conclusion that the collective bargaining process had become too remote from their day-to-day problems. Such a feeling on the part of the membership seemed to have been the major factor in the ousting of David McDonald from the presidency of the United Steelworkers of America in 1965. And it was in order to advance the cause of regional autonomy that the pulp and paper workers on the Pacific Coast split off from the existing national unions to form a new independent national union.

The problems stemming from centralized bargaining are not easily solved, however. Neither unions nor most companies would seem desirous of scrapping multiplant bargaining, but both unions and managements will have to pay increasing attention to the specific concerns of various groups of workers and to the noneconomic concerns of all workers. In order to counter a threat by the minority of skilled workers to secede from its ranks because of their feeling that centralized negotiations were ignoring their interests, the United Automobile Workers have given the skilled workers a veto power over agreements. Thus, before an agreement can be officially entered into, a majority of the entire membership involved must ratify it, and a majority of the skilled members, voting separately, must approve those terms that apply specifically to them.

Managements, too, have begun to pay greater attention to local plant conditions. Workers are particularly unhappy with plant regulations that they believe unnecessarily restrict their freedom, with working conditions they regard as oppressive, and with jobs that they consider dull and unworthy of the abilities and capacities of intelligent beings. No easy remedies offer themselves, but some companies—notably Texas Instruments, International Business Machines, Polaroid, and Maytag—have experimented with enriching jobs, giving employees more freedom in carrying out their assigned tasks, and liberalizing rigid organizational structures. Such experimentation has been easier to undertake in nonunion situations, because collective bargaining often rigidifies conditions still further, especially with respect to job content. Unions, however, are as much under pressure as managements to find ways to meet the noneconomic needs of workers.

Weber discerns four alternative methods of solving the decentralization-within-centralized-bargaining dilemma.[15] The first involves measures to im-

---

[14] *Ibid.,* p. 42.

[15] Arnold R. Weber, "Stability and Change in the Structure of Collective Bargaining," in Lloyd Ulman (ed.), *Challenges to Collective Bargaining* (Englewood Cliffs, N.J.: Prentice-Hall, 1967), pp. 13–36.

prove the grievance procedure in large negotiating units, so that more prompt attention is given to concerns that workers have over working conditions. Second is the joint labor-management study committee, which discusses common problems outside the adversary context of formal negotiations, as has taken place in basic steel, meatpacking, glass containers, and agricultural implements. Third is the attempt to bring representatives of the locals more directly into the central bargaining sessions. Fourth has been the effort actually to transfer some issues from the central negotiations to the local level. It may very well be that collective bargaining in the future will become a formally two-tiered structure—centralized bargaining over economic matters and local bargaining on noneconomic matters—with the latter becoming more important than the former.

Industrial Conflict

The public becomes aware of the institution of collective bargaining when the news media report impending disputes or actual strikes. It tends to overlook, therefore, the fact that the vast majority of labor-management negotiations proceed relatively amicably and agreements are reached without recourse to strikes or even serious threats of strikes. Yet unions contend, and most students of labor-management relations would agree with them, that the union's ability to strike, and thus halt the employer's production, is essential to the collective bargaining process. In this view it is the potential of a disruption in production that induces employers to strive to effectuate agreement with the union.

The Strike as a Method of Bargaining

An analogy has been drawn, in fact, between labor-management relations and the relations between nations, and just as Clausewitz referred to war as a continuation of diplomacy by other methods, so some observers have called the strike a continuation of collective bargaining by other methods. This analogy, however, is a most unfortunate one, for the strike is not an equivalent to war either in purpose or consequence. War involves destruction and the killing of human beings, but the typical strike is a peaceful exercise in the withdrawal of labor, for a temporary period, from the employer. In war, moreover, one side attempts to defeat the other, but the aim of each party in collective bargaining is not to defeat the other but to secure more favorable terms on which to continue their collaboration in producing or distributing goods or services.

Although the analogy to war is fallacious, the statement that the strike is a continuation of collective bargaining by other means is correct, for the aim of every strike is to achieve labor-management agreement, though on terms other than management desires. In the United States the vast majority of strikes arise when labor and management cannot agree on the terms of a new contract at the time that the old one reaches its expiration date.

Unions are almost always loath to call a strike, and management is equally loath to have one occur. After all, the very nature of the strike makes it costly to both parties: union treasuries are depleted, workers' earnings are cut off, and management's sales disappear. The aim of both parties in collective bargaining, therefore, is to reach agreement without recourse to strike, and it is only when all hopes of doing so have been abandoned that a strike actually takes place.

The fact that the union takes the action in calling the strike should not be interpreted to mean that it is necessarily the cause of the strike. Only in one sense can the union be termed the aggressor, and that is that in almost all cases it is the union that is making demands upon the employer, and it is his failure to concede to them that prompts the union to strike. There have been instances, however, of strikes resulting from employer demands for changes in the collective agreement that the union has refused to accept. Moreover, even though the union may be the demander, the employer may very well be the precipitator of the shutdown because of his refusal to agree to demands that are reasonable in terms of both his ability to grant them and what is transpiring in other firms and industries.

The employer's counterpart of the strike—the lockout, by which he shuts down his facilities—is no longer very popular in this country. For one thing, employers do not relish the idea of cutting off production, even for achieving some tactical bargaining advantage over the union. More important, however, has been the attitude of the NLRB and the courts, which do not see the lockout as the counterpart of the union's strike weapon but, in most cases, as an unfair labor practice, and consequently employer use of the lockout has been severely restricted.

The Effectiveness of Strikes

The objective of any strike, of course, is to halt the employer's operations, thus causing a loss to him that he may come to recognize as being greater than the benefit of resisting the union's demands. In most instances today strikes are quite peaceful, and management makes no attempt to operate its plants. In fact, labor and management will negotiate concerning the dimensions of the strike and the process of halting production: in the steel industry, for example, elaborate procedures for banking furnaces so that no permanent damage is done to them are worked out, and, in the 1970 strike at General Motors, company management and the UAW leadership agreed upon which plants would continue to operate in order not to disrupt the flow of parts to other manufacturers. It is only when management attempts to continue operating despite the strike that the danger of violence, by strikers attempting to prevent nonstrikers from entering the plant, exists.

In most industries the ability of employers to operate their plants during a strike, even if they wanted to, is severely limited. The bulk of their employees are loyal union members, so there is little point in asking them to disregard the call to strike, and the absence of a pool of unemployed makes it nearly impossible to recruit other workers in their stead. In some industries, however, automated technology has severely reduced the effectiveness of the strike. The manpower requirements for some highly automated continuous process industries, such as a power plant, petroleum refinery, or chemical works, have been reduced in some instances to the point where supervisory personnel could run an operation at near peak efficiency for sustained periods.[16] There has been experience along these lines in telephone service, which has been maintained despite strikes.

The Extent of Strikes

Even so, the strike remains a formidable weapon in most industries, and there is little evidence to suggest that the strike is disappearing from the labor-management scene. The data on strikes, year by year, from 1945 to 1972, are presented in Table 6.1. They show that in the twenty-eight-year period, on the average, 4,270 strikes, involving 2.27 million workers, occurred each year. Although this may sound like a large figure, it caused an average of only 37 million man-days of idleness, equivalent to only 0.26 percent of estimated working time; only in 1946, which witnessed a wave of strikes as wartime controls approached their end, did the losses due to strikes equal one percent of total working time. Thus, in the aggregate, strikes do not result in any serious disruptions in national production, though, of course, specific disputes may have significance.

There is a tendency for strikes to fluctuate with the business cycle. Certainly, workers are more willing to strike when jobs are plentiful than when unemployment is high, and disruptions of production are more effective in inducing employer concessions when orders are flowing in than in periods of reduced volume. Periods of rapidly rising prices are also more conducive to strikes, as workers seek to have their wages keep pace with or surpass prices. Thus we see that, following a period of reduced strike activity, the number of strikes began to rise in the late 1960s, as a new period of rapid rises in prices began.

In a comparison of strike experience in eleven industrialized countries, Kerr and Siegel found some industries to be more strike prone than others.[17] They found strikes to be high in mining, shipping, longshoring, lumber, and textiles, but to be low in clothing, public utilities, hotels, trade, railroads, and agriculture. Among the reasons advanced for the high strike experience in some industries was the isolated position of the worker in society; thus, the miner or lumberjack lives in a community made up of other miners and lum-

---

[16] Richard A. Beaumont and Roy B. Holfgott, *Management, Automation, and People* (New York: Industrial Relations Counselors, 1964), p. 293.

[17] Clark Kerr and Abraham Siegel, "The Interindustry Propensity to Strike—An International Comparison," in A. Kornhauser, R. Dubin, and A. M. Ross (eds.), *Industrial Conflict* (New York: McGraw-Hill, 1954).

Table 6.1 Work Stoppages Resulting from Labor-Management Disputes, 1945–1972[a]

Year	No. of Stoppages Beginning in Year	No. of Workers Involved (in thousands)	Man-Days Idle During Year	
			No. (in thousands)	Percentage of Estimated Working Time
1945	4,750	3,470	38,000	0.31
1946	4,985	4,600	116,000	1.04
1947	3,693	2,170	34,600	.30
1948	3,419	1,960	34,100	.28
1949	3,606	3,030	50,500	.44
1950	4,843	2,410	38,800	.33
1951	4,737	2,220	22,900	.18
1952	5,117	3,540	59,100	.48
1953	5,091	2,400	28,300	.22
1954	3,468	1,530	22,600	.18
1955	4,320	2,650	28,200	.22
1956	3,825	1,900	33,100	.24
1957	3,673	1,390	16,500	.12
1958	3,694	2,060	23,900	.18
1959	3,708	1,880	69,000	.50
1960	3,333	1,320	19,100	.14
1961	3,367	1,450	16,300	.11
1962	3,614	1,230	18,600	.13
1963	3,362	941	16,100	.11
1964	3,655	1,640	22,900	.15
1965	3,963	1,550	23,300	.15
1966	4,405	1,960	25,400	.15
1967	4,595	2,870	42,100	.25
1968	5,045	2,649	49,018	.28
1969	5,700	2,481	42,869	.24
1970	5,716	3,305	66,414	.37
1971	5,135	3,263	47,417	.26
1972 (p)[b]	5,100	1,700	26,000	.14

[a] The data include all known strikes or lockouts involving six workers or more and lasting a full day or shift or longer. Figures on workers involved and man-days idle cover all workers made idle for as long as one shift in establishments directly involved in a stoppage. They do not measure the indirect or secondary effect on other establishments or industries whose employees are made idle as a result of material or service shortages.

[b] p=preliminary.

SOURCE: U.S. Department of Labor, Bureau of Labor Statistics.

berjacks, and he places great stress on group solidarity to win what he considers his due. "The strike for this isolated mass is a kind of colonial revolt against far-removed authority, an outlet for accumulated tensions, and a substitute for occupational and social mobility."[18] They also attributed strike-proneness to the nature of the work and the workers, believing that tough jobs recruit tough workers, who are more willing to engage in struggle than are other workers.

There are differences in aggregate strike-propensity among nations, too.

---

[18] *Ibid.,* p. 193.

Table 6.2 presents data on strikes in sixteen Western industrialized nations that have been compiled by Professor Turner of Cambridge University.[19] The statistics indicate that although the number of strikes is not particularly high in the United States and Canada, the number of working days lost due to strikes is higher in North America than in all other countries, except Ireland and Italy.

Table 6.2 International Comparisons of Statistics Relating to Stoppages Due to Industrial Disputes in Mining, Manufacturing, Construction, and Transport (Average annual figures for 1964–1966 inclusive[a])

Name of Country	No. of Stoppages Per 100,000 Employees	No. of Working Days Lost Per 1,000 Employees
United Kingdom	16.8	190
Australia[b]	63.8	400
Canada	15.8	970
Denmark[c]	5.5	160
Finland	10.8	80
Federal Republic of Germany	n.a.	*
Japan	7.6	240
Norway	0.6	*
United States[d]	13.2	870
Belgium	7.0	200
France	21.8	200
Republic of Ireland	25.6	1,620
Italy	32.9	1,170
Netherlands	2.2	20
New Zealand	26.8	150
Sweden[e]	0.5	40

[a] Based on information supplied by the International Labour Office. For fuller description, see *Report of Royal Commission on Trade Unions*, etc., p. 95.
[b] Including electricity and gas.
[c] Manufacturing only.
[d] Including electricity, gas, water, and sanitary services.
[e] All industries.
n.a. = figures not available.
* = fewer than ten working days lost.
SOURCE: Turner, H. A., *Is Britain Really Strike Prone?* (Cambridge: Cambridge University Press, 1969), p. 7.

Great care is needed in explaining these international differences, for more strikes do not necessarily mean greater union power. On the contrary, Ross and Hartman have attributed low strike activity in some countries in which the unions are very powerful, partly to the fact that strikes become less necessary because the very threat of them is effective.[20] They also suggest that,

[19] H. A. Turner, *Is Britain Really Strike Prone?* (Cambridge: Cambridge University Press, 1969), p. 7.
[20] Arthur M. Ross and Paul J. Hartman, *Changing Patterns of Industrial Conflict* (New York: Wiley, 1960), p. 19.

as unions and managements mature in their relationships, as evidenced by the Scandinavian countries, strike activity tends to decline.

The Social Cost of Strikes

The relatively high loss of working time in the United States compared with most other industrial countries, however, tends to exaggerate the losses in national production from strikes. Very often there is no real loss in output, even by the direct participants in the dispute, because the time lost is made up by increased activity following the settlement. In other cases, customers who anticipate the possibility of a strike in a supplying industry stock up on its products in advance, and so the time lost was made up before the strike even began; this has been the case in some steel strikes. Also, losses to those involved in an industrial dispute do not necessarily mean losses to the national economy; if one firm in an industry is struck, customers can merely shift their purchasing to those companies which continue to operate.

Although the losses from strikes may be exaggerated in the public's mind, there is growing evidence that public opinion has begun to look less favorably on the disruptions in production and services that result from industrial disputes. Part of the reason for this is that the issues in dispute between labor and management have become more complex, and the man in the street can less easily understand them or why they cannot be settled without resort to force. This has been particularly true in periods of rapid technological change that has seriously disrupted the existing labor-management relationships in some industries.

Declining public tolerance of strikes also stems from the fact that workers' living standards have risen and arbitrary treatment by management has declined. When oppressed workers were battling giant corporations for union recognition and some reduction in arbitrary management behavior, the general public could rally to their side. Today, however, the issues are less clear and not of the sort to evoke public sympathy. Thus, the union representing workers who earn $5.00 per hour that calls a strike because management offered them only a $.40 per hour increase in wages and they want $.50 cannot expect the general public, many of whom are also union members and many of whom themselves earn less money, to rally to its side. This does not mean that the public necessarily sides with management—it rarely does— because the reports on company profits figures may indicate that it could afford to grant its employees more money; in most cases of this sort, the public tends to take a "plague on both your houses" attitude.

Another heavy contributor to a declining tolerance of strikes is the fact that they have spread to groups that provide services to the public. Unlike automobiles or washing machines, services cannot be stored up beforehand or compensated for with overtime later. A strike in the automobile industry has little immediate impact on the general public, but a strike of hospital workers, of teachers, or of employees in the transit system does.

Of course, some strikes may cause more than inconvenience, and seriously affect the well-being of the community. The problem of such emergency disputes, however, will be left for discussion in the next chapter. Meanwhile, let us continue our analysis of collective bargaining.

Theories of Collective Bargaining

The institution of collective bargaining can be conceived of in different ways, depending largely upon the interpreter's own scholarly discipline and the factors that he tends to stress. To the economist, collective bargaining is what its name implies—a device through which employees sell their labor power in combination with one another instead of as separate individuals. As the introduction to the Wagner Act stated, it was necessary for workers to combine because the individual worker was at an extreme disadvantage dealing with his employer, and collective bargaining allows him to gain a balance of power.

To other observers, however, this view of collective bargaining as a means of establishing the price at which labor would be supplied to a firm ignored the fact that the labor-management relationship continued beyond the period of negotiations. Viewing this continuity in the relationship, William M. Leiserson advanced the view of collective bargaining as a form of industrial government.[21] Building on this concept, Professor Slichter saw collective bargaining as establishing a system of industrial jurisprudence:

> Through the institution of the state, men devise schemes of positive law, construct administrative procedures for carrying them out, and complement both statute law and administrative rule with a system of judicial review. Similarly, laboring men through unions, formulate policies to which they give expression in the form of shop rules and practices which are embodied in agreements with employers or are accorded less formal recognition and assent by management; shop committees, grievance procedures, and other means are evolved for applying these rules and policies; and rights and duties are claimed and recognized. When labor and management deal with labor relations analytically and systematically after such a fashion, it is proper to refer to the system as "industrial jurisprudence."[22]

Rejecting the governmental theory because it depends upon drawing an analogy between state government and the relationship between labor and management, Chamberlain has proposed what he terms a "managerial theory" of collective bargaining.[23] In his view the union, through collective bargaining, becomes involved in the management of the enterprise with respect to

---

[21] William M. Leiserson, "Constitutional Government in American Industries," *American Economic Review*, 1922 (Supplement).

[22] Sumner H. Slichter, *Union Policies and Industrial Management* (Washington, D.C.: Brookings, 1941), p. 1.

[23] Neil W. Chamberlain, *Collective Bargaining* (New York: McGraw-Hill, 1951), pp. 130–136.

joint decision-making in the areas of wages, hours, and most other matters dealing with the employment of manpower. Collective bargaining, thus, has become one method of management.

Each of these theories contains elements of truth, yet none by itself is satisfactory to explain the process of collective bargaining. Some economists, viewing collective bargaining as the process through which the level of wages and employment are determined, treat it as a form of bilateral monopoly. According to this view, the employer is a monopsonistic buyer of labor; that is, he has monopoly power in contracting for its purchase. If, however, the labor supply organizes into a union, that union will possess monopoly power in the sale of labor.[24] Under bilateral monopoly the actual wage rate is indeterminate, but one will be decided upon through the bargaining process.

Models other than those relating to bilateral monopoly have been constructed to explain the bargaining process. As early as 1932, Sir John R. Hicks of Oxford University attempted to explain the bargaining process in terms of employer concession schedules and union resistance curves.[25] Figure 6.1 demonstrates Hicks' concept, which is basically a theory of strikes. If there were no union, the employer would pay a wage of OZ, but, since there

Figure 6.1

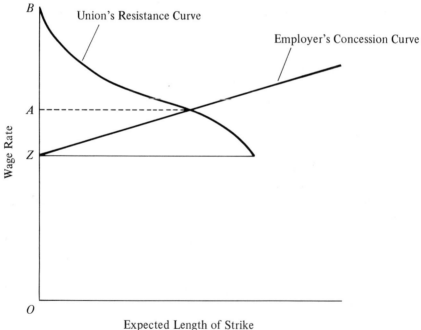

_____

[24] An analysis of bilateral monopoly theory of collective bargaining can be found in Bevars D. Mabry, *Labor Relations and Collective Bargaining* (New York: Ronald Press, 1966), pp. 189–202.

[25] J. R. Hicks, *The Theory of Wages* (New York: Macmillan, 1932), pp. 141–144.

is a union, he will be willing to pay more in order to avoid a strike of a particular duration. How much more he is willing to pay is shown in his concession curve. Similarly, the union would like to obtain as high a wage as possible (OB) for its members, but it will accept less in order to avoid having to strike. How much less it will accept is shown by the union's resistance curve. If the negotiators were skilled enough they would arrive at a settlement at wage OA, where the employer's concession curve and the union's resistance curve intersect. Strikes do occur, however, because neither party knows the shape of the other's concession or resistance schedule.

Chamberlain criticized this and all other models that focus strictly on prices and wages, and he elaborated a model of bargaining power related to each party's cost of agreeing relative to the cost of disagreeing with the other's terms, encompassing in costs more than monetary costs, but also matters of principle, prestige, and sentiment.[26] Each party's bargaining power, therefore, is determined by the economic, political, and psychological context within which negotiations take place. According to Chamberlain's model, moreover, bargaining power is relative to one's demands: a union seeking a 10 cents per hour wage increase has greater bargaining power than if it requested 50 cents per hour, because the cost to the employer of acquiescing to the union's demand for 10 cents is smaller than his cost of disagreeing, which would mean a strike and a shutdown of his facilities. Each party, of course, attempts to strengthen its bargaining power vis à vis the other. Unions attempt to strengthen their bargaining power by having agreements expire in the busiest periods of production, building large strike funds, and whipping up membership enthusiasm for the demands being put forth, thus indicating to employers the greater cost of resisting than acquiescing to their demands. On their side, employers attempt to strengthen their bargaining power by seeking to have agreements expire in slow periods, by having alternative sources of production where bargaining is on a plant-by-plant basis, and by threats to relocate or close down operations.

Pen attempted to improve the Chamberlain model of bargaining power by introducing the concept of conflict evaluation.[27] Based upon a psychological model of tension avoidance, Stevens described a model of collective bargaining as a conflict situation in which the parties must choose between undesirable alternatives: settlement upon the other's terms or a strike.[28] Mabry proposed a net gain theory, which evaluated the benefit levels to the parties in terms of pain and pleasure functions.[29]

The proliferation of bargaining models, many of which employ sophisti-

---

[26] Chamberlain, *op. cit.*, pp. 218–236.

[27] J. Pen, "A General Theory of Bargaining," *American Economic Review,* March 1952.

[28] Carl M. Stevens, *Strategy and Collective Bargaining Negotiations* (New York: McGraw-Hill, 1963).

[29] Bevars D. Mabry, "The Pure Theory of Bargaining," *Industrial and Labor Relations Review,* July 1965.

cated mathematical formulations, is an attempt to find a general theory of collective bargaining. Unfortunately, none of them yet provides an adequate explanation of this complex human relationship. Meanwhile, unions and managements will continue to engage in collective bargaining, setting the terms and conditions of employment and establishing a web of rules, as Dunlop has called them, by which they will live together, and, on occasion, when they cannot amicably reach agreement, there will be temporary disruptions of production until the two can find a mutually acceptable solution.

Summary

Collective bargaining between labor and management in the United States takes place under rules established by law and custom. Government control of the collective bargaining system derives from the legal compulsion that employers and unions "bargain in good faith" concerning wages, hours, and other terms and conditions of employment. National Labor Relations Board decisions on what constitutes "other terms and conditions of employment" have expanded the mandatory area of collective bargaining to the point that many managements believe their prerogatives have been invaded. Even so, wages remain the key issue in collective bargaining, but in the last two decades "fringe benefits" have risen in importance as unions have sought to protect their members against the insecurities of old age, sickness, and unemployment.

The periodic negotiation of terms of employment is not the only important part of collective bargaining, for any agreement reached must be administered, and the grievance procedure provides the means by which employees may contest management actions which they believe violate the agreement. Employee grievances are handled by elected shop stewards who take them up with the foremen. If no solution is formed at this level, the matter goes up the steps of the grievance ladder, with arbitration by an impartial third party as the final step if the parties themselves cannot resolve it.

A major trend in labor-management relations has been toward the centralization of collective bargaining, largely because of union desires to equalize wages and working conditions. Thus, as product markets have spread, unions have attempted to spread the negotiating unit so that their members do not compete against each other for available work. The unions' drive for centralization of collective bargaining, however, has collided with the desire of their members to have a say in the bargains that are effected.

National bargaining, moreover, tends to concentrate on economic matters, but workers are becoming ever more concerned with noneconomic questions, particularly plant working conditions. In recent years, as a result, there have been revolts of locals against national union domination and a rise in the number of agreements that the members refuse to ratify. Most managements and unions do not want to abandon multiplant bargaining, but they will be forced to pay greater attention to local plant conditions or face increasing local restiveness, which could undermine leadership and disrupt plant operating efficiency.

When the parties to collective bargaining cannot reach agreement on the terms of a new collective agreement, the almost inevitable result is a strike. There is, however, a growing body of public opinion that looks unfavorably on the disruptions in production and services that result from industrial disputes, and which believes that "there must be a better way" of resolving labor-management differences. Unless unions and employers can devise their own procedures for reducing strike activity, or at least its adverse impact on the public, they may find themselves saddled with new laws restricting the strike weapon.

A number of theories of collective bargaining and models of its operation have been advanced by students of industrial relations. Although no one of these adequately explains collective bargaining, they do help us better understand the process. Collective bargaining, however, has become an established institution in the United States, and unions and managements will continue to use it as the means of effecting accommodation between the conflicting interests of workers and employers.

BIBLIOGRAPHY

Chamberlain, Neil W., and James W. Kuhn. *Collective Bargaining.* New York: McGraw-Hill, 1965.

Chernick, William N. *Coalition Bargaining.* Philadelphia: University of Pennsylvania Press, 1961.

Dunlop, John T., and Neil W. Chamberlain (eds.). *Frontiers of Collective Bargaining.* New York: Harper & Row, 1967.

Hicks, J. R. *The Theory of Wages.* New York: Macmillan, 1932.

Kornhauser, A., R. Dubin, and A. M. Ross (eds.). *Industrial Conflict.* New York: McGraw-Hill, 1954.

Kuhn, James W. *Bargaining in Grievance Settlement.* New York: Columbia University Press, 1961.

Leiserson, William M. "Constitutional Government in American Industries," *American Economic Review,* 1922 (Supplement).

Lester, Richard, and Joseph Shister (eds.). *Insights into Labor Issues.* New York: Macmillan, 1948.

Mabry, Bevars D. "The Pure Theory of Bargaining," *Industrial and Labor Relations Review,* July 1965.

Pen, J. "A General Theory of Bargaining," *American Economic Review,* March 1952.

Ross, Arthur M., and Paul J. Hartman. *Changing Patterns of Industrial Conflict.* New York: Wiley, 1960.

Slichter, Sumner H. *Union Policies and Industrial Management.* Washington D.C.: Brookings, 1941.

Slichter, Sumner H., James J. Healy, and E. Robert Livernash. *The Impact of Collective Bargaining on Management.* Washington, D.C.: Brookings, 1960.

Stevens, Carl M. *Strategy and Collective Bargaining Negotiations.* New York: McGraw-Hill, 1963.

Torff, Selwyn H. *Collective Bargaining—Negotiations and Agreements.* New York: McGraw-Hill, 1953.

Turner, H. A. *Is Britain Really Strike Prone?* Cambridge: Cambridge University Press, 1969.

Ulman, Lloyd (ed.). *Challenges to Collective Bargaining.* Englewood Cliffs, N.J.: Prentice-Hall, 1967.

Weber, Arnold R. (ed.). *The Structure of Collective Bargaining.* New York: Free Press, 1961.

7 PUBLIC POLICY AND COLLECTIVE BARGAINING: UNRESOLVED ISSUES

As we have seen, government plays an important role in the industrial relations system of the United States, particularly with respect to collective bargaining between labor and management. Since there is a public interest in labor-management relations, we want a national labor policy that is responsive to and serves the overall, long-range interests of the public and the national economy. There is wide disagreement, however, on what exactly the public interest is in any situation. Furthermore, while there is wide agreement on broad principles regarding collective bargaining, there is disagreement on their implementation, and there remain many issues on which there is no consensus, even on principle. In this chapter, therefore, we shall focus on some of the unresolved issues of public policy with respect to collective bargaining, including the means of dealing with industrial conflict, the question of the applicability of the antitrust laws to union activities, the role of the National Labor Relations Board in applying national labor policy, proposals for labor law reform, and recent developments in public employment labor relations.

The Emergency Disputes Issue

The growing public concern with the impact of strikes that was discussed in the last chapter is a very real phenomenon that prompts periodic suggestions for new national policy to halt or control industrial conflict. Although the cost of strikes to the national well-being in aggregate may be small, some strikes do have immediate and significant impact.

The problem of the industrial dispute that could seriously interfere with the nation's economy did not arise until a generation ago, because until then both unions and collective bargaining were weak.[1] The occasional significant dispute that did arise was dealt with on an ad hoc basis by the incumbent president, from Cleveland on. Since unionism was strong in the railroad industry, and disruptions of rail service could cause serious losses to the economy, special railway labor legislation was enacted back as far as 1888, culminating in the Railway Labor Act of 1926.

The passage of the National Labor Relations Act in 1935, however, changed the picture. By encouraging unionism and collective bargaining, it set the stage for impasses in bargaining that could result in strikes that had

---

[1] This section relies heavily on the report the author prepared, *Emergency Disputes: A National Labor Policy Problem* (New York: Industrial Relations Counselors, 1961).

significant impact on the economy. The danger of "emergency" disputes was particularly acute during World War II, when any strike could be regarded as an emergency because of its interference with the production of material needed by our fighting men. The tripartite War Labor Board, therefore, was empowered to settle all labor-management disputes. The Board, however, did not have the power to enforce compliance with its decisions, and a bituminous coal strike prompted Congress, in 1943, to pass the War Labor Disputes Act, which empowered the President to seize struck facilities and run them under government control.

With the return of peace the War Labor Disputes Act lapsed, and the 1946 strike wave prompted Congress to include procedures for dealing with emergency disputes in the Labor-Management Relations Act of 1947. Those procedures are still the law of the land, but they have been attacked since their enactment as unfair to labor by some and as too ineffectual by others. The critics, however, have been accused by Cullen of using a double standard in their evaluation of Taft-Hartley by comparing it with an "ideal and abstract standard of a law that would prevent all emergency strikes while simultaneously exerting only a beneficial effect upon bargaining practices and relationships."[2]

The fact that the nation must have some means of dealing with labor-management disputes that create or threaten to create an emergency does not imply that all strikes are necessarily evil. On the contrary, strikes are the ultimate means of settling labor-management disputes in a system of free collective bargaining. But a national labor policy of seeking to promote free collective bargaining can conflict with other national policies, and in the case of some strikes the overriding interest for government may be its responsibility for ensuring the general welfare, with which the strikes may interfere. In attempting to define the public interest, two questions arise: (1) How do you keep the essential production or service operating? (2) How do you settle the dispute from which the threatened cessation arises?[3] As long as national labor policy seeks to promote free collective bargaining, the public interest must be confined to keeping the operation going, and not to the terms of the settlement, which is the preserve of the parties. There is no doubt, however, that any government intervention can affect the outcome of the dispute.

Definition of an "Emergency Dispute"

Under what conditions does a strike become of such importance that it could be considered to threaten a national emergency and require government action to head it off? Obviously, a distinction must be made between war- and peace-

---

[2] Donald E. Cullen, "The Taft-Hartley Act in National Emergency Disputes," *Industrial and Labor Relations Review*, October 1953, p. 29.

[3] John T. Dunlop, "The Settlement of Emergency Disputes," *Proceedings of the Fifth Annual Meeting* (Madison, Wisc.: Industrial Relations Research Association, 1952), p. 120.

time, because in the former almost any disruption of production and distribution could be regarded as threatening an emergency. What about peacetime? Cyrus Ching, who had been director of the Federal Mediation and Conciliation Service, claimed in 1953 that there had never been a strike that caused a true national emergency.[4] Hildebrand. however, suggested that there were four preconditions of a true emergency: (1) the strike must have a national rather than a local impact, (2) it must affect essential products, (3) it must involve all or a substantial part of an industry, and (4) it must be actual rather than merely speculative.[5] Based on these criteria, he identified five industries as ones in which strikes could cause national emergencies: critical defense products; mining, smelting, and refining of fissionable materials; railroads; bituminous coal mining; and basic steel products.

Some of these industries have declined in importance since the mid-1950s, but the impact of strikes in them, even at that time, was a matter of debate. Studies by Christenson, comparing coal output and man-days lost in strikes over thirteen years, showed that output increased shortly before and after each strike, thereby offsetting lost production.[6] Similarly, in a study for the U.S. Department of Labor, Livernash found that damage to the economy through lost production was offset in steel, as in coal, by added output just before and after five strikes.[7] He concluded that "most strikes can last much longer . . . than is generally believed before the economy will be seriously hurt." A Labor Department study of the economic effects of national emergency disputes concluded that three longshore strikes in which Taft-Hartley procedures were invoked had minimal impact nationally.

Whether a strike creates a real national emergency or merely severe inconvenience, however, may be less important than the public reaction to it and the outcry for government action to end it. Furthermore, a strike of local dimensions can create a serious situation for a given community, as has been demonstrated by a 1949 Hawaiian dock strike that cut off the islands' food supply and by a strike by a small group of tugboat workers that threatened to tie up the entire port of New York, and thus create a threat to the health and safety of the residents of the metropolis. Also, there are strikes that, while not directly affecting the health and safety of the community, could adversely affect national policy. A strike that delayed delivery of foreign aid materials might cause loss of confidence abroad in the United States, for instance, and the nation's balance of payments problems could be aggravated by strikes that forced domestic consumers to look to imports in order to keep supplied, as

[4] Cyrus S. Ching, *Review and Reflections* (New York, B. C. Forbes, 1953), p. 103.
[5] George H. Hildebrand, "An Economic Definition of the National Emergency Dispute," in Irving Bernstein, Harold L. Enarson, and R. W. Fleming (eds.), *Emergency Disputes and National Policy* (New York: Harper & Bros. 1953), pp. 6–15.
[6] C. L. Christenson, "Theory of the Offset Factor," *American Economic Review*, September 1953, pp. 513–547.
[7] *Collective Bargaining in the Basic Steel Industry*, U.S. Department of Labor (Washington, D.C.: Government Printing Office, 1961), pp. 3–18.

happened during the 1959 steel strike, the 1958–1959 flat glass strike, and the 1967–1968 copper strike.

The Railway Labor Act

The nation, however, is not defenseless against strikes that create emergencies, having two lines of defense, one dealing with railroads and the other with the rest of interstate commerce. Under the Railway Labor Act, which covers railroads and airlines, disputes that threaten substantially to interrupt interstate commerce progress through mediation, voluntary arbitration, a thirty-day freeze on changes in wages and working conditions, and finally submission to an ad hoc emergency board appointed by the President. The emergency board investigates the dispute's causes and makes recommendations for a settlement, but the parties do not have to accept them.

At one time the Railway Labor Act was viewed as a model labor-management relations law, but its procedures have broken down in the last two decades. Indeed, many observers have concluded that the disputes-settling machinery merely deters serious bargaining between railway management and labor. As a result, Congress was forced in 1963, 1967, and 1970 to enact special legislation to settle disputes and prevent nationwide rail stoppages.

The Taft-Hartley Act

The Taft-Hartley Act applies to all other interstate commerce, and under its procedures, if the President believes that a strike "affecting an entire industry or substantial part thereof" will imperil the national health or safety, he can appoint a board of inquiry to investigate the dispute but not make recommendations. He may then direct the Attorney General to seek an eighty-day injunction to prevent or terminate the strike. The strike is suspended, and for the next sixty days the parties negotiate with the assistance of the Federal Mediation and Conciliation Service. Then the board of inquiry reconvenes to report on the parties' current positions, and the National Labor Relations Board polls the employees to ascertain their willingness to accept the employer's last offer. At the end of eighty days the injunction is dissolved, and, if the strike then takes place or is resumed, the President can recommend additional action to Congress.

Between 1947 and 1970 the emergency disputes procedures had been invoked twenty-nine times, and in all but six cases the disputes were settled within the eighty-day injunction period—and three of those within a few days after. Even the exceptions, according to the National Association of Manufacturers, resulted primarily from confused representation situations which could well have been resolved earlier through more adept NLRB action. In the view of the NAM, which speaks for the nation's large industrial corporations, the Taft-Hartley emergency disputes procedures have attained their basic objectives.

Others are less sanguine concerning the success of the Taft-Hartley emergency procedures, believing that they are too slow to halt a strike. Unions have attacked them as one sided, claiming that employers often refuse to compromise in the expectation that the government will seek an eighty-day injunction to halt the strike, should one occur. Some observers see the procedure for polling employees on the employer's last offer as ineffective, being used by union leaders to bolster the confidence of striking members; and expecting that the last offer will be rejected, management keeps something in reserve to be offered later. All these maneuvers, it is contended, delay the reaching of agreement. Critics of Taft-Hartley, therefore, have proposed a number of alternative procedures, which we shall examine next.

Compulsory Arbitration

Under compulsory arbitration, the parties would have to abide by a settlement determined by an impartial third party. Since a settlement would be imposed, compulsory arbitration is seen as the antithesis of free collective bargaining, and it is opposed by both unions and most management officials. Yet newspaper editorials and public opinion surveys disclose a growing support for it among the general public, and even a decline in labor and management opposition.

A major drawback of compulsory arbitration is that it may inhibit collective bargaining: the parties may be afraid to make concessions to each other lest they weaken the case that may have to be presented in arbitration later. Agreeing with this view, a tripartite commission appointed by the governor recommended repeal of the New Jersey Public Utility Labor Disputes Act, which permitted seizure in form and compulsory arbitration.[8] On the other hand, the congressional solution to the railroad work rules dispute was a 1963 law to settle it by compulsory arbitration. Again, in 1967 a form of compulsory arbitration called by the euphemism of "mediation to finality" was legislated to settle a railway labor-management dispute.

Government Seizure

A second proposal for dealing with emergency disputes is to have the government seize the struck facilities and thereafter deny the employees the right to strike, on the theory that they are government employees. When President Truman attempted to seize the struck steel mills in 1952 under the general powers of the President, the Supreme Court declared his action unconstitutional, but Congress could pass legislation authorizing peacetime seizure. Even so, the effectiveness of seizure is questionable. In a study of federal government seizures of struck facilities, Blackman found that, in forty-six out of seventy-one cases since 1864, one of the parties rejected the President's authority, usually by stopping production.[9]

Seizure, moreover, can take different forms, from just flying the United

---

[8] "Governor's Committee Report on New Jersey Public Utility Labor Disputes Act," *Industrial and Labor Relations Review,* April 1955, pp. 408–427.

[9] John L. Blackman, Jr., *Presidential Seizure in Labor Disputes* (Cambridge, Mass.: Harvard University Press, 1967), p. 23.

States flag over facilities but permitting the management to continue to operate them as before to instituting changes in the terms of employment during government operation. If the former is done, it may amount to little more than the use of government power to break a strike. If the latter is done, seizure comes close to being another form of compulsory arbitration. In the 1946 seizure of coal mines, for example, a new labor contract was negotiated between the Secretary of the Interior and the United Mine Workers, which the mine owners had to accept when the mines were returned to them.

The Statutory Strike

One of the most novel proposals for dealing with emergency disputes is the statutory or nonstoppage strike, by which, if an impasse in bargaining were reached, one of the parties could declare a "statutory strike," during which operations could continue, but both parties would suffer penalties in the form of partial losses in wages and profits. The theory is that "the bargaining function of the strike would be preserved, yet the conflict with the public interest would be avoided."[10]

Despite its seeming attractions, the statutory strike idea has serious limitations. The means of imposing penalties can shift the bargaining power between the parties; withholding wages from workers would affect them more than withholding profits from management. In fact, the entire concept of withholding profits ignores the nature of profits, which do not flow in a regular stream but may be concentrated in one part of the year and absent in another, and may not even exist at all; thus, depending upon when the statutory strike was invoked, the penalty on the firm could be totally meaningless or terribly costly. Whether the government is to keep the penalty funds permanently or in temporary escrow has an impact on the strike's effectiveness, for, if the funds are to be returned, the parties may treat them as deferred income and feel no serious bite from failing to reach agreement. Finally, the statutory strike could be administratively impractical, difficult to police, and a source of interminable litigation.

Recommendations by Fact-Finding Boards

It has also been advocated that the presidential boards of inquiry appointed under the Taft-Hartley Act in emergency disputes be authorized to make recommendations for their settlement. The boards were not empowered to make recommendations because it was believed that these would resemble arbitration awards that management would be forced to accept, but labor would go along only with those that it liked. The arguments in favor of allowing the boards to make recommendations are that it would lengthen the period of negotiations, bring a disinterested point of view to bear on the

---

[10] Leroy Marceau and Richard A. Musgrave, "Strikes in Essential Industries: A Way Out," *Harvard Business Review*, May 1949, p. 287.

issues, allow both sides to hear the other present a reasoned case calmly, and serve as an agency for the formation of public opinion.[11]

This claim rests on the assumption, however, that if the facts are known, a just settlement becomes obvious and blame can properly be placed on the recalcitrant party. But facts are open to different interpretations, "facts" are mental references to specific past experience, and there is no assurance that third parties can make better estimates and devise better policies and programs than labor and management.[12]

Despite these criticisms, there is considerable support for repeal of the Taft-Hartley prohibition against board of inquiry recommendations for settlement of emergency disputes. Fact-finding boards that offered recommendations for settlement of disputes in 1946 and early 1947 were credited with having been helpful in curtailing the length of many strikes.[13] Even though presidential boards of inquiry are not authorized to make recommendations, this, in fact, was done in the case of the 1967–1968 copper strike, and it served as the basis for finally bringing the dispute to an end. According to the chairman of that board, Professor George W. Taylor, fact-finding with recommendations in the copper strike halted what he called the "enervation of collective bargaining by an insistence of unilaterally imposed preconditions."

Choice of Procedures

One of the major objections to all of the proposals for dealing with emergency disputes is that they allow the parties to plan their strategies in the light of them. If the parties were uncertain as to what action the government were going to take, they would be under pressure to reach agreement. Such an approach to handling emergency disputes came into being right after the war, when Professor Sumner Slichter headed a tripartite board that studied industrial relations problems in Massachusetts, and was embodied in a 1947 Massachusetts law dealing with public utility disputes.

The Massachusetts law makes available to the governor four procedures that may be used as alternatives or in series:

1. The governor may order both labor and management to appear before a moderator to show cause why they should not submit the dispute to arbitration. The moderator may also act as mediator. If an agreement is not reached, the moderator makes public his findings, placing blame on either or both parties for failure to agree on arbitration.
2. The governor may request the parties to voluntarily submit their dis-

---

[11] *Emergency Disputes Settlement*, U.S. Senate, Subcommittee on Labor-Management Relations (Washington, D.C.: Government Printing Office, 1952), p. 23.

[12] Bryce M. Stewart and Walter J. Couper, *Fact Finding in Industrial Disputes* (New York: Industrial Relations Counselors, 1946), p. 50.

[13] "Governor's Committee Report on New Jersey Public Utility Labor Disputes Act," *op. cit.*, p. 412.

pute to a three-man emergency board empowered to recommend terms for settlement.

3. In the event that these procedures are ineffectual, the governor may enter into arrangements with either or both parties for the continuance of part of the production or distribution of goods and services.

4. The governor may also seize all or part of the essential plant or operation, and put into effect changes in conditions of employment recommended by the emergency board.

Although many labor-management experts find the choice of procedures (or "arsenal of weapons," as it is sometimes called) approach attractive, a number of objections to it have been raised. It is argued, for instance, that if the objections raised against the injunction, compulsory arbitration, and seizure are valid, and if these measures are individually undesirable, no one of them becomes acceptable when it is combined with others. Furthermore, the choice of procedures approach may not work; as veteran labor reporter A. H. Raskin has put it, "If you give the President an infinite range of things he may or may not do, in a crisis most of the bargaining by the parties will not be with one another but with the White House on what route to choose."[14]

Mediation and Conciliation

Others would continue to rely solely upon mediation and conciliation (in which a third party attempts to bring the conflicting parties together) to control situations in which labor and management (essentially sensitive to public reaction and reluctant to precipitate disputes inimical to the general welfare) become embroiled in difficult negotiations and assume positions from which they cannot easily extricate themselves. In such instances, they stress, mediation can provide the parties with a way out of difficult negotiations without "losing face."

Certainly, no one would quarrel with the idea of improving mediation services, publishing more factual information—such as wage, productivity, price, and profits data—to guide negotiators and the public, and the establishment of investigatory panels to explore labor-management relations in various industries. But mediation efforts, while desirable, are not always effective, and experience with mediation under Taft-Hartley indicates that it is no bar to emergency disputes.

Individual Industry Machinery

Professor Dunlop has argued that our national industrial relations system suffers from seeking solutions to problems in terms of legislation and litigation, formal arbitration, and public pronouncements; instead, greater reliance should

---

[14] A. H. Raskin, "Collective Bargaining and the Public Interest," in Lloyd Ulman (ed.), *Challenges to Collective Bargaining* (Englewood Cliffs, N.J.: Prentice-Hall, 1967), p. 166.

be placed upon the development of consensus.[15] Both Professors Dunlop and Cox have advocated that all industries in which a labor dispute might affect the national health or safety should create their own specialized machinery and procedures for resolving disputes that will not yield to the ordinary processes of negotiation.[16] Such machinery might include "voluntary arbitration," whereby the parties would agree in advance that issues that cannot be settled through normal collective bargaining would be turned over to a mutually acceptable third party for resolution.

This type of approach has achieved some success in a number of industries, including some in the building trades, utilities, and needle trades. To a large extent, however, joint industry procedures work most effectively in those industries in which labor-management relations are good to begin with, but, where relations are strained and therefore greater dangers of strikes exist, the mere establishment of new machinery is no answer. Nevertheless, if labor and management wish to avoid further government intervention in collective bargaining, they should explore the possibilities of establishing in each industry their own disputes procedures.

The Nixon Proposals

In 1970 President Nixon proposed a new approach to controlling emergency disputes in the five industries affecting transportation: airline, railroad, longshore, maritime, and trucking. His proposed Emergency Public Interest Protection Act would, first, eliminate the emergency strike provisions of the Railway Labor Act and transfer jurisdiction for railroads and airlines to the Taft-Hartley Act. Secondly, it would amend Taft-Hartley so the President could invoke one of three new weapons in a major transportation dispute that went beyond the current eighty-day nonstrike injunction period. The act would:

1. Extend the cooling-off period for as long as thirty days if a settlement is near.
2. Require part of a struck industry to operate for six months while negotiations continue. This would make it possible to minimize the tieup of an essential industry without interfering with the lawful strike or lockout rights.
3. Require the parties to submit final offers to the Secretary of Labor within three days and bargain over these offers for another five days. If no agreement were reached within that time, a panel of three neu-

---

[15] John T. Dunlop, "Consensus and National Labor Policy," *Proceedings of the Thirteenth Annual Meeting* (Madison, Wisc.: Industrial Relations Research Association, 1960), p. 2.

[16] John T. Dunlop, "The Settlement of Emergency Disputes," *Proceedings of the Fifth Annual Meeting* (Madison, Wisc.: Industrial Relations Research Association, 1952), p. 120; and Archibald Cox, *Law and the National Labor Policy* (Los Angeles: Institute of Industrial Relations, University of California, 1960), p. 54.

trals, selected either by the disputants or the President, would decide which of the final offers should be selected. This would rule out mediation and would force the bargainers to make the most realistic final offer—one that they could both live with if the panel chose it.

Neither labor nor management welcomed the President's proposals, particularly the "Russian roulette" feature of getting an all-or-nothing settlement. Both AFL-CIO president George Meany and John P. Hiltz, Jr., chairman of the National Railway Labor Conference, declared them to be less favorable than existing laws, and the President subsequently withdrew his proposal.

Labor and the Antitrust Acts

There are those who see emergency disputes merely as a symptom of a much deeper malaise: monopoly power in the hands of labor unions, which permits them to shut down large segments of the economy or to wrest gains for their members at the expense of other members of society. To the late Professor Henry Simons of the University of Chicago, any degree of bargaining power was equal to monopoly power in that it implied group restraint over individualistic action.[17] The solution often proposed to this "monopoly power" of unions is to subject them to the Sherman and Clayton Anti-Trust acts.

Such a proposal would call for a reversal of national policy, for, as we saw in Chapter 4, unions had been subject to the antitrust acts until the 1930s, and were convicted of violations of them. By 1940, after national labor policy had changed, by virtue of the National Labor Relations Act, to that of promoting unionism and collective bargaining, the Supreme Court did an about-face with respect to the applicability of the antitrust laws to unions. Although the Norris–La Guardia Act no longer permitted employers to obtain federal injunctions to bar union actions, they could still sue a union for damages under the antitrust acts. Even this remedy, however, was virtually barred to employers as a result of Supreme Court decisions in the Apex and Hutcheson cases.

The 1940 case of *Apex Hosiery Co. v. Leader* grew out of an organizational effort by the Hosiery Workers' Union, which was accompanied by a sit-down strike. The company was prevented from shipping its products, and it sued the strikers for illegal restraint of trade under the Sherman Act. The case was similar in essence to the Danbury Hatters case in that the union activity restrained interstate trade, but whereas a quarter of a century before the Supreme Court had found the union guilty, in 1940 it held that the union action did not violate the antitrust laws. In the opinion of the majority of the justices, the purpose of the Sherman Act was to prevent suppression of commercial competition, but union actions to eliminate price competition based

---

[17] Henry C. Simons, *Economic Policy for a Free Society* (Chicago: University of Chicago Press, 1948), chap. 6.

upon differences in labor conditions were not in this category. Thus, the activities of unions would not violate the law unless the primary intention of their activities was to restrain product market competition through the fixing of prices.[18]

The Supreme Court went even further in granting unions immunity from the antitrust acts the very next year in its decision in *United States v. Hutcheson*, which arose from a jurisdictional dispute between two craft unions—the Carpenters and Machinists—over construction work at the St. Louis brewery of the Anheuser-Busch Brewing Company. When the company awarded the work to the Machinists, the Carpenters instituted a national boycott of Anheuser-Busch products, in violation of their own agreement to arbitrate the dispute. The government, at this point, charged the Carpenters' Union with restraint of trade.[19]

Again, the case resembled a previous one—Duplex—but in this instance, the Supreme Court found the union activity not in violation of the Sherman Act. By linking the Clayton and Norris–La Guardia acts the Supreme Court found that a jurisdictional strike, or picketing and boycotting in its support, did not constitute a violation of the Sherman Act. Furthermore, it declared the antitrust laws to be unsuited for the regulation of labor relations. According to Professor Gregory, the effect of the Hutcheson decision is to allow unions strong enough to control the marketing of products in a region "to exclude competing goods and to promote unreasonably high noncompetitive prices, thus insuring their restricted memberships steady employment at attractively high wage rates."[20]

Indeed, this was the case: unions were free to attempt to exert control of product markets, but, as was decided in 1945 in *Allen-Bradley Company v. Local 3, International Brotherhood of Electrical Workers* (IBEW), only if they did so on their own and not in collusion with employers. The New York City local of the electrical workers, Local 3, had negotiated closed-shop contracts with the electrical contractors in which the latter agreed to purchase supplies only from other companies that also had agreements with Local 3. Thus, manufacturers located in New York City had a local protected market, immune from outside competition, even from firms organized by other locals of the IBEW. Both employers and employees benefited from this arrangement, the former through higher prices and profits, the latter through higher wages and employment, and only New York City consumers suffered by footing the bill for these monopoly benefits.

The Allen-Bradley case grew out of a suit by out-of-state manufacturers of electrical equipment against the union and its officers under the Sherman

---

[18] Herbert F. Northrup and Gordon F. Bloom, *Government and Labor* (Homewood, Ill.: Richard D. Irwin, 1963), pp. 25–26.

[19] George H. Hildebrand, "Collective Bargaining and the Anti-Trust Laws," in Joseph Shister, Benjamin Aaron, and Clyde Summers (eds.), *Public Policy and Collective Bargaining* (New York: Harper & Row, 1962), p. 168.

[20] Charles O. Gregory, *Labor and the Law* (New York: Norton, 1958), p. 279.

Act. In the Supreme Court's view the New York employers were clearly in violation of the antitrust acts, but the union, had it acted alone to bar out-of-state products from the market, would not have been. However, the fact that the union had acted in concert with the employers made it also guilty of a violation.

In fact, in a number of cases unions, acting on their own, were allowed to undertake activities that would have been denied to employers. In *United States v. American Federation of Musicians*, the union was permitted to use a boycott to prevent the use of recorded music by radio broadcasting stations. In *United States v. International Hod Carriers' Union*, the Supreme Court ruled that the union could bar the use of cement-mixing trucks in its jurisdiction except under conditions that made their use as costly as under the former technology. The Court also permitted a union to boycott materials that were prefabricated or produced by a company organized by a rival union. The Court even permitted a union to drive an employer out of business, simply because it harbored a grudge against him.

Since then the Congress has attempted to deal with some of these union activities through legislation. Both the Taft-Hartley and Landrum-Griffin acts have tightened the restrictions against secondary boycotts, and jurisdictional disputes have been brought under more stringent control under Taft-Hartley. There are those, however, who believe that union actions to control product markets should be subject to the same standards that apply to employer behavior.

In 1965 the Supreme Court attempted anew to balance the conflicting aims of the law: through the antitrust acts, to promote competition, and through the labor relations acts, to promote collective bargaining, the goal of which is to eliminate competition among workers. In *United Mine Workers v. Pennington*, the charge was that the union and the major coal producers had conspired to drive smaller, less efficient producers out of business by fixing uniform, industry-wide labor standards that the small producers could not afford.[21] The Supreme Court stated that a union retains its exemption from the antitrust laws when it bargains with a particular employer, but not when it is clearly shown that it has agreed with one group of employers to impose a certain wage scale on other bargaining units. Although the union was found guilty of conspiracy, upon reargument the Court ruled, in 1967, for the union. The matter was further complicated in 1970, when the Supreme Court upheld a jury award in a similar case of triple damages of $1.5 million to the Tennessee Consolidated Coal Company. The net result of this series of decisions was that unions were liable to antitrust prosecutions.

The other 1965 case, *Local 189, Amalgamated Meat Cutters v. Jewel Tea Company*, involved a union prohibition on the hours that stores might

---

[21] For a full review of the Pennington and Jewel Tea cases, see Theodore J. St. Antoine, "Collective Bargaining and the Anti-Trust Laws," *Proceedings of the Nineteenth Annual Winter Meeting, 1966* (Madison, Wisc.: Industrial Relations Research Association, 1967), pp. 66–75.

sell fresh meat, which, the company charged, was a restraint on the product market. The Court ruled, however, that the marketing-hours restriction was "intimately related" to wages, hours, and working conditions, and thus exempt from the antitrust laws. The Court intimated, however, that it would have ruled against the union had the public interest in competition outweighed the workers' stake in their job standards. Had the self-service supermarkets been able to operate without substantially affecting the workload of butchers, the Court intimated that it would have ruled against the union. The Court is thus attempting to balance the public's stake in competition versus the workers' stake in their job standards.[22]

Others would go further in the application of the antitrust laws to unions, and apply them to union attempts to control labor markets as well as product markets. Agreeing with the Simons view that union power is monopoly power per se, they would severely restrict, even beyond the Pennington ruling, the ability of unions to establish uniform labor standards across an industry. Some would, for instance, ban multi-employer bargaining. Such a proposal, however, might very well backfire on its proponents. Its purported aim would be to reduce the power of national unions to push up wage rates, but, in practice, employers in large-scale industries might find themselves the victims of union whipsawing tactics, as local unions vied with each other for higher settlements. At the same time it could create chaos in small-scale industries, in many of which—for example, the garment trades—unionism and multi-employer collective bargaining have brought a degree of stability not formerly known.

Even aside from these practical objections to banning the labor market activities of unions, making them violations of the antitrust laws would return labor-management relations to the point that they were under the common law in the early nineteenth century. Unions would once again be subject to conviction as conspiracies in restraint of trade because they attempted to improve the conditions of their members. The courts, moreover, would again become the arbiters of what union actions were permissible and which were illegal. It is doubtful that the status of labor-management relations in the United States in the 1970s is so bad as to demand such overhaul; besides, the remedy proposed for some of our current problems is probably too drastic to command popular support.

The Role of the National Labor Relations Board

Criticisms of the Board

While few observers of our system of industrial relations favor subjecting unions to the antitrust acts, many are of the opinion that there are other avenues for reform. One continuing source of criticism is the National Labor Relations Board, which has been accused of being too political to fill the needs

---

[22] *Ibid.*, p. 75.

of a stable labor-management relations system. Some critics accuse the NLRB of being too responsive to the party in power. During Democratic administrations employers tend to complain of NLRB prejudice in favor of unions, and during Republican administrations it is the unions who charge the board with being pro-management. This is inevitable, since any agency of government is inclined to follow the theories of the administration in power.

In the case of labor-management relations this tendency is even stronger, because there are conflicting aims in national labor policy: it favors both furthering union organization and protecting the rights of employers to resist unions through legal means. The differences in view that a majority of the National Labor Relations Board may take on any specific matter will reflect the emphasis that it gives to one of these aims of public policy against the other.

The NLRB has been accused of having a pro-labor bias in that, for most of its history, it has tended to emphasize the first of the aims of national labor policy—furthering union organization—at the expense of the other—the legal right of employers to resist organization of their work forces by unions. While such a policy may have been eminently fair in the days when unions were struggling to gain recognition, and may make sense in some sectors of the economy today, it ignores the reality of a large portion of the economy of the 1970s. In fact, the U.S. Supreme Court in 1970 accused the board of emphasizing the protection of a nascent labor movement, when in fact unions had become powerful institutions in their own right by then.[23]

From the point of view of all parties involved in our industrial relations system, there is need for continuity and consistency in the application of the law. Philip Ross has defended the NLRB in this respect, claiming that it has had a fairly consistent record in a very difficult field of applying and interpreting the intent of Congress as expressed in not always clearly worded legislation, in a changing environment.[24] Others, however, believe that, as an administrative agency, the NLRB is ill equipped to carry out quasi-judicial functions as well. In order to better understand the criticisms of the National Labor Relations Board, let us briefly review its structure and operation.

Structure of the Board

The NLRB is composed of five members (three from the majority political party and two from the minority party), each appointed by the President for a five-year term of office. It is responsible for administering national labor policy as defined in the Taft-Hartley and Landrum-Griffin acts, with respect to both hearing and deciding cases involving unfair labor practices and repre-

---

[23] *Boys Market, Inc., v. Retail Clerks Union, Local 770*, U.S. 235, 257, 62LC 10,902 (1970).

[24] Philip Ross, *The Government as a Source of Union Power* (Providence: Brown University Press, 1965).

sentation questions. At least three members must hear a case, but often all five do, and decision is by majority.

Prosecution of cases is not in the hands of the five-member board, but is vested in a general counsel, who is also a presidential appointee and whose term of office is four years. He is the official charged with supervision of the NLRB regional offices, which are located in the major industrial cities of the nation.

It is through the regional offices that much of the board's work is transacted, though there is a large backup staff in Washington. The field offices conduct elections to determine collective bargaining representation rights in their regions. Their decisions, however, may be appealed by either party, within twenty days of issuance, in which case they are reviewed by the NLRB in Washington.

The NLRB has sought congressional approval to delegate decision-making authority on unfair labor practices complaints to the regional offices, but this has been refused. Between 1948 and 1970 the board's case load increased 450 percent, making it difficult—since each case must be investigated, hearings on it held, and then board orders issued—for the board to handle the total load. According to the NLRB, for fiscal year 1969 the median time, from the filing of a representation petition to the actual holding of an election to determine if the employees wish union representation, was 49 days. The median time required to process an unfair labor practice charge was considerably longer: from the filing of a charge to the date of NLRB decision took 319 days.

This time-consuming process has led to severe criticisms, particularly from unions such as the Textile Workers, which have alleged that, by the time a board cease-and-desist order against an unfair labor practice has been issued, the union organizing effort has been killed. In an attempt to circumvent this type of problem, the NLRB has ordered employers to bargain with unions in cases where it believed that the employer's action had undermined the union's majority. This in turn has brought the wrath of employers down upon the NLRB.

The NLRB can issue a cease-and-desist order, but it does not have the power to enforce that order, and if it is disobeyed it must proceed to the federal courts. If the board's order is upheld by the court, it will be enforced through contempt-of-court proceedings and, if necessary, the issuance of a temporary injunction. It has been suggested that much time could be saved if the NLRB were permitted to issue self-enforcing orders that would be final unless appealed within limited time periods.

There are those, on the other hand, who would completely separate the administrative and quasi-judicial functions of the NLRB. They charge that at the present time the NLRB is district attorney, judge, and jury, all at the same time. Management critics, moreover, charge the NLRB with holding a pro-labor bias, permitting unions wide latitude of action while severely restricting what employers are permitted to do. They point to the relatively high number of NLRB decisions that have been reversed by the courts as proof of the board's bias.

Proposals for Change

Many of the critics see little value in attempting to reform the NLRB, seeing the basic problem in the fact that the board functions in a political atmosphere. The Chamber of Commerce of the United States, therefore, has proposed limiting the board's function to that of conducting representation elections, and transferring all unfair labor practices cases to the federal courts. A counterargument to this proposal is that labor-management relations is a highly specialized field, requiring more intimate knowledge of its workings than the typical federal judge possesses; moreover, this would only add further burdens to already crowded court dockets.

Bearing this in mind, former NLRB chairman Guy Farmer and others have proposed the establishment of a special labor court, which would combine the expertise of the present NLRB with the alleged greater impartiality of an independent judiciary.[25] Since the judges on the labor court would be appointed for life, presumably they would be free of the changing whims of political administrations. This would enable them to administer the law in a logical and consistent manner, so that both labor and management would know what types of behavior were sanctioned or not, whereas now one may find himself guilty of committing an unfair practice for an action that last year was considered fair.

Opponents of emasculating the powers of the NLRB counter these arguments with the observation that the labor-management relations field is a dynamic one: since the context in which it takes place—technological and economic—tends to change, it, too, must be capable of adapting to new circumstances. In their view, therefore, attempting to assure continuity and consistency could result in so rigidifying national labor policy administration as to weaken its ability to fashion new responses to an altered environment.

Proposals for Labor Law Reform

Aside from proposals to place union activities under the antitrust acts or to replace the National Labor Relations Board with a special labor court, other ideas have been advanced for changes in national labor policy. Most of these are far less drastic than the two discussed so far; they would not basically alter present policy but would correct what some people consider to be imbalances that exist. Obviously, we cannot examine all the proposed avenues of reform, but let us focus on a few key ones.

---

[25] See, for example, Guy Farmer, *Collective Bargaining in Transition; (2) Restoring the Balance* (New York: Industrial Relations Counselors, 1967), p. 16. For a review of many suggestions, including establishment of a labor court, see Fritz L. Lyne, "The National Labor Relations Board and Suggested Alternatives," *Labor Law Journal,* July 1971, pp. 408–423.

Good-Faith Bargaining

One area of national labor policy that has been subject to criticism concerns the legislative requirement that the parties bargain in good faith over wages, hours, and other terms and conditions of employment. Management representatives claim that the good-faith requirement has been used to widen the scope of compulsory bargaining far beyond that intended by Congress, and as a consequence unions have been enabled to invade areas of decision-making that clearly belong solely to management.

A simple solution to the problem of the uses of the law to widen the scope of negotiations would be to eliminate from the law the duty to bargain. Professor William Gomberg has called for an end to the requirement, because the good-faith bargaining clause has made the NLRB an extension of the tactics of the parties. "It provides a whipping boy for the frustration of a party to the bargain who refuses to face the consequences of overplaying his hand and then goes running to papa government."[26] The Independent Labor Study Group, a body of outstanding scholars and arbitrators assembled by the Committee for Economic Development, also endorsed this approach.[27]

Professor Douglas V. Brown has suggested that if the legal requirement of good-faith bargaining is not totally repealed, it should be applied only to new bargaining situations, and not to negotiations occurring after the first agreement.[28] In his view there is evidence that labor and management, once they have survived their first encounter, learn to live together without the compulsion of law.

Yet it is most unlikely that Congress would seriously consider repealing the good-faith requirement. For one thing, it simply has become too institutionalized for most lawmakers, the NLRB, and many employers and unions to be able to contemplate life without it. Beyond that, its repeal could seriously undermine collective bargaining in some industries. Although the vast majority of collective bargaining relationships would be little, if at all, affected by such a move, a few, in which unions are very weak, could experience unnecessary employer intransigence.

Recognizing the problem that would be posed by the repeal of the requirement of good-faith bargaining, others would seek instead to revise the concept of compulsion, strengthening the wording of the law that neither concessions nor agreement are necessary. Another approach would be to amend the law to redefine the bargaining obligation to exclude essential managerial decisions relating to the conduct of the business.[29] Management operating

---

[26] William Gomberg, "Government Participation in Union Regulation and Collective Bargaining," *Labor Law Journal*, November 1962, p. 944.

[27] *The Public Interest in National Labor Policy* (New York: Committee for Economic Development, 1961), p. 82.

[28] Douglas V. Brown, "Legalism in U.S. Industrial Relations," *Proceedings of the Twenty-Third Annual Meeting, 1970* (Madison, Wisc.: Industrial Relations Research Association, 1971), pp. 2–10.

[29] For an exposition of this point of view, see Farmer, *op. cit.*, p. 19.

decisions—such as subcontracting, introduction of technological change, and termination of operations—would not fall within the scope of wages, hours, and other terms and conditions of employment. Unions, of course, could use their bargaining power in an effort to get employers to bargain over such matters, but employers could refuse without being considered in violation of the law.

Such an amendment of the law would mean that if an employer's operating decision were based on economic criteria, and not on any desire to undercut the position of the union, he would be free to undertake it. Management would still be required to inform the union and to bargain with it over the job effects, but not over the decision itself. Thus, the union would still be able to bargain for protection of affected employees through such devices as severance pay, early retirement, retraining, and relocation. It is claimed that such a narrowing of mandatory bargaining subjects would be to the long-term interests of both employees and employers, for in the final analysis it is the efficient operation of the enterprise that ensures the viability of the concern and the jobs and incomes of its employees.

There are, of course, equally cogent arguments against restricting the subject matter of bargaining, and, as one observer has put it, "One can defend either view, depending upon his convictions about the relative importance of 'management prerogatives' versus 'employee interests.' "[30] As in most issues in labor relations, there is a genuine dilemma: to restrict employer freedom to act could threaten the viability of a firm, but to grant management complete freedom to act can adversely affect employees, and should hence be a matter for collective bargaining. One partial solution to this dilemma has been offered by Nelson, who would agree that subjects such as subcontracting are mandatory subjects of bargaining, but would couple that with a recognition of the residual-rights theory of managerial prerogatives. In other words, the union could insist in negotiations on bargaining on the subject, but, if it did not secure a contract clause covering the subject, management would be free to act in that area without consulting the union.

Employer Free Speech

A second area in which some observers of the labor-management scene see need for legislative reform concerns the right of employers to make statements to their employees concerning union representation. From 1935 to 1941 the NLRB banned virtually all employer statements; mere expressions of opinion and simple statements of fact were held to violate the Wagner Act.[31] While such a position may have been justified at that time because unions were weak and struggling for recognition from openly hostile employers, it became

---

[30] Wallace B. Nelson, "Through a Looking Glass Darkly: Fibreboard Five Years Later," *Labor Law Journal*, December 1970, pp. 755–761.

[31] Benjamin Aaron, "Employer Free Speech: The Search for a Policy," in Shister, Aaron, and Summers, *op. cit.*, p. 29.

less so as union power expanded. The changed situation was recognized in the Taft-Hartley Act, which expressly authorized employer speech so long as the employer's statement contained no threat or promise of benefit. Yet it has been charged that the NLRB continues to impose restrictions on employer speech, both in pre-election organizing campaigns and in collective bargaining disputes, while continuing to expand opportunities for unions to proselytize employees.[32] Indeed, during Mr. Farmer's tenure as chairman of the NLRB, employers were permitted wide latitude in speaking to their employees against union representation, but this policy was reversed under Democratic administrations.

Professor Bok, while not seeking new legislation, believes that the area of free speech as patrolled by the NLRB is in need of new ground rules.[33] In his view, instead of restricting employer free speech in a representation election campaign, the NLRB should simply make sure that there is sufficient opportunity for the union to rebut his statements. Bok disagrees with the NLRB view that intemperate speech tends to undermine the reasoning process of voters; the NLRB, therefore, should rely less on the substance of what the parties are allowed to say and more on whether there is time for rebuttal.

Defenders of present policy express fear of opening the floodgates to employers to speak against union representation. In their view this would lead to subtle, and possibly not so subtle, forms of coercion of employees, and thus denial of the free choice of union representation. The danger would not be the same for all unions, but would be most pronounced for the weak ones still struggling to organize workers in nonunion sectors of the economy.

In fact, the entire issue of coerciveness of employer statements tends, in practice, to ignore the context in which they are made. An analysis of contested NLRB election cases found that the unemployment in the local labor market had an influence on the impact of employers' statements.[34] The higher the unemployment rate, the easier it was for the employer to arouse job security fears when he talked about the possible loss of jobs and plant shutdown if the employees voted for union representation. Indeed, it was found that employers in high unemployment areas conducted more intensive antiunion campaigns. Similarly, employers in small communities, where they can act as monopsonistic buyers of labor, also resorted to propaganda campaigns designed to arouse employee concern about job security if they voted for union representation.

It would be very difficult, however, to frame legislation concerning representation election campaign statements that would take differences in environmental factors into account. It would still be necessary for the NLRB to interpret the events when attempting to balance freedom of employee choice and freedom of employer speech.

---

[32] Farmer, *op. cit.*, p. 27.

[33] Derek C. Bok, "The Regulation of Campaign Tactics in Representation Elections under the National Labor Relations Act," *Harvard Law Review*, 1964.

[34] John E. Drotning, "The Union Representation Election," *Monthly Labor Review*, August 1965.

Problems in Labor Law Reform

Numerous additional changes in the law governing labor-management relations have been advocated, such as tightening up the restrictions on union picketing and secondary boycott activities. As in the case of the other proposals for labor law reform, there is sharp disagreement on the need for change, and the differences of opinion stem from differences in outlook. Those who defend the present policy point out that the struggle for union organization is not yet completed in the United States, and that indeed what is needed is more government encouragement of unionism and stricter legal safeguards against employer antiunion tactics.[35] Those who call for reform are more concerned with the plight of small employers facing powerful unions, such as the Teamsters, or with the interests of those workers who do not want union representation.

The problem is that one basic law for labor-management relations may not be able to protect both the weak union, such as the Textile Workers, in its dealings with powerful antiunion employers, and small employers confronting giant unions that may be more concerned with their institutional position than with the survival of that particular firm. It has been proposed, therefore, that what is needed is more diversity in labor laws so that they can take into account the heterogeneous nature of unions and employers.[36] Some start in this direction has been made: the Landrum-Griffin restrictions on boycotts, for instance, exempt the clothing and construction industries, because to have applied them there would have upset existing collective bargaining arrangements and seriously weakened legitimate union activities.

Finally, it should be recognized that no law or series of laws governing labor-management relations will satisfy everyone. The American economy, moreover, is a dynamic one, and changes that occur may strengthen employers in one industry, while unions may gain the upper hand in others. National labor policy, therefore, must continually be reevaluated to determine if it is meeting its goals, not merely from the viewpoints of labor and management, but also from the point of view of the public at large.

Collective Bargaining in Public Employment

In Chapter 4 we saw that the most dramatic event on the labor-management scene in decades has been the recent eruption of unionism among public employees, the fastest growing sector of the labor force. Now let us examine the spread of collective bargaining among public employees, including the problems it has given rise to and some of the dilemmas it has posed.

---

[35] Archibald Cox, *op. cit.*, p. 22.

[36] For discussion of this idea, see Northrup and Bloom, *op. cit.*, pp. 484, 485; and Solomon Barkin, "New Labor Relations Policies and Remedies Suggested by Different Industrial Settings," *Proceedings of the Fifteenth Annual Meeting, 1962* (Madison, Wisc.: Industrial Relations Research Association, 1963).

Federal Employment

In the federal government, employees have belonged to employee organizations for more than one hundred years, but until recently the activities of those organizations have been narrowly circumscribed.[37] Unions had depended upon lobbying as their main activity, but in 1902 President Theodore Roosevelt issued a "gag rule" forbidding employees and their associations from petitioning Congress for salary increases or other improvements except through department channels. In 1912 Congress reversed this rule through the Lloyd–La Follette Act, which not only permitted individual or group petitioning of Congress, but also formally extended the right of postal employees to join unions, if those organizations renounced the right to strike against the government. The prohibition against strikes was strengthened in 1947, for the Taft-Hartley Act contained a section forbidding federal employees to participate in any strike, and in 1955 Public Law 330 made it a felony to strike and required new federal employees to sign affidavits that they would not strike.

Thus, while the United States government in the 1930s began to foster union growth and collective bargaining in private industry, it continued to ignore them within its own house for three decades. Then, in early 1962 President Kennedy issued an executive order, which led to dramatic changes. That executive order—10988, "Employee-Management Cooperation in the Federal Civil Service"—was designed to facilitate collective bargaining among federal employees. By its terms all federal agencies except those that already had their own programs, such as the Tennessee Valley Authority, and those involved in national security, such as the Central Intelligence Agency, were required to recognize unions representing the majority of employees in appropriate units and bargain with them.

While Executive Order 10988 spurred union growth among federal employees, it severely restricted the scope of collective bargaining. The role and authority of management were explicitly preserved: management officials of an agency retained control over direction of employees; hiring, promotion, and transfer; discharging because of lack of work; maintaining efficiency; and the like. Employee organizations could be recognized only if they did not discriminate on the basis of race, creed, color, or national origin, and if they did not assert the right to strike against the United States government. Implementation of the order, moreover, was left largely to the heads of individual executive agencies. Finally, an executive order is not the same as legislation enacted by Congress, for it remains in effect only as long as the President so desires.

Within these limitations, collective bargaining in the federal service made significant progress, and it was further strengthened by a new executive order,

---

[37] For this discussion of the development of government labor relations, the author has relied heavily on Michael H. Moskow, J. Joseph Loewenberg, and Edward Clifford Koziara, *Collective Bargaining in Public Employment* (New York: Random House, 1970).

11491, issued by President Nixon, effective January 1, 1970. The new executive order established the Federal Labor Relations Council, to administer and interpret the order, decide major policy issues, and report and make recommendations to the President. Such matters as determination of appropriate bargaining units, supervision of representation elections, decision as to eligibility of labor organizations, and ruling on complaints of unfair labor practices, which had formerly been in the domain of individual agency heads, were assigned to the Assistant Secretary of Labor for Labor-Management Relations.

New criteria for unit determination were promulgated, including those of ensuring community of interest among the employees concerned and promoting effective dealings and efficiency of agency operations. Also, the concept of exclusive bargaining agent, which governs representation in private employment, was extended to federal unions that were chosen by secret ballot by a majority of the employees in the unit. The scope of bargaining was widened to cover such matters as employee adjustment to technological change, a negotiated grievance procedure, and arbitration of unresolved grievances. When impasses in collective bargaining occur, the Federal Mediation and Conciliation Service is authorized to assist in resolving them. Finally, the unfair labor practice of refusing to "consult, confer, or negotiate" was extended to unions as well as federal management, thus bringing federal practice still more in line with that in private industry.

According to the U.S. Civil Service Commission, in 1969 1.4 million federal employees were covered by exclusive recognition: 600,000 postal employees, 400,000 blue-collar workers, and 400,000 white-collar employees. By 1970 the American Federation of Government Employees reported that it represented 325,000 federal employees in 1,300 locals in the United States and overseas. While it represents workers in many agencies and occupations (approximately 55 percent of them blue-collar workers), its strength has traditionally been among white-collar workers in such federal departments as Labor, Defense, and Health, Education, and Welfare.[38] In addition, many federal blue-collar employees belong to unions that represent mainly private industry workers, such as the International Association of Machinists. The Postal Service is almost completely unionized, and the eventual merger of all the postal unions into one powerful organization became a distinct possibility.

Frustrated by the long delay in congressional action to grant them a wage increase—due, they believed, to political maneuvering between the White House and Capitol Hill—postal workers went on strike in 1970 and tied up the nation's mails. Despite the ban on strikes, and the calling up of the National Guard to move the mails, the federal government negotiated a wage increase with the postal unions. Since then the U.S. Post Office has been converted from a federal department run by a member of the President's cabinet to a quasi-independent public corporation, the U.S. Postal Service, capable of bargaining directly with unions representing its employees. The Postal

---

[38] "Union Conventions," *Monthly Labor Review*, October 1970, pp. 33–39.

Reorganization Act of 1970 authorizes collective bargaining on wages and working conditions under the laws applying to private industry, but retains the ban on federal employees' strikes, providing instead for binding arbitration in the event of negotiation impasses.

State and Local Government Employment

While not quite as old as unionism among federal employees, state and local government employee unionism goes back some time. The International Association of Fire Fighters, AFL-CIO, perhaps the oldest of local government unions, was organized in 1918. Even policemen organized very early, as the famous Boston police strike of 1919 attests. The American Federation of Teachers, AFL-CIO, was established in 1919. The largest union of state and local government workers, the American Federation of State, County, and Municipal Employees, AFL-CIO, had originally been part of the American Federation of Government Employees, but received its own charter in the mid-1930s. Other unions that have sizable numbers of state and local government employees include the Laborers International Union, AFL-CIO, the Service Employees International Union, AFL-CIO, the unions in the skilled trades, and the International Brotherhood of Teamsters.

The most rapid organizing success, however, has been achieved in recent years, encouraged by the growing militancy of public employees who believed that they were failing to keep pace with the gains being achieved by unionized workers in private industry. Executive Order 10988 also helped to influence events at the state and local government levels. Prior to 1962 no state had passed a law permitting or requiring government agencies to bargain with employee organizations. Most state and local governments, in fact, adhered to the idea that, since the government represents the sovereign power, it must reserve the sole right to determine the terms and conditions of employment under which its employees work. Some state and local governments even prohibited their employees from organizing, but recent court decisions have declared it unconstitutional to prohibit an employee from joining a union.

Despite the absence of laws governing collective bargaining, some state and local governments had, in fact, been negotiating with unions for many years, basing their actions on the idea that the essence of sovereignty includes the right to delegate authority. The influence of Executive Order 10988 can be seen in the fact that today more than twenty states have legislation extending bargaining privileges to public employees. The trend here is to parallel private collective bargaining even more than does the federal government. Recognition of unions as exclusive bargaining agents is becoming common, and in some jurisdictions the scope of bargaining is almost as broad as that in private employment. Interestingly, Jerry Wurf, president of the American Federation of State, County, and Municipal Employees, AFL-CIO, has reported that there is no correlation between union activity and state laws.[39]

---

[39] "Collective Bargaining in the Public Sector" (Highlights of the Collective Bargaining Forum, May 1969), *Monthly Labor Review,* July 1969, pp. 60–69.

Although neither the federal government nor some state and local governments will bargain on wages, forcing employee organizations to rely on lobbying as their chief weapon, others do negotiate on money matters. Collective bargaining among municipal employees in New York City and Philadelphia, for instance, differs little from that in private employment, for it has become the institution through which their wages, hours, fringe benefits, and other terms and conditions of employment are determined. Grievance procedures have become very widespread in public employment, and even arbitration as the final step in the procedure is gaining ground.

The Problem of Strikes

As collective bargaining spreads, so do the problems common to it. The enactment of legislation in New York State in 1967, the Taylor Act, so named because it followed the recommendations of a commission of distinguished labor-management experts headed by Professor George W. Taylor, who had been chairman of the War Labor Board during World War II, was supposed to serve as a model for other states to follow. The Taylor Act not only assured unions of their collective bargaining rights, but set up mediation and arbitration procedures according to which strikes of public employees would be unnecessary. Despite the establishment of alternative procedures, however, public employee strikes have occurred in New York, and unions have been fined and their leaders jailed for violation of the provision prohibiting strikes.

In fact, a basic dilemma of public collective bargaining arises from the fact that giving public employees a voice in the determination of the conditions under which they work is supposed to further better relations between management and employees, but strikes of public employees are becoming more numerous and frequent. In 1968 over 200,000 employees struck against state and local governments in 254 work stoppages, and days lost due to those stoppages equaled half the rate in private industry. And, just as in private industry, most strikes resulted from an impasse in contract negotiations.

Not all states bar all public employee strikes. Vermont, Montana, Hawaii, and Pennsylvania extend a modified right to strike, that is, if there is no serious threat to public health or safety. The well-known labor arbitrator Theodore Kheel, believing that collective bargaining cannot exist if employees cannot withdraw their services, supports the legal right of public employees to strike. Even Kheel, however, would bar strikes by those employees whose absence would endanger the health or safety of the public. The problem, however, is determining what public activities can be interrupted without creating a threat to health or safety. Strike activity, moreover, has been particularly pronounced precisely in these services that the public believes to be essential. Strikes by sanitation workers in New York, Memphis, Atlanta, and other cities have seen the garbage pile up in the streets, threatening the health of the local populations. Strikes by hospital employees can also be injurious to health and safety. Even teacher strikes are regarded by many, particularly working mothers who must either stay home or let their children roam the streets unattended, as threatening the health and safety of the community.

Strikes, moreover, are not the only weapon of unions when encountering an impasse in negotiations with public managers. In order to circumvent the prohibition against strikes by federal employees, the air traffic controllers have employed the tactic of calling in sick. Another euphemism for the strike has been mass resignations, a tactic that has been employed by organized teachers in some communities. In other cases employees have worked according to the rule book, thus causing slowdowns; such a tactic has been utilized by bus drivers, for example, who refuse to move their vehicles until they can see that all passengers are standing three feet back from the doors.

What, however, are the alternatives to strikes, calling in sick, mass resignations, and slowdowns? Professor Taylor believes the best alternative is the appointment of a neutral third party to investigate disputes, determine the facts, and make recommendations. In his view neutrals "have the function of insuring that, in the budgetmaking process, the claims of public employees do not become inequitably subordinated to the myriad other claims for public funds."[40]

A tripartite panel of experts assembled by the Twentieth Century Fund has proposed that disputes be subject to intense and continuing negotiations between the parties, followed by mediation, and if that fails it should be followed by fact-finding that will recommend the terms on which the parties should end their dispute.[41] Those who propose third-party resolution of public labor-management impasses also usually favor placing severe penalties on those who refuse to abide by the prohibition against strikes.

Other Problems Posed by Public Collective Bargaining

Even aside from the strike, many new issues are posed when government recognizes the right of employees to organize and bargain collectively. These issues concern the methods by which recognition would be given to employee representatives, if there would be elections similar to those conducted by the National Labor Relations Board in private industry, how bargaining units would be determined, and what issues are subject to bargaining.

A second set of questions revolves around the process of collective bargaining. How, for instance, can a union negotiate on wages, hours, and working conditions if these are set by the legislature or a civil service commission? To date, the federal government and some state and local jurisdictions have simply excluded economic matters from bargaining, and the unions have continued to rely on lobbying in the legislative halls to secure higher wages, pensions, and other benefits. Even when local governments do engage

---

[40] *Ibid.*

[41] *Pickets at City Hall, Report and Recommendations of the Twentieth Century Fund Task Force on Labor Disputes in Public Employment* (New York: Twentieth Century Fund, 1971), p. 21.

in collective bargaining over economic matters, the very process of bargaining inevitably becomes enmeshed in political considerations. Since the managers of public agencies often lack the authority that private managers enjoy, are they in a position to reach binding agreements with union officials or are all decisions ultimately in the hands of the mayor or the governor?

A third set of questions involves structural and conceptual problems. What impact does collective bargaining have on the merit system common in public employment, and are the two compatible? The merit system would seem to frustrate some basic concepts of union organization: unions, for example, put great stress on seniority as a criterion for promotion, whereas the merit system emphasizes ability. A cardinal principle of civil service has been equal pay for equal work, but this could be contravened if one group of employees, through union organization, obtained higher salaries than a similar group who remained unorganized.

The Economic Impact of Public Collective Bargaining

There is one final question that may be the most difficult to resolve, and it looms very large for those jurisdictions in which the scope of bargaining includes wages and fringe benefits. Public employees cannot be treated as second-class citizens and denied the right to a voice in the determination of the conditions under which they work, a right that has been granted in private industry, but there are significant differences between private and public negotiations. First of all, public bargaining is, of necessity, enmeshed in politics to a much greater degree than are private negotiations. Secondly, the parties to collective bargaining in private industry are subject to economic constraints: management is concerned with the impact of any proposed settlement on its profits; for labor, there are the considerations of the impact upon the competitiveness of the firm, and hence upon the employment of its members. A recent study of public collective bargaining in New York City, for example, claims that city officials have viewed municipal strikes as involving prohibitive political costs.[42] As a result, labor peace became the primary goal of public management, with economic or managerial costs secondary.

In the absence of consumer sovereignty and choice with respect to most public services, it has been argued that these economic constraints do not operate as forcefully upon public employees and managements. Union bargaining power is greatly strengthened in public employment when it can ignore the price elasticity of demand for the service.[43] Of course, a local government could attempt to meet increased labor costs by the same means as private employers, that is, by contraction and substitution: reducing the

---

[42] Raymond D. Horton, *Municipal Labor Relations in New York City: Lessons of the Lindsay-Wagner Years* (New York: Praeger, 1973).

[43] George H. Hildebrand, "The Public Sector," in John T. Dunlop and Neil W. Chamberlain (eds.), *Frontiers of Collective Bargaining* (New York: Harper & Row, 1967), p. 149.

amount of service and laying off workers, or substituting machines for labor. The absence of a profit motive, and a political concern for unemployment, however, may severely limit the government's ability to do this.[44] There are, therefore, the decided dangers that government budgets will be pushed up faster than the ability to raise revenues, and that the potential for improvement in public services will decline sharply as the bulk of the extra dollars added to an agency's budget go for higher salaries and improved working conditions. The dilemma that presents itself is that, in the absence of collective bargaining, public employees may in effect subsidize public services through low wages, but, in the presence of collective bargaining, public employees may be able to wrest more than "fair pay" from the citizenry. In the latter case the spread of public collective bargaining, despite its other merits, might only add to the problems of our cities, already staggering under the burdens of declining tax bases and mounting costs.

There is a related question of equity, too. In many communities public employees receive decent earnings, their salaries sometimes being at least comparable with and even higher than in private industry. For example, in New York City in 1971, city maintenance workers were being paid considerably more than those in private industry, garbage collectors having a base pay of over $12,000 per year and transit workers being able to retire at half pay after twenty years of service. Even so, the appetites of these workers were hardly satisfied, and their unions continued to press for still better conditions.

Of course, public employee unions were acting no differently than those of workers in private industry in seeking to win as much as they could for their members, and there is little objection to private employee gains, even when this means higher prices for consumers. Why then should there be objection to gains for public workers, even if they require higher taxes? Aside from the fact that no one likes to pay higher taxes, the question of equity arises from the sources of local tax receipts. The taxing abilities of local communities are highly restricted, and much of their revenues come from regressive types of taxes, such as the sales tax, which fall most heavily on people at the lower end of the income scale. This means, in effect, that uncontrolled public collective bargaining could lead to a redistribution of income from lower income groups to higher ones.

The consequences of union bargaining power and private collective bargaining settlements upon the national economy in terms of distortion of the wage structure and the impact upon the price structure are serious enough, but they may be even greater in public employment. Since the consumers of public services cannot choose to reduce their consumption of most services, are they to be forced to pay continually higher prices or, in the case of subsidized operations, continually higher taxes? Are taxpayer revolts

---

[44] Harry Wellington and Ralph K. Winter, Jr., "The Limits of Collective Bargaining in Public Employment," *Yale Law Journal*, June 1969, p. 1121.

the only solution to the problem of the lack of sufficient economic constraints in public collective bargaining? This in turn raises the question of who suffers the most when taxpayers refuse to vote needed revenue. A number of communities have already experienced the need to shut down their school systems for periods of time when the citizenry has refused to tax itself to meet the educational budget needs. In these cases, those who have suffered most have been the children.

The Future of Public Collective Bargaining

The die, however, has been cast, and there is little likelihood of a return to unilateral management authority in public employment. As in private industry, public employees legitimately claim a voice in the decision-making with respect to the conditions under which they work. Many of the problems discussed will undoubtedly be worked out in time, but the intervening period of turmoil may be a most difficult one. Many observers fear a repetition of the acrimonious labor-management relations experienced in private industry in the early years of collective bargaining.

Certain steps could be taken immediately to straighten out some of the confusion arising from the unionization of public employees. First of all, there is the need for clearer legislation governing labor-management relations among government employees that would specify rights and obligations, the means of a union's gaining recognition, and the mechanics of the bargaining process. The Twentieth Century Fund Task Force, for example, recommends that the responsibility for the administration of public employment relations policies be placed in an independent agency.[45] An agency like this would have functions similar to those of the National Labor Relations Board in private industry, and a number of states—for example, New York, New Jersey, and Pennsylvania—have established such types of agencies.

There is also a need to sharpen the role of management in government service so that it has the authority and capability to deal with unions and can be held responsible for its actions. The National League of Cities, the United States Conference of Mayors, and the National Association of Counties have proposed a plan for helping to train public managers in labor matters. At the same time the role of civil service commissions in setting employment standards will have to be clarified. Budget-making processes must also be altered and speeded up if public management is to be able to pay salaries agreed to in negotiations with unions.[46]

Whether its employees are unionized or not, government has a responsibility to provide efficient service to the public and decent working conditions to its employees. Most of these suggestions, therefore, would be in order

---

[45] *Pickets at City Hall, op. cit.*, p. 27.
[46] Harry P. Cohany and Lucretia M. Dewey, "Union Membership Among Government Employees," *Monthly Labor Review*, July 1970, p. 20.

under any circumstances. With public employees joining unions and bargaining collectively, however, they become imperative.

Summary

Government plays a very important rule-setting role in the relationships between labor and management in the United States, but there are many areas in which there is disagreement with respect to what the proper national labor policy should be. One very important area concerns the means of dealing with strikes in private industry that assume such proportions as to threaten health or safety. At the present time the Railway Labor Act and Taft-Hartley Act provide procedures by which such strikes can be controlled, but some observers believe that these procedures are not sufficient. Critics of Taft-Hartley, therefore, have proposed a number of alternative procedures, including compulsory arbitration, government seizure of struck facilities, the statutory strike, recommendations by fact-finding boards, a choice of procedures, intensified mediation and conciliation, and mandating that each industry set up its own disputes-settling machinery.

A second area of disagreement with respect to national labor policy revolves around the applicability of the antitrust laws to labor unions. Although these laws were used against unions until the 1930s, after that the Supreme Court granted unions virtual immunity from prosecution unless they engaged in collusion with employers to restrain trade. In the last few years, however, the Supreme Court has attempted anew to balance the conflicting aims of the law—through the antitrust acts to promote competition, and through the labor relations acts to promote collective bargaining, the goal of which is to eliminate competition among workers.

A third area of disagreement concerns the role of the National Labor Relations Board, which is charged with administering the nation's labor-management relations laws. The board is accused of unnecessary delays in effectuating its role, of having a pro-labor bias, or of a lack of consistency in the application of the law. Proposed solutions range from increasing the power of the NLRB so that it can act more effectively and speedily to emasculating its power and transferring all unfair labor practices cases to the federal courts. Others, however, believe that this would tend to rigidify national labor policy administration and thus weaken its ability to fashion new responses to a changing environment.

Proposals for reform of the labor laws in other areas have also been prolific. Management has been very concerned with the application of the duty to bargain in good faith, which, it claims, has enabled unions to encroach upon areas of decision-making that rightfully belong solely to management. Controversy also rages around employer free speech with respect to union attempts to organize their employees.

An entirely new area of labor relations has arisen with respect to the rights of employees of government—federal, state, and local—to organize and bargain collectively. Unionism and collective bargaining have spread rapidly in the federal service since President Kennedy's Executive Order 10988, issued in 1962. The subject matter of bargaining in the federal service, however, is severely constrained.

Some state and local governments, on the other hand, bargain over all matters, including wages and benefits, very much as private industry does. This has raised serious questions about the right of public employees to strike and the economic impact of public collective bargaining. Many observers believe that the normal economic constraints upon the parties do not operate sufficiently well in public employment, and that uncontrolled bargaining could cause serious fiscal problems for local communities. Although many of these problems of public collective bargaining will be worked out in the long run, in the meanwhile this will be an arena for intensified conflict.

BIBLIOGRAPHY

Bernstein, Irving, Harold L. Enarson, and R. W. Fleming (eds.). *Emergency Disputes and National Policy.* New York: Harper & Bros., 1953.

Blackman, John L., Jr. *Presidential Seizure in Labor Disputes.* Cambridge, Mass.: Harvard University Press, 1967.

Cox, Archibald. *Law and the National Labor Policy.* Los Angeles: Institute of Industrial Relations, University of California, 1960.

Cullen, Donald E. *National Emergency Strikes.* Ithaca: New York State School of Industrial and Labor Relations, 1968.

Dunlop, John T., and Neil W. Chamberlain (eds.). *Frontiers of Collective Bargaining.* New York: Harper & Row, 1967.

Emergency Disputes: A National Labor Policy Problem. New York: Industrial Relations Counselors, 1961.

Farmer, Guy. *Collective Bargaining in Transition: (2) Restoring the Balance.* New York: Industrial Relations Counselors, 1967.

Gregory, Charles O. *Labor and the Law.* New York: Norton, 1958.

Lyne, Fritz L. "The National Labor Relations Board and Suggested Alternatives," *Labor Law Journal,* July 1971.

Marceau, Leroy, and Richard A. Musgrave. "Strikes in Essential Industries: A Way Out," *Harvard Business Review,* May 1949.

Moskow, Michael H., J. Joseph Loewenberg, and Edward Clifford Koziara, *Collective Bargaining in Public Employment.* New York: Random House, 1970.

Pickets at City Hall, Report and Recommendations of the Twentieth Century Fund Task Force on Labor Disputes in Public Employment. New York: Twentieth Century Fund, 1971.

Ross, Philip. *The Government as a Source of Union Power.* Providence: Brown University Press, 1965.

St. Antoine, Theodore J. "Collective Bargaining and the Anti-Trust Laws,"

Proceedings of the Nineteenth Annual Winter Meeting, 1966. Madison, Wisc.: Industrial Relations Research Association, 1967.

Shister, Joseph, Benjamin Aaron, and Clyde W. Summers (eds). *Public Policy and Collective Bargaining.* New York: Harper & Row, 1962.

Wellington, Harry, and Ralph K. Winter, Jr. "The Limits of Collective Bargaining in Public Employment," *Yale Law Journal,* June 1969.

8 THE LABOR MARKET

This book opened with a description of the emergence of a free labor market, that is, one in which employees could make their own individual choices as to jobs and employers could hire whom they wanted. In this chapter we shall examine that labor market more carefully. First we shall review some basic economic theory as it applies to the demand for and the supply of labor. Then we shall analyze types of labor markets, both in theory and in actual practice, attempting to determine in the process why the reality does not conform to basic economic hypotheses. Since economics is concerned with the allocation of scarce resources, our attention shall next be focused on labor mobility, which is essential if an economy is to maximize its income; again, our concern will be with the conformity between theory and actuality. That there are impediments to mobility will become evident in our discussion of depressed areas—those in which unemployment has remained above the national average for long periods of time.

The Demand for and Supply of Labor

The labor force was described in Chapter 1 in terms of its aggregate size and the shifting numbers and percentages in different industries and occupations. These movements of workers obviously imply changes in demand by employers and a responsiveness on the part of people in the labor force to them. Before we can focus on such aggregate movements, we must first examine the demand for a specific kind of labor and the supply of that labor.

The demand for labor of any type arises from the fact that labor is a factor of production; that is, it can be combined by employers with the other factors of production—land and capital—to produce goods and services that can be sold to consumers. Except in the case of some personal services—as, for example, a valet—labor by itself can produce nothing; it must have tools and raw materials with which to work. Similarly, capital by itself is useless, but, with raw materials to feed a machine and a worker to operate it, it can help to produce goods. Each of the factors of production is vital to the production process, but we shall examine only the labor factor of production.

To explain the demand for labor, we shall assume that the labor market is a competitive one, by which we mean that:

1. Workers are able to move easily from one employment to another.
2. There are many prospective buyers of their services, each of whom

uses such a negligible portion of the total type of labor that he cannot influence its price.

3. Workers and employers have adequate information about each others' offers.

The Demand for Labor

The demand for labor or, more accurately, for the productive services that human beings can perform, refers to the various quantities of it that employers will purchase at various prices (wage rates). Thus, in a particular community, which constitutes a distinct labor market, employers would hire only 10 first-class machinists if their wage rate were $6 per hour, 65 machinists if their wage rate were $4 per hour, and 120 if their wage rate were only $2 per hour. By the demand for first-class machinists in this community we mean the entire schedule representing the relationship between wages (the price of labor) and the number of machinists who would be hired. The line D_1D_1 in Figure 8.1 illustrates this labor demand schedule. Given this schedule, we can see that if the actual wage rate were $3, 90 machinists would be employed in the community.

Figure 8.1 Labor Demand Schedule

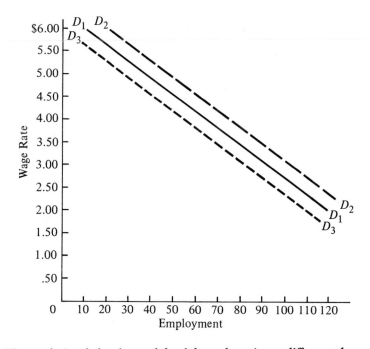

The analysis of the demand for labor, then, is no different than that for any other factor of production or commodity. The demand curve has a negative slope, which means simply that, *ceteris paribus* (other things being

Figure 8.2 Labor Supply Schedule

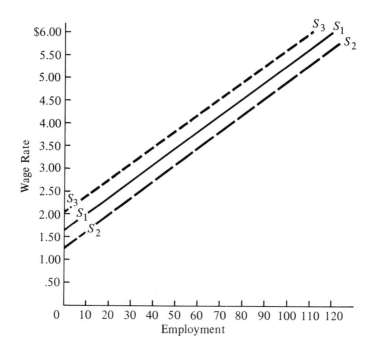

equal), the lower the wage rate, the more labor is hired. Similarly, the higher the wage rate, the less labor is used.

Demand for labor is not constant, but shifts in response to price changes in the economy and fluctuations in demand for products. A change in the demand for machinists, however, does not refer to movement along the demand curve, but requires an entirely new schedule. An increase in demand means that more machinists would be hired at each wage rate: 20 machinists would be hired at a wage rate of $6, 76 at $4, and so on, as shown by the demand curve D_2D_2 in Figure 8.1. Thus at the wage rate of $3 about 103 machinists would be hired. A decrease in demand means that fewer would be hired at each wage rate, as shown by D_3D_3. In this case, at a wage rate of $3 only 82 machinists would be hired.

The Supply of Labor

Now let us turn to the supply side of the labor market. The supply of labor, in this case first-class machinists, means the various numbers of machinists who will be willing to accept jobs at the various wage rates that may be offered by employers. The supply schedule S_1S_1, in Figure 8.2, shows that at $2 per hour only 10 first-class machinists would be willing to accept jobs in this community; at $4, 65 machinists; and at $6, 120 machinists. Supply represents a relationship between wage rates (the price of labor) and the amount of labor (number of workers) available. The supply curve has a positive slope, that is, the higher the wage, *ceteris paribus,* the greater the number of workers offering their services.

As in the case of demand, a change in supply requires a shift in the entire curve, not movement along the same one. An increase in the supply of first-class machinists, which might have come about as a result of a community training program, would shift the supply curve downward and to the right, as shown by S_2S_2 in Figure 8.2. An increase in supply means that more machinists would be available for hire at each wage rate; at $2, twenty machinists would be available; at, $4, seventy-five; and so on. A decrease in supply, that is, a shift in the supply curve upward and to the left, means that fewer machinists would be available for hire at each wage rate, as shown in S_3S_3. Such a decline in supply might come about as a result of migration of machinists to other communities.

Equilibrium in the Labor Market

Having examined the demand for and supply of labor, let us now see how the two interact to determine the number of workers who will be employed in an occupation and at what wage rate. Continuing with our example of first-class machinists in our mythical community, we can plot our original demand and supply schedules, D_1D_1 and S_1S_1 from Figures 8.1 and 8.2, as is done in Figure 8.3. The actual number of machinists who will be employed is deter-

Figure 8.3 Labor Market Equilibrium

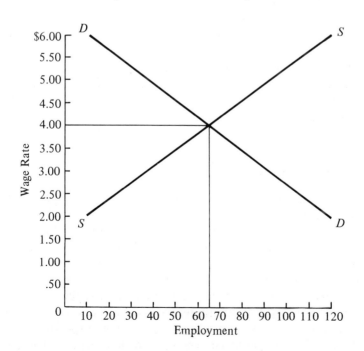

mined by where the supply and demand curves intersect. We can see that in our example sixty-five machinists would be employed, and that their wage rate would be $4 per hour.

When supply and demand are in balance we say that we have equilibrium in the labor market, by which we mean that there is no tendency for the number employed or the wage rate to change. We are, of course, assuming that this is a situation of pure competition.

To understand why this is so, let us see what would happen if, for some reason, the wage rate were different. If the wage rate for first-class machinists were, say, $4.50, a look at Figure 8.3 would show us that 78 machinists would be available for hire, but at that wage employers would only hire 51 of them. Thus, the 27 surplus machinists would start to underbid each other for the available jobs until the wage rate was pushed back down to $4.00, at which point job offers and available machinists would be equal. Similarly, if the wage rate were $3.50, we would also have a situation of disequilibrium, which would right itself. At that wage rate the employers in the community would seek to hire 79 machinists, but only 51 would be available, leaving a shortage of 28. In order to attract more workers in this "tight" labor market, employers would begin to offer higher wages, and the wage rate for machinists would climb to $4.00, at which point there would be neither a shortage nor a surplus.

Equilibrium, it also must be kept in mind, exists as of a given time, and our analysis is based upon a *ceteris paribus*, other things being equal, assumption. But in practice other things may not be equal. In a dynamic economy, such as ours is, the situation is always changing: shifts in consumer demand for products may lead to changes in employer demand for machinists, and deaths and retirement, education and training, and in- and out-migration in a community may lead to changes in the supply of this type of labor. Equilibrium, therefore, represents a tendency of supply and demand to "clear the market," that is, to match job offers and available workers. Even to the extent that competitive conditions are violated in real labor markets, equilibrium analysis will enable us to understand better the deviations and their consequences.

Determinants of the Demand for Labor

Next let us examine the demand for, and supply of, labor more fully. A demand for any particular type of labor will depend partly on the ability of employers to substitute some other type of labor or another factor of production for it. A rise in the wage rate for first-class machinists may lead employers to use fewer of them and rely more on lesser-skilled machinists. Another alternative for employers may be to substitute capital for labor: this might be done by using more numerically controlled machines and fewer machinists. Employers will be inclined to substitute machines for workers because the increase in the wage rate has made labor relatively more expensive.

The demand for any particular type of labor also depends partially on the demand for products. The demand for labor is a derived demand; that is, the number of first-class machinist jobs available depends upon the demand for the goods that they help to produce. An increase in wage rates, therefore, can mean that the price of the product will also be increased, relative to the prices of other goods, and as a result fewer units will be sold. Thus, an increase in wages can lead to less employment via a contraction effect.

A decrease in the wage rate, on the other hand, will lead to greater employment as employers substitute that type of labor for other types of productive services, and/or the price of the final product is lowered, thus inducing consumers to buy more units of it. In practice, of course, wage rates seldom go down, but workers, and even unions, have agreed to decreases in wages on occasion, precisely in order to save and possibly increase the number of jobs in a plant that is in serious economic difficulties. More usually, a decrease in the wages of a particular type of labor is achieved through having its wage rates go up more slowly than others; thus, they decline relatively.

In the final analysis, therefore, the slope of the demand curve for any particular type of labor will reflect two things: (1) the elasticity of demand for the products it is engaged in producing, and (2) the substitutability of other types of labor or factors of production for it.

Changes in the Supply of Labor

At this point, one may understand how demand shifts but still wonder about the process by which the supply changes in response. After all, is not the supply of labor of any particular type fixed in any given period of time? This is quite true, and labor, being inseparable from the human beings who perform it, cannot be reduced or increased in quantity as easily as tons of steel. Surpluses or shortages of particular types of labor, therefore, can persist, but in time equilibrium will reassert itself; if there is a surplus, some people will be induced to shift to other types of work, and others may drop out of the labor market altogether; and if there is a shortage more people will enter that type of work. These adjustments may take time to accomplish, many years in some cases, but they will take place.

Reductions in the demand for a particular type of labor, moreover, may entail human suffering. Thus, as demand declines workers will be laid off, and, unless their skills are easily transferable, many of them will endure long periods of unemployment, and others will have to accept new jobs that are significantly worse than their former ones. The reduction in demand will also lead some workers to drop out of the labor force, either through retirement in the case of older workers, by returning to full-time schooling in the case of young workers, or by returning to the status of housewife in the case of some women workers. Young people getting out of school, meanwhile, will shun this occupation, and the places of those who left the trade will not be refilled. Thus, within time the supply of this type of labor will fall until it is again in balance with the demand for it.

Now let us trace the process of adjustments in the supply of a given type of labor by referring to an actual example, that of college teaching. Due to the low birthrates experienced during the depression period in the 1930s, college enrollments actually fell in the mid-1950s, and since colleges and universities had little trouble finding teachers in many disciplines, increases in faculty salaries lagged behind most others. Since the salaries of college professors were relatively low compared with those in private industry and even government employment, many people who were qualified for college teaching chose instead to take research jobs in industry and government. At the same time many persons who would otherwise have continued their educations in pursuit of a doctorate, the basic requirement for professorships, did not do so, preferring to take jobs immediately in industry and government, which did not demand the degree.

By the 1960s, however, the demand for college professors increased, because, as a result of the increased birthrates of the 1940s and 1950s and the fact that a larger proportion of young people chose to continue their educations beyond high school, there were more college students. This increase in demand is illustrated, in Figure 8.4, by the shift in the demand curve from D_1D_1 to D_2D_2. This shift in demand increased the employment of college professors from OE to OF. But where did EF professors suddenly come from?

Figure 8.4   Wage Change in Response to a Shift in Demand

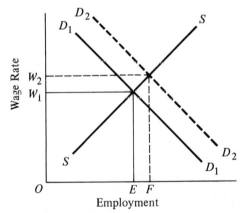

The answer is, first of all, that they did not all immediately appear, since shifting takes time to accomplish, and for a period of time there was a critical shortage of professors. But the increase in demand raised academic salaries, in Figure 8.4, from OW_1 to OW_2, and this encouraged people to shift from private and government research to the college campuses and more students to continue their educations in graduate school. In 1959 the total number of people awarded Ph.D. degrees by American universities was 9,400, but by 1969 the total had jumped to over 26,000.

At any given moment of time, however, the supply of a particular type of labor is limited. Thus, as academic salaries rose and people moved into college teaching, private and government employers found that the supply available to them had decreased, with the result that the salaries of professionals in private industry and government rose. In fact, the general increase in demand for professional manpower during the 1960s led to a rapid rise in professional salaries. By the early 1970s there were clear signs, however, of the achievement of a new equilibrium, and possibly even a reversal of the 1960s situation: the higher salaries had augmented the supply of college teachers while tight college budgets were holding down the demand, with the result that new Ph.D.s were finding college teaching openings scarce.

The Principle of Equal Advantage

It is a basic assumption of economic theory that people behave rationally and attempt to maximize their advantages in terms of income and working conditions. This being the case, workers will tend to gravitate toward those occupations, industries, and areas which offer the highest wages, other things being equal. A second assumption is that labor can be shifted from one employment to another. In fact, labor should continue to shift from lower-paying to higher-paying employments until real returns are equalized: this is the principle of equal advantage. (This does not mean that all workers must be willing to move, but only a large enough minority of workers to ensure that labor is allocated most efficiently.)

We have actually already illustrated the principle in operation through our example of the augmenting of the supply of college professors during the 1960s. As college teaching became more desirable—through higher salaries; the reduction of time required in the classroom, thus leaving more time for scholarly research; and the expansion of research funds—people moved out of other occupations into teaching. Although the principle of equal advantage states that labor should move from one employment to another until the returns are equalized, this shifting is only a tendency, and it is not always easy to accomplish. As a result, wage differences may persist. Let us next examine the factors that explain the persistence of these differences.

Nonmonetary Advantages

People do not find all jobs to be equally desirable, and nonmonetary advantages, often called "psychic income" by economists, may compensate for lower salaries in some employments. A few years ago someone observed that truck drivers were earning more than many college professors, yet few of the latter sought jobs driving trucks. Obviously, the higher status accorded by society to professors, the freedom to pursue one's own scholarly interests, and the leisure time in which to do so compensated for money differentials.

Nonmonetary advantages are actually equalizing differences, and do not represent a deviation from the theory of a competitive labor market, which states that workers will attempt to maximize their net advantages from em-

ployment. In the case of the professors and the truck drivers, the nonmonetary
aspects of the job offset some of the monetary ones. This illustration, therefore, does not violate the principle of equal advantage but only indicates that
the total configuration of employments, including the monetary as well as the
nonmonetary aspects, must be taken into consideration.

Nonmonetary Disadvantages

Another equalizing difference, reflecting the fact that employments are un-
equally attractive, is the existence of nonmonetary disadvantages. Some jobs,
because they involve such adverse working conditions as dirt, noise, heat,
tension, or peculiar hours, must have higher wage rates if workers are to be
induced into accepting them. Thus, those who work the "swing" and "grave-
yard" shifts (4 P.M. to midnight and midnight to 8 A.M.), which prevent them
from leading normal biological and social lives, generally receive shift differentials as a compensation.

Another example of nonmonetary disadvantages of jobs is offered by the
automobile industry. In recent years, when labor markets have been tight,
automobile manufacturers have complained about their inability to recruit
and retain workers for their assembly lines, even though straight-time average
hourly earnings in the automobile industry were almost 25 percent higher
than in all manufacturing. Many studies have reported workers' dissatisfaction with the monotony and repetitiveness of assembly-line jobs, the inability
to exercise control over them, and the lack of opportunity for advancement.[1]
When job opportunities are plentiful, therefore, better conditions elsewhere
are valued more highly by some workers than $.70 to $1.00 an hour more
working on an automobile assembly line.

Costs of Entry

Another explanation of the persistence of earnings differences are differences
in cost of entry among occupations. Undergoing a five-year apprenticeship to
become a skilled worker, during which the individual receives considerably
less than the journeyman's rate of pay, may mean sacrifice of income that
could have been immediately available had he taken an unskilled job. Becoming a physician requires some ten years of education and training beyond high
school—four years of college, four years of medical school, and two years of
interning—and not everyone in the society is either willing or can afford to
pay the tuition costs and the sacrifice of ten years of earnings.

Indeed, there is a direct correlation between lifetime earnings and the

---

[1] Daniel Bell, *Work and Its Discontents* (Boston: Beacon Press, 1956); Charles R.
Walker and Robert H. Guest, *The Man on the Assembly Line* (Cambridge, Mass.: Har-
vard University Press, 1952); Eli Chinoy, *Automobile Workers and the American Dream*
(Garden City, N.Y.: Doubleday, 1952); and William E. Faunce, "The Automobile In-
dustry: A Case Study in Automation," in H. B. Jacobson, *Automation and Society* (New
York: Philosophical Library, 1959).

amount of education people have. Despite some invidious comparisons between the earnings of truck drivers and college professors, it is a fact that the average college graduate can expect to earn about $160,000 more than the average high-school graduate over his working career. His prospective lifetime earnings, in 1966 dollars, of $508,000 is double that of the average grade-school graduate.[2]

This does not mean that a family's investment in a college education for a child is always necessarily financially worth it. The costs of education are very high, as we shall see right away, and, depending upon the occupation for which the student prepares himself, a higher return might be earned by investing an equivalent amount of money in stocks, bonds, or real estate with the son becoming a skilled production worker instead.[3] Of course, education is valued for more than financial returns, and, moreover, on the average a college degree does pay off.

Higher prospective earnings are, of course, a major explanation of the boom in education. Yet a college education is very costly: four years at a prestigious private college can cost the student and his parents $50,000; tuition, books, travel, and the like will cost them directly $3,500 to $4,000 per year, and to this amount must be added opportunity costs, the $6,000 to $6,500 above summer employment earnings that the individual could have earned had he not gone to college. Even this figure tends to understate the true cost of a bachelor's degree, since tuition fails to cover the entire cost of educating the student. The cost of an education at a public institution is not much different, but the student and his family bear less of a share of it, receiving instead a large subsidy from society in the form of government financial support of higher public education.

Costs of entry, thus, are quite high, and lower-income persons are less able to bear them; even low tuition at public colleges and universities does not enable them to go to college, because poor families cannot afford to sacrifice their children's earning power for four years.

Inequality of Abilities

The fact that differences in native ability prevent equalization provides another explanation for the persistence of differences in net advantages among employments. People are not alike and each is uniquely endowed, but some of these endowments, such as rare beauty, brawn, or brains, may be pecuniarily more valued by society than others. Even if society made college and medical school education free to individuals and provided them with income while they pursued their training, we should find that not everyone was

---

[2] *Current Population Reports*, Bureau of the Census, Series P-60, No. 56, August 1968.

[3] See, for example, Arthur Carol and Samuel Parry, "The Economic Rationale of Occupational Choice," *Industrial and Labor Relations Review*, January 1968, pp. 183–196.

qualified to become a physician. Human resources are simply not completely transferable among employments.

Geographical Immobilities

Another factor explaining earnings differences is that geographical immobilities exist. People who have been born and bred in a community are often loath to leave it, even for higher earnings elsewhere, and for various reasons business may not move into the community to take advantage of its lower wages. (We shall examine the questions of labor mobility and depressed areas following this discussion of the demand for and supply of labor.)

Man-Made Restrictions on Entry

An important explanation of the failure to achieve equalization of net advantages among employments is that man-made restrictions have been placed on entry into some of them. Occupational licensing has become a chief means of restricting entry into trades and thus preserving higher earnings for those in them, and this has been demonstrated for occupations as diverse as barbers[4] and physicians and dentists.[5] By varying the standards that new entrants must meet, the licensing board, which is invariably dominated by members of the occupation, can keep the total labor supply in such relation to the demand as to ensure higher earnings.

Discrimination by race, religion, sex, and age also serves to limit entry into various occupations. In many labor markets blacks, Chicanos, and Puerto Ricans have found skilled jobs in the building trades blocked to them. Similarly, women have complained bitterly about their being denied access to managerial positions in most companies. And Jewish groups have charged that, despite the high educational attainment within the Jewish community, the executive offices of leading corporations have been barred to them. All these forms of discrimination prevent augmentation of the labor supplies in the various occupations and thus act to maintain earnings above competitive levels.

Union practices in some of the skilled trades are designed basically to restrict entry and thus boost the earnings of those already in them. These practices include charging high initiation fees, requiring long apprenticeship periods, limiting the number of apprentices, closing the union books to new members except for sons of present members, and, of course, discrimination against minority groups.

---

[4] Simon Rottenberg, "The Economics of Occupational Licensing," in *Aspects of Labor Economics* (Princeton: Princeton University Press, 1962).

[5] L. Benham, A. Maurizi, and M. Reder, "Migration, Location and Remuneration of Medical Personnel: Physicians and Dentists," *Review of Economics and Statistics*, August 1968.

Lack of Knowledge

One final barrier to the movement of labor from one employment to another is simply the lack of knowledge on the part of workers about opportunities. Workers might be willing to shift to higher-paying occupations, industries, and geographic areas if they knew that they were higher paying, but they often do not. Contrary to the assumption underlying a competitive labor market, information in the labor market is far from perfect, so differences in net advantages can exist. An automobile mechanic in Rhode Island is not likely to be aware of job possibilities in his field in California, or realize that his skills can be used by an industrial plant even closer to his home. Reynolds has shown that, even within a local labor market, the same type of job can be paid significantly different wages because workers have little knowledge of alternatives.[6]

The Backward-Bending Supply Curve of Labor

Before examining labor markets in practice, one issue with respect to the supply of labor merits attention: the so-called backward-bending supply curve of labor. According to this concept, the supply curve of labor was positively sloping only up to a point, beyond which it became negatively sloped, as shown in Figure 8.5a. The reasoning behind the backward-bending supply curve of labor was as follows: workers will offer more labor in response to the opportunity for higher earnings up to the point where their needs are so well satisfied that they prefer additional leisure to additional money.

Figure 8.5a The Backward Bending Supply Curve

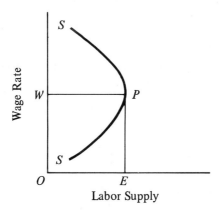

Labor Supply

---

[6] Lloyd G. Reynolds, *The Structure of Labor Markets* (New York: Harper & Bros., 1951).

[7] Harold G. Vatter, "On the Folklore of the Backward Sloping Supply Curve," *Industrial and Labor Relations Review,* July 1961, pp. 580–582.

[8] F. Aldrich Finegan, "Comment: The Backward Sloping Supply Curve," *Industrial and Labor Relations Review,* January 1962, p. 230.

Such behavior on the part of workers is explainable in very underdeveloped countries, where people find a paucity of additional goods and services that they might purchase with additional income. Once their appetites have been whetted by exposure to the myriad products that are available in the industrialized countries, however, people in developing countries do begin to manifest a desire for additional income, as witness the "revolution of rising expectations" throughout the so-called third world.

If additional income is becoming highly prized by workers in less developed countries, does the concept of the backward-bending labor supply curve have any relevance in the United States, where human wants seem insatiable and the mind of man able to continually invent new goods and services? Vatter, for one, has argued that only at an unrealistically high wage could the labor supply curve of the individual worker begin to bend backward.[7] His contention, however, has been subjected to severe criticism.[8]

The logic of the backward-bending supply curve becomes more apparent if we remember that labor also involves sacrifice: a surrender of leisure in exchange for money with which to purchase goods and services. Each of these —income and leisure—is valued by a person, but as we can recall from introductory economics courses, the more of anything that a person acquires, the less each additional amount of that is worth to him (decreasing marginal utility). A person with low earnings, therefore, is very desirous of earning more income, but at some point the marginal utility of money will be less than that of additional leisure. We can see that the aggregate supply curve of labor can slope backward in that people work shorter hours today than in the past and the number of holidays and weeks of vacation have increased. After all, if everyone worked longer the gross national product could be higher, but leisure, as well as goods and services, makes up a part of the American standard of living.

But our analysis does not stop here, for the reluctance to offer more

**Figure 8.5b   The Labor Supply Curve Taking Account
of the Leisure-Income Tradeoff**

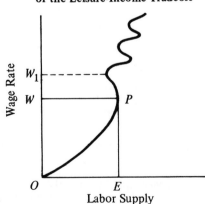

labor can be overcome by the offering of still more income. The marginal utility of an hour of leisure may be greater than that of an hour of labor if the wage rate is $4, but at $6 the opposite may be the case. Thus, employers, in order to induce workers to offer more labor, must pay them one and a half times their normal rates of pay for overtime hours, double those rates for work on Saturdays, and triple those rates for work on Sundays and holidays. In other words, at some point workers value leisure more than income and the labor supply curve slopes backward, but then, as leisure increases, at another point additional income becomes more valuable, and so on. Beyond a certain point, therefore, the labor supply curve would look more like a corkscrew, as shown in Figure 8.5b.

Labor Markets in Practice

Our discussion up to this point indicates that the labor market in practice differs from the labor market in theory. In fact, one cannot speak of *the* labor market, for many different types of labor markets exist. Let us now distinguish some of these.

Labor Markets by Degree of Structuring

A century ago Cairnes observed that barriers to movement created noncompeting groups of workers, and thus that many different labor markets existed.[9] Clark Kerr has elaborated on this theme, claiming that labor markets are continually being "Balkanized," that is, broken up into smaller, noncompeting units.[10]

Kerr distinguishes between "structureless labor markets" and "institutional labor markets." The former is exemplified by the harvest labor market in California, but even that is becoming institutionalized as unionism spreads within it. The structureless labor market is typified by the absence of unionism and its seniority and other rules governing hiring and firing; by being transitory in nature, with impersonal employer-employee relationships; by being composed of unskilled workers who are paid by the amount produced; and by the use of little capital or machinery. Farmers hire people to harvest their crops, not caring who the people are, pay them for what they produce, and may never see them again as they drift on to other work; meanwhile, the farmers will hire a new group of people on the same basis. This structureless labor market is governed by a cash nexus, pretty close to the economic theory concept of a labor market.

Institutional labor markets, on the other hand, create noncompeting groups, which are governed by rules as to which workers are preferred.

---

[9] J. E. Cairnes, *Some Leading Principles of Political Economy Newly Expounded* (New York: Harper & Bros., 1874), pp. 64–68.

[10] Clark Kerr, "The Balkanization of Labor Markets," in E. Wight Bakke *et al.*, *Labor Mobility and Economic Opportunity* (New York: Technology Press of MIT and Wiley, 1954), pp. 92–110.

Kerr distinguishes two types of institutional markets. The first, which he calls "command ownership," is typified by the craft union that asserts proprietorship over jobs in a defined occupation and geographic area. Here the worker movement is horizontal, from job to job, with the worker's security emanating from his skill and his union's control of the competitive supply of labor. The second type exists in the industrial enterprise, in which the worker asserts his private property claim to a particular job. The employer does the initial hiring, but the union bargains for the order of moving up and down the occupational ladder within the plant. Government policy, moreover, supports both types of institutional markets.

In operation, institutional labor markets differ considerably from unstructured ones. Entry is not always easy, mobility is reduced, and the impact of the forces of supply and demand is blunted. Oversupply, for example, does not bring down the price of labor, as has been shown by such industries as steel and automobiles during periods of economic recession, and undersupply in the crafts does not bring more workers into the trade.

Geographical Extent

Labor markets can also be distinguished by the size of the area that they cover. In this respect we can distinguish among local, regional, national, and even international labor markets. The most important of these, in terms of the number of exchange relationships affected between workers and employers, is the local labor market.

The vast majority of nonprofessional, nonmanagerial jobs are transacted within the local labor market. At one time the local labor market was severely restricted in geographic scope, being limited to within walking distance of workers' homes. With improvements in transportation, particularly the intraurban trolley line, its area spread. Today, with so many workers owning automobiles and driving them to and from their jobs, it can be defined as the normal commuting radius of an urban center.

"Americanization" has also helped to extend the scope of the local labor market. In the late nineteenth and early twentieth centuries, individual immigrant groups tended to cluster in tight neighborhood communities within a city and not to venture very far from home in search of work. The children of immigrants, educated in the public schools, were willing to venture further from home neighborhoods and even to move to new neighborhoods, so the labor market covered a wider geographic area.

The labor market tends to expand in geographic scope as one ascends the occupational ladder. Thus, while most unskilled and semiskilled workers seek jobs, and are recruited by employers, within a normal commuting radius of home or establishment, some skilled worker labor markets are regional in character. Operating engineers, for instance, will seek employment in a broad region that may cover a number of states.

For many types of professional and managerial jobs, competition among workers for jobs and among employers for workers is national, and the entire country becomes the labor market. Companies with facilities spread across the nation recruit engineers, business administration graduates, and other young professionals from college campuses that are also spread across the country. The graduates recruited, moreover, come from many different parts of the country, and they accept the idea that their employment may be very far from their parents' homes. College faculties are also recruited from all over the country.

For very rare types of talents, the labor market becomes the entire world. At the end of 1970, following a wide search for a successor to the retiring Sir Rudolph Bing, the Metropolitan Opera Company, in New York City, announced that Goeran Gentele, head of the Royal Opera in Stockholm, Sweden, had been named its general manager.

In a sense the whole world has always been the labor market for the United States. After all, even unskilled labor was actively recruited in Europe in the nineteenth century, but the passage of restrictive immigration legislation in the 1920s limited the geographic scope of the labor market for blue-collar workers. But the world still remains the labor market for many professional occupations: the hospitals of New York City, for example, would not be able to operate except for the large number of medical interns from India and other less developed countries. Indeed, the movement of foreign professionals to the United States, to take advantage of its higher salaries and more generous research facilities, became known as the "brain drain." Many of the sending countries complained that the United States was reaping the advantages of their expenditure in educating people in such professional occupations as engineering.[11] Of course, this illustrates the workings of a free labor market, with labor gravitating to those employments and geographic areas in which it can maximize its advantages.

Labor Markets in Operation

While the Metropolitan Opera may have recruited its new general manager through a careful search of all the leading opera companies in the world, in most instances the actual process of job placement is a rather haphazard affair in the United States. This is particularly true for the less-skilled occupations and local labor markets. Normally, for most jobs, employer recruiting hardly goes beyond posting a notice of job openings at plant gates or, more likely today, placing an advertisement in the local newspaper. The majority of employees, both in blue-collar and lower white-collar positions, learn of their jobs through word of mouth: a neighbor or relative who works in the plant or office informs them that there are openings, and they apply for them.

More systemized job placement is typical of the labor markets for pro-

---

[11] See, for example, John R. Niland, *The Asian Engineering Brain Drain: A Study of International Relocation into the United States from India, China, South Korea, Thailand and Japan* (Lexington, Mass.: Heath Lexington Books, 1970).

fessional personnel. Each recognized discipline—for example, economics, physics, and mechanical engineering—has a professional association, which publishes journals that in addition to learned articles contain listings of job vacancies and members of the profession available for jobs. Also, their annual meetings serve as a national labor market at which prospective employers and employees interview each other and exchange information on jobs and qualifications.

The persistence of high rates of unemployment in the late 1950s and early 1960s focused a good deal of attention on the actual operations of labor markets. Professor E. Wight Bakke called attention to the inadequacies of the labor market in fulfilling its function of providing workers and employers with free choice. In a call for a program for the maximum development and employment of the nation's manpower, he pointed out that free choice was being blocked for most workers by ignorance of the general conditions of demand and supply, their trends, and their probable future; by the absence of opportunities to receive training in new skills; and by the restrictive costs of movement.[12] Some of his proposals have since been enacted, and we shall examine them in greater detail in Chapter 18.

Internal Labor Markets

A third distinction of labor markets can be made between "internal" and "external" ones. Up to this point we have been concentrating on external labor markets, that is, community ones in which all employers and employees participate. But in recent years we have begun to recognize the importance of the labor markets that are internal to large companies.[13] These internal labor markets have always been important for managerial and professional personnel, but in many organizations the concept of career employment encompasses employees at all levels, including those in production jobs.

The importance of the internal labor market can be seen from the size of some large employers: the United States government has 2.7 million civilian employees and General Motors has 350,000 employees; both thus have larger internal labor markets than many community labor markets. To most of the employees within an organization future job movement is seen as taking place within the organization. Usually one looks forward to vertical movement, that is, to promotions to higher job categories, but many people are also subjected to, or seek, lateral moves, to different departments and different locations.

Not only the employee, but the large employer also places great stress on the internal labor market for meeting its needs for personnel. Typically, new

[12] E. Wight Bakke, *A Positive Labor Market Policy* (Columbus: Charles E. Merrill, 1963), pp. 64, 65.

[13] An excellent source of information on internal labor markets is Peter B. Doeringer and Michael J. Piore, *Internal Labor Markets and Manpower Analysis* (Lexington, Mass.: D. C. Heath & Co., 1971).

employees are hired for entry-level jobs in their category, whether a semi-skilled job for a blue-collar production worker or a management trainee position for a recent college graduate. Dunlop has called these jobs that are filled by recruitment from the external labor market "ports of entry" into the company.[14] For higher-level jobs, however, the company usually trains present employees. Some of this training is "on the job," with the employee simply learning how to operate another machine or process, but in some cases it is quite elaborate, for example, skilled trade apprenticeship training or management development programs.

With all this movement within it, one would think that the internal labor market would function better than the external one, but some observers have concluded that it, too, suffers from lack of information and immobilities.[15] Posting of job vacancy notices so that employees may bid for them is often haphazard, supervisors tend to "hoard" good subordinates and deny them the opportunity to move on to other jobs, and one unit of the company is often unaware of what is going on within others. Professor Alfred advocates increasing the efficiency of the internal market through improved systems of job postings and providing employees with greater freedom in job bidding. Improvements in the operation of internal markets would be another important step toward improving the allocation of labor in our economy.

Labor Mobility

A free labor market has been defined as one in which employees can change jobs whenever they want to in response to pressures they may be under or desires to increase their benefits. Such a labor market implies worker movement from one job to another. Mobility is essential, not only from the individual employee's point of view, but also from that of the entire economy. Mobility is essential to the efficiency of the economy, for in a dynamic economy some firms, industries, and areas will be declining, others growing slowly, and still others growing rapidly. If the economy is to achieve its highest potential output, differentials in growth rates necessitate the movement of workers away from the declining firms, industries, and areas to those that are growing. In this section, therefore, we shall examine how mobile workers really are and the influences on labor mobility.

The Extent of Job Changing

Labor mobility means that workers change their jobs, and, in fact, each year approximately one out of every ten people who work changes his job, and

[14] John T. Dunlop, "Job Vacancy Measures and Economic Analysis," in *The Measurement and Interpretation of Job Vacancies* (New York: National Bureau of Economic Research, 1966), pp. 27–48.
[15] See, for example, Theodore M. Alfred, "Checkers or Choice in Manpower Management," *Harvard Business Review*, February 1967, pp. 157–169.

about one-third of that 10 percent change jobs more than once.[16] While many of these job changes are "simple," that is, they involve shifting within the same job category from one employer in an industry to another, most job changes are "complex"; that is, the worker also changes his occupation or industry or both.[17]

Occupational Shifts

During 1966, for example, one out of every eleven workers changed his occupation.[18] Five out of six of these occupational changes also involved a change in employer. Among professional and technical workers, however, fully one-third of those who changed occupations remained with their same employers, thus illustrating the importance of the internal labor market for such workers. Not all the occupational changes, however, represent great differences in the type of work done: about one-quarter of the men and half of the women who make such changes remain within major occupational groups.

Economic theory postulates that workers should be moving from slow-growing to rapidly expanding occupations, and there is evidence to show that this does happen. There has been a large shift from blue-collar to white-collar types of jobs, and a surprisingly high proportion of men who moved into white-collar work in 1966 had been blue-collar workers: better than one out of four in the case of professional and technical workers; better than one out of three for managers, proprietors, officials, and salesworkers; and almost two out of five for clerical workers.

Interindustry Shifts

Workers who change jobs may also move from one industry to another. Using Social Security Administration data, Gallaway found that one out of four workers who had changed jobs between 1957 and 1960 had moved to a different industry.[19]

Geographic Mobility

Not only do people change employers, occupations, and industries, but some of them also change their locations. Although interregional mobility is lower

---

[16] See, for example, Gertrude Bancroft and Stuart Garfinkle, "Job Mobility of Workers in 1961," Special Labor Force Report No. 35 (Washington, D.C.: Bureau of Labor Statistics, 1963); and "Job Mobility of Workers in 1955," *Current Population Reports,* Bureau of the Census, Series P-50, No. 70, February 1957.

[17] Herbert S. Parnes, "Labor Force Participation and Labor Mobility," in Woodrow L. Ginsburg *et al., A Review of Industrial Relations Research*, Vol. 1 (Madison, Wisc.: Industrial Relations Research Association, 1970), p. 40. This review of the literature has been relied on heavily for the material in this section on labor mobility.

[18] Samuel Saben, "Occupational Mobility of Employed Workers," Special Labor Force Report No. 84 (Washington, D.C.: Bureau of Labor Statistics, 1967).

[19] Lowell E. Gallaway, *Inter-Industry Labor Mobility in the United States 1957 to 1960*, Research Report No. 18 (Washington, D.C.: Social Security Administration, 1967), p. 29.

than other types, still one out of fourteen workers moves from one county to another each year. According to Lansing and Mueller, two out of every three family heads live in a different labor market from the one in which they were born; and close to six of ten in a different one from that in which they had graduated from or left high school.[20]

Trends in Mobility

Ignoring the depression decade of the 1930s, when quit (as opposed to layoff) rates were understandably very low, the data for recent decades on quits in manufacturing, compared to the 1920s, seem to disclose a long-term downward trend in labor mobility. These data prompted Professor Ross to ask if we were approaching a form of industrial feudalism, whereby workers would be tied to their jobs the way the feudal serfs had been tied to the land in medieval times.[21] But mobility itself is no virtue. In fact, it can be a decided hindrance to individuals, employees, and the national economy if it simply means that workers are aimlessly leaving jobs for other, similar ones.

Too much mobility can cause as great inefficiencies as too little. Mobility has costs. The employee who leaves one job, voluntarily or involuntarily, surrenders accumulated seniority, the progression he may have achieved within his job grade, his accumulated pension rights, and his association with a work group in which he has felt at home. In a new job he usually starts at the bottom of the rate range for the job, must make new associations with workmates, has no seniority and thus little job security, and must work for a number of years before becoming eligible for a pension.

Mobility is also costly to employers and to the entire economy. When an experienced worker quits a job and must be replaced with a less experienced one, the employer faces training costs and a period in which the new worker does not produce as efficiently as the man he replaced. Similarly, when the worker who quits takes another job, he, too, will have to be trained to fit the specific requirements of his new job, and it will take him a period of time to become fully efficient.

We need only enough mobility to ensure economic efficiency by shifting workers out of declining or slow-growing occupations, industries, and regions to the more rapidly growing ones, and to provide people with freedom of choice in the labor market. The decline in mobility, therefore, may not have seriously interfered with these objectives. Yet the fact that some communities throughout the nation have experienced long periods of above average unemployment, while in others certain types of jobs have been readily available while unemployment has been a problem, indicates that improved mobility is needed. Let us now turn our attention to the factors that influence labor

---

[20] John B. Lansing and Eva Mueller, *The Geographic Mobility of Labor* (Ann Arbor: Institute for Social Research, University of Michigan, 1967), p. 17.

[21] Arthur M. Ross, "Do We Have a New Industrial Feudalism?" *American Economic Review*, December 1958.

mobility so that we may better understand the reasons for unnecessary immobilities.

Influences on Labor Mobility

The Rate of National Economic Growth

Not all labor mobility is voluntary, for workers are forced to change jobs when they lose their present ones. The influence of the business cycle on the demand for labor, and hence on mobility, becomes clear. If jobs are scarce, workers are not likely voluntarily to give up the ones they have in search of better prospects. But when unemployment rates are low and employers are actively seeking new workers, one is more willing to quit his present job, since prospects of finding another one seem good.

Age

Probably the most important influence on mobility is age: young workers engage in a disproportionate amount of the total job changing, but with advancing age every type of mobility declines beyond the early twenties.[22] The importance of age is readily understandable. Young workers, particularly those without specific skills, often merely drift into their first job. When this turns out to be unsatisfactory, they move on to another one, and another one, until they find a niche that is satisfying to them. Early jobs also provide the type of training and experience that enable young workers to move on to better jobs. Few young people are so set in their attitudes toward work and life that they are ready to settle down in a job; most are groping toward careers and life styles. This is true even for young professionals and managers, and many companies have been quite concerned in recent years at high turnover among such employees, who leave one company in search of more challenging opportunities in another. Having fewer family responsibilities, young workers are less concerned with security and are more willing to gamble by giving up good jobs for other prospects. As workers grow older, however, they are likely to become more settled, have a firm attachment to the labor market, and, because of growing family responsibilities, be more concerned with job tenure and income security.

Geographic mobility is even more affected by age. Reynolds, in his study of worker attitudes and behavior in relation to mobility, stated: "Younger workers showed a greater willingness to move than did older workers, and tenants were more willing to move than were home owners."[23]

Older workers, moreover, are more likely to be homeowners than younger ones, and to have sunk roots in a community; hence, it is more costly for them to migrate to other regions. Also, since employers generally prefer to hire young workers, their job prospects in new areas are lower; even when

[22] Parnes, *op. cit.*, p. 44.
[23] Reynolds, *op. cit.*, p. 78.

older workers are unemployed, therefore, they prefer to take their chances in the home community, where they have friends and relatives, than go off to a strange city.

Job Tenure

Another important influence on a worker's mobility is the length of time he has been in his present job: the longer the time, the less likely he will change jobs. This is to be expected, because one has a heavy investment, both financial and emotional, in a position in which he has spent a good share of his working life; he is familiar with the organization's procedures and has built relationships with the members of his work group, which he is reluctant to sever. According to Gallaway, other things being equal, long tenure in a job increases both the pecuniary and psychic costs of leaving it.[24]

Sex

Job changing is more pronounced among males than females, but it is not clear to what extent this is due to sex or to other factors, such as occupational differences and differences between the two sexes in their continuity of labor force exposure.[25] Although the overall mobility rates are higher for men than women, within specific occupations—such as professional and technical workers and managers, proprietors and officials—these differences tend to disappear. Female geographic mobility, at least among married women, however, seems to be much lower than that of males.

Race

Race is another factor that plays a role in mobility. Gallaway found that black men changed employers and industries more than did white men, but that the reverse was true in the case of women.[26] Much of the black male mobility, however, is involuntary, for recessions normally lead to a greater proportionate permanent displacement of black than white men. A disproportionate number of the blacks who lose their jobs in relatively high-paying industries are forced to settle for new ones in lower-paying industries.

Occupation

Occupation is a further influence on mobility, with job-changing rates inversely correlated with degree of skill. Thus, among men, the rate of job changing in 1961 was highest among laborers and farm laborers, followed by operatives, craftsmen, and salesworkers; distinctly fewer changes were made by clericals and professionals; at the bottom of the list were managers, officials, and proprietors, and farmers and farm managers, many of whom own

---

[24] Gallaway, *op. cit.*, p. 61.
[25] Parnes, *op. cit.*, p. 46.
[26] Gallaway, *op. cit.*, p. 29.

their own businesses and thus would not be expected to change jobs.[27] On the other hand, geographic mobility is highest among the best educated and, in occupational terms, among professional and technical workers.[28]

Unionism

A number of institutional factors also help to explain variations in labor mobility. The spread of unionism, for example, has been held responsible for a decline in mobility. The development of the seniority concept, which seeks to protect long-service employees against layoff, has had some effect on reducing voluntary quits, but the ones who benefit most are older workers, who are less inclined to leave jobs anyway. Thus, there is no firm evidence that unionism has had any appreciable effect on mobility.

Pensions

The development of fringe benefits, particularly pensions, has been seen as a deterrent to mobility, but, as with the impact of unions, there is conflicting evidence here, too. A study by Parnes of male workers in two Columbus, Ohio, plants, one with a pension plan and the other without, found that pensions were not important in explaining immobility.[29] The findings of a Bureau of Labor Statistics study directly contradict the thesis that pensions make workers less mobile.[30] Folk, on the other hand, has presented theoretical arguments suggesting that pensions do reduce mobility.[31]

The Rationality of Labor Mobility

A final aspect of the mobility question that must be dealt with concerns the rationality of labor mobility, that is, the movement of workers to jobs that have greater advantages. A number of labor market analysts have suggested that workers do not move according to the postulates of economic theory, from jobs with less to jobs with more advantages. Rottenberg has countered, claiming that research does confirm, rather than deny, the postulates of neoclassical economic theory.[32]

According to Parnes, several studies have shown that white-collar workers behave somewhat more like "maximizers" than blue-collar workers.[33] But

---

[27] Bancroft and Garfinkle, *op. cit.*

[28] Parnes, *op. cit.*, p. 48.

[29] Herbert S. Parnes, "Workers' Attitudes to Job Changing," in Gladys L. Palmer *et al., The Reluctant Job Changer* (Philadelphia: University of Pennsylvania Press, 1962), pp. 45–80.

[30] *Labor Mobility and Private Pension Plans*, Bureau of Labor Statistics Bulletin 1407, June 1964.

[31] Hugh Folk, "Private Pensions and Labor Mobility," in *Old Age Income Assurance*, Part IV: Employment Aspects of Pension Plans, U.S. Congress, Joint Economic Committee, December 1967.

[32] Simon Rottenberg, "On Choice in Labor Markets," *Industrial and Labor Relations Review*, January 1956.

[33] Parnes, "Labor Force Participation and Labor Mobility," *op. cit.*, p. 55.

there is also evidence that blue-collar workers act more rationally than some people think. According to Gallaway's study of interindustry mobility, men tended to remain more in those industries in which earnings were higher and unemployment lower.[34] The fact that many production workers move to lower-paying industries is not a matter of choice on their part, but a reflection of displacement from higher-paying ones with the only job opportunities available being lower-paid ones. Occupational movement, too, conforms to economic theory, for the empirical evidence shows that workers do tend to shift into higher-paying occupations.[35]

Further evidence of rationality in labor mobility is the fact that people tend to move geographically to areas of greater opportunity, either in terms of the job vacancies available or earnings levels. Raimon found a very direct correlation between net migration during the decade of the 1950s and employee earnings by state.[36] The continual movement of people from farms to urban areas and from the South to the North cannot be explained except as a response to better opportunities. Through multiple regression analysis, Gallaway examined the effect of five variables on interstate migration since 1850: per capita income levels, job opportunity, distance between states, population density, and the cultural affinity between states.[37] Although each variable was of some significance in explaining migration, the economic ones were the most important.

Thus, despite the contentions of some labor market specialists, the preponderance of empirical evidence is that worker mobility occurs in response to economic factors. We can conclude, therefore, that economic theory of labor market behavior is roughly in accord with actual behavior. Even so, there is also sufficient evidence to indicate that there is a good deal of room for improvement in the actual functioning of the labor market.

The Problem of Depressed Areas

The question of labor mobility must inevitably also involve concern with the problem of "depressed" areas: communities that have become areas of "substantial and persistent labor surplus." Many depressed communities are located, as one would expect, in the older centers of economic activity, some of which have lost their earlier locational advantages. For example, former textile manufacturing centers—such as Fall River, Lowell, and New Bedford, Massachusetts—and railroad and coal towns—such as Altoona, Johnstown,

---

[34] Gallaway, *op. cit.*, pp. 29–32.

[35] See, for example, A. H. Jaffe and R. O. Carleton, *Occupational Mobility in the United States, 1930–1950* (New York: Kings Crown Press, 1954); and Robert L. Aronson, *Components of Occupational Change in the United States, 1950–1960,* Technical Monograph Series No. 1 (New York: New York State School of Industrial and Labor Relations, 1969).

[36] Robert L. Raimon, "Interstate Migration and Wage Theory," *Review of Economics and Statistics,* November 1962, pp. 428–438.

[37] Lowell E. Gallaway, *Manpower Economics* (Homewood, Ill.: Richard D. Irwin, 1971), pp. 48–53.

and Scranton, Pennsylvania; and Huntington, Ashland, and Wheeling, West Virginia—have had unemployment rates well above the national average for long periods of time.

Differential rates of growth by region are to be expected in a dynamic economy in which new products and markets arise as old ones decline; natural resources are depleted and new ones discovered; population moves from rural to urban, from city to suburb, and from east to west; the structure of freight rates changes; new forms of transportation are developed; and new technology emerges. A region tends to become depressed, therefore, as a result of structural changes in the economy that lead the industries located there to decline or relocate. Thus, with the rise of petroleum and natural gas, the decline of coal as a source of fuel resulted in large sections of West Virginia and Pennsylvania becoming depressed, and the relocation of the textile industry from the North to the South left New England mill towns in a depressed condition.

Is there any justification for national concern with the problem of local areas declining because they are no longer as economically attractive to industry as they once were? The answer is yes, because, as Gallaway points out, the causes of depressed area unemployment are extralocal in character, and thus outside the scope of control of the particular area.[38] The reallocation of resources that causes some areas to become depressed benefits the entire society in that it enjoys a greater level of social welfare from its given resources. But while the entire community benefits from the reallocation, the depressed area is left to bear the burden of the cost. Thus, public policy that embraces some type of social aid for depressed areas is highly appropriate.

The next question that arises concerns the type of aid to be given depressed areas. Basically, the question is a "classic" one in location theory: whether to move industry to people or people to industry. The case for migration of people rests on the assumption that retardation of a region's growth is due to its being an uneconomic location, and emigration, therefore, permits taking advantage of superior productive possibilities in other regions. By following this strategy we would allow depressed areas to decline and transfer their surplus populations elsewhere.

The case for moving industry to where the people are is based on the claim that planned reductions of population through emigration are most difficult to achieve and require more social overhead investment, such as in building housing in the areas to which people move while allowing old housing within former communities to remain unused. It is further claimed that it is more economical to revitalize depressed areas and attract new industry to them, because a good deal of social capital is already invested in these communities in the form of homes, schools, and highways; to allow the communities to decline, therefore, would mean forfeiting a return on those investments.

---

[38] Lowell E. Gallaway, "An Economic Analysis of Policy for the Depressed Areas," *Industrial and Labor Relations Review*, July 1962, pp. 500–509.

This strategy was actually embodied in the Area Redevelopment Act of 1961, which provided for financial aid to depressed communities to revitalize their public facilities, for retraining of workers, and for low-interest loans to build plants in those regions.

The only real test of subsidizing a movement of industry to the people is the same as that applied to "infant industry" arguments for a protective tariff: Can the subsidy be temporary?[39] The very limited success of the Area Redevelopment Act that was designed to help depressed areas would seem to indicate that it is not easy to induce industry to move to an area that lacks basic locational advantages, though some of the failures of ARA have been ascribed to the fact that it tried to aid too many areas at once: over one thousand were so defined as to come under its jurisdiction.[40]

To the contention that planned reductions of population through emigration are most difficult to achieve can be counterposed the diennial census data, which do show not only relative drops in population, but even absolute ones, for depressed areas. Of course, these are net figures, for population movements are two way, with some people moving into a community while others move out, but the net, as indicated, is from depressed to better-off communities.

Part of the reluctance of people to move out of depressed areas is that they lack the skills that would help them to acquire jobs elsewhere. An analysis of eastern Kentucky, a very badly depressed area, by Bowman and Haynes advocated public policies designed to give potential migrants skills and training to match job opportunities elsewhere, as well as comprehensive relocation assistance.[41] Research by Hansen and Yukhin adds further support for such a policy, for they show that although family considerations are still important in influencing migration paths, especially for those who do not go to college, there is considerable sensitivity to relative wages in location preferences and expectations.[42] Hansen and Yukhin found that people in depressed areas are not only ready and willing to move to areas offering better economic opportunities, but that they would prefer to go to intermediate areas, such as (in their case study) Lexington and Louisville, Kentucky, instead of northern metropolitan areas in Ohio and Michigan. Based on this finding, they advocate policies that would divert out-migrants from big cities toward intermediate areas through training in job skills needed in those areas.

To summarize our discussion of depressed areas, their very existence indicates that there is considerable labor immobility. Yet there is also evi-

---

[39] Edgar M. Hoover, *The Location of Economic Activity* (New York: McGraw-Hill, 1963), p. 276.

[40] Sar A. Levitan, *Federal Aid to Depressed Areas: An Evaluation of the Area Redevelopment Administration* (Baltimore: Johns Hopkins Press, 1964).

[41] Mary Jean Bowman and W. Warren Haynes, *Resources and People in East Kentucky* (Baltimore: Johns Hopkins Press, 1963).

[42] Niles M. Hansen and Richard Yukhin, "Locational Preferences and Opportunity Costs in a Lagging Region: A Study of High School Seniors in Eastern Kentucky," *The Journal of Human Resources*, Summer 1970.

dence that many people do move and that many more would be willing to if they were provided help in relocating and received training in skills that are in demand elsewhere. The United States has made progress along these lines in recent years, through the Manpower Development and Training and other acts, but we shall wait until Chapter 18 before exploring these policies more thoroughly.

Summary

Labor is a factor of production. As a result, there is a demand for labor by employers who want to combine it with the other factors of production to produce goods and services. Under the assumptions of competition, the demand for labor varies inversely with its price (the wage rate). A shift in demand means that, at every wage rate, employers would hire more of it (in the case of an upward shift) or less of it (in the case of a decline in demand).

The supply of labor varies directly with its price, that is, the higher the wage, other things being equal, the greater the number of workers offering their services. The actual employment of a given type of labor in a particular labor market will be determined by the interaction of supply and demand. When supply and demand are in balance, the labor market is in equilibrium, and there is no tendency for the number employed or the wage rate to change.

The actual demand for labor is a derived demand; that is, it depends upon the demand for the goods and services that labor helps to produce. An increase in the wage of a particular type of labor, which would lead to a higher price for the product, by which the employer would be able to sell fewer units of it, would lead to a contraction in the amount of labor used. Also, since the factors of production are substitutable for one another, within limits, an increase in the wage rate could lead to less employment as another factor is substituted for it.

Since labor cannot be separated from the human beings who perform it, adjustments in the supply of labor take longer to work out and may entail human suffering. Nevertheless, supply does adjust upward and downward in response to shifts in employer demand.

According to the postulates of economic theory, labor should gravitate to those employments that offer the highest wages, other things being equal, and should continue to shift until real returns are equalized in all employments. This is the principle of equal advantage. Wage differences persist, however, due to nonmonetary advantages of some jobs, nonmonetary disadvantages of other jobs, costs of entry into certain occupations, inequality of abilities among people, geographic immobilities, man-made restrictions on entry into various employments, and lack of knowledge about job opportunities.

A seeming deviation from economic theory is the backward-bending supply curve of labor, that is, workers offering more labor in response to higher wages up to a point, after which, as the wage rises further, they offer less labor. The concept is not illogical, however, if we remember that labor also involves a sacrifice: a surrender of leisure in exchange for income with which to purchase goods and services. It is possible, therefore, that as people obtain more income, additional amounts of it would become less valuable than additional leisure; then, as they obtained more leisure, they might come to value income more, and so on. As a result, beyond a certain point the labor supply curve would look like a corkscrew.

Labor markets in practice may differ from the labor market in theory. In fact, labor markets may be classified by their degree of structuring, by their geographical extent, and as between those "internal" to the individual firm or external to it.

A free labor market implies worker mobility, which is also necessary from the points of view of individual workers, employers, and the efficiency of the economy. About one out of every ten workers changes his job each year, but it is difficult to classify this as "a lot," "a little," or "just enough." These job shifts involve changes in occupation, industry, and geographical regions.

The major influences on mobility are the rate of national economic growth, age, job tenure, sex, race, and occupation. A number of labor market specialists have claimed that labor mobility has not been in accord with economic theory. The empirical evidence, however, does indicate that worker mobility occurs in response to economic factors. This does not preclude the need for improvements in the actual functioning of the labor market.

One indication of a lack of sufficient labor mobility has been the existence of "depressed areas," or labor markets that have suffered from substantial and persistent labor surplus. Differential rates of regional growth are to be expected in a dynamic economy, but the fact that some regions become and remain depressed indicates that there are immobilities with respect to either labor or capital, or both. Greater mobility of labor could be achieved if people were aided in relocating and received training in skills that are in demand elsewhere, and progress has been made along those lines.

BIBLIOGRAPHY

Aronson, Robert L. *Components of Occupational Change in the United States, 1950–1960.* Technical Monograph Series No. 1. New York: New York State School of Industrial and Labor Relations, 1969.

Bakke, E. Wight, *et al. Labor Mobility and Economic Opportunity.* New York: Technology Press of MIT and Wiley, 1954.

Bancroft, Gertrude, and Stuart Garfinkle, "Job Mobility of Workers in 1961," Special Labor Force Report No. 35. Washington, D.C.: Bureau of Labor Statistics, 1963.

Berg, Elliot. "Backward Sloping Labor Supply Functions in Dual Economies —The African Case," *Quarterly Journal of Economics,* August 1961.

Bowman, Mary Jean, and W. Warren Haynes, *Resources and People in East Kentucky*. Baltimore: Johns Hopkins Press, 1963.

Gallaway, Lowell E. *Inter-Industry Labor Mobility in the United States 1957 to 1960*. Washington, D.C.: Social Security Administration, Government Printing Office, Research Report No. 18, 1967.

——. "An Economic Analysis of Policy for the Depressed Areas," *Industrial and Labor Relations Review,* July 1962.

Ginsburg, Woodrow I., E. Robert Livernash, Herbert S. Parnes, and George Strauss. *A Review of Industrial Relations Research,* Vol. I. Madison, Wisc.: Industrial Relations Research Association, 1970.

Jaffe, A. H., and R. O. Carleton. *Occupational Mobility in the United States, 1930–1950*. New York: Kings Crown Press, 1954.

Lansing, John B., and Eva Mueller. *The Geographic Mobility of Labor.* Ann Arbor: Institute for Social Research, University of Michigan, 1967.

Levitan, Sar A. *Federal Aid to Depressed Areas: An Evaluation of the Area Redevelopment Administration*. Baltimore: Johns Hopkins Press, 1964.

National Bureau of Economic Research. *Aspects of Labor Economics.* Princeton: Princeton University Press, 1962.

——. *The Measurement and Interpretation of Job Vacancies*. Princeton: Princeton University Press, 1966.

Palmer, Gladys L., Herbert S. Parnes, Richard C. Wilcock, Mary W. Herman, and Carol P. Brainerd. *The Reluctant Job Changer*. Philadelphia: University of Pennsylvania Press, 1962.

Reynolds, Lloyd G. *The Structure of Labor Markets.* New York: Harper & Bros., 1951.

Vatter, Harold G. "On the Folklore of the Backward Sloping Supply Curve," *Industrial and Labor Relations Review,* July 1961.

9 WAGES

Having examined the labor market in theory and practice, and having seen that the wage for any occupation is determined by the balance of supply and demand, let us now look more closely at the phenomenon of wages. We shall start by examining the nature of wages, finding, in the process, that it may mean many different things, depending upon who is looking at it and for what purpose. Next, we shall review some of the theories that were put forth to explain why wages were what they were, and why these earlier theories were discarded by later economists. Our major focus will then turn to the explanation of wages that became the most widely accepted among economists: the marginal productivity theory of the demand for a factor of production. We shall, however, also review the criticisms of this theory, which, some students of the labor market contend, does not jibe with reality. Since much of the criticism, as we shall see, stems from the theory's neglect of the rise of trade unionism, we shall briefly consider some institutional theories of wages. Finally, we shall make an attempt to integrate these institutional theories with the marginal productivity theory.

The Nature of Wages

Wages mean different things to different people. To the economist they are a necessary payment to one of the factors of production for its contribution to the production process. To the worker they are a source of income with which he can purchase goods and services to satisfy his wants. To the employer they are a cost of production. Despite these seemingly conflicting views of wages, all of them agree that wages are the price of labor. Yet, when people talk about "wages," they may actually be referring to a number of different things.

Wage Rates

When a job is advertised as paying $3 per hour, this refers to the "wage rate," that is, the amount or pay per time. In actual practice, however, the worker who accepts that job may receive more than the base rate of $3. In addition to the base rate, the job may have incentive features, whereby the worker will be paid more if he exceeds a certain quota of output; how much more will depend upon how many units above the standard he produces. If he works the lobster or night shifts, the worker will receive a differential to compensate for the strange hours, and, if he works more than forty hours per week, he will receive premium pay for the overtime hours.

Most blue-collar workers are paid hourly rates of wages. A large number of blue-collar workers, however, are paid on some sort of incentive basis. More than 60 percent of the workers in such industries as apparel and basic steel are paid either straight piece rates (common in the former) or some sort of incentive rate. A comprehensive survey of the prevalence of wage-incentive systems disclosed that in May 1958 as high a proportion as 27 percent of the nation's 11.5 million production and related workers in manufacturing were paid on an incentive basis.[1] A more recent Labor Department study, conducted between 1968 and 1970, however, found a trend away from incentive payments toward wider prevalence of time payments.[2] Only 20 percent of manufacturing plant workers in metropolitan areas were paid by incentive methods.

Earnings

Obviously, our discussion so far tells us that workers, whether they are paid on an hourly or incentive basis, will have earnings that may differ substantially from their base wage rates. "Earnings," therefore, refer to the total remuneration that they receive, including overtime rates of pay, shift premiums, and bonuses. Each month the Bureau of Labor Statistics publishes data on the average weekly earnings, weekly hours, and hourly earnings of production and nonsupervisory workers on private nonagricultural payrolls. In 1972, for example, the gross average hourly earnings in all private industry were $3.65, but they varied by industry, from $3.02 in wholesale and retail trade, to $3.18 in services; $3.45 in finance, insurance, and real estate; $3.81 in manufacturing; $4.38 in mining; $4.64 in transportation and public utilities; and $6.06 in contract construction.

Within each major industry category, earnings also vary sharply. In manufacturing, for example, average hourly earnings ranged in 1972 from $2.61 in apparel to $4.95 in petroleum and coal products. Similarly, within each of these industries, as one divides it into finer categories, there are further variations. Thus, within the apparel category, average hourly earnings were only $2.16 in men's and boys' work clothing, but they were $3.26 in men's and boys' suits and coats.

Hourly earnings, however, only partially determine a worker's total earnings, because the number of hours that he actually works is also important. Let us compare two manufacturing industries—machinery and printing and publishing—to see the influence of the number of hours worked on earnings. In 1972 average hourly earnings in printing and publishing were higher than

---

[1] E. Earl Lewis, "Extent of Incentive Pay in Manufacturing," *Monthly Labor Review*, May 1960, p. 460.

[2] John Howell Cox, "Time and Incentive Pay Practices in Urban Areas," *Monthly Labor Review*, December 1971, pp. 53–56.

in machinery: $4.48 versus $4.27. If both industries had averaged 40.0 hours per week of work, those in printing and publishing would have had a $8.40 weekly differential. The workers in the machinery industry, however, had an annual average of 42.0 hours of work each week as against only 37.9 hours in printing, with the result that the machinery workers had average weekly earnings of $179.34 and the printing and publishing workers only $169.79.

Typically, white-collar workers do not suffer these variations in weekly earnings because they are paid "salaries"; that is, they are paid by the week, regardless of the amount of work the employer has for them. Even high weekly earnings may not ensure the blue-collar worker income security, because he may be laid off for a number of weeks during the year. Some industries are particularly seasonal, due either to the weather, as in the case of construction, or to fashion, as in the case of women's clothing. White-collar workers have also enjoyed much greater security because they have typically had full work years, but of late some large companies have begun to "furlough" office staffs, too, during slack periods.

Take-Home Pay

When workers talk about their earnings, they do not normally mean their gross weekly earnings, but their "take-home pay," that is, the amount of money they have left after the deduction of federal and state income and social security taxes, any contributions they may be required to make toward company retirement and health and welfare plans, and union dues. The progressive nature of federal income taxes means that, as earnings rise, a greater proportion of the increase is taken in taxes. This fact, plus increases in social security taxes, means that increases in earnings are not equally reflected in take-home pay. Thus, between 1967 and 1972 gross average weekly earnings of production workers in private industry rose $33.94, but spendable average weekly earnings (gross less federal social security and income taxes) rose only $27.99 for the single worker and $29.93 for the worker with three dependents.[3] In recent years, the greater imposition and rise in rates of state income taxes have also served to keep increases in take-home pay much smaller than the increases in gross earnings.

Real Earnings

This section opened with the statement that, to the worker, wages are a source of income with which to purchase goods and services. But earnings are only a partial determinant of how much he can purchase, because this also depends upon the prices of those goods and services. When the price level is rising, workers may find that their "real earnings," that is, the amount of goods and services that their dollar earnings will buy, have declined.

---

[3] *Monthly Labor Review*, May 1972, p. 103.

Real earnings can be determined by dividing money earnings by an index of prices. The Bureau of Labor Statistics compiles such an index, the Consumer Price Index for Urban Wage Earners and Clerical Workers (CPI), and publishes the changes in it monthly. The CPI measures the average change in prices of goods and services purchased by families and single workers, and it represents all U.S. urban places having populations of more than 2,500. Separate indexes are compiled for twenty-five metropolitan areas.

The impact of price changes can be seen by comparing what transpired between 1969 and 1970. Gross average weekly earnings of production workers rose from $114.61 to $119.46, a gain of $4.85 in the period. However, although gross earnings rose 4.2 percent, real earnings actually declined, because the CPI rose even more, 5.9 percent. Measured in terms of 1967 dollars (the period used as the base óf 100 for computing changes in consumer prices), gross average weekly earnings declined 1.6 percent, from $104.38 in 1969 to $102.72 in 1970. It is no wonder that unions attempt to obtain automatic cost-of-living wage adjustments in collective bargaining with employers, as discussed in Chapter 6.

Real Take-Home Pay

The CPI also allows the computation of real take-home pay. As we saw a few paragraphs back, gross weekly earnings rose almost $18 in the three-year period from 1967 to 1970, but the gains in spendable earnings were much less. In terms of constant dollars, however, there was actually hardly any gain at all, as can be seen from Table 9.1. In fact, as shown in Table 9.1, in the

Table 9.1 Gross and Spendable Average Weekly Earnings of Production and Nonsupervisory Workers on Private Nonagricultural Payrolls, in Current and 1967 dollars, 1960–1972

| | Gross Average Weekly Earnings | | Spendable Average Weekly Earnings | | | |
| | | | Workers with No Dependents | | Workers with 3 Dependents | |
Year	Current $	1967 $	Current $	1967 $	Current $	1967 $
1960	$ 80.67	$ 90.95	$ 65.95	$73.95	$ 72.96	$82.25
1961	82.60	92.19	67.08	74.87	74.48	83.13
1962	85.91	94.82	69.56	76.78	76.99	84.98
1963	88.46	96.47	71.05	77.48	78.56	85.67
1964	91.23	98.31	75.04	80.78	82.57	88.88
1965	95.06	100.59	78.99	83.59	86.30	91.32
1966	98.82	101.67	81.29	83.63	88.66	91.21
1967	101.84	101.84	83.38	83.38	90.86	90.86
1968	107.73	103.39	86.71	83.21	95.28	91.44
1969	114.61	104.38	90.96	82.84	99.99	91.07
1970	119.46	102.72	95.94	82.49	104.61	89.95
1971	126.91	104.62	103.51	85.33	112.12	92.43
1972	135.78	108.36	111.37	88.88	120.79	96.40

Source: U.S. Department of Labor, Bureau of Labor Statistics.

entire period from 1965 to 1970, despite a $25 increase in gross average weekly earnings, real spendable earnings of workers, with either no or three dependents, failed to grow at all, and even declined a bit. The wage-price spiral, induced by the escalation of the Vietnam War, was clearly a treadmill on which workers pressed employers for higher wages only to find that taxes and higher prices left them in the same place they had been at the start. Only in 1971 did real earnings begin to rise once again.

Whose Average Earnings?

At this point, however, we must introduce a note of caution. Average earnings data can be misleading, because they lump together part-time workers and secondary wage earners with full-time workers who head families. If only family breadwinners were studied, it would disclose a significant increase in real earnings. A special tabulation of census data, prepared for a study of blue-collar workers by Professor Sar Levitan of George Washington University, shows that from 1965 to 1969 the average white married man, employed in a blue-collar job, had a 15 percent real increase in his annual income.[4] During the entire decade of the 1960s, white men in blue-collar jobs had real gains of 25 percent, which was about equal to the gains made by whites in all occupations.[5] Finally, income—which includes earnings from second jobs and from second earners, such as wives—rose still more. According to this study, at the start of the 1960s, white families headed by blue-collar workers had average incomes of $8,236, measured in 1969 dollars, and by the end of the decade this had risen to $10,731, a real gain of 30 percent. Although taxes took a bigger bite out of incomes by the end of the decade, blue-collar workers, as compared to other elements of American society, had not suffered disproportionately from increased tax burdens.

Family Budgets

Blue-collar discontent may become more understandable, however, if we examine family budgets prepared by the Bureau of Labor Statistics. In the autumn of 1967 the Bureau published the *City Worker's Family Budget for a Moderate Living Standard, Autumn, 1966* (CWFB), according to which the annual cost of a moderate living standard for a "well-established" family of four in urban areas of the United States averaged $9,191.[6] Geographic variations, however, were considerable, ranging from a high of $11,190 in Honolulu, Hawaii, to a low of $7,855 in nonmetropolitan areas in the South.

The bureau has also issued a lower, more minimum budget and a higher,

[4] Sar A. Levitan and Robert Taggart III, "Has the Blue-Collar Worker's Position Worsened?" *Monthly Labor Review*, September 1971, pp. 23–29; adapted from Sar A. Levitan (ed.), *Blue-Collar Workers* (New York: McGraw-Hill, 1971).
[5] Leonard S. Silk, "The Blue-Collar Blues," *The New York Times*, September 9, 1970, pp. 65, 73.
[6] *City Worker's Family Budget for a Moderate Living Standard, Autumn, 1966*, Bureau of Labor Statistics Bulletin 1570-1, October 25, 1967.

comfort-standard budget for the same type of four-person family: a thirty-eight-year-old man, his wife who is not employed outside the home, and two children, an eight-year-old girl and a thirteen-year-old boy. It has periodically updated the cost of each of these budgets, and by the spring of 1970 the lower budget had an annual cost of $6,960; the intermediate, $10,664; and the higher, $15,511. The average blue-collar family had an income on par with the intermediate budget level, but only a minority were at the higher budget level.

Yet the CWFB can also be a misleading indicator of a family's well being. Since the CWFB represents a "goal," to which people aspire, the Bureau of Labor Statistics cautions that "the budget total should not be compared directly with general levels of industrial wages and wage rates or with average family income of all urban families." Yet it is equally obvious that, if the budget represents a "goal" to which people aspire, blue-collar workers also aspire to that goal, and they will use the bargaining power that unionism provides them in an attempt to reach it. Thus, even increases in real income, if they fall short of aspirations, will leave workers unhappy and prepared to seek still more.

Wages as a Cost of Production

But let us return to the question of wages, exploring them now from the employer's point of view. As was stated at the beginning, wages, to the employer, are part of the cost of production. In this respect the employer is concerned with more than hourly wages: he is concerned with the entire payroll cost of each hour, which includes his contributions for old age, survivors, health, and disability insurance (Social Security); unemployment insurance; possible state disability insurance; private pension and health and welfare insurance; and an allocation of payments for time not worked (vacations, holidays) to the hours actually worked. According to the United States Chamber of Commerce, such payments were 30.8 percent of payroll in 1971 ($1.223 cents per payroll hour), ranging from 24.2 percent in department stores to 35.7 percent in the petroleum industry.[7]

But the most important concern of the employer is the labor cost per unit of output. In this respect high-paid workers may be relatively cheap if their "productivity" is high. Productivity refers to the output per unit of input of labor. Over the long run, productivity, as measured by the average annual increase in output per man-hour in the private economy, rises at a rate of about 3 percent.

Wages and Productivity

Unions that bargain with employers in industries that have been experiencing high rates of increase in output per man-hour sometimes use the rising pro-

---

[7] *Employee Benefits, 1971*, Chamber of Commerce of the United States, Washington, D.C., 1972.

ductivity as a basis for demanding above-average wage increases; their excuse is that the employers "can afford it." This, however, may not be the case, for output per man-hour is only a partial measure of productivity, ignoring the contribution of other factors of production, particularly capital. Indeed, the use of one input per unit of output may be reduced merely because the use of another is increased: less labor may be needed per unit of output because more capital equipment has been substituted for labor. As Professor Rees has stated, "If output per man-hour rises because more capital is used, the added output is not available for raising real wages until the costs of using this additional capital have been met."[8]

Increases in labor productivity in a particular industry, moreover, cannot be used as the basis for wage adjustments. If this were to be the case, then industry A, with a 2 percent increase in output per man-hour, would pay a 2 percent increase in wages, but industry B, which had a 4 percent increase in output per man-hour, would grant a 4 percent increase in wages. At compound interest, in time the workers in industry B would be earning fantastically more than those in A, and the nation would have a completely distorted wage structure. In terms of equity, moreover, the workers in the industries experiencing less rapid increases in productivity cannot be expected to accept a situation in which their real incomes would trail far behind what other workers were enjoying.

In the long run, of course, increases in national productivity (the average for all industries) are the source of real wage increases and the nation's rising standard of living. Taking the two decades from 1950 to 1970, we find that compensation per man-hour rose 190 percent: the increase in wages was more than twice as great as the increase in output per man-hour, which was only 75 percent. Workers, however, were not 190 percent better off, because the price level had also risen in the period. Taking account of the changes in the Consumer Price Index, we find that real compensation per man-hour rose 80 percent, pretty much in line with the increase in output per man-hour.

By now it has become obvious that if compensation rises faster than productivity, unit labor costs must rise. In the period 1950–1970, unit labor costs rose 70 percent. In fact, over the long run money wages do tend to rise faster than productivity, which leads to an increase in unit labor costs. Employers facing higher costs of production will, to the degree possible, try to pass them on to the consumers of their products through increases in prices, in order to maintain their profit margins. Thus, the fact that worker compensation tends to increase faster than labor productivity is part of the explanation of the tendency of prices to rise over the long run. At this point we shall only note this tendency, but we shall explore its implications more fully in Chapter 13; we turn now, instead, to theories of wage determination.

---

[8] Albert Rees, "Patterns of Wages, Prices and Productivity," in *Wages, Prices, Profits, and Productivity* (New York: American Assembly, 1959), p. 23.

The History of Wage Theory

With the advent of capitalist industrialism and the free labor market, under which the productive services of human beings were bought and sold in the same way as commodities, economists began to try to explain why wages were what they were. In order to do so they had come up with a "theory" of wages. But what is a theory? In simple terms, it is nothing more than a general principle that helps to explain a phenomenon. For a theory to be accepted as correct, it must be supported by evidence.

A theory, therefore, gives one the ability to predict what will occur as a result of certain actions. This is most obvious in the physical sciences, where other things can be held constant; thus, the chemist can predict with accuracy that mixing two parts of hydrogen with one part of oxygen will produce water. Theorizing in the social sciences presents greater difficulties, however, because other things cannot be held constant. Economic theory may tell us that, if wages go up in a given industry, employment will decline, other things being equal; but other things may not remain equal, consumer tastes may shift and consumers may be willing to buy more of the product, even at a higher price.

Despite these problems of the absence of laboratory conditions, economists must evolve explanations of economic phenomena. With respect to wages, this means explaining differences in wages for different groups and the general level of wages, in both the short run and the long run. As we shall see, a wage theory would be advanced and accepted for a period of time because it seemed to explain events in the real world, but then evidence would begin to accumulate that would seem to contradict important elements of the theory. At this point a new theory would have to be advanced, and it would gain acceptance as long as it was supported by evidence from what actually was taking place in the labor market.

The Subsistence Theory

In the early days of capitalist industrialism, wages were extremely low and the lot of the workers very harsh. The task of economists, therefore, was to explain why this was so, and the explanation that they came up with was far from optimistic, helping to earn for economics the appellation "the dismal science." The first generally accepted explanation was the subsistence theory of wages put forth by the English economist David Ricardo in 1817.[9] According to Ricardo, "the *natural price* of labour is that price which is necessary to enable the labourers, one with another, to subsist and to perpetuate their race, without either increase or diminution."

---

[9] David Ricardo, *The Principles of Political Economy and Taxation* (New York: Dutton, 1911; original edition, 1817). An excellent source of readings on wage theory, historical and modern, is Campbell R. McConnell (ed.), *Perspectives on Wage Determination: A Book of Readings* (New York: McGraw-Hill, 1970). A selection from Ricardo's work can be found on pp. 7–10.

By adopting the Reverend Robert Malthus' principle of population, that population tends to press upon the means of subsistence, Ricardo's theory became an "iron law" of wages. If the interaction of supply and demand were to push the market price of labor—the actual wages paid to workers by employers—above the "natural price," then the high wages would induce workers to have more children. The subsequent increase in population would, within a few years (this was a period in which children went to work before the age of ten), augment the supply of labor, thus driving the market price of labor back down to its natural price. On the other hand, if the short-run wage were to drop below the subsistence level, starvation and increased infant mortality would reduce the supply of labor, and in time the long-run natural price of labor would reassert itself.

Ricardo's iron law of wages was a most harsh doctrine, for it left no room for any improvement in the conditions of workers' lives. Ricardo himself recognized this, and tried to fit the higher wages that English workers enjoyed as compared to workers in less developed countries into his theory by asserting that the subsistence wage "depends on the habits and customs of the people." Yet the theory was unable to explain the rise in real wages that English workers experienced over time: to assert that this was due to a change in "habits and customs" would have explained nothing, for in that case the subsistence theory would merely have said that wages are whatever they are.

The Wages-Fund Theory

The secular rise in real wages, therefore, demanded a new theory. If the old theory—Ricardo's iron law—could not explain a real increase in wages, the new one would, but not at the price of a reduction in capital formation. If we recall from Chapter 5, when we examined early legal attitudes toward trade unionism, we saw that in the early period of a nation's economic development, the stress is on capital formation. The way in which a nation can accumulate capital is to consume less than it produces, save the surplus, and then convert it into capital goods to be used in further production. Immediate increases in consumption, therefore, would be at the expense of capital formation and detract from a nation's ability to increase real incomes in the long run.

The new theory of wages that gained dominance in the middle of the nineteenth century—the "wages-fund" theory—was based on this concept of the need for capital formation, and its leading exponent was the liberal economist and philosopher John Stuart Mill.[10] The wages-fund theory was integrated within classical economic doctrine, and viewed "supply and demand" as determining the average wage rate. But, as McConnell points out, "the concepts of supply and demand were envisioned crudely as absolute

---

[10] John Stuart Mill, *Principles of Political Economy* (New York: Appleton, 1923; original edition, 1848).

amounts of stocks."[11] There was a fixed fund of capital from which employers could pay wages, and the average wage could be determined simply by dividing the wages fund by the number of workers.

The wages-fund theory can be explained in terms of a simple functional relationship: $W = f(C)$, wages are a function of capital. Out of each year's production, certain amounts must go for equipment, raw materials, and the entrepreneur's profits; the remainder is available for labor. If more were to go to labor, then there would be less to reinvest, and the decline in the rate of capital growth would undermine the size of the wages fund.

The critics disagreed with the theory's central notion that there was a fixed stock, no matter how defined, from which to make wage payments. Instead, they viewed production as a flow of goods and services; workers were paid out of this current flow rather than from a fixed fund deriving from production in a previous period. Thus, there was no predetermined wages fund, and an increase in the current flow of production, through an increase in the supply of the factors of production or through their more efficient use, could lead to higher wages.

The Surplus-Value Theory

Before examining the theory that arose to replace the wages-fund doctrine, let us look at one theory of wages that gained adherents among the opponents of the private market economy but was never accepted by the dominant school of Western economics. This was Karl Marx's "surplus value" theory of wages, which we referred to in our review of theories of unionism. Following in the tradition of the classical economists—Smith, Malthus, and Ricardo—Marx identified human effort as the source of all value. To Marx, the other factors of production only represented the labor that was embodied in them; the value of capital (e.g., machinery) was determined by the amount of labor that had been required to produce it. Any product, therefore, was simply an embodiment of current and past labor power and nothing more.[12]

The employers' greater bargaining power, however, enables them to "exploit" the workers by paying them less than the full value of their daily output. Thus, in the Marxian view, profit is "surplus value" that is withheld from the workers: it is not earned by the capitalist, but simply expropriated from the workers. The Marxian theory of wages was even more dismal than the subsistence doctrine, because, while the latter did not leave room for higher wages, the exploitation theory posited a deterioration.

According to the wages-fund theory, a growth in the capital stock could lead to higher wages, but Marx saw capital accumulation as actually hurting labor. It did so, first, by its substitution of capital for labor, which led to

---

11 McConnell, *op. cit.*, p. 11.

12 Karl Marx, *Capital, The Communist Manifesto and Other Writings* (New York: Modern Library, 1932), pp. 20–47. These selections are extracted from his famous work, *Capital*, which was originally published in 1867.

technological unemployment and the creation of an "industrial reserve army." This industrial reserve of unemployed, its members anxious to get jobs at any wage, only served to strengthen the employers' bargaining position vis à vis labor and drive down wages. Furthermore, since labor is the sole source of value, increased use of capital cannot increase profits, and there is, therefore, a natural tendency for the rate of profit to decline. In order for the capitalists to maintain their profits, they would have to take more and more "surplus value," resulting in the increasing impoverishment of the working force.

History, of course, has proved Marx's exploitation theory as wrong as the subsistence and wages-fund theories, for real wages have risen, and very dramatically, in the past century. All of these theories stressed the supply of labor but overlooked the role of demand in the determination of wages, and Marx's theory suffered most from its insistence on labor as the source of all value. Indeed, Marx himself had trouble handling it, and he could do so only by distinguishing between what he called "value in use" (the labor embodied in a commodity) and "value in exchange" (the price at which the commodity is sold), the difference between the two being "surplus value." With the development of the concept of marginal utility, the problem of "value" was resolved, and from this flowed a new theory to explain the level of wages, the "marginal productivity" theory, which we shall now examine.

The Marginal Productivity Theory

The marginal productivity theory is essentially a demand theory, in that the value of a commodity depends upon what consumers pay for the last unit of it. It is, at the same time, a theory of income distribution, because it determines the share that each of the factors of production is to receive. The theory was developed in the late nineteenth century, essentially by John Bates Clark in the United States and Alfred Marshall in England; its most elaborate restatement was made by Professor Hicks of Oxford University in 1932.[13]

The marginal productivity theory is part and parcel of the generally accepted theory of pricing under competitive conditions. Let us, therefore, examine it very closely. As was stated in the last chapter, the wage rate of any group of workers will be determined by the interaction between demand and supply. Now the question that arises is, "What determines the demand for labor?"

In a profit-motivated economy, it is quite obvious that employers do not hire workers because they want to be good citizens and provide them with jobs. Private businessmen, who must be concerned with competition in the sale of the goods and services they produce, will hire workers only if thereby they can increase their own earnings. The proprietor of a retail store, for

---

[13] John Bates Clark, *The Distribution of Wealth* (New York: Kelley & Millman, 1956; original edition, 1899); Alfred Marshall, *Principles of Economics* (London: Macmillan, 1947; original edition, 1890); and John R. Hicks, *The Theory of Wages* (New York: Macmillan, 1932).

example, would hire an additional salesman only if this would increase the volume of his sales to the point that it would add to the owner's profit; he would not hire him at $100 per week if this added only $90 per week to his net earnings, because then he would have suffered a diminution of $10 per week in profits. If the additional salesman could sell enough goods to increase the employer's profit by more than $100 per week, however, he would not only hire him, he would continue to add more salesmen as long as they increased his net earnings. In the more precise language of economics, a firm would hire additional labor if the added cost (marginal cost) of that additional labor were less than the added money returns (marginal revenue) that its hire would generate.

This, of course, leads to another question: "What determines the marginal revenue product of labor?" Two things determine it: (1) the additional, or marginal, product that will be produced with the additional labor; (2) the price at which the product can be sold. Since at this point we are discussing a competitive product market, in which no producer is large enough to affect the price of the commodity by variations in the total of his output, the second factor—price—is assumed to be constant.

Competitive Conditions

In a competitive market, therefore, in which the price of the product is given, the demand for labor by a firm is determined basically by consumer demand for the product and the marginal product of labor (the addition to total product resulting from the employment of additional workers). As more workers are hired the total product rises at an accelerating rate, but beyond a certain point the total product will increase at a decelerating rate, and eventually even decline. This is an application of the principle of diminishing returns, and can be stated as follows: for the individual firm, the addition of labor to a fixed quantity of capital (or land) will yield increasing returns up to a point, beyond which the returns will diminish. That is, if an employer has a plant with a certain number of machines, he can increase the number of units of product by hiring more workers, until all machines are manned; by adding still more workers to service the machine operators (bringing them raw materials, taking away finished units, repairing broken machines, and so forth) he can increase total output further, but at a slower rate. If he hired too many men, they would eventually begin to get in each other's way, and total product would actually decline.

Figure 9.1 depicts the rise in total product as more units of the variable resource, in this case labor, are used. We can see that total output rises rapidly at first, then more slowly, and that it eventually declines. Average product is obtained simply by dividing total product by the number of units of output. Marginal product is the amount that total product changes when one unit more, or less, of the variable resource is used. Marginal product is largest when total product is rising most rapidly, it is 0 when there is no rise

Figure 9.1 Total, Average, and Marginal Product

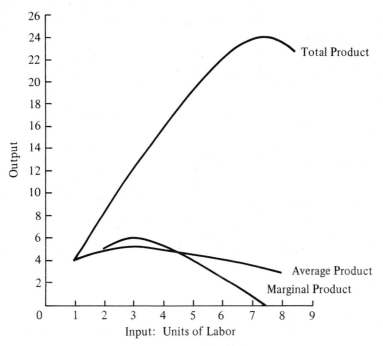

in total product, and it is negative when total product declines. When the average product curve is rising, marginal product is greater than average, but when the average product curve is falling, marginal product is less than average.

Table 9.2 Marginal Productivity Calculations under Perfect Competition

(1)	(2)	(3)	(4)	(5)	(6)	(7)
Units of Labor	Total Product	Price of Product	Value of Total Product	Marginal Physical Product	Value of Marginal Product	Marginal Revenue Product
1	4	$15	$60	—	—	—
2	8	15	120	4	$60	$60
3	11	15	165	3	45	45
4	13	15	195	2	30	30
5	14	15	210	1	15	15
6	13	15	195	−1	−15	−15

An example of marginal productivity is presented in Table 9.2, which gives a daily production and cost schedule for a hypothetical factory. The example shows that as more units of labor are applied to a given amount of capital, the total product rises, from 4 to 8 to 11 to 13 and to 14, but as each succeeding unit of labor is added, the total product increases by a smaller amount—this is marginal physical product (shown in Column 5). Beyond five units of labor, moreover, total product actually falls, and the marginal product thus is negative.

Continuing with our example, let us try to see how many workers the employer would actually hire, given this schedule of output and the fact that the product sells in the competitive market for $15 each. As can be seen in Table 9.2, if the price of labor were $3.50 per hour (or $28.00 for an eight-hour day), the employer would hire four workers, for this would enable him to maximize his revenues. If he hired only three workers, he would be sacrificing $2 per day in additional earnings, because a fourth worker would cost him only $28, but he could sell what that worker added to total output (two units of the product) for $30. The employer, however, would not hire a fifth worker, because he would have to pay him $28, but the value of the additional product would be only $15. Thus, the principle of marginal productivity tells us that employers will hire units of labor up until the point at which the value of their marginal product (MVP) is equal to the cost of the labor.

Labor Market Equilibrium

While the principle of marginal productivity tells us how many workers the individual firm will hire, it also becomes an explanation of the wage rate in the entire economy. Again, assuming a competitive situation, that is, both employers and workers seek to maximize their advantages—homogeneity of a given grade of labor, labor mobility, and sufficient information—then labor must be allocated in the most efficient manner possible and the market must be cleared. Each firm in every industry hires labor up to the point where the value of its marginal product is equal to the wage. The wage rate of labor of a given quality will be the same in all industries; otherwise, based upon the maximizing assumption, workers will leave lower-paying industries for higher-paying ones (those where products are more desired by consumers), and labor will continue to shift until the marginal value product of labor is the same in all industries. This serves to ensure the most efficient allocation of labor, because the lower-paying industries are those in which labor MVP is lower, and the shifting results in the highest possible value of output per input of labor.

Not only must labor MVP be the same in all industries, but all demands for labor at the market price must be filled, and all workers willing to work at the market wage must be hired. Let us assume that, for some reason, the wage rate is set too high, that is, above the marginal value product of labor. If this were the case, some labor would not be hired. Under these conditions the unemployed workers would be willing to accept jobs at a lower wage rate, and their competition for existing jobs would drive the wage rate down until it was equal to the value of the marginal product at full employment. At that point there would be full employment.

Monopoly

The marginal productivity principle has been subjected to a good deal of criticism because of its assumption of competitive equilibrium when markets are actually far from perfect. Yet the principle is not obviated because of the existence of noncompetitive conditions in product markets. There is a difference, however, which we shall try to illustrate in Table 9.3. In this case we assume that there is imperfection in the product market. A firm might, through control of patents, have a monopoly in the production of a particular good; a complete monopoly, however, is extremely rare. A more likely situation in some industries is oligopoly, in which a few large companies dominate production: such a situation arises largely as a result of economies of scale and the need for huge agglomeration of capital in order to produce efficiently. Oligopoly is typical in such industries as automobiles, rubber tires, steel, and electrical equipment. A third type of imperfection is monopolistic competition, whereby each producer differentiates his particular product, either through styling or advertising, to the point where consumers regard it as different from other, similar products. Soap and cosmetic manufacturers expend large sums of money in the attempt to differentiate their products.

Table 9.3 Marginal Productivity Calculations under Imperfect Competition

(1)	(2)	(3)	(4)	(5)	(6)	(7)
Units of Labor	Total Product	Price of Product	Value of Total Product	Marginal Physical Product	Value of Marginal Product	Marginal Revenue Product
1	4	$15	$60	—	—	—
2	8	14	112	4	$56	$52
3	11	13	143	3	39	31
4	13	12	156	2	24	13
5	14	11	154	1	11	− 2
6	13	10	130	−1	−10	−14

Under perfect competition, each individual firm has no influence over price because consumers can turn to another seller for their purchases, the products of all the firms in the industry being substitutable for each other: for example, one farmer's bushel of wheat is the same as the next farmer's bushel of wheat. Imperfection in a product market, of whatever type, however, implies that there is a lack of substitutes for the employer's product, either because he supplies a significant proportion of the total output of that product or because his product is in some way differentiated from those of other firms. The employer, therefore, faces a typically downward-sloping demand curve, the same way that an individual industry does. This means that in order to sell more units of his product, the employer must continually lower the price. Thus, although the marginal physical product of labor remains the same as under competition, its value does not. Under monopolistic conditions, then, the value of the marginal product (MPP times the price of the product) does not indicate the change in the employer's revenues, for the price at which that output is sold declines as more units are produced. To determine the change in employer revenues—the marginal revenue product —we must multiply marginal physical product (MPP) by the marginal revenue (MR) arising from the sale of an additional unit of output.[14] In our example, therefore, at a daily wage of $28 the employer would hire only three workers.

The essential difference between the competitive and monopolistic situations is that in the former the value of the marginal product is equal to the marginal revenue product, but in the latter it is not. Thus, under competition the employer will hire workers up to the point at which the value of the marginal product is equal to the wage rate, but under imperfect competition the employer would hire workers up to the point at which the marginal revenue product was equal to the wage.

Factor Proportions

In the last chapter we talked about the substitution of machinery for labor when the latter became too expensive relative to the former. To fully understand what this means, we must again use marginal analysis, for the marginal productivity principle also explains the amount of one factor of production as compared to another that an employer will utilize in the production process. This flows from the fact that labor and capital are to some extent substitutes, and employers can use different proportions of each to obtain the same output. This is called a "production function," and a simple production function with two factors (labor and capital) can be depicted graphically by an "isoquant" map, that is, a set of lines showing equal product for varying combinations of inputs. Every point on a given isoquant represents the same output, although the latter can be produced with different combinations of capital and labor. In Figure 9.2 QQ is an isoquant that represents the various combinations of capital and labor that would produce ten units of a product. The employer, therefore, could use OB amount of labor with OM amount of capital, or he could use more capital, ON, and less labor, OC, to produce the same ten units. Which combination of factors will an employer actually select? The answer is obvious: he will choose that combination of labor and capital that costs the least money.

Since employers can use different factor proportions to obtain the same output, and since they seek to obtain the largest possible output, they will tend to use more of the less expensive inputs than of the expensive ones. This is readily observable by comparing a highly industrialized country, such

---

[14] For an excellent presentation of the marginal productivity principle under imperfect competition, see Allan M. Cartter, *Theory of Wages and Employment* (Homewood, Ill.: Richard D. Irwin, 1959), pp. 29–31.

Figure 9.2   A Simple Production Function

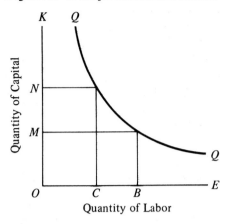

Quantity of Labor

as the United States, with industrially underdeveloped China or India. In the United States capital is plentiful and relatively cheap, but labor is relatively expensive; in India or China, capital is very scarce, but there is an abundance of labor, with the result that capital is very expensive relative to labor. When building roads in the United States, therefore, construction contractors use heavy earth-moving equipment and few workers, but in India they would tend to rely much more on the use of lots of people working with picks, shovels, and wheelbarrows.

The relative expensiveness of a factor of production depends upon its output relative to its price as compared to the output of another factor relative to its price. If an employer could obtain two more units of output for an expenditure of a dollar on capital, and only one more unit for a dollar spent on labor, he would, of course, spend the extra dollar on capital. The profit-maximizing employer would thus substitute one factor of production for another until the relation between the marginal product and marginal cost of any factor would be the same as the relation between the marginal product and marginal cost of any other factor; or where:

$$\frac{\text{mp (labor)}}{\text{mc (labor)}} = \frac{\text{mp (capital)}}{\text{mc (capital)}}$$

At this point there would be equilibrium, and hence no tendency to replace one factor by the other, because no additional profits could be made by further substitution.

Once a particular production function is chosen it cannot be quickly changed. Thus, in the short run we assume constancy of the production function, and this comprises part of what is meant by "other things being equal." In the long run, however, as new technology and organizational structures are introduced into an operation, the production function can be altered.

That this principle works in practice is clearly evident when viewing American industry, where tens of thousands of engineers are employed for the purpose of devising new machinery and methods of manufacture that economize on the use of labor in the production process. Not all new techniques, however, are actually put into operation, because many of them are deemed to be too expensive, which means simply that the increased output of the capital is less than could be secured by an equal outlay on labor. As wages rise, a point is reached at which the increased output of the capital is greater than could be achieved by an equal outlay in wages, and the machine is substituted for labor.

The Supply of Labor Under Competition and Monopoly

One other aspect of wage determination that deserves exploration, in which there again is deviation between competitive and noncompetitive conditions, is the supply of labor to the individual firm. We have seen that the demand for labor is indicated by the marginal revenue product curve. But what about the supply?

In a perfectly competitive situation we need not worry about the supply, because it is given: the supply curve of labor to the firm is horizontal; that is, the single employer hires such a small part of the total supply that he cannot affect its price. Let us take as an example a small machine shop employing half a dozen machinists at $4 per hour each. If this firm experiences a large pickup in business (15 to 20 percent), it would probably have to hire one more machinist, which it would do without having to pay the extra man a wage any different than that being paid its present complement (which is the going rate in that labor market). Labor supply to the individual firm under perfect competition is infinitely elastic, as depicted in Figure 9.3a.

The large firm employing a few hundred machinists may not, however, find this to be the case. Since it employs a large portion of the machinists in the particular labor market, any significant increase in its output would necessitate the adding of many additional machinists. The result would be a tendency to push up the wage rate for machinists in the labor market. While one more machinist would be available at the going rate of $4.00 per hour, attracting fifty more might require offering $4.50 an hour. The supply curve of labor to the large firm, therefore, tends to slope upward. Labor supply under imperfect competition is depicted in Figure 9.3b.

This upward slope of the supply curve introduces a further complication. The firm cannot hire additional workers at a wage rate higher than the one it pays its present employees, who would regard such action as intolerable discrimination; besides, since their employer has driven up the machinist wage rate, they would tend to quit unless he paid the higher rate to them, too. As a result, the cost of additional workers to the large firm will be the wage it must pay the additional workers ($4.50 per hour), plus the increase ($.50 per hour) that it must add to the wage of its present employees.

Figure 9.3a   Labor Supply to the Firm: Perfect Competition

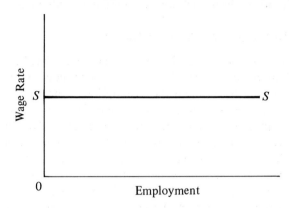

Figure 9.3b   Labor Supply to the Firm: Imperfect Competition

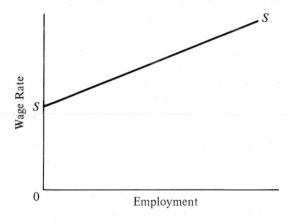

Recapitulation

At this point let us summarize some of our main points about the marginal productivity principle. We have said that it is a part of general equilibrium price theory. In this case, we are dealing with the price of labor, but the same type of analysis would apply to the other factors of production, capital and land. Factor substitutability, moreover, means that the price of labor is related to the price of the other factors, and in an industrialized country this particularly means capital. Marginal productivity determines the demand for labor by the individual firm, and it governs wages for the entire economy. In the latter sense it is a long-run theory, because it takes time to work out deviations: the movement of workers from lower- to higher-paying industries, or the competition from the unemployed to force the wage rate down to the marginal revenue product. Obviously, then, wages may not be equal to marginal productivity at any given moment of time, but they tend toward it.

Furthermore, to the extent that there are digressions, these will activate the forces that will move wages back toward marginal productivity.

Criticisms of the Marginal Productivity Theory

As in the cases of the other theories explaining wages that have been examined, marginal productivity has also never been without its critics. Part of the criticism has been based upon the assumptions concerning a competitive situation, but, as has been indicated, the principle of marginal productivity still applies, though in a different manner, to noncompetitive situations.

Another type of criticism has dealt with what was alleged to be the inapplicability in practice of marginal productivity because employers cannot determine the value productivity of labor. In an empirical attempt to test the applicability of marginal productivity, Professor Lester surveyed businessmen, and their responses indicated that they rarely made any changes in employment because of changes in wages.[15] According to employers, employment was adjusted in conformance with sales volume, not the level of wages. To Lester this meant that wages were not determined by marginal productivity.

Professor Cartter has attempted to refute this seeming denial of marginal productivity analysis by questioning the accuracy of the employers' answers. He does not doubt their honesty, but contends that they confuse symptoms with causes in explaining their troubles. His explanation runs along the following lines:[16] following a wage increase that increases the cost of production, the employer does not reduce employment, but when the occasion arises he raises his prices in order to restore his markup. The higher price of his product means that fewer units of them can be sold, and in time inventories pile up until he is forced to cut back production and reduce employment. Employment is reduced until the equality between labor's marginal value product and the wage rate is restored. "If we now approach this employer, or for that matter, his employees, they will almost invariably say that the decline in employment was 'caused' by a decline in market demand."[17] Demand, however, did not decrease, the amount demanded did, and the reason was the price increase, which was necessary to take account of the upward shift in marginal costs resulting from the wage increase.

While not rejecting marginal productivity analysis as explaining long-run adjustments, Professor Reynolds contends that it is inadequate to explain the behavior of wages and employment in short periods of time.[18] In the short run production functions are often discontinuous; that is, production processes are "lumpy" and employers cannot quickly substitute capital for

---

[15] Richard Lester, "Shortcomings of Marginal Analysis for Wage-Employment Problems," *American Economic Review*, March 1946, pp. 63–82.

[16] Cartter, *op. cit.*, pp. 40, 41.

[17] *Ibid.*, p. 40.

[18] Lloyd G. Reynolds, "Toward a Short-Run Theory of Wages," *American Economic Review*, June 1948, pp. 289–308.

labor when wages rise. Furthermore, if profit margins are reduced by the resulting higher costs, employers will find other ways to reduce costs, such as through better routing and holding down scrap wastage, than through substituting machinery for labor. But such improvements might very well affect the amount of labor relative to capital that the firm does employ.

The argument concerning the inability to substitute capital for labor in the short run depends very much upon the industry and the technology being used. Obviously, very expensive, highly automated processes, which have only recently been introduced in a plant, cannot easily be changed overnight. Yet many plants have found that labor costs can be significantly reduced, not necessarily through the purchase of vast new amounts of equipment, but through simple modifications of existing equipment, for example, adding another jigger to a particular machine. These simple, day-to-day changes, while they do not show up in the data as significant substitutions of capital for labor, in their aggregate may be quite significant changes in production functions.

Another type of serious criticism of the marginal productivity theory of wages arises from the fact that continuous full employment of labor has not been achieved. This used to be blamed on the obstinacy of workers, who were charged with being unwilling to accept wages commensurate with MVP. In the 1930s, however, John Maynard Keynes revised economic theory by showing that it was possible to have equilibrium in the labor market at below full-employment levels.

The lack of conformity of the actual operation of the economy with the competitive ideal has been a source of severe criticisms. It is true that monopolistic power in product and labor markets can inhibit the most efficient allocation and utilization of labor. Rigidities and immobilities in the labor market, as explained in the last chapter, do prevent equalization of wage rates, which marginal productivity analysis purports should occur. Its model of an "ideal" world must be an abstraction from reality, but the theory can be used to understand that reality better.

Indeed, as a society we may want to have deviations from the competitive model. The competitive model, for example, postulates a free labor market of atomized workers. Through experience, society concluded that this was not a good situation, so it permitted, and indeed encouraged, the banding together of workers into trade unions. Similarly, society has not taken the position that workers should be paid only what the free labor market decrees, for it has legislated minimum wages that may be above the value of the marginal product in some cases. Marginal productivity analysis, however, provides a basis for judging what may be the consequences of these actions.

The Institutional Approach to Wage Determination

The rise of powerful trade unions engaged in collective bargaining with employers, large and small, in a host of industries, has led some observers to conclude that more can be learned about wage determination from a study of the institutions of unions and collective bargaining than from marginal productivity analysis. After all, about one-third of employees have their wage rates set through collective bargaining, and an even larger percentage are influenced by the results of major negotiations. Attempts, therefore, have been made to explain the behavior of unions.

Unions as Political Institutions

These critics of marginal productivity analysis, led by Kerr and Ross, focus on the nature of unions.[19] In their view economists have erred in picturing unions as sellers of labor or attempting to maximize something, whether the wage bill, employment, or what have you. Unions are seen rather as political, not economic, institutions.

In Kerr's view a union can be analyzed as an institution separate and apart from its members. While the members may be interested in wealth maximization, the union pursues its own goals, which include its sovereignty, its survival, and its growth. Moreover, the goals of the members and of the union can conflict, and in those cases the union will act on its own behalf, not on the behalf of its members. "When the 'chips are down' it is more concerned with the power of the institution than the wealth of its members. It will sacrifice the latter for the former both in the short run and the long run."[20]

Ross also sees the union as a political institution, but he believes that it is more responsive to the membership than does Kerr. Union wage policy, in fact, is not based upon any considerations of its effect on employment, but is purely a reaction to the members' feelings about the equity of their wages. Workers judge the rightness of their pay by reference to that of other workers to whom they normally compare themselves. For example, when a city's policemen receive an increase in salary, the firemen are convinced that they deserve a similar raise.

Wages won by one group of workers, therefore, become a "coercive comparison" that must be won by the other group, which compares itself to the former, regardless of its economic impact. Since the union representing the workers is so concerned with the force of equitable comparisons, it gives no consideration to the employment effect of a wage increase. Besides, as a political institution the union will cater to the majority, who will continue to support it on the basis of its having won a large wage increase even at the expense of the jobs of a minority of the members.

Evidence of the coercive comparison effect of wage increases won by one union upon another can be found in the competition that was exhibited

---

[19] Clark Kerr, "Economic Analysis and the Study of Industrial Relations," in Mc-Connell, *op. cit.*, pp. 81–84; and Arthur M. Ross, *Trade Union Wage Policy* (Berkeley: University of California Press, 1948).

[20] Kerr, *ibid.*, p. 83.

by rival AFL and CIO unions in the years preceding the merger of the two federations. Even unions that are not rivals, and that organize workers in entirely different industries, are highly influenced by what another achieves in collective bargaining: whatever the Autoworkers win in their negotiations with the automobile manufacturers becomes a compelling target for the Steelworkers in their subsequent bargaining with the major steel producers. The force of equitable comparison thus links together separate wage bargains into an interdependent system, and pattern setting, whereby one union after another gets pretty much the same wage/fringe package, is the order of the day, even though economic conditions may differ by industry.

To Ross it appeared that "impersonal market forces" were no longer operative in wage determination, having been supplanted by "conscious human decisions." This being the case, he saw economic theory as having little to offer in studies of the labor market. He advocated instead that scholars adopt an interdisciplinary approach, integrating political science, psychology, law, and economics, in order to arrive at a realistic and meaningful explanation of wages under collective bargaining.

As was to be expected, few economists were prepared to agree with Ross on the irrelevancy of their discipline to the analysis of labor market behavior. Without demeaning the contributions that might be made by other disciplines in explaining human behavior, they reacted sharply to the idea that marginal productivity analysis was obsolete. Let us, therefore, examine some of the rejoinders to the Kerr-Ross position.

Unions as Economic Institutions

Obviously, any answer to their position had to begin with an analysis of the labor union. To the claim that the unions pursued policies inimical to their members' interests and desires, McConnell argued that unions are essentially democratic institutions, and in most cases, therefore, they will act in accord with the major interests of their members.[21] Should they fail to do so, members may desert them for rival unions or for nonunion status, or, even more likely, change the leadership. There are numerous examples in recent years of union leaders having been deposed because the members believed that the policy the union was following was wrong.

Professor Dunlop has posed a model of a trade union that is very different from the Kerr-Ross model. To him the union is "composed of wage earners in a particular market, either actually employed or willing to work under some conditions, who have formed an enterprise with leadership to act as their collective agent."[22] Recognizing that some of the criticism of economic

---

[21] Campbell R. McConnell, "Institutional Economics and Trade Union Behavior," *Industrial and Labor Relations Review*, April 1955; reprinted in McConnell, *op. cit.*, pp. 85–87.

[22] John T. Dunlop, *Wage Determination under Trade Unions* (New York: Augustus M. Kelley, 1950).

analysis of union behavior may have stemmed from a concentration on one type of behavior, which could be shown not to exist in another case, Dunlop offers a number of different things that unions may attempt to maximize under varying conditions. One union may attempt to achieve the largest possible wage bill, in which case it is concerned with the employment effects of its policy, but is willing to sacrifice some workers to unemployment if the wage increases of the remaining workers are greater than the lost wages of those laid off. Another union may take account of unemployment benefits and attempt to maximize the wage bill it can extract from the employers, but include in that the funds for the support of the unemployed. In still another case the union will be responsive only to the employed majority of the members and attempt to maximize the wage bill of employed workers. Or a union may attempt to maximize employment.

A particular union's objectives, moreover, may change from one time period to another. In a period of economic expansion, when the demand for labor is rising, the union will likely be more concerned with wage increases than any adverse effects these may have on employment. On the other hand, in periods of economic decline, when the demand for labor is falling, pursuing the objective of maximizing the wage bill would necessitate the union's giving much greater consideration to the employment effects of any wage increase.

The important point to Dunlop's work is that by postulating these varying maximizing objectives, wage-employment behavior can be predicted from each of them. In other words, economic analysis can be applied to wage determination under trade unions.

The Interaction of Institutional and Economic Forces

One problem with debates among scholars is that one tends to attempt to demolish everything that his "opponent" says in defending his own position. This is indeed unfortunate, because there may be elements of truth in each party's arguments. Thus, Kerr and Ross have offered valuable insights, though far from universal in application, into some trade union behavior, without necessarily undermining marginal productivity analysis.

In fact, Professor Reder claims that the disagreement reflects, in good part, a difference in viewpoint. "Students of labor problems are concerned with the *process* by which wages are set; e.g. they are concerned with the effect one collective bargaining agreement has upon another signed soon after; how temporary product market situations influence the terms employers offer unions, or how internal union politics influence union demands."[23] The institutional approach has much to say about such matters, and marginal productivity analysis much less. On the other hand, however wages are determined,

---

[23] Melvin W. Reder, "Wage Determination in Theory and Practice," in Neil W. Chamberlain, Frank C. Pierson, and Theresa Wolfson (eds.), *A Decade of Industrial Relations Research, 1946–1956* (New York: Harper & Row, 1958), p. 71.

their behavior in the long run will conform to the marginal productivity theory.

Thus, it is obviously true that groups of workers tend to compare their situations with those of other groups. And if a group with which you compare yourself gets a wage increase, you conclude that you are entitled to a similar increase. This is so whether one is a union member or not, but if he does belong to a union, he will expect its leadership to secure this "justice" for him. There is sufficient evidence that pattern bargaining has been a phenomenon in the labor market.

Where the institutionalist approach has erred, however, has been in making the coercive comparison a new "iron law" of wages. If the institutionalists have objected that "reality" has not conformed to marginal productivity analysis, there is also a great deal of empirical evidence that undermines their claims. Shultz and Myers, for example, have found evidence that unions do take into account the probable effect of wage demands on employment of their members when formulating their wage policies.[24] They found that unions were most inclined to do this in industries in which there was strong competition in the product market and a nonunion sector in the industry.

But the empirical evidence indicates that unions in industries in which the product market is not competitive and in which there is no threat of the growth of a nonunion sector will also take cognizance of the economic situation and the possible impact on employment of their wage demands. For example, Seltzer has shown that the powerful United Steelworkers did not make the same settlement with small producers that had been won from the giant, fully integrated steel companies, and that patterns were followed more rigorously when the economy was booming and less closely when the economy was weaker.[25] Even if unions attempted to impose high settlements, regardless of economic conditions, employers are more inclined to resist high union demands when product market conditions are not good and sales and profits are falling. This was clearly visible in the late 1950s and early 1960s, when many managements, fearful that higher wages would further undermine their companies' competitive positions, adopted a stance of "hard bargaining" in their negotiations with unions. With workers on layoff, unions facing tough management bargaining positions recognized that the prospect of winning a strike had diminished, and were more inclined to moderate their demands.

Further empirical evidence of the interaction of economic and institutional forces in wage determination has been found by Eckstein and Wilson in a study of the behavior of money wages in American manufacturing industry from 1948 to 1950.[26] Focusing on industry in a "key group" (high-wage

---

[24] George P. Shultz and Charles A. Myers, "Union Wage Decisions and Employment," *American Economic Review*, June 1950, pp. 362–380.

[25] George Seltzer, "Pattern Bargaining and the United Steelworkers," *Journal of Political Economy*, August 1951, pp. 319–331.

[26] Otto Eckstein and Thomas A. Wilson, "The Determination of Money Wages in American Industry," *Quarterly Journal of Economics*, August 1962, pp. 379–414; reprinted in McConnell, *op. cit.*, pp. 108–124.

industries, with strong industrial unions, dominated by large corporations with considerable market power, and geographically concentrated in the midwestern industrial heartland), they found that wage changes could be explained primarily in terms of two standard economic variables: profit rates and unemployment rates. The statistical evidence led to finding that "the economic variables enter into wage determination differently than they would under pure supply and demand mechanisms, with both product and factor market conditions influencing the outcome of the bargaining." They concluded that both economic and political factors play a role in wage determination.

At this point, therefore, we can begin to summarize this discussion of wage determination. The attacks upon the marginal productivity theory appear to be quite premature, for marginal analysis still enables us to understand events in the labor market. This does not mean, however, that we can afford to ignore the institutional forces, for it is obvious that significant wage rates in the economy are established through collective bargaining.

But to focus solely on the "politics" of collective bargaining would be an even more serious mistake, for the results of the negotiations that take place between unions and managements are heavily influenced by economic conditions. Ross was correct in pointing to the existence of coercive comparisons that help to determine union goals in collective bargaining, but the ability to achieve those goals depends upon the economic situation that a particular union faces. Patterns are established, but they are not followed automatically, and, in fact, in the 1960s, when unemployment rates were high and consumer demand for many industrial products sluggish, pattern bargaining broke down.

The same company that quickly concedes to union demands when labor markets are tight and customer orders are rolling in adopts a hard bargaining stance when orders decline and it is no longer as easy to pass cost increases on to consumers in the form of higher prices. Under these conditions, unions recognize that strikes have less chance of success, and they are willing to trim their demands to avoid them; even if they do not, the ensuing strike may be long and end on terms that are not favorable to the union position. When large numbers of their members are on layoff, moreover, unions pay greater attention to the possible employment effects of their demands.

Finally, to the degree that institutional forces are weighted more heavily than the economic, the "victory" of the union may be very short lived. Higher wages that are converted into higher prices reduce the demand for the employer's product, which, in turn, reduces his demand for labor, and the wage is brought back in line with marginal revenue product. In other cases higher wages may end the equality between factor prices relative to product and lead to a substitution of capital for labor. Thus, the post-World War II policy of the United Mine Workers to make the coal miner one of the highest-paid production workers was quite successful, but in the process coal mining employment dropped in half and hundreds of thousands of miners lost their jobs.

In conclusion, therefore, we can say that institutional forces have become important in the labor market, but that these forces face the constraint of economic reality. Marginal productivity analysis enables us to understand how institutional forces must bend and, to the extent that they do not bend, to judge what the consequences will be.

Summary

In this chapter we have seen that "wages" may refer to different things, such as wage rates, earnings, take-home pay, real earnings, and real take-home pay. Whichever measure is used, workers obviously think of wages in terms of the incomes they provide. To the employer, on the other hand, wages are a cost of production, and thus he is concerned, not only with the amount of money paid out for labor's contribution to the production process, but also with how much output he receives for those wages.

Since the advent of the free labor market, economists have attempted to explain why wages were what they were. The first widely accepted doctrine was the subsistence theory, according to which wages would tend to a level that would enable workers to subsist and perpetuate the race. Since this theory could not explain the rise in real wages over time, it gave way to the wages-fund theory, which saw wages as being simply a function of the amount of capital available. The surplus-value theory of Karl Marx viewed the exchange relationship between worker and employer as one in which the latter exploited the former by not paying him the full value of his labor. All of these theories, however, neglected the demand side of the employer-employee relationship.

The theory that arose which gained widest acceptance in capitalist economies was the marginal productivity theory. According to this theory, the wage rate is determined by equality between the marginal cost and the value of the marginal product of labor. Under competitive conditions, therefore, labor should be allocated in the most efficient manner and equilibrium should occur at full employment.

The marginal productivity theory has also been subject to criticisms. It has been attacked for its assumption of competition, but it still applies, in a different manner, to noncompetitive situations. The charge that employers really do not apply the theory has also been leveled and basically refuted. And even though Keynes proved that equilibrium could be achieved at below full-employment levels, this did not undermine marginal productivity analysis.

An important line of criticism of the marginal productivity theory has centered on its complete neglect of unions and collective bargaining. According to this line of thinking, wages are politically determined, by dint of coercive comparisons, irrespective of particular economic situations. The empirical evidence, however, indicates that institutional forces cannot act independently of economic reality. Thus, there must be an interaction of economic and institutional forces in wage determination. Marginal productivity analysis helps to explain how institutional forces must bend and, to the extent that they do not bend, to judge what the consequences will be.

BIBLIOGRAPHY

Cartter, Allan M. *Theory of Wages and Employment.* Homewood, Ill.: Richard D. Irwin, 1959.

Chamberlain, Neil W., Frank C. Pierson, and Theresa Wolfson (eds.). *A Decade of Industrial Relations Research, 1946–1956.* New York: Harper & Row, 1958.

Clark, John Bates. *The Distribution of Wealth.* New York: Kelley & Millman, 1956.

Dunlop, John T. *Wage Determination under Trade Unions.* New York: Augustus M. Kelley, 1950.

Hicks, John R. *The Theory of Wages.* New York: Macmillan, 1932.

Lester, Richard. "Shortcomings of Marginal Analysis for Wage-Employment Problems," *American Economic Review,* March 1946.

Levitan, Sar A. (ed.). *Blue-Collar Workers.* New York: McGraw-Hill, 1972.

Marshall, Alfred. *Principles of Economics.* London: Macmillan, 1947.

Marx, Karl. *Capital, The Communist Manifesto and Other Writings.* New York: Modern Library, 1932.

McConnell, Campbell R. (ed.). *Perspectives on Wage Determination: A Book of Readings.* New York: McGraw-Hill, 1970.

Mill, John Stuart. *Principles of Political Economy.* New York: Appleton, 1923.

Reynolds, Lloyd G. "Toward a Short-Run Theory of Wages," *American Economic Review,* June 1948.

Ricardo, David. *The Principles of Political Economy and Taxation.* New York: Dutton, 1911.

Ross, Arthur M. *Trade Union Wage Policy.* Berkeley: University of California Press, 1948.

Rothschild, K. W. *The Theory of Wages.* Oxford: Basil Blackwell, 1960.

Seltzer, George. "Pattern Bargaining and the United Steelworkers," *Journal of Political Economy,* August 1951.

Shultz, George P., and Charles A. Myers. "Union Wage Decisions and Employment," *American Economic Review,* June 1950.

Wages, Prices, Profits, and Productivity. New York: American Assembly, 1959.

10 WAGE STRUCTURE

Theories abound as to how wages are determined, as we have seen, but what is the actual process by which a firm determines the wages that it will pay its employees, and what are some of the results of the process? We shall begin by examining the internal wage structure, that is, how a firm establishes pay scales for its work force. Next we shall turn to the external wage structure: the relationship between the wages paid by the different firms within an industry, as well as relationships among different industries. Wage supplements and their impact on intra-industry and interindustry comparisons will also be of interest to us. Following that, we shall probe the question of differentials in wages by region and skill, examining the empirical evidence, determining the role of unions, and comparing the evidence to the theory of marginal productivity. Finally, we shall examine the role of unions with respect to relative wage rates and the distribution of the national income, attempting to answer the question, "Do unions really raise wages?" Although that question may sound naïve at this point, we shall find that economists are of varying opinions as to its answer.

Internal Wage Structure

Any organization—be it a private corporation, a nonprofit institution, or a government agency—when opening a plant, office, or warehouse must establish a structure of wages by which to remunerate its employees. In a perfectly competitive situation, the firm would not have to worry about its wage structure because the pay of each grade of labor would be determined by the market, but, to the degree that there are frictions and imperfections in the labor market, the firm has the power to exercise discretion with respect to whom to hire and what wages to offer. Therefore, the organization must determine what its wage policy will be—and so let us begin our discussion with wage policy.

Establishing a Wage Policy

The purpose of any establishment is to produce or distribute goods or services, and this requires the employment of labor. A major function of a wage policy is to enhance the ability of the establishment to attract and retain qualified and efficient personnel. Moreover, wage and salary programs, which are the embodiments of policy, control the total compensation dollar and its distribution: they are designed to assure a "fair wage for a fair day's work" and to keep labor costs within an established budget. A wage policy provides a firm with an enduring basis against which to determine whether a proposed, or existing, practice veers toward or away from stated objectives.

Traditionally, wage policy embraces both the relation of one organization's wage policy to those of others and the internal job-pay relationships, in order to ensure that there is a proper relation between job content, recognition, and reward. Let us start with the first of these: relation of one firm's wages to those of others.

The Relation of Wages to Those of Other Firms

No firm can operate very long if its costs are greater than its income. From the employer's point of view, wages are costs: the ratio between costs and prices is almost always direct, and, if costs increase, this will eventually be reflected by an increase in prices, unless there is a corresponding increase in productivity. As a consequence of this relationship, the careful control of labor costs within a firm is particularly important.

Increased costs, resulting from higher wages, cannot always be shifted to consumers. Under competitive conditions a firm has no control over product price, which is determined in the market, so it cannot raise its price above those of its competitors, for if it did so it would cease to sell any of its output. Thus, firms in competitive industries attempt to ensure that the wages they pay their employees are in line with those of their competitors.

Even under imperfect competition, the firm does not have undisputed ability to pass increases in costs on to consumers, for its ability to do so depends largely on the elasticity of demand for its products. Elasticity refers to the change in the quantity demanded relative to the change in its price, that is:

$$\text{Price elasticity of demand} = \frac{\text{Percentage change in quantity demanded}}{\text{Percentage change in price}}$$

If the elasticity is greater than 1, then the demand is said to be elastic; that is, a small increase in price will lead to a large drop in the quantity demanded. This is shown in Figure 10.1a, where at price OA a total of OC units of the product is demanded, but, when the price is raised slightly to OD, only OF is demanded. Under elastic demand the firm's total revenue drops as a result of a price increase, as shown in Figure 10.1a, where the area of the rectangle ODEF, which represents the firm's revenue (number of units sold times the price) after the price increase is smaller than that of the rectangle OABC, which represents its revenue under the original price. If elasticity is equal to 1, the demand is said to have unitary elasticity, and the firm's revenue will be the same as before, as shown in Figure 10.1c, where OABC=ODEF. If elasticity is less than 1, demand is said to be inelastic; in this case a large rise in price will reduce the quantity demanded relatively slightly, as shown in Figure 10.1b, and the firm's revenue increases, ODEF>OABC.

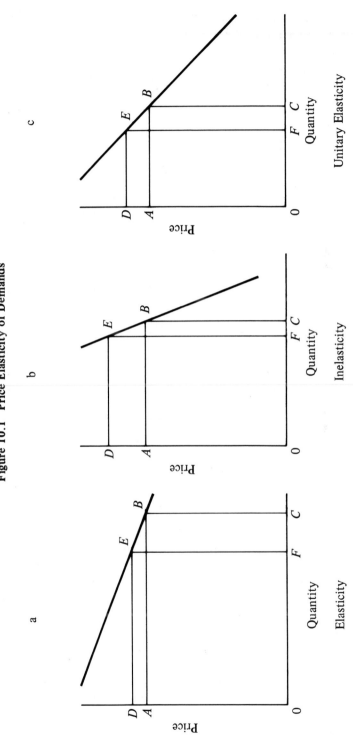

Figure 10.1 Price Elasticity of Demands

Elasticity of demand is determined basically by the availability of substitute products or services. Under perfect competition demand is perfectly elastic; that is, if the firm raises its prices above those of its competitors, it will sell nothing, because its product is the same as that of its competitors and consumers will not pay more for it when they can get it for less from someone else. Under pure monopoly, demand would be perfectly inelastic, and the monopolist should be able to raise his price as high as he wants without fear of losing business. More realistically, however, at some price all products have substitutes.

Under other types of imperfect competition, there are more substitute products to which consumers can switch if the price of a particular product is raised. In the case of monopolistic competition, the manufacturer has been able somehow to differentiate his product from that of competitors, thus giving him some discretion in price policy. That discretion, however, is within certain bounds: for example, automobile purchasers who prefer Chevrolets would begin to buy more Fords and Plymouths if the price of comparable Chevrolets was significantly higher.

It is quite clear, therefore, that firms in an industry, even one operating under imperfect competition, must be concerned with controlling their wage rates and keeping them in line with those being paid by the other firms in the industry. But what of the case where all the firms in an industry raise their wages at the same time and pass the increase in costs on to consumers in the form of higher prices: do they have to worry about elasticity of demand? The answer is definitely yes, as the steel industry discovered by the 1960s, for users of steel had begun to substitute plastics, glass, aluminum, poured concrete, and the like for steel as its price was raised relative to the other products. Thus, the firm producing items that are price elastic must be concerned with the wages being paid by firms that manufacture products that can be substituted for its own.

Competition in the labor market, as well as in the product market, is also a factor in shaping an organization's wage policy. Wage rates and personnel practices that are prevalent in the community in which the establishment is located must be taken into consideration. Competition in the labor market is a fact of life, and it operates for buyers as well as sellers. The wage structure of a firm, therefore, must take into account the wages being paid in firms and industries that compete with it for similar types of labor. Maintaining parity with comparable employers would presumably permit a firm to attract and keep qualified personnel.

Wage surveys of prevailing rates of pay in a community for certain key jobs are the major source of information for the firm in determining the comparability of its wages and salaries with those of its competitors for labor. Such surveys, both of community wage practices and of particular industries, are made periodically by the United States Bureau of Labor Statistics. Wage surveys are also conducted by some employer associations, and a few large firms conduct their own.

Some large firms follow the practice of not merely meeting prevailing wages in a community, but of surpassing them. Their aim is to be able to attract the best qualified workers available, and they therefore follow the policy of being the highest wage employer in a community. Adhering to such a policy, however, is possible only in those industries in which wages have not been standardized across the country, for such a policy implies different rates of pay in company plants in different locations.

Finally, it is obvious that the wage policy of a firm will be governed, at least in part, by the factor of unionism. If the employees of the firm are organized, the union, or unions, will play a very important role in helping to shape the wage structure. But organizations whose employees are not organized are also cognizant of gains won by unions. If the wages that they pay are low in comparison to what unionized workers are receiving, employee dissatisfaction would undoubtedly lead to their joining the union, too.[1]

Another factor in determining a firm's wage structure may be its desire to be considered a good employer that deals fairly with employees. Such considerations will lead the firm to establish a wage structure by which its employees not only maintain the purchasing power of their earnings, but also achieve increases in their real earnings commensurate with the general rise in standards of living in the society.

Job Evaluation

Company wage administrators must also ensure that the internal wage structure is a rational one, that is, that those whose jobs are more important, require greater skill, and entail greater effort are rewarded commensurately. This is not easily accomplished, for the company may have thousands of employees performing hundreds of different jobs. The first step in creating a rational wage structure, therefore, is adequate description of all the jobs in an operation. When this is done a way must be found to rate these jobs, and, finally, wage rates must be attached to the jobs.

Although not all companies use it, job evaluation has become widespread in the United States. Job evaluation entails the establishment of a hierarchy of jobs according to such constituent factors as education, skill, experience, working conditions, responsibility, and effort. A job classification system would entail analysis of work being performed, establishing major job classes or grades, and then assigning the various jobs to these grades.

Job evaluation, which has developed largely through management initiative, has been an outgrowth of the expansion of the staff functions of personnel and industrial engineering. According to Slichter and his associates, job evaluation became important in the 1930s, when organizations such as the American Management Association and Industrial Relations Counselors

---

[1] For an analysis of the "threat effect," that is, unionism's impact on wages in non-union establishments, see Sherwin Rosen, "Trade Union Power, Threat Effects, and the Extent of Organization," *Review of Economic Studies,* April 1969, pp. 185–196.

early saw its significance as a device both to improve company wage structures and wage administration and to maintain management control of the
wage structure under collective bargaining.[2] As one would expect, the unions'
response to job evaluation has not been one of overwhelming enthusiasm, but
they have learned to live with it. In a few cases unions have even cooperated
in establishing job evaluation, as was done jointly by the United Steelworkers
and the major steel producers in the basic steel industry following World
War II.[3]

External Wage Structure

While the internal wage structure refers to the hierarchy of pay within the
firm, the external wage structure refers to the distribution of pay within the
larger environment, be it local labor market, region, or the entire nation.
That wage structure can be analyzed in terms of differences within an industry, among industries, among occupations, and among geographic regions. In
the course of this chapter we shall look at each of these, but first let us
examine the subject broadly, starting with a model of wage structure.

Job Clusters and Wage Contours

One most interesting attempt to explain wage structure, both internal and
external, is offered by Professor Dunlop's concepts of job clusters and wage
contours.[4] A job cluster is defined as a stable group of job classifications or
work assignments within a firm (wage-determining unit) that are so interconnected by technology, administrative organization of the production process
—including policies of transfer, layoff and promotion, or social custom—that
they have common wage-making characteristics. An example of such a job
cluster would be all the employees of a plant's tool room.

   In Dunlop's typology the wage structure of a plant is comprised of a
limited number of job clusters, each with a number of wage rates. Ordinarily
a job cluster contains a key wage rate and a group of associated rates. The
key rate helps to relate the exterior—that is, labor market influences, union
wage policies, and product market forces—to the internal wage structure.

   A wage contour is defined by Dunlop as a stable group of wage-
determining units that are so interconnected by (1) similarity of product
markets, (2) resort to similar sources for a labor force, or (3) common labor
market organization (custom) that they have common wage-making characteristics. A contour for particular occupations is defined in terms of both
product market and labor market, and a contour has three dimensions: (1)

---

   [2] Sumner H. Slichter, James J. Healy, and E. Robert Livernash, *The Impact of
Collective Bargaining on Management* (Washington, D.C.: Brookings, 1960), p. 561.

   [3] See, for example, Jack Stieber, *The Steel Industry Wage Structure* (Cambridge,
Mass.: Harvard University Press, 1959).

   [4] John T. Dunlop, "The Task of Contemporary Wage Theory," in John T. Dunlop
(ed.), *The Theory of Wage Determination* (New York: St. Martin's Press, 1957),
chap. 1.

particular occupations or job clusters, (2) a sector of industry, and (3) a geographic location. Following Dunlop's typology, we see that a change in compensation is highly interrelated among occupations and industries.

Stability of the Wage Structure

Economic theory tells us that, other things being equal, the forces of supply and demand are supposed to operate to allocate labor in an optimum fashion. We should therefore expect that, over time, shifts in consumer tastes, the rise of new products and technologies, the movement of population geographically, and the like should operate to cause significant changes in a nation's wage structure. Those industries, occupations, and regions in which employment is growing rapidly should increase their wages relative to others, while those that are declining in employment should experience a relative decline in wages.

Certainly changes do take place, yet a study by an expert group for the Organization for Economic Co-operation and Development (OECD) on wages and labor mobility in a number of countries, including the United States, found that there was a high degree of stability in the wage structure over long periods of time.[5] In a study of fifty-seven United States manufacturing industries for the period 1948 to 1960, Ulman found a weak relationship between industry changes in employment and earnings.[6] The railroad industry, for example, in which employment dropped by one-half during that period, experienced an increase in earnings comparable to that of most other industries, including those in which employment was growing. Findings such as these imply a strong central tendency in wage movements, with only modest changes in industrial, occupational, and regional differentials.[7]

We must not jump to the conclusion, however, that wages play no role in allocating labor among different employments, but only recognize that the role is a limited one. The OECD expert group, for instance, did not find that relative wages were completely independent of changes in employment, though there were many examples of very large increases in employment in low-wage occupations and industries. There was evidence, however, that changes in wages and employment were related among broad industry sectors, among broad industry groupings within manufacturing, between salaried employment and earnings, and for a number of professional groups. These findings would seem to imply that unionism has an important impact on the wage structure, for strongly organized workers seem to be able to keep their

---

[5] P. de Wolff *et al., Wages and Labour Mobility* (Paris: Organization for Economic Co-operation and Development, 1965). A summary of these findings and others with respect to wages can be found in E. Robert Livernash, "Wages and Benefits," in *A Review of Industrial Relations Research*, Vol. 1 (Madison, Wisc.: Industrial Relations Research Association, 1970), pp. 79–144.

[6] Lloyd Ulman, "Labor Mobility and the Industrial Wage Structure in the Postwar United States," *Quarterly Journal of Economics*, February 1965, pp. 73–97.

[7] Livernash, *op. cit.*, p. 106.

wages relatively constant with respect to other workers, despite declines in employment in their occupations or industries.

Another explanation of the lack of conformity between the data on wages and employment and economic theory may lie in the inadequacy of the studies. Livernash criticizes the studies of industry and regional wage levels because they typically have not been corrected for differences in occupational mix.[8] In other words, wages may go up in an industry, despite a decline in its total employment, because skilled workers comprise a larger proportion of its smaller work force. This is particularly true of industries that have been subject to a good deal of technological change, because such change tends to eliminate the least skilled jobs the most. Studies of the impact of automation on the work forces of automated continuous process operations, such as chemical plants and petroleum refineries, have disclosed that, following automation, the majority of employees have been in the skilled maintenance and technical work occupations. This may help explain why, despite a drop in production, worker employment in petroleum refining, from 123,000 in 1958 to 86,000 in 1969, average hourly earnings remained about one-third higher than the average for all manufacturing. If the changes in occupational mix were taken into account, however, we might find that petroleum refining earnings had declined relatively, but, since we do not have the data, we cannot reach any firm conclusion.

Wage Supplements

Another explanation of the divergence of the wage structure from the competitive model might lie in the distribution of wage supplements, that is, some groups of workers, instead of receiving higher wages, might be receiving higher fringe benefits instead. The facts are to the contrary, however, for to a very large degree high fringe benefits go together with high wage rates. If we look at the highest-wage manufacturing industries, such as petroleum refining and automobiles, we find that they are also the industries that devote the highest percentage of payroll to various fringe benefits. In fact, to a considerable extent it is the industries that can afford to pay high wages and benefits that do so. Why some industries can afford to pay more than others will be examined shortly, but first let us continue our discussion of fringe benefits.

The overall wage structure has changed significantly over the past quarter of a century, precisely as a result of the increase in fringe benefits. There is no question but that pay for time not worked, premium pay for time worked, and retirement, health, and supplementary unemployment benefits have become an important part of the wage structure. In fact, they have become such an integral part of the wage structure that it hardly seems right to continue to refer to them as "fringes." Almost all workers are covered by government old age and unemployment insurance, and the majority, in addition, are under employer pension plans. Most workers also have employer-

---

[8] *Ibid.*, p. 107.

financed life insurance, accident insurance, and hospital and surgical insurance. Paid holidays and vacations are also common. According to the Bureau of Labor Statistics, wage supplements, which hardly existed four decades ago, now total more than 20 cents of each compensation dollar (see Table 10.1 and Figure 10.2).[9]

Table 10.1 Level and Structure of Employer Expenditures for Employee Compensation, Private Nonfarm Economy, 1968

Compensation practice	All employees	
	Percent of compensation	Dollars per hour of work
Total compensation	100.0	$3.89
Pay for working time	82.8	3.22
Straight-time pay	80.4	3.13
Premium pay	2.4	.09
Overtime, weekend, and holiday work	2.1	.08
Shift differentials	.3	.01
Pay for leave time (except sick leave)	5.3	.21
Vacations	3.1	.12
Holidays	2.0	.08
Civic and personal leave	.1	.01
Employer payments to vacation and holiday funds	.1	(a)
Employer expenditures for retirement programs	6.0	.24
Social security	3.3	.13
Private pension plans	2.7	.11
Employer expenditures for health and insurance programs[b]	3.7	.15
Life, accident, and health insurance	2.2	.09
Sick leave	.6	.03
Workmen's compensation	.9	.03
Employer expenditures for unemployment benefit programs	.9	.04
Unemployment insurance	.8	.03
Severance pay	.1	(a)
Severance pay funds and supplemental unemployment benefit funds	(a)	(a)
Nonproduction bonuses	1.0	.04
Savings and thrift plans	.2	.01

a Less than 0.05 percent or $0.005.
b Includes other health benefit programs, principally state temporary disability insurance not presented separately.

SOURCE: Alvin Bauman, "Measuring Employee Compensation in U.S. Industry," *Monthly Labor Review*, October 1970.

[9] Alvin Bauman, "Measuring Employee Compensation in U.S. Industry," *Monthly Labor Review*, October 1970, pp. 17–24.

Figure 10.2 The Structure of Compensation, Selected Worker Groups and Industries, 1968, and Manufacturing Production Workers, 1959–68

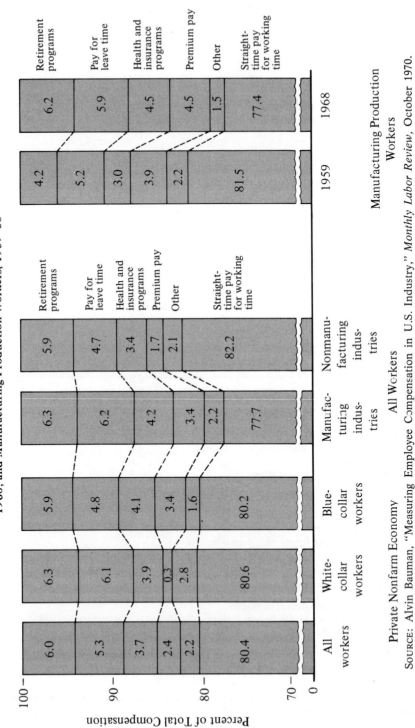

SOURCE: Alvin Bauman, "Measuring Employee Compensation in U.S. Industry," *Monthly Labor Review*, October 1970.

258

Benefits and other supplements have not only become an important part of the nation's wage structure, but the trend has been for them to increase in importance. Gordon and LeBlue found that after adjustments for the effects of increased price levels, employee benefits for the years 1929–1967 increased at the rate of 9.6 percent per year while wages and salaries rose at only a 3.9 percent rate.[10] There are no signs of any diminution in this trend, as more paid holidays are added, vacation periods are lengthened, health and medical benefits spread, and pension payments are raised. In fact, Gordon and LeBlue see wage supplements rising to 50 percent of payroll by 1985.

Differentials in Wages

At this point let us return to our discussion of differentials in wages. We shall examine the empirical evidence in terms of differentials among industries, occupations, and regions. We should keep in mind, however, that all three may be interrelated; that is, high-wage regions may have a higher proportion of high-wage industries, and high-wage industries may have a higher proportion of high-wage occupations. To aid our analysis, however, we shall examine each of them separately.

Interindustry Wage Differentials

The discussion of wage structure showed that wages, whether measured in terms of rates or earnings, differ among industries. Since average hourly earnings data are the most readily available, we shall use them in our analysis of these interindustry wage differentials. Table 10.2 presents gross average hourly earnings of production workers in major industries, plus a breakdown within manufacturing, and indicates very wide variations. Among major industry groups in 1971, average earnings ranged from $2.57 per hour in retail trade to $5.72 per hour in contract construction. The table also constructs an index of average hourly earnings, using the $3.43 in the total private economy as the base of 100, and compares all the other industries to it.

The obvious question that comes into mind at this point is, "What distinguishes the high-wage industries from the low-wage ones?" There is no simple answer to this question, for there are a number of factors that influence the differences, and these do not operate in all cases. Nevertheless, let us try to isolate those factors which help to explain the interindustry earnings differentials.

First of all, the proportion of an industry's labor force that is skilled is an important influence. That contract construction is the highest-paid industry, therefore, does not come as a complete surprise, for a very large proportion of the industry's labor force is composed of skilled electricians, carpenters,

---

[10] T. J. Gordon and R. E. LeBlue, "Employee Benefits, 1970–1985," *Harvard Business Review,* January–February 1970, pp. 93–107.

Table 10.2 Gross Average Hourly Earnings of Production or Nonsupervisory Workers on Private Nonagricultural Payrolls, by Industry Division and Major Manufacturing Group, 1971

Industry	Annual Average	Index
Total Private	$3.43	100
Mining	4.05	118
Contract construction	5.72	167
Manufacturing	3.57	104
Durable goods	3.80	111
Ordnance and accessories	3.85	112
Lumber and wood products	3.14	92
Furniture and fixtures	2.90	84
Stone, clay, and glass products	3.66	107
Primary metal industries	4.23	123
Fabricated metal products	3.74	109
Machinery, except electrical	3.99	116
Electrical equipment and supplies	3.50	102
Transportation equipment	4.44	129
Instruments and related products	3.53	103
Miscellaneous manufacturing industries	2.93	85
Nondurable goods	3.26	95
Food and kindred products	3.38	99
Tobacco manufacturers	3.15	92
Textile mill products	2.57	75
Apparel and other textile products	2.49	73
Paper and allied products	3.68	107
Printing and publishing	4.20	122
Chemicals and allied products	3.94	115
Petroleum and oil products	4.58	134
Rubber and plastics products	3.41	99
Leather and leather products	2.59	76
Transportation and public utilities	4.21	123
Wholesale and retail trade	2.87	84
Wholesale trade	3.67	107
Retail trade	2.57	75
Finance, insurance, and real estate	3.28	96
Services	2.99	87

SOURCE: U.S. Department of Labor.

masons, plumbers, and the like. Since these occupations are highly paid, the industry average is also high. At the other extreme, the lowest-paid industry is retail trade, and obviously part of the explanation lies in the fact that the vast majority of the employees are not skilled; in most cases it takes very little training to become a stock clerk or a salesclerk in a retail establishment.

Just as there is interaction between occupational and industrial wage differentials, so there is also interaction between regional and industrial wage differentials, and a second explanation is location of an industry. The high-wage industries are more concentrated in high-wage areas and the low-wage industries in low-wage areas. The differences among manufacturing industries makes this most clear. Among the high-wage industries are primary metals and transportation equipment (steel, automobiles, and so forth), which are highly concentrated in the high-wage East North Central region (Illinois, Indiana, Michigan, Ohio, and Wisconsin). On the other hand, the low-wage textile industry is very highly concentrated in the low-wage South.

A third and extremely important explanation of interindustry wage differentials, particularly within manufacturing, has to do with the technical-economic nature of industries. The high-wage industries tend to be large-scale, high-capital-investment-per-worker industries. The high-capital-investment requirement tends to restrict the entry of new firms into an industry, which develops an oligopolistic structure: dominance by a few large firms that have some degree of discretion in pricing and production policies. At the same time the high capital-labor ratio means that labor compensation tends to be a relatively small proportion of total operating expenses. Industries that fit this description include flat glass, steel, automobiles, tires and tubes, and petroleum refining, all of which are high-wage industries.

In contrast, industries that are typified by low-capital investment requirements, ease of entry of new firms, competitive market structure, and in which labor costs are a high proportion of total costs tend to be low-wage industries. Typical of such industries would be apparel and other textile products and leather and leather products, and, as can be seen from Table 10.2, they are among the lowest paid manufacturing industries, their average hourly earnings being only 73 and 76 percent respectively of the average of the total private economy.

A fourth factor in explaining interindustry wage differentials is the extent of unionism, for high-wage industries also tend to be relatively highly organized. The role of unionism as an independent force in boosting an industry's wages, however, is open to serious question. Undoubtedly, unions have been most important in winning construction workers very high wage rates, but in this case union strength comes from their monopoly control of a scarce resource: the skills of their members. That there is no clear-cut distinction among industry wage rates on the basis of degree of unionism can be seen from a comparison of the textile and the apparel industries. Both industries are low wage, having almost identical average hourly earnings, but textiles is very poorly organized while apparel is fairly well unionized.

The failure of apparel manufacturing to be a high-wage industry, despite a relatively high degree of union organization, can be explained in terms of the third factor: the technical-economic structure of the industry. Even when the unions (mainly the International Ladies' Garment Workers in women's apparel and the Amalgamated Clothing Workers in men's) organize a major center of production, their ability to push up wages is constrained by the fact that the industry is characterized by very low capital requirements and ease of entry of new firms. In the cheaper price lines, moreover, skill requirements are not very high, and workers can be easily trained, especially since many women have a familiarity with the sewing machine. As a result, the industry is very mobile: present firms can move without undue expense and new ones can open in new locations. Since employers are subject to interregional competition based upon low wages, the problem from the national unions' point of view is to raise wage standards in organized areas as fast as they can, but not so fast as to drive producers into unorganized territory.[11]

The impact of mobility can be seen in what transpired two decades ago in the hosiery industry. The industry had been concentrated in the Northeast, where it was highly unionized, and the union was able to win relatively high wages for its members through collective bargaining. New plants were built in the South, however, where wages were considerably lower. Although the union was able to maintain its high wage standards in the Northeast, the competitive pressure from the southern plants led to the eventual destruction of the northern industry.

Occupational Wage Differentials

We shall return to the question of the independent force of unionism in explaining relative wage differentials, but let us now examine some of the empirical evidence with respect to occupational differentials. Since there are thousands of different occupations, what determines why one is paid more than another and what relationship occupational earnings have to one another? We discussed this subject in Chapter 8, when we probed the factors that explained why wages did not tend to conformity in all employments, but let us examine it more thoroughly now.

Economists have always been interested in this topic, and two hundred years ago Adam Smith advanced five explanations of occupational wage differentials, as follows:[12]

1. Wages will vary with the ease or hardship, the cleanliness or dirtiness, the honorableness or dishonorableness of the employment.
2. Wages will vary with the easiness and cheapness, or the difficulty and expense of learning the trade.
3. Wages in different occupations will vary with the regularity or irregularity of employment.
4. Wages will vary with the degree of trust reposed in an occupation.
5. Wages will vary according to the probability of success in the occupation.

As we saw earlier, skilled workers earn more than unskilled construction workers who have irregular employment have higher wages than those who work more regularly; physicians, who must undergo many years of rigorous training and whose work entails great responsibility, earn more than

---

[11] For a full explanation of this dilemma, see Roy B. Helfgott, "Women's and Children's Apparel," in Max Hall (ed.), *Made in New York: Case Studies in Metropolitan Manufacturing* (Cambridge, Mass.: Harvard University Press, 1959), esp. pp. 88–92.

[12] Adam Smith, *The Wealth of Nations* (New York: Modern Library, 1937; original edition, 1776), pp. 99–106; abridged and reprinted in Campbell R. McConnell (ed.), *Perspectives on Wage Determination* (New York: McGraw-Hill, 1970), pp. 187–190.

truck drivers; and so on. There is evidence, however, that over the long run differentials in earnings among occupational groups have been narrowing. During the first decade of this century skilled workers in manufacturing had median earnings double those of unskilled workers, but by the 1950s their median earnings were less than 40 percent higher. Similarly, in that period the earnings of full professors in colleges and universities had declined from three and one-half times average wages in manufacturing to about one and three-quarters times, and college instructors, who had earned almost 50 percent more than the average manufacturing wage were, by the 1950s, actually earning about 10 percent less.[13]

There have been a number of attempts to explain the secular decline in skill differentials. One set of explanations relates to education and training. Concentrating on the skilled-unskilled wage differentials in manufacturing, laundries, and agriculture, Reder has put major emphasis on the rising level of educational attainment of the American labor force, which has increased the supply of skilled workers relative to unskilled workers.[14] Keat explains the declining skill differentials as a reflection of the reduced cost and time required to educate and train skilled workers.[15]

Differential sensitivity to the business cycle has been another explanation offered for the decline in skill differentials. Reder, for example, claims that the wages of unskilled workers are more cyclically sensitive than those of skilled workers.[16] In periods of labor shortage, employers raise unskilled wage rates faster than skilled rates in order to attract more workers. They need not raise skilled wage rates as much, because they can promote less skilled workers into the skilled ranks. Differentials start widening again in periods of recession, but the widening is not as great as the narrowing in the boom periods.

The role of government policy has also been important in explaining the narrowing of skill differentials. As American society has become wealthier, it has become more concerned with the plight of its less fortunate members. Through government, therefore, steps have been taken to aid those people at the bottom of the socioeconomic ladder. In terms of wages, public policy has sought to boost the standards of the lowest-paid members of the work force through legally established minimum wages. Not all unskilled workers have been covered by minimum wage legislation, and this helps to explain why not all of them have gained relative to the more skilled.

Unionism has been given a good deal of credit (or blame, depending upon one's point of view) for the narrowing of wage differentials between

[13] P. G. Keat, "Long-Run Changes in Occupational Wage Structures, 1900–1956," *Journal of Political Economy*, December 1960.

[14] Melvin W. Reder, "Wage Differentials: Theory and Measurement," in *Aspects of Labor Economics* (Princeton: Princeton University Press, 1962), pp. 257–299.

[15] Keat, *op. cit.*

[16] Melvin W. Reder, "The Theory of Occupational Wage Differentials," *American Economic Review*, December 1955.

skilled and unskilled workers. This is true, of course, only of the industrial unions, for the craft unions obviously attempt to preserve the advantages of their members relative to other workers. The industrial unions, on the other hand, being composed mainly of semiskilled workers, have had more egalitarian philosophies. With skilled workers comprising only a minority of thei memberships, moreover, industrial unions have, until recently, catered mainl, to the interests of the majority of semiskilled members.

To a very considerable degree this is precisely what happened in most industries following unionization in the 1930s: the unions bargained for across-the-board, cents-per-hour wage increases. The result was a sharp narrowing of skill differentials. To use a hypothetical example, if, in an industry, skilled workers—for example, maintenance electricians, machinists, and millwrights—were earning $1.00 per hour and semiskilled machine operators $.50 per hour in 1940, and during the next twenty-five years, through collective bargaining, all workers had received a total of $3.00 per hour in wage increases, by 1965 the skilled workers would have been earning $4.00 per hour and the semiskilled $3.50. Although there still would have been a $.50 per hour differential between them, the skill margin would have narrowed very considerably in relative terms: in 1940 skilled workers earned twice the semiskilled rates, but in 1965 the skilled would have been earning only 14.3 percent more.

A pattern such as this did indeed occur, but by the 1960s the skilled workers were no longer content to abide by it, and began to revolt against the industrial unions. In some cases skilled workers actually split off from existing industrial unions to form new independent unions or to join craft unions. In other situations the mere threat of secession by the skilled workers induced the industrial unions to reverse their policies and to win special, higher wage increases for their skilled members. As a result, during the 1960s skill differentials in manufacturing began to widen once again. Similarly, various professional groups, such as college professors, also received differential salary increases. Whether these changes will mean a permanent reversal of the long-run trend for skill differentials to narrow remains to be seen.

Interregional Wage Differentials

Wages vary not only by industry and occupation, but also by region. Michigan, for example, is a high-wage state, and North Carolina is a low-wage one. Most differences in wage rates among locations, however, can be easily explained. They are due to such factors as industry mix (Michigan's major industry is automobiles and North Carolina's textiles), skill mix of the labor force, and various characteristics of the labor force such as age, sex, and race.

Major concern with interregional differentials has been focused on the historical fact that wages in the South have been lower than in the rest of the nation. Based upon a sample from the 1960 Census of Population, Fuchs estimated that average hourly earnings of nonagricultural workers were about

20 percent lower in the South than in the rest of the nation.[17] Some of this difference could be explained by adjusting for labor force composition and city size, but, even after doing this, some differential still remained.

Further evidence of a North-South wage differential has been found by Gallaway. He standardized the wage data to eliminate the differences that could be accounted for by differences in interregional industry mix. Even after doing this, however, he found that there still existed a sizable—about 15 percent—difference in wages between the North and South.[18]

The persistence of lower wages in the South would seem particularly perplexing, since in some industries regional wage differentials have been sharply reduced or even eliminated entirely through collective bargaining. For example, Lester and Robie found that, by World War II, flat glass industry wage rates had been fairly standardized throughout the country, though because of incentive pay systems differentials in straight-time hourly earnings existed.[19] Following World War II a number of other unions used their bargaining power to eradicate interregional, mainly North-South, wage differentials. Regional differentials were eliminated mainly in those industries characterized by large, capital-intensive firms, in which southern plants formed a small percentage of the firms' total number of plants. The basic steel and automobile industries are the prime examples of such industries.

In most industries, however, straight-time average hourly earnings in southern plants continue to lag behind those in the rest of the nation, and almost all economists who have studied interregional wage differentials have explained this by the fact that the South is a region of labor surplus. It could be expected, therefore, that the market mechanisms would operate to reallocate labor out of the South and capital into the South to bring the South's capital-labor ratio into equality with the rest of the country. This indeed has tended to occur. There has been a net migration of population to the North and West in search of better-paying jobs, and industry has been moving into the South, raising its share of the nation's manufacturing employment. Yet North-South wage differentials continue to exist, and Douty explains this by what he calls offsetting factors: "Labor force migration to higher paying areas has been offset by a higher natural rate of population increase in the South and by a heavy flow of largely unskilled labor out of an increasingly mechanized agriculture into urban employments."[20]

Since unskilled and semiskilled labor is in greatest surplus in the South, wage differentials based upon skill are higher in the South than in other

---

[17] Victor R. Fuchs, *Differentials in Hourly Earnings by Region and City Size, 1959,* Occasional Paper 101 (New York: National Bureau of Economic Research, 1967).

[18] Lowell E. Gallaway, "The North-South Wage Differential," *Review of Economics and Statistics,* August 1963.

[19] Richard A. Lester and Edward A. Robie, *Wages Under National and Regional Collective Bargaining* (Princeton: Industrial Relations Section, Princeton University, 1946), pp. 74, 75.

[20] H. M. Douty, "Wage Differentials: Forces and Counterforces," *Monthly Labor Review,* March 1968.

regions. For the same reason regional wage differentials between the South and other regions are least pronounced among skilled workers, but most highly pronounced among unskilled manufacturing workers. A 1969 Labor Department survey disclosed that regional wage differentials were considerably less pronounced for either the professional and administrative or the clerical occupations than they were for blue-collar jobs.[21] As Table 10.3 shows, regional pay variations were particularly pronounced for unskilled plant workers: the southern average was 20 percent below that for the nation, while the averages in the West and North Central regions were 9 percent above. Regional differentials were much narrower for skilled maintenance workers, and even narrower still for clerical occupations. For professional and administrative occupations, regional wage differentials hardly existed.

Table 10.3 Regional Wage Differentials among Occupations, June 1969

Groups of Occupations	United States	Northeast	South	North Central	West
Unskilled plant	100	102	80	109	109
Clerical	100	101	96	100	105
Skilled maintenance	100	95	94	105	106
Technical support	100	101	97	101	101
Professional & administrative	100	101	99	99	102

SOURCE: *Monthly Labor Review,* January 1971, p. 53.

What about the role of unions? As indicated before, some unions have been able to narrow interregional wage differentials in multiplant industries operating in national product markets. Segal found that this was the case in the period 1947–1954 in such industries, but that industries operating in local product markets did not exhibit such narrowing.[22] Similarly, the more competitive industries exhibited less narrowing, and these industries were characterized by varying degrees of unionization. Segal concluded, therefore, that the failure of unions to narrow differentials was due to the surplus of labor in the South and the absence of collective bargaining in some areas.

The persistence of a North-South wage differential should not obscure the long-run trend of a narrowing of interregional wage differentials, evidence of which has been accumulated by Easterlin.[23] He attributes this largely to the migration of labor from low- to high-income areas. Capital, at the same time, has tended to move into the less industrially developed regions, and there is today a more equal distribution of manufacturing throughout the nation than there used to be. Federal minimum wage legislation and the spread of col-

---

[21] Harry F. Zeman, "Regional Pay Differentials in White-collar Occupations," *Monthly Labor Review,* January 1971, pp. 53–56.

[22] Martin Segal, "Regional Wage Differences in Manufacturing in the Postwar Period," *Review of Economics and Statistics,* May 1961, pp. 148–155.

[23] R. A. Easterlin, "Regional Income Trends, 1840–1850," in Seymour E. Harris (ed.), *American Economic History* (New York: McGraw-Hill, 1961), chap. 16.

lective bargaining have also contributed somewhat to the narrowing of differentials.

What of the future? Will labor continue to flow out of surplus labor regions and capital into them until interregional wage differentials disappear, as is posited by economic theory? Will institutional forces, such as collective bargaining, become more significant?

Most economists would answer yes, though they might concede that it will still take a long time to accomplish. For example, the labor force in the South continues to grow faster than in the rest of the nation. But at some point in the future this will no longer be the case, for, as Douty points out, as the South becomes increasingly urban, demographic factors will become less powerful in the perpetuation of wage differentials.[24] As per capita income rises in the South, the market for many products will expand to the point where production in the South will be justified in terms of economies of scale; a major trend in industrial location, moreover, is to put plants closer to their consumer markets. Southern industry, therefore, will become more like industry in the rest of the country. Also, unionism is growing in the South, and collective bargaining, too, will become more prevalent and a powerful factor toward reducing regional wage differentials.

Do Unions Raise Real Wages?

The final question in relation to wage structure that we shall concern ourselves with is, "Do unions raise real wages?" This may sound like a strange question, particularly since in our discussions of unionism we had concluded that their role was to improve the lot of their members. Yet many economists seriously doubt that unions do improve the position of their members relative to that of nonunion members, and the empirical evidence is mixed.

Considering the long struggle that unions had to conduct to be able to organize, one would expect that through collective bargaining, they would have won for their members wages that exceeded those of nonunion workers. In a study conducted four decades ago, Douglas concluded that unions, through collective bargaining, could raise their members' earnings in the early stages of organization, but that, after an initial gain, nonunion wages kept pace with what unions won for their members.[25] Douglas reached this conclusion based on the data for the period 1890–1926. Using data for a later period, Ross and Goldner reached a very similar conclusion.[26]

Unions as Enders of Economic Exploitation of Labor

Both the Douglas and Ross and Goldner findings can be explained in terms of the economic theory of exploitation. According to this theory, employers,

---

[24] Douty, *op. cit.*

[25] Paul H. Douglas, *Real Wages in the United States, 1890–1926* (Boston: Houghton Mifflin, 1930), p. 562.

[26] Arthur M. Ross and William Goldner, "Forces Affecting the Inter-industry Wage Structure," *Quarterly Journal of Economics*, May 1950.

having greater bargaining power than unorganized workers, enjoy monopsonistic power in the labor market. Just as pure monopoly means that there is
only one seller of a given product, pure monopsony would mean that there
is only one buyer for a particular commodity. Of course, pure monopsony
is a rarity (the U.S. government is the only purchaser for certain types of
armaments), and only the one-industry company town approximates it in the
labor market. The fact that a surplus of labor exists in some areas, however,
does give employers a degree of monopsonistic power.[27]

Having a degree of monopsonistic power, an employer, as the purchaser
of labor, is able to set a price for it (wage rate) that is below its marginal
value. The difference between the wage rate and labor's marginal value represents the degree of exploitation. (This concept of exploitation should not
be confused with the Marxian idea of labor exploitation.)

Figure 10.3   The Wage Rate in the Monopsonistic Labor Market

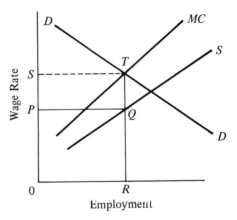

The case of the monopsonistic buyer of labor is illustrated in Figure 10.3.
DD is the labor demand curve, and is equal to the value of labor's marginal
product. Marginal cost and value of the marginal product are equal at the
intersection of MC and DD, and the employer maximizes his profits. At this
point he will hire OR number of workers. If the labor market were competitive he would pay them OS, but the competition among workers for the
jobs that he is offering enables him to pay only OP. The rectangle PQTS,
therefore, would represent the excess profits earned by the employer because
of his monopsonistic power, and it is equal to the economic exploitation that
his workers suffer.

Now if the workers organize they increase their bargaining power vis à
vis the employer. The fact of unionization thus enables the pushing up of the
wage rate from OP toward OS. Once the wage rate equals OS and the exploitation has been eradicated (the wage is equal to labor's marginal revenue
product), the union cannot push wages up further without causing unemploy-

_____
   [27] See, for example, Robert L. Bunting, *Employer Concentration in Local Labor
Markets* (Chapel Hill: University of North Carolina Press, 1962).

ment; so, following this initial period of unionism, union wage gains will be no higher than nonunion wage gains, since both depend upon increases in the value of labor's marginal product.

Empirical Studies of Unionism and Relative Wages

A number of economists, in comparing interindustry wage differentials, have attempted to isolate those variables that explain why some industries pay higher wages than others. Dunlop has argued that high wages are linked mainly with large increases in productivity, and increases in industry production, the small proportion of total costs that labor costs form, the absence of competitive conditions in the product market, and the skill content of the industry's job also have an effect.[28] Slichter included other variables, such as high capital investment per worker, high value added by manufacturing per worker, and a low percentage of women workers in the industry.[29]

These explanations of interindustry wage differences thus stress technical-economic factors, not unionism. But Garbarino, who like Dunlop emphasized technological change and product market structure as the major factors in interindustry wage differentials, also saw unions as being of importance.[30] His analysis, therefore, merits special attention. Technological change raises labor productivity, and, if the industry is a competitive one, the gains are shared with consumers in the form of lower prices, but, if the industry has a concentrated structure, the gains need not be shared. The gains in productivity also provide the means for increasing wages, but only if the workers are organized into unions that can exert bargaining power can they force employers to pass some of the gains on to them.

Research by Weiss, however, tends to question the association between interindustry wage differentials and employer concentration in the product market.[31] He found, for example, that employers in concentrated industries hired higher-quality workers than employers in more competitive industries. According to him, "The laborers in concentrated industries seem to receive no more for their services than they might in alternative employments for persons with similar personal characteristics." Even so, he concluded that unions did raise worker earnings a little over those of workers in poorly organized industries.

Another approach to comparing union and nonunion wages has been to compare different periods of time. Ozanne, for example, compared the earnings of production workers in manufacturing in the period 1923–1939, when a very small percentage of the workers were organized, with the period 1947–

---

[28] John T. Dunlop, "Productivity and the Wage Structure," in *Income, Employment, and Public Policy* (New York: Norton, 1948).

[29] Sumner Slichter, "Notes on the Structure of Wages," *Review of Economics and Statistics*, February 1950.

[30] Joseph W. Garbarino, "A Theory of Interindustry Wage Structure Variation," *Quarterly Journal of Economics*, May 1950, pp. 282–305.

[31] Leonard W. Weiss, "Concentration and Labor Earnings," *American Economic Review*, March 1966, pp. 96–117.

1957, when a significant portion was. Since he found that real compensation per worker went up almost twice as fast in the unionized period as in the nonunionized, he concluded that collective bargaining had had a substantial influence on wages.[32]

Using the same type of approach, that is, comparing two periods of time, Rees reached the opposite conclusion. He compared the behavior of wages in the steel industry following World War I, when the industry was not organized, with their behavior after World War II, when a powerful union existed,[33] and found that wages rose less in the unionized period. He attributed this to collective bargaining, as follows: When the steel industry was not unionized, management would raise wages whenever the industry was booming and more labor was needed; wage changes thus took place fairly often. Under collective bargaining, however, wages become sticky; that is, they are fixed for a period of time and are not changed until the existing agreement comes up for renewal, and as a result long periods of time may elapse before wages are changed.

Research by Levinson also found a small differential in the wages of unionized workers over unorganized ones.[34] He found that unions were better able to resist downward pressures on wages during periods of economic decline and labor surplus. In his view, unions are best able to widen the union-nonunion wage differential in periods of unemployment, for in periods of high employment it is the level of employment that determines relative wage changes, and nonunion workers share equally in wage gains.

The most comprehensive recent study of union-nonunion wage differentials has been conducted by Lewis.[35] His data show that there is a correlation between the degree of unionism in an industry and its wages, and that unionized workers receive 10 to 15 percent higher pay than unorganized workers. Like Levinson, he found that the impact of unions is strongest during periods of unemployment and weakest during periods of inflationary boom. During an economic downturn the union is better able to protect wage rates, but during a boom employers seeking labor bid up its price without the encouragement of unions.

Conclusion

All the studies keep coming back to the fact that unions do exert bargaining power, but that their ability to win more for their members depends upon

[32] Robert Ozanne, "Impact of Unions on Wage Levels and Income Distribution," *Quarterly Journal of Economics*, May 1959, pp. 177–196.

[33] Albert Rees, "Wage Determination in the Basic Steel Industry," *American Economic Review*, June 1951, pp. 389–404.

[34] Harold M. Levinson, *Unionism, Wage Trends, and Income Distribution: 1914–1947*, Michigan Business Studies, No. 10 (Ann Arbor: University of Michigan Press, June 1951).

[35] H. Gregg Lewis, *Unionism and Relative Wages in the United States* (Chicago: University of Chicago Press, 1963).

economic circumstances. That unionism is not an independent force in winning wage differentials is implicit in Segal's study, which related union impact and market structure.[36] His classification of product markets by scope and competitive characteristics, along with an analysis of related degrees of union organization, supports the finding that unions can take advantage of employer discretion in the pricing of products to win gains for their members. Where product markets are competitive, however, employers have no price-setting ability, for prices are determined by supply and demand; so unions, too, are severely limited in their ability to set wages at levels other than what they would be without them.

At this point some students, on the grounds that such a conclusion ignores the dynamics of the situation, may be ready to object to the conclusion that, based on union-nonunion differentials, collective bargaining has had relatively minor impact on wages. Some claim that the fact that unions achieve wage increases for their members through collective bargaining forces nonunion employers also to raise the wages of their workers. Unorganized firms may follow the collective bargaining pattern simply to remain nonunion, for if their wages lag too far behind those of unionized firms, their employees will see the advantage of joining unions themselves. Even in the absence of a fear of unionization, nonunion employers would have to keep their wages in line with what was being paid by organized firms simply to be able to compete in the labor market for capable workers.

Labor's Share of National Income

The fact that labor, unionized or not, has enjoyed rising real wages is obvious. The rise in workers' living standards is due to the growth in the American economy. As was indicated back in Chapter 2, this has been true over the long run: we bake a bigger pie, so everyone gets a bigger piece. But do workers get a bigger share of the pie now than they used to?

Empirical Findings

In a study of money and real wages in five countries (France, Germany, Sweden, United Kingdom, and United States) for the century from 1860 to 1960, E. G. Phelps Brown and Margaret H. Browne found that the increase in real wages over the period was based primarily upon increasing productivity.[37] Workers were able to obtain very substantial rises in real wages because, as a result of technological change and other factors, the value of the product

---

[36] Martin Segal, "The Relations Between Union Wage Impact and Market Structure," *Quarterly Journal of Economics,* February 1964, pp. 96–114.

[37] E. H. Phelps Brown with Margaret Browne, *A Century of Pay* (New York: St. Martin's Press, 1968), p. 334.

of the marginal unit of labor also increased substantially. Phelps Brown has also concluded that the proportionate share of the product going to labor has not changed.[38]

The seeming constancy of labor's share of national income has puzzled economists for many years. The empirical evidence is not clear cut, however, for a problem arises in determining how to measure labor's share. One of the most usual techniques is to take the proportion of national income that is distributed as compensation to employees. This seems to indicate a fair degree of constancy, with employee compensation accounting for about two-thirds of national income, but as Table 10.4 shows, there does seem to be a gradual rise in the employee compensation percentage of national income during the past four decades.

Table 10.4 National Income and Compensation of Employees, 1929–1972, Selected Years (in billions of dollars)

Year	National Income	Compensation of Employees	Compensation as Percent of National Income
1929	86.8	51.1	58.9
1930	75.4	46.8	62.1
1933	40.3	29.5	73.2
1935	57.2	37.3	65.2
1940	81.1	52.1	64.2
1945	181.5	123.1	67.8
1947	199.0	128.9	64.8
1950	241.1	154.6	64.1
1955	331.0	224.5	67.8
1960	414.5	294.2	71.0
1965	564.3	393.8	69.8
1966	620.6	435.5	70.2
1967	653.6	467.2	71.5
1968	711.1	514.6	72.4
1969	766.0	566.0	73.9
1970	798.6	603.8	75.6
1971	855.7	644.1	75.3
1972p[a]	934.9	705.2	75.4

[a] p = preliminary.

SOURCE: U.S. Department of Commerce.

Even these data, however, may understate the share going to labor, when labor is considered not as employees but as a factor of production. Some economists contend that the categories for which national income data are reported—compensation of employees, corporate profits, income of unincorporated businesses, rental income of persons, and interest—do not accurately reflect the returns to the factors of production. Haley, for example, argues

---

[38] E. H. Phelps Brown, *The Economics of Labor* (New Haven: Yale University Press, 1962), p. 220.

that the "incomes of unincorporated enterprises" consist of both returns to the owners for the capital that they have invested and for the work that they have performed.[39] In national income accounts, however, all the income of unincorporated enterprises is treated as if it were a return to property, and none of it is allocated to labor.

In an attempt to overcome this problem, Kravis split the reported incomes of unincorporated enterprises between labor and capital, allocating a constant 65 percent to the former and 35 percent to the latter. On this basis he found the property share of national income declining, from 30.6 percent in the period 1900–1909 to 23.8 percent for 1949–1957.[40] Kravis also split the unincorporated enterprise income in slightly different ways, which offered somewhat different property shares, but they all indicated decline over time. It is not very easy to determine precisely what share of the income of unincorporated enterprises should be allocated to labor, but Haley concludes that on any basis on which entrepreneurial income is split between labor and property shares, the share to national income attributable to labor has increased since 1900. Increasing shares to labor have also been referred to by Kendrick and Dennison.[41]

Other studies, however, continue to discern constancy of labor's share. Weintraub, in particular, offers evidence of the near constancy of the wage bill in gross business product for the period 1929–1957.[42] He explains this largely in terms of a near constancy in the wage-cost markup factor (k). Thus, if wages are boosted the wage share of the product value is not increased, because the price of the product is increased proportionately.

Other explanations of the constancy of labor's share are based primarily on the constancy of the production function (the functional relation between inputs and output); that is, total output shows constant returns to scale. Brown, for example, maintains that the marginal product of each factor of production is a constant proportion of its average product regardless of the quantity of each factor that is employed.[43] Thus, if labor and capital are paid in accordance with their marginal productivities, their shares will be a constant proportion of total output.

Unions and Labor's Share of National Income

All of these explanations are solely in terms of the economics of factor share distribution and ignore the role of trade unions. Even those, such as Haley

[39] Bernard F. Haley, "Changes in the Distribution of Income in the United States," in Jean Marchal and Bernard Duclos (eds.), *The Distribution of National Income* (New York: St. Martin's Press, 1968), pp. 21–28.

[40] Irving B. Kravis, "Relative Income Shares in Fact and Theory," *American Economic Review*, December 1959, pp. 917–949.

[41] John W. Kendrick, *Productivity Trends in the United States* (Princeton: Princeton University Press, 1961); and Edward F. Denison, *The Sources of Economic Growth in the United States* (New York: Committee for Economic Development, 1962).

[42] Sidney Weintraub, *A General Theory of the Price Level, Output, Income Distribution and Economic Growth* (Philadelphia: Chilton, 1959), pp. 13–15.

[43] Phelps Brown, *op. cit.*, pp. 219–230.

and Kravis, who have reported a rise in the labor factor's share of national income do not ascribe it to the activities of unions. If we examine the functional distribution of national income, we find that the rising share being distributed as compensation to employees has not been achieved at the expense of corporate profits, but reflects a decline in the percentages going to unincorporated enterprises and interests and rents. Much of "labor's" gain, therefore, may merely reflect the decline in unincorporated enterprises, mainly farms, and the conversion of a larger proportion of the labor force to employee status.

An elaborate attempt to explain the constancy of labor's share through the interrelation of economic and institutional forces has been offered by Kerr.[44] Unions, he says, are unable to increase labor's share of national output, basically because they cannot exert control over employer pricing policy. If the union pushes up the wage rate, the employer may raise his price or introduce labor-saving devices that raise productivity. Either way, he returns labor's share to what it had been before the wage increase. In fact, Kerr believes that unions, through collective bargaining, cannot increase labor's share more than temporarily, and that "only through quite deep penetration into economic decision-making, either directly or indirectly through government," can unionism do so. Since unions have been accorded a voice in industry pricing and production policies in very few instances, and they are not that actively involved in government (there is no "labor" party in the United States), their ability to affect income distribution is severely limited.

Even if unions are unable to increase their members' real wages, this does not mean that they may not be of value to workers. Unions, as we should recall from earlier discussions, perform other functions for their members, such as winning them grievance procedures, which permit them to protest and win adjudication of arbitrary management decisions. Also, they win workers a voice in the determination of both working conditions and the form in which they wish to take advances in productivity, whether in wages, pensions, health benefits, or leisure. So, even if unions are not as powerful with respect to wages as one sometimes thinks, they still may be very important to their members.

Summary

In this chapter we have examined wage structure, internal and external. Any organization that hires workers establishes some sort of wage structure by which to remunerate its employees. Its wage policy relates its wages to those of other employers, in order to assure its competitiveness both in terms of costs of production and its ability to attract and retain workers. The firm also seeks to have a rational wage structure that assures proper relationship

---

[44] Clark Kerr, "Labor's Income Share and the Labor Movement," in George W. Taylor and Frank G. Pierson (eds.), *New Concepts in Wage Determination* (New York: McGraw-Hill, 1957), pp. 260–299.

between job content and recognition and reward, and job evaluation is increasingly being used to achieve this goal.

While the internal wage structure refers to the hierarchy of pay within the organization, the external wage structure refers to the distribution of pay within the larger environment, and Dunlop's concept of job clusters and wage contours seeks to relate the two. Despite vast changes in the economy over time, empirical evidence discloses that there is a high degree of stability in the wage structure over long periods of time.

Differentials in wages among industries can be explained in terms of different skill proportions, location, and the technical-economic nature of industries. High-wage industries tend to be large-scale, high-capital-investment-per-worker, oligopolistic ones. Low-wage industries, in contrast, tend to be typified by low capital investment requirements, ease of entry of new firms, competitive market structure, and relatively high labor costs. High-wage industries also tend to be relatively highly unionized, but the high wages seem to be linked to their technical-economic characteristics rather than to the fact of unionism as an independent force.

Occupational wage differentials are explainable mainly in terms of skill requirements. Over the years, however, there has been a marked reduction in skill differentials. This has been attributed partly to the rising level of educational attainment of the labor force, which has increased the supply of skilled workers relative to unskilled workers; to the fact that unskilled workers' wages are more cyclically sensitive; to government policy that seeks to boost the wages of the lowest-paid workers; and to union wage policies that have stressed across-the-board cents-per-hour wage increases.

Interregional wage differential analysis has focused mainly on the historic North-South differences. The major explanation of lower earnings in the South has been the fact that it has been a region of labor surplus. Even so, there is evidence of a long-run trend of a narrowing of interregional wage differentials, as surplus labor flows out of low-wage regions and capital into them. It will be a long time, however, before wages are equalized in all regions.

Various studies also indicated that in their early stages of organizing, unions were able to win higher wages for their members, but that after an initial gain, nonunion wages kept pace. These findings could be explained largely in terms of recouping for workers the full value of their marginal product, which monopsonistic power of the employer in the labor market had formerly denied them. More recent studies give evidence of some slight advantage in wages for unionized workers, but unionism did not appear to be an independent force in winning these wage differentials. Market structure appears to be the key determinant, for when employers exercise discretion in pricing of products, unions can take advantage of this to win gains for their members.

Unions have also not been very successful in increasing labor's share of national income. This has been attributed largely to the fact that they cannot exert control over employer pricing policy, and higher wages won by unions are usually converted into higher product prices, which keep real wages down.

BIBLIOGRAPHY

Aspects of Labor Economics. Princeton: National Bureau of Economic Research and Princeton University Press, 1962.

Burton, John F., Jr., Lee K. Benheim, William M. Vaughn III, and Robert J. Flanagan (eds.). *Readings in Labor Market Analysis.* New York: Holt, Rinehart and Winston, 1971.

Douglas, Paul H. *Real Wages in the United States, 1890–1926.* Boston: Houghton Mifflin, 1930.

———. *The Theory of Wages.* New York: Macmillan, 1934.

Dunlop, John T. (ed.). *The Theory of Wage Determination.* New York: St. Martin's Press, 1957.

Fuchs, Victor R. *Differentials in Hourly Earnings by Region and City Size, 1959.* Occasional Paper 101. New York: National Bureau of Economic Research, 1967.

Ginsburg, Woodrow L., E. Robert Livernash, Herbert S. Parnes, and George Strauss. *A Review of Industrial Relations Research,* Vol. I. Madison, Wisc.: Industrial Relations Research Association, 1970.

Keat, P. G. "Long-Run Changes in Occupational Wage Structures, 1900–1956," *Journal of Political Economy,* December 1960.

Kravis, Irving B. "Relative Income Shares in Fact and Theory," *American Economic Review,* December 1959.

Levinson, Harold M. *Unionism, Wage Trends and Income Distribution: 1914–1947.* Michigan Business Studies, No. 10. Ann Arbor: University of Michigan Press, 1951.

Lewis, H. Gregg. *Unionism and Relative Wages in the United States.* Chicago: University of Chicago Press, 1963.

Phelps Brown, E. H. *The Economics of Labor.* New Haven: Yale University Press, 1962.

Phelps Brown, E. H., with Margaret Browne. *A Century of Pay.* New York: St. Martin's Press, 1968.

Reder, Melvin W. "The Theory of Occupational Wage Differentials," *American Economic Review,* December 1955.

Rees, Albert. "Wage Determination in the Basic Steel Industry," *American Economic Review,* June 1951.

Ross, Arthur M., and William Goldner. "Forces Affecting the Inter-industry Wage Structure," *Quarterly Journal of Economics,* May 1950.

Segal, Martin. "The Relations Between Union Wage Impact and Market Structure," *Quarterly Journal of Economics,* February 1964.

Taylor, George W., and Frank G. Pierson (eds.). *New Concepts in Wage Determination.* New York: McGraw-Hill, 1957.

11 WAGES AND INFLATION

Since World War II inflation has been endemic in the Western world. This inflation has not been the hyper type that plagued Germany in the 1920s when prices rose astronomically within a short period of time; it has, rather, been characterized by a fairly steady rise in prices and depreciation of the value of money. The United States did not escape this trend, but it enjoyed much greater stability of prices than did most other Western industrial nations.

The rapid annual rise in the level of prices in the United States that began in the latter half of the 1960s, therefore, led to a renewed national debate with respect to its causes. Classically, inflation could be explained in terms of demand-pull: too many dollars were chasing too few goods and, in the process, bidding up their prices. But by 1970, in the face of unused resources, both capital and labor, prices were rising, and in view of this some people contended that the nation was suffering from cost-push inflation, that is, rising costs were forcing businessmen to jack up the prices that they were charging for goods and services.

In this chapter, therefore, we shall examine the problem of inflation and its relationship to the labor market, but before doing so we shall focus attention on the relationship between productivity and wages, and following that we shall turn to the problem of inflation, particularly as it relates to productivity, wages, unemployment, and the role of unions. In so doing we shall examine both theoretical arguments and empirical evidence relating to wages, employment, unions, and prices.

Productivity

Definition of Productivity

Throughout this book the importance of rising productivity as the source of the nation's continually rising standard of living has been stressed. That this is so should be obvious from the very definition of productivity: output per unit of input. If, over time, a greater output is achieved with the same input, then there are more units of output to distribute. Thus, in an economy that consisted of only two people (Robinson Crusoe and Friday), if the two could pick a pound of berries a day, they would have half a pound each, but if they could pick two, and they did pick two, then they could have one pound each.

It is feasible to measure the output per each type of input—land, labor, and capital—and come up with a measure of productivity for each of them. Attempts have been made to measure total factor productivity. Kendrick, for example, has measured output against a combination of the capital and labor inputs.[1] Since the concern of labor economics is with the labor factor in the production process, we shall concentrate on labor productivity.

The usual measure of labor productivity is the output per man-hour, and responsibility for gathering the data belongs to the Bureau of Labor Statistics of the U.S. Department of Labor. BLS data generally give output per man-hours paid for, which would include sick leave, vacations, and holidays when pay is directly from the firm. Output information is usually collected by the Department of Commerce and other government agencies.

Data are collected for the total private economy, the total nonfarm private economy, major sectors of the economy, and a selected group of individual industries. Output in the economy is based upon dollar value deflated for changes in prices, but for individual industries, such as electric and gas utilities, physical output is measured. By dividing output by the figures available on man-hours worked, the BLS comes up with the data on output per man-hour.

Having to collect all these data presents conceptual and practical problems, and the data, therefore, represent only very good estimates of changes in output per man-hour over time. For example, it is most difficult to measure the output of government services. To a very large degree, therefore, no productivity growth is imputed to the government sector or, for that matter, to many service industries. Attempts are under way, however, to measure productivity in government by use of the same statistical tools that are applied to private industry. A special task force funded by the President's Productivity Commission was, in 1972, constructing an index that could measure productivity performance of about half of the federal government's civilian labor force.[2]

Another set of problems arises with respect to whose man-hours are included. We can, for example, distinguish between the total private economy, including agriculture, or simply the total nonfarm private economy. Another distinction can be made between output per man-hour of all persons, including the owners of businesses, and simply the employees. Table 11.1 presents the data, using an index, with 1967 = 100, of output per man-hour of all persons, including the self-employed, for both the total private and total private nonfarm sectors of the economy for the years 1947 through 1972.

The Historic Record

From Table 11.1 we learn that output per man-hour in the nonfarm private sector went up 96.3 percent in this twenty-five-year period, but that for the

---

[1] John W. Kendrick, *Productivity Trends in the United States* (Princeton: Princeton University Press, 1961). The Bureau of Economic Analysis of the U.S. Department of Commerce in 1972 published a combined labor and capital productivity index.

[2] *Business Week*, May 13, 1972.

Table 11.1 Indexes of Output Per Man-Hour, All Persons, in the Private Sector of the Economy, 1947–1972 (1967 = 100)

	Output Per Man-Hour	
Year	Total Private	Nonfarm
1947	51.3	57.1
1948	53.6	58.8
1949	55.3	61.1
1950	59.7	65.0
1951	61.5	66.3
1952	62.7	66.9
1953	65.3	68.9
1954	66.9	70.5
1955	69.9	73.6
1956	70.0	73.2
1957	72.0	74.8
1958	74.3	76.7
1959	76.9	79.3
1960	78.2	80.3
1961	80.9	82.7
1962	84.7	86.4
1963	87.7	89.1
1964	91.1	92.4
1965	94.2	95.1
1966	98.0	98.4
1967	100.0	100.0
1968	102.9	102.9
1969	103.4	102.7
1970	104.3	103.5
1971	108.1	107.1
1972	112.7	112.1

Source: U.S. Department of Labor, Bureau of Labor Statistics.

total private economy the increase was even greater, 119.7 percent. We should have anticipated this difference, for, as was pointed out in the very first chapter, productivity in agriculture has been rising faster than in the rest of the economy. The table also shows us that the gains in productivity do not occur with precise regularity: for the nonfarm sector, for instance, there was an actual drop from 1955 to 1956 but a gain of more than 6.0 percent from 1949 to 1950.

To a considerable degree the trends in productivity tend to follow the pattern of the business cycle. At the peak of an economic boom, productivity increases tend to become smaller as full utilization of plant capacity is reached, production bottlenecks appear, and marginal workers and machinery are employed. Productivity is even more adversely affected as the economy slides into a recession, because sales and production are cut back faster than the work force. But, as the economy picks up once more, the increase in production results in the fuller utilization of plant capacity and labor force, and, consequently, productivity tends to increase at a rapid rate.

Productivity increases vary not only by year but also among industries.

Figure 11.1 indicates a wide variation in labor productivity increase among thirty-eight industries from 1957 to 1970. At one extreme, petroleum pipelines experienced an almost 10 percent average annual growth in output per man-hour, while, at the other, footwear had a less than 1 percent a year increase.

Returning to the total economy and averaging out the year-to-year fluctuations reveals that the trend for the period 1947–1972 was about 3.25 percent annual increase in output per man-hour for the total private economy and 2.75 percent for the nonfarm sector. The 3.25 percent rate for the total private economy is somewhat higher than the rate for an even longer period of time, for data tracing labor productivity changes back to the early years of this century indicate a rate of slightly under 2.5 percent annual increase.[3]

Explanations of Rising Productivity

Although labor productivity figures relate output to the one input, they do not measure the specific contribution of that factor of production. "Rather they express the joint effect of a number of interrelated influences on the use of the factor in the production process—such as changes in technology, substitution of one factor for another, utilization of capacity, layout and flow of material, the skill levels and efforts of the work force, and managerial and organizational skills."[4] Obviously the whole set of attitudes—competition in a free market, getting ahead, the idea of "progress"—ushered in with capitalist industrialism in the eighteenth century has underlain the long-run trend of productivity rise. More directly, three factors generate labor productivity improvement in the economy at large: the quality of the labor input, the quantity of the capital input, and innovations that permit more efficient use of the labor input.

With respect to the quality of the labor input, a better-trained, more skilled worker can produce more units of output within a given time period than a less skilled, poorly trained worker. Thus, the increasing number of years of schooling that workers undergo, and the vast training and development programs that industry conducts, have been extremely important in increasing the efficiency with which labor works. The declining percentage of the labor force that comprises unskilled laborers and the increasing percentage of professionals, such as engineers and scientists, is indicative of the improved quality of the labor force. Scientists can make new discoveries, engineers can convert them into new machinery and methods of operation, and well-educated workers can operate the new, sophisticated systems. Im-

---

[3] *Trends in Output Per Man-Hour in the Private Economy, 1909–1958*, Bureau of Labor Statistics Bulletin 1249, December 1959, p. 16.

[4] Jerome A. Mark, "Concepts and Measures of Productivity," in *The Meaning and Measurement of Productivity*, Bureau of Labor Statistics Bulletin 1714, September 1971, p. 7.

Figure 11.1 Growth in Output per Man-Hours in Selected Industries, 1957–1970

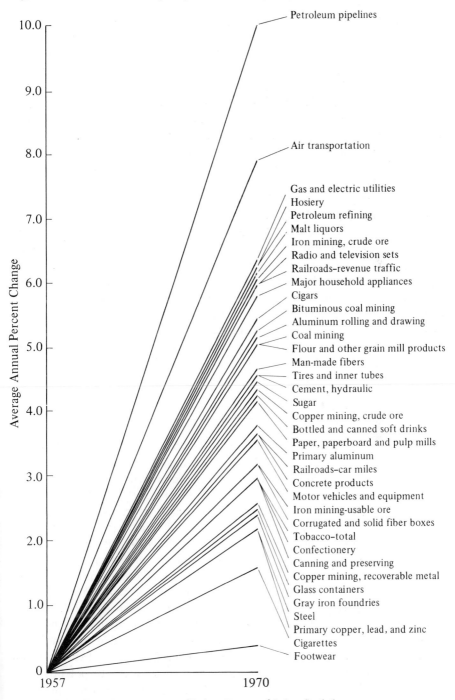

SOURCE: U.S. Department of Labor, Bureau of Labor Statistics

proved quality of the labor force is also partially attributable to its health, which, in turn, is a result of better living conditions, sanitation, medical advances, and proper nutrition. Two-fifths of the increase in labor productivity has been attributed to the improvements in the quality of the labor force.[5]

The importance of the quantity of the capital-input contribution to productivity growth also should be apparent. A carpenter using an electric saw can cut more boards of wood in a given time than if he used a hand saw. The entire history of the Industrial Revolution has been a continual process of increasing the amount of capital equipment with which industry operates. The capital invested per employee in manufacturing, for example, is more than $20,000.

More efficient utilization of labor is the third factor contributing to the growth in labor productivity. Economies of large-scale production, which the growing market for goods and services has permitted, has been a major part of this more efficient utilization. The mass production techniques of the automobile industry, with its very specialized division of labor, is an example of such economies of scale. New technology, such as better plant layout and more efficient equipment, has been an even more important factor in terms of more efficient utilization of the labor force. Technological change encompasses more than better machinery, for advances in managerial control systems and in organizational behavior techniques have also been part of it. Improvements in transportation and developments in communication are also elements comprising technological innovation.

Unions and Productivity

The increase in the rate of productivity improvement in the recent period above its historic rate of 2.5 percent per year has occurred despite the claims of some people that unions retard the rate of productivity growth. Those who level this charge at unions point to union work rules, which often restrict the efficient utilization of manpower, and so-called featherbedding practices, whereby workers get paid even though no work is performed. Even where work is performed, it may be unnecessary, such as the rethreading of pre-threaded pipe by plumbers at building sites and the setting of bogus type by printers. Another example of the adverse impact of unions on productivity that is pointed to is the insistence that employers use work crews that are larger than necessary to perform a job: outstanding instances of this practice are the fireman in the diesel locomotive and the refusal of the longshoremen on the East Coast for many years to agree to a reduction in the traditional work gang size, despite the use of improved machinery. A further example of union action that prevents the realization of productivity potentials has been the refusal of some unions to allow the use of more efficient equipment,

---

[5] Edward F. Denison, *The Sources of Economic Growth in the United States and the Alternatives Before Us* (New York: Committee for Economic Development, 1962), p. 73.

for example, the fact that painters for many years were not allowed to use spray guns, or even wider paintbrushes.

Even when unions do not directly restrict output, some observers are of the opinion that their very existence serves to retard productivity improvement. In their view, the general effect of unions is to reduce work standards and to restrict management's ability to discipline the work force when it fails to meet standards that have been established. They also point to the fact that unions have, on occasion, disciplined their members for "producing too much." Fines levied by unions on members for exceeding union-imposed output quotas have even been upheld as legal by the Supreme Court.[6]

But the fact that output per man-hour has continued to rise in the same period that unionism and collective bargaining have become widespread would seem to cast doubt on the contention that unionism has retarded productivity growth. First of all, the ability of unions to set restrictive work rules and crew sizes has been limited to certain industries. In large sections of basic manufacturing, employers have never agreed to joint determination of plant operating decisions, such as speeds of operation or work crew sizes, and so unions have been unable to restrict productivity, assuming that they might have so desired.

Secondly, and more importantly, unions may actually encourage productivity improvement without actually intending to do so. This phenomenon takes place through the normal activities of unions in trying to win higher wages, benefits, and improved working conditions for their members. By their pressure on wages, unions may force managements to seek ways of operating more efficiently in order to absorb the wage increases and prevent them from being converted into higher labor costs. In other words, the unity between the value of labor's marginal product and its marginal cost is maintained by increasing the former in line with the rise in the latter. As long as employers have the freedom to innovate—that is, to introduce new machinery, plant layout, and systems of control—and most employers have that freedom, they can increase labor productivity. Indeed, the continual pressure of unions on labor costs may cause employers to expend greater efforts to introduce labor-saving techniques.

Neither the case for or against unions with respect to their impact on productivity can be considered proved. No one can deny that some unions have restricted productivity improvement. On the other hand, other unions, such as the United Mine Workers, have deliberately encouraged technological innovation so that their members, even though there would be fewer of them, would have higher wages. The general impact of unionism, by protecting workers against management discipline, may very well have retarded somewhat the rate of increase in output per man-hour. At the same time, however, through their pressure on labor costs, unions have encouraged employers to utilize labor more efficiently. Thus, there is no proof that unions have had any net impact on productivity.

---

[6] *Scofield v. NLRB* (Wisconsin Motor Corp.) SC-'69, 70 LRRM 3105.

Wages and Productivity

If productivity rises 2.5 percent per year over the long run, then members of the society should be able to enjoy increases in their real incomes of about the same amount. This could be achieved by holding payments to the factors of production steady, and converting the improved productivity into lower prices charged to consumers. Such a procedure would spread the benefits of improved technology among all members of society, including those who are not currently contributing to economic growth, as for example, retired workers, as well as to those who are currently economically active.

Some sectors of the economy do distribute productivity gains in the form of lower prices today, but as a total economy we have not done so for a long time. Instead, we have chosen to distribute the gains of productivity in the form of higher payments to the factors of production. Thus, real wages and real returns to property have been increasing, raising the living standards of those who are economically active, but ignoring those who, because of age, sickness, unemployment, or death of the family breadwinner, are not economically active. The needs of these people have to some extent been met in other ways—higher transfer payments (for example, social security, private pensions and disability payments, unemployment compensation, and welfare); these have been financed through the collection of taxes from the economically active. All in all, despite its shortcomings, this method of distributing the gains from productivity has been fairly well accomplished.

Another problem, however, presents itself. Since the real gains in income are limited by the gains in productivity, what if more is paid to the factors of production than their output has increased? For example, the increase in wages can be greater than the increase in productivity. When this happens, employers find that their labor costs have gone up, despite increasing output per man-hour, and, to the degree that they can (depending upon elasticity of demand for their products), they pass the increased costs on to the consumers in the form of higher prices. If money wages continually rise faster than productivity, the price level will also continually rise, and it is this problem that concerns us in this chapter.

Before further analyzing the problem, let us examine the data with respect to trends in money wages. Table 11.2 presents indexes of compensation per man-hour, in current dollars, for the private sector of the economy. Once again, using the year 1967 as the base (equal to 100), we find that compensation rose 291.4 percent from 1947 to 1972 for the total private economy and 266.6 percent for the nonfarm part of it. By referring back to Table 11.1, we can see that compensation per man-hour has grown much more rapidly than output per man-hour; the rate of increase in compensation has been about 5.5 percent per year, as against 3.0 percent for output per man-hour.

The fact that compensation increased much faster than productivity meant that unit labor costs were rising, and as costs rose so did the prices that businesses charged for their goods and services. As a result, the price level, as measured by the Consumer Price Index, rose 87.3 percent, about 2.5 percent per year, from 1947 to 1972. When the increase in the price level is removed from the increase in compensation, we find that the increase in real compensation per man-hour, therefore, was roughly equivalent to the increase in output per man-hour.

Table 11.2 Indexes of Compensation Per Man-Hour, All Persons, in Current Dollars, in the Private Sector of the Economy, 1947–1972 (1967 = 100)

Year	Compensation Per Man-Hour	
	Total Private	Nonfarm
1947	36.2	38.3
1948	39.5	41.8
1949	40.1	43.0
1950	42.8	45.3
1951	46.9	49.3
1952	49.8	52.0
1953	52.9	54.9
1954	54.5	56.6
1955	55.9	58.6
1956	59.5	62.0
1957	63.3	65.5
1958	66.0	68.1
1959	69.0	71.0
1960	71.7	73.9
1961	74.4	76.3
1962	77.7	79.3
1963	80.8	82.2
1964	84.9	86.1
1965	88.4	89.2
1966	94.5	94.6
1967	100.0	100.0
1968	107.6	107.3
1969	115.6	114.7
1970	124.0	122.7
1971	133.4	131.8
1972	141.7	140.4

SOURCE: U.S. Department of Labor, Bureau of Labor Statistics.

Some observers are quick to place the blame for the fact that money wages outstripped productivity gains upon the spread of unionism and collective bargaining. But, before jumping to such a conclusion, we must examine what the situation was before unionism and collective bargaining became so prevalent in the American economy. Bowen has done this, and the data indicate that since 1900 wages have been rising faster than productivity.[7] Since unions and collective bargaining have been important institutions for fixing money wages only since the mid-1930s, the phenomenon cannot be attributed solely to them.

The fact that money wage increases have outstripped productivity gains

[7] William G. Bowen, *Wage Behavior in the Post-War Period: An Empirical Analysis* (Princeton: Industrial Relations Section, Princeton University, 1960).

for as far back as data are available does not mean that the wage pressure on prices has not intensified in the period since unions have become important. Indeed, there is evidence that the problem has become more pronounced since collective bargaining became a major influence in the economy. In former times employer demand for labor tended to bid up wages in boom periods, but wage increases would slacken, and occasionally wages would even go down, during periods of economic decline. In more recent times, however, the pattern has been for unions to secure annual increases in wages and to eliminate wage reductions totally in recessions. The trend in collective bargaining toward long-term contracts, usually for three years' duration, makes wages still more recession proof, for such agreements normally contain built-in wage increases. Moreover, as we saw earlier, many unions have secured protection for their members against declines in real wages through escalator clauses that automatically result in higher wages when prices rise.

The change in the behavior of money wages has had its impact on price behavior. Whereas formerly the price level would rise during periods of prosperity, it also tended to decline during periods of recession, but this is no longer the case. Thus, for the past three decades prices have continued to rise, though at varying rates, through prosperity and recession.

Again, we should be on guard against reaching a conclusion that this is necessarily bad. Periodic deflations can be as bad as, and indeed even worse than, a steadily rising price level. It does indicate, however, that if the nation does not want a persistent rise in the price level, the problem of preventing it may have been compounded by the spread of unionism and collective bargaining.

The Problem of Inflation

What Is Wrong with Rising Prices?

Perhaps at this point we should inquire into what, if anything, is wrong with a rising price level. Not everyone is in agreement that rising prices are a serious problem, and some economists are of the opinion that society has been much too concerned about attempting to achieve price stability at the cost of failing to realize other national objectives. Indeed, Slichter argued that a moderately rising price level was a good thing, because it encouraged businessmen to invest in new capital and to increase production.[8]

Others, however, are less sanguine about rising prices. Some argue that a little inflation is like being "a little pregnant." The analogy, however, is hardly accurate, for there is no evidence that rising prices must build up momentum and eventually result in a runaway inflation. On the contrary, consumer prices rose at an annual rate of about 2.5 percent from 1947 to 1972, and the periods of greatest increase were wartimes (Korea and Vietnam), when special pressures were present.

---

[8] Sumner H. Slichter, "On the Side of Inflation," *Harvard Business Review*, 1957.

A rising price level, however, does present society with problems, and how deep those problems will be will depend upon whether prices are rising at 1 to 2 percent per year or 5 to 6 percent. Rapidly rising prices complicate the problems of making rational spending and investment decisions.[9] In an effort to protect the value of their money, people tend to direct into more speculative pursuits, and resources are channeled away from productive pursuits. The major domestic problem, however, stems from the fact that inflation results in a redistribution of income within the population, for not everyone's income keeps pace with the rise in prices. As the incomes of some people rise even faster than prices, they may become better off, but the income of others will fall behind, and consequently these people will suffer a reduction in living standards. Of course, people living on fixed incomes, whether they be bondholders or retired workers on pensions, suffer the most from inflation.

But inflation can also pose difficulties for the nation with respect to the rest of the world. If the prices of American products rise faster than those of other nations, then the United States could find its goods losing out in world market competition. Not only would exports decline as consumers abroad cut their purchases of American products, but as the prices of the imports dropped relative to American goods and services, American consumers would also be tempted to turn to imports in place of domestically produced goods. For example, the American merchant marine has declined sharply, because it is much more expensive to ship cargo by American than by foreign carriers. The concern with the adverse balance of international payments that developed in the late 1950s has been a major factor in stirring efforts to contain rising prices within the United States.

The Data on Prices

Having established that inflation can have very bad consequences, particularly if the rate of price rise is high, let us examine the record, not only for the United States, but for all the major industrial nations. From Table 11.3, we can quickly see that inflation has been a problem plaguing all of them. In fact, looking at the long run, we find that the United States has suffered less from inflation than any other major industrial nation.

Although the U.S. record may be better than that of other nations, there is no question but that price inflation has intermittently plagued the economy since World War II. At the war's end powerful consumer demand, which had been restrained during the war by the absence of most types of durable goods (no automobiles for civilian use were produced for four years, for example), was suddenly unleashed. Price and wage controls were also removed, and the consumer demand that had been built up during the war years carried the economy to new highs, but it also unleashed inflationary

---

[9] Jerry E. Pohlman, *Economics of Wage and Price Controls* (Columbus, Ohio: Grid, 1972), p. 45.

Table 11.3 Decline in the Value of Money in Industrialized Countries

	Average Annual Percentage of Decline		
	1959–1969	1968–1969	1969–1970
Australia	2.4	2.8	3.1
Canada	2.4	4.3	4.0
France	3.7	5.7	5.4
Italy	3.6	2.5	3.7
Japan	5.0	4.9	7.5
Sweden	3.7	2.6	5.8
Switzerland	3.0	2.5	2.5
United Kingdom	3.4	5.1	5.3
United States	2.2	5.1	5.7
West Germany	2.4	2.6	3.6

SOURCE: *Monthly Economic Letter,* First National City Bank, September 1970.

pressures. The rapid rise in prices of the years 1946–1948 was repeated in 1950–1952 during the Korean conflict, and much of the postwar rise in prices could be traced to those two periods. From 1952 to 1964, however, prices rose at an annual rate of only 1 percent. Then, with the escalation of the Vietnam War in 1965, a new period of rapid rise in prices was inaugurated.

Inflation: Demand-Pull or Cost-Push?

To a great extent the wartime inflationary periods conformed to the classic definition of inflation: prices rose because of a rise in demand relative to supply. Such a "demand-pull" inflation has been common to war periods because of society's unwillingness to pay for the costs of war through higher taxes; it inevitably ends up paying for them instead through higher prices. Of course, the two different methods of financing a war shift the burden of the cost to different groups in the population: the price rise approach tends to shift the burden to those least able to pay.

Very few economists would quarrel with this explanation of inflation as being related to very ebullient periods of economic growth, but some would disagree with it as an explanation of rising prices in other periods. For example, in the mid-1950s, following the end of the Korean War, expanded production appeared to be sufficient to meet consumer demand, yet prices continued to rise. Similarly, by the late 1960s and early 1970s the nation was actually suffering from underutilization of its physical and human resources, but prices continued to rise, and at an accelerating rate.

A number of economists diagnosed this situation as a new form of inflation, calling it "cost-push" inflation.[10] In their view, prices were not

---

[10] Some of the tendency toward higher annual increases in the price level has also been attributed to a shift in demand toward services, as was discussed in Chapter 1. Since output per man-hour tends to rise more slowly in service-producing than goods-producing industries, yet the incomes of the employees in these industries must generally keep pace with those of workers in other sectors, service prices tend to rise faster. Thus, between 1949 and 1971 the prices of commodities that consumers purchased rose 50 percent, but the prices of services went up 125 percent.

rising because of an excess of money chasing a shortage of goods, as according to classical economic theory, but because competitive forces were not strong enough to prevent unions and companies from negotiating big wage settlements. As we have seen, wage increases that outstrip gains in productivity increase unit labor costs of the companies and industries involved, and these increased costs are then passed on to consumers in the form of higher prices for the goods produced.

When the cost-push theory was first advanced, many economists denied its validity. They continued to insist that inflation was related to the supply of money, and to the relationship between aggregate demand and the supply of goods and services.

The defenders of the cost-push hypothesis were equally vociferous. They pointed to the growing power of organized labor to push up money wages beyond productivity advances, even in the absence of excess demand for labor. To the power of organized labor was added that of giant corporations, operating under oligopoly or monopolistic competition, to raise prices regardless of the demand for their products.

As in most debates there was merit to both arguments, and they could not be considered in isolation. Bowen's work, for example, pointed to a very complex interaction between demand-pull and cost-push in the inflationary process.[11] What transpired starting in the middle of the 1960s illustrates this interaction. Following a prolonged period of slow economic growth that had set in during the latter part of the 1950s, and during which the rise in prices had been moderate, the United States, under the impetus of the tax cut of 1964, was once again approaching a full employment level. The very next year, however, the American involvement in Vietnam had escalated into a full-scale war; the economic impact of this was to add $20 billion of federal spending without reducing the spending capabilities of business or consumers. Had taxes been raised in 1966 the Vietnam War might not have caused inflation, but President Johnson waited a year before he asked for a tax increase to cover the costs of the war, and then Congress dragged its feet for another year before enacting one—and by that time inflation was well under way.

Once inflation was under way it became very difficult to arrest, and as workers saw prices rising they put pressure on their union leaders to win them larger wage increases from employers. As employers found their labor costs rising, they in turn raised prices. The unions that bargained in subsequent periods, therefore, demanded still higher wage increases, which were followed by even larger price increases. The all-too-familiar wage-price spiral was in operation, and it can be seen in the figures for annual rises in the Consumer Price Index: from 1.3 percent in 1964 to 1.7 percent in 1965, 2.9 percent in 1966, 2.9 percent in 1967, 4.2 percent in 1968, 5.4 percent in 1969, and 5.9 percent in 1970. Only starting in 1971, with the imposition

---

[11] William G. Bowen, *The Wage-Price Issue* (Princeton: Princeton University Press, 1960).

of a freeze and then wage and price controls, did the rate of rise in the CPI start to drop, to 4.3 percent in 1971 and to 3.4 percent in 1972. With the easing of controls at the start of 1973, in the midst of an economic boom, price rises accelerated once again.

This period is a clear illustration of the interaction of demand-pull and cost-push as factors in inflation. The original cause of rising prices was the excess demand generated by the Vietnam War, but once inflation was under way it continued, even though excess demand had been dissipated by the end of the 1960s.

Hypotheses with Respect to Rising Money Wages

Before turning to the question of how to handle the problem of the wage-price spiral, which we shall take up in the next chapter, let us focus on the research that has been conducted concerning it. Much of the early research on the problem was conducted in the United Kingdom, and this was not unexpected, since the British had become aware of the problem earlier than we and had suffered, as a major world trader, from price increases more than we had.

The Phillips Curve

Studying the course of wage changes in the United Kingdom from 1861 to 1957, Professor Phillips of the London School of Economics found that there was a correlation between the rate of change of money wages and the unemployment rate.[12] His findings are demonstrated in Figure 11.2, which has the rate of unemployment on the horizontal axis and the rate of change of money wages on the vertical. The rate of unemployment and the rate of

Figure 11.2   The Phillips Curve Model

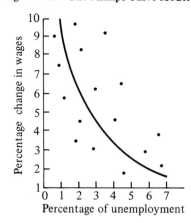

12 A. W. Phillips, "The Relation Between Unemployment and the Rate of Change of Money Wage Rates in the United Kingdom, 1861–1957," *Economica*, November 1958, pp. 283–299.

change in money wages for each year are shown by a dot, and as one looks at the dots they seem to form a pattern: when unemployment was high, wage increases tended to be low, but when unemployment was low, wage increases were high. Phillips drew a line showing the relationship between unemployment and wages, and the "Phillips curve" became a household term.

Other economists quickly turned to testing Phillips' findings in other situations. Garbarino found that for all leading Western industrial nations there is an inverse relationship between wage increases and unemployment, thus tending to confirm the Phillips curve hypothesis.[13] Next, researchers turned their attention to attempting to estimate equations that would determine money wages and prices. Using data for the United States economy since World War II, these equations generally implied that it required an unemployment rate of between 6 and 8 percent to keep increases in money wages within the bounds of increases in productivity, and thus to avoid price inflation. If unemployment, however, were to be at what is considered to be close to a full employment level, then wage increases would outstrip productivity gains at a rate that would boost prices about 3 percent.

Unemployment Plus Other Factors

Further research in both the United Kingdom and the United States began to raise doubts that the unemployment rate by itself could explain changes in money wages. While not rejecting the importance of unemployment, other studies indicated that it was only a partial explanation for advances in wage rates, but that other factors, such as changes in the cost of living and changes in the rate of corporate profits, also exert strong influence on wage rates. Reviewing the data for the United Kingdom, Dicks-Mireaux and Dow concluded that rising prices, as well as the demand for labor, caused increases in money wages.[14] Perry studied the United States economy during the period 1948–1960 and concluded that wage changes were related to changes in the Consumer Price Index, the corporate profit rate, and the change in the rate of corporate profits, as well as being inversely related to the rate of unemployment.[15]

Upon analysis, the fact that researchers have found that wage rate changes are linked with changes in prices, profits, and the rate of unemployment seems eminently reasonable. Workers are quite aware that dollars alone do not make one rich, but that what is important is the buying power of money. (A trip to the supermarket is an eye-opener for those unaware of

---

[13] Joseph W. Garbarino, "Income Policy and Income Behavior," in Arthur M. Ross (ed.), *Employment Policy and the Labor Market* (Berkeley and Los Angeles: University of California Press, 1965), pp. 56–88.

[14] L. A. Dicks-Mireaux and J. C. R. Dow, "The Determinants of Wage Inflation: United Kingdom, 1946–1956," *Journal of the Royal Statistical Society*, Series A, February 1959.

[15] George L. Perry, *Unemployment, Money Wage Rates, and Inflation* (Cambridge, Mass.: MIT Press, 1966).

this.) When consumer prices rise, therefore, workers will attempt to compensate for the shrinking value of their paychecks by securing higher wages from their employers. High and rapidly advancing employer profits tend to trigger higher union wage demands, because of their belief that the workers deserve to share in the gains. High profits, moreover, mean that employers can afford bigger wage increases, and their desire to avoid shutdowns of operations at times when profits can be earned encourages them to grant the union demands. On the other hand, falling profits and high unemployment rates are indicative of slack in the economy, and the excess of labor tends to discourage union demands for very high wage increases while encouraging employer resistance to such demands.

Perry's analysis of the data on the United States economy led him to conclude that an unemployment rate of a little over 6 percent would have been necessary to hold wage changes down to the level of productivity improvement from 1948 to 1960. Such a rate of unemployment was clearly unacceptable to the American people, so the nation experienced a rising price level that averaged a little under 2 percent per year. The net impact, therefore, of the Phillips curve hypothesis was that the nation faced a cruel dilemma in having to choose between unemployment and rising prices. Much analysis went into trying to determine what the precise trade-offs between the two would be. We shall return to this question of trade-off between unemployment and inflation very shortly, but first let us examine some other ideas with respect to the causes of changes in money wages.

Union Power

Phillips' linking of wage changes with the rate of unemployment did not go unchallenged. Another British economist, A. G. Hines, subjected wage data for the United Kingdom to other statistical tests, from which he concluded that it was union "pushfulness," and not the rate of unemployment, that was most closely associated with changes in wage rates.[16] His measure of pushfulness was the rate of change of unionization. In Hines' view, moreover, unions affected wage changes independently of the demand for labor. In other words, according to his hypothesis aggressive union activity could push wages up even if unemployment were growing.

Gallaway has, in effect, merged the Phillips and Hines approaches. According to his statistical studies of the United States economy, the rate of change in money wage rates can be explained by variation in unemployment levels. He is thus in agreement with Phillips, but he also found a shift in the Phillips curve relationship after public policy toward unions and collective

---

[16] A. G. Hines, "Trade Unions and Wage Inflation in the United Kingdom 1893–1961,"*Review of Economic Studies*, October 1969, pp. 221–251. Excerpts of his article are reprinted in B. J. McCormick and E. Owensmith (eds.), *The Labour Market* (Baltimore: Penguin, 1968), pp. 284–319.

bargaining changed in the mid-1930s.[17] The Wagner Act of 1935, which granted exclusive collective bargaining rights, imparted an upward bias to wage levels, which, according to Gallaway, has introduced a much more substantial inflationary bias in the American economy.

Labor Market Conditions

Another explanation of rising money wages in terms of the demand for labor has been expounded by Behman, but instead of linking wages to the rate of unemployment, she links them to the rates of rehiring, new hiring, and quits.[18] In her model, when there are large numbers of workers on layoff, they can be rehired as the economy picks up, without any increase in wage rates, but when this supply of laid-off workers is exhausted and firms must begin to hire new workers, they start to offer them higher wages in order to attract them. As wage rates rise in the firms that have expanded employment, workers in other firms become dissatisfied with their wages and tend to quit, forcing their employers also to raise wages. In a later study Behman also assigned institutional forces—unions—a role in changes in money wages in those industries in which union power is combined with employer market power, that is, industries with high concentration ratios (oligopolies).[19]

Can the Various Hypotheses Be Integrated?

The assigning of different causes for wage gains that are higher than productivity increases cannot be dismissed as being only of "academic interest," for in this case what is of interest to academicians is also of vital interest to the entire society. In this instance, where economists are analyzing employment, unemployment, union power, and inflation, the importance of the subject should be obvious to everyone. The different hypotheses, however, lead to entirely different policy actions. Assuming that the nation wished to hold down inflationary pressures, then agreement with the Phillips curve hypothesis would lead to a policy of finding the proper level of trade-off between unemployment and price rise; the union pushfulness hypothesis, on the other hand, would lead to policy designed to control union power.

By 1970 the United States government had apparently concluded that the Phillips curve approach was the correct one. The Nixon administration, therefore, deliberately adopted the policy of slowing down the economy in order to halt the inflation that had been plaguing the nation, in the hopes that after a brief respite, economic growth could start again without being accompanied by inordinately rising wages and prices. The results of the

---

[17] Lowell E. Gallaway, *Manpower Economics* (Homewood, Ill.: Richard D. Irwin, 1971), pp. 80–108.

[18] Sara Behman, "Labor Mobility, Increasing Labor Demand, and Money Wage Rate Increases in United States Manufacturing," *Review of Economic Studies,* October 1964.

[19] Sara Behman, "Wage Changes, Institutions, and Relative Factor Prices in Manufacturing," *Review of Economics and Statistics,* August 1969, pp. 227–238.

administration's "game plan," as its policy was called, were other than it had anticipated, for rising unemployment was not accompanied by lower increases in wages, but by even higher ones. The best term to describe the situation in 1970 was the one concocted by the influential British magazine, *The Economist*—"stagflation"—output was flat, profits falling, unemployment rising, and wages going up at a rapid rate.

Clearly, this large-scale test of the Phillips curve hypothesis had failed, and it became necessary to explain why. First of all, it is only fair to state that the events of 1970 did not lead all economists to abandon the Phillips curve hypothesis. A later analysis by Perry did not contradict the hypothesis, but claimed that there had been a worsening of the "trade-off" between unemployment and inflation because of structural changes in the labor force.[20] According to Perry, young workers (those under twenty-five years of age) and females now comprise a much larger proportion of the labor force than formerly, but they also have relatively high unemployment rates. But when a teen-ager who might work twenty hours per week for $2 an hour becomes unemployed, this does not exert as much downward pressure upon wages as when a thirty-five-year-old male worker loses his job. In Perry's opinion it is the tightness of the demand for prime-age males that determines the rate of wage rise, and not union-bargained wage settlements. The labor market for prime-age males in 1970 was about as tight when the overall unemployment rate was 5.5 percent as it had been a decade earlier when the unemployment rate was 4.0 percent. The implications of Perry's findings are that a given "tightness" of the labor market is now associated with a higher level of unemployment, and policy designed to restore full employment will lead to greater inflation, while policy designed to hold prices in check will result in higher unemployment.

While there is disagreement with Perry's conclusions, his analysis did successfully predict the large rise of 7 percent in average hourly compensation that accompanied the rising unemployment that averaged 5 percent in 1970. Others, however, believed that it was overly simplistic to assume that a rise in the rate of unemployment would be accompanied by a decline in the rate of wage increase. Phillips and the others who had found the inverse relationship between unemployment and wage changes had observed it after the fact, and as a statistical tendency. In other words, the relationship *usually* existed, and one could therefore be correct in pointing out the significance of the relationship. But it was also true that individual years deviated quite sharply from the overall trend. The data for the United States economy, for example, disclose that unemployment of about 5 percent has been accompanied by variations as wide as zero wage increase in one year to 6 percent wage increase in another[21] (and even 7 percent in 1970).

---

[20] George L. Perry, "Changing Labor Markets and Inflation," *Brookings Papers on Economic Activity,* No. 3 (Washington, D.C.: Brookings, 1971).

[21] Paul Samuelson and Robert Solow, "Analytical Aspects of Anti-Inflation Policy," *American Economic Review,* May 1960, pp. 177–194.

A second problem with attempting to effect a trade-off between unemployment and wage rises is that instantaneous results cannot be achieved. There is always a time lag between the rise in unemployment and the decline in the rate of wage rise. As previously discussed, unions enter into long-term agreements with employers providing for deferred wage increases; thus, an agreement concluded in a prosperity year will also call for wage hikes during the next two years, but by then general economic conditions may have deteriorated and unemployment risen. In the early stages of the 1957–1958 recession, too, wages continued to go up despite rising unemployment. It is only after unemployment persists for some length of time that Phillips curve effects can be expected to operate. Having experienced a relatively long period of slow economic growth and high unemployment the previous decade, the American people were not prepared to pay this price for price stability again, as the election results of 1970, in which the Democrats made gains, disclosed.

The factor of union power, moreover, cannot be entirely dismissed. The Phillips curve effect can work fairly quickly in the nonunion sector of the labor market, and did in 1970, when the rate of pay increase for nonunionized employee groups was only 3.5 to 4.0 percent. But rising unemployment had no impact on existing long-term collective bargaining agreements, which contained built-in wage increases negotiated earlier. Moreover, unions were winning their members an average of 8.5 percent in first-year wage increases in 1970, justifying them on the basis of past increases in prices.

Another reason advanced for the failure of the administration's policy of reducing the rate of wage rise through an increase in unemployment is that it ignored the role of expectations. Many people assumed, as the administration asserted, that the economic slowdown would be short lived, and they acted accordingly. For unions this meant largely ignoring the slowdown when making demands upon employers, and the deferred increases of previous settlements again became a floor for the wage increases of new agreements.

Expectations are not only important in terms of what people assume will be the length of a downturn in production, but also with respect to what they think will happen to prices and wages in the future. When prices have been rising rapidly for any length of time, people begin to assume that they will continue to rise in the future. Workers then demand higher wages to compensate for the expected higher prices; the higher wages they win inevitably lead to higher prices; and thus, once an inflationary wage-price spiral is under way, expectations of its continuance become a form of self-fulfilling prophecy.

The Dilemma of Wage Policy

If a 5 percent unemployment rate would not moderate the pace of wage rise in 1970, either because of the role of expectations or union power or, as claimed by Perry, because of structural changes in the labor force, then the nation faced a cruel choice. In order eventually to change expectations and reduce union power, it might have to suffer a much longer period of less than full employment and even much higher unemployment than has been experienced since the Great Depression. (According to Bowen, since 1900 wages have risen faster than output per man-hour whenever nonfarm unemployment has been less than 9 percent.) [22] Indeed, this remedy, no matter how distasteful, has been recommended by many people.

Others, encountering the same cruel choice, conclude that, no matter how unfair inflation is, unemployment is still worse. In their view, while many people suffer from reductions in their real incomes as a result of rising prices, they are still better off than those who would be unemployed. Those who hold this opinion, therefore, say that if a choice between the two must be made, then it is preferable to have high price increases and low unemployment.

All the hypotheses advanced to explain the wage-price spiral—government fiscal and monetary policy, union power, labor supply and structure, and unemployment—may have degrees of truth to them, and may be interrelated. In order to explore this possibility, let us engage in some economic analysis and construct a model of the inflationary process. [23] Let us assume that the economy, following a period of slack, in which physical and human resources were not fully utilized and prices were relatively stable, begins to expand once again.

As demand for goods and services increases, output and employment also begin to increase, but as the economy begins to approach full employment, prices and wages also begin to rise, because of increasing costs. Costs of production will rise because manufacturers start operating less efficient plants and equipment that formerly had been idle, and because labor costs rise even without an increase in wages when members of the secondary labor force must be hired. More money must be spent, for example, on recruitment, as the reserves of primary labor force members are depleted, and upon training, as less skilled and experienced workers are hired.

Not only may costs be rising, but, since demand is also increasing, selling prices also start to rise. At this point, workers begin to find that their actual real wages are falling below those which had been anticipated on the basis of the previously stable price level, and, when they find prices rising, they begin to put pressure on their union leaders to win them higher wages. Union appetites for higher wages are also whetted by the rising profits

---

[22] Bowen, *Wage Behavior in the Postwar Period, op. cit.,* p. 18.

[23] This model incorporates elements from various others, including cost-push elements from Bowen (William G. Bowen, "Wage Behavior and the Cost-Inflation Problem," in William G. Bowen [ed.], *Labor and the National Economy* [New York: Norton, 1965], pp. 78–87), and demand-pull elements from "Has Mr. Phillips Thrown the Policy Makers a Curve?" *Monthly Economic Letter* (New York: First National City Bank, February 1971), pp. 10–12.

that the firms with which they bargain are enjoying. With demand for industry's products expanding, unions find that their bargaining power has increased, because employers are reluctant to suffer strikes at a time when orders are flowing in and profits can be earned. The unions' demands, therefore, are met, even though this will add further to costs, and, since businesses price on some cost-plus basis, they raise the prices of their products.

Thus, the closer the economy comes to a full employment level, the greater the tendency for wages and prices to rise. This results from the fact that there are no longer underutilized resources that can be brought into operation. In the case of labor this means fewer unemployed workers to be hired, and so wages go up and this helps to push up prices.

The process cannot go on forever, however, because as prices rise the amount of goods and services that can be sold declines. The demand for labor, being derived from the demand for the goods and services it helps to produce, also declines. This is illustrated in Figure 11.3, in which, assuming OC to be an almost-full employment level, at which the wage rate is OA, if the wage rate climbs to OE, employment will fall to OG.

Up to this point there is nothing unusual in our analysis, for according to traditional theory, the resulting unemployment should push the wage rate back down again to OA, as workers compete for existing jobs. But, as we have seen, wages tend to be sticky, a fact that is even more true with unions on the scene, so the unemployment tends to persist. Unemployment, however, tends to be regarded as unnecessary and a waste of resources, so public demands for restoring full employment arise.

If unemployment cannot be gotten rid of through a reduction in wages, an alternative policy that the government can pursue is to attempt to shift the demand curve for labor upward and to the right. Through fiscal and monetary policy—increased government spending, tax cuts, increased money

**Figure 11.3 The Effect of a Wage Increase on Employment
and the Restoration of Full Employment**

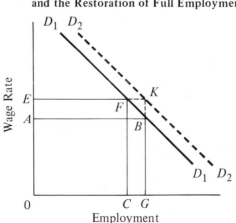

supply, or lower interest rates—the government can try to increase the aggregate demand for goods and services. Increased demand leads to higher production and the hiring of additional workers. In Figure 11.3, D_2D_2 represents the new demand curve for labor, which permits restoration of near-full employment at the wage rate OE.

This may sound like a very good solution to the problem, but it must be recognized that, in the process of increasing aggregate demand to accommodate the higher wage rate, the price level has been raised. At this point all the forces that had caused the original jump in wages from OA to OE start to operate once more, and prices and wages start to rise once more. Unless still further boosts in aggregate demand are forthcoming, there will again be an unemployment problem. But further increases in aggregate demand spell a further rise in the price level, and thus there emerges the problem of secular inflation.

Can the Dilemma Be Solved?

The problem of secular inflation at full employment was not unforeseen. One of the earliest advocates of government action to ensure full employment, Sir William Beveridge, recognized it.[24] Beveridge had defined full employment as an excess of job vacancies as compared to unemployed persons, which almost by definition means pressure on wages. The only thing new in our analysis, therefore, is that the pressure on wages sets in even before the economy reaches such a point of labor scarcity.

Thus, this analysis of the inflationary process allows room for all the explanations: government fiscal and monetary policy, the rate of unemployment, union pushfulness, and corporate pricing power. It does so, however, without clearly labeling anyone as a villain. In the absence of perfect competition in product markets, corporations can establish pricing policies that serve to raise the price level. Unions may have intensified the problem of the secular rise in the price level, but they do not appear to be the initiating agent: prices first begin to rise, then unions demand higher wages. This also is not new, for, as we saw in Chapter 3, in the review of union history, workers always tended to join unions in periods of rising prices in order to win some degree of protection for themselves. Of course, the ability of unions to win wage increases, to compensate for and even surpass rising prices, only serves to push prices up faster and to shift the burden of inflation from the backs of their members to less well-organized segments of the society, such as nonunionized workers, the retired, and those on welfare. But to ask unions to forego wage increases when prices are rising is no more reasonable than to ask employers to forego price increases when wages are rising.

We have come full circle back to our starting point of the question of choice between nearly full employment and more stable prices. Although the

---

[24] Sir William Beveridge, *Full Employment in a Free Society* (New York: Norton, 1945), p. 199.

problem of wage pressure on prices has been widely recognized, Douty, for one, says that an answer to the problem within the context of full employment has proved elusive. In his view:

> Given the existence of strong trade unions in strategic sectors of the economy, and government policy calculated to support employment at a high level, the process of wage determination can plainly exert secular pressure on the price level, and, if not in some way counteracted, may actually frustrate the basic goal of high employment and economic growth.[25]

More Responsible Behavior

Is there no way out of this dilemma? Some say that the solution lies in "responsible" behavior on the part of labor and management; this, for instance, was the essence of Beveridge's prescription.[26] But who determines when behavior is responsible and not? After all, management sees its responsibility as achieving as high a profit as possible for its owners and unions see theirs as winning as much as they can for their members.

Curbing Union and Corporate Power

Since union power to increase money wages and corporate power to set prices are part of the inflation dilemma, some people contend that a solution lies in reducing their power and restoring market conditions more in line with the competitive model of the economy. Such a policy would involve government in an active program of "trust-busting," that is, breaking up large corporations that have monopolistic power in particular sectors of the economy. To explore the possibilities and implications of such a policy is byond the scope of this book, but we can note that the antitrust acts have been in existence for more than eighty years and yet giant corporations are still with us; moreover, economies of scale serve to limit the extent to which we could re-create an economy of small-scale producers and at the same time maintain high levels of efficiency.

The problems with respect to reducing union power are equally great. Some would prohibit unions from engaging in industry-wide bargaining, but this would not necessarily reduce their ability to win higher wages and, in fact, might even strengthen it, as unions would be able to whipsaw employers into granting bigger and bigger settlements. Others believe that the answer lies in the opposite direction: toward greater centralization of bargaining on the assumption that it could reach agreements that would be in the national interest, and thus in the interest of most workers and employers, rather than in the sectional interests of particular groups of workers and employers.

Institutional reform, however, is not easily accomplished, and, moreover,

---

[25] H. M. Douty, "Some Problems of Wage Policy," *Monthly Labor Review*, July 1962, pp. 733–741.

[26] Beveridge, *op. cit.*, pp. 23, 199–207.

its desirability has also been questioned. As Bowen has warned, weakening a union's bargaining power in the wage area may also weaken its ability to defend workers against arbitrary treatment.[27] National labor policy has been predicated on the belief that workers have the right to organize and bargain collectively, and we should not rush into a reversal of that policy without considering all its possible consequences.

Improving the Functioning of the Labor Market

In the next chapter we shall examine proposed remedies to the problem of rising prices that involve government regulation of wages. At this point, however, let us look at proposals that are concerned with the correction of some of the imperfections of the labor market.

Economists who have studied the relationship between unemployment and inflation have been convinced that persistent attempts to reduce unemployment to a full employment level by means of general expansionary fiscal and monetary policies lead to sizable inflation. Part of the reason for this is that "bottlenecks," which develop because different grades of labor are not easily substitutable for others, begin to appear the closer the economy is to a full employment level. These bottlenecks usually take the form of shortages of skilled labor, such as engineers, construction craftsmen, and tool and die makers, before the pool of unemployed unskilled workers is absorbed. It is these types of shortages, moreover, which tend to bid up the price of labor. (Such bottlenecks also apply to the other factors of production, but we are concentrating only on the labor input to the production process.)

The proposed solution to the problem of wage pressure on prices, therefore, focuses on the supply of labor. During the discussions in the mid-1960s on how the economy might reach full employment without unleashing inflation, Barbara Berman Bergmann, for example, advocated expanding aggregate demand only until bottlenecks appeared. At that point, however, she would have had government policy shift to retraining programs, in order to increase the supply of the types of labor that were scarce, and to provision of relocation assistance, in order to get the labor to where it was needed, "giving at the same time some additional cautious increment to demand so that jobs opened up for the retrained."[28]

Treating the structural aspects of unemployment recognizes that not all workers are the same and that shortages of some types of labor can exist while the unemployment rate remains above a satisfactory level. Under these conditions, emphasis on better matching of jobs and workers through retraining programs, expanded hiring of blacks for jobs from which they have been historically excluded, youth employment programs, relocation assistance, and the providing of better labor market information may be the best means of

---

[27] Bowen, "Wage Behavior and the Cost-Inflation Problem," *op. cit.*, p. 87.
[28] Barbara Berman Bergmann, "An Approach to an Absolute Measure of Structural Unemployment," in Ross, *op. cit.*, p. 257.

mopping up excess unemployment. Such efforts would increase the size of the effective labor supply and the productivity of the labor force.

The idea of increasing the supply of labor to counteract inflationary tendencies is not novel, but merely a recognition that supply as well as demand is a determinant of price. If a shortage of certain key types of workers threatened, it could be countered by shifting the supply curve for those occupations, thus preventing the bidding up of the wage rate. Two purposes could thus be accomplished: (1) by overcoming bottlenecks toward the expansion of production, we could proceed to expand that production; (2) we could continue to use fiscal and monetary policy further to increase aggregate demand without putting as much pressure on prices. Both of these accomplishments would permit an expansion of total employment.

This type of proposal—to counter wage pressure on prices through the upgrading of worker skills and increasing of labor mobility—can also be stated as one of shifting the Phillips curve in order to secure a more favorable trade-off between inflation and unemployment. The importance of an active manpower policy has been recognized since the mid-1960s, and we shall return to it later, but before concluding our discussion of inflation let us examine briefly the notion that it cannot easily be dealt with unless we are prepared to make fundamental changes in our thinking and institutions.

Is Inflation Inevitable?

One view of inflation in the United States in the 1970s sees it as inherent in the way of living common to all the Western "mixed economies." Inflation is endemic to these economies, according to Sommers, because:

> We set our targets at full employment, and chase the ensuing inflation with restraints that can only induce unemployment; then we chase the unemployment with stimuli that can only produce inflation.
> We commit ourselves as a nation to a public guarantee of jobs for all, and then leave wages to be resolved by private parties whose legitimate private responsibilities prevent them from consulting the public interest.
> We exalt consumption while we decry the deterioration of our cities, as though we had infinite resources for both consumption and public investment.
> We will not ask ourselves to accept the tax rates necessary to meet our own insatiable demands for public services and social spending.
> We attempt to remove the risk and uncertainty which were the controlling disciplines of the free market, but we are reluctant to put anything in their place to serve the purpose of allocation and control.[29]

Sommers' indictment is indeed a formidable one, and we can hardly hope to discuss its manifold ramifications, but we have partially examined his first two points. With respect to them, he believes that "the deliberate achieve-

---

[29] Albert T. Sommers, "The Sources of Inflation in a Mixed Economy," *Conference Board Record*, September 1971, pp. 7–14.

ment of full employment must ultimately involve us with controls over wages." In the chapter that immediately follows, therefore, we shall explore those solutions to inflation that entail government interference with the wage-setting procedures of the labor market.

Summary

In this chapter we have more carefully examined the concept of productivity, which, as we have seen, is the source of gains in real wages. Output per man-hour has risen historically about 2.5 to 3.0 percent per year, due to improvement in the quality of the labor force, increase in the quantity of capital, economies of large-scale production, and technological innovation. There is no evidence, moreover, that unions have had any net impact on the rate of productivity increase.

Since money wages have risen faster than productivity, this has served to increase unit labor costs, which, in turn, have been reflected in higher prices for goods and services. Money wage increases outstripped productivity gains long before unions became important factors in the wage-setting process, but since then the wage pressure on prices has been intensified. This problem has not been a peculiarly American one, but is common to all the Western industrial nations.

This phenomenon of rapid rise in the price level, even in periods of undcrutilization of physical and human resources, has been diagnosed as a new form of inflation. As opposed to the traditional concept of "demand-pull" inflation, in which prices rise because of an excess of demand relative to supply, people now talk of "cost-push" inflation. According to this view, prices rise because competitive forces are not strong enough to prevent unions and companies from negotiating big wage settlements, which are then converted into higher prices.

Empirical research with respect to the wage-price relationship has produced a number of hypotheses to explain rising money wages. The most famous has been that of Phillips, who found that there was an inverse relationship between wage increases and the rate of unemployment. Others added the changes in consumer prices and corporate profits to the rate of unemployment as explanations of rising money wages, thus producing a different type of "Phillips curve." Still other explanations have been offered, including union power and labor market conditions, particularly the rates of rehiring, new hiring, and quits. A model was presented that attempted to integrate the various hypotheses with respect to money wage increases.

Between 1969 and 1971 an attempt was made in the United States to put the Phillips curve into practice by deliberately increasing the rate of unemployment in order to reduce the rate of inflation. The actual result, however, was that both unemployment and inflation increased. Some attributed failure to time lags, to an ignoring of the role of expectations, and to the factor of union power. Perry, on the other hand, believed that the policy did not work because of structural changes in the labor force that had shifted the trade-off position between unemployment and inflation.

If a 5 percent unemployment rate would not moderate the pace of wage rise, either because of the role of expectations or union power or structural changes in the labor force, then the nation faced a cruel choice: either more unemployment or more inflation. Solutions that have been offered to this dilemma include more responsible behavior on the part of labor and management, placing curbs on union and corporate power, and improving the functioning of the labor market. Others, however, believe that the problem of inflation is so deeply rooted in the institutions of Western mixed economies that it can only be solved by draconian measures; in terms of wages, the solution proposed most often has become government control, which will be examined in the next chapter.

BIBLIOGRAPHY

Behman, Sara. "Labor Mobility, Increasing Labor Demand, and Money Wage Rate Increases in United States Manufacturing," *Review of Economic Studies,* October 1964.

────. "Wage Changes, Institutions, and Relative Factor Prices in Manufacturing," *Review of Economics and Statistics,* August 1969.

Beveridge, Sir William. *Full Employment in a Free Society.* New York: Norton, 1945.

Bowen, William G. *The Wage-Price Issue.* Princeton: Princeton University Press, 1960.

────. *Wage Behavior in the Postwar Period: An Empirical Analysis.* Princeton: Industrial Relations Section, Princeton University, 1960.

Denison, Edward F. *The Sources of Economic Growth in the United States and the Alternatives Before Us.* New York: Committee for Economic Development, 1962.

Dicks-Mireaux, L. A., and J. C. R. Dow. "The Determinants of Wage Inflation: United Kingdom, 1946–1956," *Journal of the Royal Statistical Society,* Series A, February 1959.

Douty, H. M. "Some Problems of Wage Policy," *Monthly Labor Review,* July 1962.

Gallaway, Lowell E. *Manpower Economics.* Homewood, Ill.: Richard D. Irwin, 1971.

Kendrick, John W. *Productivity Trends in the United States.* Princeton: Princeton University Press, 1961.

McCormick, B. J., and E. Owensmith (eds.). *The Labour Market.* Baltimore: Penguin, 1968.

Perry, George L. "Changing Labor Markets and Inflation," *Brookings Papers on Economic Activity,* No. 3. Washington, D.C.: Brookings, 1971.

————. *Unemployment, Money Wage Rates, and Inflation.* Cambridge, Mass.: MIT Press, 1966.

Phillips, A. W. "The Relation Between Unemployment and the Rate of Change of Money Wage Rates in the United Kingdom, 1861–1957," *Economica,* November 1958.

Sommers, Albert T. "The Sources of Inflation in a Mixed Economy," *Conference Board Record,* September 1971.

12 GOVERNMENT REGULATION OF WAGES

As we have seen from the very opening of this book, the free labor market was supposed to be one in which wages were determined by the forces of supply and demand unfettered by any interference from outside forces. But it was equally true that no sooner had the free labor market made its appearance on the social scene than people reacted against its operation and sought to protect themselves from its consequences. For workers this meant to combine in order to take themselves out of competition and, thus, to try to affect wage rates that would differ from those that supply and demand would have established.

But not all workers had the ability to combine effectively, and many of them labored for extremely low wages. For a long time these workers were forgotten, but as standards of living rose there was a growth in social concern over the plight of those workers who were very poorly paid. At first this concern was limited to the weakest members of the labor force—women and children—but it eventually spread to male workers as well. Thus, government came to interfere with the workings of the free labor market through the establishment of legal minimum wages, and in this chapter we shall examine such legislation and its impact.

Government has also interfered with the workings of the free labor market to prevent wages from going too high. Such efforts have been put forth in emergency periods, specifically wartime, when the extraordinary demands of the war effort spelled problems so grave that society was willing to forego its belief in "free enterprise" and to substitute government coercion in its place, at least for the duration of the conflict. In this chapter we shall also focus attention on government wage controls of wartime periods.

Finally, as we were discussing in the last chapter, the full employment–money wage dilemma has prompted its own type of government interference in the wage-setting process. There have been advocates of outright wage and price control to deal with inflationary problems, and a very vocal chorus that has demanded the establishment of an "incomes policy," which is something less than outright controls. Indeed, during the first half of the decade of the 1960s, the United States had a type of incomes policy in the form of government-established wage and price guidelines. This form of government wage regulation will occupy us also in this chapter, as we attempt to explain its genesis, operation, and effectiveness. And before closing the chapter we shall briefly discuss the type of government regulation of wages that was introduced in 1971 in order to curb rising prices. First, however, let us turn to minimum wage legislation and its impact.

Minimum Wage Legislation

History

At the turn of the century a great outcry arose in Britain against labor conditions in a number of industries, which were very low paid and employed large percentages of women workers. The industries in which labor conditions were very poor became known as "sweated" industries. The sweated industries were small-scale, low-capitalized, highly competitive ones, in which employers vied with one another for business by offering lower prices, but in order to do so they had to drive wages and labor standards down as well. Because of the fierce competition, if one employer paid low wages the others had to follow suit or be driven out of business.

But to cry out against the situation was not enough. A solution also had to be found, and the one that gained dominance called for the establishment of legal minimum wages below which no worker could be remunerated. In 1909 Winston Churchill was able to pilot a bill through the House of Commons that established boards to set minimum wages in four trades in which wages were considered to be unduly low: chain making, machine-lace making, paper-box making, and tailoring.[1]

Small-scale, highly competitive industries in the United States also suffered from very poor labor conditions, and such industries as clothing became known as "sweatshop" industries. As in Britain, and in part, inspired by it, a social reform movement also arose in the United States, among its aims the enactment of minimum wage legislation. The movement, led by such groups as the National Consumers' League, achieved its initial victory in 1912, when Massachusetts enacted the first minimum wage law in the nation. Although the Massachusetts act only authorized a commission and wage boards to recommend minimum wages for women and children, it marked the breaking of new ground. Indeed, within the two-year period 1912–1913, eight other states also enacted minimum wage laws in order to protect the health and morals of women workers.

By 1923 six more states, the District of Columbia, and Puerto Rico had also enacted such legislation, but the drive for minimum wage legislation was frustrated by challenges in the courts to the constitutionality of government regulation of wages. The definitive judicial decision was rendered in 1923, when the United States Supreme Court reviewed the District of Columbia statute. By a 5 to 4 decision, the Supreme Court, in *Adkins v. Children's Hospital*, declared minimum wage legislation unconstitutional as depriving an

---

[1] See Roy B. Helfgott, "Minimum Wages as a Deterrent to Union Organization: Experience in the British Clothing Industry," *Current Economic Comment*, May 1959, pp. 47–58.

individual of his freedom to take whatever job he chose, on such conditions as were acceptable to him. This ruling arrested the movement toward minimum wage legislation.

The Fair Labor Standards Act of 1938

The first federal attempt at general minimum wages came with the New Deal and its National Industrial Recovery Act of 1933. The NRA codes of fair competition, which individual industries were adopting, provided for the establishment of minimum wages and maximum hours. But the Supreme Court struck down the act in 1935, and did likewise with a New York State minimum wage law in 1936. By 1937, however, the Court's majority had swung to a more favorable view of social legislation, and a Washington State minimum wage act was upheld as constitutional.

The way was now cleared for action on both state and federal levels, and in 1938 a special session of Congress enacted the Fair Labor Standards Act (FLSA), known popularly as the Wage-Hour Act. The fact that the nation was in the midst of a recession influenced the aims and contents of the new law: as in the case of the NRA codes of fair competition, it sought to put a floor under wages in order to boost employee income and purchasing power, reflecting President Roosevelt's policy of "reflation," and a ceiling to work hours in order to create more jobs for the nation's unemployed.[2]

The original FLSA provided for an immediate minimum for workers engaged in interstate commerce, with the exception of agriculture, most retail trade, and some other industries, of 25 cents an hour, with the figure rising to 30 cents in 1939 and to 40 cents by 1945. (The act also provided for workers to be paid one and one-half their normal wages for all hours over forty worked within a week, but we shall leave the examination of the hours part of the law to a later chapter, and confine ourselves here to the wage aspects.) Under the Fair Labor Standards Act, moreover, tripartite industry committees could recommend putting the 40-cent minimum into effect before the 1945 date, as long as that would "not substantially curtail employment in the industry," and the committees could also recommend reducing the minimum in order to curb a substantial reduction of employment.[3]

The rise in the general price and wage level during and following World War II made the 40 cents per hour minimum meaningless, but it took until 1949 to secure amendment to the FLSA to raise the minimum to 75 cents per hour as of 1950. As a price for securing a congressional majority to raise the minimum, its supporters had to agree to further restriction of its coverage. The 1949 amendments also did away with the industry committees for the continental United States, and applied the 75-cent minimum uniformly to all covered employments.

---

[2] Richard A. Lester, *Labor and Industrial Relations* (New York: Macmillan, 1951), p. 371.

[3] *Ibid.*, p. 372.

The original purpose behind the drive for minimum wage legislation was to boost the earnings of the very low-paid workers to some decent "minimum" standard. As the nation's standard of living rises, however, the concept of what constitutes an acceptable minimum also changes. By 1949 the 40-cent minimum had declined to 29 percent of average hourly earnings in manufacturing, but the 75-cent minimum that went into effect in 1950 brought it up to about half the average hourly earnings in manufacturing. As wages continued to rise, however, the minimum kept slipping relative to average earnings. As Table 12.1 indicates, by 1955 the 75-cent minimum was equal to only 40 percent of average hourly earnings in manufacturing.

Table 12.1 Federal Minimum Wage and Average Earnings in Manufacturing, 1949–1972

Year	Minimum Wage as of March 1	Average Hourly Earnings in Manufacturing	Minimum Wage as Percentage of Average
1949	$0.40	$1.38	29
1950	.75	1.44	52
1951	.75	1.56	48
1952	.75	1.65	45
1953	.75	1.74	43
1954	.75	1.78	42
1955	.75	1.86	40
1956	1.00	1.95	51
1957	1.00	2.05	49
1958	1.00	2.11	47
1959	1.00	2.19	46
1960	1.00	2.26	44
1961	1.00	2.32	43
1962	1.15	2.39	48
1963	1.15	2.46	47
1964	1.25	2.53	49
1965	1.25	2.61	48
1966	1.25	2.72	46
1967	1.40	2.83	49
1968	1.60	3.01	53
1969	1.60	3.19	50
1970	1.60	3.36	48
1971	1.60	3.57	45
1972	1.60	3.81	42

Source: U.S. Department of Labor.

Under these conditions a new drive was launched to get Congress to again raise the minimum, and it was hiked to $1.00 per hour in 1956, bringing it back up to half of average hourly earnings. As wages continued to rise, the minimum was pushed up to $1.15 in 1961 and $1.25 in 1963. The 1961 amendments, moreover, extended coverage to another 4 million workers, mainly in retail and service trades, but started them off at a $1.00 minimum wage in 1962, rising to $1.15 in 1964 and $1.25 in 1965.

As prices and wages began to mount with the escalation of the Vietnam War, Congress voted a further increase in the legal minimum, boosting it to $1.40 in 1967 and $1.60 in 1968. Again, additional workers were brought under coverage—about 8 million in smaller trade and service establishments, in government, in hospitals, and on large farms—but only by February 1, 1971, did the minimum for them reach the $1.60 level.[4]

Arguments for and against Higher Minimum Wages

The reasoning behind proposals to increase the minimum wage is simple: people are poor because they are low paid; therefore, by raising their wages you increase their incomes. In the words of the AFL-CIO: ". . . programs to lift the incomes of the low-paid workers must be an integral part of the campaign to eradicate the sources of poverty. Extension of minimum wage coverage and an increase in the minimum hourly rate are essential. . . ."[5]

A diametrically opposed view is that the minimum wage itself can be a breeder, rather than a preventer, of poverty. Clarence Long, formerly of Johns Hopkins University and now a member of the United States House of Representatives, has seen the social minimum wage—"the wage below which custom, employer ethics, or law forbids workers to be employed"—as pricing marginal workers out of jobs.[6] A similar view has been expressed by Demsetz, who sees the low-productivity workers—the unskilled, the poorly educated, the young, and the old—in the economy as being structurally unemployed because they are hindered by minimum wage laws and union wage rates from offering their services at wage rates reflecting their low productivity.[7] Finally, Stigler, echoing his earlier arguments on the subject,[8] has charged that minimum wage rates have been a serious barrier to the employment of unskilled young workers.[9]

Those who contend that minimum wages can harm more than they help low-paid workers base their arguments on economic theory. In their view, attempting to eradicate poverty through higher minimum wages treats wages only as income. Wages, however, are also a cost of production, and, since the demand curve is normally downward sloping, a large increase in the price

---

[4] In 1973 the Congress passed a new set of amendments to the FLSA that would have increased the federal minimum to $2.00 in 1973 and to $2.20 per hour as of July 1, 1974. Coverage was also to be extended to include about 1 million household domestics (though they would not receive the $2.20 until 1975), 5 million government employees, plus some others who had previously been excluded. President Nixon vetoed the proposal legislation because of the size of the increase.

[5] *AFL-CIO American Federationist*, April 1964.

[6] Presented in a talk to a seminar on "Manpower Trends and Labor Market Research in the 1960s," Cornell University, Ithaca, New York, December 13, 1960, at which the author was present.

[7] Harold Demsetz, "Structural Unemployment: A Reconsideration of the Evidence and the Theory," *Journal of Law and Economics*, October 1961, pp. 90–92.

[8] George J. Stigler, "The Economics of Minimum Wage Legislation," *American Economic Review*, June 1946, pp. 358–365.

[9] *The New York Times*, June 12, 1964.

of labor leads to a drop in the quantity of it that is demanded. But this type of argument holds against all nonmarket-induced wage increases, such as those won by unions for their members through collective bargaining. If society is willing to allow unions to interfere with the market setting of wages for their members, why can it not use the force of law to protect the most downtrodden members of the labor force?

Society, of course, can use the force of law in order to protect the lowest-paid workers, but there is disagreement as to the efficacy of minimum wages in accomplishing this objective. In those cases in which poorly organized workers are low paid because their employers enjoy monopsonistic power in the purchase of labor, legal minimum wages can be used to end economic exploitation, that is, paying wages that are below labor's marginal value product. As long as the legal minimum merely restores the equality between the value of the marginal product and the wage, it will not result in any reductions in employment. When workers are extremely low paid, establishing a higher minimum wage could improve their standard of living to the point where they could increase their productivity. In such a case the minimum wage would have the effect of increasing the workers' marginal value product so that it would be equal to the legal minimum.

In other cases, however, workers may be low paid because the value of their marginal product is low. If employers are forced to pay higher wages, that is, wages above labor's marginal value product, they will lose money. Employers faced with such a predicament will take steps to bring the marginal value product and the wage into alignment again, either by becoming more efficient through the substitution of machinery for labor or by raising the prices of their products and services. Thus, an increase in the minimum wage will have both substitution and contraction effects, and some low-paid workers will be worse off than before because they will lose their jobs and have no wages. The precise effects in any industry of an increase in the minimum wage will depend upon the elasticity of demand for labor, and demand will be more elastic the higher the percentage that labor is of total costs and the more elastic the demand for the industry's products.

Again, however, society has a right to determine that no worker should be paid below a certain amount, even if some workers will lose their jobs as a result, preferring instead to maintain the displaced people through government transfer payments. The proponents of higher minimum wages rarely present such arguments, however, being unwilling to admit that adverse consequences might result from the minimum wage. In fact, society might even want to shut down some very low-wage employments and move the low-paid workers into industries that are paying better wages.[10] Such a policy, however, would require programs to retrain the workers and provide them with skills that are in demand elsewhere, and these could be undertaken without closing out their present employments. The empirical evidence, moreover, indicates

---

[10] K. W. Rothschild, *The Theory of Wages* (Oxford: Basil Blackwell, 1960), pp. 150–151.

that workers who have been driven out of jobs through minimum wages generally end up in still lower-paying jobs, not in higher-wage ones.

The Impact of Minimum Wages

The evidence seems to indicate that minimum wages do raise the wages of workers, and that the periodic increases in the federal minimum wage since 1938 have not resulted in the dire employment consequences that some economists have been predicting for so long. Some workers, however, have lost their jobs and been forced into unemployment, out of the labor force, or into even lower-wage jobs in industries not covered by the FLSA. The studies by the Department of Labor have indicated that the direct employment effects of the periodic increases in the FLSA minimum have been minor, although the increase from $.75 to $1.00 had a somewhat greater impact than that from $.40 to $.75.[11] In about 15 percent of the plants studied by the Department of Labor, some workers were discharged because of the $1.00 minimum wage, basically because of their low productivity and inability to meet new production standards.[12] Labor Department studies of the impact of the $1.60 minimum in 1968 also indicated minimal adverse effects.[13]

There are those, however, who contend that the employment effects of minimum wage legislation have been greater than indicated by the BLS studies. Using more sophisticated statistical analysis, the studies by these others of the impact of higher minimum wages indicate more severe reductions in jobs.[14] Adie and Chapin's study of youth unemployment concluded that increases in the federal minimum wage cause unemployment among teen-agers, that the effects persist for a long time, and that they become greater as coverage is extended and enforcement made more vigorous.[15] Similar conclusions

---

[11] Various studies by the Bureau of Labor Statistics, as reported in *Monthly Labor Review*, January, June, and August 1951, March 1955, March, September, and November 1957, May, July, and October 1958, and March, May, and June 1960; and H. M. Douty, "Some Effects of the $1.00 Minimum Wage in the United States," *Economica*, May 1960, pp. 137–147.

[12] Norman J. Samuels, "Plant Adjustments to the $1 Minimum Wage," *Monthly Labor Review*, October 1958, pp. 1137–1142.

[13] *Minimum Wages and Maximum Hours Standards under the Fair Labor Standards Act*, U.S. Department of Labor, Wage and Hour and Public Contracts Divisions (Washington, D.C.: Government Printing Office, 1969).

[14] John M. Peterson, "Employment Effects of Minimum Wages, 1938–50," *The Journal of Political Economy*, October 1957; and "Employment Effects of State Minimum Wages for Women: Three Historical Cases Re-examined," *Industrial and Labor Relations Review*, April 1959. For a critique of Peterson's view, see comment by Richard A. Lester and rejoinder by Peterson in *Industrial and Labor Relations Review*, January 1960. See also John M. Peterson and Charles T. Stewart, Jr., *Employment Effects of Minimum Wage Rates* (Washington, D.C.: American Enterprise Institute for Public Policy Research, 1969); David E. Kaun, "Minimum Wages, Factor Substitution, and the Marginal Producer," *Quarterly Journal of Economics*, August 1965, pp. 476–486; and George Macesich and Charles T. Stewart, Jr., "Recent Department of Labor Studies of Minimum Wage Effects," *Southern Economic Journal*, April 1960, pp. 281–290.

[15] Douglas K. Adie and Gene L. Chapin, "Teenage Unemployment Effects of Federal Minimum Wages," *Proceedings of the Twenty-Third Annual Winter Meeting* (Madison, Wisc.: Industrial Relations Research Association, 1970), pp. 117–127.

were reached by Kosters and Welch in a study of the impact of minimum wages on employment patterns.[16] They found that minimum wage legislation did result in higher wages for some relatively low-productivity workers, but that the primary beneficiaries were adults, particularly white males. On the other hand, increased minimum wages made it more difficult for teen-agers, particularly nonwhite youth, to obtain jobs during periods of normal employment growth and to hold on to jobs when employment declined.

All studies of the impact of minimum wages are hindered by the fact that the economy is dynamic, and, since "other things" do not remain equal, it is difficult to isolate the effect of increases in the minimum wage (though the Kosters-Welch study was based on a model that tried to take other influences into account). Based upon their review of the studies conducted up to 1967 of the minimum wage impact, Kaufman and Foran concluded that minimum wages raise the wages of workers and may, in fact, redistribute income in favor of labor.[17] On the negative side, minimum wages did have adverse employment effects, but they could not find strong evidence that the resulting unemployment was disproportionately borne by the disadvantaged groups in society. Although they concluded that pushing up the minimum wage in some plants and industries does lead to a relative decline of employment in them, the displaced workers are often able to find alternative jobs in industries not covered by the Fair Labor Standards Act. The adverse effects of the legislation would be further reinforced, however, if minimum wage coverage were made universal, as the AFL-CIO proposes, for then there would be no alternative low-paying jobs to which low-productivity workers could turn.

Solving the Minimum Wage Dilemma

This analysis indicates that the nation faces another wage policy dilemma, this one with respect to the minimum wage. On the one hand, society wants to ensure that workers are paid some decent minimum wage relative to the nation's standard of living, and that employers, because of monopsonistic power, cannot pay them less than the value of their marginal product. On the other hand, society does not want, in the name of helping low-paid workers, to make their situation actually worse by destroying their jobs entirely.

In this case, however, the dilemma may be soluble. One type of solution would lie in introducing greater flexibility into minimum wage legislation. It is contended that because the law now establishes one uniform rate for all covered industries, the minimum is never raised high enough to satisfy the desires of the unions in the low-wage manufacturing industries that could

[16] Marvin Kosters and Finis Welch, "The Effects of Minimum Wages on the Distribution of Changes in Aggregate Employment," *American Economic Review*, June 1972, pp. 331–332.

[17] Jacob J. Kaufman and Terry G. Foran, "The Minimum Wage and Poverty," in Sar A. Levitan, Wilbur J. Cohen, and Robert J. Lampman (eds.), *Towards Freedom from Want* (Madison, Wisc.: Industrial Relations Research Association, 1968), pp. 189–218.

afford higher minimums, but it is raised too high to permit extension of protection to the even lower-wage excluded industries, for fear of disastrous employment effects in them. According to Rothschild, "the social advantages that can be derived from a minimum wage and its effectiveness will be greater the more flexible it is."[18] Such flexibility could be achieved through allowing the minimum to vary in conformity with industrial productivity and having separate minima for individual industries, areas, occupations, or age groups.

One approach that has been suggested for achieving greater flexibility would be to have a lower minimum for youth so that they could obtain jobs commensurate with their low productivity. Others recommend abandonment of the one, uniform minimum wage and substitution of individual industry boards. These boards could then establish specific minimum rates for their own industries, based upon the realities of their specific situations.

This approach to minimum wage regulation would permit minimum rates to be set based on the economic situations of particular industries. Those industries which could afford higher minimum rates could have them without, at the same time, endangering employment opportunities in other industries. It would, moreover, tend to relieve the current problem of driving more workers out of covered employment into noncovered employment, and offer some degree of protection to all employees in interstate commerce.

Whatever approach to the establishment of minimum wages that is taken—one national uniform minimum or separate industry minima—it must be recognized that low-productivity workers may still not earn enough to support themselves or their families. In 1966, a prosperous year, the Bureau of the Census reported that close to 2 million family heads with full-time jobs earned so little that their families were classified as "poor." Another solution to the dilemma, therefore, might lie in government-provided income supplements rather than boosting the wage so high that the worker loses his job and his entire income.[19] This type of subsidy is not new: during the period 1945–1955 more than 2 million persons received income supplements under the G.I. Bill of Rights while enrolled in on-the-job training programs. Such supplements have also been available to workers undergoing training under various federal acts of the past few years. Payment of similar income supplements to low-productivity workers would permit maintenance of minimum living standards without interfering with market processes. This should not increase the costs to society, since the nation would otherwise have to foot the bill for those persons if they were unemployed.

The Davis-Bacon Act

The Fair Labor Standards Act is not the only federal law regulating wages in private industry. The Davis-Bacon Act of 1931 requires construction contrac-

---

[18] Rothschild, *op. cit.*, pp. 154–155.

[19] For an exposition of how such wage supplements might work, see Edgar K. Browning, "Alternate Programs for Income Redistribution: The NIT and the NWT," *American Economic Review*, March 1973, pp. 38–49.

tors who receive federal funds in excess of $2,000 to pay at least the prevailing wages in their area, as determined by the Secretary of Labor. In practice this has meant the extension of the building trade union rates to all federal government construction. By a 1964 amendment, fringe benefits are included in the definition of prevailing wages.

The Davis-Bacon Act, passed in the depths of the Great Depression, was designed to halt a downward spiral in the wages of construction workers. In recent years, however, it has come under severe criticism, and charges have been leveled that it contributes to inflationary pressures. There is valid reason to question the need for government support of construction wages, for in October 1970 the average of hourly rates for all building trades in cities was reported as $6.27, and ranged from $4.84 for laborers to $7.12 for plumbers. Construction wages, moreover, were rising more than twice as fast as those of other workers; in 1970 average hourly earnings in construction went up 46 cents, and in 1971 another 47 cents. In early 1971 President Nixon temporarily suspended the Davis-Bacon Act, in order to slow skyrocketing wages and prices in the construction industry and to end federal encouragement of inflation.

The Walsh-Healy Act

What the Davis-Bacon Act did for construction wages, the Walsh-Healy Public Contracts Act of 1936 tried to do for all other industries. The Walsh-Healy Act provides that prevailing minimum wages, as established by the Secretary of Labor, be paid in all government-let contract work exceeding $10,000. These prevailing minimums for government work are determined for about thirty industries on the basis of wage surveys conducted by the Bureau of Labor Statistics. Given the importance of federal government work in many of these industries, such as electronics, they become virtually a minimum wage for the entire industry.

Since in some industries Walsh-Healy rates are no higher than those mandated by the Fair Labor Standards Act, many people have questioned the need to perpetuate the act. An analysis by Morton of the operation of the act led him to conclude that it is a far from effective instrument for combatting substandard wages, and that its repeal would not detract from government protection of worker welfare.[20] Similar conclusions were reached by Christenson and Myren, who suggest repeal of the Walsh-Healy Act, since the FLSA provides ample protection against low wage rates being an important factor in the assignment of government contracts.[21]

[20] Herbert C. Morton, *Public Contracts and Private Wages: Experience under the Walsh-Healy Act* (Washington, D.C.: Brookings, 1965), pp. 126–131.
[21] Carrol L. Christenson and Richard A. Myren, *Wage Policy under the Walsh-Healy Act* (Bloomington: Indiana University Press, 1966), p. 227.

Wage Controls during National Emergencies

Aside from attempting to ensure that workers are paid certain minimum rates, the government normally has not attempted to regulate wages in private industry, leaving this to either the free labor market or free collective bargaining between labor and management. In times of severe national emergency, however, the nation has decided that neither the free market nor free collective bargaining can be relied upon to accomplish the national goals. Thus, in three wartime periods—World War I, World War II, and the Korean War—wages, along with prices of goods and services, have been regulated.

The justification for price and wage controls during wartime is that, with a major share of production going for armaments, severe shortages would develop and prices would be driven up, because the supply of civilian goods cannot be increased. Of course, the government could tax away the excess income of consumers, thus obviating the danger of demand pulling up prices, but the people have never been willing to be taxed that heavily. The other alternative would be simply to allow prices to rise until a new equilibrium was achieved. There are two faults with this proposal, however: (1) if it did work, it would channel all goods in short supply to upper-income groups who could afford the higher prices; but (2) it probably could not work, because as prices rose workers would demand higher wages, landlords higher rents, and so on, and an inflationary spiral would ensue.

Thus, to prevent inflation, price and wage controls have been imposed during war periods. It is beyond the scope of our interest to examine price controls and the need for rationing of goods that develops when prices are held below an equilibrium level. We shall instead focus only on wage regulation in the Second World War and Korean War periods.[22]

World War II

In January 1942 a national War Labor Board was established to settle labor-management disputes in the interests of keeping all vital production going. By mid-1942 the nation's stock of physical and human resources was being fully utilized, and in order to prevent runaway inflation, price and wage controls were enacted in October, and the WLB was also given the task of controlling wages. According to Executive Order 9250, wages were to be stabilized at the levels prevailing on September 15, 1942.

The board evolved what became known as the "Little Steel Formula," because it was first applied to the steel industry aside from the very largest companies. According to this formula, wages were to be allowed to rise 15 percent over their levels of January 1, 1941. The 15 percent figure paralleled the rise in living costs between January 1941 and May 1942.

---

[22] Much of the analysis presented here is based upon B. C. Roberts, *National Wage Policy in War and Peace* (London: Allen & Unwin, 1958), chaps. 3, 5.

Wages, however, were not completely frozen beyond the 15 percent increase. The WLB permitted the maintenance of established differentials between groups of workers, and special increases were allowed to correct interplant and intraplant inequities, to raise substandard wage rates, and to aid effective prosecution of the war by allowing vital industries to pay higher wages in order to attract labor. Fringe benefits, which did not result in immediate increases in income, were also permitted. Wages and prices thus were never frozen; indeed, they continued to creep upward.

The War Labor Board was a tripartite agency, being composed of representatives of labor, management, and the public. In 1943 the national board was supplemented with thirteen tripartite regional boards and seventeen industry agencies. According to Gitlow, its three basic organizational principles were (1) voluntarism, (2) tripartition, and (3) a centrally developed set of general principles on substantive issues.[23]

Since the War Labor Board was at the same time both a wage control and disputes settling agency, it encountered a conflict between its two functions. The easiest way to settle a labor-management dispute would have been to allow the workers to receive a higher economic package. To have done so, however, would have run counter to the desire to hold wages down, but to concentrate on the latter aim might have helped to breed labor disputes. Despite this inherent conflict, the WLB is considered by almost all who have studied its operations to have worked well in both preventing interruptions in production due to labor disputes and in controlling wages.

Part of the reason why the WLB worked well was that the price and wage control policy was a flexible one; it was never intended to "freeze" the status quo, but only to limit the upward movement. Moreover, the WLB was concerned only with wage rates, not weekly earnings. Thus, while the rise in wage rates was limited, worker earnings soared due to the fact that there were vast opportunities for working overtime. Had there not been this rise in earnings, worker discontent would have risen with a policy that held down wage rates despite increases in prices.

The Korean War

Although the Korean War hardly had the impact on the American economy that World War II had had, it nevertheless produced inflationary pressures. Part of the reason for this lies in expectations: since prices had always risen in war periods, people assumed that they would do so this time, and in order to beat the price rise they ran out to buy goods as fast as they could. The spurt in demand, of course, led to higher prices, and the expectations of the population became a self-fulfilling prophecy.

The government was slow to act in stemming the new inflation through the invoking of controls. The General Ceiling Price Regulation was not issued

---

[23] Abraham L. Gitlow, *Wage Determination Under National Boards* (Englewood Cliffs, N.J.: Prentice-Hall, 1953), p. 127.

until January 26, 1951, and wages and prices were frozen the same day. However, the Consumer Price Index had risen 8.0 percent in the eight months between June 1950, when hostilities commenced, and February 1951, when the stabilization program got underway. From February 1951 to February 1952, a period during which prices and wages were under control, the CPI rose only 2.2 percent.

Since the Korean conflict was far from all-out war, the experience with wage and price stabilization is of particular interest. The stabilization process had begun in December 1950, when President Truman, acting under the powers granted to him by Congress in the Defense Production Act, established the Office of Defense Mobilization. Immediately under this agency was the Economic Stabilization Agency with two subdivisions, the Office of Price Stabilization and the Wage Stabilization Board (WSB). The WSB, therefore, was a wage control and not a disputes settlement agency. In addition, the compensation of executives and professionals was regulated by the Salary Stabilization Board, and employees subject to the Railway Labor Act were under the jurisdiction of the Railroad Price and Wage Board.[24]

The Wage Stabilization Board was modeled on the War Labor Board in that it was tripartite in composition. Under the order of January 26, 1951, a temporary freeze on wages was maintained until wage control policies could be formulated. The fact that prices had been rising so rapidly until then had led to union demands for substantial wage increases. The WSB, therefore, devised a new "Little Steel Formula," allowing wages to rise 10 percent above their level of January 1950.

The unions believed that the 10 percent limit on wage increases placed too much of the burden of the war effort on workers' shoulders, and their disagreement led to a walkout of the labor members from the Wage Stabilization Board in February 1951. President Truman then constituted a new Wage Stabilization Board, which was more like the old War Labor Board in that it had a dispute-settlement function as well as wage stabilization. The WLB's regional boards and industry agencies, however, had no authority to settle disputes.

One of the major problems facing this new board was the fact that a number of labor-management agreements, such as the General Motors–UAW pact, contained escalator clauses according to which wages were to be raised as prices went up. Recognizing that not permitting these previously agreed-to increases would upset existing labor-management relations, the WSB went along with them, but in fairness to other workers, it had to allow all workers to receive wage increases to compensate for rising prices. In fact, the cost of living became the basic factor in determining future wage changes.

The WSB did not attempt to impose any predetermined wage pattern upon the nation, preferring to leave room for collective bargaining between labor and management. It permitted unions and managements to negotiate

---

[24] *Ibid.*, p. 201.

special increases to correct interplant and intraplant inequities, fringe benefit improvements, incentive payments, and annual productivity gains along the lines of those that were also contained in the GM-UAW agreement.

In its second year of operation the WSB ran into the same obstacle that the War Labor Board had encountered a decade before: John L. Lewis. The United Mine Workers had negotiated a wage increase that went beyond what the stabilization program allowed, and when the WSB refused to approve it Lewis called a strike. President Truman, on the eve of the 1952 presidential elections, personally intervened to overrule the WSB in Lewis' favor. At this point the Chairman of the WSB resigned, and he was quickly followed by the industry representatives. For all intents and purposes the Wage Stabilization Board was dead, but it was continued on a temporary arrangement until the newly elected president, Eisenhower, ended all controls early in 1953 as a cease-fire was effected in Korea.

Appraisal of the Korean War Controls

Experience with controls during the Korean War foretold many of the problems that would be encountered when the United States undertook another effort at wage and price regulation two decades later. In the opinion of the public members of the Wage Stabilization Board, in the absence of really effective measures by Congress to control inflation, the WSB could do no more than prevent the movement of wages from adding much to inflationary pressures. From 1950 to 1952 wages rose about 14 percent, about 8 percent before controls were imposed and about 6 percent afterward. Clearly, wage stabilization was only of limited success.

In contrast to World War II, there was an absence of a true wartime psychology, with everyone willing to subordinate his own interests to the cause of victory. Even though the Korean War had only incidental impact on the economy, price pressures built very rapidly because, unlike World War II, the United States had no large body of unused resources to bring into play. Another factor was the institutionalization of collective bargaining, as a result of which, in Roberts' opinion, wage stabilization policy was set by General Motors and the United Automobile Workers, not by the United States government.

Based upon his study of wage controls, B. C. Roberts concluded that as a temporary expedient wage restraint may be of great significance, but the crisis psychology tends to dissipate rapidly. A wage stabilization policy, thus, ultimately rests on the willingness of employers and unions to accept it. The United States policy during the Korean War was basically a voluntary policy of wage restraint, in spite of its legalistic framework, and it was abandoned by both sides when it failed to suit their economic interests.[25]

---

[25] Roberts, *op. cit.*

An Incomes Policy

A Different Trade-Off

It is time to return to the question that occupied us in the last chapter: how to deal with the wage-employment dilemma in nonwar periods. On the one hand, excessive monetary and fiscal restraint to curb rising prices can lead to intolerable levels of unemployment, but, on the other, monetary and fiscal promotion of economic expansion to ensure low levels of unemployment can result in unacceptable rates of rise in the price level. One set of proposals for solving this dilemma has been against trading off between low unemployment and minimal inflation, but, instead, trading both of them off against the freedom of unions and management to set wages and companies to set prices.

Although Roberts reached the general conclusion that a centralized system of wage controls is ill fitted to cope with the complex problems of a modern industrial economy, there have been advocates of such a solution. In their view, it is the power wielded by many unions and corporations to set wages and prices that undermines price stability. In the absence of competitive product and labor markets, therefore, public power must be wielded to check the exercise of private power by unions and corporations. John Kenneth Galbraith has been for many years the leading advocate of government intervention into wage and price setting as the only alternative to inflation or unemployment.[26] As the inflationary problem worsened in 1970, while unemployment rose, many more people were converted to this position. For example, Dr. Arthur Burns, chairman of the Federal Reserve, a former opponent of government intervention, proposed the establishment of a wage-price review board as part of an "incomes policy" to halt inflation.

What exactly an incomes policy is no one is quite certain, but in general it is a form of controls that may be somewhat less than compulsory. Presumably, national targets of production, price, and wage movements are set, usually with the cooperation of labor and management representatives, and everyone tries to adhere to the parameters established. The Organization for Economic Cooperation and Development (OECD) has defined an incomes policy as follows:

> . . . that the authorities should have a view about the kind of evolution of incomes which is consistent with their economic objectives, and in particular with price stability; that they should seek to promote public agreement on the principles which should guide the growth of incomes; and that they should try to induce people voluntarily to follow this guidance.[27]

---

[26] See, for example, his comments in John Kenneth Galbraith, *American Capitalism: The Concept of Countervailing Power* (Boston: Houghton Mifflin, 1952), p. 205; and Galbraith, "Inflation: What it Takes," chap. 4, *The Liberal Hour* (Boston: Houghton Mifflin, 1960), pp. 63–76.

[27] *Policies for Price Stability* (Paris: Organization for Economic Cooperation and Development, 1962), p. 23.

The Wallich-Weintraub Proposal

One form of incomes policy that has been proposed would minimize government interference in product and labor markets and rely instead on its taxing power to force companies and unions to behave in a noninflationary manner. Professor Wallich of Yale and Professor Weintraub of the University of Pennsylvania independently have suggested that the government each year prescribe a noninflationary level of wage increase. Labor and management would be free to bargain for any level of increase that they wanted, but those corporations that granted wage increases above the allowable amount would have a special surtax imposed upon them.[28]

Weintraub contends that placing the full burden of policing anti-inflation wage increases upon the business firm would stiffen management's resistance in collective bargaining to very high union demands. Unions, in turn, would come to recognize that excess wage demands would increase management's bargaining power, since the cost of agreement would outweigh that of holding firm. The net result would be collective bargaining settlements more in line with increases in national productivity, obviating the need for direct government intervention into labor and product market pricing.

Many people, however, question the efficacy and fairness of this idea. First of all, it is based upon the assumption that it is union wage policy that initiates and perpetuates inflation, but this is far from proved. Second, the remedy might not even be effective in curbing a price rise in response to a large wage settlement. A corporation might simply treat the tax as part of the cost of achieving a settlement with the union and pass it, along with the wage increase granted to labor, on to consumers in the form of higher prices. Third, if the tax were really to hurt, then corporations would be forced to bargain harder with unions, but the net result might be a wave of long, bitter strikes that could wreak havoc with the economy. Finally, under the Wallich-Weintraub proposal, the firm would suffer doubly: union bargaining power would wring a high settlement from it, and on top of that the government would penalize the company, even though it is national labor policy that gives unions bargaining power to wrest large wage increases from companies.

The United States' Wage-Price Guideposts

Background to the Wage-Price Guideposts

The United States actually had its own form of incomes policy from 1962 to 1965, in the form of guideposts for noninflationary wage and price behavior that were issued by the President's Council of Economic Advisers.[29] The

---

[28] See, for example, Sidney Weintraub, "An Incomes Policy to Stop Inflation," *Lloyds Bank Review*, January 1971, pp. 1–12.

[29] Many of the ideas expressed in this section are taken from a memorandum of Industrial Relations Counselors, Inc., written by Richard A. Beaumont, Robert R. Reichenbach, and the author in 1964. The author, however, assumes full responsibility for the interpretation expounded here.

wage-price guideposts emerged from the price inflation that had intermittently plagued the United States economy after World War II. Since peacetime wage and price controls were abhorrent to the American people, an alternative to direct government controls was sought.

Some students of the problem believed that the answer lay in more "responsible" behavior on the part of the parties to collective bargaining. Thus, the initial effort to clamp a lid on inflationary pressures took the form of appeals to both sides to voluntarily exercise restraint in reaching economic settlements, and to relate wage increases and prices to changes in productivity. In 1952 the Council of Economic Advisers saw the need for including "productivity allowances" within the framework of "a well-rounded wage stabilization program." It cautioned, however, that "these increases should be held to the likely productivity increases for the economy as a whole—that is, in the neighborhood of 2 to 3 percent—instead of being allowed to reflect in particular cases a higher rate of productivity increase in particular industries." This rationale was to play an important part in the development of subsequent wage-price guideposts.

The classical solution to inflation would have been fiscal and monetary restraint, and such a policy was actually followed in the late 1950s by the Eisenhower administration. The cure turned out to be worse than the disease, because this policy checked economic growth and caused high rates of unemployment. When President Kennedy assumed office in January 1961, unemployment was approaching 7 percent, and he quickly sought to stimulate the economy. To solve the basic inflation-unemployment dilemma, he resorted to his predecessors' use of moral suasion to moderate wage and price movements, while he pursued expansionist economic policies. This was later supplemented by a form of incomes policy known as the "wage-price guideposts."

Wage-Price Guideposts, 1962

In January 1962 the Council of Economic Advisers enunciated guideposts for noninflationary wage and price behavior, according to which wage-rate increases, including fringe benefits, should be equal to the trend rate of productivity change in the economy at large. Productivity, as measured by the average annual increase in output per man-hour, was figured to be 3.2 percent. Thus, wage increases were not to be greater than 3.2 percent a year.[30] For those sectors of the economy operating at lower rates of productivity, this meant raising prices to accommodate the rise in labor costs; for those enjoying above-average productivity increases, lowering prices; and for those at the average,

---

[30] The council later elaborated a set of exceptions to the average-productivity norm to take account of such considerations as the need to attract sufficient labor, exceptionally high or low wages in particular situations, and unemployment in an industry. Similarly, it recognized that price adjustments might be necessary where the level of profits was insufficient to attract the capital necessary to finance expansion, where costs other than labor had changed, where overcapacity made an outflow of capital desirable, or where profits were too high.

maintaining stable price levels. Thus, increases and decreases in prices in the various sectors would average out, and the nation would enjoy price stability.

Many critics, however, raised serious questions as to whether the guideposts provided a sound basis for the conduct of a free economy. Some observers objected that there was a confusion between cause and effect. According to their view, the competitive process does result in an averaging of productivity benefits, but after it has served its role of allocating resources. The guideposts, however, by attempting to achieve the same end in advance, would tend to misallocate resources. If the guideposts were to achieve full compliance, the economic effect would be the same as that resulting from the imposition of wage and price controls.[31] Wages and prices would move only as directed by the productivity formula, and not in response to supply and demand conditions in a particular industry, free collective bargaining, or the need for more workers because of increased product demand.

According to Arthur F. Burns, adherence to the guideposts would result in automatic annual increases in wages being built into the economy, regardless of the stage of the business cycle, the level of unemployment, or the state of the balance of international payments.[32] Furthermore, "black wages" might become common, as they have in some European countries that have attempted to control wages and prices, and voluntary price reductions for competitive reasons would seldom, if ever, occur. Another complaint concerning the guideposts was that they froze labor's share of total output. Finally, the 3.2 percent guidepost made no allowance for increases in the cost of living, and, indeed, the guidepost approach broke down in 1966, when the price level began to rise.

All the arguments concerning the desirability of the guideposts died out of active discussion when the new inflationary period ushered in by the escalation of the Vietnam War broke the back of the stabilization effort in 1966. This was not the fault of the guideposts; they had been designed to curb cost-induced inflation resulting from union power to win large wage increases, regardless of the demand for labor in an industry, and corporate power to raise prices, regardless of the demand for their products. The guideposts, however, had not been intended to deal with inflation caused by excess demand in the economy. After that, the debate turned to the question of the effectiveness of the guideposts in holding down wages during the period 1962–1965.

Were the Guideposts Effective?

When the guideposts first emerged, the consensus in labor and management circles was that they would not work. It was considered unrealistic to assume that either unions or managements would accept the concept that wages and

---

[31] *Morgan Guaranty Survey,* October 1964.

[32] Arthur F. Burns, "Wages and Prices by Formula?" *Harvard Business Review,* March–April 1965.

prices should move in inverse relationship to their bargaining or marketing power in a given situation. Professor Rees likened the situation to a baseball game played in a park with a very short right-field fence, in which the umpire urges all of the left-handed pull hitters, for the sake of sportsmanship, to bunt rather than try for home runs.[33] He, along with others, believed that experience indicated that unions would take advantage of favorable economic circumstances to press for gains that would outstrip the guideposts prescriptions. Similarly, there was no assurance that employers who enjoyed above-average increases in productivity would actually pass the benefits on to consumers in the form of reduced prices.

While the guideposts were operative, neither all unions nor all managements adhered to them. In many cases, moreover, it required a great deal of pressure from the White House to achieve compliance. Overall, however, there is no question but that wage movements were moderate and prices remained remarkably stable during the early 1960s. But many people argued that this was due less to adherence by labor and management to the guideposts than a reflection of economic conditions in which unemployment was relatively high and excess plant capacity existed. On the other hand, some statistical analyses, using the tests of expected versus actual wage increases, support the hypothesis that the guideposts did exert a moderating influence on United States wage advances after 1962.

According to Pierson, the annual rate of change in wages was reduced by about one percentage point during the period in which the guideposts were operative, and the presence of the guideposts eliminated the influence of union strength on the trade-off between the rates of inflation and unemployment.[34] Even stronger evidence on the effectiveness of the guideposts was offered by Perry, who, applying data for the years 1947–1960 to the period from the third quarter of 1962 to the first quarter of 1966, found fifteen successive quarters in which actual increases in straight-time earnings were below the expected increase.[35] Perry found that the wage slowdown was most pronounced in what he termed "visible" industries, that is, those characterized by a high degree of concentration and unionism, and which are subject to most government scrutiny, such as steel and automobiles. The most comprehensive analysis of the guidepost period was conducted by Sheehan, who also credited them with having held wages down below what they otherwise would have been.[36]

Not all economists agreed with these conclusions concerning the effectiveness of the guideposts. Those active in labor-management relations claimed

[33] Albert Rees, "Restraint and National Wage Policy," in William G. Bowen (ed.), *Labor and the National Economy* (New York: Norton, 1965), p. 100.

[34] Gail Pierson, "The Effect of Union Strength on the U.S. 'Phillips Curve,'" *American Economic Review*, June 1968, pp. 456–467.

[35] George L. Perry, "Wages and Guideposts," *American Economic Review*, September 1967, pp. 897–904.

[36] John Sheehan, *The Wage-Price Guideposts* (Washington, D.C.: Brookings, 1967).

that they had observed few instances in which the guideposts had played a role in collective bargaining.[37] Sheehan's work has been a particular target of attack, based on his claim that automobile and steel negotiations were affected by the guideposts. Livernash, for one, contends that wage determination in the automobile industry tends to support minimal or zero guidepost influence, while the low settlements in the steel industry during the guidepost period largely reflected the reduced power position of the union in the wake of its 1959 strike.[38]

The 1971 Wage-Price Controls

Although there is no consensus on the effectiveness of the guideposts, and no way of "proving" conclusively who is right, the arguments are important in evaluating later attempts at adopting an incomes policy in the United States. In a comprehensive study of the European incomes policy experience for the Economic Council of Canada, Smith concluded that Canada should not adopt one.[39] A study of four nations—Italy, West Germany, Britain, and the Netherlands—by Edelman and Fleming concluded that although such methods as exhortation, establishment of wage and price guidelines, and outright controls were not very effective, governments would continue to use them because the public and public officials alike find them reassuring.[40]

Construction Industry Controls

In fact, the first tentative steps toward a new American incomes policy were unveiled early in 1971, with the establishment, following tremendous pressure from the White House and the suspension of the Davis-Bacon Act provisions, of "voluntary" wage controls in the construction industry. President Nixon, by executive order, established a mechanism to monitor construction prices and compensation. The President issued this executive order under the Economic Stabilization Act of 1970, which gave him standby authority to invoke wage and price controls. A craft dispute board would be set up for each of the crafts in the construction industry to review all collective bargaining agreements. Each board would decide whether a wage settlement met criteria set forth in the executive order, which defines an acceptable settlement as one "not in excess of the average of median increases in wages

[37] See, for example, John T. Dunlop, "Guideposts, Wages, and Collective Bargaining," in George P. Shultz and Robert Z. Aliber (eds.), *Guidelines, Informal Controls, and the Market Place* (Chicago: University of Chicago Press, 1966).

[38] E. Robert Livernash, "Wages and Benefits," in Woodrow L. Ginsburg *et al.*, *A Review of Industrial Relations Research*, Vol. 1 (Madison, Wisc.: Industrial Relations Research Association, 1970), pp. 102, 103.

[39] David C. Smith, *Income Policies, Some Foreign Experience and their Relevance for Canada*, Economic Council of Canada, Special Study No. 4 (O'Hara: Queen's Printer, 1966).

[40] Murray J. Edelman and Robben W. Fleming, *The Politics of Wage-Price Decisions, 1946–1963: A Four-Country Analysis* (Urbana: University of Illinois Press, 1965).

and benefits over the life of the contract in major construction settlements in the period 1961 to 1968."[41] These settlements averaged increases of 6 percent. The criteria would make certain allowances for trends in the cost of living, improvements in productivity, and other factors.

If a craft dispute board found a wage settlement to be unacceptable, it would notify a second new group, the Construction Industry Stabilization Committee. This committee, appointed by the Secretary of Labor, was tripartite, with four representatives each from labor, management, and the public. The committee would have fifteen days in which to deliberate as to whether or not the particular settlement had violated the criteria.

The New Economic Policy

The wage stabilization procedures in the construction industry were indicative of what lay in store for the rest of the economy. By the summer of 1971 it was apparent that the United States was facing increased economic difficulties, both at home and abroad. Collective bargaining wage settlements were growing larger, prices continued to mount, there was growing pressure on the dollar throughout the world, and the nation was experiencing its first deficit in the balance of international trade (imports exceeding exports) since 1888. In a dramatic reversal of policy, President Nixon decided to impose wage and price controls as part of a new economic policy designed to deal comprehensively with domestic inflation and monetary and trade problems abroad.

Phase I of the new program was a ninety-day freeze on wages, salaries, prices, and rents, beginning on August 15, 1971. The objective of the freeze was to immediately break the spiral of wage and price increases, while allowing time for the formulation of a more long-range but less drastic incomes policy; it was generally successful in halting the rapid escalation of wages and prices.

On the whole, Phase I was relatively uncomplicated. Problems were encountered for those organizations which had scheduled pay and price increases; teachers, whose annual salary increments went into effect on September 1, were particularly perturbed at the loss of their pay hikes. In the main, however, the freeze had public support: as long as everyone was being penalized, people were willing to suffer a short-run sacrifice in order to assist the effort to curb inflation.

At the end of the ninety-day freeze period, a more long-range and flexible program for controlling wages and prices went into effect. Phase II of the New Economic Policy, which went into operation on November 14, 1971, allowed for wage and price increases in line with guides that were to be formulated by newly created public bodies.

The new controls program was under the supervision of a council, the Cost of Living Council. Operating under the council were the seven-member

---

[41] *The New York Times*, March 30, 1971.

Price Commission, to monitor price increases, and the fifteen-member Pay Board, to stabilize wages. There were also a number of committees to deal with special areas, such as interest and dividends and the health services industry. The Internal Revenue Service was given the task of administering the program and monitoring compliance with it.

As with previous wage control agencies, the Pay Board was tripartite, with five representatives each of the public, business, and labor unions. From the outset the Pay Board's operations were marked by confusion, administrative problems in quickly gearing up for its task, and conflict between the labor members and other members. Four of the five union representatives resigned from the board in March 1972, charging that it represented government control and business and political interests. President Nixon then converted the Pay Board into a wholly public seven-member body, though one representative each of labor and business was included within the seven.

Differing regulations were formulated depending upon the size of the business involved.[42] Firms employing more than five thousand workers had to obtain permission from the Pay Board before implementing a collective bargaining agreement. Those with one thousand to five thousand employees simply had to report any increases, and those with under one thousand employees were only subject to spot checks to ensure that they were complying with the established guidelines. By the spring of 1972 very small businesses—those with fewer than sixty employees—were exempted from wage and price controls, on the assumption that they wielded too little economic power to be a major contributor to inflationary pressures. As a result, 5 million firms and 19 million employees, constituting over 25 percent of the economy, were exempted from controls.

The Pay Board set the figure of 5.5 percent as the guideline for wage and salary increases, reasoning that holding wage increases to that level would substantially reduce inflation in 1972. Workers earning under $1.90 per hour were permitted higher percentage increases, and, later, those earning under $2.75 per hour were exempted from the guideline.

In January 1973 President Nixon announced Phase III of his incomes policy, which amounted to a switch from mandatory controls to voluntarism. The Pay Board and the Price Commission were abolished, and the controls apparatus was put under the direction of the Cost of Living Council. Aside from firms in the food processing and retailing, health, and construction industries, all others were freed from having to seek government approval of wage and price changes. They were expected, however, to abide voluntarily by the wage and price guidelines. Firms employing five thousand or more workers still had to report wage rate changes, and those with one thousand or more employees had to keep records of rate changes. In order to ensure "voluntary" compliance, the government reserved the right to roll back in-

---

[42] Jerry E. Pohlman, *Economics of Wage and Price Controls* (Columbus, Ohio: Grid, 1972), p. 195.

creases that were inconsistent with the standards established. In addition, the Labor-Management Advisory Committee was organized to work with the Cost of Living Council on modifications of general wage standards.

Effectiveness of the New Economic Policy

The mandatory phases of the Nixon administration's New Economic Policy were of such short duration—seventeen months (three months of a freeze and fourteen months of mandatory controls)—that it is difficult to reach definitive conclusions on its effectiveness. In 1972, the one full year in which mandatory controls operated, the economy expanded rapidly, yet inflation subsided somewhat. Although collective bargaining settlements continued at a high level, they were lower than before the controls program went into effect. How much of this was due to the controls program was an open question, for 1972 was regarded as an off-year for collective bargaining, in that it involved more of the less powerful unions representing workers in more competitive industries. According to studies of the Price Commission and the Brookings Institution, however, inflation under the controls program was 1.5 to 2.0 percentage points lower than it would have been had controls not existed.

Despite the seeming success of Phase II, the administration apparently feared that its continuation would spell possible confrontation with organized labor and Congress. The unions, which were of the opinion that the Phase II program was not adequately controlling prices and was therefore inequitable, wanted mandatory wage controls dropped. Government economists also feared that, with unemployment declining and utilization of available plant increasing, the continuation of rigid controls would distort the allocation of resources, produce serious inequities, and create "gray" and "black" markets. In order to avoid such problems and secure labor peace and cooperation, the government abandoned Phase II. In its stead came Phase III, which decreed "voluntary" controls but gave the government power to upset wage and price increases in violation of established guidelines.

Phase III proved to be totally ineffective in controlling inflation. There was a sharp rise in prices, particularly of food products (raw food prices were never brought under the controls program), as a result of the sudden lifting of mandatory controls and a spurt in demand because of the economic boom and sales of grain to the Soviet Union and China. Consumer prices, therefore, were rising at about an 8 percent rate under Phase III, despite relatively moderate collective bargaining settlements, largely in line with the prescribed guidelines. The inflation had turned from one of cost-push back to the demand-pull variety, which is more difficult to control through incomes policy.

In a new attempt to bring inflation under control, President Nixon decreed another price freeze in June 1973. Retail prices, though not wages and rents, were to be frozen for sixty days. It quickly became apparent, however, that shortages of some food products would develop if their prices did not rise, so President Nixon ended the freeze on prices of health care and food, except beef, in July. At the same time, he announced a Phase IV to go into effect August 12, 1973, which was to be a return to some of the types of mandatory controls of Phase II. The 5.5 percent wage increase guideline, for example, was to be continued.

Even Phase IV was expected to be of only limited effectiveness in curbing the rate of inflation, with major emphasis being placed again on slowing down the rate of economic expansion. Clearly, this series of attempts to curb inflation through government controls had not been very successful. The President, in fact, still looked forward to an eventual abandonment of incomes policy and a return to free markets and free collective bargaining.

Summary

Government has, at times, interfered with the workings of the free labor market both to put a floor under and a ceiling over wages. Minimum wage legislation was evolved to protect the lowest-paid, least-protected members of the labor force. Such workers were usually employed in the small-scale, highly competitive industries, in which employers were able to offer lower prices for their products by driving down wages. For many decades, however, minimum wages were blocked by adverse Supreme Court decisions.

When the attitude of the Court changed, Congress enacted the Fair Labor Standards Act of 1938, establishing a 25 cents per hour minimum. Over the years, the minimum has been raised, and more workers have been brought under coverage. In addition, three quarters of the states have their own minimum wage laws covering intrastate commerce, but millions of workers have no coverage whatsoever.

Proponents of a higher minimum wage contend that it helps to fight poverty, but others believe that, on the contrary, it leads to greater poverty. The latter claim that the low-wage workers are also low-productivity ones, and that, if the wage is set above the marginal value product, workers will become unemployed, either through substitution of capital for labor or through contraction of demand for the employers' products as a result of higher prices.

Various studies of the impact of minimum wage increases have come up with conflicting conclusions. BLS studies have indicated minimal adverse effects upon employment, but private studies disagree. Two mitigating factors with respect to the effects of minimum wage increases are that they have been moderate, bringing the minimum back up to about half the average earnings in manufacturing, and that displaced low-productivity workers have been able to find other low-paying jobs in noncovered industries. Proposed solutions to the minimum wage dilemma include setting different minimums by industry to take account of differing economic circumstances, and leaving the minimum wage alone but having the government pay income supplements to low-wage workers.

The government has attempted to hold wages down during periods of inflation. War periods are marked by excess demand, which unleashes inflationary pressures, and the United States resorted to wage and price controls during World War I, World War II, and the Korean War. Although problems were encountered, wage stabilization in these war periods worked rather well and helped to prevent more serious inflations.

The growing concern with cost-push inflation has led to proposals for a national "incomes policy," which would be something less than outright controls. Most western European countries have had incomes policies at one or another time since World War II, and the United States had its own version of it in the early 1960s in the form of wage-price guideposts. Wage movements were moderate and prices remained fairly stable during that period. There is disagreement, however, as to the role of the guideposts in this achievement, because it was also a period of underutilization of plant, equipment, and human resources.

The acceleration of inflation during the early 1970s, in the face of mounting unemployment, led to the imposition of new wage-price controls in mid-1971. Phase I was a freeze on wages and prices. Phase II was characterized by a Pay Board to establish guidelines for wage increases. Phase III replaced mandatory controls with voluntary compliance, but a new spurt of inflation in 1973 led to another freeze of prices, plus a Phase IV of the control effort.

BIBLIOGRAPHY

Bowen, William G. (ed.). *Labor and the National Economy.* New York: Norton, 1965.

Christenson, Carrol L., and Richard A. Myren. *Wage Policy Under the Walsh-Healy Act.* Washington, D.C.: Brookings, 1965.

Edelman, Murray J., and Robben W. Fleming. *The Politics of Wage-Price Decisions, 1946–1963: A Four-Country Analysis.* Urbana: University of Illinois Press, 1965.

Galbraith, John Kenneth. *American Capitalism: The Concept of Countervailing Power.* Boston: Houghton Mifflin, 1952.

————. *The Liberal Hour.* Boston: Houghton Mifflin, 1960.

Ginsburg, Woodrow L., E. Robert Livernash, Herbert S. Parnes, and George Strauss. *A Review of Industrial Relations Research,* Vol. 1. Madison, Wisc.: Industrial Relations Research Association, 1970.

Gitlow, Abraham L. *Wage Determination Under National Boards.* Englewood Cliffs, N.J.: Prentice-Hall, 1953.

Levitan, Sar A., Wilbur J. Cohen, and Robert Lampman (eds.). *Towards Freedom From Want.* Madison, Wisc.: Industrial Relations Research Association, 1968.

Morton, Herbert C. *Public Contracts and Private Wages: Experience under the Walsh-Healy Act.* Washington, D.C.: Brookings, 1965.

Perry, G. L. "Wages and Guideposts," *American Economic Review,* September 1967.

Peterson, John M., and Charles T. Stewart, Jr. *Employment Effects of Minimum Wage Rates.* Washington, D.C.: American Enterprise Institute for Public Policy Research, 1969.

Pohlman, Jerry E. *Economics of Wage and Price Controls.* Columbus, Ohio: Grid, 1972.

Roberts, B. C. *National Wage Policy in War and Peace.* London: Allen & Unwin, 1958.

Rothschild, K. W. *The Theory of Wages.* Oxford: Basil Blackwell, 1960.

Sheehan, John. *The Wage-Price Guideposts.* Washington, D.C.: Brookings, 1967.

Shultz, George P., and Robert Z. Aliber (eds.). *Guidelines, Informal Controls, and the Market Place.* Chicago: University of Chicago Press, 1966.

Ulman, Lloyd, and Robert J. Flanagan. *Wage Restraint: A Study of Incomes Policies in Western Europe.* Berkeley: University of California Press, 1971.

13 THE PROBLEMS OF UNEMPLOYMENT

In discussing the inflation-unemployment dilemma up to now, we have concentrated on the inflation part of the equation; it is time, therefore, to examine the unemployment side. Looking at the neoclassical economic theory of the labor market, we again find that it was inadequate in that it did not allow for the persistence of unemployment. While unemployment might occur in the short run, its existence would set into motion forces that would lead to its elimination. According to the neoclassical theory, the market was supposed to clear itself; that is, there would be a balance between all who wanted jobs and all who wanted to hire workers for jobs. If anyone was left without a job, this was due to the fact that he was not willing to offer his services at the market price, and hence he was voluntarily unemployed. Thus, involuntary unemployment was not really possible.

The reality, as we shall see, and as everyone well knows, has turned out to be quite different than neoclassical theory postulated. In this chapter, therefore, we shall examine the problem of unemployment in terms of its extent and distribution within the work force, its impact on the individual worker, the relationship between unemployment and poverty, the types of unemployment to which people are subjected, and what society has attempted to do about unemployment. We shall examine the nation's system of unemployment insurance, which was designed to alleviate the impact of joblessness on individuals, and the Employment Act of 1946, which was aimed at ensuring high levels of production so fewer people would suffer from unemployment. Then we shall turn to a debate that engulfed economists a few years back as to the cause of the unemployment then plaguing the nation: whether it was due to structural changes in the economy, such as automation, or to insufficient aggregated demand. Although the debate may seem dated, the problem of unemployment persists, so the debate may shed light on current and future difficulties. Finally, we shall return to the problem of the trade-off between inflation and unemployment.

What Is Unemployment?

In 1970 the average unemployment rate was recorded as 4.9 percent of the labor force; that is, during the course of the year one out of every twenty people who sought jobs could not, on the average, find any. While this may sound like a high percentage, it is not much above the average for the twenty-six-year period, 1947–1972, of 4.7 percent of labor force unemployed. In fact, in that entire period unemployment dipped below 3.0 percent, to 2.9 percent, in only one year, so we can conclude that unemployment is a seemingly natural phenomenon of the U.S. economy.

Unemployment should not be identified with idleness, for, as we saw back in Chapter 1, a person is considered unemployed only if he has been actively looking for a job but unable to find one. The person who is without a job, but has not been seeking one, is simply not counted as being in the labor force. The fact that some people may have quit looking for work because they have become too discouraged about the prospects of finding a job means that, at times, some unemployment may be "hidden" and not reflected in the monthly data.

The Impact of Unemployment and Its Duration

The Definition of Unemployment

Data on unemployment are compiled from the monthly sample of the working age population that was described in Chapter 1. Counted as in the labor force are the employed—that is, anyone who worked for pay for as much as one hour during the survey week—and the unemployed. The unemployed are those persons without jobs who are actively seeking work, persons who would have been seeking work except that they were temporarily ill, individuals on temporary layoff awaiting a call to return to work, persons who are waiting to start on new jobs, and workers who have not actively sought work because of a belief that none is available in their communities or lines of work. Obviously, an element of judgment on the part of the persons asking the questions enters into the respondent's being classified as unemployed or not, but the sample surveyers are trained, and no question of bias in the survey has arisen.

Not everyone is satisfied with the government's definition of unemployment. Some claim that it counts too many people as jobless, because it counts many people as unemployed who have only a tenuous attachment to the labor market and are only vaguely seeking work. Others charge that the current way of counting grossly underestimates the number of unemployed because it excludes from the labor force those who would like to work but have become so discouraged about finding jobs that they cease active search. There is obviously hidden unemployment, especially when unemployment rates are up, but a looser definition might simply lead to an exaggeration of unemployment.

The number unemployed during a given month is divided into the total civilian labor force to yield the unemployment rate, and then the rate is adjusted to account for seasonal variations (rises and declines in the size of the labor force, as when students flood into the labor market in the summer). When the economy is declining the unemployment rate may not accurately reflect the dip, because some of the employed may have been reduced to part-time work, which is not reflected in the unemployment data, and others may have become too discouraged about the prospects of finding work to actively seek it and are counted as not being in the labor force. Similarly, when the economy picks up, unemployment does not drop as rapidly, because many of the discouraged now return to active job seeking.

The monthly data are averaged to give the number unemployed for the year and the average rate of unemployment for the year. As can be seen from Table 13.1 and Figure 13.1, since 1947 the number of people unemployed has ranged from 1.9 million in 1953 to 5.0 million in 1971. But absolute numbers can be misleading, because the size of the civilian labor force grows over time; we look, therefore, at the percentage of the civilian labor force that the unemployed comprise. The annual rate of unemployment has fluctuated from a low of 2.9 percent in 1953 to a high of 6.8 percent in 1958.

Table 13.1 Employment and Unemployment, Persons Sixteen and Over, 1947–1972 (in thousands)

Year	Civilian Labor Force[a]	Employed	Unemployed	Percentage of Labor Force
1947	59,350	57,039	2,311	3.9
1948	60,621	58,344	2,276	3.8
1949	61,286	57,649	3,637	5.9
1950	62,208	58,920	3,288	5.3
1951	62,017	59,962	2,055	3.3
1952	62,138	60,254	1,883	3.0
1953	63,015	61,181	1,834	2.9
1954	63,643	60,110	3,532	5.5
1955	65,023	62,171	2,852	4.4
1956	66,552	63,802	2,750	4.1
1957	66,929	64,071	2,859	4.3
1958	67,639	63,036	4,602	6.8
1959	68,369	64,630	3,740	5.5
1960	69,628	65,778	3,852	5.5
1961	70,459	65,746	4,714	6.7
1962	70,614	66,702	3,911	5.5
1963	71,833	67,762	4,070	5.7
1964	73,091	69,305	3,786	5.2
1965	74,455	71,088	3,366	4.5
1966	75,770	72,895	2,875	3.8
1967	77,347	74,372	2,975	3.8
1968	78,737	75,920	2,817	3.6
1969	80,733	77,902	2,831	3.5
1970	82,715	78,627	4,088	4.9
1971	84,113	79,120	4,993	5.9
1972	86,542	81,702	4,840	5.6

[a] Figures in this column will not always exactly total figures in the next two columns because of rounding.

SOURCE: U.S. Department of Labor, Bureau of Labor Statistics.

Figure 13.1   Percent Unemployment, 1947–1972

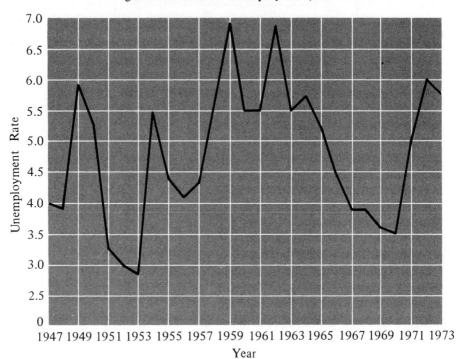

Figure 13.1   Percent Unemployment, 1947–1972

Duration

Unemployment in 1970 averaged a little over 4 million, almost 5 percent of the civilian labor force. Too often, people who read in the newspaper that 4 million are unemployed picture to themselves that throughout 1970 4 million specific individuals had no jobs. In reality, most of the unemployed are without jobs for short periods of time and most of the workers who are reported as unemployed one month will be back on a job the next; their places, however, have been taken by others who have been laid off or quit during the next month. To get an average unemployment of 4 million in 1970 means that during the course of the year many more millions suffered some period of joblessness. The number of persons who are unemployed a week or more during the course of a year, therefore, is three to four times the monthly average. For example, in 1970 14.6 million were unemployed at some time during the year and they comprised 15.3 percent of the labor force.[1]

Table 13.2 shows that more than half the spells of unemployment

---

[1] Anne M. Young and Kipp Michelotti, "Work Experience of the Population in 1970," *Monthly Labor Review*, December 1971, pp. 35–44.

**Table 13.2 Duration of Unemployment,
1970 (in thousands)**

Period	Number
Less than 5 weeks	2,137
5 to 14 weeks	1,289
15 weeks and over	662
15 to 26 weeks	427
26 weeks and over	235

SOURCE: U.S. Department of Labor.

during 1970 were for less than 5.0 weeks at a time. Close to one-third were from 5.0 to 14.0 weeks, and only 15 percent for 15.0 or more weeks. The mean duration of unemployment in 1970 was 8.8 weeks, about one week higher than in 1969 and below the levels of the early 1960s, when unemployment levels were comparable to that of 1970.[2]

A recent analysis by the Department of Labor that utilized a new estimating procedure has found that average jobless spells are shorter than had been assumed previously, but that there are more of them.[3] During 1969, according to the study, on the average a person who became unemployed remained so for 4.6 weeks. But only half of those leaving unemployment found work, and the remainder left the labor force; in the latter group were mainly people who wanted to work for only a short period, such as students and mothers of young children. At low unemployment rates, the percentage of newly unemployed changes more rapidly than the average spell length, but above an unemployment rate of 5.5 percent, the length of the average spell of unemployment increases faster than the unemployment rate.

The average length of a spell of unemployment, however, does not give a true picture of its impact on individual workers, because a person may suffer more than one spell of joblessness during the course of a year. A person may be laid off from one job, be unemployed for a few weeks before finding another job, only to be laid off from that one; thus, though each spell of unemployment may have been only a few weeks, two or three spells during the year will mean that he was without work for a number of months in total. Persons unemployed for fifteen weeks or more—whether for consecutive weeks or the aggregate of several spells of unemployment—are called "long-term" unemployed, and there were approximately 4.5 million persons in this category in 1970.[4]

Impact

Unemployment is rarely pleasant: one's normal income is cut off, and unemployment compensation makes up for only part of that loss. Some workers,

---

[2] *Manpower Report of the President*, 1971 (Washington, D.C.: Government Printing Office, 1971), p. 17.

[3] Hyman B. Kaitz, "Analyzing the Length of Spells of Unemployment," *Monthly Labor Review*, November 1970, pp. 11–21.

[4] Young and Michelotti, *op. cit.*

moreover, do not even qualify for unemployment compensation, and this is particularly true of those who have not had steady jobs for a sufficient number of weeks. But the person who is unemployed for a couple of weeks can not be said to have suffered greatly. Many of the unemployed, moreover, are only secondary workers, and the family, while experiencing a diminution in income, does not suffer from privation as long as the primary breadwinner is still employed. The situation is different, however, when the primary earner loses his job and remains unemployed for a long period of time. In an attempt to maintain customary standards of living, the unemployed worker will dip into his savings, and, if he cannot find a job soon, his savings will be depleted. If at the end of twenty-six weeks he still has no job, his unemployment benefits usually run out, and the next step may be having to go on welfare.

But unemployment that persists is more than an economic catastrophe: it also affects a worker psychologically, particularly if he has been a family breadwinner. Since in our society a person's status is still largely determined by his work and earnings, unemployment can undermine his self-respect and self-confidence. If his wife becomes the family's major provider, he loses status in the eyes of his children. Long-term unemployment can also mean having to borrow money from relatives and friends, avoiding those to whom one owes money, and a general restriction of normal social life. Children may be particularly affected, as they become ashamed to bring friends into a home that is becoming increasingly shabby, and plans for going to college may have to be canceled because the family needs their immediate earnings.

Those who are unemployed for long periods of time, moreover, get out of the habits associated with work—getting up early in the morning, keeping oneself well groomed, and the like—and in time become unemployable. As they lose hope they may turn to alcohol in order to drown their sorrows, and by so doing they take another step on the road to unemployability. Under such circumstances people seek someone or something to blame for their miseries, and they become susceptible to extremist causes that promise a way out of their troubles. Experience in Germany in the early 1930s indicates that both the Communists and the Nazis fed on unemployment.

Fortunately, this dismal picture of the effects of long-term unemployment applies to very few people today, for as we have seen, most of the unemployed are without jobs for relatively short periods of time, and very often they also receive unemployment compensation that at least partially sustains normal living standards. The problem of widespread long-term unemployment, however, continues to exist in some communities in which the former major industries have either declined or relocated; we examined some of the difficulties of such depressed areas in Chapter 8.

Long-term unemployment, however, tends to become a relatively greater problem as total unemployment rises. In 1961, when the unemployment rate was 6.7 percent, one out of six of the jobless suffered twenty-seven weeks or more of unemployment. In very sharp contrast was the situation in 1969, when the unemployment rate was down to 3.5 percent; in that year only one out of twenty-seven of the unemployed was without work for twenty-seven weeks or more.

These figures on the duration of unemployment bring home ever more forcefully the dilemma of the inflation-unemployment trade-off. An exchange of more unemployment for less inflation (the Phillips curve trade-off) is not simply an increase in the average rate of employment, but involves a whole shift in the structure of unemployment. It means moving from a situation in which, although people are unemployed, it is for relatively short periods of time for most of them, without undue hardship, to one in which very large numbers are jobless for relatively long periods of time, with extreme hardships being visited upon them and their families. When the duration dimensions of the unemployment problem are brought into the picture, the costs of higher unemployment begin to outweigh the benefits of lower increases in prices.

The Distribution of Unemployment

Not all workers are equally liable to unemployment, and there are marked differences according to race, age, sex, education, industry, and occupation.

Race

Starting first with race, we find that blacks and other nonwhite workers have much higher rates of unemployment than do white workers. In most years the nonwhite unemployment rate is about double that of the whites. Blacks, moreover, suffer disproportionately from multiple spells of unemployment.

How much of this racial differential is due to race itself is open to serious question, for to a very large degree blacks are in the occupations, industries, and educational attainment brackets that are subject to greater unemployment. Nevertheless, even holding all the other characteristics of the unemployed constant, the nonwhite unemployment rate is higher, thus indicating that racial discrimination is itself a cause. The fact, moreover, that blacks are less skilled and less educated than whites, and thus subject to greater unemployment, is itself a reflection of racial discrimination. We shall examine the problems of blacks in the labor market in greater depth in Chapter 17.

Age

Differences in rates of unemployment are even sharper among different age groups. Overall teen-age unemployment was more than 12 percent in every year of the decade of the 1960s. The gap between the unemployment rates

Figure 13.2   Ratio of Youth/Adult Unemployment Rates, 16–19/25+, 1960–1969

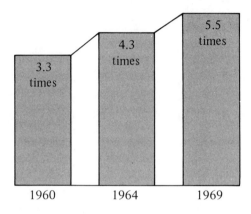

SOURCE: U.S. Department of Labor, Bureau of Labor Statistics

of youths (sixteen to nineteen years of age) and adults (twenty-five years and older), moreover, widened. As Figure 13.2 shows, at the beginning of the decade youth unemployment was 3.3 times adult unemployment. At the end of the decade it had risen to 5.5 times.[5]

A good part of the explanation of the deterioration of the position of teen-agers in the labor market during the 1960s lies in the supply of such workers. The high birthrates of the 1940s and early 1950s were reflected eighteen years later in large numbers of youths flooding into the labor market. Since the birthrate has tapered off in recent years, it should be easier to absorb young workers into employment in the future.

Not only are youth unemployment rates high, but they are still higher for black youth. In 1970, a year in which unemployment averaged 4.9 percent of the entire civilian labor force, the white youth (sixteen–nineteen years) unemployment rate was 13.5 percent, and the black youth rate, 29.1 percent. The dimensions of the youth unemployment problem are seen even more clearly when one focuses on urban poverty neighborhoods of the nation's metropolitan areas with populations of 250,000 or more. In the fourth quarter of 1970, when the overall unemployment rate was 5.4 percent, the rate for white youth in urban poverty neighborhoods was 27.6 percent, and for black youth in such neighborhoods, 42.2 percent.

The fact that unemployment rates tend to decrease with age, largely because seniority protects older workers against layoff, obscures a real problem facing older workers. Older workers who do lose their jobs find it very difficult to find alternative employment. In 1970, 42 percent of those fifty-

---

[5] *"The Manpower Posture of the Seventies,"* mimeographed (New York: U.S. Department of Labor, Bureau of Labor Statistics, Middle Atlantic Regional Office, 1971).

five years of age and over who were unemployed were jobless for at least fifteen weeks.

Sex and Marital Status

Unemployment is also not evenly distributed between male and female workers. When unemployment is low, the female rate tends to be considerably higher than the male rate; in 1969, when the overall rate was 3.5 percent, the male rate was 2.8 percent, only three-fifths of the female rate of 4.7 percent. When unemployment rises, however, it increases faster among men: in 1970, when the overall rate rose to 4.9 percent, the male rate of 4.4 percent was four-fifths of the female rate of 5.9 percent. As the overall unemployment rate rises, moreover, men tend to suffer more from multiple spells of unemployment than do women. The disproportionate increase in male unemployment when the economy turns downward largely reflects the layoff of full-time workers in manufacturing and other cyclically sensitive industries. Women, moreover, have a greater tendency to leave the labor force when jobs become scarce.

There is also a correlation between marital status and unemployment. A glance at Table 13.3 shows that unemployment, regardless of its overall level, is highest among single workers and lowest among married workers whose spouses are present in the household. In fact, unemployment among males is three to four times higher for single men than for those who are married and whose wives are present. These differences can be interpreted in two ways: (1) either more stable workers tend to get married and be more stable husbands; or (2) more likely, the fact that a man heads a household puts extra pressure upon him to find and hold a job. Age, too, plays a role in explaining the differences: young workers, who suffer much more unemployment, tend to be single much more than do older workers, who do not experience as much unemployment.

Table 13.3 Unemployment By Sex and Marital Status, January 1970 and January 1971

	Percent Unemployed	
Category	January 1970	January 1971
Male workers	3.9	6.4
Married, wife present	2.4	4.2
Widowed, divorced, separated	6.0	8.7
Single	9.9	14.8
Female workers	4.8	6.8
Married, husband present	4.0	6.1
Widowed, divorced, separated	4.2	6.2
Single	7.1	9.2

SOURCE: U.S. Department of Labor, Bureau of Labor Statistics.

Industry and Occupation

The type of job one has, both in terms of the industry and the occupation, is important with respect to his susceptibility to unemployment. If we look at Table 13.4 we see that the workers from the construction industry and agriculture experience the highest rates of unemployment, due largely to seasonal factors. Although construction unemployment is normally high, because outdoor work is sharply curtailed in the bad weather months, during a recession it usually rises even faster than other unemployment as business cuts back expansion of new plant facilities and new housing starts decline. Workers in agriculture and construction, moreover, are more susceptible to long-term unemployment than are those in other industries. Durable goods manufacturing is an industry that is highly cyclical sensitive; thus, in 1969, a good year, unemployment among workers from durable goods industries was lower than the overall average, but in the recession year 1970 it was higher.

In contrast, government workers experience the lowest rates of unemployment, and they have the greatest job security even in periods of economic recession. Workers in transportation and public utilities are also subject to less unemployment than other workers, since the demand for these types of services tends to be quite steady and workers are rarely laid off.

Very pronounced differences in unemployment liability also accompany the occupation a worker follows. As Table 13.4 shows, white-collar workers

Table 13.4 Unemployment by Industry and Occupation, 1969 and 1970 (in percentage)

Industry	1969	1970
Nonagricultural private wage and salary workers	3.5	4.9
Construction	6.0	9.7
Manufacturing	3.3	5.6
Durable goods	3.0	5.7
Nondurable goods	3.7	5.4
Transportation and public utilities	2.2	3.2
Wholesale and retail trade	4.1	5.3
Finance and service industries	3.2	4.2
Government wage and salary workers	1.9	2.2
Agricultural wage and salary workers	6.1	7.5
Occupation		
White-collar workers	2.1	2.8
Professional and managerial	1.2	1.7
Clerical	3.0	4.0
Sales	2.9	3.9
Blue-collar workers	3.9	6.2
Craftsmen and foremen	2.2	3.8
Operatives	4.5	7.1
Nonfarm laborers	6.7	9.5
Service workers	4.2	5.3

SOURCE: U.S. Department of Labor, Bureau of Labor Statistics.

generally experience less unemployment than do the blue-collar workers. Some of these differences are due largely to institutional arrangements. Thus, blue-collar workers have traditionally been paid by the hour or by the amount of output, and their services dispensed with whenever there was insufficient work for them. White-collar workers, on the other hand, have been on weekly salaries and, historically considered part of "management," were consequently not laid off when there was insufficient work for them. However, as the number of white-collar workers has grown relative to total employment, companies have begun to lay them off when less work has been available, and this trend may be accelerated as office work is mechanized and subject to more precise measurement. Thus, in 1950 and 1960 unemployment among clerical workers was only 68 percent of the overall unemployment rate, but by 1970 it had risen to 80 percent of the overall rate.

Differential unemployment rates among occupational groups can be viewed also as variations by level of skills. Among white-collar workers, rates of unemployment of managerial and professional employees are much lower than for clerical workers, and among blue-collar workers the skill differential is very apparent: the most skilled group, craftsmen and foremen, are subject to much less unemployment than the semiskilled operatives, but they in turn experience less unemployment than the unskilled laborers.

There are a number of reasons for these differential rates of unemployment. In the first place, there is a relative shortage of workers as one ascends the skill ladder, so one would expect the more skilled to experience less unemployment; even if one employer is willing to lay them off, another will be ready to hire them. Second, even when employers do not have sufficient work to keep their highly skilled employees fully occupied, the fact that they have invested in their training makes employers reluctant to let them go for fear that they will not be able to get them back when business picks up again. Third, when workers must be laid off, it is easier to let the less skilled go first and have the more skilled employees do some of their work: engineers, for example, can be utilized in doing drafting, while draftsmen can be laid off. Fourth, when employers start hiring again, they prefer to hire those with greater skills before those who are unskilled.

Poverty and Unemployment

There is disagreement on whether or not unemployment is a major cause of poverty. As we have seen, the majority of the unemployed are without work for relatively short periods of time, and, while these periods of joblessness reduce annual incomes, they do not push the unemployed workers down to a poverty level. Indeed, the average unemployed person has annual earnings that are well above the $3,000 considered to be the borderline of poverty.

Those unemployed who are without jobs for long periods of time, however, are likely to be reduced to poverty, but they usually comprise a small proportion of the total unemployed. Of course, when high unemployment rates persist for long periods of time, the ratio of long-term to total unemployment rises, and unemployment does become a significant breeder of poverty. Most of the time, however, the link between unemployment and poverty is rather tenuous. In fact, it is claimed that over half of those classified as "poverty stricken" are employed.[6] These people, of course, hold low-paying jobs and are called the "working poor."

An unemployed worker is a member of the labor force who has lost his job, or, in the case of youth, a new entrant into the labor force who has not found a job yet and is seeking employment. But most of the heads of poor families are not even counted in the labor force, because they are not seeking work. In some cases their unemployment may be hidden; that is, they are discouraged workers who have dropped out of the search for work because of their inability to find it. Gallaway had concluded that hidden unemployment is a significant phenomenon, even for prime labor force groups, and that, therefore, it is necessary to maintain high levels of aggregate demand and employment in order to improve the economic status of relatively low-income groups.[7]

High levels of employment, however, are only a partial solution to the problem of poverty, because many of the poor are not in the labor force because they are not able to work. This does not mean that some of these poor could not be converted into productive citizens, and much of the original conception of former President Johnson's "war on poverty" was designed to accomplish that aim. The setting up of day-care centers for working mothers, the provision of adequate medical care, education, and training, and the like could go a long way to making some of the poor employable. We shall explore some of these matters more fully in later chapters.

Types of Unemployment

Having examined who becomes unemployed, now let us begin to explore the question of why people become unemployed. Traditionally, the explanations have been made in terms of descriptions of the types of unemployment that beset the labor market.

Frictional Unemployment

The conceptual view of neoclassical economic theory is that of a perfectly functioning labor market: through bidding and offering, employers and workers should be able to effect their exchange relationships and "clear the market"; that is, all jobs should be filled and all workers who want jobs (at the market-determined price of labor) should be able to find them. According to this view, therefore, any worker who does not have a job is

---

[6] Robert E. Klitgaard, "The Dual Labor Market and Manpower Policy," *Monthly Labor Review*, November 1971, pp. 45–48.

[7] Lowell E. Gallaway, *Manpower Economics* (Homewood, Ill.: Richard D. Irwin, 1971), pp. 142, 143.

voluntarily unemployed in that he has not chosen to accept one at existing wage rates.

But any theoretical framework, while it may be an excellent tool for analysis, does abstract from reality, and the same is true of the neoclassical conception of the labor market. For all workers and employers to be able to offer and accept jobs simultaneously would require that they know of the existence of each other and that they be immediately able to get together. But, just as with the operation of physical forces we recognize the existence of "friction," so we have come to realize that there are frictions in the operation of the labor market.

Frictional unemployment, therefore, may be defined as that amount of unemployment that exists at all times because of "imperfections" in the workings of the labor market. Frictional unemployment is compatible with full employment in that jobs exist, but it takes time for workers to move into them. In a dynamic economy such as ours, change is always taking place. Given consumer sovereignty and consumer choice and the fact that tastes change over time, a product or service that was very much in demand yesterday may be less so today, but meanwhile other goods and services will be gaining greater consumer favor. The excess labor in the declining industries must shift to the growing ones. Technological changes also take place, but at different rates in different industries and establishments, with the result that some employers need fewer workers today than yesterday, while others seek more.

If there were perfect knowledge and perfect mobility in the labor market, then as a worker left one job he would immediately report to a new one, but in reality it takes time to find a job, even when it exists. Thus, frictional unemployment is that temporary unemployment resulting from a dearth of information, a lack of conformity between the skills of the workers and the requirements of the jobs available, and the costs of moving from one occupation, industry, or location to another.

Precisely how much unemployment is frictional is difficult to estimate. In 1944, at the height of the World War II labor shortage, when some 15 million people were in the armed forces, and when industry was willing to hire and train retired people and housewives for existing jobs, unemployment was still over 1.0 percent. But since the war unemployment has dipped below 3.0 percent only once, and then, in 1953, it was 2.9 percent. Even in the boom years of the late 1960s, unemployment never dropped below 3.5 percent. If in a period of very high demand for labor, the unemployment rate has been about 3.5 to 4.0 percent, it may be assumed that such a rate is roughly equivalent to the frictional unemployment level. Rees has suggested an alternative measure of frictional unemployment—all those who are temporarily unemployed—which he equates with that portion of the unemployed who have been jobless for ten weeks or less.[8] According to Rees'

---

[8] Albert Rees, "The Meaning and Measurement of Full Employment," in *The Measurement and Behavior of Unemployment* (Princeton: Princeton University Press, 1957), p. 27.

definition, about two-thirds of the unemployed would normally be considered to be frictionally unemployed.

The degree of frictional unemployment depends upon what individuals and the total society do to reduce the frictions. Persons seeking jobs could send resumes to thousands of potential employers, and companies seeking workers could engage in extensive advertising via newspapers, radio, and television. The costs of such a search, however, might far outweigh the benefits of finding a job or, in the case of the employer, a worker, a week or two sooner than would occur under the normal means of search.

Society in general can take steps designed to reduce the level of frictional unemployment. If, at one time, frictional unemployment exists at a 4 percent level, government—through the provision of better labor market information, the training of workers in skills that are in demand, and the provision of relocation assistance—might be able to reduce the frictional rate substantially, possibly to 3 percent. Again, however, society weighs the cost of such programs against the benefits that would be derived from them; such measurements can be made by comparing the losses in gross national product from unemployment of a given amount against the cost of programs that would reduce unemployment by that amount. Most cost-benefit analyses that have been conducted indicate that there would be a net benefit from greater efforts to reduce frictional unemployment.

Seasonal Unemployment

A second type of unemployment, which can also be considered to be "normal," may be classified as seasonal; that is, it is recurrent and periodic within one year. There is no constancy in levels of production and employment—nor, for that matter, in the size of the labor force—over the course of the year, and to compensate for the differences the data are reported on a deseasonalized basis. In some industries the differences in levels of production and employment during the course of the year are quite pronounced, and few workers can anticipate fifty-two weeks of employment. This is most obvious in the case of such summer camp jobs as counselors, waiters, and the like, which exist only during the months of July and August, but other industries are also subject to seasonal peaks and valleys of activity, though not as drastic as those of summer camps.

The basic cause of seasonal fluctuations is the buying habits of the public, and these in turn are related to changes in the weather. In some cases weather and the sowing-harvest cycle, such as in agriculture, are the major factors in causing seasonal patterns of work. Similarly, consumers buy heavy clothing for the winter and not for the summer, but with clothing fashion also plays a role in seasonality. Construction is another industry that is heavily influenced by seasonal variations in the weather, as outdoor work falls off during the cold and snowy winter periods: construction activity, for example, is more regular throughout the year in the more even climate of southern California than in the cold-winter state of Minnesota.

Individual workers can try to some extent to compensate for seasonal variations in available work by either following the seasons or dovetailing work in one industry in one period of the year with work in another during the slack period. The former is evident in the annual trek of migrant farm workers, who pick one crop early in the harvest period and work their way northward picking other crops as their harvest periods follow. Similarly, workers in resort hotels may be employed in the north in the summer and then move to Florida for its busy winter season. Dovetailing different seasonal peaks of activity between industries is more difficult, but a few workers have managed it.

Not all seasonal variation is due to natural conditions; much of it stems from patterns of human behavior, which can be changed. Automobile production, for instance, used to be much more seasonal than it is today: the companies used to concentrate production early in the year, then shut down for a good part of the summer before retooling for the start of the new model year production late in the summer. The ability to carry inventory, plus some change in consumer buying habits, however, have led to greater regularization of production over the year.

An even more dramatic illustration of regularization of production is offered by the soap industry. Despite fairly constant demand on the part of ultimate consumers (people wash all year round), the production of soap used to be highly seasonal because the wholesalers purchased from the manufacturers in bulk at particular times during the year and then sold from their inventory. In the interests of regularizing production and employment, Proctor and Gamble worked with the wholesalers to change their purchasing patterns, and as a result P & G was able to inaugurate a guaranteed annual wage for the employees in its soap plants.[9]

There is, in fact, evidence of a general reduction in seasonal variations in production and employment in recent years. Even so, many industries— those subject to climatic variations and that can not inventory output easily— remain highly seasonal. To a large degree the unskilled workers in these industries are most affected by seasonality, because employers tend to keep on at least skeleton forces of skilled workers during the slow periods.

Communities that have an industrial mix that is heavily weighted with seasonally oriented industries are also likely to have higher annual average unemployment rates than other areas. The resort town of Atlantic City, New Jersey, for example, has suffered from substantial and persistent unemployment largely because the workers needed in the resort hotels and restaurants during the summer season can find little alternative employment during the rest of the year. Technically, one could define seasonal unemployment as a

[9] A. D. H. Kaplan, *The Guarantee of Annual Wages* (Washington, D.C.: Brookings, 1947), p. 76.

part of frictional unemployment, but, since methods of dealing with the problem would differ, there would be little point in doing so.

Cyclical Unemployment

If production and employment are not steady within a year, we also know from history that there are recurrent expansions and contractions of economic activity of longer than one year. This expansion and contraction of economic activity has been named the "business cycle," and hence the unemployment associated with it is called "cyclical." As in the case of seasonal fluctuations, not all industries are equally affected by the business cycle, either.

Cyclical unemployment is basically due to a deficiency in overall demand, and the degree to which an industry is exposed to cyclical fluctuations depends largely on the income elasticity of demand for its products; the more postponable are purchases of those products, the more income-elastic is the demand. The investment goods industries are the most seriously affected by the business cycle. As production and sales drop during a recession, businessmen find that their plants are operating at far below capacity, so they are less inclined to add further capacity through investment in new plant and equipment. Furthermore, if we recall from our introductory economics course the principle of the accelerator, we recognize that the fluctuations in the production of investment goods, such as machine tools, can be quite severe. One form of investment—construction—is both seasonally and cyclically sensitive.

The durable goods manufacturing industries, almost by definition, are also cyclically sensitive, in that the purchase of their products may be postponed. The person who was going to trade in his old car for a new one can try to make it last another year, and when income drops, as it does during a recession, many people do precisely this. Sales of domestically produced automobiles, for example, dropped from 9.0 million in the boom year of 1969 to 7.2 million in the recession year of 1970.

In contrast, the purchase of the products of the nondurable goods manufacturing industries can less easily be postponed, and hence they are much less cyclically sensitive. Demand for the products of these industries is less income-elastic, and so production in many of them, particularly food products, continues at close to normal levels even in periods of recession. From 1969 to 1970, while employment in durable goods manufacturing dropped more than 5.5 percent, employment in nondurable goods manufacturing was down only 1.5 percent.

Very significant progress in moderating the downswings of economic activity associated with the business cycle has been achieved in the past three decades. Where once society took a very fatalistic view of depressions—assuming that they had to run their course—today, largely because of the "Keynesian revolution," we know much more about the causes of economic fluctuations and what to do about them. Even more important is the fact that as a society we have decided that we want to do something about such downswings and have used the instruments of government fiscal and monetary policy to prevent their worsening and to restore economic expansion.

Success in dealing with the business cycle does not mean that it has been eliminated, but rather that it is controlled much better. Since World War II five mild business downturns have occurred—in 1948–1949, 1953–1954, 1957–1958, 1960–1961, and 1970—none of them coming close to being as severe and prolonged as those of prior American history. Thus, while unemployment in the depths of the Great Depression was 25.0 percent of the labor force in 1933, and 12.5 percent in the much milder primary post-World War I depression of 1921, the highest it has been in any post–World War II year was 6.8 percent in 1958. The rate of unemployment for each of the twelve years from 1930 through 1941, moreover, was higher than in any single year since then.

Technological Unemployment

Traditionally, a fourth type of unemployment has been classified as "technological." Such unemployment is obviously attributed to changes in industrial techniques, that is, the introduction of labor-saving machinery and processes into industry, or to the rise of new products that make existing ones obsolete. According to this reasoning, capital is substituted for labor, and hence workers become unemployed.

But the concept of technological unemployment is a highly dubious one. Technological change takes place all the time, as the data on labor productivity show, but there are long periods in which there is no national concern with "technological" unemployment. These are periods in which production is growing at least as rapidly as productivity, and there need be no one who is unemployed as a result of the greater efficiency. Let us examine this idea, first with respect to an individual establishment, and then for the entire economy.

A worker may very well be displaced from his particular job by the introduction of a labor-saving device, but if the plant's total production is increasing, his services may be of value elsewhere in the plant. Furthermore, even if he is laid off from that plant he may not become unemployed, at least not for more than a frictional period, for overall expansion in the economy may allow him to find a new job in another plant. A problem arises, however, when a worker displaced by technological innovation cannot find another job because not enough new jobs are being generated. But is this worker technologically unemployed or is his lack of work due to insufficiency in aggregate demand, which is independent of innovation? We shall examine this question more closely in short order.

Denying the applicability of technological unemployment to the general level of unemployment within the economy does not mean that individual workers may not be unemployed as a result of technological change. This can occur, even when the economy is growing rapidly, if the skills that a displaced worker possesses are no longer in demand. This may help to explain the great resistance on the part of locomotive firemen to their being dropped from railroad employment even though they were no longer needed because of dieselization, for their skills were not easily transferable to other types of employment.

Thus, while technological change may not be responsible for higher levels of unemployment in the economy, it definitely can cause severe distress for particular workers. When displacement occurs, workers who have become highly specialized in a specific skill that is not needed in other types of employment, older workers, and those with poor educational backgrounds find it very difficult to locate new jobs, and even when they do it is usually at wage rates far below what they had earned before. This, however, is a price that must be paid for economic progress.

But this does not mean that these individuals must bear the entire burden of that price while the rest of society enjoys the benefits. As in the case of depressed areas, there is justification for special efforts to aid those who have been displaced by technological change. Indeed, many employers have attempted to cushion the shock of technological change for employees by attempting to help them find alternative employment, training the displaced for alternative jobs, and providing various forms of special payments upon termination to tide them over periods of unemployment. In the mid-1960s the federal government also began to act, through the provision of better labor market information, educational and training programs, and relocation assistance.

Programs to aid those who are unemployed, whether for technological or other reasons, are justifiable on economic and humanitarian grounds. On humanitarian grounds, of course, the aim is to prevent people from undue suffering. On economic grounds, providing them with some income helps to maintain consumer purchasing power, and retraining or relocating them enables them to contribute to national production. Let us turn next, therefore, to our major type of aid to the unemployed: unemployment compensation.

Unemployment Insurance

Background

Although unemployment has been a concomitant of an industrial society, economic theory and Puritan attitudes would not allow society to take measures to aid those who suffered from it. It was generally believed that any man "with get up and go" would be able to find a job; hence, those without work were shiftless and lazy. The economist did not necessarily think in these terms, but his view of the jobless was equally devastating: they were without jobs because they would not work for low enough wages; and since by definition they were "voluntarily" unemployed, there was no need to provide them with any aid. Thus, while most of the other industrial nations had adopted systems of unemployment insurance (the Belgian system had gone into effect as early as 1901), the United States continued to allow the unemployed to fend for themselves as best they could.

The Great Depression of the 1930s, however, destroyed this notion of large-scale voluntary unemployment along with many other ideas associated with a laissez-faire economy. The Social Security Act of 1935 established old-age insurance, a system of aid to the needy, and unemployment insurance. It was intended to provide greater security for workers subject to the vicissitudes of an industrial order by providing them with insurance against the risks of old age and unemployment. Cash benefits were to be provided regularly employed members of the labor force who became involuntarily unemployed, but who were willing and able to accept suitable jobs.

The program itself was supposed to help prevent the snowballing of unemployment caused by a decline in income and consumer spending. Thus, when one worker lost his job and his income was entirely cut off, the reduction in demand that resulted from his not having money to spend could lead to a second worker's losing his job, and so on. Unemployment compensation was one form of "automatic stabilizer" of the economy in that it provided people with some income, thus maintaining consumer spending when the economy declined.

The Social Security Act of 1935

According to the Social Security Act, all employers of eight or more employees, in covered employments, were required to contribute 3 percent of payroll (as of 1938) on the first $3,000 of each worker's earnings toward an unemployment insurance fund. But the law stated that if the state in which the establishment was located adopted its own system, the federal government would remit 90 percent of the money to the state fund. Each of the states thereupon adopted an unemployment insurance system, but a different one for each state, operating only under very broad federal guidelines. How the system was financed, what employments were covered, which workers were eligible, and the amount of benefits the unemployed would receive, therefore, differed from one state to another. Generally, the northern industrial states were more liberal and the southern and midwestern agricultural states less liberal, both in coverage and in providing benefits to the unemployed.

Originally, only about one-third of the labor force was covered by unemployment insurance, but the percentage has gone up dramatically, and by the Employment Security Amendments of 1970, as of January 1, 1972, close to 65 million were covered under federal and state unemployment insurance laws. Coverage has been extended through the process of bringing more employments, formerly excluded, under coverage, and by lowering the size of the firm subject to the tax to four employees by the 1954 amendments, and to one by the 1970 amendments. The federal act still excludes agricultural workers, family workers, domestic servants in private homes, the self-employed, state and local government employees, and most employees of non-profit organizations operated for religious or educational purposes, but some states extend coverage to various of these groups.[10] Close to 12 million employees, thus, are still without unemployment insurance coverage.

Besides working in covered employment, to be eligible for unemployment compensation a worker must have had some minimal past earnings and/or employment. Recent entrants into the labor force, such as college and high school graduates, therefore, cannot collect unemployment benefits while they search for their first jobs. Even experienced workers who have gone through a period of erratic employment may find that they are not eligible. Very short periods of unemployment are not covered either, because in most states there is a waiting period, usually of one week, before an unemployed worker can begin to collect benefits. The requirements beyond these are that the worker be available for work and not disqualified for having voluntarily left his former job or having been discharged for misconduct. The grounds for disqualification, and the severity of the penalty imposed, vary among the states. No state, however, can deny benefits to a worker if he refuses to accept a new job under substandard labor conditions, if there is a labor dispute involved, or if he is in an approved training program.

A payroll tax on employers is the source of the unemployment compensation funds in all states but three, which also have employee contributions. The 1970 amendments raised the taxable wage base to $4,200 as of 1972, and increased the tax to 3.2 percent of taxable wages, with the federal government retaining 0.5 percent for administrative purposes. Three states have higher taxable wage bases and some have tax rates that are above 3.2 percent. The actual amounts that employers pay, however, vary in all states according to their unemployment experience, that is, industries and/or employers whose employees suffer less unemployment pay a smaller tax than do those with higher rates of unemployment.

The justification for experience rating is that it encourages employers to stabilize employment, but critics contend that employers cannot be blamed for unemployment, because it is a social risk out of the control of the individual employer. Critics also charge that experience rating encourages states to compete for industry through lower unemployment insurance tax rates and employers to contest employee claims for benefits, since this worsens their experience. It is further charged that experience rating operates in such a manner that it intensifies rather than counters the business cycle, in that it lowers employer payments in boom periods, when they can best afford to pay more, and raises them in recessions, when employers are suffering from declining sales and profits. The fact that experience rating lowers the average

---

[10] *Social Security Programs in the United States*, Social Security Administration, U.S. Department of Health, Education and Welfare (Washington, D.C.: Government Printing Office, April 1971), p. 56.

employer contribution—in 1970 it was only 1.3 percent of taxable payroll—continues to attract employer support.

Weekly Compensation

Unemployment benefits were originally supposed to be 50 percent of the worker's full-time wages, but this too has varied among the states. All states, however, have a maximum benefit, as a result of which high-wage workers may receive substantially less than half their former earnings. As of December 1, 1972, the minimum weekly benefit varied from $5 in Hawaii to $25 in California, and the maximum from $45 in Indiana (for those with no dependents) to as much as $138, including dependents' allowances, in Connecticut.[11] In 1970 the actual weekly compensation received was less than half of previous earnings for the majority of recipients.

Duration of benefits also varies among the states. In 1938 twenty weeks was the typical maximum duration of benefits, but by 1971 the standard was 26 weeks, with nine states above it. In periods in which the unemployment rate has been high, the federal government has intervened to provide additional aid to the long-term unemployed. During the depths of the 1958 recession, Congress enacted the Temporary Unemployment Compensation Program, and in 1961 the Temporary Extended Unemployment Compensation Act.

The 1970 amendments established a new permanent federal-state program to pay extended unemployment insurance benefits to workers who exhaust their regular state unemployment insurance benefits during periods of high unemployment. Such extended benefits go into effect when the national seasonally adjusted rate of insured unemployment equals or exceeds 4.5 percent in each of the three most recent calendar months, or when an individual state's rate averages above 4.0 percent for any thirteen-consecutive-week periods and is 20 percent higher than the average rate for the corresponding thirteen-week period in each of the two preceding years. With extended benefits a worker could receive unemployment compensation for up to thirty-nine weeks in all states, and even longer in some.

The Employment Act of 1946

Neoclassical economic theory made no allowance for the persistence of involuntary unemployment, though the concept of frictional interferences with the workings of the labor market could be accepted. Unemployment above the frictional level, however, could not be accommodated within the theory, because the market was supposed to clear. Indeed, there was no room for the business cycle within neoclassical general equilibrium theory, for full production and employment were supposed to be assured by Say's Law of Markets, which,

---

[11] "State Unemployment Insurance Laws: A Status Report," *Monthly Labor Review*, January 1973, pp. 37–44.

in essence, claimed that "supply creates its own demand." In terms of the labor market, this meant that labor determined the volume of its own employment, because, if unemployment occurred, workers without jobs would be willing to accept employment at lower wage rates, and as their competition drove down wage rates, more workers could be hired; and the fact that prices of goods and services would be reduced in the process would restore full production and employment.

Given this view of general equilibrium, economists tended to define unemployment as "voluntary"; that is, it persisted simply because workers were not willing to accept low enough wages. This view of unemployment as voluntary was upset by what transpired during the Great Depression of the 1930s, when unemployment averaged 17.2 percent for the twelve years 1930–1941. The idea that workers were without jobs because they wanted too much money was patently ridiculous, for it was evident that workers were willing to accept jobs for less pay; many were willing to work for just about anything, including a sandwich and a cup of coffee. Yet heavy unemployment continued, because employers whose inventories were already at excessively high levels, and without new orders coming in, had no need to add to their labor forces.

The Great Depression was so devastating, not only in the United States but in every industrial capitalist nation, that neoclassical economic theory was shaken to its foundations. Yet it was not until 1935 that a new theory was advanced that could explain reality, and this came about with the publication of John Maynard Keynes' *The General Theory of Employment, Interest and Money.*[12] We cannot here trace Lord Keynes' theory, but only point out that he discovered that equilibrium at full employment was only a special case and that there could be situations in which the economy was in equilibrium but high levels of unemployment existed.

The individual firm facing lower purchases of its products may be able to solve the problem by cutting costs, including wages, and thus be able to lower its prices and win back its customers. It need not be concerned with the effect of the reduced incomes of its employees, because they constitute an infinitesimal proportion of the total population. An economy-wide reduction of wages, on the other hand, reduces consumer purchasing power as well as costs, and this is what happened during the Great Depression.

Economists continued to call for wage cuts after the depression set in, and employers did reduce wages, but more, rather than less, unemployment resulted. As consumer purchasing power fell, demand for goods and services dropped, too, and production and employment dropped still lower. Keynes argued for increases in aggregate demand, rather than wage reductions, in order to restore prosperity.

According to Keynes, the level of total output depends upon the spend-

---

[12] John Maynard Keynes, *The General Theory of Employment, Interest and Money* (New York: Harcourt, Brace, 1936).

ing of consumers, business, and government $(Y = C + I + G)$. The most vola-
tile of these was business spending for investment, and problems could arise
because actual savings exceeded actual investment. In the neoclassical model,
excess savings would drive down the interest rate and lead to additional
investment, but Keynes demonstrated that this was not necessarily the case;
with plenty of excess capacity on hand, businessmen were not going to invest
in building new plants, no matter how low the interest rate might be. What
emerged from Keynes' formulations, therefore, was the need for an active
government policy—both fiscal and monetary—to ensure high levels of
aggregate demand.

Keynes' theory did not gain many adherents immediately, nor did the
governments of the industrial nations change their policies in conformity with
his proposals. Very high rates of unemployment, therefore, did not disappear.
In the United States, unemployment hovered at the 10 percent level in 1941,
but once we were fully involved in World War II, not only did excess unemployment disappear, but the nation experienced severe labor shortages from
1943 through 1945.

The contrast between mass unemployment in the 1930s and full employment during the war years convinced many Americans that unemployment
was not a necessary concomitant of a capitalist industrial economy. According
to the Employment Act of 1946, the federal government is charged with the
responsibility of promoting high levels of production and employment. This
indeed was a revolution, for the United States, along with the other capitalist
industrial nations, had moved from a position of fatalism with respect to
unemployment to one of active intervention into the economy through fiscal
and monetary policy to maintain high levels of production and employment.
Over the years, moreover, the Keynesian theory became the dominant one
among economists, and many of them expanded on Lord Keynes' ideas and
devised new techniques for ensuring full employment.

The Structural Unemployment Thesis

The goals of the Employment Act were fairly well achieved during its first
decade, but in its second problems were encountered. A glance back at Table
13.1 will quickly show that for the seven-year period 1958–1964, unemployment remained above the 5.0 percent level, averaging 5.8 percent as against
only 3.9 for the preceding seven-year period. This far-from-satisfactory performance evoked demands for all sorts of government action to counter it.
But there was disagreement on what types of government action were needed,
largely because of disagreement as to the basic cause of high unemployment.
Two theories predominated, one focusing on a shortage in aggregate demand,
and the other blaming higher unemployment upon structural transformation
of the economy. Let us examine the second theory first.

The onset of the period of high unemployment coincided with a new
phase of the continual process of technological change, which was popularly

called "automation." Many observers saw automation as qualitatively and quantitatively different from previous technological innovation, and some identified it as the cause of the higher unemployment. The public concern with the problem was fed by newspaper, magazine, and television reports about the plight of workers who had been displaced as a result of automation, and the specter of mass unemployment began to haunt the nation.

The concept of structural unemployment, however, need not be limited to changing technology as a cause. It could result also from foreign competition, shifts in demand resulting from altered consumer tastes, declines in the manufacture of particular products because of the exhaustion of raw materials, or government action in the forms of taxation, contract letting, and fiscal and monetary policy.[13] The unemployment of depressed areas that have seen their former major industries decline because of shifts in consumer tastes or relocation is an example of such structural shifts. Similarly, the decline of the American hand-blown and pressed glassware industry has resulted from a series of structural shifts, including the rise of competition from imports and from machine-made products.

In fact, a new form of structural transformation was being blamed for high unemployment in the 1970s, only this time the villain was foreign trade and investment. Just as labor unions claimed that "automation" was taking away the jobs of their members in the 1960s, so, in the 1970s, they said that imports and investment abroad by American corporations (multinational companies) was exporting American jobs. The AFL-CIO gave all-out support to legislative proposals, such as the Burke-Hartke Bill, which would place quotas on imports and restrict investment abroad. In view of this, it is important to focus attention on the structural transformation arguments of the past decade.

The structural transformation theory of unemployment thus attributes high unemployment to changes in the economy, whether resulting from new forms of technology, foreign competition, or shifts in consumer tastes, which destroy jobs once held by workers who cannot qualify for the new jobs that are emerging. It is a fact that unskilled workers with low levels of educational achievement, and those whose work experience is limited to a specific skill, are at a disadvantage in the labor market when they are displaced. With improvements in plant technology, for example, job requirements change, and some displaced workers lack the skills and versatility to meet new job demands. In the early 1960s, therefore, some observers viewed the restructuring of the labor force by recent technological change as buttressing their contention that the unemployment of the period was structural in nature.

The leading spokesman of this viewpoint was Charles Killingsworth, who saw the presure for automation as creating an insoluble unemployment

---

[13] A more detailed discussion of these points is contained in *Unemployment and Structural Change*, Studies and Reports, New Series No. 65 (Geneva: International Labour Office, 1962), pp. 11–14.

bottleneck.[14] The key aspect, in his opinion, was labor market imbalance: too many unskilled workers competing for ever fewer unskilled jobs. Furthermore, the shortage of skilled workers created a bottleneck that, even if aggregate demand were increased, would prevent the reemployment of the unskilled.

For those who saw the unemployment problem as being due to structural transformation the solution lay in the labor market, not in the market for goods and services. They urged massive governmental programs to retrain workers, relocate the unemployed, and provide subsidies for distressed communities.

Aggregate Demand and Unemployment

The other major explanation of high unemployment flowed from a Keynesian framework of analysis, and it became known as the "aggregate demand theory." It was well defined by the Joint Economic Committee of Congress, as follows:

> The aggregate demand theory maintains that recent unemployment rates are explainable by traditional supply and demand analysis. . . . unemployment has been quite high since mid-1957, because the rate of growth in final demand has been low relative to the actual and normal rates of growth in potential supply made possible by increases in capital stock, labor force, and productivity.[15]

The Joint Economic Committee concluded that there was little evidence for the structural transformation hypothesis, and supported the contentions of the aggregate demand theory. The leading exponent of this viewpoint, however, was the President's Council of Economic Advisers, which stated its position in these words:

> Higher unemployment is explained by the shortage of new job opportunities. . . . The source of the high unemployment rates in recent years, even in periods of cyclical expansion, lies not in labor market imbalance, but in the markets for goods and services.[16]

The council advanced the idea that there had developed a gap between actual national product and the national product that was needed to provide full employment. Walter Heller, who was the chairman of the Council of Economic Advisers at the time, argued that both the "accelerator" and

---

[14] Charles Killingsworth, "Automation, Jobs, and Manpower," in *Nation's Manpower Revolution*, Part 5, Hearings before the Subcommittee on Employment and Manpower of the U.S. Senate Committee on Labor and Public Welfare, 88th Congress, First Session (Washington, D.C.: Government Printing Office, 1963).

[15] *Higher Unemployment Rates, 1957–60; Structural Transformation or Inadequate Demand*, U.S. Congress, Subcommittee on Economic Statistics of the Joint Economic Committee (Washington, D.C.: Government Printing Office, 1961), p. 6.

[16] *Economic Report of the President*, transmitted to the Congress, January 1963 (Washington, D.C.: Government Printing Office, 1963), p. 25.

"multiplier" effects were needed to bring about an increase in total spending of about $35 billion, in order to close the gap that lay between capacity and spending and to achieve a potential output at 4 percent unemployment.[17] The Council championed the idea of a "full employment budget," that is, a federal government budget that would be balanced if the economy were operating at full employment. Even though there was a budgetary deficit at that time, it argued that the federal budget was restricting expansion, and in the hope of spurring a more rapid rate of economic growth, the administration proposed an $11.5 billion tax cut for both individuals and corporations.

The debate between the structural transformation and inadequate aggregate demand theories was determined by the outcome of events, and experience has thrown new light on both arguments. The tax cut was enacted in 1964, and with more money available for spending on the part of both business and consumers, aggregate demand did increase. Moreover, the increase in aggregate demand proved effective in getting unemployment down toward the level of 4 percent.

Everything seemed fine: unemployment in 1965 had been brought down to a 4.5 percent level and consumer prices were rising at only a 1.7 percent rate. It seemed as if the nation were on the threshold of achieving close to full employment with price stability, but before 1965 was over a stepped-up Vietnam War was superimposed upon an already-booming economy. Starting in 1966, therefore, inflationary pressures accompanied the further reduction in unemployment.

With the growing fear of inflation, there was a shift in emphasis with respect to the unemployment problem, from a stress on pushing up aggregate demand to treating the structural aspects of the problem. As the wartime boom continued, even advocates of the aggregate demand theory recognized that there was a growing shortage of skilled labor, even while the unemployment level remained near 4 percent. A panoply of government programs emphasizing the matching of jobs and workers through retraining programs, attempts to expand black hiring, and youth employment programs emerged. They, too, played a role in reducing the unemployment rate, as long as the economy was expanding rapidly enough to create new jobs for those who were being trained.

The Situation in the 1970s

As the nation entered the decade of the 1970s, the rate of unemployment was down to 3.5 percent, but prices were rising at a rapid rate, and government policy shifted from concern with unemployment to an attempt to moderate the rate of price rise. The Nixon administration, therefore, adopted its famous "Game Plan," to slow the rate of economic expansion and thus to reduce the

---

[17] Walter W. Heller, *Address to Conference on Fiscal and Monetary Policy*, sponsored by the President's Advisory Committee on Labor-Management Policy (Washington, D.C.: Government Printing Office, 1962), pp. 7–11.

rate of inflation through the Phillips curve effect. It discovered, however, that although the economy slowed down, the inflation did not. The civilian labor force grew by 2.0 million (1.0 million males, 1.0 million females) during 1970, but employment rose only 0.7 million; thus, unemployment shot up 1.3 million to an average of 4.1 million for the year, or 4.9 percent of the labor force. In 1971, the discouraged worker effect of slow economic growth could be seen in the fact that the labor force expanded by only 1.4 million. Since employment grew by only 500,000, unemployment jumped 900,000, to a rate of 5.9 percent, the highest it had been since 1961. At this point government policy abruptly shifted, to stress once again economic growth and a reduction of unemployment, and to curb inflation through wage and price controls.

The situation in the early 1970s brought to the fore another interpretation of structural unemployment. During the structural transformation-aggregate demand debate of the 1960s, the British economist R. G. Lipsey had defined structural unemployment as "that part of frictional unemployment which is not acceptable either because there would be a net money gain in removing it or because the social gains of removing it are judged to outweigh the *net* money cost of so doing."[18] Lipsey, therefore, advocated that "the rational policy in the present situation would clearly be to increase aggregate demand progressively until unacceptable degrees of inflation are encountered."

The definition of structural unemployment as that level of unemployment at which prices start to rise at an "unacceptable" rate would put most stress on labor market policies, such as worker training and relocation. But it must be emphasized again that workers must be trained or relocated for jobs, and jobs will be opening up only if aggregate demand is growing. A second problem that this definition of structural employment presents is that of securing agreement on what constitutes an "acceptable" rate of inflation, and in this respect there will be a clear difference of opinion between those who have jobs and those who do not. Since the employed are far more numerous, the level of inflation that they would find acceptable might be so low as to condemn a minority of the labor force to long periods of unemployment and thus to bear an inordinate share of the burden of solving the employment-inflation trade-off.

A second aspect of the structural unemployment concept refers to the structure of the labor force itself. In fact, a shift in the composition of the labor force in the direction of those groups with the highest unemployment rate was advanced as a reason for higher unemployment a decade ago, but this was regarded by the Joint Economic Committee of Congress as having had only a minor effect.[19] This idea, however, has been reintroduced by Perry in his explanation of why the trade-off between unemployment and the rate of

---

[18] R. G. Lipsey, "Structural and Deficient-Demand Unemployment Reconsidered," in Arthur M. Ross (ed.), *Employment Policy and the Labor Market* (Los Angeles: University of California Press, 1965), pp. 210–255.

[19] *Higher Unemployment Rates, 1957–60, op. cit.,* p. 6.

wage rise has worsened in recent years.[20] Perry finds that young persons now form a much higher proportion of the labor force than they used to, but, as we have seen, they are also subject to much higher rates of unemployment.

Perry concludes that, if the economy should stabilize at 4.0 percent unemployment in the 1970s, the resulting inflation would be 4.5 percent per year. It is quite possible that such a rate of inflation might not be found acceptable by the majority of people, so unemployment might very well stabilize at a higher level, possibly 5 percent, or even more. Among the groups that would carry the major share of the burden of holding down inflation, therefore, would be the nation's youth, and this is hardly an appetizing prospect for the student who will be graduating from high school or college in this period. Since black youth have poorer educational backgrounds and less skills than whites, they would be hit even worse by relatively high unemployment, and this would create a very dangerous situation in the nation's urban areas.

Domestic tranquility may very well depend upon full employment. Ethnic minorities, such as blacks, American Indians, Mexican-Americans, and Puerto Ricans, who have stood at the back of the hiring line, want to move up, and rightfully so. Their ability to do so, however, depends upon how fast jobs are growing, for it is easier for them to make breakthroughs when workers are in demand than when unemployment is rife. Under the latter condition the workers who have jobs will guard them jealously and attempt to prevent newcomers from entering their trades. Existing racial strife, therefore, would only be exacerbated by unemployment.[21]

Summary

Unemployment as a major social problem arose with the emergence of a free labor market. To be counted as unemployed a worker must be actively seeking a job but unable to find one. In the last quarter of a century, unemployment in the United States has ranged from an average of 2 to 5 million a year, and from 2.9 to 6.8 percent of the labor force.

The yearly average, however, means that during the course of a year many more millions of workers will experience some unemployment, since most of the unemployed are without jobs for relatively short periods of time. When the rate of unemployment rises, however, the number of workers experiencing long-duration unemployment rises sharply. Workers who are unemployed for long periods of time suffer psychological as well as economic deprivation.

Not all workers are equally liable to unemployment, for there are marked differences according to race, age, sex, education, industry, and occupation.

---

[20] George L. Perry, "Changing Labor Markets and Inflation," *Brookings Papers on Economic Activity*, No. 3. (Washington, D.C.: Brookings, 1971).

[21] The economist's championing of growth as the means to improve the lot of the disadvantaged is akin to Paretian optimality, whereby one should undertake actions that make some people better off but no one else worse off than he was before.

Blacks usually experience twice as much unemployment as whites, and teen-agers three to five times more than older workers. Women experience more unemployment than men, but the male rate increases faster during recessions. Married workers experience considerably less unemployment than do single ones. Workers in agriculture, construction, and durable goods manufacturing are more prone to unemployment, while those in government and transportation and public utilities have the least unemployment. The rate of unemployment is also inversely correlated with degrees of skill, with professional workers having the lowest rates and laborers the highest.

With respect to the causes of unemployment, traditional explanations have run in terms of descriptions of four types of unemployment. The first, frictional, refers to the amount of unemployment that exists at all times because of imperfections in the workings of the labor market. The second, seasonal, arises from seasonal fluctuations in the buying habits of the public, which are related in turn to climatic variations within the year. The third, cyclical, is that unemployment which arises from downturns in the level of national economic activity. The fourth, technological, has been attributed to changes in industrial techniques, but there is sharp disagreement as to the legitimacy of such a designation.

In order to protect workers against severe deprivation because of unemployment, the nation has created a system of unemployment insurance, financed through a payroll tax on employers. Not all workers, however, qualify for benefits when they lose their jobs, because some are in noncovered employments and others have not had sufficient previous employment and earnings.

Neoclassical economic theory made no allowance for unemployment as a major problem because it assumed that the labor market would automatically clear, and all who wanted jobs would be able to find them. The Great Depression of the 1930s proved this not to be the case, and John Maynard Keynes provided the theoretical underpinnings of a new view of economics, which demanded an active government policy to ensure high levels of aggregate demand. In the United States this was embodied in the Employment Act of 1946, which charged the federal government with responsibility for promoting high levels of production and employment.

The goals of the Employment Act were fairly well achieved during its first decade, but after that unemployment rose and remained above a 5 percent level for a number of years. Two theories emerged to explain excess unemployment: (1) the structural transformation theory and (2) the inadequate demand theory. The structural transformation theory attributed the problem to changes in the economy, largely resulting from new forms of technology, which destroy jobs once held by workers who cannot qualify for the new jobs that are emerging. The aggregate demand theory, on the other hand, claimed that unemployment had risen because final demand for goods and services had not grown as rapidly as the nation's productive capacity; in other words, there was a shortage of job opportunities.

The nation followed the inadequate demand theory and enacted a tax cut in 1964 to spur faster economic growth, as a result of which the high unemployment rate began to melt. Then, the Vietnam War was superimposed on an already booming economy. As the fear of inflation mounted, there was a shift in emphasis with respect to the unemployment problem, from a stress on increasing aggregate demand to treating the structural aspects of the problem through manpower training, labor information, and antidiscrimination programs.

As inflation increased in pace, the nation switched its economic policy to one of attempting to slow the economy and trade higher unemployment for less inflation. Unemployment did rise sharply but inflation failed to abate, and the government policy shifted again, this time to pushing economic growth but trying to deal with inflation through wage and price controls.

BIBLIOGRAPHY

Gallaway, Lowell E. *Manpower Economics.* Homewood, Ill.: Richard D. Irwin, 1971.

Gordon, Robert A., and Margaret S. Gordon (eds.). *Prosperity and Unemployment.* New York: Wiley, 1966.

Haber, William, and Merrill G. Murray. *Unemployment Insurance in the American Economy.* Homewood, Ill.: Richard D. Irwin, 1966.

Keynes, John Maynard. *The General Theory of Employment, Interest and Money.* New York: Harcourt, Brace, 1936.

Lester, Richard A. *The Economics of Unemployment Compensation.* Princeton: Industrial Relations Section, Princeton University, 1962.

Levy, Michael E. "Full Employment and Inflation: A 'Trade-Off' Analysis," *The Conference Board Record,* December 1966.

Manpower Report of the President, 1971. Washington, D.C.: Government Printing Office, 1971.

National Bureau of Economic Research. *The Measurement and Behavior of Unemployment.* Princeton: Princeton University Press, 1957.

Perry, George L. "Changing Labor Markets and Inflation," *Brookings Papers on Economic Activity,* No. 3. Washington, D.C.: Brookings, 1971.

Ross, Arthur M. (ed.). *Employment Policy and the Labor Market.* Los Angeles: University of California Press, 1965.

————. *Unemployment and the American Economy.* New York: Wiley, 1964.

Social Security Administration, U. S. Department of Health, Education and Welfare. *Social Security Programs in the United States.* Washington, D.C.: Government Printing Office, 1971.

Unemployment and Structural Change. International Labour Office, Studies and Reports, New Series No. 65. Geneva: 1962.

U.S. Congress, Subcommittee on Economic Statistics of the Joint Economic Committee. *Higher Employment Rates, 1957–60; Structural Transforma-*

tion or Inadequate Demand. Washington, D.C.: Government Printing Office, 1961.

U.S. Congress, Subcommittee on Employment and Manpower of the U.S. Senate Committee on Labor and Public Welfare. *Nation's Manpower Revolution,* Part 5. Washington, D.C.: Government Printing Office, 1963.

Young, Anne M., and Kipp Michelotti. "Work Experience of the Population in 1970," *Monthly Labor Review,* December 1971.

14 WORKING TIME

Early in this book, when we discussed the supply of labor, we said that it was determined by the size of the population and the labor force participation rate of the various segments of that population. A third ingredient—how much time people put into working—is also a determinant of the supply of labor. In this chapter, therefore, we shall examine working time, starting with a brief history of it, proceeding to government regulation of it, and to the activities of unions, through collective bargaining with respect to the work week and "overtime" hours of work. In the course of our discussion we shall reflect upon the fact that the number of hours worked per week is only part of the determination of working time, so we shall also examine trends with respect to vacations, holidays, and sabbatical leaves.

The History of Hours of Work

The Agricultural Work Time Pattern

According to the Book of Genesis, man's punishment for having disobeyed God's injunction against eating the forbidden fruit was expulsion from the Garden of Eden and having henceforth to earn his daily bread through the sweat of his brow. If the Book of Genesis condemned man to an existence of toil, it also detailed the first personnel policy with respect to working time, because it provided that man should work only six days of the week and that on the seventh he should rest. Throughout the millennia, man, or at least Western man, has lived according to the biblical prescription of the standard work week. He worked six days each week, generally from sunup to sundown, tending his flocks, and sowing and tilling his fields.

Man in an agricultural economy was thus guided largely by nature in his working time. The seasons dictated when he would sow and when he might harvest, and the hours of daylight, in which he could see what he was doing, the time during the day that he worked. Man's own physical needs played their role in his working time and pattern, for it was necessary to reserve certain hours of each day for eating, sleeping, and other bodily functions. But the social needs of man were also important, and certain days within the year, besides the Sabbath, became nonwork days, usually "holy days" on which to propitiate the gods on behalf of a good crop.

This nature-determined pattern of working time persisted as long as the economy remained basically agricultural. With the rise of industry, however,

362

there no longer was a "natural" pattern to follow, but in the absence of any new pattern the old agricultural one was adopted. Workers reported to their factory jobs at sunup and labored all day, with short breaks for eating, until sundown.

But there was no longer any logical reason for following such a working time pattern, and, indeed, the pace and conditions of factory work indicated that the agricultural pattern was injurious to workers' health. Workers, therefore, soon began to rebel against it. Moreover, the very success of the Industrial Revolution, with innovations and the application of capital in the process of production, enabled the achievement of a greater output within a given period of time. The impact of the Industrial Revolution, of course, went far beyond merely an increase in productivity, for it caused an even greater revolution in the way men thought about life and its meanings. Traditional modes of thought and behavior crumbled under the new type of society, and it was inevitable that ideas about work and leisure would also be altered.

Early Moves for Shorter Hours

The first significant manifestation of a demand for a shorter work week in the United States occurred in the 1830s, when a fledgling labor movement started agitation for the ten-hour day. The Philadelphia carpenters proclaimed, "All men have a just right, derived from their creator to have sufficient time each day for the cultivation of their mind and for self-improvement; Therefore, resolved, that we think ten hours industriously imployed are sufficient for a day's labor."[1] Employers, on the other hand, continued to proclaim the Puritan virtues of hard work and to warn that men would be led into dangerous temptations if they had "idle" time. Although employers resisted the union demands, strikes and the threat of strikes were largely successful in reducing working time, and by the end of the decade the ten-hour day had become common for the skilled artisans and mechanics in American cities.[2]

An executive order of President Van Buren in 1840 established the ten-hour day for workers on government projects, and more craftsmen also won the shorter hours. Yet, for most of the workers in the nation's factories, the twelve-hour day continued to be the norm until after the Civil War. But even the twelve-hour day represented a reduction from the more universal thirteen-hour day that had prevailed in 1840.

Having largely secured the ten-hour day, the labor movement next set its sights on a further reduction, this time to the eight-hour day. The motivation for labor's seeking shorter hours was different, however, than it had been a generation earlier. In the 1830s shorter hours of work had been justified on the basis of providing workers with sufficient time for self-improvement, but

---

[1] Foster Rhea Dulles, *Labor in America* (New York: Crowell, 1954), p. 60.
[2] Richard L. Rowan, "The Influence of Collective Bargaining on Hours," in Clyde E. Dankert, Floyd C. Mann, and Herbert R. Northrup (eds.), *Hours of Work* (New York: Harper & Row, 1965), p. 19.

in the post–Civil War period the motivation was essentially economic: to alleviate the problem of unemployment. The postwar depression led to a new shorter-hours movement based on the theory that if those with jobs worked fewer hours, the unemployed would have to be hired to bring the labor supply up to where it had been.

The eight-hour day movement was sparked by Ira Steward and the National Labor Union founded in 1866.[3] Steward recognized that an economy characterized by advancing technology and productivity had the capacity to use some of the gains of increased productivity in the form of reduced working time. He coupled this observation with the idea of rising expectations; that is, if workers had more leisure time, their wants for goods and services would expand, and they would demand higher wages. Rising wages, in turn, would lead to the use of more machinery and, hence, higher productivity, which would provide a new basis for a further reduction in working time.

The eight-hour day movement not only had a different basic motivation than that of the ten-hour day, but it also sought to accomplish its goal through a different means. The craftsmen of the 1830s had attempted to win the ten-hour day through economic action—collective bargaining and the use of the strike weapon—but Steward put his emphasis on political action—securing legislation that mandated shorter hours. The movement had very little success, and had little impact on the length of the work week in private industry.

The drive for the eight hour day was renewed in the 1880s by the Knights of Labor, but the means used were economic: the use of bargaining power of organized workers. Some successes were achieved, but in many cases the results were only temporary. After 1890 the American Federation of Labor became the dominant trade union federation, and its constituent unions continued the drive for shorter hours for their members via collective bargaining, and gradual reductions were achieved. The AFL, however, was opposed to legislating shorter hours, fearing that government action would make workers feel less need for unionization. Others, however, continued to seek state laws mandating shorter hours, regardless of AFL attitudes.

Voluntary Reductions in the Work Week

Despite the failure—or, at best, limited success—of the eight-hour day movement politically and economically, the daily hours of work were being gradually reduced throughout large sectors of the American economy. Employers themselves began voluntarily to cut the length of the work day. Of course, some of their action was sparked by the agitation for shorter hours and designed to strengthen their hands against unionization. More important, however, was the fact that increasing productivity enabled them to reduce

---

[3] Ray Marshall, "The Influence of Legislation on Hours," in *ibid.*, pp. 43–44.

hours without suffering diminutions in profits. Moreover, American industry was being rationalized in this period, and employers began to discover that better flows of production, more efficient scheduling, and the like enabled them to achieve better utilization of their work forces. In effect, much of the workers' wasted time that had characterized the longer work day was eliminated, so hours actually in the plant could be reduced without any loss of output. Thus, the actual average hours worked per week in 1890 were fifty-eight and one-half, or about nine and one-half per day and considerably lower than the twelve-hour day of thirty years earlier.

It must be remembered, however, that averages tend to hide significant variations, and this is especially true in the case of hours of work. The nation's basic steel industry, for example, remained on the twelve-hour day until 1923. On the other hand, in the industries in which unionism was strong, such as printing, the building trades, and apparel, the work week was substantially reduced through collective bargaining.

Part of the explanation for the reduction in the hours of work must also be sought in the changing composition of the labor force, particularly the entrance of women in greater numbers. Under their police powers, a number of states had begun passing laws limiting the hours that women and children might work. By 1889 nineteen states had passed such laws,[4] and the 1903 Illinois law establishing an eight-hour day for children was copied in other states. By 1920 maximum-hour laws for women existed in forty-three states, the District of Columbia, and Puerto Rico.

Another factor leading to hours reduction came from the application of psychology and industrial engineering in industry. Studies of fatigue revealed that very long hours of work were not necessarily efficient. In a summary of case studies on the impact of work hours on output, Brown found that in almost half the cases of comparisons of work weeks of sixty or more hours with shorter ones, total output was no greater for the longer work periods.[5]

Finally, we must not overlook the profound changes in styles of living that were taking place as the nation grew in affluence. As the nation's output of goods and services increased, there was greater stress on consumption in contrast to production. Ira Steward had indeed foreseen this quite early, and others later caught on to the idea that if people were to consume the goods being spewed forth from the nation's factories, they needed leisure time in which to do so.

All these factors led to a gradual but progressive reduction in working hours. By 1910 average weekly hours in nonagricultural industries were down to 50.3 hours; by 1920, to 45.5; and by 1930, to 43.2.[6] By the 1930s, the

---

[4] *Ibid.*, p. 46.

[5] David G. Brown, "Hours and Output," in *ibid.*, pp. 148–150.

[6] J. Frederic Dewhurst and Associates, *America's Needs and Resources* (New York: Twentieth Century Fund, 1955), p. 1073.

eight-hour day had become fairly standard, and in addition Saturday had become largely a half day in terms of work.

Impact of the Depression of the 1930s

The depression of the 1930s paved the way for the universalization of the shorter work week. With millions of people unemployed, many saw in reduced working time a means of sharing available work. The AFL urged adoption of a national thirty-hour week in order to combat unemployment. All the codes of fair competition adopted by various industries under the National Industrial Recovery Act of 1933 provided for limitations on hours.[7] Many of these shorter work weeks were continued voluntarily, even after the act was declared unconstitutional. In 1936 Congress passed the Walsh-Healy Act, which, in addition to minimum wages, established a forty-hour standard for government contract work. Under Walsh-Healy workers had to be paid one and a half times their normal wage rates for any hours beyond eight in a day or forty in a week.

There is little evidence to indicate that the shorter work week contributed to economic recovery, and some even claim that it retarded it. Although the concept of shorter hours as a means of combating unemployment may have been economically unsound, it played no small part in inducing Congress to enact the Fair Labor Standards (Wages and Hours) Act in 1938. We previously examined the FLSA with respect to its wage provisions, but now let us see what it said about hours of work.

The FLSA established the forty-hour week as the standard work week in American industry. Unlike the NRA codes, no limit was placed on the number of hours that people might work, but the act required that workers, at least nonmanagerial ones, be paid at one and one-half their normal rates for all hours above forty. (Unlike Walsh-Healy, however, overtime rates do not apply on a daily basis.) As we have seen, not all industries were covered by the FLSA, but, with a few exceptions, the eight-hour, five-day work week became standard throughout most of the economy. By 1940 actual average hours worked per week in nonagricultural industries stood at 41.1. Figure 14.1 depicts the trend in the work week since 1850.

The War and Postwar Periods

The forty-hour week came under severe criticism during World War II when the nation needed all the workers and output it could get. The FLSA, however, did not prevent employees from working more than forty hours, but merely provided that workers be paid overtime rates for hours beyond forty. Indeed, Meyers contends that the overtime premium pay provisions of the FLSA permitted the nation to obtain more hours of labor at a lower average

---

[7] Marshall, *op. cit.*, p. 48.

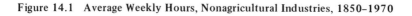

Figure 14.1 Average Weekly Hours, Nonagricultural Industries, 1850–1970

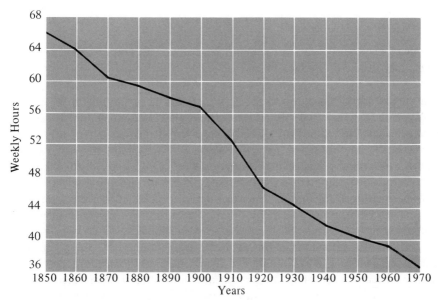

SOURCE: 1850–1940, Dewhurst and Associates, *America's Needs and Resources,* 1955; 1950–1970, U.S. Bureau of the Census and U.S. Department of Labor, Bureau of Labor Statistics

cost than it could have had overtime rates been abolished.[8] In his view, in the absence of time and one-half rates for hours beyond forty, average wages would have had to rise to the levels available with the premium arrangements if the same total supply of labor were to be obtained.

The actual work week did rise substantially during World War II, reaching 49.3 hours in 1944 (60.2 hours in agriculture and 46.9 in nonagricultural industries). There is general agreement, moreover, that the opportunity to increase earnings through overtime work led workers to accept the holding down of wage rates, even though prices continued to rise. After the war, the average work week declined again and has remained very close to forty hours for the past quarter century. In manufacturing, for example, average weekly hours have fluctuated within a very narrow band, between a low of 39.1 in 1949 and high of 41.3 in 1966. In fact, the length of the average work week has become an indicator of the trends in the economy. When the economy begins to head downward, average number of hours worked declines even before unemployment begins to rise, as the reductions in output are first reflected in elimination of overtime work. Similarly, the number of hours worked rises before unemployment drops, because those on

---

[8] Frederick Meyers, "The Economics of Overtime," in Dankert, Mann, and Northrup, *op. cit.,* p. 102.

short work weeks are placed on normal schedules before those on layoff are recalled.

Recent Developments with Respect to the Work Week

Explanations for the Reduced Work Week

The steady decline in the work week, which saw it cut in half in the century between the 1830s and 1930s, is a most remarkable phenomenon. It reflected changed social values and an altered conception of the meaning of life. Where formerly life had consisted mainly of work, at least for the mass of workers, in the later period it had become but one aspect of life. Indeed, for the majority of unskilled and semiskilled workers, their attitude toward work had become instrumental; that is, instead of deriving satisfaction from their work, they accepted routine, meaningless jobs because they provided them with income with which to fulfill their needs as consumers.

The most important factor, however, in explaining the reduction of the work week was the incredible increase in productivity that additional capital, improved technology, and a better educated and trained labor force brought. As incomes have risen, people have come to value extra leisure more than additional income, so they have substituted leisure for income. As a society, in the century from the 1830s to the 1930s, the United States chose to take a major share of the increased productivity that capital, technology, and a more efficient labor force had made possible in the form of increased leisure.

Shorter Hours as a Means of Spreading Employment

Amazingly, however, in the last four decades the forty-hour work week has persisted as the basic standard for the nation, and only in periods of unemployment has there been any significant agitation for shorter hours. In 1962, the fifth year in succession that the unemployment rate had averaged 5.5 percent or higher, the AFL-CIO Executive Council unanimously decided to press for a reduction in the basic work week to thirty-five hours.[9] The Federation contended that shorter working hours would spread employment. Most economists, however, would not agree that shorter working hours can be a solution to unemployment. As Dankert has pointed out, the long-run reduction in the length of the work week has not eliminated the problem of unemployment, and there seems to be no particular relationship between the two.[10]

The notion that shorter hours mean more employment is based on the long-discredited "lump-of-labor" theory, that is, that there is just so much

---

[9] American Federation of Labor and Congress of Industrial Organizations, "Shorter Hours: Tool to Combat Unemployment," in William G. Bowen (ed.), *Labor and the National Economy* (New York: Norton, 1965), pp. 152–162.

[10] Clyde E. Dankert, "Hours of Work," in *ibid.*, pp. 162–170.

work to be done in the economy, and the less time spent doing it by workers, the more workers are needed to complete the task. By now, however, the concept of aggregate demand as determining the level of output and employment should be apparent. This is not an argument against reducing working time, but only a caution that the rationale for it should not be a faulty one. Society, for example, may decide that in the future we must slow down the rate of economic growth and increase in affluence in order to preserve the environment. One way of doing this could be through reduced working time.

The Costs of Shorter Hours

Arguments in favor of reduced working time in order to spread employment usually contain the implicit assumption that the cut would actually increase aggregate demand because wage rates would be raised accordingly to maintain the purchasing power of workers who had jobs. Such arguments, however, focus on wages solely in terms of income and ignore the fact that they are also a cost of production. In order to understand this, let us assume that the standard work week is to be reduced to thirty-two hours throughout the economy.

Since employees working a forty-hour week do not want to have their hours reduced to thirty-two unless their wage rates are raised to bring their total earnings up to where they had been, very heavy costs would be involved. Simple arithmetic will disclose that such a reduction in the work week would require an increase in wage rates of 25 percent: a worker earning $120 per week on a forty-hour schedule would have to have his hourly wage increased from $3.00 to $3.75 in order to maintain his total earnings. Since there is no reason to assume any concomitant increase in productivity, labor costs would rise by an equal amount. In fact, labor costs in the short run would rise even more, because employers would have to recruit new workers and train them, and until all shortages were remedied they would have to work present employees overtime at premium rates.

The increase in the costs of production would force employers to raise prices; thus, the real cost of the reduction in hours would be shifted to the consumer, who would bear it in the form of higher prices. Since all the members of society are its consumers, all would have suffered diminutions in real income. No increase in aggregate demand would have resulted from the reduction in the work week; in fact, it is more likely that the increase in the price level would result in a new equilibrium at an even lower level of national output.

If the economy were operating at a full employment level and we cut the work week, the net effect would be a reduction in the total amount of goods and services that we could produce, and the populace would suffer a reduction in living standards. If the citizens of the United States want a shorter work week because they desire to have more leisure, that is a choice that they can make, but they must recognize that more leisure means less income. Gradual reductions in line with increases in productivity, however, can be achieved without giving up any of present income, as has been true over the long run. Historically, between one-third and two-fifths of the total rise in productivity has been taken in the form of increased leisure. Thus, hours of work can be reduced, but they should be reduced only when, as a society, we have determined that we prefer to take more of the gains in productivity in the form of leisure and less in the form of income.

Factors against Shorter Hours

The fact that during the past forty years we have not continued to take part of our increased productivity in the form of a shorter work week, however, is puzzling. Even the AFL-CIO dropped its campaign for the thirty-five hour week once high levels of employment returned in the second half of the 1960s. Perhaps forty hours is about right for the average person, leaving him as much free time as he wants. Fatigue that significantly lowers output per worker, moreover, only seems to set in at work weeks well beyond forty hours and, equally, does not decline significantly at shorter work weeks.

Probably more important has been the general desire of people to achieve higher standards of living as measured by the amount of goods and services that they can consume. The desire for an automobile, refrigerator, washing machine, a house in the suburbs, and the ability to send one's children to college has placed the stress in recent decades on earning more money, rather than on securing shorter hours of work. The fact that, at least until recently, many workers actively sought overtime work and millions even moonlighted, that is, they held second jobs in their "free" time, is indicative of the marginal utility of income.

The moonlighting phenomenon is clearly indicative of the fact that there are distinct differences in individual preferences as between more income and more leisure. According to a U.S. Labor Department study, in 1966 a little over 3.5 million people, equal to about 5 percent of the total employed, held two jobs.[11] Some of these people undoubtedly held second jobs because of the need for additional income, at least in terms of the desire to attain and retain certain levels of living. Thus, moonlighting was found to increase with size of family, from 5.4 percent of married men with no children to 10.3 percent for those with five or more children. Also, the higher one's income, the less likely is it that he will hold a second job. For example, among married men earning less than $60 per week from their primary jobs, 12.5 percent held second ones, but for those earning more than $200 per week, only 5.5 percent moonlighted. Ability to qualify for other work and having a work schedule on the primary job that permits part-time work elsewhere also are factors in moonlighting: teachers, for example, are very prone to moonlighting.

---

[11] Harvey R. Hamel, "Moonlighting—An Economic Phenomenon," *Monthly Labor Review*, October 1967.

People's attitudes, however, change over time. The present young generation, which has been most voluble in denouncing the "materialness" of its parents, may value leisure more highly. It is possible, therefore, that there will be a renewed drive for a shorter work week in the future. But we may also discover that, as today's youth grow older and assume the burdens of raising families, they too may prefer more income to time off, much in the same way their parents did.

Shorter Hours in Some Sectors of the Economy

Even today, many millions of people, probably about 15 percent of all employees, have a standard work week of less than forty hours. Unions in the printing, brewing, and building trades have, through collective bargaining, won shorter work weeks in many labor markets. Rubber workers in Akron worked a thirty-six hour week (six hours, six days) for many years. The most dramatic reduction in the work week was the twenty-five hour week negotiated by Local 3, International Brotherhood of Electrical Workers with construction contractors in New York City in 1962. The shorter standard work week was only partially intended to reduce actual working time, however, for the union also sought it as a device to boost pay. The agreement establishing the five-hour day also contained a guarantee of at least one hour of work above that at premium rates of pay.

Various sections of the women's apparel industry have had a standard thirty-five hour week since the mid-1930s, and in recent years the International Ladies' Garment Workers' Union has spread the thirty-five hour week to most other sections of the industry. Significantly, the garment industry has an 80 percent female labor force, and the shorter hours undoubtedly are most appealing to the wives and mothers who work in the industry.

Another sector of the economy in which shorter work weeks have become common are the service, trade, and finance industries. By 1963 one-third of all clerical workers had a work week of less than forty hours.[12] Work weeks of thirty-five or thirty-seven and one-half hours in stores and offices are quite common in many large cities, particularly New York. Again, the fact that a large percentage of these workers are women, who are attracted into the labor force partially through the reduced hours, is an important factor. Also, commuting time to work in large urban conglomerations such as New York must be compensated for to some degree by a reduction in actual working time.

The Ten-Hour, Four-Day Week

One very recent innovation with respect to the work week deserves special consideration. In the last few years a number of companies have adopted the

---

[12] Dean F. Berry, "Automation, Rationalization, and Urbanization: Hours of Work in the Office," in Dankert, Mann, and Northrup, *op. cit.*, pp. 128–147.

four-day, forty-hour work week, and others have experimented with flexi-time, whereby employees can choose their own hours of work as long as they add up to forty for the week. Glowing reports on the benefits of the four-day week to both employers and workers have begun to appear.[13] To the employee it is supposed to bring the benefits of reduced time and costs of commuting to work and of a three-day weekend in which to enjoy leisure-time activities. For the employer the four-day week is supposed to cut costs and increase productivity through a reduction in absenteeism and a cutting of personnel turnover.

In 1971, according to the Bureau of Labor Statistics, the four-day, forty-hour week had actually been implemented in over 650 companies.[14] Most of these companies were nonunion and had relatively small numbers of employees. Only 80,000 employees, or .001 percent of the labor force, were working under a four-day week arrangement.

So far the move to the four-forty week has been very small. Workers are divided on its desirability, and many unions and managements remain quite dubious about it. Objections by the Teamsters' Union led to the end of a two-month experiment with the four-day week at the Intercontinental Steel Corporation in Michigan in 1971.[15] Basically, the unions see the four-day, forty-hour week as no gain whatsoever for workers, but merely a reshuffling of existing work schedules, largely for the employer's benefit. The unions, more-over, fear that the four-forty week would deflect worker interest from the struggle for a reduction in the standard forty-hour week.

Most employers, particularly the large corporations, are equally unen-thusiastic. Many managements believe that the ten-hour day would interfere with schedules for receipt of shipments from suppliers and shipments of fin-ished products to customers. The fact that some employees must be in on the fifth day might tend to create jealousies within the work force. Industries that operate their facilities around the clock, twenty-four hours a day, would find it extremely difficult to adjust to a ten-hour working day. Furthermore, there are serious questions of the effect of long hours on employee fatigue, which could not only cut efficiency but also lead to more industrial accidents. For many workers, moreover, a three-day weekend may simply provide greater opportunity to engage in moonlighting, that is, accept a second job.

Even so, a younger work force and changing attitudes toward work and leisure may promote the four-day week. Legislative changes, however, may have to be made before employers in many industries could undertake the four-day, forty-hour week, even if they wanted to do so. The Walsh-Healy Act, covering firms with government contracts, for example, stipulates that time-and-one-half wage rates be paid for work over eight hours in any day.

[13] See, for example, Riva Poor, *Four Days, Forty Hours* (Cambridge, Mass.: Burch and Poor, 1970).
[14] Janice Neipert Hedges, "A Look at the 4-Day Workweek," *Monthly Labor Review*, October 1971, pp. 33–37.
[15] *Wall Street Journal*, April 15, 1971.

In the long run experiments and studies, plus shifting attitudes, will help to determine how widespread the four-day week will become.

Overtime Hours

Despite the fact that employers must pay premium rates for hours beyond forty per week, a surprisingly large amount of overtime work exists in American industry. In May 1966 17.0 million out of a total of 71.0 million people at work actually worked overtime, and 6.5 million of them received premium pay. Those receiving premium pay were mainly blue-collar and clerical workers, for extra compensation is not as common among higher level white-collar workers, such as managers, foremen, and professionals. Four distinct groups of overtime workers were found to exist: (1) professional and managerial employees who often work extra hours regardless of their pay status; (2) craftsmen and other blue-collar workers who do receive premium pay, and put in extra hours because of shortages in their skills; (3) an amorphous group of workers who were temporarily on overtime, for which they are paid premium rates, in response to temporary spurts in demand, as from seasonal factors; and (4) a relatively large group of low-paid marginal workers who often work excessive hours but rarely receive premium pay.[16]

More than one-third of the overtime workers were in manufacturing, one-quarter were in service and finance, and better than one-fifth were in trade. Most of those receiving premium pay for the overtime hours, however, were in manufacturing, reflecting the limited coverage of the FLSA in other industries.[17]

In the 1960s a controversy arose concerning the use of overtime in a period when unemployment rates were rather high. Organized labor sought legislation that would raise the premium for overtime from one and one-half times normal rates of pay to double in order to discourage employers from scheduling overtime and encourage them to hire more workers instead.

Many of those who analyzed the overtime situation identified a structural change in the nature of employee compensation as the cause of employers preferring to work present employees longer, even at premium rates, than to hire additional employees. Fringe benefits have become a major component of the total compensation packet, but the costs of most fringes, such as hospitalization, do not go up if the employee works more hours, but only if more employees are hired. Similarly, state unemployment compensation systems, through their provisions for merit rating, that is, determining what percentage of payroll the employer must pay according to his unemployment experience, encourage employers to reduce turnover. A means of reducing

---

[16] James R. Wetzel, "Overtime Hours and Premium Pay," *Monthly Labor Review,* May 1967.

[17] A revolt against having to work overtime, however, has been brewing among factory workers. The United Auto Workers, for example, made the employee's right to accept or refuse overtime work an issue in its 1973 negotiations with the automobile manufacturers.

employee turnover, of course, is not to hire additional workers for temporary spurts in output but to work present employees longer hours.

In an attempt to assess the validity of these arguments, Garbarino used an algebraic model by which to measure the cost of fringe benefits for additional employees against that of overtime for present workers. Through the use of this model, he hoped to see if fringe benefit costs actually did restrict new hires. His findings indicated, that, to the contrary, in manufacturing the cost of overtime exceeded that of fringe benefits, and that the absolute dollar differential between the two had been increasing at least until the 1960s.[18] He conceded, however, that if turnover costs and the long-run effects of irregular employment could have been taken into account, then for some companies the differential would have been much reduced, and for them fringe costs might truly have been a cost barrier to expanding employment. Garbarino also suggested that the structure of both public and private fringe benefits and their financing may discourage expanding employment without necessarily having a direct effect on the amount of overtime worked. By implication, he suggested that even increasing the premium rate for overtime might not have the effect of substituting additional workers for overtime.

Others contended that the real barrier to hiring additional workers was the costs of doing so. It is very costly to recruit, select, and train new workers, and if the period of time for which they will be needed is short, it will be cheaper to work present employees overtime, even at premium rates of pay. On the other hand, Joseph has argued that the alternatives are not limited to the hiring of new employees as against working overtime, and that the relevant comparative costs are not just those associated with new hires.[19] In his view, very often the only real alternatives to overtime work are either curtailment of production or extensive capital expenditures. To substantiate his point, he cites the results of a survey of the Department of Labor as to why employers schedule overtime hours, which disclosed that availability of skilled labor and additional equipment, cost of training and length of training period, reduction in output of inexperienced workers, adverse effects of subsequent layoffs on unemployment experience ratings, and employees' willingness to take a job of limited duration were more important than the cost of fringe benefits.

Usually, employers faced with increased production of short or uncertain duration used overtime work to meet it, but those who expected a long period of increased production hired additional workers. Thus, in periods of economic sluggishness and uncertainty, relatively more overtime tends to be worked, whereas, in periods of rapid and sustained economic growth, employer optimism leads to the expansion of hiring. Thus, if employers were

---

[18] Joseph W. Garbarino, "Fringe Benefits and Overtime as Barriers to Expanding Employment," *Industrial and Labor Relations Review*, April 1964, pp. 426–442.

[19] Myron L. Joseph, *Hours of Work Issues*, Vol. II (Appendix), *Technology and the American Economy*, The Report of the National Commission on Technology, Automation, and Economic Progress, 1966, p. 334.

using "excessive" overtime in a period of high unemployment, it was a result, rather than a cause, of depressed economic conditions.

Technical factors also play a role in the use of overtime. A typical plant problem is that one department falls behind in its work relative to the others. Since balancing production may not require adding workers for a full work week, the easiest solution is to have the department that is behind in its schedule put in overtime hours in order to catch up. In fact, scheduling problems, whether due to cyclical factors, emergency problems, or seasonal variations, all of which are temporary, are a major reason for overtime work in large-scale industry.

Although many economists contended that increasing the premium pay for overtime work would not lead to substantial additional hiring, President Johnson did propose such a move to Congress. The fact that the majority of people who work overtime do not receive premium pay at all would seem to have strengthened the case against increasing premium payments under the Fair Labor Standards Act. At any rate, following the President's proposal, the economy began to grow at a more rapid rate, new hiring increased substantially, and Congress never acted on the proposal.

The Shorter Work Year

Historically, between one-third and two-fifths of the total rise in productivity has been utilized by American society in increased leisure, and over the period of a century the average work week was reduced by two and one-half hours each decade. No basic change in the work week, however, has been made since the 1930s. Does this indicate that Americans are less interested in additional leisure? The answer must be no.

The fact that the basic forty-hour work week has persisted for four decades does not mean that workers do not want to take some of the increase in national productivity in the form of increased leisure. In recent years, however, the reduction in working time has been accomplished through an increase in the number of paid holidays and length of vacation periods. Let us, therefore, examine these two means of reducing the total time during the year that people work.

Holidays

At one time the only days off that industrial workers received were when they were laid off the job, but they received no pay and, until a generation ago, no unemployment compensation for these periods of forced idleness. By the 1920s some large nonunion employers, under the inspiration of "welfare capitalism," began to provide a few paid holidays to their work forces. A few unions were also able to negotiate paid holidays for their members, but the big breakthrough for blue-collar workers did not come until 1947, when the United Automobile Workers negotiated agreements with the automobile manufacturers providing for six paid holidays. After that, paid holidays for blue-collar as well as white-collar workers became common, with over 90 percent of them receiving paid holidays today.

The trend since 1947 has been for a continual increase in the number of days off with pay that are provided workers. Blue-collar workers, moreover, are closing the paid-holiday gap between themselves and white-collar workers. Between 1960 and 1968 paid holidays for office workers increased by three-tenths of a day on the average, but for plant workers, by seven-tenths of a day.[20] According to the Department of Labor, by 1970 the latter averaged 7.5 paid holidays, compared with 8.0 for office workers.

In 1955 six holidays per year was the typical number, but by 1970 half of all collective bargaining agreements provided for nine or more, and 23 percent of major contracts called for ten or more. There is also a trend toward combining extra days off with traditional holidays, in order to provide long weekends. This trend is being reinforced by the legislation, which went into effect in 1971, that had five national holidays fall on Monday. In their 1970 negotiations the automobile manufacturers and the UAW agreed to a paid-holiday break of four days during the Christmas period.

In addition to such standard holidays as Washington's Birthday, Memorial Day, Independence Day, Thanksgiving, Christmas, and New Year's, new holidays in some collective bargaining agreements include the day after Thanksgiving, Martin Luther King's birthday, the Friday before Labor Day, and a "travel day" taken on the last working day before or the first working day after vacation.[21] Some industries now provide a "floating" holiday which is sometimes used as a day off for each individual on his birthday or to commemorate an occasion that is important to the individual; the extra day may also be used to create another long weekend.

Not only is there a distinct trend to more holidays, and to cluster them around weekends, but workers are becoming increasingly loath to work on holidays, even at premium rates of pay. With respect to holidays the marginal utility of leisure seems to clearly outweigh that of income. As a result, half of all collective bargaining agreements provide that, for holiday work, employees will receive their holiday pay plus either time-and-one-half or double their normal rates of pay.

Vacations

Paid vacations for industrial workers are also of relatively recent origin, although a few of them have been receiving paid vacations for decades and vacations have been part of the white-collar workers' schedule even longer. In 1940 only 25 percent of workers covered by collective bargaining agreements received paid vacations, by 1944 the percentage had risen to 85, and

---

[20] Geoffrey H. Moore and Janice Neipert Hedges, "Trends in Labor and Leisure," *Monthly Labor Review*, February 1971, pp. 3–12.

[21] *Basic Patterns in Union Contracts* (Washington, D.C.: Bureau of National Affairs, 1971).

today virtually all have them. Paid vacations, even in nonunion establishments, have spread rapidly since 1960. In 1968 two-thirds of all workers in the private nonfarm economy received a paid vacation.[22] Of the remainder, some were newly hired workers who had not been on the job long enough to qualify for a vacation that year, and the rest worked in firms that made no provision for paid vacations.

There is a definite trend toward longer vacations. In fact, the increase in the number of weeks of paid vacation in recent years has been nothing short of spectacular. Between 1960 and 1969 the total number of weeks that workers spent on vacation increased almost 50 percent, from 87 to 129 million. In the latter year, full-time workers averaged 2.2 weeks of paid vacations, compared with 1.8 in 1960.

The number of weeks of paid vacation to which workers are entitled depends upon their length of service with the company. Long-service workers, therefore, are entitled to much longer vacations than indicated by the average. By 1970 the typical collective bargaining agreement provided for vacations of one week after one year's service, two weeks after three years, three weeks after ten years, and four weeks after twenty years of service. Nearly one-quarter granted up to five weeks of vacation each year, and 5 percent provided six weeks or more for very long-service employees. As the large percentage of young workers hired in recent years begins to accumulate more years of service, the additional weeks of vacation eligibility will be reflected in much longer vacations on the average.

Not only are vacations becoming longer, but the annual period during which they may be taken is also being extended. It used to be the rule to limit the time during which vacations might be taken to very short periods— July and August or the plant's slack period—but there appears a trend toward a fifty-two-week vacation season.

The can, steel, and aluminum industries have pioneered the concept of the extended vacation or sabbatical leave for industrial workers. Under the steel industry arrangements, workers with fifteen years' seniority are entitled to thirteen weeks of vacation every five years. This extended vacation is similar in concept to the sabbatical leave in colleges and universities, whereby every seven years or so professors are supposed to be able to take one semester off with pay in order to pursue research in their field.

The extended vacation concept, however, has not spread widely beyond the industries that originally adopted it, and in the aluminum industry the actual extended vacation has been cut to ten weeks with thirteen weeks of pay. In other areas widespread worker enthusiasm for the sabbatical plan has not developed, because the sabbatical must be taken all at once, and many workers do not know what to do to fill this extra time. For example, when, in the mid-1960s, Armco Steel Corporation gave its white-collar employees a choice between extra vacation and extra pay, 80 percent chose to take the money.

---

[22] Moore and Hedges, *op. cit.*

The Increase in Leisure during One's Lifetime

When we review the history of the cutting of the work week, the introduction of paid holidays, and the increase in vacation time, we recognize how much of the gains in productivity have been taken in the form of more leisure rather than more income. But even these changes fail to tell the whole story, for the growth in leisure has not been limited to the individual's work life.[23] Retirement on a pension has been another form of leisure that has spread very widely through the American economy.

In terms of total life expectancy, the United States has been using only half of the additional years in work time, the other half being taken as time out of the labor force. Between 1900 and 1960 average life expectancy at birth for men rose from 48.2 to 66.6 years, but only nine of the additional years of life are devoted to work, the other nine being devoted to increased schooling before entering the labor force and retirement in the later years. There is, moreover, also a trend toward earlier retirement, which will serve still further to augment the leisure proportion of people's lives.

Looking back over the past century, we find that there has been a most significant increase in the amount of time free from work that Americans have. The reduction in the average work week of about 13 hours gives the individual about 675 hours of free time annually. Time spent on vacation provides another 70 hours of free time. Paid holidays actually not worked equal about 45 more hours. The total of the three, therefore, is nearly 800 hours per year, which is about equal to one month out of twelve. As Moore and Hedges point out, "The additional hours of nonworking time in youth and old age represent a further gain of about 18,000 hours during a man's lifetime. Altogether, the lifetime gain for all workers in the past 100 years comes to about 50,000 hours free of work."

Two factors have enabled American society to achieve this very substantial increase in nonworking time while at the same time raising the standard of living to new heights. First and foremost, of course, has been the increase in productivity that has come from the use of a greater quantity of capital, the improvement of the quality of the labor input to the production process, and technological innovations that have permitted more efficient utilization of the factors of production. But a second factor should not be overlooked, and this is the continual growth in the number of people in the labor force. Not only population growth, but also the increasing percentage of women working or looking for work, has served to keep up the supply of labor and for the nation to allow all workers more time off the job without creating labor shortages.

The Future

A continued growth of productivity at the rate of 2.5 to 3.0 percent per year will provide even greater opportunity for taking some of it in the form of

---

[23] *Ibid.*

increased leisure. Based on the trends of the past decade there is every reason to expect that there will be even more emphasis on additional free time. Undoubtedly, much of the increase in nonworking time will continue to come in the form of more holidays, longer vacations, and earlier retirement.

One should not, however, discount possibilities of a renewed thrust toward a shorter work week. There are many indications that workers prefer to take free time in lumps, as, for example, the drive for Monday holidays, the concentration of absenteeism on Mondays and Fridays, and longer vacations. By working fewer days within the week, the worker saves commutation costs and has the ability to spend a few days "out in the country." As incomes rise, many are also able to afford to purchase and operate second homes in more rural areas, even if these homes are only log cabins or bungalows.

So far the movement to the four-day week, which is still too small to be considered a trend, has entailed the concentration of forty hours of work within the fewer days. Should the four-day week become widespread, however, there will be renewed agitation for the eight-hour day. It is not inconceivable, therefore, that within a decade or so many industries will have adopted the four-day, thirty-two hour week, and a three-day weekend. (The tremendous increase in employee absenteeism, most of which occurs on Mondays and Fridays, is an indication that many workers have already opted for the shorter work week, even, as now, when it means less weekly pay.) The continuous process industries might even prefer such a work schedule to any other nonmultiple of eight, because it would permit them to maintain three eight-hour shifts around the clock.

Time off from work might also be taken in other forms. Given the rapidity of technological change, it may be desirable to provide many workers with the opportunity to undergo retraining in new skills before their old ones become obsolete. Many engineers, for example, have encountered the problem of not being able to keep up with the latest developments in their fields after a number of years on the job. The sabbatical leave, whereby they could take off half a year or a year to return to college for further education, might be of great value not only to them, but also to their employers and the entire society, because of their having become more valuable employees.

Finally, it must be recognized that not all people have the same preferences, and that, while some will seek more leisure, others will be interested in still greater income. As more free time is provided from a given job, some workers will use it in order to take a second job. Moreover, as longer weekends develop, the pressure will be on the service industries to provide more services all week long, so some workers will actually find greater opportunities for moonlighting. As a total society, however, the United States probably will opt for more leisure.

Summary

For many millennia men worked from sunup to sundown six days a week. Although this agricultural pattern of work time was adopted when industry first arose, workers quickly demanded shorter hours. Through both union activity and legislative efforts they sought to attain first the ten-hour day and later the eight-hour day. The rationalization of industry also led many employers voluntarily to reduce daily hours of work.

The Fair Labor Standards Act of 1938 established the forty-hour week as the standard work week in American industry. Employees may work longer than that, but they must be paid time-and-one-half their normal rates of pay for the overtime hours.

The major explanation of the reduction in working time is the tremendous increase in productivity that the nation has enjoyed. Economists have rejected the idea, however, that shorter hours are an effective means of reducing unemployment. They point to the fact that shorter hours of work are costly and are purchased at the price of the ability to earn more income and thus to enjoy a higher national output. While some workers may prefer more leisure, others prefer higher incomes, as is evidenced by the fact that about 5 percent of the employed hold second jobs. On the other hand, some sectors of the economy, such as the building trades, printing, the clothing industry, and office work, generally have work weeks under forty hours.

In recent years a number of small companies have experimented with a ten-hour day, four-day week. Although the move in this direction is much too small to be labeled a trend, it does indicate a desire on the part of some for longer weekends.

About one-fourth of the labor force, on the other hand, works overtime hours. Only a minority of these workers, however, receive premium pay for the extra hours. In the 1960s the AFL-CIO supported a move to raise over time premium pay rates in order to encourage the hiring of additional workers. Economic analysis, however, indicated that increasing the premium pay for overtime work would not lead to substantial additional hiring. When the labor market situation changed to one of shortage, rather than surplus, of labor, the agitation concerning overtime work subsided.

Historically, between one-third and two-fifths of the total rise in productivity has been utilized by American society in the form of increased leisure. Although the standard work week has remained at forty hours for four decades, additional leisure has been taken in that period in the form of more holidays and longer vacations. Furthermore, only half of the years of increased life expectancy are used in working, the other half being devoted to increased schooling before entering the labor force and retirement in the later years.

The continued growth in productivity, when combined with new attitudes toward life on the part of younger workers, will probably mean an intensified interest in more leisure in the future. It is quite possible that the thirty-two-hour week, plus sabbatical leaves every few years, may become the pattern of the future.

BIBLIOGRAPHY

Becker, Gary S. "A Theory of the Allocation of Time," *Economic Journal,* September 1965.

Bowen, William G. (ed.). *Labor and the National Economy.* New York: Norton, 1965.

Dankert, Clyde E., Floyd C. Mann, and Herbert R. Northrup (eds.). *Hours of Work.* New York: Harper & Row, 1965.

De Grazia, S. *Of Time, Work and Leisure.* New York: Twentieth Century Fund, 1962.

Dewhurst, J. Frederic, and Associates. *America's Needs and Resources.* New York: Twentieth Century Fund, 1955.

Garbarino, Joseph W. "Fringe Benefits and Overtime as Barriers to Expanding Employment," *Industrial and Labor Relations Review,* April 1964.

Hamel, Harvey R. "Moonlighting—An Economic Phenomenon," *Monthly Labor Review,* October 1967.

Moore, Geoffrey H., and Janice Neipert Hedges. "Trends in Labor and Leisure," *Monthly Labor Review,* February 1971.

Poor, Riva. *Four-Days, Forty-Hours.* Cambridge, Mass.: Burch and Poor, 1970.

Technology and the American Economy. Report of the National Commission on Technology, Automation, and Economic Progress, Washington, D.C.: Government Printing Office, 1966.

Wetzel, James R. "Overtime Hours and Premium Pay," *Monthly Labor Review,* May 1967.

15 ACHIEVING ECONOMIC SECURITY FOR WORKERS

Throughout this book it has been emphasized that workers did not originally greet the free labor market with joy, because its initial impact on them was far from favorable. In no area was this more true than with respect to security—of employment or income. Under a contract relationship the employer owed the worker nothing except payment for work actually performed, and when there was no work or the individual could not perform labor because of illness or old age, the employer had no responsibility toward him.

The situation would not have been all that bad had someone else been willing to assume responsibility for aiding the incapacitated. In a modern industrial society only the state could be that somebody, but the concepts of laissez faire dictated that the government stay out of any interference with the normal workings of the market, even when this resulted in suffering for many people. Workers who became injured, sick, or too old to work, therefore, had to rely upon their own meager resources or upon charity in order to survive.

The United States continued to cling to laissez-faire precepts until the Great Depression of the 1930s, when it adopted "social security." In this chapter, therefore, we shall examine the problem of economic security in an industrial society, the emergence and expansion of social security legislation in the United States, employer programs for pensions and health and welfare, workmen's compensation and occupational health and safety legislation, and current proposals for guaranteeing a minimum of well-being to all citizens.

Problems of Economic Security in an Industrial Society

When the United States was founded in the late eighteenth century it was basically an agricultural nation, and the problems of economic security are far different for an agricultural society than for an industrial one. As late as 1880 72 percent of the U.S. population was still rural, so farm attitudes still predominated. Some of these differences with respect to the problem of unemployment were examined previously, but they also applied with respect to other risks that confronted workers. Let us examine some of these as they applied to the problem of old age, which is a prime cause of interruption of earning power and therefore of want. While it is true that the aged have always existed, certain modern phenomena have made old age a national problem in an urban industrial society.

Changes Wrought by an Urban Industrial Order

First of all, the dimensions of any old-age problem were far smaller in an agricultural than a modern industrial society. Improvements in public sanitation and in diet, plus advances in medicine, have increased longevity. This fact does not mean that older people live much longer today than two hundred years ago, but that a larger percentage of the population lives to be old. In 1880 there were only 1.7 million persons sixty-five years of age or over in the United States, and they comprised 3.4 percent of the population. By 1970 there were 20 million older citizens, and they made up 10 percent of the total population.

Second, the shift from agriculture to industry has changed the nature of work, particularly with respect to older persons. In an industrial economy there is a sharp dichotomy between working and not working: a person usually puts in full time on a job, and when he can no longer work full time, he cannot continue to hold a job. Life on a farm, however, was decidedly different. The farm tended to be family owned, and as the father grew older his sons took over doing more of the arduous tasks, but, even as he grew still older, father could continue to earn his keep by performing some of the chores that needed to be done. In other words, the phenomenon of "retirement" was much less common in an agricultural setting, and one worked until he was completely bedridden or died, but at a gentler pace as age and physical stamina dictated.

Third, the shift from agriculture to industry has also resulted in a dramatic change in the nature of the family. On the farm the family was an economic unit, but this was no longer the case under industrialism. The family farm was also multigenerational, but with the spread of industry and urbanism the nuclear family became dominant. Under the former setup, while some children moved westward or sought their fortunes in the city, others remained on the farm to help run it and eventually to take over its management. In the city, however, children almost invariably moved out of their parents' households when they went to work, married, and raised their own families. Concepts of responsibility changed in the process: one's primary responsibility was to the rearing of his own children, and aging parents could not depend upon their grown children for support when they could no longer hold down jobs. The size of the family, moreover, was contracting, and whereas a relatively small contribution each from a number of children, which each could afford, could sustain aging parents, it required very substantial contributions from only two children, and such contributions were usually beyond the children's financial abilities. Many aged, moreover, lack family units altogether. Thus, the disappearance of the extended family served to increase the insecurity of old age.

Fourth, all these changes also served to alter the economic needs of older persons. In the farmhouse there was always a bedroom available for the old folks, and, if not, an extension to the house could be built in spare time without incurring any great expense. In the city, with people living in small apartments, there simply was no room for parents, and so an additional rent had to be paid in order for them to maintain their own apartment. Similarly, the total cost of food is smaller when the same number of people live in one household than when they maintain two separate ones. The shift to the nuclear family, therefore, raised the income requirements of aged persons.

Finally, the very rise in living standards that industrialism brought called attention to the plight of the aged. When most people were relatively poor, the poverty of the aged was just a part of the general situation. But as real wages rose, the relative status of the aged who were no longer capable of working became sharply distinguished.

What has been said of old age also applied with respect to other disabilities. Thus, the farmer who lost the use of a hand or an arm as a result of an accident could still perform some work on the farm, but the industrial worker who suffered such an accident could rarely find an employer willing to hire him. And, of course, the extended family concepts applied to the sick and disabled as well as to the aged.

Personal Savings for Retirement

Thus, the shift from an agricultural to an industrial society has brought forth the problem of insecurity. But, if the employer was not responsible for his workers, the state eschewed responsibility, and relatives were unable to assume it, how was the individual supposed to manage? In a society rooted in the concept of the "rugged individualist," the answer was that he was supposed to save for his own "rainy day."

Again, let us look at this reasoning with respect to old age. On the face of it, the idea that workers should, on their own, save money to provide for their needs when they became too old to work seems reasonable, but, historically, it has proved to be impossible for workers and other low- or moderate-income groups to provide for their own hours of need.

To begin with, while it is true that real wages were rising, the wages of most industrial workers were, at least until rather recently, not high enough to allow them much discretionary income: wage income could cover food, clothing, and shelter (and sometimes barely that), but left little over for saving. Even if one were able to save from his earnings, adversity usually intervened to deplete those savings. Any illness in the family would quickly eat up savings, for there was no Blue Cross or Blue Shield to cover any part of hospital and physician bills. Probably most inimical to savings was a period of unemployment, and it must be remembered that economic depressions with widespread unemployment were a regular phenomenon until World War II. Thus, the ability to save enough money to live on in old age was simply beyond the capabilities of most people who worked for a living, whether in white-collar or blue-collar jobs.

Social Insurance

The obvious solution to the problem of insecurity in old age would have been a governmental program of social insurance. In fact, by the mid-1930s twenty-seven countries had well-developed national retirement systems.[1] The United States, however, continued to act as if its economy was still an agricultural one and to uphold the principles of laissez faire and individual responsibility.

The Great Depression of the 1930s, however, finally made the nation responsive to the needs of the aged. Although all segments of the population were affected by the depression, the aged suffered the most. In a situation of mass unemployment, they were the least able to find jobs, saw the depletion of any savings they might have accumulated, and could not, as private charity funds disappeared because of the immensity of the burden, even depend upon charity. Public pensions became the hope of the aged, and many younger people also began to favor them as a means of getting the older people out of the labor force and thus reducing the competition for scarce jobs. Millions of people joined the Townsend Crusade, which proposed to solve the depression by paying pensions of $200 per month and requiring the recipients to spend the money and thereby create additional purchasing power and stimulate the economy. Under this political pressure, President Roosevelt in 1934 created the Committee on Economic Security, and its studies and recommendations led to the passage of the Social Security Act of 1935.

The Social Security Act contained three major sections: (1) Old Age Insurance (OAI), which was to be an entirely federal system; (2) Old Age Assistance (OAA), which was to be state administered with partial federal financing; and (3) Unemployment Insurance (UI), which was to be a state-run system. We have already examined the unemployment insurance system, so now let us turn to the old-age features, starting with old-age assistance.

Old-Age Assistance

A system of old-age insurance requires that people work for a period of time during which they accumulate rights to a pension when they retire. Its adoption in 1935, however, did little good for those persons who were already aged. Providing income to the needy aged immediately was to be accomplished through a system of old-age assistance.

Actually, old-age assistance laws were in existence in a number of states by 1935. Since the Social Security Act provided for federal grants to state systems, it induced all the states to set up old-age assistance programs. Old-age assistance provided cash income to the needy aged, as determined on the basis of minimum standards established by each of the states. Federal requirements set a standard of old-age assistance that, while not high, was more liberal than that which had hitherto existed in most state laws.[2]

---

[1] Joseph A. Pechman, Henry J. Aaron, and Michael K. Taussig, *Social Security: Perspectives for Reform* (Washington, D.C.: Brookings, 1968), p. 48.

[2] Eveline M. Burns, *The American Social Security System* (Boston: Houghton Mifflin, 1949), p. 297.

For many years OAA was actually more important than old-age insurance in terms of the number of aged helped, because the original coverage of old-age insurance was restricted, few people had worked long enough to accumulate benefit rights, and benefits were quite low. Recipients of old-age assistance reached a peak of 2.8 million in 1950, but as old-age insurance coverage was extended and the system matured, OAA declined in relative importance, becoming largely a supplement to low social security benefits. By 1969 there were only 2.1 million OAA recipients, even though the number of aged had increased by 7.0 million since 1950.

The Social Security amendments adopted in the fall of 1972 (H.R. 1) replaced the state programs of aid to the aged, blind, and disabled with a new federal program of supplemental security income that guarantees at least $130 monthly for an individual and $195 for a couple.

Old-Age Insurance

In 1935 coverage for old-age insurance was limited to employees in interstate commerce, except for agriculture. Also excluded were workers in intrastate commerce; employees of local, state, and federal governments; domestic workers; and the self-employed. As a result, only about five out of ten workers were covered, but coverage has been extended gradually to more groups, to the point at which nine out of ten are covered and the system is virtually universal. With the inclusion of the special retirement systems for railroad workers and for federal, state, and local government employees, 96 percent of the working population have retirement protection through public programs.[3]

The scope of the social security system has also been broadened over the years. When it was first enacted it provided for old-age insurance (OAI), but in 1938 survivor benefits were added (OASI), in 1956 permanent disability became part of social security (OASDI), and in 1966 medical benefits for the aged were included (OASDHI). We shall leave the latter two benefits for later discussion, and concentrate now on old-age and survivors' insurance.

Financing

The social security system is financed by a payroll tax, with employers and employees paying equal amounts. When self-employed were brought under coverage they were required to pay one and one-half times the employee rate of taxation. When the tax went into effect in 1937, employers and employees had to pay 1 percent each of the first $3,000 of an employee's earnings. By 1974 the social security contribution was to be 5.85 percent each of the first $12,600 of an employee's earnings. After that, the taxable wage base will be automatically raised in line with wage levels.

---

[3] *Social Security Programs in the United States*, U.S. Department of Health, Education, and Welfare (Washington, D.C.: Government Printing Office, 1971), p. 1.

Benefits

Ten years of covered work makes one fully insured for benefits, but workers born before 1930 may become fully insured with even fewer years of covered experience. In 1970 66 million people were permanently insured under Old-Age Insurance, and even were they not to work another day in their lives, they would be entitled to receive monthly pensions at retirement age. About 93 percent of the people now becoming sixty-five are eligible for monthly cash benefits.[4]

The actual amount of benefit to which the individual will be entitled depends on his average earnings covered by social security. Thus, the longer a person works in covered employment and the higher his earnings, the larger will be his monthly benefit. Although workers who have earned more receive higher retirement benefits, the benefit formula and the inclusion of minimum ($84.50 in mid-1972) and maximum monthly benefits provide a higher benefit to income relationship for lower-income workers.[5] The Social Security Program, thus, has become partly a system for redistribution of income.

Retired workers with dependents receive additional benefits. If the retired worker has a dependent spouse who is sixty-five years of age or over, or if he has a child under eighteen years of age, an additional 50 percent of his primary benefit is added to his monthly social security check for each of them.

Amendments to the Social Security Act since 1935 have permitted workers to retire before they reach sixty-five. Workers could elect to retire as early as age sixty-two, but their benefits were actuarially reduced to take account of the longer period over which they will receive their monthly payments. Female retired workers, however, are not subject to the actuarial discount, since sixty-two is considered to be "normal" retirement age for women. By the 1972 amendments, men were granted the same right to retire at age sixty-two without loss of benefits. Also, extra cash benefits will be provided to those who continue working and delay receipt of social security beyond age sixty-five.

Originally, old-age insurance was thought of as providing pensions to workers who had completely withdrawn from the labor market, but many older people are capable of and desirous of working part time. Starting in 1940, therefore, the law permitted earnings of up to $15 a month without loss of benefits. The limit has been raised a number of times since then, and by 1974, a retired person could earn up to $2,400 a year without loss of

---

[4] *Ibid.*, p. 23.

[5] By further amendment in the autumn of 1972, minimum social security benefit payments were raised to $170 per month for people who have been employed for thirty years or more in low-income jobs, with lesser amounts for those who had worked between twenty and thirty years. Below twenty years of covered employment, the regular $84.50 minimum applies. Since prices were rising very rapidly in the period between enactment of these amendments and their going into effect, in mid-1973 Congress again raised social security benefits, this time by a further 5.6 percent. As a result, the minimum monthly benefit went to $89.30.

benefits. For earnings above $2,400, an individual loses $1 of benefit for every $2 of earnings. There is no earnings limitation for beneficiaries after age seventy-two.

Survivors' Benefits

The 1938 amendments to the Social Security Act added survivor benefits to those of old age, and the system became OASI in place of the original OAI. Today aged widows (or dependent widowers), younger widows who are caring for children, children under eighteen, and dependent parents of deceased workers may qualify for benefits. For widows caring for children under eighteen years of age and the children to be eligible for such benefits, the worker need not have been fully insured, but only currently insured; that is, at the time he died he had credit for at least one and one-half years of work within the previous three years.

The benefits are 100 percent of the primary insurance amount for widows or widowers at age sixty-two, 75 percent for dependent parents over sixty-two, and 75 percent for children. Widows and widowers may collect benefits at age sixty at an actuarially reduced rate, or at age fifty, if disabled. Widows of all ages with children under eighteen years of age are entitled to benefits for themselves and for each dependent child. Close to 6.5 million survivors were receiving benefits by mid-1970.

The family of an insured individual who dies is also entitled to a lump-sum death benefit designed to cover costs of burial. The payment is three times the primary insurance amount. If there is no widow or widower eligible for the benefit, the money is paid to whoever met the burial expenses of the deceased.

Issues in Social Security

Old-age and survivors' insurance has become a major feature of the American economy. By 1970 17 million, or 84 percent of all persons sixty-five years of age and over, were receiving benefits from the system, and social security had become the major factor in preventing poverty among the aged. By 1970 $29 billion was being disbursed through social security for the aged, disabled, their dependents, and their survivors. Yet many issues of public policy remained or had arisen since 1935, including adequacy of benefit payments, methods of financing, and the impact of the system on the nations's economic stability and growth. Let us, therefore, briefly examine some of the current public policy issues.

Adequacy of Benefits

Although social security benefits have been raised a number of times since the act was first passed, in 1970 the average benefit actually being paid to a retired worker with no dependents was only $114 per month. Couples received more—$197 a month—not only because of the 50 percent larger benefit for the wife, but also because married men tend to earn more than single men and thus to qualify for higher primary benefits. Even so, it is quite clear that social security hardly provided sufficient income with which to live well in our society.

A good part of the problem is that for those who are now retired, the earnings level on which benefits are computed was much lower while they were in the labor force. Of course, one might be tempted to dismiss the problem of inadequacy of benefits as ephemeral, since the wage base and the benefit formula have been raised substantially in recent years, and so future retirees will be better off. In 1972, for example, Congress raised social security benefits 20 percent, on top of a compounded increase in benefits of 26.5 percent during the previous two years. In 1973 Congress raised social security benefits a further 5.6 percent. The average retired individual in 1974, for example, would receive a benefit of $170 per month, and a couple $239. At the same time Congress acted to remove the effects of inflation, by which rising prices erode the value of the benefits that the aged receive. The 1972 amendments provide for automatic increases in benefits whenever the Consumer Price Index (CPI) rises by more than 3 percent, effective January 1, 1975.

Financing

Social security is financed through a payroll tax on employers and employees, and the monies collected go into trust funds that are earmarked for the payment of OASDHI benefits. The system supposedly works like private insurance, with the funds collected being invested and the returns from investment used to pay benefits. The analogy to private insurance, however, is far from accurate: the earmarking of trust funds for social security benefits is a pure bookkeeping arrangement, for the money collected actually goes right into the federal treasury the same way that any other taxes do. The reality is that social security benefits are a form of transfer payment: each year, part of the income received by those who are currently economically active is taken away from them and given to those who have ceased contributing to production. Social security differs from other forms of transfer payments, such as public assistance, only in that those retired from the labor force had themselves made contributions to the support of previously retired workers and, through these contributions, established their "right" to receive benefits from the next generation when they became too old to work.

Since the reality is that current benefits are financed out of current income, the question of the soundness of the present payroll tax as the best source of financing comes to the fore. The social security payroll tax has become the second largest federal tax, ranking behind only the personal income tax. An argument against the social security payroll tax is that it is regressive, falling most heavily on low- and moderate-income workers by taking a much higher share of their total incomes than it takes from those with larger salaries and incomes from property. For example, the 5.85 percent tax takes $737.10 from the $12,600-a-year worker as well as from the one who earns $25,200 (since the tax is only on the first $12,600), so the higher-paid employee pays only a 2.975 percent rate. No allowance is made for the number of dependents, either, and the employee with a family pays the same tax as a single person with the same earnings. Millions of lower-income Americans, thus, pay more in social security than in income taxes. There is evidence, moreover, that the incidence of the entire payroll tax apparently falls upon employees, because employers pay workers wages that are lower by the amount of the tax that they must pay.[6] With payroll taxes accounting for almost one-third of the federal government's revenues, it tends to make the entire tax structure more regressive.

Since the payroll tax is regressive while the income tax is progressive, it is less sensitive to fluctuations in national income and employment. On the other hand, social security payments are very sensitive, and have helped to maintain purchasing power in periods of economic decline by allowing older workers to collect benefits when jobs become scarce. The Brookings Institution study team concluded that, on balance, the social security system has contributed to the nation's economic stability since the end of World War II.[7]

Even so, some economists favor converting from a payroll tax to the use of general revenues to finance social security. Many people, however, are fearful that financing social security out of general revenues would result in a loss of "fiscal control," because Congress would no longer have to be concerned with raising the revenues to pay for higher benefits. The other major argument for maintaining the present system is the sense individuals have that they have a "right" to benefits because of their contributions while they were working. From an economic point of view, however, all benefits, as has been demonstrated, are paid out of current production and income, not out of past contributions, and so, how best to effect the transfer of income from present workers to retired ones is a legitimate question.

Finally, there is some doubt that the payroll tax by itself will be capable of financing an adequate level of benefits in the future unless the rate is pushed up still higher. This, however, would impose a still heavier burden on low-income workers. The present desire to maintain an "actuarially sound" system, that is, to put into the trust fund enough money from which to pay out benefits, when combined with a reluctance to further raise the tax rate, could serve to limit benefits in the future. But it is doubtful that anyone would want the nation's social policy in terms of treatment of the aged to be determined solely by tax and actuarial standards, for questions of fairness must also be taken into consideration. It is quite probable, therefore, that government contributions from general revenues will be needed to help finance

    [6] John A. Brittain, "The Incidence of Social Security Payroll Taxes," *American Economic Review,* March 1971, pp. 110–125.
    [7] Pechman, Aaron, and Taussig, *op. cit.,* p. 184.

social security sometime in the future. In fact, the Brookings Institution study team has recommended that the payroll tax eventually be replaced by financing through income taxes.[8]

Employer Retirement Programs

For many workers, social security benefits comprise only part of their retirement pension, for in recent years private pension plans have shown spectacular growth. By 1969 they had assets of more than $125 billion and they covered about 29 million employees, almost half the wage and salary workers in private industry. Although private pension plans go back in origin to 1875, as in the case of other "fringe" benefits, widespread provision of private pensions is of rather recent vintage. Some large companies, particularly in petroleum refining, had established pension plans for all their employees in the 1920s, but major breakthroughs in collective bargaining came after World War II. Pension plans spread widely throughout American industry as a result of the negotiations establishing them in the automobile and steel industries in 1949 and 1950. A major push in the direction came from the 1949 Supreme Court decision in the Inland Steel case that pensions and benefits commonly provided through group insurance were a mandatory subject of collective bargaining.

Most pension plans are entirely employer financed; in large companies they are almost always administered exclusively by the employer, too, but in the smaller-scale industries joint union-employer administration is more common. Even when the plan is employer administered, its rules and regulations are determined jointly with the union through the collective bargaining process.

Benefits

The most dramatic development in private pension plans, besides their spread, has been the sharp increase in the scale of benefits. When major industries first adopted negotiated plans twenty years ago, they typically tied their pensions in as a supplement to federal old-age insurance, and the collective bargaining agreement would specify that the two together should yield the worker up to $100 a month. Through collective bargaining, unions have won higher pensions for those already retired and liberalized formulas for computing pensions for workers who will retire in the future. The 1971 aluminum industry agreement, for example, provided that the pension at retirement be $9 per month times the number of years of service that the worker had had; thus, an individual with thirty years of service would receive a pension of $270 a month, exclusive of his social security benefits. (Agreements negotiated in the spring of 1973 were providing for pensions of up to $10 per month per year of service in some industries.)

---

[8] *Ibid.*, p. 222.

Not all pension plans are as liberal as that of the aluminum industry. The Bureau of Labor Statistics has analyzed private pension plans and, based upon estimates of final earnings for workers with career average earnings of $4,800 in mid-1969, has come up with figures on assumed pension benefits and retirement income after different years of service.[9] The bureau then compared the retirement income to the estimated income needs of an urban retired couple. The results are shown in Tables 15.1 and 15.2, and they indicate that workers with only ten years of service would have insufficient income to provide a lower-budget standard of living.

Table 15.1 Estimated Final Monthly Earnings, Assumed Pension Benefits, and Retirement Income of Workers Retiring after Stipulated Years of Service, with Career Average Earnings of $4,800, mid-1969

Years of service	Final monthly earnings	Assumed pension benefit		Worker's retirement income		Family retirement income [a]	
		Mean	Median	Mean	Median	Mean	Median
10	$474	$27	$27	$177	$177	$252	$252
15	519	58	63	208	213	283	288
20	566	90	85	240	235	315	310
25	615	115	111	265	261	340	336
30	667	140	135	290	285	365[a]	360[b]
				Percentage of final monthly earnings			
10	100	5.7	5.7	37.3	37.3	—	—
15	100	11.2	12.1	40.1	41.0	—	—
20	100	15.9	15.0	42.4	41.5	—	—
25	100	18.7	18.0	43.1	42.4	—	—
30	100	21.0	20.2	43.5	42.7	—	—

[a] Assuming that the wife received a social security benefit equal to one-half that of her husband.
[b] This is sufficient for the retired couple to maintain an intermediate budget ($4,192/12=$349.33 monthly).

SOURCE: U.S. Department of Labor, Bureau of Labor Statistics.

Longer-service workers, however, are more fortunate. On the average, the twenty-five-year and thirty-year service employee would receive a pension, which when combined with social security would enable him to maintain lower budget standards without further supplementation. The thirty-year worker's retirement income, when augmented by a one-half social security benefit for his wife, would be sufficient to maintain an intermediate standard of living.

Such income estimates, however, are based solely on social security and private pension benefits, and do not take into account other income that retired couples may have. While it was unrealistic to assume, in the days before social security, that workers could have enough for their retirement,

[9] Arnold Strasser, "Pension Formula Summarizations: An Emerging Research Technique," *Monthly Labor Review*, April 1971, pp. 49–59.

Table 15.2 Relationship of Pension Benefits and Retirement Income to the BLS Lower Budget Estimate for a Retired Couple in Urban Areas[a]

		Percentage of budget need					
Years of service	Budget estimate ($2,902/12)	Pension benefit		Worker's retirement income		Family retirement income[b]	
		Mean	Median	Mean	Median	Mean	Median
10	$242	11.2	11.2	73.1	73.1	104.1	104.1
15	242	24.0	26.0	86.0	88.0	116.9	119.0
20	242	37.2	35.1	99.2	97.1	130.2	128.1
25	242	47.5	45.9	109.5	107.9	140.5	138.8
30	242	57.9	55.8	119.8	117.8	150.8	148.8[c]

[a] Based on spring 1969 cost estimates of three budgets for an urban retired couple. These cost estimates are updated periodically by BLS. For a description of the budget, see *Three Budgets for a Retired Couple in Urban Areas of the United States, 1967–68* (BLS Bulletin 1570–6).

[b] Assuming that the wife received a social security benefit equal to one-half that of her husband.

[c] This is sufficient for the retired couple to maintain an intermediate budget ($4,192/12=$349.33 a month).

SOURCE: U.S. Department of Labor, Bureau of Labor Statistics.

it is reasonable to assume that today they can save enough to supplement their pension and social security benefits so as to provide a decent retirement standard of living. In fact, there is evidence that workers covered by social security and private pension plans tend to save more than those who are not covered.[10] As the standard of living has risen, people have been able to save more, and this has been reflected in a rise in personal savings relative to disposable income. The combination of social security, private pension, plus personal savings would thus provide many retired people with adequate retirement incomes.

Early Retirement

Another trend in private pension plans, which has already been referred to, has been the lowering of the normal retirement age. According to the Bureau of Labor Statistics, in 1969 only about 70 percent of the workers under private pension plans had to be sixty-five to retire, compared with approximately 90 percent in 1962.[11] In 1969 about 25 percent of workers were in plans that permitted normal retirement prior to age sixty-five, usually at sixty or sixty-two, and 6 percent were in plans with no age requirements. In plans

[10] See, for example, Phillip Cagan, *The Effect of Pension Plans on Aggregate Saving: Evidence from a Sample Survey*, Occasional Paper 95 (New York: National Bureau of Economic Research, 1965).

[11] Harry E. Davis, "The Growth of Benefits in a Cohort of Pension Plans," *Monthly Labor Review*, May 1971, pp. 46–50.

with no age requirement, normally the individual must have completed thirty years of service with the company.

A dramatic development in recent years has been the growth of special early retirement provisions in private pension plans. About 90 percent of workers are now in plans that provide for such early retirement. Early retirement provisions were originally inserted in pension plans to provide income to disabled workers who were below normal retirement age, but many large companies have extended the privilege to workers displaced by technological change or plant closings. Normally, the early-retired worker receives a pension for the rest of his life that is less than he would have received at age sixty-five.

In more recent years, unions in both private and public employment have been seeking earlier retirement. In private industry such as automobiles, the cry has been "thirty and out," meaning that any worker with thirty years of service might retire with a pension regardless of his age. In New York City unions representing municipal employees have secured retirement at half pay after twenty years of service regardless of age.

Early retirement has also been encouraged by the federal government through the social security system. Beginning in 1956 women were allowed to start collecting old-age insurance benefits at age sixty-two instead of the normal sixty-five, and in 1961 the eligibility age for men was also lowered to sixty-two. Although benefits were actuarially reduced for men (until the 1972 amendments), there has been definite encouragement for workers to retire earlier. Since many private pension plans tie their benefits in with social security, the effect of this legislation has been to give added impetus to include early retirement provisions in private pension plans. The widespread use of early retirement, particularly after having completed a fixed number of years of service, would mean that more people would spend the remaining fifteen to thirty-five years of their lives drawing pensions. Of course, most of the people who opt for early retirement will not spend it in idleness, but will take new jobs and enjoy the combined income that their wages plus pensions provide. This use of pensions to supplement earnings from other jobs, however, is a complete travesty of the concept of pensions as a means of ensuring the aged an income when they are no longer capable of working. In addition, it would greatly increase the burden on the rest of the population of maintaining a greater number of retired persons.

Problems in Private Pension Plans

Coverage

While private pension plans are an excellent supplement to social security, and some of the major corporate programs are quite liberal in the pensions provided retired workers, the fact is that only a small minority of the retired are actually receiving pensions from them. In 1970, only a little over 4 million persons or about one out of five persons sixty-five years of age or older, were receiving a pension from a private plan, and the average pension was about $1,400 per year. With the spread of pension coverage, more workers will receive them when they retire, but by 1980 only two out of five will. About 30 million workers, particularly in smaller companies and outside of manufacturing, are still not covered by private pension plans.

Even coverage by a private pension plan does not mean that a worker will actually receive a pension when he reaches retirement age. A major assumption of most private plans is that the individual will have career employment with the company (or industry, in the case of multi-employer plans), but turnover often means that few employees actually ever become eligible to collect pensions. The major solution to this problem that has been proposed is vesting of pension rights.

Vesting

Vesting establishes the right of an employee to the pension benefits paid for by his employer even if, at retirement time, he no longer works for that employer. Vesting rights have been increasing rapidly, and, according to the Bureau of Labor Statistics, three out of four workers were covered by vesting provisions in 1969. Vesting, however, was much more typical of single employer programs than multi-employer plans, and hence, of larger rather than smaller companies. Even plans with vesting provisions normally require at least ten years of service, or even fifteen or twenty, for full vesting of pension rights, and thus many workers still cannot qualify. A study of pension plans by the Labor Committee of the United States Senate showed that in fifty-one plans with no vesting or vesting with eleven or more years of service, only 4.5 percent of 6.9 million employees participating since 1950 have drawn retirement benefits; 70 percent forfeited their rights, and 25 percent were still in the plans.

Many proponents of vesting favor it, not only because of individual equity, but also because they claim it would benefit society by promoting labor mobility. According to them private pension plans that do not provide vesting retard mobility by tying the worker to the company. Many companies, on the other hand, fear that liberal vesting would lead to too much labor turnover.

In December 1971 President Nixon proposed to Congress legislation mandating vesting of private pension rights. The President proposed a "rule of fifty," whereby an employee's right to 50 percent of his pension benefits would be vested when he achieved a combination of fifty years of age and service. Thus, a worker who entered a pension plan at age thirty would begin to vest at age forty, when his years of participation (ten) coupled with his age (forty) would total fifty. An additional 10 percent would accrue in each of the five following years of service to a maximum of 100 percent.[12]

---

[12] "News and Background Information," *Labor Relations Reporter*, December 13, 1971, p. 292.

Solvency of Private Pension Plans

Added to the question of worker rights to the monies set aside in a pension plan is that of the very solvency of private programs. Almost all pension plans today have funding arrangements. Funding a private pension plan is the process of accumulation, over a period of many years, of assets in a fund irrevocably earmarked to pay future retirement benefits. Certain minimum funding standards are set by law as a requirement for employer contributions to a pension plan to be tax deductible, but since there have been cases in which plans did not have sufficient monies with which to pay the pensions that had been promised, some observers believe that those standards must be tightened.

Appraisal

Whatever their shortcomings, there is no doubt but that private pension plans are a major second line of defense for worker protection against insecurity in old age. The leading problem with private pensions is that so few of the aged actually receive them, largely because they do not remain with one employer long enough to qualify for benefits, but also because of plan terminations. Under the circumstances, additional federal government regulation of private pension funds seems inevitable. Such regulation will probably provide for: (1) more liberal vesting arrangements; (2) more stringent funding provisions; and (3) the ensuring of the fulfillment of pension expectations through some form of reinsurance of pension funds, possibly through a federal reinsurance fund.[13] The price for more people receiving pensions, however, will probably be some check on the escalation of benefits and a holding back from a general reduction in the retirement age.

Private Health and Welfare Programs

Another type of insecurity facing the worker in an industrial society was that occasioned by illness, and as in the case of old age, there was no one ready and able to help the family that was beset by sickness. Illness, moreover, could be a double blow to a family: first, if anyone in the family became ill, medical expenses had to be borne, but second, if the breadwinner was the sick one, the family's source of income was cut off at the same time. After family savings were used up and ability to borrow from friends and relatives exhausted, there was only private charity to be sought.

As in the case of old age, the idea advanced in the heyday of laissez-faire economics was that each family should set aside some savings to take care of interruptions of income and medical expenses due to illness. If one averaged the total medical bill of the nation, then most people could afford to meet their share, but it is unfeasible for a family to budget for medical expenses,

---

[13] Patrick J. Davey and Mitchell Meyer, "More Regulation for Pension Funds?" *Conference Board Record*, July 1972, pp. 13–18.

for these costs do not hit families on the average. Four decades ago the Committee on the Cost of Medical Care showed that the costs of medical care in any one year fell very unevenly upon different families in the same income and population groups. For instance, for one year studied 58 percent of the families had 18 percent of the costs, while 10 percent of the families had 41 percent of the costs.[14]

Yet the total amount of sickness within the population is predictable, so, actuarially, it presents the type of risk that is very adaptable to the insurance principle. Not everyone will be sick in any year, but the person who does become sick may face catastrophic costs that he will be unable to meet, and insurance becomes the means of spreading the risk.

As in the case of old age, the United States lagged far behind the other capitalist industrial nations in dealing with the problem of insecurity caused by illness. Indeed, it still eschews treating the problem as a social one requiring government action. While most other industrial nations have had health insurance or national health services for many decades, the United States has only begun to take the first tentative steps in such a direction.

One form of medical expense was particularly costly and beyond the means of most families: hospitalization. While the poor might be treated in the charitable wings of private hospitals or in public hospitals, those above the poverty level—workers and middle-class families who did not want or could not qualify for free care—were very hard hit financially when major illness required a stay in the hospital. The voluntary hospitals themselves recognized this problem, and in 1933 they began to organize nonprofit hospital service plans (Blue Cross) on a community basis. Blue Cross applied the principle, on a group basis, of prepaid insurance to meet the costs of hospital care. As demands for government health insurance mounted, the American Medical Association finally began in 1945 to advance its own system of prepaid insurance for physicians' services, known as Blue Shield. In addition, many private insurance companies have, for many years, been offering commercial hospital and medical insurance.

In the absence of government programs, it was virtually inevitable that as unions gained power they would use it in collective bargaining with employers to secure protection of their members against the financial burdens of sickness. The wage controls of World War II, from which fringe benefits such as hospital and medical insurance were excluded, fostered the movement. The existence, moreover, of private insurance plans, of Blue Cross–Blue Shield, and the development of more elaborate prepaid medical insurance programs, such as the Health Insurance Plan of Greater New York (HIP) and the Kaiser Foundation Health Plan, provided services that could be utilized.

When health and welfare programs were established through collective bargaining in the automobile and steel industries in the late 1940s and early

[14] *Medical Care for the American People*, Committee on the Costs of Medical Care (Chicago: University of Chicago Press, 1932), p. 2.

1950s, the pattern was set for most other organized industries. In time, most organized workers were entitled to hospital, medical, and surgical care, weekly cash benefits for periods of incapacity due to sickness or accident, life insurance, and accidental death and dismemberment insurance.

The growth of health and insurance plans through collective bargaining has been quite phenomenal: in 1948 only 18 percent of the workers covered by union contracts were in such plans, but by 1966 91 percent were.[15] Over the years, moreover, plans have been greatly liberalized: benefits have been raised and paid for longer periods, they have been extended to workers' dependents and to the retired, and they have been broadened to include new features, such as optical, dental, and even psychiatric care. Another major trend has been toward noncontributory financing of health and welfare, with the employer bearing the entire cost of the program. (A major reason for this trend is the fact that employer contributions for health and welfare are tax deductible as a business expense, but employee contributions are not.)

Health and welfare plans have become so popular that they have expanded far beyond organized workers. By 1969 two-thirds of all wage and salary workers were covered by life insurance and death benefits, half by accidental death and dismemberment benefits, three-quarters by hospitalization and surgical insurance, two-thirds by regular medical insurance, one-third by major-medical-expense insurance, and half the workers in private industry for temporary disability benefits.[16] Contributions for health benefits (hospitalization, surgical and medical, major medical expense) totaled $11 billion in 1969. Obviously, individuals covered by such benefits had a modicum of protection from the economic insecurity caused by illness.

Public Health Insurance

Medical Expense Problems of the Retired

The adoption of old-age and survivors' insurance and the gradual improvement in benefit levels provided Americans with a modest degree of security in old age, except for one problem: medical expenses. The problem was very grave, and became increasingly so, for three reasons. First, older people are subject to more illness than younger ones. Beyond the age of fifteen there is a direct relationship between age and the frequency of disability lasting seven days or more. In fact, those sixty-five and over suffer more than 60 percent more illnesses than the average for all ages combined. Furthermore, there is a striking increase in the severity of illness with increasing age, and those sixty-five and over are subject to more than twice as many days of disability per case than are those under sixty-five.

Since older people have less income, and at the same time are more

---

[15] Dorothy R. Kittner, "Negotiated Health and Retirement Plan Coverage," *Monthly Labor Review*, December 1968, pp. 24–28.

[16] Harry Gersh (ed.), *Employee Benefits Factbook, 1970* (New York: Fleet Academic Editions, 1970), pp. 379–381.

prone to sickness, medical expenses become a much greater proportion of their budgets. But, while voluntary health insurance became the chief way in which medical expense problems were resolved for those in the productive ages and their dependents, a second explanation of the inability of older people to adequately handle medical expenses was that most private health insurance programs excluded those sixty-five and over from coverage. Just as automobile insurance companies drop from coverage persons with bad accident records as poor risks, so private health insurers did the same with their poor risks: the elderly. Only after the movement for governmental medical insurance for the elderly developed did the private insurance carriers begin to set up special plans for them, and then at rather high premium rates.

The third factor compounding the medical expense problem of the aged was that the prices of medical services were rising much more rapidly than those of all other goods and services. While the overall Consumer Price Index rose 61.6 percent from 1946 to 1965, the prices of medical care services jumped 117.6 percent, and the daily service charges of hospitals skyrocketed 314.3 percent. Clearly, the medical expense problem for the retired was becoming unmanageable, and causing many of them either to neglect proper medical attention or to be driven into poverty.

Medical Assistance for the Aged

The first step toward governmental medical aid for the aged was taken in 1960, with the passage of the Medical Assistance for the Aged (Kerr-Mills) Act. Under this act, federal grants were made available to the states in order for them to provide medical assistance to low-income aged persons who were not receiving old-age assistance. Experience under the Kerr-Mills Act was far from satisfactory, with only twenty-two states having MAA plans in operation by 1963, and benefits going to people who would probably have qualified for them under some other program in the absence of the new legislation. The nation, therefore, turned from a public assistance to a social insurance approach.

Medicare

By the 1965 amendments to the Social Security Act, health insurance was added to the existing old-age, survivors, and disability insurance (it now became OASDHI). In 1972 the benefits included: (1) up to ninety days of inpatient hospital care for each illness, with $68 deductible, and after sixty days the beneficiary pays a coinsurance payment of $17 a day; (2) up to one hundred days of posthospital care in an extended care facility—for example, a nursing home—with $8.50 per day deductible after the first twenty days; and (3) up to one hundred home health "visits" by nurses, physical therapists, home health aides, or other health workers. In addition, for a monthly premium of $5.80 the aged may secure medical insurance that will pay 80 percent, beyond the first $50, of physicians' services, diagnostic services, medical supplies, and outpatient physical therapy services. Since 1967 each Medicare beneficiary has also been allowed a "lifetime reserve" of sixty hospital days beyond the ninety days of "spell of illness," with $34 a day deductible.

Almost every person sixty-five and over (20.4 million as of July 1, 1970), working or not, has hospital insurance protection under Medicare (Part A), and 95 percent (19.4 million) are also protected under the voluntary medical insurance part of Medicare (Part B).[17] For the year July 1, 1969–June 30, 1970, social security paid more than $4.8 billion in hospital bills on behalf of 4.4 million elderly people, and $2.0 billion in supplementary medical insurance benefits for 9.3 million people.

The hospital insurance part of Medicare is financed by special contributions from employees and their employers of 0.9 percent each of the taxable base earnings, and this will rise to 1.2 percent by 1993. Medical care insurance is financed from monthly premiums paid by each person who enrolls in that program. The 1972 Social Security amendments extended Medicare coverage to those persons receiving Social Security disability benefits and to those suffering from acute kidney disease.

Medicaid

The great increase in the demand for medical services throughout the population and the escalation of their costs has caused financial problems for people under sixty-five as well as for the aged. Title XIX of the 1965 Social Security amendments provided for helping people of all ages who are too poor to pay for medical care. The program, known as Medicaid, is financed out of general revenues and provides federal financial assistance to states that provide medical assistance to low-income groups.

National Health Insurance Proposals

Some people believe that Medicare and Medicaid are only partial solutions to the problems of financing health care. They point out that the United States remains the only industrial nation in which the government does not operate either a system of health insurance or a health service. The original Social Security bill in 1935 called for the Social Security Board to study the question of health insurance and report its findings and recommendations to Congress, but this roused so much opposition that it was dropped from the bill that eventually became law.[18]

Almost four decades later the situation had not yet changed, but seemed to be in the process of doing so, as numerous proposals for national health insurance were put forth. There were, however, two basically different ap-

---

[17] *1970 Annual Report*, U.S. Department of Health, Education and Welfare (Washington, D.C.: Government Printing Office, 1970), p. 276.

[18] Domenico Gagliardo, *American Social Insurance* (New York: Harper & Bros., 1949), p. 458.

proaches to the government role in the health field, as typified by legislative proposals sponsored by President Nixon and Senator Kennedy.

President Nixon's proposed national health insurance partnership act of 1971 was designed to strengthen the nation's "present system of joint cooperation between the public and private sectors" by integrating within it the private carriers, such as Blue Cross and Blue Shield. Under the Nixon plan every employed person and his family would be given a private health insurance policy, with the premium costs being shared by the employer and employee, and federal funds would buy policies for the poor. Senator Kennedy (D., Mass.), on the other hand, was leading the fight for a different plan, which would establish a direct government health insurance program for the entire population, financed by a payroll tax. One of these proposals, or some compromise between them, seemed likely to become law before long.

Workmen's Compensation

Industrial Injury Hazard

One of the major hazards facing production workers in factories was the possibility of industrial accidents. Those who were injured on the job, moreover, had no source of help to which to turn, and their only recourse was to sue the employer for damages. Even this route offered little promise of financial recompense because of certain common-law doctrines. One was the concept of "contributory negligence," by which the employer could claim lack of responsibility if the injured worker could be shown to have in any way neglected to take proper precautions. A second doctrine that employers used in defense against employee suits for industrial injuries was that of "assumption of risk," by which, if an employee continued to work for any period of time under unsafe conditions, he was deemed as a matter of law to have assumed the risk of injury from such deficiency or defect. Also, according to the "fellow servant doctrine," by which if an injury were due to actions taken by another worker, rather than directly to employer action, the employer was not responsible.[19] As a result of these legal doctrines, workers injured on the job rarely received any financial compensation.

Evolution of Workmen's Compensation

In 1902 Maryland became the first state to adopt a workmen's compensation law, which was limited to a few very hazardous employments and applied only to a payment of $1,000 to the dependents of workers who were killed without having to prove employer negligence. Gradually other states also adopted workmen's compensation laws, but it took until 1948, when Mississippi finally adopted workmen's compensation, for all the states to have such legislation. In the intervening years, the existing laws were improved by extending coverage to more employments, making coverage compulsory rather

---

[19] *Ibid.*, pp. 368–374.

than elective, including industrial diseases as well as accidents as compensable, improving cash and medical benefits, and introducing rehabilitation programs.

Workmen's Compensation in Practice

Today there are fifty-four different state and federal workmen's compensation programs in operation, and there are great variations among them. By 1972 thirty-three of the state laws were compulsory for most of the private employments covered. The laws in the other seventeen states are elective; that is, the employer may accept or reject the legislation, but if he rejects it he loses the customary common-law defenses against lawsuits by employees if they are injured on the job.

In almost all cases workmen's compensation is financed entirely by employers, who do so by purchasing insurance from private carriers, state funds, or through self-insurance. Some states have state funds exclusively, while others allow the employer a choice of insuring with the state fund, a private carrier, or self-insurance. Most states also operate "subsequent injury funds" that cover workers who were previously disabled by an industrial injury; in this way, they attempt to encourage employers to hire permanently, but partially, disabled workers.

Workmen's compensation benefits include periodic cash payments and medical services to workers during periods of disablement, and death and funeral benefits to survivors of those who are killed in industrial accidents. Weekly cash benefits to workers disabled because of occupational accident vary among states, and, given the slowness of state legislatures to raise benefits periodically, they tend to fall behind advances in wages and living costs. By 1972, however, fourteen states had adopted "flexible maximum" benefit provisions, whereby weekly benefits can be adjusted annually without further legislative enactments.[20] Such maximum benefits are tied either to changes in the Consumer Price Index or to the average weekly wage in the state. Even so, in 1971 only nine states paid benefits equal to at least two-thirds of the states' average weekly wage, a standard recommended by many authorities on workmen's compensation laws. In fact, the median ratio of maximum weekly benefits to average weekly wages was 55 percent.

The number of weeks for which a worker may receive benefits also varies, depending upon the particular type of injury and the state. Some states also provide additional benefits when the injured worker has dependent children. Most states, however, provide for full payment of medical care expenses.

At the beginning of 1970 an estimated 60 million workers, 80 percent of the employed labor force, were covered by workmen's compensation laws. During 1969 $2.6 billion were paid in benefits, $1.7 billion in cash compensation to injured workers, and $0.9 billion in medical and hospital care. The

---

[20] Florence C. Johnson, "Changes in Workmen's Compensation in 1971," *Monthly Labor Review*, January 1972, pp. 51–55.

cost of workmen's compensation was equal to 1.07 percent of covered payroll and benefits to 0.63 percent.

Although workmen's compensation continues to have many serious faults,[21] such as inadequate benefits and/or rehabilitation programs in some states, its major accomplishments have been a marked reduction in worker insecurity resulting from industrial injury and a spur to industrial safety. The latter has come about largely as a result of the experience rating features of workmen's compensation insurance. Since employers who suffer more accidents must pay higher premiums, they are induced to improve work place safety. Federal legislation in 1970 will prove a further spur to occupational safety, but let us defer discussion of that until we examine disability that is not job related.

Disability Insurance

Temporary Disability

According to statistics, most accidents occur in the home, not on the job. The toll of automobile accidents that are not job related is also staggering. People also become too sick to work for periods of time. Yet none of these nonwork-related disabilities were covered by governmental insurance programs until Rhode Island adopted the first temporary disability insurance program in 1942. Since then only three other states—California, New Jersey, and New York—have adopted such laws to pay weekly benefits to workers who are temporarily disabled because of illness or accident. However, many workers have such protection through private employer insurance programs, and it is estimated that in 1969 almost two-thirds of all private employees had some protection against loss of earnings caused by short-term nonoccupational disaster.[22]

The failure of most states to adopt temporary disability insurance has been attributed to fears of legislatures that by so doing they would put local employers at a competitive disadvantage with employers in states that do not have such legislation.[23] The solution that has been proposed is federal legislation to provide national coverage against the risk of temporary disability. Such legislation could either establish a federal temporary disability program or mandate that the states adopt them as part of their unemployment insurance systems. As yet, however, there is no large campaign afoot for federal action in this area.

---

[21] See, for example, Earl F. Cheit and Margaret S. Gordon (eds.), *Occupational Disability and Public Policy* (New York: Wiley, 1963), and the more recent *Report of the National Commission on State Workmen's Compensation Laws* (Washington, D.C.: Government Printing Office, 1972).

[22] *Social Security Programs in the United States, op. cit.*, p. 87.

[23] Wilbur J. Cohen, "Economic Security for the Aged, Sick and Disabled: Some Issues and Implications," in Sar A. Levitan, Wilbur J. Cohen, and Robert J. Lampman (eds.), *Towards Freedom from Want* (Madison, Wisc.: Industrial Relations Research Association, 1968), p. 79.

Permanent Disability

Although the nation has not seen fit to adopt any program with respect to temporary disability, it has acted with respect to permanent disability. The 1956 amendments to the Social Security Act added the feature of permanent disability insurance for workers between the ages of fifty and sixty-four. Since then the age limit has been dropped, and benefits have been extended to dependents and disabled widows and widowers.

A person is considered "disabled" if he cannot work because of a severe physical or mental impairment that has lasted, or is expected to last, for twelve months or longer. Payments can continue as long as the disability continues to prevent the individual from working. In addition, vocational rehabilitation, through state rehabilitation agencies, is partially paid for by social security. In mid-1970, 2.6 million disabled workers and their dependents were receiving benefits totaling nearly $2.8 billion a year.

Occupational Safety and Health

Industrial Injury and Illness

Despite the safety movement in industry, work injuries continue to be a problem. Certain industries are, of course, more susceptible to accidents than others, and serious coal mining disasters occur from time to time as a result of cave-ins, explosions, and the like. Among major industry categories, the number of disabling injuries per million man-hours worked varied in 1968 from 1.8 in communications to 31.6 in local and long-distance trucking; the extractive industries were the most dangerous to work in, the rate for coal mining and preparation being 41.7, and for oil and gas drilling 69.1. About 2 million disabling work injuries occur each year, some 15,000 workers are killed, and about 400,000 are stricken by occupationally related diseases.

While this safety record may sound very bad, it actually marks a vast improvement over conditions that existed much earlier. In the nineteenth century industrial employers paid almost no attention to the health and safety of their employees, but a series of industrial catastrophes led to a public demand for action. As a result, several states passed legislation providing for factory inspections and for fire protection, ventilation, and sanitation regulations.[24] Furthermore, under the impetus of workmen's compensation and new attitudes toward workers and their interests, management became concerned with safety. In larger companies, for example, a full-time safety director usually reported to the vice-president for industrial relations, and plant-level safety supervisors worked closely with plant managers to record injuries and

---

[24] George C. Guenther, "The Significance of the Occupational Safety and Health Act to the Worker in the United States," *International Labour Review*, January 1972, pp. 59–67. This article by the Assistant Secretary of Labor for Occupational Safety and Health contains an excellent review of the Occupational Safety and Health Act of 1970.

accidents, to investigate their causes, and to take steps to prevent their recurrence.[25]

The growing public concern of recent years with ecology and the quality of life encompassed the problem of health hazards in the job environment. Growing dissatisfaction with state laws, many of which were out of date or poorly administered, led to pressure for federal health and safety legislation.

The Occupational Safety and Health Act of 1970

In 1970 the Williams-Steiger Occupational Safety and Health Act (OSHA), covering all employees in any business "affecting commerce," or an estimated 57.0 million in 4.1 million work establishments, was passed. The new law called for the setting of safety standards by the federal government, federal inspection of work establishments to ensure that they are meeting safety standards and the levying of fines if they are not, and the right to shut a plant down when conditions are very dangerous. Employees and unions are given the right to participate in inspections and to initiate actions on their own.

Under the pressure of organized labor, moreover, major responsibility for enforcement and administration of the new job safety act was given to the Secretary of Labor. The law created the new Occupational Safety and Health Administration, headed by an Assistant Secretary of Labor, and the tripartite Occupational Safety and Health Review Commission. Furthermore, the National Institute for Occupational Safety and Health (NIOSH) was established within the Department of Health, Education, and Welfare to conduct research and related functions. The OSHA allows the states the option of developing and enforcing their own plans, as long as they meet federal standards. In order to prevent state administration from being weaker than federal, the AFL-CIO has drafted model state laws along the lines of the federal act, and has been attempting to have them adopted by the various states.

During its first six months of operation, the OSHA had conducted 9,300 inspections, but only 1,842 establishments were found to be in compliance with the standards of the act. As a result, the offenders were fined a total of $361,692. The OSHA also launched a Target Health Hazards program aimed at improving work place conditions with respect to five toxic substances: asbestos, cotton dust, silica, lead, and carbon monoxide.[26]

Clearly, occupational health and safety is becoming a major element in labor-management relations. It will take a number of years, however, for the Labor Department to work out all the standards and procedures required by the law. In the meantime, unions can be expected to become increasingly vocal and active in the protection of their members against the safety and health hazards attendant on modern technology.

---

[25] Leo Teplow, "New Dimensions for Management in Occupational Safety and Health" (New York: Organization Resources Counselors, November 1970).

[26] "News and Background Information," *Labor Relations Reporter,* January 10, 1972, p. 30.

Guaranteed Income for All

The major insecurity of an industrial capitalist order is the absence of income
when one is not contributing directly to the nation's production. Those in the
labor force face this problem when they are unemployed, sick, or aged. But
the situation of those who are not even fortunate enough to be in the labor
force may be still more acute, because they do not qualify for the various
types of social insurance that have come into being during the past few
decades. Let us, therefore, touch on some of the income maintenance and
work proposals that have emerged in recent years.

Income Maintenance Proposals

During the Great Depression of the 1930s, the breakdown in the ability of
private charities and state governments to care for the many millions of desti-
tute Americans led to systems of work relief for the able-bodied and home
relief for others. Work relief disappeared with the labor shortages of World
War II, but public assistance—the welfare system—became institutionalized.
By 1970 14 million people were benefiting from one or more cash, food, or
housing assistance programs at a cost of $9 billion a year.[27] But over the years
the welfare system became anathema to its recipients, who viewed it as providing inadequate living standards with a loss of dignity, and came to be
regarded by many of the rest of the population as paying out money to
"lazy bums."

Besides disillusionment with the existing public assistance programs, a
second factor that played a role in the emergence of new approaches to income
maintenance for those not working was the relatively high unemployment of
the period 1957–1964. As we saw in Chapter 13, a majority of economists
attributed the unemployment to inadequate aggregate demand. Among the
minority who blamed unemployment on technological change, some foresaw
a long-run worsening of the problem and, consequently, the need to divorce
receipt of income from work. Robert Theobald became the leading champion
of the concept of the "guaranteed income": the idea that the government
should guarantee each citizen an income sufficient for him to live with dignity,
whether or not he was working.[28]

Arguments for a government guarantee of income also came from laissez-
faire economists, who saw that as highly preferable to government interference with the operations of free markets. The leading proponent of this point
of view was Professor Friedman, who advanced the idea of the "negative
income tax."[29] Basically, the plan would allow the poor to make use of tax
exemptions that, because their incomes are below their total exemptions, they

[27] Gilbert Y. Steiner, *The State of Welfare* (Washington, D.C.: Brookings, 1971).

[28] See, for example, Robert Theobald (ed.), *The Guaranteed Income: Next Step in
Socio-Economic Evolution?* (Garden City, N.Y.: Doubleday Anchor Books, 1967).

[29] Milton Friedman, *Capitalism and Freedom* (Chicago: University of Chicago Press,
1962).

now lose. Under Friedman's plan a family would receive one-half of the difference between the total exemptions and the family income if it were less than the exemptions. Briefly, Friedman's plan would operate in the following manner: Each head of a family and his dependents would continue to receive the $600 exemption (or whatever the tax laws made the exemption) and a standard deduction. If the family's total of exemptions and deductions were $3,000, but its gross income only $2,000, it would then receive negative taxes totaling $500 from the federal government.[30]

According to its proponents, the negative income tax is the most effective weapon against poverty because it strikes directly at the heart of poverty—lack of income—by providing help in the most useful form, cash. The negative income tax also provides incentive to low-income people to try to earn more money on their own by not deducting the total value of their earnings from the tax "refund" to which they are entitled. Adoption of some form of negative income tax or other type of income maintenance program would probably relieve some of the pressure increasingly to use the Social Security system as a means of redistributing income. The major impetus to pushing up benefits has been the desire to aid the aged with very low benefits, but this has disturbed the relationship between benefits and previous earnings. Income maintenance, it is claimed, could thus provide sufficient income to the poor aged while Social Security could concentrate on providing retirement benefits in line with employees' previous earnings.

Job Guarantees

Another approach to protecting people from the insecurities attendant to a dynamic capitalist industrial order would be to guarantee them jobs. Some people, including a large group in Congress, have proposed, therefore, that the federal government act as an "employer of last resort," providing work for people who cannot find jobs in the private economy.

Legislative Developments

Movements in the direction of both government as employer of last resort and income guarantees had taken place by 1972. In 1971 Congress enacted the Emergency Employment Act, which authorized $750 million to create jobs in local public services for the unemployed. Under the act, in periods in which the national unemployment rate was above 4.5 percent, cities, counties, and state governments would be able to hire jobless people for new "transitional" jobs in such areas as parks, police and fire departments, schools, public hospitals, and antipollution agencies. An additional $250 million was available for fiscal 1972 and 1973 to be spent for public service jobs in areas of substantial unemployment, those in which the unemployment rate was 6 percent

---

[30] An excellent review of negative taxes can be found in Christopher Green, *Negative Taxes and the Poverty Problem* (Washington, D.C.: Brookings, 1967).

or higher in three consecutive months, regardless of the national rate. EEA was expected to open up about 130,000 jobs for its first year of operation.[31] The hiring unit of government would pay 10 percent of the wages of the employees and the federal government the other 90 percent. The law seeks to improve local public services, while at the same time providing work for those unable to find any through the regular labor market. After it was in operation for a few months, however, the EEA was criticized for not preparing people for jobs in the normal labor market.

Welfare reform, incorporating the philosophy of the negative income tax, by which the federal government would guarantee a $2,400 annual income to a family of four, including the "working poor," was proposed by President Nixon. The maximum that any family could receive under the proposed welfare reform would be $3,600, but states would be permitted to supplement the federal benefit levels. Incentive-to-work features would be built into the legislation, because benefits for the working poor—those with very low incomes—would not be cut off entirely but tapered off as income rises, with federal assistance stopping only when total earnings reached $4,320 a year. Under the proposed Family Assistance Plan, those who are employable would be required to register for work and accept training, but no one would be required to accept work at less than 75 percent of the federal minimum wage. The federal government, at the same time, would develop training, counseling, and employment programs for those receiving benefits and establish day-care centers for children of beneficiaries. The bill, however, failed to pass, and President Nixon dropped its espousal.

Summary

An industrial capitalist order brought forth problems of economic security for workers when they were unable to work because of illness, disability, or old age. The United States, however, continued to act as if it were still an agricultural society, clinging to the tenets of rugged individualism long after the other capitalist industrial nations had recognized the social nature of these risks. It was not until the Great Depression of the 1930s that the United States moved decisively in this direction.

The Social Security Act of 1935 provided for old-age insurance, old-age assistance, and unemployment insurance. Old-age assistance provided cash income to the needy aged. Old-age insurance provides retirement pensions to the aged who have worked in covered employment, and they receive their benefits as a right, without having to prove need.

Old-age insurance, which is almost universal in coverage today, is financed by a payroll tax, whereby employers and employees contribute 5.85 percent each on the first $12,600 of the employee's earnings (as of 1974).

---

[31] Darold Powers, "Bridge to a Better Future," *Manpower*, October 1971, pp. 2–5.

After ten years of contributions a worker is permanently insured, but his retirement benefit depends upon his career average earnings. Survivors of covered employees have also been entitled to benefits since 1938.

A major issue with respect to social security is the sole reliance upon the payroll tax as the method of financing. Since benefits, in reality, are paid out of the nation's current income, proposals have been made to add a subsidy from the federal treasury to the trust funds or to pay benefits directly from general revenues.

In addition to federal social security, many workers also receive private pensions from their employers. Most private pension plans are entirely employer financed, and in recent years benefit levels have gone up sharply. Yet many workers never collect their private pensions because they do not remain with the same employer. It has been proposed, therefore, that the law mandate vesting of employee pension rights.

Although most other capitalist industrial nations have also adopted social insurance or national health services to deal with the problem of insecurity caused by illness, the United States still has not done so. Today, however, many workers have such protection through private health and welfare programs, which have become quite widespread as a result of collective bargaining.

A government program of health insurance for the aged was adopted by the 1965 amendments to the Social Security Act. Medicare provides hospital and posthospital care for the retired, and Medicaid provides assistance to the medically indigent of all ages. There are now a number of proposals before Congress that would extend health insurance to the entire population.

One of the major hazards facing workers is the possibility of industrial accidents. All the states, therefore, have adopted workmen's compensation laws, whereby employers must insure themselves against the costs associated with employee injury. Workmen's compensation benefits include periodic cash payments and medical services to workers during periods of disablement, and death benefits to survivors of those killed in industrial accidents.

Four states also provide cash benefits to workers who are temporarily disabled because of illness or accident that is not job related. Since 1956 the federal government has provided benefits for workers who are permanently disabled. In 1970, moreover, Congress adopted the Occupational Safety and Health Act, by which the federal government will set safety standards in industry and inspect work establishments to ensure that they are being met.

Today, as a result of both public and private programs, members of the labor force have a fair degree of protection against the insecurities associated with a dynamic economic order. Those who are not members of the labor force, however, are much less secure. Recent proposals to aid them include income maintenance through a form of negative income tax, the government's guaranteeing jobs to those who cannot find them through the normal workings of the labor market, and welfare reform, which would provide a basic guaranteed income to everyone.

BIBLIOGRAPHY

Bowen, William G., Frederick H. Harbison, Richard A. Lester, and Herman M. Somers (eds.). *The American System of Social Insurance.* New York: McGraw-Hill, 1968.

Brinker, Paul A. *Economic Insecurity and Social Security.* New York: Appleton-Century-Crofts, 1968.

Brittain, John A. *The Payroll Tax for Social Security.* Washington, D.C.: Brookings, 1972.

Cheit, Earl F., and Margaret S. Gordon (eds.). *Occupational Disability and Public Policy.* New York: Wiley, 1963.

Gersh, Harry (ed.). *Employee Benefits Factbook, 1970.* New York: Fleet Academic Editions, 1970.

Green, Christopher. *Negative Taxes and the Poverty Problem.* Washington, D.C.: Brookings, 1967.

Levitan, Sar A., Wilbur J. Cohen, and Robert J. Lampman (eds.). *Towards Freedom from Want.* Madison, Wisc.: Industrial Relations Research Association, 1968.

Old Age Income Assurance, A Compendium of Papers on Problems and Policy Issues in the Public and Private Pension System. Washington, D.C.: Government Printing Office, 1968.

Pechman, Joseph A., Henry J. Aaron, and Michael K. Taussig. *Social Security: Perspectives for Reform.* Washington, D.C.: Brookings, 1968.

Report of the National Commission on State Workmen's Compensation Laws. Washington, D.C.: U.S. Government Printing Office, 1972.

Somers, Herman M., and Anne R. Somers. *Doctors, Patients, and Health Insurance.* Washington, D.C.: Brookings, 1961.

Steiner, Gilbert Y. *The State of Welfare.* Washington, D.C.: Brookings, 1971.

Teplow, Leo. "New Dimensions for Management in Occupational Safety and Health." New York: Organization Resources Counselors, November 1970.

Turnbull, John G. *The Changing Faces of Economic Insecurity.* Minneapolis: University of Minnesota Press, 1966.

U.S. Department of Health, Education and Welfare. *Annual Report.* Washington, D.C.: Government Printing Office, 1971.

———. *Social Security Programs in the United States.* Washington, D.C.: Government Printing Office, 1971.

16 LABOR IN AN URBAN ENVIRONMENT

A major theme that has run through this book is that the rise of a capitalist industrial order has changed man's whole way of life: where he resides, the kinds of work he does and how he does it, the nature of the family and other social institutions, and his very concepts of the meaning of life. Nothing symbolizes all these changes more than the shift from a rural agricultural economy and way of life to that of an urban industrial economy and its very different modes of living. In this chapter, therefore, we shall focus on labor in an urban environment. We shall examine first the rise of the city as the central place of work and residence under industrialism, and the attractions that urban areas hold for industry and commerce. We also shall view cities as labor markets and make some comparisons among them, attempting to explain why people earn more in one than another. Finally, we shall look at some major changes that have been taking place within urban areas, particularly the movement of some people and jobs from central cities to suburban fringes and the movement of other people from rural areas into the central cities. The problems, particularly in terms of the urban labor market, that have flowed from these changes, as well as possible solutions to them, will then be discussed.

Rise of the City as the Central Focus of Economic Life

When the United States was founded, 90 percent of the people lived in rural areas, following predominantly agricultural pursuits. By 1970, barely two centuries later, 70 percent of the people lived in urban areas, and by the year 2000 90 percent will. Urban areas, moreover, keep growing in size with the result that six out of every ten Americans live in metropolitan areas of more than 250,000 population.

Cities as Economic Centers

As we saw in Chapter 1, the cities of medieval Europe, many of which had been established as military fortifications, began to expand with the development of commerce and handicrafts. Because of the need for location along a stream for water power, the initial impact of industrialization was back to the countryside. But when steam power became dominant, factories were built in cities because people could be concentrated there and enable the factories to obtain a sufficient labor supply. That labor supply became available, moreover, because people were migrating from the rural countryside to the cities in search of work.

But labor is not the only factor that has made urban areas attractive for the location of economic activities. The question of location is essentially one of movement of goods and services, and consequently transport is a key element in the determination of the proper location of industry. In the early days of a nation's industrialization there is no transport network spanning the entire nation, and there is a resulting locational bias in favor of those areas that are better serviced by transportation, with industry gravitating toward the nodes of the network. Thus, seaports such as New York, and port cities at river junctions such as Pittsburgh, became early economic centers. And with the advent of the railroad, major rail junction points, such as Chicago (a lake port), also became very attractive to industry.

Growth of Cities in the United States

As the United States became a major industrial power during the second half of the nineteenth century, transportation, agglomeration, and urbanization economies helped to make the cities grow and become the home of industry. Different cities might specialize in the manufacture of different products: Pittsburgh, because of its proximity to the mining of coking coal and its location at the junction of the Monongahela and Allegheny rivers (the gateway to the West), became a steel-producing center; New York, because of its great seaport, particularly once the Erie Canal gave it easy access to the West, became the great commercial and cultural center of the nation; Chicago, as a lake port and rail terminus, with proximity to the midwestern agricultural heartland, became a center for meat packing and grain trading.

Although the products that each urban area "exported" to the rest of the nation were specialized, the internal economy of the city was diversified. The rise of industrial plants in a city induced expansion of the construction industry to build factories, warehouses, and stores, plus homes for the workers who flocked to the city for jobs in the new establishments. As the population expanded, still more wholesale and retail establishments came into being to service it. All sorts of service types of business grew, some to service business —lawyers and accountants, for instance—and others to service people— doctors, dentists, repairmen.

As the cities grew, they became the places where the action was. Agglomerations of people and, as the pace of immigration increased, people of diverse cultures and backgrounds, made the cities "interesting." The sheer number of people and the development of a small group of very wealthy patrons enabled the establishment of theaters, symphony orchestras, opera houses, and art museums in the large cities. Their presence in turn enhanced the attractiveness of the city to others. The youngster in the rural area or small town who was bored with its tranquil but pedestrian life yearned for the opportunity to go to the city to make his fortune or just enjoy the excitement of its dynamism. As the popular song of World War I asked, "How are you going to keep them down on the farm after they've seen Paree?"

Importance of the Central City

In those days, moreover, the city meant just that: the central city. "It was the place where business was concentrated. It was the place where the people who worked in the businesses lived. It was, in short, metropolitan America. The outlying towns were largely self-sufficient communities. Only a wealthy few could afford the train fare and the time required to commute from country to city."[1]

Transportation and manufacturing technology were the most important factors tying industry and people to the central cities. Manufacturing plants were typically multistoried buildings located along a railroad siding for receipt of raw materials and shipping out of finished products. Given the level of mechanization at the time, these plants employed large numbers of unskilled and semiskilled workers and had, therefore, to be near large concentrations of people. Since first walking, and later the trolley line, were the chief means of transporting people to work, the factories and the people had to be close to each other, and this meant a location in a densely populated area: the central city.

The cities, as a result, became the nation's major labor market areas. The mechanization of agriculture that reduced the proportion of the population needed to produce the nation's food supply, plus the fact that the birthrate was higher on the farms, created a surplus farm population that tended to gravitate toward the cities, in which expanding industry offered jobs. But as the United States became a great industrial power in the last third of the nineteenth century, even that supply of labor was not sufficient to meet the needs of employers, so immigrants from rural areas of eastern and southern Europe were attracted.

The lot of urban workers was not easy—work was hard, hours long, and pay relatively meager—but jobs were available. Housing was far from good, but as builders rushed to put up row houses or tenements at rentals that the new arrivals in the city could afford at the going rate of industrial wages, it was adequate. The clustering of people of various immigrant groups or from particular rural areas in specific neighborhoods, moreover, allowed the maintenance of kinship and cultural ties, and thus eased the adjustment to the new urban industrial environment. The free public school system provided the education that "Americanized" the children of immigrants and provided them with opportunity to move up the occupational ladder. The streets of the cities were not paved with gold, but the growth of the urban economy did afford opportunities for the advancement of many.

Cities as Labor Markets

Labor as a Locational Factor

The industrial development of the nation made its cities become the leading labor markets. In fact, as a leading book on urban economics states, "the

---

[1] David L. Birch, *The Economic Future of City and Suburb*, CED Supplementary Paper No. 30 (New York: Committee for Economic Development, 1970), p. 1.

urban economy is above all else a labor market."[2] The location of industry is partially conditioned by availability of labor, and many industries are attracted to cities because they offer large labor markets. This is of particular importance to enterprises characterized by uncertainty of production schedules, since they must be able to hire additional workers on short notice.

For industries whose products are made by relatively unskilled workers and that are highly competitive in regard to price, labor cost differentials become a significant influence on location. These generally more labor-intensive industries, in which labor costs comprise a significant part of the total cost of production, also tend to have low transport costs (for example, textiles and apparel). Their tendency, therefore, is to seek locations offering sources of cheap labor supply, and smaller cities in relatively backward or depressed regions have attracted them in recent years.

Since skills are not evenly distributed within nations, industries requiring skilled workers tend to concentrate where they are most available. Such areas are generally those where the educational level is high and where activities requiring special skills have been concentrated for a long time.[3] The larger cities, therefore, are usually the most attractive to those activities needing skilled labor.

Diversity of labor supply, which is also important to many types of economic activity, is also most characteristic of the large labor markets of intensively urban regions. New York is probably the example par excellence of this, for New Yorkers work as actors, barbers, diplomats, educators, fishermen, lathe operators, masons, neurologists, radio and television technicians, sewing machine operators, typesetters, union officials, writers, and at thousands of other jobs. Thus, activities needing highly diverse types of skills—corporate headquarters, research and development laboratories, business service establishments, publishing houses—find New York and a few other very large metropolitan regions very attractive.

Many types of economic activities—retail trade and local services are the chief examples—are located in cities simply because the market for their products and services consists of the people who live there. For example, a city's newspaper cannot relocate because labor is cheaper or more typesetters are available elsewhere.

For most jobs and workers, therefore, the local labor market—the commuting radius around a district of concentrated employment—is the only labor market, at least in the short run. As we saw in Chapter 8, only the more skilled professional and managerial jobs are involved in a national labor market, and, while businesses and people can and do relocate from one local labor market to another, these are not everyday decisions, and once the relocation has taken place the new local area becomes the labor market.

---

[2] Wilbur R. Thompson, *A Preface to Urban Economics* (Baltimore: Johns Hopkins Press, 1968), p. 67.
[3] Edgar M. Hoover, *An Introduction to Regional Economics* (New York: Knopf, 1971), p. 187.

The economic status of the citizens of a community, therefore, will depend upon the status of the local labor market. How well off they are will depend upon whether jobs are growing and the unemployment rate is low or the area is stagnating and the number of jobless is swelling, and if wages and salaries are low or high relative to other communities.

Earnings and Income Differentials Among Urban Labor Markets

The first step in exploring these differences is to compare urban with non-urban areas. All the data indicate quite clearly that people in urban areas have higher incomes, on the average, than do those in rural areas. Fuchs, moreover, has found a strong and positive relation between earnings and city size. Average hourly earnings tend to rise with city size in every region of the nation and for every color-sex group.[4] He was able to account for one-third of the South–non-South wage differential, which was discussed in Chapter 10, by regional differences in city size. Total family income, not merely wages, is linked to city size, and, as demonstrated in Table 16.1, there is a direct correlation between size of community and median income.

Table 16.1 Median Income of Families and Unrelated Individuals by Size and Type of Community, 1959[a]

Size and Type of Community	Median Income
In urban areas of	
3,000,000 or more	$5,831
1,000,000 to 3,000,000	5,656
250,000 to 1,000,000	5,170
Less than 250,000	4,903
Outside urban areas, in places of	
25,000 or more	$4,441
10,000 to 25,000	4,327
2,500 to 10,000	4,328
Rural nonfarm	4,013
Rural farm	2,951

SOURCE: *United States Census of Population, 1960*, U.S. Department of Commerce, Bureau of the Census, Report PC(3)-1B (Washington, D.C.: Government Printing Office, 1964), Table 1, pp. 10–12.

[a] From Edgar M. Hoover, *An Introduction to Regional Economics* (New York: Knopf, 1971), Table 7-3, p. 164.

There are many factors that explain the differences in income by size of community. Fuchs suggests that higher earnings may reflect differences in labor quality not captured by standardization for color, age, sex, and education. Thus, larger urban areas may provide better-quality schooling and more on-the-job training, and may benefit from selective in-migration of the most ambi-

[4] Victor R. Fuchs, *Hourly Earnings Differentials by Region and City Size, 1959*, Occasional Paper 101 (New York: National Bureau of Economic Research, 1967),

tious people. Alonso argues that, even if urban costs rise after a certain point in size is reached, productivity may rise even faster (by reason of external economies or economies of scale) and "big cities may yield a greater net return per worker or inhabitant than smaller ones."[5] The community with the highest income—the large metropolitan area—has been described by Hanna as a place with a high labor force participation rate, a high proportion of multiple-income families, manufacturing specialization, a high ratio of males to females, and a high population growth rate.[6]

The fact that money incomes are higher in larger communities does not necessarily mean that real incomes are, because living costs may also be higher. Indeed, the City Worker's Family Budget figures of the U.S. Department of Labor reveal distinctly higher costs to maintain the same level of living in metropolitan areas than in nonmetropolitan areas: in the autumn of 1966, the budget costs were $9,376 in metropolitan areas and only $8,366 in nonmetropolitan areas. Yet careful analysis of the data indicates that real incomes are higher, despite higher living costs, in larger urban areas. A glance at Table 16.1 will show that the median incomes in urban areas average more than 20 percent higher than those in nonurban areas of 2,500 or more, or more than twice the difference in living costs. The net real income advantage of the urban community exists, and helps to explain why the nation has become increasingly urban.

Explanations of Higher Earnings in Different Urban Labor Markets

While on the average urban areas have higher earnings and incomes than nonurban ones, and larger urban areas than smaller ones, there are differentials among urban areas, even those of comparable size. The major reasons lie in variations among urban areas in "industry mix," "occupational mix," rate of growth, impact of trade unionism and collective bargaining, and labor force participation rates.

Industry Mix

To begin our analysis of intercity earnings and income differentials, let us look at Table 16.2, which shows 1971 average hourly earnings of production workers in manufacturing in a selection of urban areas. Back in Chapter 10 we saw that there were interregional differentials in wages and that the South still lagged behind the rest of the nation. This would seem to be borne out by the $2.90 average hourly earnings in Greensboro–Winston-Salem–High Point, North Carolina, but another southern area—Beaumont–Port Arthur–Orange, Texas—with average earnings of $4.40 per hour ranks among the

---

[5] William Alonso, "Location, Primacy and Regional Economic Development," in *Annals of the Second Inter-American Congress on Regional Planning* (Rio de Janeiro: Escritorio de Pesquisa Economica Aplicada, 1967).

[6] Frank A. Hanna, *State Income Differentials* (Durham, N.C.: Duke University Press, 1959), pp. 204–214.

Table 16.2 Average Hourly Earnings of Production Workers on Manufacturing Payrolls, Selected Areas, 1971

Area	Average Hourly Earnings
Akron	$4.42
Baltimore	3.75
Beaumont–Port Arthur–Orange	4.40
Boston	3.75
Chicago	3.97
Cleveland	4.17
Cincinnati	3.88
Detroit	4.80
Greensboro–Winston-Salem–High Point	2.90
Houston	3.93
Los Angeles–Long Beach	3.87
Milwaukee	4.18
Minneapolis–Saint Paul	4.03
Newark	3.74
New York City	3.63
Philadelphia SMSA[a]	3.80
Pittsburgh	4.06
St. Louis	4.09
San Diego	4.25
Seattle-Everett	4.36
Youngstown-Warren	4.45

[a] SMSA = Standard Metropolitan Statistical Area.

SOURCE: U.S. Department of Labor.

highest-paying areas. Although the South, on the average, has low wages, some southern communities have high earnings, so there must be a more fundamental reason for differentials among urban communities.

The major explanation becomes apparent when we pinpoint all the high-wage areas in our sample, those with over $4.20 average earnings: each of them has a concentration of high-wage industries. Thus, the highest wage area—Detroit—is the center of the high-wage automobile industry. Similarly, Akron is the center of tire and tube production; Beaumont–Port Arthur–Orange, of petroleum and chemicals production; San Diego and Seattle-Everett, of aircraft production; and Youngstown-Warren, of steel production. At the other extreme, Greensboro–Winston-Salem–High Point is a center for the manufacture of tobacco and textile products, both of which are low-wage industries.

From this analysis we can conclude that an area's industry mix is a major factor in determining its wage level, and that differences in industry mix are extremely important in explaining interarea wage differentials. Once we know a community's industry mix we can begin to determine whether, given that mix, it really is a high-, medium-, or low-wage center. This can be done by "standardizing" the data (multiplying national average wage rates for each industry by the number of workers engaged in each in the local area) and then seeing if the community's actual average wage is above or below the hypothetical one. About a decade ago, for example, a controversy took place concerning whether or not New York City was becoming a low-wage center. Those who claimed this pointed to the fact that New York ranked nineteenth among twenty major cities in average hourly earnings in manufacturing. Yet the fact, paradoxically, was that New York City was not a low-wage center, but rather a center of low-wage manufacturing industries, for which New York City was a high-wage area.

Analysis of an area's industry mix, however, should not be limited to manufacturing, which today accounts for only a minority of employment in the nation: about 27.5 percent in 1970, and a number of urban areas have even smaller percentages. For example, only about 20.5 percent of New York City's employment was in manufacturing, 16.0 percent of San Francisco–Oakland's, 15.0 percent of Miami's, 14.0 percent of New Orleans', and a bare 7.5 percent of Honolulu's. Whether or not this will mean high average earnings or low ones, however, still depends on the mix of economic activities that the urban area contains. Miami, which is so heavily dependent upon its role as a resort, will not have particularly high average earnings, because earnings in hotels and restaurants are not very high. Great commercial centers, such as New York and San Francisco, with very high concentration of business service establishments and financial institutions, which employ large percentages of managerial and professional personnel, will be high-earnings centers.

Occupational Mix

This last point—the occupational mix—is, therefore, a second important explanation of income differentials among labor markets. Urban areas with high concentrations of high-paid skilled workers are obviously going to have higher average earnings than those with very high proportions of lower-paid semi- and unskilled workers. Earnings data for occupational mix can be standardized in the same way as are those for industry mix, but we should keep in mind that, given greater mobility among skilled workers, interarea earnings differentials are much narrower for them than for the lesser skilled workers. The proportion of lesser skilled workers in different areas and their relative earnings, therefore, become important determinants of inter-area earnings differentials.

Economic and Institutional Factors

The fact that neither capital nor labor is perfectly mobile, but is tied for long periods of time to its present location, means that local labor markets are partially autonomous. A third explanation of interarea labor income differentials, therefore, lies in differences in the economic and institutional forces among labor markets. A community suffering persistent unemployment, which indicates labor surplus in relationship to job opportunities, will generally find its wage rates declining relative to other communities as workers compete for available jobs. On the other hand, growing communities, dependent upon attracting more labor to fill the expanding number of jobs, will be enjoying a relative rise in average wages. Labor surplus, of course, helps to explain the generally lower wages in the South and in depressed communities in the North, and the rapid expansion of job opportunities in California, at least until recently, was very important in boosting earnings levels in California urban areas.

Institutional forces—largely collective bargaining—also play a role in determining an area's labor earnings. When a community has a high concentration of a well-unionized industry there is bound to be some spillover of its wage rates to other industries. The spillover effects, however, can be much wider than into an industry organized by the same union, for a high-wage manufacturing center sets a standard for workers and even employers in other sectors of the community's economy, such as the service industries and retail trades, to try to emulate. The spillover effects tend to operate also when the community's export industry is a low-wage one, thus reinforcing the low-wage character of the local labor market.

The effects of collective bargaining on a community's labor income, however, need not be limited to spillovers from basic export industries, but may be independent. Local government employees, for example, are overwhelmingly involved in performing functions that are intracommunity oriented. The unionization in recent years of municipal employees in New York City has seen their salary scales escalate quite considerably. Similarly, hospital employees in New York City, who used to be very low paid, have enjoyed phenomenal increases in wages since the advent of large-scale unionization. The collective bargaining agreement provided for a minimum salary of $130 per week in 1971 in New York. hospitals, and this was far above what unskilled workers earned elsewhere. These collective bargaining gains among groups of employees who are not highly organized in most other communities raised New York City's relative labor earnings.

Collective bargaining is not the only institutional force in operation that affects a community's labor earnings. Industries characterized by oligopoly have a degree of price and wage setting that is independent of the forces of supply and demand, and this, of course, reinforces the industry-mix explanation of interarea labor earnings differentials. Thompson has coined the phrase "political productivity" to refer to such things as the protective tariff and the oil depletion allowance of our tax laws as contributing to the high incomes of some communities.[7]

The Labor Force Participation Rate

The spillover effects, however, need not be universal within a community. In most high-wage manufacturing industries and construction in Pittsburgh,

---

[7] Thompson, *op. cit.*, p. 82.

wages are particularly high, but, in the lower-wage retail and service industries, wages in Pittsburgh tend to be lower than elsewhere.[8] The major explanation of this seeming paradox is that Pittsburgh is a man's town and men earn considerably more there than they do in other cities. Given the heavy industry character of the Pittsburgh economy, there are relatively few jobs available for women, so their paychecks are lower than those of women in most other large metropolitan areas. The relative scarcity of female jobs in Pittsburgh, moreover, discourages women from participating in the labor force.

Industry mix, thus, is tied in with a fourth factor that helps to explain family income in an area: the labor force participation rate. In those communities in which other family members besides the principal breadwinner can readily find jobs, the combined family income is likely to be higher than those in which only the husband works. In contrast to Pittsburgh, New York with a high concentration of office work has a high female labor force participation rate, and this helps to boost the median family income of New Yorkers.

Narrowing of Intercity Earnings Differentials

The fact that there are wide disparities in income among local labor markets does not mean that it must always remain so. As economic growth continues, beyond a certain point there is a renewed interregional decentralization trend, because of changes in transportation, the declining importance of raw materials, and the growth of demand in many more regions of the country up to the point necessary to provide sufficient markets for plants of efficient size. This decentralization trend in the United States is making all regions more diversified and alike, rather than specialized and different, as they had been historically.

For at least a century all areas of the United States have been gaining in manufacturing at the expense of the early heavily industrialized Northeast. In 1860 72 percent of manufacturing employment was concentrated in the Northeast, with only 16 percent in the North Central and 12 percent in the South and West; by 1899 the Northeast's percentage had declined to 52, the North Central's had risen to 29, and the South and West's to 20; and by 1954 these three major divisions of the nation were almost equal, the Northeast with 35 percent, the North Central with 35, and the South and West, 30.

As regions become more alike, interregional income disparities narrow. According to Easterlin's data for the nine regions of the United States, the arithmetic mean deviation of regional per capita income from national levels (in percentage) had declined steadily, from 45.6 in 1880, to 36.6 in 1940, and to 16.9 in 1950.[9] By 1970 the average deviation of regional per capita income from the national level had dropped to 11.3 percent.

---

[8] *Region in Transition*, Report of the Economic Study of the Pittsburgh Region Conducted by the Pittsburgh Regional Planning Association (Pittsburgh: University of Pittsburgh Press, 1963), p. 80.

[9] R. A. Easterlin, "Long Term Regional Income Changes: Some Suggested Factors," *Papers and Proceedings* (Philadelphia: Regional Science Association, 1958), p. 315.

Income differentials have not only narrowed among the broad regions of the country, but also between metropolitan and nonmetropolitan areas. In 1929 people in nonmetropolitan areas had, on the average, only 43 percent of the per capita income of those in metropolitan areas, but by 1966 the ratio had risen to 68 percent.[10] Similarly, there has been a substantial convergence of per capita incomes among the standard metropolitan areas of each region. In other words, all the differences in income that we have reviewed—between broad regions, between metropolitan and nonmetropolitan areas, and between large metropolitan areas and smaller ones—persist, but the differentials in each case are narrowing as labor and capital move in response to economic opportunities.

Changes within Metropolitan Areas

Actually, the most dramatic changes in urban labor markets are those that have been taking place within each of them. Whereas an urban area and the local labor market used to be confined to the central city, today they encompass a much broader physical area, including the central city and vast new outlying suburbs. Jobs and people have been flowing out of the central city so fast that the typical central city finds itself with a declining tax base at the same time that the needs of its remaining citizens have increased, and this has become a major portion of what is commonly referred to as the "urban crisis." In this section, therefore, let us trace some of the major factors— technological and demographic—that have contributed to the changes that have taken place within urban areas, with particular reference to their impact on the local labor market.

Technological Changes

Changes in technology have had a profound effect upon the urban economy. Strangely enough, however, we must look first not at manufacturing technology, but at that of agriculture. The application of science and technology to agriculture has made the American farmer enormously productive. At the end of the twenty-year period 1950–1969, American farmers produced more than triple the amount of goods per man-hour that they had at the beginning Since the demand for agricultural products is inelastic, output did not expand as rapidly as productivity, with the result that fewer people were needed in agriculture and less than one out of ten people is involved in growing our food supply today.

This is progress of which the nation can justly be proud, but in the process of achieving that progress it forgot all about the people who were being displaced as a result of this greatly increased efficiency. Instead of devising programs to aid them, it simply left them to fend for themselves. This is another case in which, while the majority enjoys the benefits of increased

---

[10] Hoover, *op. cit.*, p. 206.

efficiency, the minority that is directly affected suffers all the costs.

When driven from the land, they, as surplus farmers always had, flocked to the cities. The nation's urban centers, particularly in the North, had to absorb millions of people displaced from southern farms. Many of these people, particularly blacks, had suffered from neglect and discrimination, and were ill-prepared for the transition to urban industrial life. They possessed neither the education nor the skills that industry was seeking. Moreover, new technology in industry had raised the requirements for jobs. Migrants to the cities in former periods came when industry required masses of unskilled labor, but this was no longer the case, because new technology had raised requirements for jobs, with the result that many of the displaced agricultural people could not qualify for the jobs that were available.

To further complicate the situation, the need for new types of physical plants and changes in modes of transportation led industry to forsake the central cities for the suburbs. A sample of seventy-three metropolitan areas, containing 75 percent of the total metropolitan area population in 1960, disclosed that the central cities' share of the areas' manufacturing employment had dropped from 65.9 percent in 1947 to 57.6 percent in 1963 as old plants were relocated or new plants opened in the suburbs.[11]

A major explanation of the outward migration of manufacturing is the character of the older, built-up areas. Manufacturing today requires long, one-story structures with more space per worker, thus rendering old factory buildings obsolete. A combination of zoning problems, the lack of available large tracts, and the high cost of sites in the central cities drives firms to erect new plants in the considerably less-congested suburbs.

In addition to changes in plant layout, suburbanization of manufacturing and related activities has also been due to changes in transportation technology, most importantly the improvement of the motor truck and the spread of the highway system.[12] In the days when inputs and outputs moved mainly by rail, a company was restricted in its choice of plant locations, but since the road network is much finer than the rail network, its choice of locations has been widened. Traffic congestion in the central cities, which were built in premotor-vehicle times, also means that an outlying plant is more accessible for speedy delivery and receipt of goods.

Demographic Changes

Furthermore, as people moved to the suburbs, the labor supply of the outlying areas increased to the point where still more plants could be located there. Continual change in the capital-output ratio, moreover, means that new plants do not normally use as much total labor as old ones did. The increasing affluence of the population played its role in suburbanization, for more people could afford to buy houses in the suburbs and to drive automobiles, thus mak-

---

[11] Birch, *op. cit.*, p. 11.
[12] Hoover, *op. cit.*, p. 330.

ing them no longer dependent upon public transportation into the central city. Furthermore, the reduction in the length of the work day and work week has enabled people to commute longer distances without adding to their total time away from home. As a result, the geographic extent of the local labor market was widened, and as more people moved to the suburbs some of them opted for employment closer to home rather than driving into the city. In turn, the location of new plants in the suburbs induced more people to move there to take advantage of the job opportunities. As people moved to the suburbs many types of businesses, such as retail stores and service establishments (restaurants, beauty parlors, etc.), followed their customers there.

Other technological changes undermined the central city's domination of activities. The locations of airports and residences of employees, and improved communications systems, have made it practical in some cases to locate the headquarters offices of some companies that had traditionally been located "downtown," in the suburbs. Even when headquarters are kept in the central city, pieces of the operation may move to the suburbs. A company's computer center, since it is engaged in performing more standardized tasks, need not be within the company headquarters, and many have been built in suburban locations, which offer sufficient labor supply and space for one-story buildings with adjoining parking lots.[13]

Decline of the Central City

The decline of the central city relative to the suburbs in every type of economic activity is documented in data gathered by Birch, which are shown in Table 16.3. Only those activities which are highly dependent upon face-to-face communications and external economies, such as finance and insurance, remain dominant in the central city, but those which involve more standardized production or procedures tend to move out. By 1970 half of all employment in the fifteen largest metropolitan areas was in the suburbs. As a result, many of the older central cities of the nation have actually declined in population since 1950.

As the central city lost economic activities relatively, and in some cases absolutely as well, to the suburbs, the well-being of its residents vis à vis those in the suburbs deteriorated. In 1960 median family income in the central cities of urbanized areas was $5,945, compared with $7,144 in the suburban portions of these areas. The central cities had almost twice the percentage of poor that the suburbs had. The unemployment rates of the central cities were higher, 5.5 percent as compared with 4.1 percent in the suburbs. The people in the central cities, moreover, were less well educated than those in the suburbs; median years of schooling were only 10.7, whereas in the suburbs the median was 12.0.[14]

[13] See Roy B. Helfgott, "EDP and the Office Work Force," *Industrial and Labor Relations Review*, July 1966, pp. 503–516.
[14] Lowell E. Gallaway, *Manpower Economics* (Homewood, Ill.: Richard D. Irwin, 1971), p. 203.

Table 16.3 The Central City's Changing Share of Urban Employment, 1948–1967*

Employment Category	Percentage				
	1948	1956	1958	1963	1967
Sample of 73 SMSAs					
Retail trade	78.9		72.4	64.0	
Wholesale trade	87.3		82.4	78.5	
Manufacturing (1947 data)	65.9		60.8	57.6	
Selected services	88.6		79.5	75.0	
Sample of 8 SMSAs					
Other services	81.4	83.6			72.1
Finance	90.4	86.8			82.9
Insurance and Real Estate	92.7	89.2			80.2
Government	n.a.	66.0			59.7

SOURCES: *Economic and Demographic Projections for Two Hundred and Twenty-Four Metropolitan Areas,* National Planning Association, Regional Economic Projection, Report No. 67-R-I, Vols. I, II, and III; *County Business Patterns,* U.S. Department of Commerce, Bureau of the Census, 1948, 1956, and 1958; and *Census of Manufactures* and *Census of Business,* U.S. Department of Commerce, Bureau of the Census, selected reports for various years, 1954–1963.

* From David L. Birch, *The Economic Future of City and Suburb,* CED Supplementary Paper No. 30 (New York: Committee for Economic Development, 1970), Figure 5, p. 11.

The lower educational attainment of the central city population was not necessarily due to inferior school systems, but to selective migration out of and into the central city. The better-educated, higher-income people tended to leave and the newcomers, consisting largely of those displaced from southern agriculture, brought poorer educational backgrounds. Once the latter group became significant, however, the quality of the central city's school system as compared to that of suburban communities did deteriorate, because the central city no longer had a tax base with which to support good schools. This in turn induced more higher-income groups to move out, and thus intensified the disparities between city and suburb.

Race, too, has been a factor in the growth of urban problems. As the poor blacks increased in number in the central city, fear, prejudice, and a combination of the two encouraged the more affluent whites to flee to the suburbs. As a result, the central city was tending to become a poor black ghetto surrounded by a ring of affluent white suburbs. With the central cities largely abandoned to the poor, the urban crisis arose, with crime, decay, unemployment and underemployment, declining tax base, rising welfare rolls, and the like. The problem is exacerbated by ethnic conflict and a heritage of treating black people as inferiors.

Labor Market Imbalances and Explanations of Them

The decline of the central city and the rise of the suburbs would not necessarily have had to cause labor market problems. But problems have arisen because of an imbalance in the location of jobs and people, and the inability of people in the central cities to qualify for the jobs that do exist there.

People and Jobs

The central cities have continued to draw in the unskilled surplus agricultural population while the industries that traditionally provided jobs for these people—primarily manufacturing—have been declining relative to others and, moreover, moving out of the central cities. The urban labor market, as a consequence, suffers from a large measure of structural unemployment.

Indicative of structural problems has been the high rate of labor force nonparticipation on the part of males in central cities. Yet many of the non-participants are discouraged workers, those who have simply given up the pursuit of jobs. A survey of the poverty areas of six major cities (Atlanta, Chicago, Detroit, Houston, Los Angeles, and New York) for the period July 1968–June 1969 found that the proportion of nonparticipants wanting a job was larger than the comparable proportion nationally.[15] Forty percent of the men in the poverty areas who were not in the labor force but wanted a job, however, cited health problems as their major obstacle to employment. Another 7.3 percent suffered from a lack of skill, education, or experience, which severely limited their chances of ever finding jobs and discouraged them, hence, from active pursuit of work.

Census data for a number of predominantly black areas of Los Angeles disclosed significant declines in the male labor force participation rate between 1960 and 1965: in Watts, for example, it dropped from 69.9 percent to 57.9. Gallaway has shown that this decline in male labor force participation rates is the product of a selective exodus of individuals from these areas.[16] His statistical tests disclose that this is not an exit of whites, but of the economically more competent blacks.

In other words, large numbers of blacks, as they obtain decent jobs and income, also join the flight from the central city, or at least from its poorest areas. Since those left behind are the least economically competent—the ones with the worst health, poorest educations, and least skills—signs of human decay begin to appear and, in time, to multiply. As the most capable leave, businesses are also induced to relocate to outlying areas in order to obtain efficient work forces, thus compounding the structural problems of the urban labor market.

Housing

But, if the jobs have been moving out, why have the people who might qualify for some of those jobs come to the central city? As usual there are a number

---

[15] Harvey J. Hilaski, "Unutilized Manpower in Poverty Areas of 6 U.S. Cities," *Monthly Labor Review*, December 1971, pp. 45–52.

[16] Gallaway, *op. cit.*, pp. 209–214.

of factors explaining this phenomenon, but the most important relate to the market for housing. The simple fact is that the private construction industry cannot build houses at prices that the lower-income groups can afford to pay, and the only access that they have to private housing is through a filtering-down process; that is, they move into the housing that higher-income groups have abandoned. The central city, being older, has neighborhoods in which the housing has deteriorated, and the poor, therefore, are better able to afford the rents charged there than they could afford to buy or rent housing in the newer suburbs.

Even if there were housing available in the suburbs at prices that low-income groups could afford, they would find it difficult to live in the suburbs because of the absence of mass transit facilities. Since the poor cannot afford automobiles, they are very dependent upon public transportation, which the central city still provides, for access to jobs.

Discrimination has also played an important role in barring low-income groups from the suburbs. In order to keep the costs of local services down, communities have practiced economic discrimination through zoning requirements that do not permit housing sites of less than one acre, two acres, or even eight acres. It must also be remembered that blacks have comprised a large proportion of displaced agricultural people, and racial discrimination has barred them from purchasing suburban homes, even when they could afford them.

Other factors, too, have contributed to the concentration of the poor in the central city. Migrant groups—whether immigrants from abroad or in-migrants from other parts of the United States—have always tended to cluster together for mutual protection and sharing of a culture, and this is most feasible in the central city. But it should not be thought that the continual black concentration there is a purely voluntary affair, because as some members of previous slum areas advanced economically they were able to move out, but this has been most difficult for blacks.

Transportation

Transportation has also played an important role in the problem of imbalance in the urban labor market. If the poor could not find jobs in the central city near where they lived, why could they not travel to the suburbs where the jobs were? The fact is that, to the degree possible, this is what the people confined to the central city do. More than a decade ago the New York Metropolitan Region Study revealed that there was a daily two-way rush hour traffic flow over the George Washington Bridge; while suburban whites were going to their midtown Manhattan offices, blacks from Harlem were headed for their jobs in industrial plants in northern New Jersey.[17]

Reverse commuting, however, is far from easy for the slum dwellers,

---

[17] Edgar M. Hoover and Raymond Vernon, *Anatomy of a Metropolis* (Cambridge, Mass.: Harvard University Press, 1959), p. 176.

who have the lowest degree of automobile ownership. Even where public transportation is available, it is very roundabout, hence time-consuming, and usually very expensive. Detailed fare schedules from the American Transit Association show that in 1967 fares on public transit lines from the central city to the closest suburban area ranged from 30 cents one way in one of the fourteen SMSAs studied to 65 cents in another.[18] (Fares have gone up considerably since 1967.) Rush hour schedules, moreover, are normally adjusted to serve the needs of those commuting from the suburbs to the central city, not the other way around. Numerous studies have produced evidence that central city residents using public transportation have to spend more money and time to reach their suburban jobs than those commuting to the city. A resident of the Bedford-Stuyvesant section of Brooklyn would have to spend about $50 in commutation each month to travel by public transportation to a job in a Long Island aircraft plant, a Westchester parts plant, or a Staten Island chemical plant. Even for a $3-per-hour job, transportation would take a hefty percentage of the worker's pay check. As a result, relatively few people—less than 10 percent of all workers—commuted from central city to the suburbs, and most of them were better-paid workers, not the least skilled.

The imbalance in the urban labor market, therefore, can be broken down into three elements: (1) a movement of unskilled workers into the central city at the same time that many of the types of jobs for which they might qualify moved out to the suburbs; (2) a housing market that, for reasons of economics plus discrimination, did not permit the unskilled to move to the suburbs to be closer to those jobs; (3) an inadequate and costly public transportation system that denied central city residents access to suburban jobs.

The Plight of the Black Ghetto

The urban problem, moreover, was still further compounded by the fact that the central city poor were increasingly becoming black. This was the result of two trends: blacks moving into the central city and whites moving out. Between 1950 and 1968 the percentage of the population of the central cities of all the SMSAs that was nonwhite had risen from 13.1 to 21.8. By 1970 sixteen cities—including Atlanta, Georgia; Gary, Indiana; Newark, New Jersey; and Washington, D.C.—had majority black populations. Meanwhile, the nonwhite percentage outside the central cities—5.7 in 1950 and 5.5 in 1968—had not changed.[19] The blacks, moreover, were crowded into the most decayed neighborhoods of the central cities and the term "urban ghetto" (the ghetto was the section of the medieval cities of Europe to which Jews were confined) was devised to describe this situation.

Residential racial discrimination was bad enough, but in this case differ-

[18] Dorothy K. Newman, "The Decentralization of Jobs," *Monthly Labor Review*, May 1967, pp. 7–13.

[19] Hoover, *op. cit.*, p. 336.

ences in income level also existed. The central city was becoming the preserve of the poor, plus a few rich who wished to remain close to the cultural amenities it offered, while the suburbs became the preserve of the middle classes. On the average, however, the incomes of suburbanites were decidedly higher than those of the city dwellers, and within the central city the blacks were poorer than the whites.

The plight of the black ghetto residents is well illustrated by the unemployment and welfare data. The unemployment rate for adult males in urban poverty neighborhoods has run consistently between 60 and 90 percent higher than in other urban neighborhoods. The situation of the black youth has been particularly desperate, with the unemployment rate among those in poverty neighborhoods remaining above 25 percent in periods of low national unemployment and climbing close to 50 percent in periods of high unemployment.

The labor market situation in the black ghettos has been reflected in a growth in the number of welfare recipients. While historically welfare cases rose and fell with unemployment, this pattern was broken in 1963, with new cases increasing rapidly as unemployment fell. The result was an explosion in welfare costs.[20]

The nation, however, remained oblivious to these urban developments until the riots of 1966–1967 abruptly awakened it. The National Advisory Commission on Civil Disorders, appointed by President Johnson, reported: "Unemployment and underemployment are among the most persistent and serious grievances of our disadvantaged minorities. The pervasive effect of these conditions on the racial ghetto is inextricably linked to the problem of civil disorder."[21]

The commission surveyed the people in the riot areas and found that 20 to 30 percent of the rioters were unemployed. Although the majority of rioters were employed, their jobs were mainly unskilled to semiskilled and their employment was often intermittent. Many of them were convinced that their present jobs reflected neither their capabilities nor rewarded their hopes.

The term "subemployment" came into use. The subemployed consisted of the unemployed plus the number of people who were working part time but wanted full-time jobs; those full-time workers earning less than $3,000 per year; and a portion of those not in the labor force, on the assumption that they had dropped out because of frustration at being unable to find work. The commission estimated that, including the totally unemployed, the subemployment rate for the available nonwhite labor force was about 33 percent and that about 1 million nonwhite subemployed were living in poverty sections of central cities in 1967.

---

[20] "The Manpower Posture of the Seventies" (New York: Bureau of Labor Statistics, Middle Atlantic Regional Office, February 1971).

[21] *Report of the National Advisory Commission on Civil Disorders* (New York: Bantam, 1968), p. 413.

Dual Structure of the Urban Labor Market

Concentration on the plight of the black ghetto has led some economists to develop a somewhat different view of urban labor market problems. They see them less as a result of deficiencies on the part of the labor supply than as defects in the structure of urban labor markets themselves that serve to constrain the poor from realizing their potential. This view, championed by Bennett Harrison, builds on the concept of differentiated labor markets discussed in Chapter 8, and posits a model of the urban labor market that is composed of a core, which provides stable jobs with adequate wages, surrounded by a periphery of less stable activities.[22] Figure 16.1 presents Harrison's model of the structure of urban labor markets.

The core, or primary labor market, is characterized by high productivity, decent wages, and relatively stable employment. This results from the fact

Figure 16.1   The Structure of Urban Labor Markets

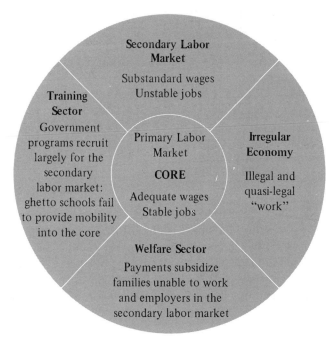

Secondary Labor Market
Substandard wages
Unstable jobs

Training Sector
Government programs recruit largely for the secondary labor market: ghetto schools fail to provide mobility into the core

Primary Labor Market
CORE
Adequate wages
Stable jobs

Irregular Economy
Illegal and quasi-legal "work"

Welfare Sector
Payments subsidize families unable to work and employers in the secondary labor market

[22] Bennett Harrison, "Employment, Unemployment and Structure of the Urban Labor Market," reprinted with permission from the *Wharton Quarterly*, Spring 1972, pp. 4–7, 26–31, Copyright Trustees of the University of Pennsylvania. This article is based on Chapter 5 of his monograph, *Education, Training, and the Urban Ghetto* (Baltimore: Johns Hopkins Press, 1972). The concept of the dual labor market was advanced by Doeringer and Piore in Peter B. Doeringer and Michael J. Piore, *Internal Labor Markets and Manpower Analysis* (Lexington, Mass.: D.C. Heath, 1971).

that the firms in it are the larger ones that have the market power to be able to invest in both capital equipment and the development of human resources. This being the case, the workers who are hired develop behavioral traits that reinforce the basic character of the core.

The periphery of the system consists of four segments, the first and most important of which Harrison calls the "secondary labor market." It is composed of the firms in the more competitive product industries, which lack market power and thus the wherewithal to invest in either physical or human capital. Since they offer jobs that do not require great skill, pay low wages, and lack stability, they attract workers who tend to display relatively low average and marginal productivity. The workers in turn have no incentive to develop behavior patterns that would increase their productivity, and they tend to drift from one low-paying job to another or into one of the other segments of the periphery, such as the "welfare sector," the "training sector" —governmental programs and the educational system, which Harrison claims prepares workers for jobs primarily in the secondary labor market rather than the primary one—and the "irregular economy," consisting of illegal and quasi-legal work, such as narcotics distribution, numbers running, and stealing.

These then are some of the ingredients of the urban crisis. Whether stress is placed on the demand or supply side, improvements must be made in the urban labor market. Obviously it will take more than labor market policies and programs to solve the urban crisis, but such policies must be an important part of any remedial program, and so it is to that subject that we turn next.

The Urban Problem in Perspective

Yet, for all their problems, the nation's cities are still functioning and they remain major centers of economic activity. Although the poor may be concentrated in the cities, the vast majority of city dwellers are not poor. In fact, in new areas of population growth, such as the West and Southwest, central cities as well as suburban areas are growing very rapidly, as, for example, Houston, Texas, and Phoenix, Arizona. It is in the older cities, serving regions that are no longer growing rapidly in population, with high-density residency, obsolete industrial plants, decaying housing, and streets that are poorly adapted to the motor vehicle that major economic difficulties are faced.

Solutions to Urban Labor Market Problems

Proposed solutions to the urban labor market problems have taken a number of forms. One proposed remedy deals in terms of the location of jobs and is designed to get the jobs to where the people are. A second remedy deals with the location of people and is designed to get the people to where the jobs are. A third, recognizing the difficulty of physically relocating people, proposes transportation improvements that would allow people to travel more easily from where they are to where the jobs are. A fourth remedy concentrates on labor market policies and is designed to improve the skills of the central city residents. A fifth remedy would involve the demand side of the labor market by breaking down patterns of racial discrimination in hiring. Aside from the fifth remedy, which we shall examine in greater detail in the next chapter, we shall now look more closely at each of these proposed solutions.[23]

Dealing with Rural Poverty

Any program for dealing with the urban crisis must include solutions for rural poverty.[24] All of the proposed solutions to labor market imbalance—erecting new plants in the cities, building low-income housing in the suburbs, constructing new transportation networks, or training people for jobs—require time for their implementation. If in that time period, as the problems of existing city residents are ameliorated, new poor in-migrants take their places, then the cities will find themselves on a virtual treadmill. Therefore, unless the steady drift of poorly educated, unskilled surplus farm people to the nation's cities can be slowed, the cities will never be able to solve their problems.

This does not mean that people must be kept in rural areas where they have no economic future. On the contrary, they should be encouraged to move. But unless the problem of rural poverty is only to be physically trans-ferred to the central cities, the nation must undertake programs of human resource development in depressed rural areas so that people who migrate out of them will be trained to qualify for jobs in urban communities. Efforts must also be intensified to develop urban growth centers closer to such rural areas. Berry, for example, would encourage migration from rural areas to such growth centers as preferable to migration to large central cities, "where isolation in ghettos produces a parallel and perhaps more debilitating isolation than in rural areas."[25] At the same time, solutions must be found to the exist-ing labor market problems of urban conglomerations.

Moving Jobs into the Central City

Since a good deal of the high unemployment in poverty areas of the central cities stems from the fact that the type of jobs that their low-skilled residents might qualify for have been moving out, some advocate that policies should be adopted that would induce industry to locate facilities in the central city. Indeed, some manufacturing facilities have been deliberately established in

---

[23] An excellent summary analysis of most of these proposals is presented by Ben-jamin Chinitz, "Urban Economics: The Problem of the Ghetto," in Alan A. Brown, Egon Neuberger, and Malcolm Palmatier (eds.), *Perspectives in Economics* (New York: McGraw-Hill, 1971), pp. 173–185.

[24] For a thorough exposition of this thesis, see Niles M. Hansen, *Rural Poverty and the Urban Crisis* (Bloomington: Indiana University Press, 1970).

[25] Brian L. Berry, "A Summary—Spatial Organization and Levels of Welfare," *Research Review*, June 1968, pp. 1–6.

poverty areas of central cities: the Watts Manufacturing Company, a subsidiary of Aerojet General, was established and successfully operated in the Watts district of Los Angeles; International Business Machines opened a computer cable factory in the Bedford-Stuyvesant section of Brooklyn; and the Warner Swasey Company purchased a manufacturing plant in the Hough section of Cleveland. Yet our earlier analysis of the reasons for the location of industry should indicate that this proposed solution is not likely to bring dramatic reversals of trends. The construction of industrial parks within cities may allow the retention of some industry that would otherwise have moved out, but the basic economics of location will not bring manufacturing back into the central city.

Moving People to Where the Jobs Are

The second solution—moving the people to where the jobs are—is economically more sensible, though far from easy to accomplish. The central cities, being older than the suburbs, have the older housing, which the lower-income groups can best afford. The concentration of displaced people from agriculture and mining in the central cities, therefore, was almost a natural phenomenon.

But discrimination in housing does play an important role in keeping disadvantaged minorities concentrated in urban ghettos. While such variables as income, family size, and location of employment help to explain the black concentration in central cities, they also indicate that there is a large residual that cannot be accounted for by these socioeconomic factors, and that residual is discrimination. A study by the RAND Corporation of black residential patterns in Chicago and Detroit revealed that as many as 40,000 nonwhites would move out of the three inner rings if discrimination did not exist. According to calculations by Kain, moreover, black employment in Chicago would rise by more than 10 percent if the black population were distributed in a pattern consistent with its socioeconomic characteristics.[26]

Data of the late 1960s, in fact, do begin to show a movement of blacks into the suburbs. That movement, however, has been limited largely to the older, inner suburbs, where blacks have been allowed to take over decayed housing that whites, who were moving further out, were abandoning. Blacks, for example, have been able to move from Harlem in New York City to the old Westchester communities of Mount Vernon and White Plains.

The ability of blacks to move into the newer suburbs, however, is extremely limited. Communities seeking to preserve their socioeconomic, and ethnic, status will not willingly allow low-income housing to be built within them, and despite all the laws against discrimination, blacks who can afford good housing find it hard to buy in most suburban areas.

Unless the present pattern of residential segregation of the black population in the central cities is broken soon, there is the grave danger of creating

---

[26] John F. Kain, "Housing Segregation, Negro Employment, and Metropolitan Decentralization," *Quarterly Journal of Economics*, May 1968, 175–197.

what Gunnar Myrdal has called a "permanent underclass."[27] This underclass would consist of central city blacks isolated from the mainstream of American economic and social life by virtue of being cut off from the rapid expansion of economic activity in the suburbs. They would become more dependent upon government assistance, and this would further undermine the viability of the nation's central cities.

But, as important as the battle against discrimination in residence is, it is of less immediate aid to the poor in the urban ghettos than the ability to find good jobs would be. Even assuming that the battle against discrimination in housing will be won eventually, this still would only aid those who can afford to buy good housing. The plight of the unskilled would remain, so the housing front remains only a very partial solution to the urban labor market problem.

Transportation Improvements

If the people cannot be moved to live near where the jobs are, why not provide them with the means of transportation for traveling from where they live to where the jobs are? Action along these lines is certainly required. In a study undertaken for New York City, the Regional Plan Association proposed that fifteen bus system extensions be instituted to connect low-income areas with nearby manufacturing districts.[28] The federal government has funded fourteen "reverse commute" city-to-suburb projects. Although some initial successes were reported, we shall see that the basic economic facts place limits on this solution, too.

Public transportation systems are expensive, and it pays to operate them only if they enjoy a large volume of business. But the automobile is a fact of life in the United States today, and it is the means of getting to and from work that 90 percent of suburbanites use today. It may be true that, through its highway program, the nation has subsidized the private automobile driver at the expense of the user of public transportation and that this has been an important factor in the decline of public transportation, but it is most difficult, if not impossible, to undo what has been done. As more people have turned to driving to work, the existing mass transit systems have become more uneconomical, and their services have declined while their prices have risen.

A number of problems present themselves with respect to reverse-commuting mass transit. First of all, suburban manufacturing plants, unlike downtown offices, are not clustered in one central area, so users of mass transit would still face the problem of getting from the transit depot to their jobs. To build the type of transit system that could deposit people near their jobs would be very costly and require fares that few could afford. To construct a decent mass transit system would probably require subsidization, but who is to provide the subsidy? Most of the central cities cannot afford to, there are

---

[27] Gunnar Myrdal, *Challenge to Affluence* (New York: Pantheon, 1962).
[28] *The New York Times,* March 19, 1973.

no metropolitan area governments, and the states and federal government have been unwilling. So, while there is justification for improving transit service, probably more in order to preserve the downtown and prevent further central city decline than to immediately improve the access of central city residents to jobs, this, too, is only a very partial solution to the urban labor market problem.

Labor Market Policies

If people have difficulty in finding work at all, or if they do find it, they must take the lowest-paying, most menial types of jobs because they are unskilled, then the problem is basically one of structural unemployment, the answer to which lies in labor market policies: the creation of more decent-paying jobs and education and training programs to upgrade the skills of the low-income groups concentrated in the central cities. One leading urban economist—Professor Chinitz—has come out flatly in favor of programs to train people in preference to those designed to attract industry to the city or to subsidize transportation to jobs in the suburbs.[29]

A task force of the Twentieth Century Fund that investigated the employment problems of blacks recommended not only building more low-income housing for minorities outside the central city and better public transportation, but also activities to increase the number and quality of jobs. It suggested that employers improve the productivity of low-paying jobs through capital investment, job redesigns, and improved management in order to raise wage rates and earnings and to build career ladders to facilitate the movement of workers from low-paying jobs to better ones.[30]

As we saw earlier in this book, in our discussion of structural unemployment, its solution cannot be separated from the ensuring of adequate demand for labor. Therefore, an absolutely essential condition for success of an investment-in-human-resources approach to urban unemployment problems is that there be jobs for which to train people. As Chinitz points out, "First, the maintenance of a high national growth rate is the most potent weapon for offsetting influences that tend to depress central-city employment." To support this assertion he cites a study of fifteen cities in which Wilfred Lewis found a strong link between a central city's employment growth and the rate of growth in national employment in the same period.[31] According to Lewis, it requires a 4 percent annual increase in real gross national product to produce a very slight increase in central city employment.

Harrison, too, stresses the need for greater general economic growth in order to create more well-paying jobs.[32] Although he is skeptical of the value of present government training programs, he would place emphasis on other

---

[29] Chinitz, *op. cit.*, p. 183.

[30] *The Job Crisis for Black Youth*, Task Force on Employment Problems of Black Youth (New York: Praeger, 1971).

[31] Chinitz, *op. cit.*, pp. 182–183.

[32] Harrison, *op. cit.*

government labor market policies. These would include the creation of more public service jobs, tighter antidiscrimination programs, contracting with private corporations to produce quasi-"public" goods—for example, high-speed ground transportation and environmental restoration systems—and stimulation of technological developments designed to replace the most objectionable kinds of work in the periphery of urban labor markets.

But what about the contention that the jobs that the city residents might qualify for are moving to the suburbs? This is so certainly with respect to manufacturing, but that tells us little about the jobs that are growing within the central cities. To a very large degree these are jobs in the service industries, and, according to Lewis, they are as much in need of relatively low-skilled labor as is manufacturing.

Unfortunately, many of the service types of jobs are relatively low paid, and are viewed as dead ends by the people who hold them. But such jobs could be made entry-level ones, from which people could progress to higher-level positions, if training to upgrade skills were available. A few examples may indicate the possibilities. In hotels and restaurants, dishwashers could be trained to become chefs and salad men, highly skilled and well-paid occupations that are in short supply. Similarly, hospital orderlies might be trained to become medical technicians. Also, there is the whole white-collar field, for which low-paid workers could be trained as typists, stenographers, and computer programmers to work in banks and offices. Brecher has detailed how workers in low-level positions in five industries—apparel manufacturing, health services, construction, transit, and food services—might be trained for more advanced jobs.[33]

Indeed, a good deal of such training has been going on during the past decade, and progress has been made in upgrading people, including many from the disadvantaged minorities. Yet in mid-1971, during a period of high unemployment, according to a front page story in *The New York Times*: "In offices throughout the city, busy executives are answering their own telephones, filing their own memos and falling behind in their correspondence and accounts because of an acute shortage of office help."[34] This shortage of skilled office workers—secretaries, good typists, stenographers, and bookkeepers—was coincident with unemployment among less-skilled white-collar workers, such as file clerks, receptionists, and slow typists. This mismatching of labor supply and demand seemed ready made for intensified training programs to upgrade skills.

The problem of shortages of white-collar skills, moreover, is not unique to New York, but is also true of Chicago, Philadelphia, San Francisco, and other cities. Training programs that have been run have been successful. According to officials of the New York City Coalition Jobs, in the previous year 400 employers had participated in a federally sponsored training program, under

---

[33] Charles Brecher, *Upgrading Blue Collar and Service Workers* (Baltimore: Johns Hopkins Press, 1972).

[34] *The New York Times*, July 5, 1971.

which they were paid subsidies to help cover the costs of training the unskilled. As a result, these companies had hired 6,600 trainees, 65 percent of them for white-collar positions, with very satisfactory results reported by 80 percent of the employers.

There does, therefore, seem to be great potential for remedying urban labor market problems in training of the poor for better jobs. In fact, if they are not trained for the jobs that do exist in the central cities, then those jobs will also disappear. Employers unable to meet their white-collar labor needs in the central city will join the trek to the suburbs where the middle classes, which possess those skills, have been moving. Thus, greatly improved central city school systems and expanded training efforts to upgrade the skills of the present central city residents would seem to provide the best answers to the problems of the urban labor market.

By now it should be clear that the problems of the urban labor market are intermixed with problems of equal employment opportunity. The next chapter, therefore, will examine the subject in greater detail, and in the one following we shall return to the question of education and training as part of overall manpower programs.

Summary

The shift in the United States economy from an agricultural to an industrial one was accompanied by a shift from a rural to an urban way of life. Cities have been attractive to the location of economic activities because they could provide a large labor supply, facility of transportation, and external economies. Originally, the city meant just that—the central city—as need for industry to be close to its supply of labor tied it to areas of concentrated population.

As a result of the industrial development of the nation, its cities became the leading labor markets, and the urban economy is essentially a labor market. There are, however, substantial earnings and income differentials among urban labor markets. These differences can be explained in terms of industry mix, occupational mix, economic and institutional factors, and labor force participation rates, all of which tend to be interrelated. In recent decades, however, there has been a narrowing of interurban area earnings differentials as all areas tend to become more diversified and more like each other in industry mix.

The most dramatic changes in urban labor markets, however, are those that have been taking place within each of them. The urban labor market is no longer limited to the central city, but today encompasses vast new outlying suburbs as well. Indeed, the central cities have been declining, while the suburbs have grown as a result of technological and demographic changes. Increased efficiency in agriculture has led to a vast migration of poorly educated and unskilled former farmers and farm workers to the central cities, and an out-migration from them to the suburbs of the more economically competent.

As a result of these changes, the urban labor market suffers from structural imbalances. The industries, particularly manufacturing, which used to provide jobs for the unskilled, have changed in character and are also moving out of the central city. Yet the poor continue to come to the cities, because that is where they can obtain housing. Furthermore, the poor cannot easily travel to suburban jobs, because they do not own automobiles and mass public transportation is not available.

The urban problem was compounded by the fact that the central city poor were increasingly becoming black. The plight of the black ghettos did not obtain national attention, however, until the riots of 1966–1967. The national commission that studied those riots found the prime cause to be unemployment and underemployment of disadvantaged minorities.

The nation is now aware of its "urban crisis," and all is not hopeless. Many of the cities still have strong economic advantages, and many of the new types of jobs opening up are as suitable for low-skilled people as those that have moved out. Among the proposed solutions to urban labor market problems, therefore, are dealing with rural poverty, moving jobs into the central city, moving people to where the jobs are, improving metropolitan transportation so that people in the central city can get to jobs in the suburbs, and labor market policies to create more well-paying jobs and increase the employability and upgrade the skills of present central city residents. Although each of these proposed remedies would be helpful, the last mentioned solution would seem to offer the best prospects of achievement, particularly in the short run.

BIBLIOGRAPHY

Birch, David L. *The Economic Future of City and Suburb.* CED Supplementary Paper No. 30. New York: Committee for Economic Development, 1970.

Brecher, Charles. *Upgrading Blue Collar and Service Workers.* Baltimore: Johns Hopkins Press, 1972.

Brown, Alan A., Egon Neuberger, and Malcolm Palmatier (eds.). *Perspectives in Economics.* New York: McGraw-Hill, 1971.

Fuchs, Victor R. *Hourly Earnings Differentials by Region and City Size, 1959.* Occasional Paper 101. New York: National Bureau of Economic Research, 1967.

Gallaway, Lowell E. *Manpower Economics.* Homewood, Ill.: Richard D. Irwin, 1971.

Hansen, Niles M. *Rural Poverty and the Urban Crisis.* Bloomington: Indiana University Press, 1970.

Harrison, Bennett. *Education, Training and the Urban Ghetto.* Baltimore: Johns Hopkins Press, 1972.

Hoover, Edgar M. *An Introduction to Regional Economics.* New York: Knopf, 1971.

Hoover, Edgar M., and Raymond Vernon. *Anatomy of a Metropolis.* Cambridge, Mass.: Harvard University Press, 1959.

Myrdal, Gunnar. *Challenge to Affluence.* New York: Pantheon, 1962.

Region in Transition. Report of the Economic Study of the Pittsburgh Region Conducted by the Pittsburgh Regional Planning Association. Pittsburgh: University of Pittsburgh Press, 1963.

Task Force on Employment Problems of Black Youth. *The Job Crisis for Black Youth.* New York: Praeger, 1971.

Thompson, Wilbur R. *A Preface to Urban Economics.* Baltimore: Johns Hopkins Press, for Resources for the Future, 1968.

17 EQUAL EMPLOYMENT OPPORTUNITY

Efficiency and equity are supposed to flow from the workings of a free labor market, and, despite shortcomings in the operation of labor markets in practice, this has largely been true. The free labor market, in which employees and employers compete among themselves, is probably more efficient than any other system of allocating labor. A major problem that has arisen, however, is that not all workers have been treated equally in the labor market, which amounts to a very denial of the principles of a free market. Some workers have found that they could not obtain employment or wages commensurate with their skills and ability because of discrimination against them on the basis of their ethnic background, age, or sex, and others have not had access to good jobs because previous discrimination had denied them the opportunity to acquire the education and skills that would have developed their potential abilities.

In this chapter, therefore, we turn our attention to the problems of racial and sex discrimination. We shall examine the history of discrimination, the attitudes of employers and unions, and the impact of discrimination on both its victims and the total society. Attempts to achieve equal employment opportunity, both through government programs and through action by those suffering from the lack of equal treatment, will also be surveyed. Finally, we shall look at recent efforts, such as employer programs to hire and train the disadvantaged and special government policies designed to further the goal of equal employment opportunity, and how effective they have been.

The History of Discrimination in the Labor Market

Discrimination: A Contradiction to Economic Principles

Racial, religious, age, and sex discrimination are contradictions to the principles of a free labor market. After all, the employer who refuses to hire the best-qualified worker is denying himself greater efficiency and profits. For the society, the misallocation of labor emanating from discrimination results in a smaller national income than could otherwise be achieved. It would only be natural to expect, therefore, that free competition would overcome individual prejudices and result in equal employment opportunity for all. Professor Friedman, a champion of laissez faire, has in fact argued that historically capitalism has been accompanied by a major reduction in discrimination against particular religious, racial, or social groups because of the "economic incentive in a free market to separate economic efficiency from other characteristics of the individual."[1]

In general, Friedman is right, for as we saw at the very beginning of this book, the free market system broke down the status system of medieval times. Men were no longer confined to following only their fathers' occupations, but many were able to move up the occupational and income ladder. Indeed, as was shown earlier, economic and social mobility have been relatively high in the United States.

Particular groups, however, have continued to suffer from discrimination in the labor market, and it seems that prejudice can overcome economic self-interest. Professor Becker has explained this contradiction of the free market by drawing an analogy between it and international trade.[2] The economic principle of comparative advantage indicates that free trade would yield a nation the highest possible national income, yet nations impose tariffs: they are willing to pay a price in order to have domestic production of certain goods. Similarly, the American people have been willing to pay a price (the Council of Economic Advisers estimated the loss in national income resulting from racial discrimination to have been about $13 billion in 1962) for the privilege of exercising their prejudices against certain minorities.

Groups Suffering from Discrimination

Almost all minority groups have suffered from discrimination in the labor market at one time or another. Catholics, Jews, and Orientals have borne their share, but, through a combination of their own persistent efforts and a decline in discrimination against them, they have made advances to the point where they can no longer be considered "disadvantaged" minorities. Today, however, some 5.0 million Americans of Mexican descent ("Chicanos"), largely in the Southwest, 1.5 million Puerto Ricans, mainly in eastern cities, and 650,000 American Indians, concentrated in the western states, still find themselves victims of discrimination and at a serious disadvantage in the labor market. But the largest group that has consistently borne the brunt of discrimination has been the black community, comprising some 22 million members. Without intending any slight of the plight of the other disadvantaged groups, therefore, our discussion of discrimination will focus on the blacks; much of what we say, however, will also apply to the others.[3]

Unlike other immigrant groups, blacks did not come to these shores

---

[1] Milton Friedman, *Capitalism and Freedom* (Chicago: University of Chicago Press, 1962), pp. 108, 109.

[2] Gary Becker, *The Economics of Discrimination* (Chicago: University of Chicago Press, 1958).

[3] For information on Chicanos, Puerto Ricans, and other Spanish-heritage groups, see Paul M. Ryscarage and Earl F. Mellor, "The Economic Situation of Spanish Americans," *Monthly Labor Review*, April 1973, pp. 3–9. According to their findings, low pay, high unemployment, few marketable skills, and a language barrier depress the incomes of Spanish Americans.

voluntarily in search of greater freedom and economic opportunity: they were brought, first to the colonies and then to the United States itself, as slaves. Following the Civil War the Thirteenth Amendment to the Constitution ended slavery and supposedly made blacks part of the free labor supply. As a result, in the past century there has been a tremendous rise in the economic status of black Americans: they have almost completely overcome illiteracy, moved out of farming and up the ladder of urban skills, and migrated to the North.[4] Yet the promise of equality has been unfulfilled, for blacks remain poorer than whites in general, they hold jobs that are concentrated on the bottom rungs of the occupational ladder, and large numbers of them are isolated in urban ghetto slums, outside the mainstream of American economic life.

The First Half Century of Black Freedom

In order to understand why this is so, let us trace, very briefly, the history of blacks in the labor market since the Civil War. The promises of the Reconstruction Period to the newly liberated blacks were quickly forgotten as the North, for reasons of political expediency, made its deals with the southern states, and the result was that "white supremacy" became the order of the day. De jure slavery was converted into de facto economic servitude as blacks were generally confined to back-breaking types of work, household service, tenant farming or being cotton field hands. The few blacks who went North for greater opportunity encountered prejudice and discrimination there, too. In fact, blacks, both North and South, who had been craftsmen, were largely driven out of the skilled trades after slavery was ended.

Other minorities had been able to advance despite discrimination against them because they were able to throw up entrepreneurs who would hire workers from their group or because they took advantage of public education to increase their skills, but blacks could not do so. In the South, where the mass of blacks was concentrated, the educational system provided them with inferior, inadequate, segregated schooling. Unfamiliarity with business, low incomes from which to save and accumulate capital, inability to borrow from white banks, and white hostility to the concept of black business, aside from funeral parlors and insurance companies to service their own communities, made it almost impossible for a black entrepreneurial class to arise. Finally, blacks could not even accumulate the political power to change things, because the southern states found all sorts of techniques to prevent them from exercising the franchise. Blacks in the North did have political rights, but at that time few blacks lived outside the South, so their limited numbers did not allow them to exert much political leverage.

---

[4] Marion Hayes, "A Century of Change: Negroes in the U.S. Economy 1860–1960," *Monthly Labor Review*, December 1962.

Progress since World War I

A significant breakthrough for black workers came during World War I. Immigration from Europe, which had been the major source of unskilled labor for industry, was cut off, and severe labor shortages led industry to let down the bars against hiring blacks. Of course, they were employed at the least skilled jobs, but industrial jobs did represent an advance, and blacks began to migrate North to take advantage of the new opportunities. With the end of labor shortage following the war, few new opportunities presented themselves, and many blacks lost the jobs they had gotten, but many of the beachheads that had been established were maintained. The depression decade of the 1930s was disastrous for everyone, but none more so than for the blacks: under conditions of severe labor surplus, blacks, who had traditionally stood at the end of the employment queue, were never reached in new hiring.

Under the impetus of the World War II labor shortage, blacks were hired in much greater numbers by industry and moved up to semiskilled operative jobs. Based upon his study of employment opportunities for blacks, Hiestand concluded that they were able to advance only in periods of labor shortage, such as wartime, and into job categories that were being forsaken by white workers who were moving up to higher levels.[5]

Continued economic growth after World War II, supplemented by an increasingly significant black vote in the North, more aggressive attitudes on behalf of their rights among blacks, and more liberal racial attitudes among whites, led to further job advances for blacks. Their gains, however, remained highly dependent upon the overall economic situation in the nation. With the setting in of a period of slow economic growth in the second half of the 1950s, which was combined with the structural changes discussed in the last chapter (suburbanization of manufacturing, changing job requirements), the relative status of blacks began to slide.[6] However, the return of rapid economic growth in the mid-1960s, reinforced by the rise of militant black protest and business concern with social unrest, led to renewed improvement in the black situation and breakthroughs into higher job categories.

The Results of Racial Discrimination

Many blacks have "made it": they are well educated, have stable family relationships, hold well-paying, meaningful jobs with opportunities for advancement, and own nice houses, albeit in segregated communities. Economically they are part of mainstream America. A disproportionate number of blacks, however, are not in such a favorable position, and remain at the end of the hiring line and at the bottom of the occupational ladder, and this is reflected in any type of black-white comparison.

---

[5] Dale Hiestand, *Economic Growth and Employment Opportunities for Minorities* (New York: Columbia University Press, 1964).

[6] See, for example, Alan B. Batchelder, "Decline in the Relative Income of Negro Men," *Quarterly Journal of Economics*, November 1964, pp. 511–524.

Jobs

Starting with jobs, the data reveal that no matter what the general level of unemployment is, the jobless rate of blacks is about twice as high as that of whites, as shown by Table 17.1. The unemployment statistics, moreover, hardly tell the whole story, for a much larger percentage of blacks than whites are among the "hidden unemployed," those who have become so discouraged about job prospects that they no longer seek them.

Table 17.1 Unemployment Rate by Race, United States, 1954–1972 (Percentage of Civilian Labor Force)

	Unemployment Rate		
Year	White	Nonwhite	Ratio (Nonwhite to White)
1954	5.0	9.9	2.0
1955	3.9	8.7	2.2
1956	3.6	8.3	2.3
1957	3.8	7.9	2.1
1958	6.1	12.6	2.1
1959	4.8	10.7	2.2
1960	4.9	10.2	2.1
1961	6.0	12.4	2.1
1962	4.9	10.9	2.2
1963	5.0	10.8	2.2
1964	4.6	9.6	2.1
1965	4.1	8.1	2.0
1966	3.3	7.3	2.2
1967	3.4	7.4	2.2
1968	3.2	6.7	2.1
1969	3.1	6.4	2.1
1970	4.5	8.2	1.8
1971	5.4	9.9	1.8
1972	5.0	10.0	2.0

SOURCE: U.S. Department of Labor, Bureau of Labor Statistics.

Blacks, moreover, are disproportionately concentrated in the less skilled occupations. Although they made up 11 percent of the employed population in 1970, they were only 7 percent of professional and technical workers; 4 percent of managers, officials, and proprietors; 8 percent of clerical employees; 4 percent of sales personnel; and 7 percent of craftsmen and foremen. On the other hand, they were 14 percent of all operatives, 23 percent of nonfarm laborers, 42 percent of private household workers, and 19 percent of other service workers.[7]

[7] *The Social and Economic Status of Negroes in the United States, 1970,* Bureau of Labor Statistics Report No. 394, *Current Population Reports,* Bureau of the Census, Series P-23, No. 38, July 1971, p. 61.

Earnings

Those blacks who do enter higher-paying occupations earn less than whites in those categories, largely because they hold the lower-level positions within them. The incomes of black, male professional and technical employees are only a little more than two-thirds of white males, and these differentials hold for all occupational categories; the incomes of nonwhite males as a percent of white males are clerical occupations, 84; craftsmen and foremen, 66; operatives, 70; laborers, 81; and service occupations, 76.

Family Income

Their labor market status is reflected in family income, and we find that, despite all the progress, the median family income of blacks in 1970 ($6,279) was, according to the U.S. Department of Commerce, only 61 percent that of whites.[8] To earn even this median income required more black wives to work than white wives. Less than one out of every ten black families had incomes of $15,000 and over, but almost one out of four white families had such incomes.

At the other end of the income distribution, about 1.4 million black families (29 percent of all black families), comprising 7.7 million persons (34 percent of the total black population), were below the poverty line in 1970. In that same year, only 8 percent of white families, comprising 10 percent of the total white population, were below the poverty line. Thus, the rate of poverty among blacks was three and one-quarter times as great as among whites. (About one-third of Chicanos also suffer from poverty, and among American Indians fully three-quarters do.)

The Effects of Poverty

Poverty, in turn, breeds other problems. Improper nutrition and inadequate medical care cause bad health. Marital disruptions increase, and in 1969 27.3 percent of all black families were female headed. Living in substandard housing, often without fathers present to serve as models, the children of the poor tend to become so discouraged that they either do badly in school or drop out completely. Men who have not had the experience of steady work find it difficult to establish stable work habits when they do get jobs, and as a result employers begin to regard them as unemployable. Some of these men give up looking for work: they drop out of the labor force. Unable to earn a living legitimately, many turn to "hustling" (illegal or semilegal means of earning income), to the use of drugs or alcohol, and eschew permanent relationships between the sexes, thus increasing the rate of illegitimacy and female-headed families.

---

[8] *Ibid.*, pp. 25–41.

Is There a "Culture of Poverty"?

Viewing this pattern of lower-class life among Puerto Ricans in San Juan and New York, Oscar Lewis advanced the concept of a "culture of poverty," by which he meant that the poor had a different life style from the typical middle-class culture and values.[9] The culture of poverty concept became a most discouraging thesis, and social workers began to point out three-generation welfare families; if the poor, rejected by American society, in turn rejected the middle-class values, there seemed to be little hope of ever bringing them into the mainstream of economic life.

Another sociologist—Lee Rainwater—has attacked the concept of a culture of poverty.[10] In his view, the behavior pattern of the lower classes comprises a strategy for survival under the circumstances they face, but they do attempt to move toward good-life and career-success strategies common to the middle classes. Although they often cannot make it on their own, the fact that they would want a "square" life offers the promise that programs to aid them, particularly with respect to jobs, could lead to breaking the poverty cycle.

Special Problems Facing Blacks

Some people argue that in time blacks, the same as other ethnic groups that started out in poverty, will climb the rungs of the economic ladder. Indeed, despite all the difficulties facing them, the majority of blacks have raised themselves above poverty, even if, on the average, not up to comparable levels with whites. A large segment of the black population, however, has migrated to the cities just when the cities were undergoing profound change in economic structure, and blacks do have, on the average, profound deficiencies in attempting to compete for jobs in an economy demanding a higher level of skills. Gallaway and Scully have advanced the hypothesis that differences in productivity may explain white-nonwhite income differentials.[11] Productivity differentials may in turn reflect past discrimination against blacks in terms of acquiring skills, education, and motivation.

Skill Deficiencies

Blacks are less skilled than whites. This is to be expected, since until recently they were denied the opportunity to learn skills. Skilled jobs were reserved

---

[9] Oscar Lewis, *La Vida: A Puerto Rican Family in the Culture of Poverty—San Juan and New York* (New York: Random House, 1966).

[10] Lee Rainwater, "A World of Trouble: The Pruett-Igoe Housing Project," in Robert E. Will and Harold G. Vatter (eds.), *Poverty in Affluence* (New York: Harcourt Brace Jovanovich, 1970), pp. 147–155. See also Rainwater, "Crucible of Identity: The Negro Lower Class Family," in Talcott Parsons and Kenneth B. Clark (eds.), *The Negro American* (Boston: Beacon Press, 1967), pp. 160–204.

[11] Lowell E. Gallaway and Gerald W. Scully, "An Economic Analysis of Minority Group Discrimination in the United States" (Chicago: Midwest Economic Association, April 1969).

for whites, and blacks were hired only for less-skilled work, the typical pattern being for employers to hire blacks into the labor pool, from which they could not advance to higher-level jobs. Moreover, unions in the building trades excluded blacks from apprenticeship training programs. When, in recent years, some employers were willing to upgrade black employees into the skilled trades, they found that many of them lacked the educational background to qualify them for the requisite training.

Educational Deficiencies

In an economy in which education is the major road to higher job status, the lesser educational attainment of blacks becomes an important factor in preventing their rise. Although the gap in years of schooling between blacks and whites has been greatly narrowed, it still exists, and was 1.1 years in 1969. The proportion of nonwhites with a high-school education (22 percent) was only half that of whites (43 percent), and with a college education (2.5 percent) less than one-third of whites (8.1 percent).

Even comparable numbers of years of schooling completed, however, does not tell the whole story, because traditionally the education afforded blacks has been inferior to that provided white children. Based upon the findings of the Coleman Report on education, one may conclude that one year of schooling for nonwhites is roughly equivalent to only three-quarters of a year of schooling for whites.[12] It is no wonder that black students test out at substantially lower levels than white youths: a full three years less, on the average, in the twelfth grade. Migration of blacks out of the South and out of agriculture has contributed to greater equality of income by color, but Gwartney contends that, at least recently, changes in scholastic achievement differentials between whites and nonwhites have helped to offset the positive impact of migration.[13]

Educated blacks do not do as well in the labor market as comparably educated whites. The median income of black men twenty-five to fifty-four years of age who were high-school graduates ($6,192) was only 70 percent of the income of white high-school graduates and, in fact, was almost $1,000 lower than that of whites who only completed elementary school ($7,018).[14] Similarly, black college graduates earned less than white high-school graduates. This reflected in part the inferiority of the education that many blacks had received, and hence their lower productivity (the Gallaway-Scully hypothesis); but beyond that it also indicated that blacks have suffered from discrimination in employment that denied them jobs in keeping with their abilities and training.

---

[12] J. S. Coleman, *Equality of Educational Opportunity* (Washington, D.C.: U.S. Office of Education, 1966).

[13] James Gwartney, "Changes in the Nonwhite/White Income Ratio—1939–67," *American Economic Review*, December 1970, pp. 872–883.

[14] *The Social and Economic Status of Negroes in the United States, 1970, op. cit.,* p. 34.

Discrimination

The results of discrimination prior to their entering the labor market tend to lower the productivity of blacks and hence make it more difficult for them to obtain jobs comparable to those that whites hold. But, even when their productivity is as high as whites, blacks suffer from discrimination in employment that denies them jobs commensurate with their abilities. Gwartney, for example, found that one-third to three-fifths of the nonwhite-white income differential could not be accounted for after adjustment of the productivity factors, and he suggests that this residual results largely from employment discrimination.[15] In a later article, however, he contended that the magnitude of the relative income gains of nonwhite urban males since 1939 suggests a decline, though a slight one, in the intensity of employment discrimination against them.[16]

Most studies have indicated that the impact of racial discrimination is least felt in the unskilled areas relative to the skilled, managerial, and professional. Yet Taylor has shown that discrimination also operates with respect to the least skilled jobs. Taylor studied the earnings of workers in two un-skilled male occupations—material handler and janitor—in a sample of eight establishments in the Chicago labor market. He found that blacks in these jobs received substantially less pay than whites, even when characteristics of the employing establishment (industry group, employment size, and location) and of the individual worker (age, education, seniority, prior work experience) were taken into account statistically.[17] Blacks, moreover, had to travel farther to their jobs than whites, further reducing their relative wages.

The earnings of black material handlers were quite low as compared to white material handlers, because they were disproportionately relegated to low-wage establishments. Blacks were not hired by the larger, higher-paying establishments, because the material handler job was considered an entry-level job from which men were promoted up the occupational ladder, but employers did not consider nonwhites promotable. Earnings differentials were not as high in the janitor occupation, since all establishments hired nonwhites as janitors, largely because this was both a traditional occupation for them and a dead-end job, not in the line of progression to better jobs. The main impact of discrimination in this instance was that the nonwhites supplied the employer with higher-quality personal characteristics than their white counterparts at the same wage.

---

[15] James Gwartney, "Discrimination and Income Differentials," *American Economic Review*, June 1970, pp. 396–408.

[16] James Gwartney, "Changes in the Nonwhite/White Income Ratio—1939–67," *op. cit.*

[17] David P. Taylor, "Discrimination and Occupational Wage Differences in the Market for Unskilled Labor," *Industrial and Labor Relations Review*, April 1968, pp. 375–390.

Motivation

Even when employers and unions end their discriminatory policies with respect to hiring and promoting of blacks, this cannot be expected to bring immediate comparability with whites in jobs and earnings. After decades of having been denied certain types of employment, blacks have learned to shun them. To a considerable degree, blacks have been demoralized by their treatment in the labor market. Conditioned not to be "uppity" and to "stay in their place," many blacks will not immediately respond to the opening of new opportunities. Blacks are not inherently less motivated than anyone else, but it takes time to prove to a group that has been denied access to better jobs that the situation has really changed. The engineering profession provides an interesting example of this problem.

Less than 1 percent of the nation's engineers are black, reflecting the fact that job opportunities for black engineers were extremely scarce historically. By the late 1960s employer attitudes had changed drastically, and many were anxious to hire black engineers, but there just were not enough to go around. Under this set of circumstances, one might have anticipated a flood of black students into engineering schools, but, on the contrary, they made up only 2 percent of the engineering student body. Deans of engineering schools, according to a study by Kiehl, attributed this to the lack of familiarity with engineering in the black community and to the history of discrimination against blacks, which continued to discourage them from entering the field.[18] Furthermore, the inferior primary and secondary education that black children receive, particularly in mathematics and the sciences, makes them poorly prepared for engineering colleges.

Union Attitudes and Behavior

As we saw in our survey of union history, the Knights of Labor had welcomed the blacks into its ranks, but when it was replaced by the American Federation of Labor as the dominant union organization, the situation changed. The problem was not the top leadership of the AFL, which called for equal treatment of workers regardless of race or religion, but the autonomy of the national unions. The decisive moment came in 1895, when the International Association of Machinists (IAM), which formally barred blacks from membership, was admitted to the AFL.[19] By 1930 about two dozen unions formally barred blacks from membership, and, since these unions were concentrated in the skilled trades in which they controlled the access to jobs, they effectively prevented blacks from acquiring those skills. The worst record was that of the railroad brotherhoods, which were not affiliated with the AFL:

---

[18] Robert Kiehl, *Opportunities for Blacks in the Profession of Engineering*, A Study Prepared for the Manpower Administration, U.S. Department of Labor (Newark: Foundation for the Advancement of Graduate Study in Engineering, 1970).

[19] An excellent history of unions and blacks is Ray Marshall, *The Negro and Organized Labor* (New York: Wiley, 1965).

the Railroad Trainmen, Locomotive Firemen, Locomotive Engineers, and Railway Conductors did not amend their constitutions to end the bar on black members until the 1960s, and the latter two, only after the Civil Rights Act of 1964 compelled them to do so.

The majority of unions, however, did admit blacks to membership. Some, such as the United Mine Workers, practiced no discrimination and admitted all workers in their jurisdictions to membership on an equal basis. Others did not accord blacks equal treatment, often placing them in auxiliary locals, usually covering lower-level types of jobs, and without equal voting rights.

The fact that a national union had no formal bar against blacks and did not place them in special locals did not necessarily mean that it would have many black members. In craft locals applicants for membership must often be proposed by other members, but blacks did not know any white members and so were never abe to become members. Even national unions that espoused equal opportunity found that local unions, which had a large degree of autonomy, thwarted their desires.

Under these conditions, a great antipathy arose between the black community and the trade unions. The situation began to change, however, with the rise of industrial unionism in the 1930s. The industrial unions could not have barred blacks from membership, even had they wanted to, because they did not control the supply of labor. Their aim was to organize all the workers in their industries, and, if this included blacks, they, too, had to be brought into the membership. The new industrial unions, moreover, were oriented to the interests of the semiskilled workers, who made up the bulk of their members, and blacks had moved into those types of jobs. Furthermore, the CIO unions were born in a spirit of social ferment that stressed broad progressive economic and social ideas.

Another factor explaining the difference in attitude and behavior with respect to racial discrimination between the craft and industrial unions was that the locals of the latter enjoyed much less autonomy. Even so, there were instances of southern locals in the industrial unions, although not legally segregated, in effect excluding blacks from active participation. Some locals, in the North as well as the South, negotiated separate seniority rosters for the labor grade jobs, into which blacks had originally been hired, and this served to prevent blacks from rising into higher-skilled positions, for they would have had to sacrifice all their accumulated seniority in order to do so.

In the main, however, the CIO and its unions were relatively free of racial discrimination, and, as the AFL unions had to compete with them for representation rights in secret ballot elections after the passage of the Wagner Act, many of them also shifted their behavior. The leaders of many national unions, both AFL and CIO, started to support the drives of blacks for equal rights, and the antipathy between the black community and the unions moderated. Walter Reuther, late president of the United Automobile Workers, for example, was a co-leader with Martin Luther King of the 1963 "March on Washington" that led to passage of the Civil Rights Act of 1964.

When the two federations of labor merged in 1955 to form the AFL-CIO, the new organization's constitution required that affiliated unions be free of discrimination. The fact that the national unions are autonomous, however, has prevented the top leadership from eradicating covert discrimination, but it has scored some successes in getting unions to extend membership and equal treatment to blacks and other minorities. Serious problems remain in the craft unions, particularly in the building trades, and it is only under pressure from civil rights groups and the government that blacks have been making significant breakthroughs into those areas of employment.

Employer Attitudes and Behavior

If the union record with respect to racial discrimination has been poor, that of employers has not been much better. After all, aside from a few skilled trades, employers had complete control of hiring policies, and few if any blacks ever got jobs in many industries. The fear of union reaction, moreover, could not be used as an excuse for not hiring blacks, for until the 1930s basic industry remained unorganized. That is not to say that employers who pioneered in hiring blacks, such as the International Harvester Company, did not encounter strikes against their nondiscriminatory policies, but firm company policy was able to overcome the white worker opposition. To this day, moreover, it is the largely nonunion textile industry that has the worst record with respect to discrimination against blacks.

Employer behavior with respect to hiring of blacks was not due solely to racial discrimination. According to Gallaway, "Specifically, the evidence which indicates a more than passing degree of consistency between wage and productivity effects of nonwhite employment implies that there is an economic rationale on the part of employers for the exclusionary and apparently discriminatory practices in which they engaged."[20] Since blacks entered the labor market with severe educational and other deficiencies, they simply could not compete equally with white workers for available jobs.

Very often employers refrained from hiring blacks because of real or imagined fears of the reactions of white workers. As late as 1959 a study urging companies to hire more black employees was replete with advice to employers on how gradually to introduce blacks into their work forces without arousing the hostility of white workers.[21] It was only in periods of labor shortage, as we have seen, that employers sufficiently overcame their fears of white worker reaction to hire and upgrade blacks.

A few large employers, such as the International Harvester Company and the Ford Motor Company, began hiring blacks many decades ago, and over the years others also did so. In fact, black organizations, such as the NAACP

---

[20] Lowell E. Gallaway, *Manpower Economics* (Homewood, Ill.: Richard D. Irwin, 1971), p. 176.

[21] Paul H. Norgren *et al.*, *Employing the Negro in American Industry* (New York: Industrial Relations Counselors, 1959).

and the National Urban League, cemented close relationships with employer groups and looked toward them for leadership in ending discrimination in employment. But very few employers hired blacks for jobs other than in the unskilled laborer categories, and soon it became the tradition that these were the preserve of black workers while all higher-level jobs belonged to whites. Given the general tone of white attitudes, many employers undoubtedly honestly believed that such jobs represented the extent of black worker abilities, and others simply did not want to rock the boat by stirring white worker reaction, particularly when there were plenty of white workers around to fill their labor needs. Such attitudes, however, broke down further under the impetus of the labor shortages of World War II.

Attitudes and behavior toward blacks continued to improve in the postwar period, but only gradually. High levels of employment, without the interruption of prolonged or deep recessions, led employers to hire more blacks and to upgrade some of them. Then, in the 1960s, under the pressure of black protest and government coercion, employers began to adopt genuine equal employment opportunity programs, and blacks started to make rapid progress. Special programs to hire and train the disadvantaged, which we shall look at shortly, were undertaken.

Despite all these efforts, there is a long road yet to be traveled in extending equal opportunities in the labor market to blacks and other minorities; most of the efforts have come in the larger, more visible companies, which either depend upon government contracts, such as defense equipment producers, or those that manufacture consumer products for which the black market is significant. Smaller companies, which in total provide the majority of the jobs in the economy, have a much poorer record with respect to equal employment. Even the progress that has been made in hiring has been confined to the lower-level jobs, and much remains to be done to move blacks into skilled, professional, and managerial jobs.

Having examined the attitudes and behavior of labor and employers with respect to racial discrimination in employment, it is only logical to turn next to that of government, both in terms of legislation and administrative action. Before doing so, however, we must interrupt the discussion of racial discrimination to focus on another type of discrimination—sex discrimination—for women, too, have not enjoyed equal status and treatment in the labor market.

Discrimination against Women

Females can hardly be considered to be a minority, for they slightly outnumber men in the population. In the labor force, however, they have been a minority, though a rapidly growing one, and they, too, have not been accorded equal treatment, being confined to specific types of occupations, refused opportunities for advancement, and often paid less than men for similar work. The median wage or salary income of full-time year-round women workers has been only 60 percent that of men for the past decade, and this represented a

Table 17.2 Median Income in 1969 of Full-Time Year-Round Workers, by Years of School Completed (Persons 25 Years of Age and Over)

Years of school completed	Income		Women's income as percentage of Men's
	Women	Men	
Elementary school			
Less than 8 years	$3,603	$5,769	62.5
8 years	3,971	7,147	55.6
High school			
1–3 years	4,427	7,958	55.6
4 years	5,280	9,100	58.0
College			
1–3 years	6,137	10,311	59.5
4 years	7,396	12,960	57.1
5 years or more	9,262	13,788	67.2

SOURCE: U.S. Department of Commerce, Bureau of the Census, *Current Population Reports,* P–60, No. 75.

decline from 64 percent in the mid-1950s. As Table 17.2 indicates, moreover, this cannot be explained in terms of educational differentials, since women with comparable years of schooling earned considerably less than men, on the average, at all levels. Let us, therefore, explore the possible reasons for these differentials.

Role Differentiation

In an analysis of earnings differences between men and women, Fuchs found them to be much larger—about 40 percent—for equal years of schooling than the differential between whites and blacks. Even adjusting for length of trip to work, marital status, and class of worker only reduced the differential to 33 percent. Fuchs attributed little of this differential to employer discrimination in the labor market; on the contrary, he hypothesized that it could be explained by the different roles assigned to men and women, which affects their choice of occupation, labor force attachment, location of work, postschool investment, hours of work, and other variables that influence earnings.[22]

Thus, women earn less than men mainly because they are employed in the lower-paying, less-skilled job categories within all occupational levels.[23] Women tend to train for elementary school teaching rather than college professorships, for being laboratory technicians rather than research scientists, and for being nurses rather than physicians. How much of the differences are due to inherent factors and how much to social conditioning is a matter of debate, but there is no doubt that girls are virtually trained from birth by their parents and society in general for playing the role of homemaker, whereas

[22] Victor R. Fuchs, "Differences in Hourly Earnings Between Men and Women," *Monthly Labor Review*, May 1971, pp. 9–15.

[23] See, for example, Malcolm S. Cohen, "Sex Differences in Compensation," *Journal of Human Resources*, Fall 1971, pp. 434–447.

boys are trained for assumption of the role of family income provider in maturity.

Changing Attitudes

The idea of women pursuing independent careers grew only very slowly. Women even lacked the power to change their conditions, for they were economically dependent upon their husbands and were denied the right to vote. The spread of industrialism and urbanism, however, with its impact on the attitudes and values of society, started to change things. Increased schooling, smaller families, and labor-saving devices for housework, among other things, freed women for greater participation in the labor force. At the same time the rise of new fields of economic activity, particularly the growth of white-collar employment, greatly increased the demand for female workers. As more women became workers, values changed still more, and soon there arose a militant female protest movement (Suffragettes), which finally won them the right to vote in 1920.

By the 1970s there had arisen a new militant protest movement— Women's Liberation—which sought equality for women in all aspects of life. We cannot in this book concern ourselves with the broad aspects of this question, but one must recognize that there is inherent conflict between a woman as homemaker and as a pursuer of a career. Perhaps the pattern of the future will be a dual-career family, in which husband and wife work on an egalitarian basis, both at their outside jobs and at home.[24] We, however, must confine our discussion to those aspects of women's rights which relate directly to their behavior and treatment in the labor market. In this respect, there have been profound changes in the past half century.

Women in the Labor Force

Nearly 31 million, or 42 percent, of American women sixteen years old and over were in the labor force in January 1970 as compared to only 8.2 million, or 23 percent of working-age women, in January 1920.[25] The continual shift from goods-producing to the service-producing industries had expanded many times the employment opportunities of women. Another significant difference was that in 1920 the typical woman employee was single, about twenty-eight years old, and from the working class, but by 1970 most women workers were married, half were over thirty-nine years old, and they came from all social classes. Three-quarters of the women workers held full-time jobs.

There was substantial evidence, however, that despite all their progress women were not accorded equal treatment in employment. The great majority

---

[24] For interesting suggestions along these lines, see, for example, Michael P. Fogarty, Rhona Rapoport, and Robert N. Rapoport, *Sex, Career, and Family* (London: Allen & Unwin, 1971).

[25] Elizabeth Waldman, "Changes in the Labor Force Activity of Women," *Monthly Labor Review*, June 1970, pp. 10–18.

of them were concentrated in occupations in which women employees predominate over men: domestic service, teaching, clerical work, nursing, and retail sales. Of the more than 250 distinct occupations listed in Bureau of Census data, half of all women workers were employed in only 21 of them in 1969.[26] One-quarter were employed in five occupations: secretary-stenographer, household worker, bookkeeper, elementary school teacher, and waitress. To a very large degree, women were employed in jobs that amounted to extensions of the work that they had done in the home, such as instructing children, caring for the sick, preparing and serving food, textile weaving and sewing, and cleaning.

Explanations for Women's Status in the Labor Market

A number of factors help to explain this employment concentration of women. As activities such as the manufacture of clothing moved out of the home and into the factory, workers were needed, and a natural source was women who were experienced in hand and machine sewing from their home chores. While rising demand helps to explain the rush of women into occupations that amounted to extensions of home work and into clerical work, a number of factors discouraged entry of women into other occupations. Being considered the weaker sex, women neither sought nor were considered for jobs that required strenuous physical efforts; in fact, early state protective legislation did not permit the employment of women in jobs involving the lifting or carrying of heavy weights. As a result, the construction trades and all types of heavy manufacturing, such as steel production, were automatically closed to women. Since women did not seek lifetime work careers, occupations requiring long periods of preparation were not attractive to them, nor were employers willing to invest in the training of people who might soon leave.

The fact that women have, on the average, a more tenuous attachment to the labor force than men has thus deterred employers from hiring them for some types of jobs that required a heavy investment in training. When employers do hire women for jobs involving substantial training expenses, they tend to pay them less than men and, in that way, secure the same return on the investment in training. Gallaway suggests that female and male labor inputs into the productive process are not homogeneous,[27] for there are objective economic costs associated with the employment of women, thus justifying earnings differentials. Yet, the actual differential was significantly greater than the differences in productivity, which means that employers do discriminate against women solely on the basis of their sex.

Extending Occupational Opportunities for Women

Extending the occupational opportunities of women would not only fulfill the requirement of equity but also that of efficiency in the allocation of labor.

---

[26] Janice Neipert Hedges, "Women Workers and Manpower Demands in the 1970's," *ibid.*, pp. 19–29.
[27] Gallaway, *op. cit.*, pp. 197–200.

If women are capable of performing higher-level jobs, as skilled craftsmen, professionals, or managers, but are confined to factory assembly jobs or office clerical positions, then the entire economy operates below its potential level of performance. The nation, for example, is suffering from a shortage of physicians, and has had to depend on foreign-trained personnel to maintain many of its hospitals. Yet, only 21,000 physicians are women, and they comprise a bare 7 percent of all physicians, a percentage that is far below that of many other nations. Of twenty-nine nations reporting to the Tenth Congress of the Medical Women's International Association, only three (South Vietnam, Madagascar, and Spain), all at much lower levels of economic development, had smaller proportions of women physicians. In Finland, Israel, and the Philippines one-fourth of all physicians are women, and in the Soviet Union two-thirds are.

The situation with respect to other professions is still worse. Women make up only 2 percent of all dentists in the United States, and less than 1 percent of the engineers. Yet a study of eleventh-grade students conducted by the U.S. Department of Labor found that 8 percent of the girls (and 12 percent of the boys) had engineering aptitude. The situation in the skilled trades was the same, for only 3 percent of craftsmen in 1968 were women. Again, however, the eleventh-grade aptitude tests revealed that the requisite combination of aptitudes for many of the crafts occurred as frequently among girls as boys.

If we add the losses to the economy resulting from sex discrimination to those emanating from racial discrimination, we find that the nation pays a very high price for its prejudices. Attitudes with respect to both types of discrimination, however, have been changing, as reflected by the rise of movements to correct the situation and government action to further the goals of equal employment opportunity, so we shall examine these next.

The Civil Rights Movement

The first civil rights movement in the United States was that of the abolitionists, who for the three decades preceding the Civil War agitated against slavery. Only a small number of whites had been antislavery, and during the Reconstruction period following the Civil War, the number of whites committed to racial equality dwindled further.[28] The burden of the struggle fell to the blacks themselves, who in 1890 organized the Afro-American League of the United States to fight for political rights and more equitable distribution of school funds. In 1905 a group of young black intellectuals, led by W. E. B. DuBois, launched the Niagara Movement, with similar goals. From the Niagara Movement emerged the National Association for the Advancement of Colored People in 1909 and the National Urban League in 1910, both of which had white support.

While the new, militant NAACP fought for equal rights, the Urban

---

[28] John Hope Franklin, "The Two Worlds of Race: A Historical View," in Parsons and Clark, *op. cit.*, pp. 47–70.

League sought to ease the transition of southern rural blacks into an urban way of life as they began to migrate to the cities.[29] Much of its stress, therefore, was on labor market policies: securing jobs and training blacks to fill them. It courted the white community, particularly the business community, for that was the source of job opportunities.

Through his leadership of the 1955–1956 Montgomery, Alabama, boycott against segregation on buses, Martin Luther King became the outstanding spokesman of the black community, particularly in the South. The days of black passivity in the face of injustice were coming to an end, being replaced by militant protest, though under King's leadership that protest emphasized nonviolence. Although the civil rights movement emphasized protest against segregation in public facilities and denial of legal rights to blacks, it inevitably spilled over to labor market questions. The existing groups, plus many new ones that arose, conducted demonstrations against building projects that refused to employ blacks or merely employed a token number of them, and picketed the headquarters or boycotted the products of companies they believed were not being fair to blacks in employment. Some even moved into the area of labor relations, and Martin Luther King was assassinated while in Memphis, Tennessee, to rally support for striking garbage workers.

In part inspired by the blacks, other disadvantaged minorities also threw up their own protest organizations. Cesar Chavez electrified the 5 million Mexican-American community, concentrated in the southwestern states, when he led a successful strike ("La Huelga") and boycott by grape pickers in California. In addition to the union, a number of Chicano organizations, of varying degrees of militancy, are attempting to secure equal treatment for Chicanos, particularly with respect to jobs. American Indians, the original inhabitants of the western hemisphere, have also organized and are fighting for better treatment.

Women, too, are no longer accepting their status, and under the slogan of "women's liberation" have mounted a campaign for equality. The aims of the women's lib groups are quite varied, but the largest of them, the National Organization of Women (NOW), is quite active with respect to the labor market. It has a division concerned with federal contract compliance to ensure that women are accorded equal employment opportunities, and it has been putting pressure on unions as well as employers for equal treatment.

Government Actions on Behalf of Equal Employment Opportunity

Voluntary action has been important in advancing equal employment opportunity, but there is no question, however, that neither employers nor unions would have moved as far as they have without government coercion. Government action, however, was also slow in coming, and aside from the abortive attempts of the early Reconstruction period, none was forthcoming for the

---

[29] Kenneth B. Clark, "The Civil Rights Movement: Momentum and Organization," *ibid.,* pp. 595–625.

first three-quarters of a century following the Civil War. It was only as the United States tooled up for World War II that the federal government took action on behalf of equal employment opportunity, and then only under threat of black protest.

The Fair Employment Practices Committee

In the interests of utilizing all available manpower resources, the National Defense Advisory Commission in 1941 set forth a nondiscriminatory employment policy for minority groups in defense industries.[30] Since no machinery to enforce such a policy was established, many feared that industry would simply ignore it and the policy would turn out to be nothing but a pious wish. When A. Philip Randolph, president of the all-black Brotherhood of Sleeping Car Porters, AFL, began to organize a "march on Washington," the Roosevelt administration entered into negotiations with black leaders. The result was that the march was called off in exchange for Executive Order 8802, which decreed that there should be no discrimination in employment in defense industries based on race, color, creed, or national origin, and established the Fair Employment Practices Committee (FEPC) to enforce compliance.

According to Means, powerful pressures from newspapers, Congress, and government officials caused the committee to crumble from within, but counterpressures by liberal, labor, and minority groups led to Executive Order 9345 in 1943, which created a new FEPC as an independent agency. How effective the FEPC was in opening employment opportunities to blacks, Chicanos, and others is a matter of dispute, but the very existence of the committee was seen as a threat by those who wanted to prevent blacks from advancing, and by 1945 Congress appropriated only enough money for it to wind up its affairs within one year. It took another fifteen years before there was a new coordinated government-wide effort to promote equal employment.

State Legislation

With southern power in Congress blocking federal legislation, the struggle for equal employment turned to the state level. The first gains were scored in 1945, when the states of New York and New Jersey passed fair employment practices laws. By the time the federal Civil Rights Act was passed in 1964, more than half the states and more than fifty major cities had adopted fair employment practices ordinances.

Although the state laws vary in application, administration, and enforcement procedures, most of them are modeled on the original New York antidiscrimination act. Typically, therefore, they make it unlawful for an

---

[30] John E. Means, "Fair Employment Practices Legislation and Enforcement in the United States," *International Labour Review*, March 1966.

employer, labor organization, or employment agency to discriminate in hiring, in accepting into membership, or in advertising jobs on the basis of race, creed, color, or national origin. A majority of the state laws are administered by independent commissions, but only the New York commission is a full-time body.[31] The administration bodies investigate complaints of discrimination, attempt to eliminate such practices through conciliation and persuasion, hold hearings with respect to complaints, and issue cease-and-desist orders, enforceable in the Courts, against unlawful employment practices.

Many state FEPC commissions have been hampered in their work by inadequate budgets and staff to do a really effective job. Yet Norgren and Hill concluded that, if effectively administered, fair employment practices legislation could be a "potent instrument for combating discrimination in employment," pointing to the records of the long-established commissions in New York, New Jersey, Philadelphia, and other jurisdictions.

How much impact the state laws have had overall, however, is open to serious question. The burden of proof of discrimination falls upon the complainant, and in practice it is difficult to produce sufficient evidence except in cases of blatant discrimination. Finally, despite all the breakthroughs made, the data on employment, upgrading, and earnings show that blacks and other minorities continue to lag far behind whites and are yet to be accorded equal treatment in the labor market.

Federal Government Activities, 1946–1963

The demise of the federal FEPC in 1946 did not mean that the government completely abandoned fighting discrimination in employment. On the contrary, presidents Truman, Eisenhower, and Kennedy each took actions designed to further the goal of equal employment. President Truman issued a series of executive orders to ensure that the federal government itself would follow a nondiscriminatory policy with respect to employment, and as a result blacks began to find their best employment opportunities with the federal civil service. And executive orders of President Eisenhower established the President's Committee on Government Contracts, which sought to eliminate employment discrimination by private firms working for the government.

The Kennedy administration, which took office in 1961, adopted a more aggressive approach to equal employment. Executive Order 10925 established the President's Committee on Equal Employment Opportunity and put teeth into the antidiscrimination effort by providing for the use of sanctions, such as cancellation of contracts, against government contractors not complying. Even so, a recent study of the occupational standing of blacks relative to whites in 1966 found that blacks had lower than average occupation status in industries that specialize in federal government contracting, indicating that

---

[31] For a review of state laws, see Paul H. Norgren and Samuel E. Hill, *Toward Fair Employment* (New York: Columbia University Press, 1964).

enforcement of existing laws and orders "is pathetically lax."[32] President Nixon's reorganization of the Office of Federal Contract Compliance (OFCC) in 1972 brought charges from the NAACP and others that the net result was a serious weakening of the effort to enforce equal employment regulations among government contractors.

The PCEEO also undertook to promote a voluntary program (Plans for Progress) to get companies and unions to follow nondiscriminatory practices and increase the number of minority workers. More than three hundred companies participated in the program, and significant success in advancing job opportunities for minorities was reported. How much of that success was due to the program or reflected business's concern with rising black militancy, preserving social tranquility, and reaction to government pressure is difficult to determine. A comparison of minority group (black and Puerto Rican) white-collar workers employed in New York City by companies participating in the Plans for Progress program and those not participating revealed a higher increase in 1967 among the latter than the former.[33]

The Civil Rights Act of 1964

Following an August 1963 "March on Washington for Jobs and Freedom," led by Martin Luther King, Congress passed the Civil Rights Act of 1964, the most comprehensive piece of antidiscrimination legislation the nation has ever had. Title VII of the act, which became effective in mid-1965, deals with discrimination in employment. It makes it unlawful for a private employer of twenty-five or more employees to discriminate against an individual in hiring, firing, promotion, compensation, or working conditions on the basis of his race, color, religion, sex, or national origin. Labor unions were forbidden to exclude minorities from membership, or to segregate them in such a way as to deny them employment opportunities, or to cause employers to discriminate. Employment agencies were also prohibited from following discriminatory practices, such as refusing to refer minority group members for employment. Neither employers nor employment agencies, in advertising for jobs, could indicate any preference based on race, color, religion, sex, or national origin, except where that might constitute a bona fide occupational qualification, as, for example, a minister for a church.

The act created the five-man Equal Employment Opportunity Commission (EEOC) to administer the provisions of Title VII. The commission has the power to conduct studies of employment practices and to receive complaints of discrimination and attempt to settle them through informal conference, conciliation, and persuasion. If such measures are not successful, the aggrieved individual may bring a civil action in the federal district court,

---

[32] Barbara R. Bergmann and Jerolyn R. Lyle, "The Occupational Standing of Negroes by Areas and Industries," *Journal of Human Resources*, Fall 1971, pp. 411–433.

[33] "White Collar Employment in 100 Major New York City Corporations" (Washington, D.C.: Equal Employment Opportunity Commission, January, 1968).

which may issue an injunction against the discriminating party. The Attorney General may also intervene in cases of public importance. Initial compliance enforcement is left to state commissions in those states that have fair employment practices laws.

Although the enforcement procedures are cumbersome, progress has been achieved under the provisions of the Civil Rights Act of 1964. The act immediately caused the two unions that still officially barred blacks from membership—the Locomotive Engineers and the Railway Conductors—to amend their constitutions to end that exclusion. More importantly, it forced employers and employment agencies to scrutinize all their policies to make sure that they were in compliance with the law. Companies, for example, had to review their employment testing programs for relevancy and fairness.

Enforcement of Title VII

The need for review of testing programs became even more crucial as a result of the 1971 U.S. Supreme Court decision in the Duke Power Co. case, which declared illegal employment tests and practices that effectively discriminate against blacks although adopted without intent to do so. In another 1971 decision the U.S. Court of Appeals for the first time outlawed transfer and seniority provisions of labor-management collective bargaining agreements that violate Title VII. In this case the Bethlehem Steel Company and the United Steelworkers of America were ordered to permit black employees to transfer from "hotter and dirtier" jobs in the plant to higher-paying and cleaner jobs with no loss in seniority or pay.

The executive branch has played the most important role in furthering equal employment opportunity. During the Johnson administration, enforcement of Title VII and of the executive orders barring discrimination by government contractors was quite vigorous. The Nixon administration pushed further in trying to get blacks into the skilled building trades, evolving mandatory programs of the Philadelphia Plan type. Such a program, first applied in Philadelphia, requires companies bidding on federally funded construction projects to promise to try to hire a specific percentage of minority workers. In other cities demonstrations by blacks have forced the contractors and unions to voluntarily agree to hire more minority workers (Chicago Plan), but these have been reported to be less successful, inducing the government to institute mandatory programs.[34] A third approach to increasing minority participation in the construction trades is through efforts to recruit and train minority group people for entry into the skilled trades.

Despite some notable judicial and administrative victories, minority group spokesmen were dissatisfied with the cumbersome enforcement procedures of Title VII. They wanted the EEOC to be authorized to issue its own orders barring discrimination, rather than relying on lawsuits by aggrieved individuals. Compromise legislation passed in 1972 gave the EEOC the power

---

[34] *The New York Times,* June 27, 1971.

to seek federal court orders against employers or unions practicing job discrimination. The amendment also extended coverage of Title VII to 15 million more jobs by applying it to employers of fifteen or more employees.

The Law and Women

Equal employment for women has also been furthered by court interpretations of Title VII. The one legal basis allowed for sex discrimination is where sex is a "bona fide occupational qualification" for a job, but the courts have severely restricted its use. In one case, for example (*Weeks v. Southern Bell*), involving a woman who wanted a job as a switchman with a telephone company, the United States Court of Appeals for the Ninth Circuit held that the employer had the burden of proving that substantially all women could not perform the job safely and efficiently.

The courts have invalidated employer requirements that women employees in certain jobs remain unmarried. They have also held employers liable for awards of back pay to women who were prevented from working overtime or denied employment in better-paid job classifications because of their sex.[35]

Strides toward equal employment practices for women have also been achieved through the Equal Pay Act of 1963, which requires equal pay for equal work, regardless of sex. The coverage of the act is roughly equivalent to that of the Fair Labor Standards Act, and, while this restricts its scope, it gives it the advantage of the much stronger administrative and enforcement procedures of the FLSA.[36] The Wage and Hour Division of the U.S. Department of Labor treats complaints in strict confidence, and court action is not required unless an employer appeals or refuses to obey a back-pay award of the division. In the Wheaton Glass case the U.S. Court of Appeals ruled that jobs must be only "substantially equal," not "identical," to permit job comparisons under the act; there must be a rational explanation for the amount of wage differential, and the employer bears the burden of providing it; and the employer's past history, if any, of unequal pay practices is an important factor in determining whether there has been a violation of the act.

Discrimination Because of Age

Before leaving the subject of antidiscrimination legislation to examine employer programs to hire and train the disadvantaged, mention must be made of another type of discrimination: that based upon age. The statistical evidence indicates that the disadvantages of older workers in the labor market are very far from as great as those suffered by ethnic minorities or women, but that they do exist. For many reasons, such as potential years of service and, hence, return on investments in training, alleged higher pension and

---

[35] *The New York Times,* July 13, 1971.

[36] Robert D. Moran, "Reducing Discrimination: Role of the Equal Pay Act," *Monthly Labor Review,* June 1970, pp. 30–34.

insurance costs for older workers, and the claim that ability to learn new tasks declines with age, employers have tended to favor hiring younger workers for many types of jobs. Workers over forty years of age, therefore, sometimes find themselves at a serious disadvantage in the labor market, particularly when their jobs disappear and they must compete with younger workers for new employment.

These problems of older workers apply whether they are semiskilled factory operatives or highly trained professional engineers. Studies of the impact of technological change on blue-collar workers, for instance, have shown that men in their late forties and early fifties, who were too young to qualify for retirement, were rarely able to find new jobs that were comparable in pay to those from which they had been displaced. The problem may be even more acute for professionals, because they are not as up to date with the latest advances in knowledge in their fields as the younger men and women, more recently out of college. Thus, many mature engineers who were laid off as a result of the defense and aerospace cutbacks of the early 1970s concluded that they would never find new jobs as engineers and had to seek new and, almost invariably, lower-paying careers.

In order to protect older workers from outright discrimination in the labor market, a number of the state fair employment practices laws also banned discrimination on the basis of age. On the federal level, the Age Discrimination in Employment Act of 1967 protects most individuals over age forty until they reach the sixty-fifth birthday. These laws, however, are limited in their effectiveness, because it is extremely difficult to prove that one has been discriminated against in employment because of age.

Private Programs to Hire and Train the Disadvantaged

During the second half of the 1960s, the racial riots that shook the nation's cities shocked American business and union leaders into action to ameliorate the conditions confronting the disadvantaged minorities. Concern with the very viability of American society, combined with growing federal government pressure and a tight labor market, led some companies—most of them large corporations with sophisticated managements—to develop comprehensive programs to open job opportunities to the disadvantaged. A number of unions have also conducted special training programs for the disadvantaged, but, since most hiring and training is under employer control, we shall briefly review some of the corporate programs.[37]

---

[37] Most of the material in this section is based on unpublished information, compiled by the staff of Industrial Relations Counselors, Inc., which was provided by more than forty companies that were actively engaged in "equal opportunity" programs. The author expresses his appreciation to IRC for permission to use some of its source material. Other sources of information on this subject include "Management Experiences in Dealing with the Disadvantaged," *Proceedings of the 1968 Annual Spring Meeting* (Madison, Wisc.: Industrial Relations Research Association, 1968), pp. 453–481, and Peter B. Doeringer (ed.), *Programs to Employ the Disadvantaged* (Englewood Cliffs, N.J.: Prentice-Hall, 1969).

By the mid-1960s, many corporations had discovered that simply announcing a policy of hiring the best-qualified people—regardless of race, creed, or color—did not in fact result in equal opportunity. On the contrary, a true policy of equal employment called for positive actions to help disadvantaged minorities overcome the handicaps imposed by poverty, inadequate education, and cultural isolation.

Programs to Hire the "Hard Core"

Once outright discrimination was abolished, companies turned to programs to increase the proportion of blacks and other minority members in their work forces and to encourage their promotion into supervisory positions. Programs to hire qualified minority group members are of little special interest; presumably, companies should have been doing that all along. Of interest, on the other hand, are those programs to hire members of the "hard core"—chronically unemployed people, or people regarded as unemployable under normal hiring standards—and to equip them to become useful and self-supporting members of society. Companies undertaking such efforts found that extensive changes were necessary to reach the so-called hard-core unemployed and help them to overcome the emotional and practical barriers to successful employment. Companies also found that some traditional hiring standards, interviewing techniques, and preemployment tests were screening out minority applicants capable of becoming valuable employees.

To reach minority applicants, normal recruitment efforts were extended to include advertisements in black community newspapers and magazines, Spanish-language publications, and radio stations and television channels that are popular in minority communities. Recruiters also got help from public and private organizations that specialize in minority employment problems, such as the Urban League and the National Alliance of Businessmen.

The Ford Experience

Ford Motor Company, faced with an unusually large number of job vacancies at the end of the long UAW strike in the fall of 1967, conducted an extensive inner city recruiting program for its plants in the Detroit area. The labor relations staff arranged with the Mayor's Committee for Human Resources Development (MCHRD) to use interviewing and physical examination facilities at its two large employment centers on the east and west sides of Detroit, where large numbers of hard-core unemployed had already been registered under a Michigan Employment Security Commission program.

Twelve experienced company industrial relations representatives were specially trained for interviewing disadvantaged job applicants, and a written test normally required for all applicants was temporarily suspended. Interviewers spent approximately one-half hour with each applicant, personnel were made available to help applicants complete employment forms, and physical examinations were performed at the centers, at company expense.

Successful candidates were hired on the spot, and were offered a choice of plants at which there were openings. The newly hired were given bus tickets for the first two weeks of employment if they had no personal means of transportation, and those who lacked funds could obtain pay advances of $5 for each of the first two weeks to enable them to buy meals in company cafeterias.

According to company officials, the Ford program was remarkably successful. The retention rate of these former unemployables was about the same as for other employees who had applied for jobs directly at the same plants during the same period. Comments received from plant managers indicated that their attendance was as good as, and at some plants even better than, that of the rest of the production work force. Plant management found that their attitudes and abilities, in general, compared favorably with those of others hired in the Detroit area in that period. Similarly, R. Heath Larry, a U.S. Steel Corporation executive, reported favorable experience and a better retention rate for the five thousand unqualified unemployed that his company had hired and trained under the Job Opportunities in the Business Sector (JOBS) program than for gate hires.[38]

Changes in Selection Criteria

In their efforts to open more job opportunities to candidates from minority groups, many companies reevaluated their normal selection criteria, especially for entry-level jobs. There was no valid reason, for instance, why a worker engaged in a mechanical assembly operation had to be a high school graduate. Some companies also suspended long-standing rules requiring that applicants with arrest records be automatically rejected. To make sure that no part of the screening process was weighted against people who are different in skin color, speech patterns, or ways of dressing, companies also gave special attention to the selection and training of interviewers, and included minority group members among them.

Tests were scrutinized for job-relatedness, and some companies did not use them at all in selecting hard-core candidates, preferring to rely on the judgment of a skilled interviewer to identify those with the aptitude and motivation to succeed in whatever training program was contemplated. Standard Oil Company of California reported considerable success with this approach. Over a period of one year its Richmond, California, refinery hired fifty-five "hard-core unemployables," using no preemployment testing, but giving them classroom training during the first eight weeks on payroll. One year later thirty-five of the former "unemployables" were still with the company, and a number of them had already been promoted to higher-level jobs; thirteen had resigned voluntarily, and only seven had been terminated for cause.

---

[38] R. Heath Larry, "Putting Steel in the JOBS Program," *Manpower*, October 1971, pp. 6–10.

Training

A large portion of the unemployed minority groups had such severe educational deficiencies that they were unable to acquire the necessary skills without remedial education. Migrants from the rural South, Appalachia, and Puerto Rico, as well as many natives of northern cities who had grown up in poverty, were unfamiliar with the environment of factory or office and unaccustomed to working in groups and to the concept of daily work and regular working hours. Companies, therefore, had to make some provision in their training programs for orientation to industrial discipline. Bringing the most disadvantaged into the mainstream of economic life, therefore, involved industry in training of three types: (1) job skill training, (2) basic remedial education, and (3) orientation to the industrial environment. Some of these programs were aimed at high school dropouts, and combined on-the-job training and work assignments each day with classroom instruction to prepare for high school equivalency examinations.

Companies also made use of adult education facilities in local schools and other institutions in their remedial education programs. An unusual instance was the program developed by Humble Oil's Baytown, Texas, refinery, in cooperation with local unions. In order to enable men—mostly blacks and Mexican-Americans—to qualify for apprenticeship training leading to skilled craft jobs, they were sent to a local junior college for a thirty-week night school course in reading and mathematics.

Regular performance reviews, with pay increases for good performance, were included in several training programs to help develop confidence and good work attitudes. Joseph T. Ryerson & Sons, a subsidiary of Inland Steel, sent trainees—recruits from social agencies and walk-in applicants unable to qualify for jobs—to an out-of-town training site for one week, which was devoted to developing a group identity and helping them to prepare psychologically for the demands of the work environment. Later classroom instruction was aimed at the specific needs revealed by intensive testing in that period. This was followed by in-plant work experience, in which the foreman took an active role in teaching the trainee practical operations and job requirements. Another device used by a number of companies was the "buddy system," in which a regular employee—preferably of similar age and background—was assigned to each trainee to monitor his progress and act as a counselor and guide in adjusting to the job.

Companies reporting on preemployment training projects pointed out that, unless some sort of subsistence allowance was provided—whether through sponsoring companies or government financing—the training activity would have to take second place to the trainees' employment elsewhere. It was even more important to ensure that jobs would be available for successful graduates, for difficulties in placement were destructive of morale and motivation. A program of orientation to industry that was not directly job related was found to be unworkable, because participants turned bitterly against attempts to change their behavior patterns that did not seem to lead to actual jobs. That, at least according to one observer, was precisely what happened to a program in Oakland, California, which was designed to teach black youth how to get a job. Numerous practice sessions in applying for employment that were not followed up by actual job interviews destroyed the faith of the participants in the program.[39]

Upgrading Present Employees

Experience throughout industry indicates that too often blacks and members of other minority groups hold jobs below the level for which they are qualified because in the past there were ceilings, perhaps tacitly understood rather than set by official policy, on how high in the organizations such employees were supposed to move. Even a change in company policy brought little results; discouraged in the past from being too "pushy," they needed positive encouragement to take advantage of opportunities that became available. Supervisors, moreover, often had to be prodded into actively seeking minority group employees when promotions were available.

As companies expanded their programs of equal employment opportunity, they became aware of the fact that black professionals, managers, and skilled workers often could not obtain decent housing near their facilities. Discrimination forced such employees either to refuse job offers or to live in segregated housing inadequate to their needs and status. A few companies, therefore, worked with community groups to support fair housing ordinances.

Results of the Special Programs

All these special programs to train and upgrade the most disadvantaged young people from minority groups obviously touched only a very small part of the total disadvantaged population. In the main they involved only some of the larger corporations rather than the mass of smaller employers. The problem, moreover, is a national one, and cannot be solved within one local labor market, as the experience of Detroit indicates.

In the city of Detroit at the beginning of 1968 it was estimated that there were 10,000 hard-core unemployed. During that year, Detroit industry, led by General Motors and Ford, found and hired over 10,000 hard-core people. At the end of 1968 it was estimated that there were 10,000 hard-core unemployed in the city of Detroit. These seemingly contradictory statistics are explainable largely by the fact that new migrants, predominantly unskilled and poorly educated, had come to Detroit in the period in search of jobs, and they had taken the places of those whom industry had hired.

The experience of the large companies that undertook special programs, even though they made only a small dent in the problem, is of great significance. It proved that special training, although costly, could make productive

---

[39] David Wellman, "A Jobs-for-Negroes Program that Flopped," *Transaction*, April 1968.

workers out of the majority of people who suffered from severe disadvantages in the competition for jobs in the labor market.

The most serious deficiency of the program, however, was that it petered out by the end of the 1960s, as recession and slow economic growth replaced tight labor markets. With present employees on layoff, companies obviously were not going to go out and recruit and train new employees, for they had no jobs to offer them. This once again emphasizes the fact that the starting point for any national effort to extend equal job opportunity must be a high level of economic performance and low rates of unemployment. As the popular quip states, when the nation suffers a mild recession, the inner city ghettos experience a major depression. Numerous studies have shown that nonwhites make their greatest progress relative to whites in periods of rapid economic expansion and suffer relative, and possibly even absolute, deterioration in sluggish times.[40]

Summary

Racial, religious, age, and sex discrimination are contradictions to the principles of a free labor market, and they have marred the operation of the labor market in the United States. Many minority groups have suffered from discrimination, but today its chief victims are blacks, Chicanos, Puerto Ricans, and American Indians. The largest of these minorities—the blacks—have suffered from discrimination since their first arrival on these shores as slaves.

Although many blacks have made it in American economic life, blacks, on the average, suffer from twice as much unemployment as whites, and those with jobs find themselves disproportionately concentrated in the low-skilled occupations. Their earnings lag far behind those of whites, and one-third of them live in poverty. An equal proportion of Chicanos live in poverty, and fully three-quarters of the Indians do.

Part of the explanation of the earnings differential between blacks and whites lies in a productivity differential. Blacks are less skilled and have poorer educational backgrounds. Thus, discrimination that they have encountered before entering the labor market accounts for a good part of their inability to compete equally with whites. Beyond that, however, blacks have also suffered from discrimination in the labor market, at all occupational levels.

Labor unions have been a source of discrimination against blacks, though some unions have always treated all members equally. The craft unions that dominated the AFL throughout most of its history had a particularly bad record with respect to discrimination, and this served to block minorities from gaining access to skilled training and jobs. As a result, there was hostility between blacks and unions, which only moderated with the rise of industrial unionism in the 1930s. Today the AFL-CIO is firmly com-

---

[40] See, for example, Becker, *op. cit.*; Elton Rayack, "Discrimination and the Occupational Progress of Negroes," *Review of Economics and Statistics*, May 1961, pp. 209–214; and Batchelder, *op. cit.*

mitted to equal opportunity, but national and local unions continue to practice discrimination, even if only covertly.

Employer practices with respect to racial discrimination have not been any better. Most refused to hire blacks, and when labor shortages forced them to do so, they hired them only for the most menial jobs for which they could no longer recruit sufficient numbers of white workers. Again, a few employers practiced nondiscriminatory hiring very early. Only during the 1960s, under the pressure of black protest and government coercion, did many employers move significantly to hire and upgrade blacks. Even so, much remains to be done to extend equal employment opportunity to all.

Women, too, have fared poorly in the labor market, as compared to men. Their earnings are only 60 percent of those of men, largely because role differentiation has placed them in the lower-paying, less-skilled job categories within all occupational levels. Again, however, there is evidence that women are also discriminated against solely because of their sex. In this case, too, attitudes are changing and women are also fighting for equal employment opportunity through their own protest organizations.

Voluntary action has been important in advancing equal employment opportunity, but there is no question, however, that neither employers nor unions would have moved as far as they have without government coercion. The first significant step on the part of the federal government came in 1941 with the establishment of the Fair Employment Practices Committee (FEPC) to ensure that there would be no discrimination in employment in defense industries during World War II. Southern power in the Congress, however, ended the FEPC in 1946, and the states assumed the struggle against discrimination. Led by New York and New Jersey, half the states adopted antidiscrimination laws between 1945 and 1964. These laws, however, had only limited effectiveness.

More aggressive federal action on behalf of equal employment came in the 1960s. The President's Committee on Equal Employment Opportunity threatened cancellation of government contracts for firms that practiced discrimination. It also promoted a voluntary program, Plans for Progress, to get companies to increase the number of minority employees.

The major piece of antidiscrimination legislation was the Civil Rights Act of 1964, Title VII of which outlawed employment practices by employers, unions, and employment agencies that discriminated against workers on the basis of their race, color, religion, sex, or national origin. Enforcement of the act has led to the opening up of new job opportunities for blacks and women. Women have also benefited from enforcement of the Equal Pay Act of 1963. The Age Discrimination in Employment Act of 1967 sought to protect older workers against discrimination in the labor market.

The racial riots of the mid-1960s led a number of large employers to undertake special programs to hire some of the "hard-core" unemployed. Special recruitment, selection, and training programs were adopted, and a number of companies reported success in converting people who had been considered "unemployable" into well-paid, efficient, productive workers. Yet all these programs touched only a small part of the total disadvantaged population, and most of the programs petered out when labor shortages gave way to labor surplus in the early 1970s.

BIBLIOGRAPHY

Ashenfelter, Orley, and Albert Rees (eds.) *Discrimination in Labor Markets.* Princeton: Princeton University Press, 1973.

Batchelder, Alan B. "Decline in the Relative Income of Negro Men," *Quarterly Journal of Economics,* November 1964.

Becker, Gary. *The Economics of Discrimination.* Chicago: University of Chicago Press, 1958.

Bureau of the Census. *The Social and Economic Status of Negroes in the United States, 1970.* Bureau of Labor Statistics Report No. 394, *Current Population Reports,* Series P-23, No. 38, July 1971.

Fogarty, Michael P., Rhona Rapoport, and Robert N. Rapoport. *Sex, Career and Family.* London: Allen & Unwin, 1971.

Gallaway, Lowell E. *Manpower Economics.* Homewood, Ill.: Richard D. Irwin, 1971.

Gwartney, James. "Discrimination and Income Differentials," *American Economic Review,* June 1970.

———. "Changes in Nonwhite/White Income Ratio—1939–67," *American Economic Review,* December 1970.

Hiestand, Dale. *Economic Growth and Employment Opportunities for Minorities.* New York: Columbia University Press, 1964.

Kiehl, Robert. *Opportunities for Blacks in the Profession of Engineering.* A Study Prepared for the Manpower Administration, U.S. Department of Labor. Newark: Foundation for the Advancement of Graduate Study in Engineering, 1970.

Lewis, Oscar. *La Vida: A Puerto Rican Family in the Culture of Poverty—San Juan and New York.* New York: Random House, 1966.

Marshall, Ray. *The Negro and Organized Labor.* New York: Wiley, 1965.

Means, John E. "Fair Employment Practices Legislation and Enforcement in the United States," *International Labour Review,* March 1966.

Norgren, Paul H., and Samuel E. Hill. *Toward Fair Employment.* New York: Columbia University Press, 1964.

Parsons, Talcott, and Kenneth B. Clark (eds.). *The Negro American.* Boston: Beacon Press, 1967.

"Special Section: Women at Work," *Monthly Labor Review,* June 1970.

Taylor, David P. "Discrimination and Occupational Wage Differences in the Market for Unskilled Labor," *Industrial and Labor Relations Review,* April 1968.

Twentieth Century Fund. *The Job Crisis for Black Youth.* New York: Praeger, 1971.

18 MANPOWER POLICY

Having examined the impediments to efficiency and equity in the labor market, we now turn our attention to what can be done to improve the functioning of that market and to prepare people to be better able to compete within it. Our concern will be with the supply of labor, with improving its quality and providing it with proper information so that jobs and workers may be better matched. We shall, therefore, start out by analyzing the importance of investment in human resources as revealed by correlations between the level of a country's education and its economic development. Since ours is primarily a private enterprise economy, it is the manpower policies of private employers that are most important, and so we shall examine them. In recent years, however, government has also begun to play an important role in manpower policy, so we shall look at some of the public programs that have been developed. Finally, we shall probe into the success of recent manpower programs through cost-benefit and other types of evaluations that have been made of them.

Human Resources and Economic Development

Concern with human resources was a natural concomitant of industrialization. The Industrial Revolution created the need for a literate labor force, for workers had to be able to read and follow instructions in order to operate machines properly. Free public elementary schooling became a fact early in the nation's history. At the same time, employers had to provide at least some rudimentary training for their employees.

Changing technology fostered still greater concern with manpower. In the heyday of mechanization, job requirements were relatively simple, demanding mainly brawn and manual dexterity, but, as more complicated forms of technology evolved, workers had to be more skilled. Between 1880 and 1930 the free public high school arose and, by the end of that period, had also become a virtually universal form of education. In this period, moreover, private employers developed sophisticated programs of personnel selection and training.

Following World War II a number of factors added impetus to the development of manpower policy. The experience during the war in training millions of workers for new jobs was important, but beyond that the commitment to high levels of manpower utilization undertaken by the federal government in the Employment Act of 1946 required paying more attention to the functioning of labor markets. Economists, moreover, had become intrigued with attempting to explain the factors in economic growth, and their conclusions eventually centered on the importance of the quality of the human input into the production and distribution systems.

Concern with economic growth developed as a part of the effort to help the economically more backward nations start on the road toward development. Those concerned with economic development sought to isolate the main variables that lead to growth or that are obstacles to it. In the late 1940s and early 1950s the stress was placed on capital as the engine of economic progress. As experience was acquired, however, it was discovered that capital alone was insufficient, for a new factory could not be operated efficiently by workers unfamiliar with technology. In more recent years, therefore, the emphasis in economic development has shifted to the quality of the human resource input. In attempting to explain economic growth in the United States, for instance, Denison ascribed a significant share to the improvement in the quality of the labor force.[1]

Symptomatic of the shift, within economic growth theory, from concern with capital formation to emphasis on manpower development has been the work of Harbison and Myers: in it they found a high correlation (.89) between a nation's educational attainment and its national output per capita.[2]

The importance of high-quality human resources is further illustrated by what happened after World War II. The defeated nations—Germany and Japan—lay prostrate, with much of their physical capital having been destroyed by allied bombing. Fifteen years later they were both again major industrial powers, leading the non-Communist world in rates of economic growth. It is true that they both had received infusions of American economic aid, but there is no question that their technical know-how, that is, their high levels of human resource development, had allowed them to put capital into operation quickly.

Investment in Human Resources

The concern of economists in recent years with the human input into the productive process is not an entirely new one, but rather a return to older concepts. Three-quarters of a century ago, Alfred Marshall, the leading figure in neoclassical economics, stressed that the most valuable of all investment was the capital invested in human beings.[3] The concept of treating labor as a form of human capital and attempting to measure the rate of returns on the investment in it became popular in the 1960s.[4]

---

[1] Edward F. Denison, *The Sources of Economic Growth in the United States and the Alternatives Before Us* (New York: Committee for Economic Development, 1962).

[2] Frederick Harbison and Charles A. Myers, *Education, Manpower, and Economic Growth: Strategies of Human Resource Development* (New York: McGraw-Hill, 1964).

[3] Alfred Marshall, *Principles of Economics*, 8th ed. (London: Macmillan, 1947), p. 216.

[4] See, for example, T. W. Schultz, "Investment in Human Capital," *American Economic Review*, March 1961, pp. 1–17; and Gary S. Becker, *Human Capital* (New York: Columbia University Press, 1964).

The increasing importance of the human input into the productive process was demonstrated by Schultz in his comparison of changing investments in human and physical capital between 1900 and 1957. In that period the investment in physical capital in the United States rose about five times (from $282 billion to $1,270 billion 1956 dollars), but the investment in the nation's labor force rose almost nine times (from $63 billion to $535 billion).

By investment in human capital, economists refer to all types of education and training: from the costs, including foregone earnings, of formal schooling, to the costs of on-the-job training. Attempts have been made to calculate rates of return on the different forms of investment, for the individual, his employer, and the total society. We saw, back in Chapter 8, that rates of return for investments in formal education are quite high for the individual in terms of higher lifetime earnings. The studies of Schultz and others also indicate a high rate of return for the total society in terms of increased productivity. Some economists, however, contend that the correlation between higher earnings and more education does not necessarily reflect higher productivity but may be merely a result of employer use of education as a screening device in hiring.[5] In other words, people with fewer years of schooling might be as efficient workers in many types of jobs, but they are excluded from those jobs by rigid selection criteria. Even if too much education is required for some jobs, there is no question, however, that most jobs today require more education than was true in the past. As a result, the median educational attainment of the labor force is now over twelve years, and it is continuing to rise.

But formal education is not the sole means of investing in human resources. On-the-job training, including formal schooling and training in a job situation, as well as "learning from experience," is another very important form of investing in workers to improve their skills and productivity. A great deal of such training is carried on by private employers. Public agencies, particularly the military, also engage in such training. Mincer, in fact, estimated that such training was extremely important for the male labor force, and the money spent on it amounts to more than half of total expenditures on school education.[6] The rate of return on investments in such on-the-job training as apprenticeships and medical specialization was about the same as that on formal schooling, but the individual bore less of the cost of the on-the-job training.

Recognition of the value of investment in human capital has led individuals, employers, and the nation to expand programs of education and training. Today half the young people continue their education beyond high school, and in 1970 833,000 people received baccalaureate degrees, 209,000 master's degrees, and 30,000 doctorates. At the same time, all sorts of new

---

[5] See, for example, James Morgan and Martin David, "Education and Income," *Quarterly Journal of Economics*, August 1963.

[6] Jacob Mincer, "On-the-Job Training: Costs, Returns, and Some Implications," *Journal of Political Economy*, October 1962 (Supplement), pp. 50–79.

training programs have come into existence, sponsored by both government and private employers. Before turning to government efforts, however, let us look briefly at the manpower programs of private industry.

Company Manpower Policies

In a private enterprise economy the individual firm obviously will carry most of the burden of manpower development, aside from basic education, and this has been particularly true for the United States, where government played a very small part in training until the 1960s. Historically, even private industry, aside from hiring and firing, engaged in few activities that could be classified as "manpower" policies. With the mass of jobs being unskilled or semiskilled, men were hired largely on the basis of their physical strength and assigned to specific jobs on a hit-or-miss basis. Aside from some general instructions from the foreman and picking up bits of experience from fellow workers, the typical employee received scant training in job skills. Skilled craftsmen, on the other hand, were more likely to have undergone apprenticeship training under a journeyman. Even at the higher-level jobs—engineers and managers—there was little formal training, either in school or on the job, with the bright, ambitious man learning things on his own and having the daring to apply them on the shop floor.

The Development of Manpower Policies

The emergence of scientific management, under the leadership of Frederick W. Taylor, however, led to significant changes in manpower management during the twentieth century. Taylor analyzed jobs to determine how they might best be performed, and he advocated the separation of planning and control from the execution of work. He also proposed better matching of jobs and workers and motivation of workers to perform their tasks efficiently through incentive payments. The ideas of Taylor with respect to selection, training, and compensation, as later supplemented by the findings of the human relations movement and the behavioral scientists, became part of modern personnel management.

Recruitment

Thus, we find today that the private firm, particularly the larger one, engages in planned recruitment of employees to meet its personnel requirements. Even so, the bulk of blue-collar workers are still recruited through the informal channel of direct hiring at the plant gate, and most workers learn of job opportunities through friends and relatives who work at a particular plant. Large employers of white-collar workers usually engage in more organized recruitment, sending representatives to local high schools to inform the graduating class of available job openings. All companies, however, are more methodical in their recruitment of managerial and professional employees, and they send recruiters annually to college campuses to interview and hire graduates. They also recruit professionals at the annual meetings of their professional associations.

Selection

The selection process in private industry has become very sophisticated, utilizing interviews and testing of general intelligence, aptitude for specific types of work, and personality. In addition, educational and experience standards are established for jobs. As we have seen, educational requirements, such as the high school diploma, and testing procedures have recently come under fire as being unrelated to job requirements. Many companies justify the continued use of such standards and testing on the basis that they do not select employees solely for entry-level jobs, but for eventual promotion to higher-level positions.

Training

While private firms select workers on the basis of education, experience, and aptitude, they still find that they must engage in a great deal of training to fit the recruits into their specific job requirements. Training is most easily accomplished, of course, for semiskilled types of jobs, such as operating machines, and generally requires only a limited period of time, from a few days to a few weeks. Such training may be conducted right on the job or may involve some classroom lessons and a vestibule schooling process, that is, a live simulation of the actual production operation.

Developing skilled workers involves more extensive training efforts. Skilled craftsmen usually are trained through apprenticeship programs, typically of a few years' duration, that combine on-the-job training and theoretical instructions. Foremen, who are often promoted from the production worker ranks, also undergo special training in technical and human relations matters. As the technical competence required of supervisors has risen, some companies have begun to use college graduates as foremen.

Training for higher-level jobs is still more extensive. Most large companies conduct management development programs, including training under actual fire on the job, understudying present holders of higher-level positions, and short-term, intensive school programs.

Performance Evaluation

In addition to training employees to be capable of performing jobs, company manpower management must evaluate their actual performance. Employees, particularly as the occupational ladder is ascended, are periodically appraised as to their performance and potential, and such appraisal is a key factor in determining merit pay increases and promotions. In order to achieve effective utilization of manpower, companies pay a good deal of attention to communications within the organization, both downward from top management to rank-and-file employees, and upward, to keep executives informed as to what may be bothering lower-level employees, so that situations which threaten operating efficiency may be corrected.

Motivation

Motivation is another part of company programs to achieve proper utilization of manpower. Compensation, of course, has always been a technique for inducing employees to perform better, but in recent years managements have been paying greater attention to the findings of behavioral scientists, which tend to emphasize the content of jobs and the ability of employees to assume responsibility and initiative. A few companies, therefore, have experimented with enlarging and enriching jobs so that they can be more meaningful to employees. Others have attempted to evolve career paths, so that the individual employee can see a series of goals toward which he can work. Another approach toward achieving effective manpower utilization has been the use of task forces, in which a group of employees operates as a cooperative team to solve particular problems or accomplish specific projects. Such an approach has been used mainly in research and development projects involving scientists and engineers, and it has been credited with stimulating creativity and task accomplishment.[7]

Manpower Planning

The recognition in recent years of the importance of improvement in the quality of the labor force as a major contributor to economic growth has brought manpower planning to the fore. In nations with private market economies, however, the individual business unit has undertaken to conduct its own manpower planning. Thus, in recent years most American companies of any substantial size have begun to explore and anticipate their manpower needs, particularly those for high-talent personnel. This manpower planning has been designed to predict future staffing requirements, appraise the capability of present personnel, and outline programs to develop employees to meet future responsibilities.[8]

Every company has its own techniques for manpower planning, but let us highlight the features that might be included in such planning. Company planning encompasses both the demand and supply sides of the manpower

---

[7] See, for example, John G. Hoven, "The Task Force Approach to Effective Manpower Utilization," in *Manpower and Planning* (New York: Industrial Relations Counselors, 1970), pp. 161–171.

[8] For a review of manpower-planning practices of corporations, see *Manpower and Planning, op. cit.*; Eric W. Vetter, *Manpower Planning for High Talent Personnel* (Ann Arbor: Bureau of Industrial Relations, Graduate School of Business Administration, University of Michigan, 1967); and Thomas H. Patten, Jr., *Manpower Planning and the Development of Human Resources* (New York: Wiley-Interscience, 1971).

question. On the demand side, the need for managerial and technical skills may be projected one, five, and ten years ahead, taking into account such factors as expected growth of demand for products, present and possible future competition (in order to determine the company's share of the market), technological developments (in order to determine the rate of productivity increase), and collective bargaining and government regulations affecting the labor market (for example, reduction in working time). The personnel staff responsible for the manpower forecasts would work with the company's technical people to try to determine new products, materials, and processes that would be emerging during the period. Ideas that are only now on the drawing boards must be included—as, for instance, using computers for product design—because training for such work must start years in advance of actual introduction of the new technology.

On the supply side, the company would study each person in a managerial or professional position to evaluate his job performance, growth potential, mobility, and promotability in order to ascertain his immediate training needs, as well as to formulate a longer-range plan for his development. When the survey of talent has been completed, succession and progression charts can be developed, so that an attempt can be made to find candidates for each position, present and potential. At the same time, once the forecast of managerial and technical manpower requirements has been completed, the company would be in a position to measure its current supply and seek ways to fill the gaps.

Of course, this is an idealized picture of how manpower planning might work within a company; the reality is often wide of the mark. For one thing, projecting company sales, particularly for products that are subject to wide fluctuations in demand, is far from easy, and being slightly off, when compounded over a five- to ten-year planning period, could mean severe shortages or surpluses of particular skills. Companies do engage in periodic revisions of their plans, but these are confused by immediate swings in production due to the business cycle; that is, when a recession restricts budgets, companies tend to hire fewer new employees, even though this may result in shortages in some occupations—engineering, for example—when the economy picks up. Planning, therefore, is usually easier for companies in the public utility field, in which demand tends to increase at a fairly steady rate, but it becomes more difficult for manufacturers of durable goods, which are very cyclically sensitive, and still more difficult for major defense contractors, whose volume of production and employment is subject to severe swings, dependent upon the award of contracts from the Pentagon.

Government Manpower Policies

Government is also interested in the manpower field. Certainly, in the United States education always has been the responsibility of government, but this was primarily local government, and there was no attempt to coordinate nationally what went on in each community. Even when the federal government did something in the educational field, such as the Morrill Land Grant College Act of 1862 and the Smith-Hughes (Vocational Education) Act of 1917, its orientation was toward agriculture and not to the other sectors of the economy.

During World War II, however, with the vital need to bring millions of new workers into the labor force, train them, and get them into the right jobs, government had to take a much more active role with respect to the labor market. The G.I. Bill of Rights (Servicemen's Readjustment Act) of 1944, although not consciously planned as part of any overall manpower policy, was of great significance in human resource development. The G.I. Bill was basically intended to ease the readjustment of World War II veterans to civilian life and to prevent an overflooding of the civilian labor market by encouraging many of them to return to their studies. By providing financial assistance for college education and vocational training to millions of veterans, however, the G.I. Bill spurred the growth of a highly skilled labor force that helped to promote high levels of economic growth in the ensuing decades.

The development of interest in manpower policy has also been an outgrowth of the movement away from laissez faire. Intervention was first directed at the demand for labor in order to prevent a repetition of the mass unemployment that had characterized the 1930s. In the Employment Act of 1946 the federal government undertook a commitment to promote "conditions under which there will be afforded useful employment opportunities, including self-employment, for those able, willing, and seeking to work, and to promote maximum employment, production and purchasing power." Government fiscal and monetary policy was to be used to promote high levels of employment. But even the promotion of aggregate demand did not ensure the end of the problem of unemployment for all sectors of the economy.

In the early 1960s, therefore, government became concerned with the quality of the supply of labor as it attempted to deal with four structural problems confronting the economy: depressed areas, shifts in foreign trade, pockets of poverty, and technological change. The major acts adopted to deal with these problems each contained provisions for retraining workers. The Area Redevelopment Act of 1961 provided government-financed retraining of unemployed and underemployed persons residing in economically depressed areas, and according to many observers the training features of the act were the most successful of all.[9] In order to promote more liberal international trade, without having the brunt of its cost borne by the industries that would lose business as a result, the Trade Expansion Act of 1962 provided for up to 78 weeks of retraining for workers adversely affected by the results of national trade policy, and relocation allowances for those who had to move to find new jobs. The Manpower Development and Training Act of 1962 provided for

---

[9] See, for example, Seymour L. Wolfbein, *Employment, Unemployment, and Public Policy* (New York: Random House, 1965), p. 156.

retraining of workers whose skills had been made obsolete by technological change. The Economic Opportunity Act of 1964 placed great emphasis on training and retraining to allow the poor to compete effectively in the labor market.

Thus, the 1960s saw the emergence of an "active manpower policy," which Mangum has defined as "the notion that government *ought* to intervene in the labor market on behalf of those it was not serving adequately. . . ."[10] Manpower policy, however, is not limited to aiding individuals to overcome the special problems confronting them in the labor market, and a major objective has been to aid in meeting the manpower needs of the economy. To this end actions have been taken to project manpower needs of the future, to provide information on labor market trends, to develop the nation's future human resources through improved education, and to train workers for immediate job opportunities. Let us now briefly examine each of these facets of federal manpower policies.

Manpower Forecasts

Forecasts of trends in manpower requirements are essential for planning programs of government, business, and the educational system. Without some idea of what the future labor market will look like, students would have no idea of what job prospects might be in a field in which they are interested, educational institutions would not be able to keep their curriculum offerings up to date, and business would be unable to plan recruitment and training programs. The rise of new types of occupations, as occurred with the advent of the computer a decade ago, requires the education and training of people to fill them. Changes in job content, such as those which accompanied the shift from mechanical to electronic control of machine processes under automation, demand a revamping of company training programs. The Manpower Development and Training Act specifically requires a reasonable prognosis for employment before a training program can be established, and the Vocational Education Act of 1963 requires information on current and projected manpower needs as a prerequisite to approval of state grants.

The actual task of forecasting manpower trends falls to the Bureau of Labor Statistics of the U.S. Department of Labor, but the National Science Foundation conducts projections of scientific and engineering manpower. Private agencies, such as the National Planning Association, and state and local governments also engage in manpower forecasting. The Bureau of Labor Statistics, however, with the most experience in the field, remains the major forecasting agency. This type of forecast was reviewed in the opening chapter of this book, when we explored the 1980 BLS labor force projections by industry and occupation.

---

[10] Garth L. Mangum, "Manpower Research and Manpower Policy," in *A Review of Industrial Relations Research*, Vol. II (Madison, Wisc.: Industrial Relations Research Association, 1971), p. 62.

According to former BLS Assistant Commissioner for Manpower and Employment Statistics Harold Goldstein, development of the BLS occupational manpower projections comprises nine steps:[11]

1. The projection starts with breakdowns of the Bureau of Census population projections, by state, region, age, sex, and color.
2. These population projections are translated into labor force participation rates by age, sex, color, and state and region.
3. The next step is projection of the gross national product that would be generated by a labor force of the anticipated size, assuming certain hours of work and rates of productivity change.
4. That gross national product is then broken down into its major components—investment, consumption, and government expenditures—and models are developed to illustrate the effect on the economic structure of such alternatives as high investment, high consumption, or high government spending.
5. From each GNP model a bill of goods, or consumption estimate, is developed for each type of good or service.
6. These estimates of final demand are then converted into production figures for each industrial sector.
7. The production estimates in turn are translated into employment needs, taking into account technological change within an industry and the resultant change in output per worker.
8. These estimates of the total number of workers required are, at this point, broken down by occupational group, based upon studies of technological developments taking place within particular industries.
9. The final step is to project the losses in each occupation, resulting from deaths, retirements, and transfers of workers to other jobs.

This nine-step procedure of forecasting future manpower needs obviously involves a good deal of estimation, and since no planning technique can possibly foresee all future events, there is room for error. Yet to date the BLS projections have been surprisingly accurate, and, in time, better data will be collected and improved statistical techniques devised, which will allow for more accurate forecasting.

But merely forecasting future manpower needs by occupation is not sufficient, for those needs must be related to potential supply. BLS, therefore, next uses the data that are available on the numbers being trained for certain occupations. Such data are most available with respect to college and university graduates, but allowances must be made for the fact that people do not necessarily pursue occupations in their college majors. If only reasonable estimates are possible for those occupations requiring college degrees, even less accurate ones are feasible for most other occupations because of the paucity

---

[11] Harold Goldstein, "Government Techniques for Projecting Occupational Manpower Needs," in *Manpower and Planning, op. cit.*, pp. 23–35.

of data, but efforts are being extended to attempt to amass more information and to develop projections on a regional basis.

Information

Forecasts of manpower trends must be made available to the public if they are to have value for private employers, government agencies, educational institutions, and individuals, and the primary source of such information is the annual Manpower Report of the President. Title I of the Manpower Development and Training Act of 1962 requires the President to issue an annual manpower report, similar to the report on the state of the economy that he submits to Congress. The report analyzes trends in manpower requirements, resources, utilization, and training. It points up areas that need remedial action, such as expected shortages of some types of manpower and surpluses of others.

The Manpower Report is scrutinized by Congress and becomes a basis for the formulation of new legislation. It is supplemented by an annual report of the Secretary of Labor on manpower research and training under MDTA, which supplies information on the number of people and the jobs for which they have been trained.

Most of the data contained in the Manpower Report come from the regular and special studies of the Bureau of Labor Statistics, summaries of which are published in the BLS magazine, *Monthly Labor Review*. The BLS also makes available to the public copies of its full reports. The bureau, in addition, issues biannually the *Occupational Outlook Handbook*, which describes more than five hundred occupations and industries, training require ments for them, and expected employment opportunities. The handbook has become a basic tool in career guidance at the secondary school level.[12]

The United States Training and Employment Service and its affiliated state services are also very important agencies for the gathering and dissemination of manpower information. The service tests and counsels individuals, and not only helps them to find jobs but also refers them to training courses. In recent years the employment service has been using computerized systems to provide information on the labor market more readily, so that individuals may be told of job opportunities more quickly.

Education

The launching by the Soviet Union of its Sputnik in 1957, before the United States had been able to perfect its space program, caused consternation within the nation. Since such a technological feat depended so heavily on a nation's scientific and engineering capability, Americans began to question their preeminence in these fields. The American system of education came in for severe criticism, with some people complaining that we were not devoting enough resources to it and others that too much money was being spent, but

---

[12] Wolfbein, *op. cit.*, p. 141.

on the wrong things, and that more emphasis had to be placed upon the sciences. The upshot of all of this was increased federal government activity, largely through the National Science Foundation (NSF), to improve science curricula and textbooks in the secondary schools and to support study and research in science and technology at the college and university level.

On top of the Sputnik concern, there were the findings of economists on the value of investment in human resources, plus growing national concern with labor force adjustment to technological change, poverty in the midst of affluence, and the urban crisis, particularly the inadequacy of the education provided blacks and other disadvantaged minorities. All these led to greater involvement by the federal government in the nation's educational system. Until then, federal aid to education had been extended through Public Laws 815 and 864, dealing with so-called "federally impacted areas," that is, school districts overburdened by the influx of pupils as a result of national defense activities.[13] The 1960s, however, saw a whole new series of acts designed to strengthen the nation's educational system.

The Vocational Education Act of 1963 sought to shift the emphasis in vocational education from agriculture and home economics to that of providing young people with training in skills that were in demand in the current labor market, not that of half a century before. The Higher Education Facilities Act of 1963 provided aid to colleges and universities in expanding their facilities to meet enlarged enrollments. The Health Professions Educational Act of 1963 provided aid to medical, dental, and other health personnel schools to expand their facilities, plus loans to students pursuing careers in the health field.

The major federal effort came in 1965 as a result of the passage of the Elementary and Secondary Education Act, with an initial authorization of $1.3 billion. This act attempted to deal with some aspects of the urban crisis by authorizing federal assistance to educational facilities in areas with high concentrations of low-income families. It also provided aid for new and improved school libraries, textbooks, and language and science laboratories, and for expanded research in education, teaching techniques, and data storage.

One final area of education that deserves mention was the Adult Basic Education program undertaken as part of the antipoverty program. It resulted from the fact that many poverty-stricken adults had such poor educational backgrounds that they could not qualify for training programs to prepare them for jobs. Its basic aim was to remedy the lack or obsolescence of earlier schooling. As a result of all these programs, the federal government was spending close to $4.5 billion on education by 1970.

Training

Government efforts in the training of manpower are not entirely new: the Bureau of Apprenticeship and Training of the Department of Labor has been working with employers and unions since its creation in 1937 to formulate

---

[13] *Ibid.*, pp. 149–152.

apprenticeship programs in the crafts. The craft unions, which have strong influence in BAT, seek to keep apprenticeship training limited in numbers lest the supply of labor relative to jobs be increased, and, as a result, only a minority of craftsmen actually come through formal training programs, but learn the trade simply by "picking it up."[14]

The apprenticeship training program is aimed primarily at high school graduates with a background in mathematics and science, but the big push for training programs for the disadvantaged came about as part of the struggle for civil rights and against poverty. The Economic Opportunity Act (EOA) of 1964 and the 1965 amendments to the Manpower Development and Training Act emphasized remedial education, training, and work experience. According to Mangum, "Essentially, the antipoverty program was a combination of manpower programs aimed at either employing or preparing for employment the employable poor, particularly the youth."[15]

Among the remedial programs of the war on poverty was the Job Corps, which sought to provide basic education, skill training, and useful work experience to young men and women who needed a change of environment and individual help to develop their talents, self-confidence, and sense of self-improvement. Job Corps centers were established on unused federal military installations in or near urban areas, and they were operated by private and public agencies, basically as residential vocational schools. Enrollees, largely young high school dropouts, received room and board, medical and dental care, work clothing, a nominal allowance for purchase of dress clothing, a monthly living allowance of $30, and a terminal allowance of $50 for each month of satisfactory service in the Job Corps.

Following the urban riots of 1967, a cooperative effort of government and business to prepare, place, and retain the hard-core unemployed in productive work was undertaken through the National Alliance of Businessmen (NAB). The program, known as Job Opportunities in the Business Sector (JOBS), involved getting private companies to provide jobs for the disadvantaged. A company could negotiate a contract to hire and train disadvantaged workers under the Manpower Development and Training Act for a period of up to twenty-four months. Although the program offered subsidies to employers, the majority of firms undertaking JOBS programs were so-called "freebies"; that is, they did so without a federal contract and, hence, without governmental financial aid. Examples of some of these training efforts were described in the last chapter in the review of private programs to hire minority persons.

The Neighborhood Youth Corps (NYC) was another part of the war on poverty. Its in-school program provided part-time work and on-the-job train-

---

[14] George Strauss, "Apprenticeship: An Evaluation of the Need," in Arthur M. Ross (ed.), *Employment Policy and the Labor Market* (Berkeley and Los Angeles: University of California Press, 1965), pp. 299–333.

[15] Garth L. Mangum, *The Emergence of Manpower Policy* (New York: Holt, Rinehart and Winston, 1969), p. 78.

ing for high-school-age students of low-income families in order to keep them in school. A summer program provided this same group with job opportunities during the vacation. An out-of-school program provided economically deprived school dropouts with practical work experience and on-the-job training, while attempting to encourage them to return to school. An analysis of NYC's in-school and summer programs, however, revealed that they had little effect on the graduation rate from high school.[16]

The New Careers program grew out of the local aides hired as part of the Community Action Program, which had sought to obtain "maximum feasible participation" of the poor. Local projects designed to improve community health, education, welfare, and public safety could receive up to 90 percent federal financing. New Careers programs enrolled adults who were unemployed or had an annual family income below the poverty line for work on these community projects. State and local government agencies and local private organizations could receive subsidies and incentives to hire and provide prospects for advancement and continued employment opportunities for enrollees. Enrollees, however, could not be used to displace employed workers or impair existing contracts for service.

Operation Mainstream was a rural work-relief program for adults, by which they could obtain work experience and training while contributing to the betterment or beautification of the area. The programs provided federal funds and technical assistance to projects, such as the conservation of parks, highways, and recreational areas, that local groups initiate, develop, and sponsor. Most of the people employed, at minimum wages, on these projects were former farmers over forty-five years of age who could not obtain other work, but how much training they received is questionable.

The Work Experience Program sought to raise the employability of needy adults by helping them to overcome inadequate education, poor work habits, lack of motivation, and absence of marketable skills. Participants received maintenance grants, adult basic education, vocational instruction, work experience, medical care, and any supportive services necessary to make them employable. The Work Experience Program, however, was basically unsuccessful and eventually eliminated.

A similar type of program, the Work Incentive program (WIN), came into being as a result of the 1967 social security amendments. It sought to eliminate malingerers from the welfare roles by placing recipients in jobs, training them for employment, or employing them in public agencies. The Nixon administration has made concerted efforts to force public assistance recipients to perform some work in public agencies. Whether the program will be limited to "working for your relief check" or actually entail meaningful training so that some people can make a transition to full-time productive employment remains to be seen.

---

[16] Gerald G. Somers and Ernst W. Stromsdorfer, *A Cost-Effectiveness Study of the In-School and Summer Neighborhood Youth Corps* (Madison, Wisc.: Industrial Relations Research Institute, University of Wisconsin, 1970).

Matching Manpower and Jobs

A national manpower policy can be conceived of as having three dimensions: (1) the creation of new job opportunities to accommodate a growing labor force and the elimination of some jobs through technological change; (2) the training of a labor force capable of handling the jobs available; and (3) making sure that workers with the requisite skills can be easily matched with the right jobs. Theoretically, this matching function is supposed to be accomplished through the normal workings of the free labor market, but as we have seen there are frictions that prevent easy and speedy matching. The more time that elapses between recruitment and job search, on the one hand, and successful placement, on the other, the greater the loss in national income and waste of manpower. There is justification, therefore, for attempting to speed the process of successful placement through the provision of better labor market information and by establishing mechanisms by which to bring employers and potential employees into contact.

One vital piece of labor market information was never available: the number and type of job vacancies. Admittedly, such information is not easy to gather, assemble, and disseminate quickly enough to be of value to employers and workers, but in the mid-1960s a series of experiments run in a number of labor markets indicated that it was feasible to compile meaningful data on job vacancies.

This work culminated in the Labor Department's new series on job vacancies, which was introduced in 1970 and provides, for the first time, some partial information on the shape and size of unfilled demand for labor.[17] Unfortunately, the series covers only manufacturing, which is subject to fluctuations in economic activity and has not been the most rapid sector of job growth, but it will eventually be extended to include data on all industries. The series reports monthly on job vacancies, new and long term (those which continue unfilled for thirty days or more), by industry and occupation. The series, when it is extended to all industries, should become an important type of information, particularly if the reporting procedures can be speeded.

Theoretically, the offices of the state employment services act as the focal point for bringing people and available jobs into juxtaposition. In reality, however, the role of the employment service has been a relatively small one, and it places relatively few workers in jobs. In 1970 an experiment—the Comprehensive Manpower Office—was installed in ten cities and one rural area that sought to restructure the local employment service office so that each job seeker receives services tailored to his own needs. Other improved services include the establishment of interstate clearance systems for placement of personnel, development of testing programs, and the provision of manpower services to a host of public agencies under various manpower programs, as well as to private industry. The Louisville office of the

---

[17] Raymond Konstant, "Job Vacancies in 1970," *Monthly Labor Review,* February 1971, pp. 20, 21.

Kentucky Employment Service, for example, helps coordinate the activities of forty-two agencies, including eight federal ones, in the Cooperative Area Manpower Planning Systems; is responsible directly or indirectly for $15 million annually in manpower programs; and deals with more than one hundred local health, welfare, and manpower organizations.[18] The Employment Service's Automated Reporting System (ESARS) provides job and employee information on a rapid-fire basis to each of the nineteen hundred offices and thus aids in the quicker placement of people.

The process of matching workers and jobs is furthered by the information services of the Labor Department, which gathers and publishes information on trends in employment by industry, the level and rate of unemployment, the nature of local shortages or surpluses in specific occupations, and the job market situation in particular industries. Major labor markets are classified each month as to degree of labor market tightness, and in this way areas of substantial and/or persistent unemployment are identified that are eligible for selective federal assistance, including preference in the award of federal procurement contracts, public works grants, and loans and business loans under the Public Works and Economic Development acts, and low interest loans under the Small Business Administration programs. Any interested party may obtain labor market information collected through this program. In addition, information useful for manpower planning, training, guidance, and testing is regularly provided to educational systems and community groups.

The national system of public employment offices also provides any employer with technical aid such as occupational analysis and classification, labor market information, studies of the work force problems of recruitment, selection, development, utilization, and stabilization, and advice on developing manpower resources needed for technical advancement or economic expansion. Manpower advisory committees and economic development groups work on enlarging employment possibilities in urban communities, while smaller community programs service rural areas in meeting their manpower problems.

Private Organizations

The federal government, of course, carries the burden of most of the work in the manpower area that private employers do not handle, but state and local government agencies are also active. In addition, a number of private organizations play important parts in the national manpower effort. The studies of such private, nonprofit research organizations as the Brookings Institution, the National Planning Association, and the National Bureau of Economic Research provide information on trends in the economy and their labor market implications. Years before the federal government became involved in active manpower policies, research on manpower needs was conducted by

---

[18] Emil Michael Aun, "All in a Day's Work: Proliferating Programs and Pressures Keep Employment Service Manager Busy," *Manpower*, July 1971, pp. 2–8.

the Human Resources Conservation Project and the National Manpower Council at Columbia University.

Colleges and universities, of course, engage in a great deal of work that is related to manpower policy, from the formation of basic concepts, to research on labor market trends and training techniques, to actually conducting training programs. They, private employers, labor unions, state and local governments, and community organizations have contracted from government agencies for research and training under the Manpower Development and Training Act, the Economic Opportunity Act, and the like.

A number of private organizations, both profit and nonprofit, have engaged in directly training or consulting with private employers on training programs. They have developed special materials and techniques for educating the poor and disadvantaged, and have helped to train supervisors for dealing with disadvantaged employees.

Experience with Manpower Policies and Programs

The emergence of an active manpower policy amounted to a manpower revolution during the 1960s, as the nation recognized the importance of the investment in human resources and undertook one program after another to improve the operation of the free labor market, deal with a number of structural problems, and see to it that the development of trained manpower kept pace with the needs of an increasingly complex technological society. Without too much experience to serve as a guide, many of the programs obviously were experimental in nature, and mistakes and lack of coordination were bound to occur.

Administration and Coordination

Problems of coordinating the vast array of manpower programs, which were assigned to different federal agencies, begat interagency conflict and competition, as each resented anyone else muscling in on what it regarded as its area of expertise. Each program, moreover, had its own maze of regulations governing eligibility, duration, conditions of training or work, and compensation received by participants. According to Mangum, it was at the local level, where people are served or not served and programs succeed or fail, that the effects of program proliferation showed their most painful symptoms.[19] The more aggressive local governments, familiar with wending their way through the federal bureaucracy, were able to fund many programs, while others, even though their needs may have been much greater, lost out with respect to many opportunities.

A series of executive orders created presidential committees on manpower, education, and antipoverty efforts to coordinate various government programs in these fields. In 1967 and 1968 significant progress in consolida-

---

[19] Mangum, *The Emergence of Manpower Policy, op. cit.,* pp. 77–93.

tion of manpower programs was achieved. Two approaches were made to coordination at the local level: the Concentrated Employment Program (CEP),
designed to provide a mechanism for turning fragmented federal programs
into meaningful combinations of services to meet local needs, and the Cooperative Area Manpower Planning System (CAMPS), which gave the state
employment service major responsibility for coordinating manpower services.

Further attempts to streamline manpower services have been made in
recent years: in 1969, for example, the Department of Labor revamped its
Manpower Administration's organizational structure, providing for a single
direct line of authority from the Manpower Administrator to the regional
offices. A single new component, the U.S. Training and Employment Service
(USTES), combined the major program activities formerly handled by the
United States Employment Service (USES) and the Bureau of Work-Training
Programs. The USTES handles all employment, work experience, and train-
ing programs other than apprenticeship that are the responsibility of the
Labor Department.[20]

In 1972 President Nixon proposed replacing the two major pieces of
manpower legislation—the Manpower Development and Training Act and
Title I of the Economic Opportunity Act—with a new manpower revenue-
sharing act. A major goal of the proposed legislation is to decentralize major
manpower activities from the federal level to that of state and local governments. In its first full year of operation the manpower revenue-sharing act
would provide $2 billion for manpower purposes, of which $1.7 billion would
be divided among state and local units of government based on the size of
their labor forces and numbers of unemployed and disadvantaged. It would
authorize such services as: (1) classroom instruction in both remedial education and occupational skills; (2) training on the job with public and private
employers, aided by manpower subsidies; and (3) job opportunities, including work experience and transitional public service employment.

Leaders of the National Manpower Policy Task Force, composed of academic manpower experts, have defended existing programs as improving the
employability of participants and taken issue with the proposed manpower
revenue-sharing bill. Its vice-chairman, Sar Levitan, termed the bill, "a cop-
out by the feds at the expense of manpower programs."[21]

Performance

The acid test of any program lies in how well it performs its assigned task,
and here the record is mixed. Vocational education, long the stepchild of
American education, has had a resurgence since passage of the Vocational
Education Act of 1963, with enrollments expanding from 200,000 to 2 million
students by 1971, and curriculum broadened to include such up-to-date fields

---

[20] "Streamlining Manpower Services," *Manpower*, May 1969, pp. 8, 9.
[21] *Daily Labor Report*, Bureau of National Affairs, December 20, 1972.

as pollution abatement, inhalation therapy, and helicopter piloting.[22] A number of private industrial companies are establishing vocational schools, and these will supplement the training given in public high schools. Given the rise in job requirements as a result of more advanced technology, a good deal of the vocational education expansion is occurring at the post-secondary school, but short of college, level.

In the training area the Manpower Development and Training Act (MDTA) is considered to have been the most successful of the programs. In its first eight years of operation almost 1.5 million persons were enrolled in MDTA training, close to one million completed training, and more than .75 million secured employment (see Table 18.1 for details). Although the numbers of people involved cannot be considered to have dealt adequately with the problem of poverty, they did make a contribution to its alleviation and toward meeting the nation's manpower needs.

Debate has arisen as to the respective merits of MDTA institutional, formal classroom training and its on-the-job training (OJT). Some observers have claimed that OJT has been more valuable than institutional training.[23] As can be seen from Table 18.1, 61 percent enrolled in on-the-job training secured post-training employment, but only 48 percent of those involved in institutional training did. The better record of OJT, however, has been ascribed by some to its "skimming the cream off the top," that is, enrolling those among the unemployed who had the best prospects of completing training and securing jobs. Training such people is also very important, however, and manpower programs cannot be limited to the most seriously disadvantaged members of the labor force if they are to make their optimum contribution to national welfare.

More legitimate questions have been raised as to whether or not trainees would have made as much progress in the absence of MDTA enrollment. Some participating employers, for example, have provided little training or training only for low-level jobs, and might very well have hired workers for them without the MDTA program. According to Mangum, the OJT program was largely one of subsidizing the employment of the disadvantaged by private firms. Such subsidy, however, in many cases resulted in productive employment for individuals who formerly had been considered "unemployable."

Probably the most criticized program was that of the Job Corps. Although those who completed Job Corps training secured much higher paying jobs than they had had, residential training was extremely expensive (about $8,000 per enrollee), dropout rates were high, and the need to concentrate large groups of disadvantaged youth in alien surroundings was questioned

---

[22] "Blue-Collar Training Gets a White-Collar Look," *Business Week*, July 31, 1971, pp. 76, 77.

[23] See, for example, David H. Greenberg, "Employing the Training Program Enrollee: An Analysis of Employer Personnel Records," *Industrial and Labor Relations Review*, July 1971, pp. 554–571.

Table 18.1 Enrollments, Completions, and Post-training Employment for Institutional and On-the-Job Training Programs under the MDTA, Fiscal Years 1963–1970 (in thousands)

Item	Total	FY[a] 1963[b]	FY 1964	FY 1965	FY 1966	FY 1967	FY 1968	FY 1969	FY 1970
Total[c]									
Enrollments	1,451.1	34.1	77.6	156.9	235.8	265.0	241.0	220.0	221.0
Completions	987.2	20.1	51.3	96.3	155.7	192.6	164.2	160.0	147.0
Post-training employment	773.4	16.1	39.4	73.4	124.0	153.7	127.5	124.0	115.3
Institutional training[c]									
Enrollments	978.4	32.0	68.6	145.3	177.5	150.0	140.0	135.0	130.0
Completions	651.7	19.2	46.0	88.8	117.7	109.0	91.0	95.0	85.0
Post-training employment	484.3	15.3	34.8	66.9	89.8	80.0	64.5	71.0	62.0
On-the-job-training[c]									
Enrollments	473.0	2.1	9.0	11.6	58.3	115.0	101.0	85.0	91.0
Completions	335.5	.9	5.3	7.5	38.0	83.6	73.2	65.0	62.0
Post-training employment	289.1	.8	4.6	6.5	34.2	73.7	63.0	53.0	53.3

[a] FY = fiscal year.
[b] Programs became operational August 1962.
[c] Completions do not include dropouts. Post-training employment includes persons employed at the time of the last follow-up. (There are two follow-ups, with the second occurring six months after completion of training.)

SOURCE: *Manpower Report of the President, 1971*, Table F-4, p. 302.

by many. The program also suffered from unfavorable publicity about "riots" in the training camps, even though those reports were highly exaggerated.

The Job Opportunities in the Business Sector (JOBS) program scored some notable initial success, but it never reached the employment targets that had been set. The major problem facing this and all other training programs was that they could succeed only if employers needed workers, and this was the case only when the economy was expanding and labor markets were tight. When the economy turned downward and layoffs mounted, employers were hardly in a position to hire and train additional workers. If employers continued to give preference to the disadvantaged during periods of stable or declining demand for labor, they would be hiring them instead of other workers and thus merely shifting the burden of unemployment.

Do Manpower Programs Pay?

Cost-Benefit Analysis

To the economist, the measure of success of a program lies in its payoff. Having discovered that the investment in human resources has brought high returns, he applies the economic calculus in evaluating recent training and related programs. The chief technique for doing this is through cost-benefit analysis, that is, determining whether the benefits, in monetary terms, resulting from the program outweigh its costs. Applying economic reasoning, expenditures on any training program, for example, would be made up to the point where benefits and costs are equated at the margin.

There are many problems, however, with trying to apply cost-benefit analysis.[24] For one thing, the external effects of programs, both in terms of costs and benefits, are difficult to measure. For example, a particular program of getting disadvantaged youth employed may be very expensive relative to the additions to the income stream that their employment generates; the program, therefore, could be negatively evaluated. But the external benefits of that program, which could not be adequately measured, may have included the deterrence of urban riots, with their destruction of physical property and human life, and the reduction of future crimes, with their costs of apprehension, trial, and imprisonment. If such benefits could have been measured, then that program would have been evaluated positively.

Secondly, there is no preordained reason why manpower programs must conform to investment-efficiency criteria. As Weisbrod has pointed out, the cost-benefit analyses of human resource programs have given little attention to the effects on income distribution or the impact on other social goals, such as equality of opportunity. In his view, we must guard against

---

[24] For a detailed critique of cost-benefit studies, see Michael E. Borus and Charles G. Buntz, "Problems and Issues in the Evaluation of Manpower Programs," *Industrial and Labor Relations Review*, January 1972, pp. 234–245.

the error of concluding that the government should allocate resources only to those programs the productivity of which exceeds their costs.[25]

These criticisms of the use of cost-benefit analysis, however, do not obviate its value, for it can still indicate to policy makers which particular programs are economically more fruitful than others and what modifications in programs might improve their effectiveness. What it does mean, however, is that its users should attempt to perfect the technique, trying to build externalities into its calculus. It is not the function of the evaluator, moreover, to determine what the national objectives are, or what weights are to be attached to the various objectives, because in a democracy such determinations must be made by the people through their elected representatives.

Evaluation of Training

With all these caveats in mind, let us now examine some of the evaluations of recent manpower programs. Interestingly enough, most cost-benefit and regression analyses of specific training programs have found them to be quite valuable, with those who received training securing better employment than comparable non-trainees. A number of studies have even found expenditures on vocational training to be more effective than those on general education in raising the income of the poor.[26]

A simpler type of evaluation, that of comparing the status of people before and after undergoing training, has also shown positive results. Thus, the Senate Subcommittee on Employment, Manpower, and Poverty presented data that showed that MDTA trainees in 1964 and 1965 had a post-training employment rate of 75 percent, 62.5 percent were in training-related jobs, and their median earnings were 21 percent higher than before the training.[27]

Since such before and after studies do not take account of the costs of the programs to improve the labor market status of trainees, the more sophisticated cost-benefit and regression analyses are of greater interest. A study by Borus in Connecticut found a very high ratio of benefits to costs, with benefits, in terms of the trainee's increased lifetime earnings, outstripping costs by

[25] Burton A. Weisbrod, "Expenditures on Human Resources: Investment, Income Redistribution, or What?" in John A. Delehanty (ed.), *Manpower Problems and Policies: Full Employment and Opportunity For All* (Scranton: International Textbook Company, 1969), pp. 405–410.

[26] Thomas I. Ribich, *Education and Poverty* (Washington: Brookings, 1968); *Federal Poverty Programs: Assessment and Recommendations* (Arlington, Va.: Institute for Defense Analysis, 1966); and W. Lee Hansen, Burton A. Weisbrod, and William Scanlon, "Schooling and Earnings of Low Achievers," *American Economic Review*, June 1970, pp. 409–419.

[27] Gerald G. Somers, "Evaluation of Manpower Policies: Methodology and Unanswered Questions," in Delehanty, *op. cit.*, pp. 345–363, and taken from Gerald G. Somers, "Evaluation of Manpower Policies," in *Federal Programs for the Development of Human Resources*, A Compendium of Papers Submitted to the Subcommittee on Economic Progress of the Joint Economic Committee, U.S. Congress, 90th Cong., 2nd sess., Vol. 1 (Washington, D.C.: Government Printing Office, 1968), pp. 159–164.

three to six times.[28] According to Borus, moreover, if externalities could be measured—that is, the benefits to the economy as a whole—then they would be even greater than the benefits received by the individual. Similar favorable cost-benefit relationships were found in studies of training experience by Page and by Somers and Stromsdorfer, among others.[29]

These studies, however, were of the MDTA in its early period, when its major mission was to retrain workers whose skills had been made obsolete by technological change. It was charged, therefore, that these training programs skimmed the cream off the ranks of the unemployed while ignoring the plight of the most disadvantaged groups. In order to correct for this selection bias, Sewell undertook a very detailed study of later experience with the training of highly disadvantaged rural workers in programs sponsored by Manpower Improvement Through Community Effort (MITCE). He found that the training resulted in substantial increases in earnings and in productivity as measured in hourly wage rates. He thus concluded that the distributional objective of the antipoverty program had been satisfied and that the training had added more to national output than it had cost.[30]

Sewell also found that on-the-job training was a much more efficient use of society's resources than institutional training, because of the higher cost of the latter. Residential training, of course, is the most expensive form of institutional training. The average annual cost per trainee under the Job Corps program, for example, was four times that of on-the-job training (more than $8,000 for Job Corps as against only about $2,000 for OJT), with the result that Job Corps costs have exceeded its benefits. On the other hand, Sewell found institutional training (classroom instruction) was superior in training for particular occupations.

Further light on the value of different types of training was shed by a study by Hardin and Borus of occupationally oriented training courses given in Michigan under both the MDTA and the old Area Redevelopment Act.[31] They attempted to measure the effects of retraining on national product, income of trainees, and the government budget, and they found that short training (sixty to two hundred hour classes) was an excellent economic

[28] Michael E. Borus, "A Benefit-Cost Analysis of the Economic Effectiveness of Retraining the Unemployed," *Yale Economic Essays,* Fall 1964, pp. 371–430; and Borus, "The Effects of Retraining the Unemployed in Connecticut," in Gerald G. Somers (ed.), *Retraining the Unemployed* (Madison, Wisc.: University of Wisconsin Press, 1968), pp. 125–148.

[29] David A. Page, "Retraining under the Manpower Development Act: A Cost-Benefit Analysis," *Studies of Government Finance,* Reprint 86 (Washington, D.C.: Brookings, 1964); and Gerald G. Somers and Ernst W. Stromsdorfer, "A Benefit-Cost Analysis of Manpower Retraining," *Proceedings of the Seventeenth Annual Meeting, Industrial Relations Research Association* (Madison, Wisc.: Industrial Relations Research Association, 1965), pp. 172–185.

[30] D. O. Sewell, *Training the Poor: A Benefit-Cost Analysis of Manpower Programs in the U.S. Antipoverty Program* (Kingston: Industrial Relations Centre, Queen's University, 1971).

[31] Einar Hardin and Michael E. Borus, "Benefits and Costs of MDTA-ARA Retraining," *Industrial Relations,* May 1972, pp. 216–228.

undertaking in all three respects. Medium and long-term training, however, were found to be poor investments from these three points of view.

A number of studies have attempted to evaluate training by comparing those who had undertaken it with those who had not. Invariably, such studies have indicated that the job market problems of those who had completed MDTA programs were far from solved, but that they were doing better in terms of stability of employment and earnings than nonenrollees. Main, for example, studied the effect of MDTA training during the period 1963–1966 by comparing the gains of 1,200 trainees with a control group of 1,060 similar people who were unemployed about the same time as the trainees but who did not participate in the MDTA program.[32] He used multiple regression analysis to control for the effects of other factors (sex, education, age, race, previous unemployment, etc.) on weekly wages and to determine the net effect of MDTA training. With these other variables taken into account, he found that training did not help people to get better-paying jobs, but it did help them to obtain more full-time employment; he calculated the net effect of training on full-time employment at between 13 and 23 percent for the period after training for completers and between 7 and 19 percent for dropouts. The fact that they obtained steadier employment boosted their incomes, and Main estimated the net effect of training on family income to be $9.60 a week, a very high return on the investment in training these people.

Labor Mobility Project Evaluation

Training is not the only type of manpower program that has been subject to evaluation. The U.S. Department of Labor, for example, has conducted studies of labor mobility projects for the unemployed.[33] Such projects have provided relocation assistance in the form of job information and financial aid to help unemployed workers who had little prospect for steady employment in their home communities to move to regions in which jobs were available. Through the spring of 1968 about ten thousand persons were placed in full-time jobs through mobility assistance. Although many of these people might have moved on their own, it was concluded that the relocation system helped bring greater economic rationality to moves and encouraged the employment of trained or experienced workers in their highest skill area.

Labor mobility studies are more difficult to conduct than training ones. There is much less uniformity of costs, for the services necessary to create a planned move for a worker will differ according to his education, experience, family size and age, and cultural background. Benefits are still harder to measure, but there is probably a significant savings to the community to

---

[32] Earl D. Main, "A Nationwide Evaluation of MDTA Institutional Job Training," *Journal of Human Resources,* Spring 1968, pp. 159–170.

[33] Audrey Freedman, "Labor Mobility Projects for the Unemployed," *Monthly Labor Review,* June 1968, pp. 56–62.

which people move. As Freedman points out, "By providing an unemployed person with specific job offers, and some moving money, the projects have prevented the arrival of an unemployed worker, with little or no funds, at a city where it may take him weeks or months to find a job." During such an interim period, the worker would have to be maintained, probably at public expense. Furthermore, some firms will operate less efficiently in that period, because they cannot find the manpower they need.

Results of Research

No other governmental policy has been subjected to as critical an evaluation as manpower. Congressmen who are often unmindful of the waste of public funds on all sorts of projects become guardians of the taxpayers' money when it is being spent on the disadvantaged in the labor market. As a result, manpower programs from the very beginning were subjected to a great deal of study, much of which has disclosed positive benefits from programs, but this has not won more funds from Congress or the administration.

According to Mangum, research has shown that the single greatest deficiency in every manpower program has been the absence of a suitable job for the participant when he completes it.[34] "Work experience" programs, thus, have been the least effective of the programs, and the Work Experience and Training program was eliminated. Institutional training, as provided by the Job Corps and the Neighborhood Youth Corps, was cut back sharply, and Job Corps administration was transferred from the Office of Economic Opportunity to the Labor Department. Mangum, however, does not believe that cost-benefit study has had a significant impact on program modification. Apparently, politics remains a more potent force in shaping government policy than academic research.

Manpower Policy in the Future

The aim of manpower policy is not only to help individuals to be better able to compete in the labor market but also to improve the functioning of the nation's economy by creating a more skilled and versatile labor force and bringing workers and jobs into juxtaposition more quickly, while at the same time reducing the need for maintaining people in idleness. At the root of any successful manpower policy, however, must be the creation of sufficient jobs, and this requires high rates of economic growth. There is disagreement, however, on the optimum rate of growth when that is accompanied by unacceptable rates of inflation. Yet, as we saw earlier, manpower policy itself can make an important contribution to the battle against inflation; by training workers in needed skills, providing information on job vacancies and on available workers, and helping people to move to where job

---

[34] Mangum, "Manpower Research and Manpower Policy," *op. cit.*, pp. 93–101.

opportunities are located, manpower programs can reduce the trade-off between high employment and price stability.

Starting with very little in the way of public manpower programs, aside from basic education, the 1960s saw a proliferation of programs. Yet the effort has been a very modest one, for at no time was as much as half of one percent of the labor force undergoing full-time training. Although some of the manpower programs were poorly conceived, hastily put together, and overlapped with others, all studies indicate that the good ones have been eminently worthwhile. The 1960s, therefore, can be viewed as a period of experimentation, from which we can learn valuable lessons.

The fact that progress has been made in various areas does not preclude the need for further efforts, and this is particularly true with respect to labor market information and job matching. As we have seen, job vacancy data must be expanded from manufacturing to all sectors of the economy. Similarly, despite improvements in the functioning of the employment service, it is still in need of clarification of purpose, obtaining commitment to objectives from all state services, a clear ordering of priorities, and additional money and competent staff if it is to make the contribution to the manpower program of which it is potentially capable.

Above all, the nation must undertake a commitment actively to engage in manpower programs. The mere fact that mechanisms for dealing with manpower problems exist does not necessarily mean that they will be sufficiently or properly utilized when needed. For example, in recognition that changes in government military procurement programs would have enormous implications for certain occupational groups, industries, and regions where defense work is concentrated, a special presidential group, the Committee on the Economic Impact of Defense and Disarmament, made up of the chairman of the Council of Economic Advisers and representatives of nine other departments and agencies, was appointed in 1964. The committee was to make a continuing examination of the problems of changing manpower demands caused by a changing defense effort.[35] Yet, when significant reductions in defense and space programs were made in 1969–1970, virtually no attention was paid to the problem of their impact on industries, employees, and communities, and no steps were taken to cushion the impact on them. Two years later hastily prepared efforts to bail out the near-bankrupt Lockheed Aircraft Corporation and to retrain engineers and scientists had to be put forward.

Although manpower policy should aim at improving the skills of all sectors of the labor force, in the period ahead it probably will have to continue its concentration on the most seriously disadvantaged groups, particularly the youth among them. They must be aided to acquire skills that are in demand, to have open access to jobs, and to move up from entry-level to more skilled, better-paying jobs. Much of the task, therefore, must be accomplished through the educational system, but since society cannot ignore

---

[35] Wolfbein, *op. cit.*, p. 136.

those who are beyond school age and cannot compete effectively in the labor market, it will have to expand training and relocation programs for them, as well as fashioning more programs of remedial education.

An active manpower policy cannot exist in a vacuum, but must be tied in with all other policies, particularly those relating to rates of economic growth. Goals must be set that are realistic and capable of achievement, something the nation is yet to do. For example, Lecht analyzed the manpower needs that would have to have been met by 1975 for the attainment of a set of goals enunciated in 1960 by President Eisenhower's Commission on National Goals and concluded that vigorous pursuit of them would have been associated with an insufficiency of manpower, thus thwarting their attainment.[36] Since not all goals can be achieved simultaneously, an ordering of priorities must be established.

Manpower policy must also be flexible and capable of adaptation to changed circumstances. Technological innovations, not now clearly predictable, could arise to require large-scale retraining of workers. The eternal human quest for a world at peace might someday become much closer to reality, and large-scale disarmament would necessitate the reorientation of much of our economy and significant sections of the labor force. Individuals must also be flexible, being prepared to move for new job opportunities, to accept retraining when skills become outdated, and for redirection of careers in a dynamic society.

Finally, manpower programs must be administered well. To accomplish this end, more people will have to be trained in the field as labor market analysts, trainers, vocational counselors, and the like. Also, techniques for evaluating programs must be improved, so that determination can better be made of their efficiency.

The most important need is for a national resolve to expand manpower programs, for an active manpower policy is an essential feature of any national effort to deal with the urban crisis, reduce poverty, extend equal employment opportunity, and achieve a better life for everyone.

Summary

Active concern with manpower policy is of recent vintage and grew out of experience in training manpower during World War II and the postwar attempt by newly emerging nations to achieve economic development. These nations discovered that economic development required the development of human resources. Attempts to explain American economic growth also focused on the improvement of the human resource input into the production process and the need to invest in human "capital."

In market economies, such as that of the United States, the individual firm carries much of the burden of manpower development. From rudimen-

---

[36] Leonard A. Lecht, *Manpower Requirements for National Objectives in the 1970's* (Washington, D.C.: National Planning Association, 1968).

tary beginnings, this has expanded in large firms to sophisticated procedures for recruitment, selection, training, performance evaluation, and motivation of manpower. In recent years the larger corporations have also attempted to plan for future manpower needs scientifically.

Until recently the role of government in manpower development was limited largely to the provision of basic education, and this was mainly a function of local government. The commitment of the federal government to promotion of high levels of production and employment, embodied in the Employment Act of 1946, brought the federal government into the picture. At first that commitment was honored by policies designed to provide sufficient jobs for those who sought work, but by the 1960s government also became concerned with the supply side of the labor market in its attempt to deal with four structural problems confronting the economy: depressed areas, shifts in foreign trade, pockets of poverty, and technological change.

That involvement in manpower policy has encompassed forecasts of manpower requirements, provision and dissemination of labor market information, aid to education, and the training of people for available jobs. Since much of the government's efforts with respect to manpower development were new, they suffered from problems of coordination and effectiveness. On the whole, however, the efforts were effective, particularly those undertaken under the Manpower Development and Training Act.

Many manpower programs were undertaken in the 1960s, including the Job Corps, Job Opportunities in the Business Sector, Neighborhood Youth Corps, and on-the-job training. On-the-job training appears to have been the most successful. The success of all training programs, however, was linked with the state of the labor market, because workers with new skills could productively utilize them only if jobs were available.

Economists have used cost-benefit analysis to determine whether or not the investment in human resources has brought returns. Despite conceptual problems and difficulties in gathering adequate data, most studies indicate a high return on investment in manpower programs. Thus, manpower policy in the future can make an important contribution to economic efficiency and equity if it is tied in with a policy of high employment, if it is flexible and capable of adaptation to changed circumstances, and if it is administered well. In this way it can help to overcome the urban crisis, reduce poverty, and extend equal employment opportunity.

BIBLIOGRAPHY

A Review of Industrial Relations Research, Vol. II. Madison, Wisc.: Industrial Relations Research Association, 1971.

Borus, Michael E., and Charles G. Buntz. "Problems and Issues in the Evaluation of Manpower Programs," *Industrial and Labor Relations Review,* January 1972.

Comptroller General of the United States. *Federal Manpower Training Programs—GAO Conclusions and Observations.* Report to the Committee on Appropriations, U.S. Senate. Washington, D.C.: Government Printing Office, 1972.

Delehanty, John A. (ed.). *Manpower Problems and Policies: Full Employment and Opportunity for All.* Scranton: International Textbook Company, 1969.

Denison, Edward F. *The Sources of Economic Growth in the United States and the Alternatives Before Us.* New York: Committee for Economic Development, 1962.

Harbison, Frederick, and Charles A. Myers. *Education, Manpower, and Economic Growth: Strategies of Human Resource Development.* New York: McGraw-Hill, 1964.

Lecht, Leonard A. *Manpower Requirements for National Objectives in the 1970's.* Washington, D.C.: National Planning Association, 1968.

Levitan, Sar A., Garth L. Mangum, and Ray Marshall. *Human Resources and Labor Markets.* New York: Harper & Row, 1972.

———, and Robert Taggart III. *Social Experimentation and Manpower Policy: The Rhetoric and the Reality.* Baltimore: Johns Hopkins Press, 1971.

Mangum, Garth L. *The Emergence of Manpower Policy.* New York: Holt, Rinehart and Winston, 1969.

Manpower and Planning. New York: Industrial Relations Counselors, 1970.

Patten, Thomas H., Jr. *Manpower Planning and the Development of Human Resources.* New York: Wiley-Interscience, 1971.

Ribich, Thomas I. *Education and Poverty.* Washington, D.C.: Brookings, 1968.

Sewell, D. O. *Training the Poor: A Benefit-Cost Analysis of Manpower Programs in the U.S. Antipoverty Program.* Kingston: Industrial Relations Centre, Queen's University, 1971.

Somers, Gerald G. (ed.). *Retraining the Unemployed.* Madison, Wisc.: University of Wisconsin Press, 1968.

Vetter, Eric W. *Manpower Planning for High Talent Personnel.* Ann Arbor: Bureau of Industrial Relations, Graduate School of Business Administration, University of Michigan, 1967.

Wolfbein, Seymour L. *Employment, Unemployment, and Public Policy.* New York: Random House, 1965.

19 THE FUTURE

Having surveyed the field of labor economics, the time has come to take stock and discern the main threads of our discussion in terms of what the future may hold in store. The major conclusion that can be reached is that a free labor market, despite faults, has produced desirable results. From an economic point of view, it has resulted in a high degree of efficiency and equity. In the aggregate people do act in a rational economic manner and gravitate to those employments which help to create the greatest possible output and incomes. Within limitations, moreover, people are remunerated in accordance with their contribution to the society, as measured, of course, by an economic calculus. From a political point of view, the free labor market, with its contract instead of status considerations, provides individual freedom of choice of employment in line with abilities, plus the opportunity to advance economically based upon those abilities. Even in a socialist economy, with centralized planning of production, a free labor market would have tremendous advantages over any attempt to dictate the allocation of human resources.

Problems of the Labor Market

Worker Reactions

The fact that a free labor market is superior to other means of allocating labor does not mean that it has been without its faults. Among those that have been examined is the fact that labor has been reduced to a factor of production, the employment relationship has become an impersonal pecuniary one, and workers have been forced to compete among themselves for jobs. Many workers revolted against these aspects of the labor market and, through the institution of trade unionism, attempted to create a sense of community and gain a voice in the determination of the terms and conditions under which they offered their services. Unionism can be viewed as an interference with the free operation of the labor market, and many devotees of laissez-faire economics do indeed see it purely as that. Since our economy has deviated quite a bit from the purely competitive model, society has come to accept unionism in the labor market just as it has accepted the existence of large corporations in product markets, and the resulting distortions in the allocation of resources.

From another vantage point, however, unionism can be viewed as the major form of worker accommodation to the free labor market. By giving workers some degree of control over their own jobs, it allowed them to accept the basic premise that the market would be the chief allocator of labor. One could hypothesize that the absence of unionism would not have resulted in greater freedom in the labor market but in much less, for the workers would have demanded much more government interference in order to protect their interests.

Insecurity

Another major problem associated with the free labor market flowed from the fact that the employer owed the worker nothing more than remuneration for the services provided. This resulted in worker insecurity, because the vicissitudes of the business cycle, changes in tastes and technology, old age, and sickness and disability could lead to people's being without jobs and, hence, cut off from sources of income. Unionism has become one vehicle by which some of this insecurity has been reduced. Much more important, however, has been the role of government in reducing the insecurity attendant to a dynamic, industrial economy. Fiscal and monetary policies have been used to tame the business cycle; manpower policy has been developed to handle the structural aspects of unemployment; and social insurance has been devised to transfer income to those workers who are cut off from earning opportunities.

Equal Opportunity

One of the most glaring deficiencies of the free labor market has been its failure to deliver one of its major promises: equal opportunity to all participants. People have been denied access to employment and remuneration in accordance with their abilities because of discrimination based upon their race, religion, national origin, sex, or age. The picture, however, is a mixed one. Although almost all minorities have, at some time, suffered from discrimination, over the long haul the free labor market has been a major channel through which they have risen economically. On the other hand, blacks and other ethnic minorities, plus women, continue to be concentrated in jobs at the lower end of the occupational ladder.

To a very large degree the economic plight of the blacks in American society stems from discrimination prior to their entering the labor market. Denied equal educational and training opportunities, they suffer from low productivity and hence, in accordance with the precepts of the free labor market, are remunerated accordingly. Beyond that, however, blacks, other ethnic groups, and women have suffered from outright discrimination in the labor market, which has denied them jobs and earnings commensurate with their productivity.

American society is coming to recognize the contradictions between its behavior toward minorities and its political and economic ideology, and the labor market has been a major focus of corrective action. While some of the corrective action has been achieved voluntarily, most of it has come about because of legislation and government pressure, and much remains to be done.

Possible Future Trends

Before dealing with future trends with respect to the free labor market, the author feels it incumbent upon him to make clear his own bias. In his opinion, what is needed is not more interference with the operation of the free labor market, but policies and programs to help the labor market to work better and to help people to be able to compete more effectively in it. With respect to those persons who cannot be made productive because of infirmity, the need to take care of young children, and the like, the labor market does not offer a solution to their problem, which should be dealt with through provision of transfer payments.

It is most difficult to predict what the future holds in store, for so much depends upon industrial and societal decisions in a continually changing environment. In dealing with aggregate data, trends can be projected with reasonable accuracy, as has been shown with respect to the size and composition of the labor force. Attempts to fathom the directions and dimensions of individual behavior and social policy in the years ahead are much more hazardous, because they are bound up with attitudes toward life and the very value structure of our society, which are susceptible to discontinuities.

With these caveats in mind, let us try to discern possible developments in four major areas: (1) the area of collective bargaining, particularly its spread into public employment; (2) the area of productivity, especially as it is influenced by changing attitudes toward work and life; (3) the inflation-unemployment dilemma and the prospects for successfully finding a way out of it; (4) the question of manpower policy, particularly the need to bring blacks fully into the mainstream of American economic life.

The four topics are, of course, interrelated, and indeed achieving an objective in one area may result in its acting as a constraint upon attaining an end in another. There are, moreover, many other topics associated with the labor market that deserve special treatment, too, but many of these will be mentioned only tangentially. Having chosen these four as the most significant, let us proceed to examine trends with respect to them.

Collective Bargaining

The reaction of blue-collar workers to their atomization in a free labor market was the creation of trade unions through which to win a voice in the determination of the terms and conditions under which they would offer their services to employers. Following a century and one-half of struggle on their part, unions became an accepted institution in the American economy, and national policy favored collective bargaining as the means through which to establish labor standards.

Conflict between Public and Private Interests

With all its faults, collective bargaining has worked reasonably well as a method through which employees could share power with employers in the work place. The major criticism of collective bargaining is that it does not take sufficient account of the public interest. It is charged that the private bargains may hurt consumers through higher prices and restricted production, and that failures to reach agreement disrupt output and services and cause the public to suffer.

Many solutions have been proposed to these problems, ranging at one extreme from decentralization of bargaining to greater centralization of bargaining at the other. Some observers see disruptions in production and services when impasses in bargaining occur as anachronistic or too costly for society to tolerate, and they advocate substituting compulsory arbitration for the right to strike. It is doubtful, however, that these purported remedies will come about, either through government compulsion or voluntary action on the part of unions and employers, in the foreseeable future. There is an inherent conflict between collective bargaining and the "public interest," if that interest is seen as the receipt of the largest possible output at the lowest possible price. Accepting collective bargaining as a legitimate decision-making institution means that society recognizes that the specific interests of groups of employees are also encompassed within the "public" interest.

The fact that collective bargaining seems here to stay does not necessarily mean that there will be no modifications in the way it is practiced. National labor policy may, in the future, attempt to balance conflicting interests better.

Unions and employers themselves will probably modify the process of collective bargaining. They are no more happy with breakdowns in the process that result in strikes than is the general public. Attempts will be made in many industries to move away from crisis bargaining to a more rational method of reaching agreement. In some sectors of the economy "early bird" or continuous bargaining of some sort or another may replace crisis bargaining. In 1973, for example, the United Steelworkers and the major steel-producing companies agreed that there would be no general strike or industry lockout in their 1974 negotiations; steelworkers were guaranteed at least a 3 percent wage increase, and the parties agreed to arbitration of unresolved collective bargaining issues after a free period of bargaining. Collective bargaining, moreover, may be more keyed in with improvements in productivity, but it will possibly also expand to cover items at the plant level that management today considers to be solely within its prerogatives. In the main, however, collective bargaining will probably not change significantly for a long time to come unless government wage controls become a permanent feature of the labor market.

Public Sector Bargaining

The growth of collective bargaining in public and nonprofit employment has begun to present formidable problems. First of all, since in the main they involve the provision of services, disruptions of them can cause great inconvenience, and even suffering, as when hospital workers strike. Intransigence in bargaining can lie on both sides of the bargaining table, and laws prohibiting public employee strikes have not prevented them. Clearly, some better solution for impasses in collective bargaining in the public sector must be found, but as yet they are not on the horizon. The probabilities are that a very trying period will be gone through before any even partial solutions are found. Arbitration, however, may come to be favored by the parties, as well as the general public, as preferable to strikes for overcoming impasses in negotiations.

An even more troublesome problem is to accommodate collective bargaining to the economic setting of public employment. There is little direct confrontation between the public and the results of collective bargaining in the private sector. When costs go up employers raise prices, and the public's only option is to pay the increase or consume less of the product. In the public sector, however, when costs go up taxes must be raised or, less likely, services cut, and this involves the public directly because it elects the legislators and executives who are responsible for fiscal policy. It will take a Solomon to find equity between the demands of public employees for proper treatment and the insistence of the general public that taxes be held in check.

While the general public has no right to expect civil servants to, in effect, subsidize them by working for substandard salaries, it does have the right to insist that public pay scales for particular jobs be in line with those of comparable employment. Yet in the absence of effective economic constraints there is evidence that collective bargaining in public employment has produced labor standards in some cases that are far superior to what these workers could earn elsewhere. This problem is further compounded by the fact that, at least at the local government level, high salaries and generous pensions for public employees are financed through regressive taxes, thus resulting in a transfer of income from lower- to higher-income groups.

Finally, there is direct conflict between collective bargaining in the public sector and the apparently changing values of American society. In recent years the United States has become absorbed with the need to reorder its priorities so as to place greater stress on the provision of needed public services and less on the consumption of private goods. To the degree, however, that collective bargaining channels increased expenditures on public services into compensation of employees it makes it that much more difficult to achieve any significant improvement in the quantity and quality of public services.

The student who is awaiting the revelation of the solutions to these problems faces only disappointment, for none are at hand. As in the case of workers in private industry, those in public employment have also asserted a right to a voice in the determination of the terms and conditions under which they work, yet this inevitably produces conflict with the public interest. Ameliorating this conflict is a major problem with which a free society will have to wrestle, but meanwhile it must recognize that extending rights to public employees will act as a constraint upon the achievement of other societal goals.

Maintaining Productivity Improvement

If public employees want "more," they are no different than almost everyone else in our society. Historically, the nation's ability to raise the standards of living of its citizenry has been through increased productivity, but there is serious question as to our ability even to maintain our historic record of productivity gains, even with the benefits of automated technology and the computer.

The Rise of the Service Sector

First, there is the whole question of the shift from goods producing to service producing. Service industries tend to be more labor intensive and less amenable to the substitutability of capital for labor, which would increase the output per unit of labor input. Indeed, Nordhaus has produced evidence that a slowdown in the rate of increase in labor productivity to 2 percent had occurred in the period 1965–1971.[1] The rising costs of public services, particularly as collective bargaining spreads, has raised demands for greater productivity in the public sector. Undoubtedly, better organizational structures, managerial systems, and manpower utilization are possible, and these could reduce much of the waste and overlap in the public sector. There are limits, however, to how much this will accomplish, for once waste is eliminated the sources of further productivity improvement are severely limited.

The very concept of productivity in many types of services is an elusive one. No one can define how a teacher can become more productive. Teaching large lecture sections instead of small classes could result in a serious deterioration of the quality of education and thus mean really lower rather than higher productivity.

Concern with the Environment

A second constraint upon productivity improvement seems to be in the offing from new concerns with preserving the environment, which have led to

---

[1] William D. Nordhaus, "The Recent Productivity Slowdown," *Brookings Papers on Economic Activity, No. 3* (Washington, D.C.: Brookings, 1972).

demands that we cease economic growth entirely. Substituting capital for labor means continued exploitation of natural resources, which many contend must now be preserved. National concern with pollution control means a greater use of resources that, while improving the quality of life, does not add to the quantity of goods produced. Preserving the environment is a most worthy objective, but we must recognize that its pursuit detracts from the attainment of other societal goals, and hard choices will have to be made.

Changing Attitudes toward Work

Another constraint on productivity improvement that may operate in the future is the new attitude of young, better-educated workers toward work. Although automation has reduced the number of back-breaking and boring jobs, it has not eliminated them, and young workers revolt against them. Actually, their attitudes are probably not much different from those of previous generations, but high levels of employment and strong unions make them more willing to act against conditions at the work place that they believe to be demeaning.

Feeling totally alienated from uncreative, boring jobs, typified by the assembly line of the automobile industry, their rebellion takes the form of increased turnover and absenteeism, insistence upon earlier retirement, resistance to management discipline, and demands for a voice in decision-making with respect to plant rules and even methods of operation. This conflict between productivity and worker rebellion against the indignity of the assembly line was highlighted in early 1972 at General Motors' assembly plants. With small foreign imports gobbling up a significant proportion of American automobile sales, the domestic producers decided to try to win back part of that market by producing their own smaller vehicles at competitive prices. This, of course, necessitated cutting down the labor costs on American cars. The manufacturers, therefore, took steps designed to improve efficiency in their plants.

When General Motors tightened the discipline of the highly automated assembly lines and reduced the number of workers, they reacted with individual acts of sabotage, sporadic wildcat walkouts, and official strikes by the United Automobile Workers at GM plants.

The specific focus of the rebellion at GM plants was only symptomatic of the general reaction of workers against meaningless jobs, which can be expected to surface in different complaints later and at other companies. From the company's point of view, using more men in an operation adds to the production costs, which conceivably could undermine its ability to compete with foreign imports. Thus, without judging who is right and who is wrong, and to what degrees, this case illustrates very dramatically the head-on collision between the attitudes and behavior of younger workers and management's efforts to increase productivity.

At this point, both unions and managements are wrestling with how to solve the conflict. Some experimentation has been undertaken that would involve workers' being consulted with respect to plant production methods, the enrichment of jobs, and the use of teamwork in production. Each of these may have value, but there are also severe restrictions, both engineering and economic, on their feasibility. The nature of assembly-line work means that many jobs simply cannot be enriched to the point where they can be meaningful. As Malcolm Denise, vice-president for labor relations of Ford Motors, put it, "You can't stay in the auto business by throwing parts on the floor and saying to the guy, 'Make an automobile out of it.' "[2] The union was equally aware of the problems involved, for according to Douglas Fraser, head of the UAW's Chrysler department, "If you triple plant capacity and would be willing to pay $10,000 per car, then you could have teams build cars."[3]

We must conclude, therefore, that there may be no solution in the offing that will end the conflict between productivity and making work meaningful. The only hopeful area seems to lie in making workers aware of the need for productivity and giving them some voice in how it is to be pursued so that they do not see it as achieved solely at their expense. In their 1971 negotiations the steel industry and the United Steelworkers agreed to establish joint productivity committees in the mills, and Chrysler Corporation has experimented with involving workers in management decisions and consulting them on methods of production and plant organization. How workers are to be involved in decision-making and how willing managements are to consult them are serious questions, but the results of these experiments will bear watching, for they could determine future trends in labor-management relations and the American economy.

Impact on Collective Bargaining

The GM case also illustrates the conflict between centralized collective bargaining and the concerns of the workers at the work place. At the end of 1970 the United Automobile Workers, after a long strike, had negotiated what it considered to be a very satisfactory agreement with General Motors. That agreement, however, focused on economic matters, and aside from earlier retirement, which could permit workers to escape the assembly line after thirty years of service, it did not deal with the content of jobs. It is doubtful that any national collective bargaining agreement could deal with such matters. It is possible, therefore, that the major long-run change in collective bargaining may be a shift in emphasis away from centralized negotiations over economic matters to local negotiations over plant working conditions.

---

[2] *The New York Times*, April 2, 1972.

[3] Some contend, on the other hand, that if work were made more meaningful, productivity would increase because of reductions in absenteeism, turnover, sabotage, and poor quality workmanship. See, for example, *Work in America*, Report of a Special Task Force to the Secretary of Health, Education and Welfare, Prepared under the auspices of the W. E. Upjohn Institute for Employment Research (Cambridge, Mass.: MIT Press, 1972).

The Inflation-Unemployment Dilemma

Should the United States not be able to maintain historic rates of improvement in productivity, this would serve to further complicate the dilemma between holding down the rate of inflation versus the maintenance of low rates of unemployment. As yet no solution to this dilemma has been found, none seems imminent, and, indeed, none may be possible. So far we have alternated in policy, stressing price stability when inflation increased in intensity, only to shift gears to promoting economic expansion when the unemployment level mounted. It is likely that this same pattern will continue to persist for some time to come. At some point, however, we may choose one route or the other as the major aim of public policy.

Opting for Price Stabilization

Some economists, in fact, are attempting to redefine full employment to be the point at which increasing aggregate demand tends to become increasingly inflationary. By such a definition, full employment today would be somewhere at about a 5 percent level, or possibly higher. Those unemployed at this "full employment" level would be considered to be "structurally" unemployed, and their disabilities would be treated through manpower policies rather than fiscal and monetary policies designed to create additional jobs.

Defining excess unemployment as structural sounds very reminiscent of the pre-Keynesian days, in which many economists defined the jobless as "involuntarily" unemployed, arguing that they simply were not willing to work for low enough wages. Definitions, however, do not solve problems nor relieve the plight of those who cannot find jobs. Manpower programs of training and relocation can help to ensure that workers possess skills that are in demand in the labor market and that they are in the locations where jobs are available. Training and relocation assistance, however, make sense only if jobs are available.

Adopting such a definition of full employment would condemn certain sectors of the population, particularly youths and blacks, to permanently high rates of unemployment. Experience in the early 1970s shows that national unemployment rates of between 5 and 6 percent have meant double that for blacks, triple for white youth, and six times higher for black youth. In 1971, for example, one-third of black youngsters were unemployed and the rate in the poverty neighborhoods was close to 50 percent, not even taking into account the number of those who were so discouraged about job prospects that they had dropped out of the labor force.

Opting for Full Employment

It may be that the nation will have to learn to adjust to the prospect of a higher rate of annual price rise than it has experienced heretofore in order to achieve an acceptable level of unemployment. Indeed, there are many economists who argue that inflation is not so terrible, as long as the rise in the level of domestic prices does not move faster than in other industrial nations with which American products must compete. Professor Tobin, for example, argues that the real gains from additional employment far outweigh the costs of inflation.[4] From an economic point of view, having resources, including human ones, lie idle is wasteful and denies the society its greatest potential output and welfare. From a social point of view, moreover, full employment promotes greater opportunity for all and helps to ensure domestic tranquility.

Of course, even the advocates of full employment recognize that there are limits to which it would be desirable to trade inflation for lower unemployment. The plight of the extremely low-productivity workers is a real one, but can be viewed as a social problem more than an economic one. They need jobs, but to increase aggregate demand to the point where they would be reached in the hiring queue would be very inflationary, because shortages of more highly skilled workers and other types of bottlenecks, which would lead to higher prices, would be encountered long before they were reached. The better solution might be to subsidize their employment through income supplements, either directly to the individuals involved or to the employers who would be induced to hire them because the government would pay the difference between the value of their productivity and the going wage. Another approach might be for the government to employ low-productivity persons itself.

Probable Public Policy

This discussion obviously points up the fact that there remains a cruel dilemma between inflation and unemployment. What economists are arguing about is not whether or not there must be a trade-off between the two, but at what point the trade-off should be made. Some argue for less inflation at the price of more unemployment, while others contend that there are greater net social gains from lower levels of unemployment even when this means somewhat higher rates of rise in the price level.

Policy, as we have indicated, will probably continue to fluctuate between the two conflicting goals of price stability and full employment. Efforts will be made periodically to attempt to attain both objectives simultaneously through the use of such devices as guideposts and wage-price controls, but experience indicates that these will be of only limited effectiveness and for limited periods of time.

Manpower Policy

Whatever position economists take on the point at which inflation must be traded for unemployment, most would agree that manpower policy can make a contribution to the amelioration of the problem. By upgrading the skills of

---

[4] James Tobin, "Inflation and Unemployment," *American Economic Review*, March 1972, pp. 1–18.

the unemployed and lesser-skilled employed, we can break labor market bottlenecks, increase productivity, and in effect shift the Phillips curve to a more favorable position. The provision of more and better labor market information using such new devices as a computerized job bank, could hasten the process by which workers and jobs connect. In a dynamic economy tastes and technology are continuously changing, so there is need to retrain workers at all levels, from factory machine tenders to engineers with graduate degrees, whose skills have become obsolete. In a dynamic economy, moreover, some regions grow rapidly as others decline, and there is need to speed up the process by which workers move from the declining areas to those offering job opportunities.

Ensuring Equal Employment Opportunity

No item on the nation's agenda for the future takes precedence over the need to solve the "urban crisis" and bring its disadvantaged minorities into the mainstream of economic life. This requires that the labor market be freed from discriminatory practices.

Thus, another trend that can be discerned is further government involvement in the labor market to enforce Title VII of the Civil Rights Act and the other legislation barring discrimination. Debates will continue to rage, however, over the means used to achieve compliance with nondiscriminatory policies. One of the fiercest of these debates, which has already surfaced, concerns the use of minority hiring quotas to determine compliance. Such quotas have already been imposed in the construction industry, through the so-called Philadelphia Plan, whereby employers on government contracts must agree to try to reach a point in hiring at which a specific proportion of the total labor force is composed of black workers. In addition, the Equal Employment Opportunity Commission often uses a head count of minority members in an employer's work force and compares this to the percentages they make up in the community in order to determine compliance with the law.

The use of specific hiring targets has been a successful device to force employers and unions to go beyond mere tokenism in hiring minority group members. Yet many people who favor an end to discrimination honestly question the compatibility of specific quotas and truly equal employment opportunity. Quotas themselves can become a form of discrimination in employment, and they were used in the past to limit, rather than increase, the number of people from various minorities who would be hired or promoted.

Forcing the ethnic and sex composition of any individual work place to conform to some predetermined pattern is as much a distortion of a free labor market as is discrimination. Interests and talents are not distributed equally among all groups in the population, and one ethnic group may be over-represented in one sector of the economy while underrepresented in another. In fact, equal employment opportunity should mean that employers no longer think in ethnic terms, but hire and promote *individuals* based upon their abilities.

Adhering to such a concept of equal employment opportunity, however, will not, by itself, bring all segments of the black, Puerto Rican, Mexican-American, and Indian communities into the mainstream of American economic life. Since they have suffered from discrimination prior to entering the labor market, many of them are low-productivity workers. Unless specific programs are undertaken to raise their productivity, they would be automatically relegated to the end of the hiring queue and would suffer greater unemployment or, at best, hold the lowest-paid, least secure, most menial jobs in the economy.

Remedying Worker Skill Deficiencies

Thus, in order to aid the disadvantaged and thus significantly reduce poverty in the nation, the government will have to continually promote programs designed to correct the educational and skill deficiencies of people so that they may be afforded the opportunity to better compete in the labor market. Significant steps along this road were taken during the 1960s, and, based on the lessons learned, more effective programs can be fashioned in the future.

A good deal of today's training efforts are designed to correct the deficiencies with which people enter the labor market. Given the continuing problems of the nation's educational system, it is likely that remediation will continue as the focal point for some time to come.

Government manpower programs do not necessarily involve the government in the actual conduct of training, but in its promotion, coordination, and financing. Not only may government subsidize the private training of those with skill deficiencies, but, as previously indicated, it may actually subsidize the hiring of low-skilled workers. These compensation supplements would have to be continued until an individual's productivity was commensurate with the going wage rate. Such a program seems inevitable because of its greater efficiency: it costs less than maintaining an individual in idleness and it adds to the total national output. For the individual, moreover, having a regular job would be a source of greater dignity than is provided by the collection of welfare.

Government as the "Employer of Last Resort"

For some very low-productivity workers, the government itself may become the source of employment. In fact, the concept of the government as the "employer of last resort," particularly during periods of high unemployment, has gained considerable headway in recent years. The beginnings of such a program came into being in the Emergency Employment Act of 1971.

A number of operational problems, however, may present themselves with respect to government employment of low-productivity workers. The first will be the need to find meaningful jobs that these workers are capable of performing, but, given the crying need for increased public services in such areas as health care, education, public safety, and pollution control, this should be possible. A second problem will be to prevent such programs from becoming merely a source of cheap labor for local communities; the number of such jobs that are allowed any governmental unit, therefore, will have to be limited. A third problem is to ensure that most workers involved in such programs are not permanently stuck in them; a partial aim of the programs must be to help upgrade individuals so that they can qualify for regular employment, public or private.

Finally, it should be recognized that many persons in our society will not be able to hold jobs, even with subsidized compensation. Requiring the aged, the infirm, and those caring for young children to work is neither right from a humanitarian point of view nor from an economic, because the very small contribution that they could make would be outweighed by the costs of forcing them to work. For those who cannot participate in the labor force, therefore, the best solution would be to provide them with income with which to live. Some variant of a guaranteed minimum income will probably come into being eventually.

A Summing Up

Many other problems and trends in labor economics could be explored, but we have selected those that seem to be the most important for the near future. All of them, as we have seen, are interconnected and, in fact, are related to the very values of American society. Making the labor market function better and enabling each person to compete within it effectively are most worthwhile objectives, but their realization will require the allocation of resources to those ends. In simple terms, the American people will have to sacrifice other goals, such as greater private consumption by those who are better off or greater military might, in order to pursue these goals.

Events may compel the nation to move in the directions outlined, but commitments to social goals often prove to be ephemeral, as people get tired of the effort required in pursuing them. As people move into the middle-income brackets they tend to resent carrying the tax load that programs of social betterment require, and, since the middle-income recipients will be a rapidly growing sector of the population, they will have the political power to block such efforts. It is possible, therefore, that the nation may retreat into a period in which people are more concerned with maintaining the "value of the dollar" and holding down their taxes than with the plight of the unemployed and disadvantaged in the labor market.

Even if the nation does not follow such a course, we must still recognize that the achievement of goals in one area may conflict with realizing those in another. Nowhere is this more clear than in labor economics today, for the goals of high levels of employment, productivity improvement, and extension of equal employment opportunity all require high levels of national economic growth. Yet at this very time many persons concerned with the preservation of the environment are advocating that we reduce the rate of economic growth.

Again, it will be necessary to assure that the burden of pursuing ecological goals does not fall disproportionately on those least able to bear it. Since it is doubtful that a politically and economically acceptable degree of income redistribution would be sufficient to raise the living standards of the poor and near-poor significantly, continued economic growth will also be needed. Properly directed growth would make the major contribution to providing jobs and higher incomes for these less fortunate citizens. A growing economy will enable the nation actively to pursue the goals of full employment and equal opportunity for all without reducing living standards. In economic terms, these goals mean simply achieving greater efficiency and equity in the labor market, which has been the subject of this book.

INDEX

Blacks: and caste system in U.S., 38; in central cities, 427–28; educational and skill deficiencies of, 445–46; and employment discrimination, 440–41, 447; history in labor market, 441–42; in labor force, 29–30; and labor mobility, 213; status in labor market, 442–51; unemployment rates of, 337; union policy toward, 75

"Black Thursday," 65

Blue-collar occupations, changes in, 25–26

"Boulwarism," 132–33

Brotherhood of Sleeping Car Porters, 457

Bureau of Labor Statistics, 11

Business cycle: and strikes, 151; and unemployment, 346–47

Capitalist economic system: class structure in, 34–35; exchange relationship in, 8

Central city, decline of, 423–24

Chamberlain, Neil W., and collective bargaining theory, 155–56, 157

Chavez, Cesar, 456

Child labor, decline in, 13

CIO. *See* Congress of Industrial Organizations

Cities. *See* Urbanization

City Worker's Family Budget for a Moderate Living Standard, Autumn, 1966 (CWFB), 225

"Civilian labor force," 11

Civil Rights Act, Title VII (1964), 459–61

Civil rights movement, historical perspective on, 455–56

Civil War, impact on trade unionism, 57

Clark, John Bates, 231

Class conflict: factors mitigating in U.S., 37–38; in Marxist doctrine, 35

Class structure: concept of, 33–38; evolution of, 34–35; Marxist view of, 35–36

Clayton Act (1914), 63, 113–14

Coalition bargaining, 146–47

Collective bargaining, 131–58: and cen-tralization controversy, 147–49; definition of, 131; emergency disputes issue in, 161–70; extent of, 131–32; and intercity earnings and income differentials, 419; and Norris-La Guardia Act, 116; outlook for, 501–04; process, 134–35; and public policy, 169–90; structure of, 143–49; subject matter of, 133–40; theories of, 155–58; units of, 143–46; use of strikes in, 149–51. *See also* Public collective bargaining

Committee for Industrial Organization, 67

Committee on the Economic Impact of Defense and Disarmament, 495

Commodity markets, expansion of, 56–57

Common law, and unionization, 108–09

Commons, John R., theories of unionism, 79

Commonwealth v. *Hunt* (1842), 109

Communication Workers of America, 102

Compulsory arbitration, and emergency disputes, 165

Concentrated Employment Program, 487

Congress: and Adamson Act (1916), 63; and antidiscrimination legislation, 459; and antitrust legislation, 111

Congress of Industrial Organizations, 68–69

Construction employment, increase in, 18, *19t*

Construction Industry Stabilization Committee, 325

Contract administration, and grievance procedure, 140–42

Cooperative Area Manpower Planning System, 487

Coronado Coal Company cases, 114

Corporate power, and inflation policy, 299–300

Cost of Living Council, 325–26

Costs of entry, and principle of equal advantage, 200–01

Council for Scientific, Professional, and Cultural Employees, 103